GENERA LICHENUM:

AN

ARRANGEMENT

OF

THE NORTH AMERICAN

LICHENS,

BY

EDWARD TUCKERMAN, M.A.

AMHERST:

EDWIN NELSON.

1872.

B M Walton
from his friend
EPJ.

GENERA LICHENUM:

AN

ARRANGEMENT

OF

THE NORTH AMERICAN

LICHENS,

BY

EDWARD TUCKERMAN, M.A.,

PROFESSOR OF BOTANY IN AMHERST COLLEGE ; MEMBER OF THE NATIONAL ACADEMY OF SCIENCES, OF THE
IMPERIAL LEOP. CAROL. GERMAN ACADEMY OF NATURALISTS, AND OF THE AMERICAN ACADEMY
OF ARTS AND SCIENCES ; CORRESPONDING MEMBER OF THE ROYAL SOCIETY OF SCIENCES
AT UPSAL, OF THE BOSTON SOCIETY OF NATURAL HISTORY, OF THE PHILADEL-
PHIA ACADEMY OF NATURAL SCIENCES, OF THE ROYAL BOTANICAL SOCIETY
OF RATISBON, FOREIGN MEMBER OF THE BOTANICAL SOCIETY
OF EDINBURGH, ETC.

AMHERST:

EDWIN NELSON.

1872.

" Nisi æternum in continua varietate, infinitum in revelatione finita, quærimus, fragilis nostra spes et inanes nostræ contentiones." — FRIES.

JOURNAL STEAM PRESS,
LEWISTON, MAINE.

This is a final report to the friendly correspondents of the author on the specimens which, for many years, they have sent to him for determination. And such determination implying a certain arrangement, the book is further a report upon what, after much labour, has commended itself to him as the best-ascertained, systematic disposition of the Lichens. It was intended, in an introductory chapter, to attempt some reckoning of the more weighty, published opinions as to the position, and rank of these plants in nature; to review cursorily the development of the system, and several of the varying interpretations of it; and to consider finally, more at large, the systematic value of the anatomical characters, as especially of the spore characters; but prolonged indisposition, resulting from overwork, and rendering it necessary to depend upon a friend for the correction of the press, and to shorten as much as possible these prefatory observations, leaves it open only to say that the author's point of view here, remains in general the same with that indicated by him already in print, on another occasion;[1] and that the further exemplification of what is there advanced must now speak for itself.

It yet appears proper to add that the result of a long study of intertropical and related lichens, pursued by the writer, at first under the friendly direction of Fries, and Montagne, as afterwards in the light of the more recent lichenology, and, especially, of the very instructive writings of Nylander, — was a persuasion that, so far as system was concerned, the later lichenographers had scarcely the advantage which it was assumed that they had over the earlier; that not a few of the changes of form proposed by the former were either insufficiently grounded, or comparatively unimportant, if not now erroneous; and that there was, in a word, nothing as yet to compare, in solidity and thoroughness of construction, with the system (as understood in its principal outlines, and as embracing, it afterwards proved, the Collemaceous lichens) of Fries. And thus the question opened which is pursued in these pages — how far does the increase of knowledge, whether of external form or anatomical

---

[1] Lichens of California, Oregon, and the Rocky Mountains, 1866, pp. 5—11.

structure, of the last thirty years, justify the newer dispositions of the system in their departures from the older; and to what extent are the latter still adequate to the phenomena, and, for the present, preferable. The author has at least had some occasion to approve of the arrangement here set down, in his own studies, as in the requirements of teaching; and its excellence is by no means lessened, in his eyes, that it is readily intelligible.

It is admitted indeed, and by all but universal consent, that Lichens may be said to fall into two principal series, determined by ground-differences of the apothecia: — a naked-fruited (Gymnocarpous) series, of which the type is the dish-like apothecium, and a covered-fruited (Angiocarpous) series, of which the type is the mammiform apothecium. The second series, inferior in all respects to the first, offers only distinctions of very subordinate value, in the process of differentiation of its type; which yet is so marked, that these lichens (*Verrucariacei*) are kept together by all authors. In the first, however, which embraces the great mass, and the highest exhibitions of lichenous vegetation, the various modifications of the dish-like (patellæform) fruit are, in their turn, ennobled; and prove to possess a systematic importance unexplained certainly by their anatomical. We appear to be indicating but moderate, and now even slight deviations when we say that the patellæform exciple of *Biatora* being diminished (mostly) and hidden or bordered by an accessory, thalline receptacle becomes thereby scutellæform; — or simply elongated, lirellæform; — or stalked (for the most part) and the disk, at the same time, so to say, disorganized, and consisting of naked spores, crateriform; but these differences are indications, none the less, of four great assemblages, or tribes, of Lichens; assemblages which, however modified, or even perplexed, the first two may be in his classifications, no lichenographer entirely ignores, and no lichenist can afford to neglect. All lichens are then, in this view, either 1, Parmeliaceous, 2, Lecideaceous, 3, Graphidaceous, 4, Caliciaceous, or 5, Verrucariaceous. The student will find sufficient perplexities; but the advantage to him of the comparative simplicity of this first step into the system is manifest.

It appears moreover incorrect to contrast disadvantageously the arrangement to which we have just referred, with some later ones, as if the former were artificial, and the latter, so to say, natural. With whatever attempt at an universal view nature be pursued, art must supervene, would we bring knowledge to a practical systematic form; and the greater the number and diversity of the points of view embraced by the systematist, the greater the art required. The arrangement of Nylander reckons all organs as of equal value in the system; which should thus, in his hands, exhibit the same universality in form, as it certainly does in aim, and in its unequalled wealth of illustration. We find it notwithstanding at once becoming eclectical; as now one, and now another organ is assumed as determinative: and whatever the advantage of this disposition, as the means of communication of the most learned of lichenologists, it is evident that it differs from other arrangements, not so much in the exclusion of selection (that is of the ' artificial and arbitrary ') as in the use made of it.

The writer has aimed then, in the following pages, first, to simplify, and render more easily apprehensible, the larger divisions. And following still further the guiding thought of the great master of cryptogamic botany who has either defined or suggested the most of what has so far been reached, he has next attempted to simplify and reduce the genera; though here, a consideration of the spore-values has led, to a certain extent, in an opposite direction; whereby certain over-large groups are disposed in smaller ones. Massalongo[1] exhibits the extreme point reached in the externalization of the Lichen-idea by the analytical studies of the last thirty years; and he asserts or assumes the existence of at least 240 genera within the limits of study of the present volume. Noteworthy indications of a reaction from this extreme, within what may perhaps be called the same school, are afforded by the classifications of Th. Fries,[2] and Stizenberger,[3] neither of whom recognizes, it should appear, quite half of these genera of Massalongo; as by that of J. Müller.[4] And the contrast becomes marked, and the return towards Acharius and Fries distinct in Nylander, with whom only about a quarter of the genera referred to, of the Italian author, find acceptance: a proportion which is much the same with that afforded by the present treatise. It is in the same direction that we still look for the full reconciliation of the later knowledge, rich as it is in the accumulations of the past generation, with all that continues to hold its own of the earlier; and for a new and better

[1] Krempelhuber, *Conspectus Syst. Lich. Massal.* (*Gesch. d. Lich.* 2, p. 221).

[2] *Genera Heterolichenum recognita.* 1861.

[3] *Beitrag zur Flechtensystematik.* 1862.

[4] *Principes de Classification des Lichens, et Enumeration des Lichens des environs de Genève.* 1862.

statement of the idea. Lastly, it has been an object in this book to recommend, and to some slight extent at least to illustrate, a larger and better conception of species. The writer cannot now attempt to explain his meaning by figures; by a comparison of what are called species in several of the most accepted manuals of the time; but the evidence appears to be sufficient that the term referred to has come to have, often, little definite meaning; and that here the investigators of vegetable structure who decline to take an interest in systematic botany have in fact something to stand on. In this new continent, where so much is to be learned, we are less prepared indeed to enter on the long and difficult studies which should possibly tend to establish a larger conception of the term; and must remain content, for the time, if many of our species, however accepted by high authority, are perhaps only members of larger species-groups, not yet understood. And, on the other hand (as in *Verrucaria*, as we now imperfectly know it) what are called species may in part rather be groups which fuller investigation shall one day enable us to separate, satisfactorily, into smaller ones. But there can be no question, it is scarcely venturesome to say, with any competent enquirer into the prevalent and increasing laxity of conception referred to, that it foretokens unfavourable results to the future of our studies.

This is seen, at least, in the very generally assumed value of recent experiments on the behaviour of lichen-tissues with certain chemical tests; species having thus come at last to have no other meaning than a chemical one: namely that they exhibit (so far, it is important to say, as the examination has gone) a different reaction from forms with which, in every other respect, they are admitted to agree. The writer has since found no occasion to qualify the opinions expressed by him already in print,[1] on the systematic value of these experiments.

Frequent use being made, in the following pages, of some views of spore-phenomena published by the author elsewhere, and not now easily accessible, place may properly be given to them here. He conceives then that while less weight than has often been assumed should be given to spore-differences of a merely *gradal* character, or such others as depend only upon dimensions, more than has sometimes been allowed should be yielded to those that seem to be typical. Analysis scarcely indicates more than two well-defined kinds of lichen-spores, complemented

[1] American Naturalist, April, 1868.

in the highest tribe only by a well-defined intermediate one. In one of these (typically colourless) the originally simple spore, passing through a series of modifications, always in one direction, and tending constantly to elongation, affords at length the *acicular* type. To this is opposed (most frequently but not exclusively in the lower tribes, and even possibly anticipated by the polar-bilocular sub-type in *Parmeliacei*) a second (typically coloured) in which the simple spore, completing another series of changes, tending rather to distention, and to division in more than one direction, exhibits finally the *muriform* type. Differences such as these appear certainly to be significant; and to suggest a possible correlation with others, which shall leave no doubt that these types require marked expression in the system. Nor is such expression questioned in the case of the best-developed, foliaceous groups. Nobody now hesitates to distinguish *Physcia* and *Pyxine* from *Parmelia*, or *Solorina* from *Peltigera* ; and the argument from such foliaceous to the analogous crustaceous genera is impeded perhaps by nothing beside the thalline inferiority of the latter. But it is seen at once that the case is not the same with the successive steps in the process of differentiation of these types; and the value of such gradal (bilocular, quadrilocular, plurilocular) distinctions should be clearly inferior. Species which exhibit the ultimate condition of their spore-type, as here taken, exhibit also, ideally at least, the whole of the preceding process of evolution. This is still better observed in larger, natural groups, as (*exc. excip.*) *Biatora vernalis*, Fr. *L. E.*, expressing, with general congruity of structure, the whole history of the colourless spore. And the step is not a long one from such groups to natural genera; to the assumption that gradal differences of the same type of spore, displayed by species, or clusters of species, within the circuit of what is otherwise a natural genus, shall be an insufficient ground for the sundering of such genus. The consideration of the numerous, sometimes sufficiently significant instances, in which nature appears to point in this direction, will be attempted further on. Suffice it here to say that, according to these views, *Parmelia* proper, Ach., will fall into *Theloschistes*, *Parmelia*, and *Physcia* ; and *Lecanora* into *Placodium* (DC.) Naeg. & Hepp, *Lecanora*, and *Rinodina*. Excluding the biatorine forms of *Placodium* from the *Lecideei*, the latter will have no examples of the polar-bilocular sub-type; but *Heterothecium*, corresponding to *Physcia* and *Rinodina*, will be distinguishable from *Biatora ;* and *Buellia* similarly from *Lecidea*. And the whole class may be conceived, as in like manner passing into 1, a Colourless Series, especially prominent and characteristical in the higher tribes; and 2, a Coloured Series, having its chief development in the lower; series which, tabularized, so as to exhibit the sporal analogies, will be found significant as well of the relations of the genera, as of the systematic value of the spores.

It is yet important to distinguish between spores typically colourless and what are rather to be taken for decolorate conditions of spores typically coloured. There are sufficiently well-ascertained instances of such decolorate spores; and we need perhaps scarcely hesitate to argue from them to some other cases in which the evidence is possibly less clear, and thus to keep entire certain natural genera. And, on the other hand, it is conceivable that a genus may rather be referable to the Colourless Series, notwithstanding that many of its species exhibit spores which, in this respect at least of colour, look often the other way. The genus *Sticta* —in all respects remarkable—combining, says Schwendener, with a very pronounced affinity between the species, such varied transitions and gross contrasts of structure, that one might well question the systematic significance of the anatomical characters concerned,[1] is also, to no small degree, equivocal in the spores.

Difficulties of this sort are however to be expected in every stage, from the first step, of our endeavours to study the life in nature. What responds to our intelligence there is indeed of kin to that intelligence, is the ideal; but the ideal imprisoned in, and subjected to all the inordinate fortuitousness of, the natural. We cannot reach any seemingly definite result, be it the determination of what we take for a species, or the reference of such species to the higher groups to which it is assumed to belong, without becoming aware, first or last, to how great an extent whatever we have succeeded in doing is only tentative. It is enough then if the difficulties of a result, or a method, appear to be overbalanced by its advantages. To this the writer has only to add here, once more, the expression of his earnest conviction, that with all the new light which the researches of the last thirty years have thrown upon Lichenology, this study has not yet advanced so far as safely to neglect the wide views, divinations as we now know they often were, of the elder lichenog-

[1] *"Es gibt wohl wenige Gattungen, welche wie Sticta bei einer so ausgesprochenen natürlichen Verwandtschaft der zahlreichen Arten, doch so mancherlei Uebergänge und so grosse Gegensätze zeigen, dass man an der systematischen Bedeutung der betreffenden anatomischen Charactere zweifeln möchte."* (*Untersuch.* 3, p. 167.)

raphers : — or, in other words, that no structural detail, of whatever apparent value, can safely assert itself in defiance of the argument from general structure ; or otherwise than as elucidated by the subtle mediation of Habit.

A Synopsis of the North American lichens is in preparation, but, for the present, necessarily laid aside.

AMHERST, MASS.,
    June, 1872.

CONSPECTUS DISPOSITIONIS.

—◆—

Trib. 1. PARMELIACEI. Apothecia rotundata, aperta, excipulo thallino marginata (scutellæformia).

Fam. 1. USNEEI. Thallus verticalis, aut demum pendulus filamentosusve (raro dilatatus depressus) undique sub-similaris.

    1. ROCCELLA.
    2. RAMALINA.
    3. DACTYLINA.
    4. CETRARIA.
    5. EVERNIA.
    6. USNEA.
    7. ALECTORIA.

Fam. 2. PARMELIEI. Thallus horizontalis, foliaceus (raro adscendens filamentosusve) subtus normaliter fibrillosus.

    8. SPEERSCHNEIDERA.
    9. THELOSCHISTES.
    10. PARMELIA.
    11. PHYSCIA.
    12. PYXINE.

Fam. 3. UMBILICARIEI. Thallus horizontalis, umbilicato-affixus.

    13. UMBILICARIA.

Fam. 4. PELTIGEREI. Thallus plano-adscendens, frondoso-foliaceus, subtus venis cyphellisve variegatus. Stratum gonimicum indolis variæ: e gonidiis aut viridibus (solitis) aut cærulescentibus (collogonidiis) constans.

    14. STICTA.
    15. NEPHROMA.

16. Peltigera.
17. Solorina.

Fam. 5. PANNARIEI. Thallus horizontalis, frondoso-foliaceus, dein squamulosus l. crustaceo-diminutus, hypothallo insigni (nunc obsoleto) impositus. Stratum gonimicum indolis variæ; e gonidiis solitis, aut sæpius e collogonidiis constans.

18. Heppia.
19. Pannaria.

Fam. 6. COLLEMEI. Thallus frondoso-foliaceus, dein crustaceo-diminutus, humidus subgelatinosus (raro adscendens filamentosusve). Stratum gonimicum inordinatum: e collogonidiis constans.

Sub-Fam. 1. LICHINEI. Thallus fruticulosus filamentosusve.

20. Ephebe.
21. Lichina.

Sub-Fam. 2. EUCOLLEMEI. Thallus foliaceus (rarissime fruticulosus).

22. Synalissa.
23. Omphalaria.
24. Collema.
25. Leptogium.
26. Hydrothyria.

Fam. 7. LECANOREI. Thallus crustaceus, aut effiguratus aut uniformis.

Sub-Fam. 1. EULECANOREI. Apothecia scutellæformia.

27. Placodium.
28. Lecanora.
29. Rinodina.

Sub-Fam. 2. PERTUSARIEI. Apothecia composita, difformia.

30. Pertusaria.

Sub-Fam. 3. URCEOLARIEI. Apothecia plus minus urceolata.

31. Conotrema.
32. Dirina.
33. Gyalecta.

34. URCEOLARIA.
35. THELOTREMA.
36. GYROSTOMUM.

Appendix. Genus incertæ sedis.
MYRIANGIUM.

Trib. 2. **LECIDEACEI.** Apothecia rotundata, aperta, excipulo proprio (patellæformia).

Fam. 1. CLADONIEI. Thallus duplex: horizontalis, squamulosus aut crustaceus (nunc evanidus) et verticalis caulescens.
37. STEREOCAULON.
38. PILOPHORUS.
39. CLADONIA.

Fam. 2. CŒNOGONIEI. Thallus horizontalis, conferveus.
40. CŒNOGONIUM.
* CYSTOCOLEUS.

Fam. 3. LECIDEEI. Thallus crustaceus, matrici adnatus.

Sub-Fam. 1. B Æ O M Y C E I. Apothecia substipitata
41. BÆOMYCES.

Sub-Fam. 2. B I A T O R E I. Apothecia subsessilia, excipulo disco pallidiore.
42. BIATORA.
43. HETEROTHECIUM.

Sub-Fam. 3. E U L E C I D E E I. Apothecia subsessilia, excipulo atro.
44. LECIDEA.
45. BUELLIA.

Trib. 3. **GRAPHIDACEI.** Apothecia difformia excipulo proprio, sæpius elongata (lirellæformia). Thallus crustaceus.

Fam. 1. LECANACTIDEI. Apothecia subrotunda, patellata, rarius elongata.
46. LECANACTIS.
47. PLATYGRAPHA.
48. MELASPILEA.

63. SEGESTRIA.

64. STAUROTHELE.

Sub-Fam. 2. TRYPETHELIEI. Apothecia plura in stromate collecta.

65. TRYPETHELIUM.

Sub-Fam. 3. PYRENULEI. Apothecia solitaria, perithecio nigro.

66. SAGEDIA.

67. VERRUCARIA.

68. PYRENULA.

69. PYRENASTRUM.

70. STRIGULA.

AN

ARRANGEMENT

OF

THE NORTH AMERICAN

LICHENS.

———•———

Trib. I.—PARMELIACEI (Fr.) Eschw., emend.

Apothecia rotundata, scutellæformia aperta aut raro subglobosa, receptaculo thallino hymenium normaliter discoideum excipulo proprio plerumque indistincto receptum marginante.

It is perhaps not surprising that the marked particularism which has characterized the study of Lichens for the last thirty years should have tended to obstruct, or at least to embarrass those who during this period have sought to comprehend the system as a whole. And it is scarcely too much to say that with whatever acuteness of minute investigation and wealth of new material of illustration the later systematists have adorned their conceptions, they are far yet from having succeeded in invalidating the general argument which binds together, in its grand outlines, the system of Fries. Especially does this appear to be true of the distinction between near and remote affinities (Fr. *Syst. Myc.* I., p. xiv.; *Lich. Eur.* p. 198) and of the reasoning upon which the great bulk of his *Parmeliacei* is brought together, and at once distinguished from and related to his *Lecideacei.* Vast as are these assemblages, they are well defined: which is more than can be said of a large part of those which have been meant to supplant them. And if this difficulty of satisfactory characterization must be admitted to perplex some of the best efforts of recent lichenographers, there is not a little, we shall venture to affirm, in 'modern' lichenology, which fails to reach the level of thought of a Fries or an Eschweiler, on account simply of its limitations.

For reasons to be elsewhere given at length, the *Collemei* are restored here, as by Eschweiler (*Lich. Brasil.*) to the position to which their fruit-characters confessedly point. And it has been found impossible not to agree with Nylander, that however remarkable the peculiarities of *Pertusaria*, this is a type of *Lecanorei*. I deem it proper to add that the whole arrangement of Parmeliaceous Lichens, as now to be set down, was completed, before any part of the important papers of Professor Schwendener (*Untersuch. über d. Flechtenth.* in Naeg. *Beitr.* 2, 3, 4) containing, if I mistake not, much suggestive of not dissimilar results, was known to me.

The *Usneei*, as here taken, are most intimately connected among themselves; and so close is their relation to the *Parmeliei*, that I find it impossible to make these two families other than immediately contiguous. *Umbilicaria*, now generally accepted as belonging to the tribe, is also, through *Omphalodium*, brought very close to *Parmelia ;* and may be regarded as Fries (*L. E.* p. 348) foresaw, the immediate link between this and *Sticta*. It is in *Sticta*, and the other *Peltigerei*, that we reach the true centre of the tribe; which diverges in *Pannaria*, and still further, in the same direction, in *Collemei ;* and descends finally, in *Lecanorei*, to crustaceous types not easily explicable as Parmeliaceous.

There is no doubt that the ground-structure of the apothecia of Lichens is in every respect comparable with that of sporangia of Discomycetous and Pyrenomycetous Fungi (De Bary *Morph. and Phys. d. Pilze*, &c., p. 277, &c. Fr. *Lich. Eur.* p. xli. &c.). And it is scarcely less certain that in all Lichens—*Myriangium*, Berk. and Mont., being excluded—this elementary structure, which Schwendener (*Flora*, 1862-4) and Fuisting (*Dissert.*, Berol. 1865) have especially illustrated, is much the same. All apothecia exhibit, or are at least included in a variously modified proper exciple; and this proper exciple may, in any tribe, be further conditioned by an accessory margin of the substance of the thallus. In the great tribe now immediately before us, embracing so large a proportion of the most distinguished types of Lichens, the thallus assumes however, manifestly, a peculiar importance; and it is not surprising that the thalline receptacle, dignified here, for the most part, as it is, at the expense of the proper exciple, should become itself characteristical.

As respects the spores, the *Parmeliacei* are remarkable for the predominance of the colourless type; and even in the genera referable to the other, or normally coloured series, a very large part is also colourless. The case is the same with the *Lecideacei ;* and we have thus an evident distinction of these especially typical groups of true Lichens from the remaining tribes *(Graphidacei, Caliciacei, Verrucariacei)* looking often towards Fungi, in which the coloured type is predominant.

Reckoning the whole number of species of Lichens as somewhere from 1350 (Nyl. *Syn.* 1, p. 75) to 1750, *Parmeliacei*, as here taken, will include not very far from one-half of the whole; and *Parmeliacei* and *Lecideacei* together, will include not much less than two-thirds.

Fam. 2.—USNEEI, Fr.

Thallus erectiusculus, suffruticulosus, l. passim filamentosus, varie dein dilatatus l. depressus, subcartilagineus.

We can no longer attempt to distinguish sharply as a whole, the fruticulose *Parmeliacei* from the foliaceous (*Parmeliei*), and even habit, which binds together the former in a for the most part easily recognizable chain, is sometimes at fault. The genera are however well marked; and recent lichenographers have sought to turn these differences to account in the construction of higher groups. Whether they have yet succeeded in supplanting the older and simpler arrangement by one practically more useful, may be questioned; but a large amount of new and careful description has resulted, and this may well hereafter find expression in compact characters. Nylander (*Syn.*) has laid especial stress upon the anatomy of the thallus, which Schwendener, still later (*Untersuch. l. supra cit.* 2, p. 109) has further described in great detail. And the former author is here, as everywhere, the most important authority as respects the spermogones and their contents.

With the exception of a single group (*Alectoria*, as understood by Nylander) the whole family belongs to the colourless spore-series. And of this excepted group the spores of every species except two, are also without colour.

Schwendener takes the sharp difference between the symmetrically divergent filaments which constitute the cortical tissue in *Roccella* (Schwend. l. c. t. 6, f. 2. Nyl. Syn. t. 8, f. 3) and the parallel ones of that of *Alectoria* (Schwend. t. 3, f. 14, 22) as the basis of his general disposition of fruticulose Lichens; and the other genera of *Usneei* are found by him to group themselves between these extremes. *Usnea*, as respects the tips of the thallus, agrees with *Alectoria;* but this parallelism of the filaments disappears in the former, with the progress of ramification, in the older portions of the *cortex;* and we find finally a confused network, 'no one direction being predominant.' A similarly confused tissue is more or less characteristical in *Evernia, Cetraria,* and *Ramalina;* which differ, indeed, to some extent, in the predominant direction of the filaments, but exhibit notwithstanding, in the majority of types examined, that symmetrical divergence, which indicates their approach to *Roccella*.

The true place of *Siphula*, Fr., referred to his *Ramalodei* by Nylander, is in fact unknown, apothecia not having yet been seen; but the thallus may perhaps be said to resemble that of *Sphærophorus*, rather more than it does that of *Roccella*. In a not dissimilar lichen of the Sandwich Islands, described many years since by the writer as *S. Pickeringii* (Bot. Wilkes Exped. p. 124, t. 2, f. 4) what were then taken for 'abortive apothecia' are noticed, and, as figured (the specimen is not now within reach) may be said also to suggest the thalline receptacles of *Sphæropho-*

rus. Thamnolia (Ach.) Schær., associated with *Siphula* by Nylander, as by other recent writers, and indeed by Wahlenberg, and Acharius, is however, at any rate, *Cladoniine.*

I.—ROCCELLA, DC.

Ach. L. U. p. 81; Syn. p. 243. Eschw. Syst. p. 23. Fr. S. O. V. p. 237; L. E. p. 33. De Not. Framm. Lich. p. 47. Tul. Mém. sur les Lich. p. 173. Norm. Conatus redact. nov. Lich. p. 13. Mass. Mem. p. 68. Nyl. Syn. 1, p. 257, t. 8, f. 2–5. Schwend. Untersuch. üb. d. Flechtenth. in Naeg. Beitr. 2, p. 165, t. 6, f. 2-17. Th. Fr. Gen. p. 50. Parmeliæ sect., Mey., Wallr. Everniæ sp., Eschw. in Mart. Fl. Bras. 1, p. 219. Roccella sect. B, Stizenb. Beitr. z. Flechtensyst. in Bericht. üb. d. St. Gall. Gesellsch. 1861, p. 175.

Apothecia scutellæformia, lateralia, disco nigricante, hypothecio nigro. Sporæ dactyloideo - fusiformes, quadriloculares, incolores. Spermatia acicularia, arcuata; sterigmatibus sub-simplicibus. Thallus fruticulosus dein pendulus, cartilagineo-coriaceus, intus stuppeus.

Maritime rock - lichens of the warmer regions of the earth, reaching northward as far as the southern coasts of England; nearly related (*affines*) to *Ramalina;* and more remotely (*analogi*) to *Sticta* and *Dirina;* as also, in other tribes, to *Stereocaulon, Platygrapha,* and *Chiodecton.* The type, whether we regard habit, or anatomical characters (upon which compare especially Schwendener, l. c.) is a remarkably distinct one; but the species, even after Nylander's revision, are by no means well - defined. It is in fact still questionable, whether *R. fuciformis* (*Lichen fuciformis,* L.) is properly to be separated from *R. tinctoria* (*Lichen Roccella,* L.) and, in this view, Wallroth's reduction of all the forms known to Acharius to a single species, in which he is followed by Eschweiler (*Bras.*) will appear less strange. The *Roccellæ* are found also, but more rarely, on trees; and our own form, *R. leucophæa,* Tuckerm. Suppl. 1 (Amer. Journ. Sci. 25) p. 423, from the coast of California, — nearest without doubt to the South American *R. intricata,* Mont., and related through that to *R. tinctoria*—has only occurred as yet on the shrub (*Obione*) upon which it was discovered.

Nylander points out the often curious variations of the apothecia of *Roccella,* suggesting now *Platygrapha,* and now even simulating *Lecidea;* it is impossible, however, to question that their type is scutellæform. Of the six species reckoned in the Synopsis of the author last cited, three are inhabitants of Europe, and all but one of South America. A sterile *Roccella,* with the aspect of *R. phycopsis* (Nyl. in *Prodr. Fl. N. Gran.* p. 12) was found by Mr. Wright in Cuba; and reference has been made elsewhere (Syn. Lich. N. Eng. p. 13) to similar specimens seen by the writer in the British Museum, the collection of which they were part purporting to be made "in Carolina, Bermudas, and the Caribbees."

II.—RAMALINA, Ach., De Not.

De Not. Framm. Lich. p. 33. Tul. Mém. p. 26, 168, t. 2, f. 13-15. Mass.
Mem. p. 63. Speerschneid. in Bot. Zeit., 1855, p. 345. Koerb. Syst.
p. 38. Nyl. Syn. 1, p. 287, t. 8, f. 24–31. Schwend. Untersuch. 1. c.
2, p. 155, t. 5, f. 7-11. Th. Fr. Gen. p. 50. Stizenb. Beitr. 1. c. p. 176.
Ramalina, Borreræ sp., and Alectoriæ sp., Ach. L. U. pp. 122, 93, 120;
Syn. pp. 220, 291, 293. Ramalina, et Usneæ sp., Fr. S. O. V. p. 237;
L. E. p. 28. Mont. in Ann. Sci. Nat. 1834. Tuckerm. Syn. N. Eng. p. 12.
Everniæ spp., Eschw. Syst, p. 23. Parmeliæ sect., Mey. Entwick. p. 335.
Wallr. Fl. Crypt. Germ. 1, p. 533. Eschw. Bras. p. 220. Ramalina et
Everniæ dein Desmazieriæ sp., Mont. Bonite Crypt. p. 159; in Ann.
t. 18; Syll. p. 318.

Apothecia scutellæformia, thallo subconcoloria. Sporæ oblongæ,
biloculares, incolores. Spermatia oblonga l. bacillaria; sterigmatibus
pauci-articulatis. Thallus fruticulosus dein pendulus filamentosusve,
plerumque compressus cartilagineo-rigescens, pallidus.

A widely diffused, and difficult genus, of which about half the best
distinguished forms occur within our limits. *R. scopulorum* (Retz) Ach.,
found on maritime rocks throughout Europe, and extending to Iceland
(Th. Fr. *Lich. Arct.*) is however unknown to me as North American;
though reckoned as such by Nylander. But some of the most remarkable
species are peculiar to this continent. *R. reticulata* (Noehd.) Krempelh.
(*R. Menziesii*, Tayl. *R. retiformis*, Menz. *hb.* Tuckerm. Syn. N. E.) is
confined to the coasts of California and Oregon, reaching northwards as
far as Vancouver's Island.——*R. Menziesii*, Tuckerm. Syn. N. E. (*R. lepto-
carpha*, Tuck., Suppl. 1858) is another, large and pendulous Californian
species, also discovered by Menzies, which has added a very unexpected
character to *Ramalina;*—the young fronds being, as it certainly appears,
puberulent! Fronds now sparingly foraminous; and at length sorediiferous. The species is closely akin to *R. reticulata.*——*R. lævigata*, Fr. *S.
O. V.* (Tuck. in Bot. Wilkes exp. *R. Eckloni*, &c., Auctt.) a very wide-
spread lichen throughout the warmer regions of the earth, and often
approaching though pretty readily distinguishable from *R. calicaris*, has
occurred here in Louisiana, Texas and New Mexico.——*R. tenuis*, Tuck.
Suppl., another southern *Ramalina*, with the same range as the last,
must be distinguished, by the spores, into two, otherwise most nearly
related forms, which now grow intertangled together, and can scarcely be
discriminated but by the microscope. One of these forms, with small,
ellipsoid spores, evidently approaches *R. rigida*, Ach. The spores of the
other are fusiform, and at length much elongated, reaching even 0,030-32^{mm}
in length. A nearly terete, torulose, *Usnea*-like *Ramalina*, with conspicuous apothecia, and ellipsoid spores, has occurred lately so far north
as the Pines of New Jersey (Mr. Austin) and belongs without doubt to

the cluster included in *R. tenuis.*——*R. rigida* (Pers.) Ach., Mont. Cuba, p. 234, is a tropical *Ramalina*, disposed by Nylander, together with *R. complanata*, Ach., under the polymorphous *R. calicaris*. It has occurred here, in the marked, compressed state (like Montagne's Cuban lichen) at Key West, Florida (Herb. Torrey). The much slenderer, finally terete lichen also referred to the present place (as by the writer in Wright *Lich. Cub.* n. 51, and by Nylander in *Prodr. Fl. N. Gran.*) should perhaps be further compared with certain supposed states of *R. tenuis.* ——*R. inflata*, Hook. f. and Tayl. Antarct. Voy. Crypt. p. 82, t. 79, f. 1, abundantly collected by Mr. Wright (U. S. N. Pacif. exp.) in China, Japan, and the neighbouring islands, as also at the Cape of Good Hope, and the specimens agreeing with those of Mont. and V. d. Bosch! *Lich. Jav.* p. 3, has much the habit of *R. calicaris* v. *fastigiata*, though differing in the remarkable feature indicated by the name, and is perhaps as widely distributed. A specimen from Arctic America, collected in Franklin's first voyage (*R. fastigiata, Herb. Hook.*) proves to belong to it, and it passes (in the Bonin islands, and in China) into a slender, more elongated, sometimes channelled state (f. *tenuis*) which has occurred to me in New England (trees in the White Mountains, and in Mount Desert, Maine) being readily distinguishable by the more or less evident inflation and sieve-like perforation of the fronds. Nor will a remark of Fries (*L. E.* p. 30, under the already cited variety of *R. calicaris*) on '*specimina in sylvis densis abiegnis lecta, quæ tubulosa, gracilia, ramosissima, cribroso-pertusa,*' permit us to doubt that the lichen is also an inhabitant of Europe. It is certainly interesting as indicating the subordinate systematic value of the tubulose, or cladonioid variation of the Parmeliaceous thallus. Fries has often suggested this, and he calls *R. pusilla* a *Dufourea* in *Ramalina;* and Nylander has taken a similar view of *R. inanis* (Mont.) Nyl., the position of which as a member of the genus is indeed fully mediated by the present, which sometimes (Cape of Good Hope, Mr. Wright) so much resembles the South American species, as to be scarcely distinguishable, but by the spores. I have not been able to observe quite so close a resemblance in R. *inflata* to the Portuguese *R. pusilla* (Welwitsch. *Cr. Lusit.* n. 40, and 43, pr. p.) with its softer and more membranaceous, sometimes gaping but hardly cribrose thallus, but Nylander has not hesitated (*Syn.* l. c.) to throw both lichens together as an extreme variation of *R. calicaris.*——*R. pollinaria*, Ach. (on which see Synops. N. Eng. p. 12) has occurred on stones in New England, and on rocks in New Mexico (Mr. Fendler).——*R. homalea*, Ach., a very distinct and conspicuous, Usnea-like species growing upon rocks on the coast of California, where Menzies discovered it, has long been known; but the nearly akin, South-American *R. ceruchis* (Ach.) De Not., from trees in the same State, has only recently been added to our Flora; my specimens being from Live Oaks at Alcatraz (Mr. Wright) and from St. Angelo (Herb. Russell.) Both of these species, while strikingly anticipating the habit of *Usnea*, may also be regarded as indicating (Fr. *S. O. V.* p. 235, where the former is referred to *Usnea;* Mont. *Diag. Phycol.* p. 2) the close relationship of the present genus to the preceding.

III.—DACTYLINA, Nyl., emend.

Tuckerm. Obs. Lich. in Proceed. Amer. Acad. 5, p. 396. Dufoureæ sp. dubia, Ach. L. U. p. 525; Syn. p. 246. Dufoureæ spp. Hook. Append. Parry's 2 Voy.; et in Richards. Append. Frankl. Narr. p. 762. Dufoureæ spp., Laur. in Sturm D. Fl. 2, 24, p. 27, t. 11, 12. Koerb. Parerg., p. 15. Cladoniæ dein Cetraria sp., Schær. Spicil. p. 43; Enum. p. 14. Everniæ sect. 2, sp., Fr. L. E. p. 24. Everniæ sect. 2, Tuck. Syn. N. Eng. p. 11. Dactylina et Dufourea, Nyl. Syn. 1, p. 286-7. Stizenb. Beitr. l. c. p. 176. Cladoniæ? sp., et Pycnothelia, Th. Fr. Lich. Arct. p. 160; Gen. p. 112.

Apothecia (quantum observ.) scutellæformia, subterminalia, disco thallo discolore. Sporæ sphæróideæ, simplices, incolores. Thallus erectus, dactyloideus ramosusve fruticulosus, turgidus, fragilis, intus stuppeus l. subinanis.

Needle-shaped, straight spermatia, on nearly simple sterigmas (Nyl.) have been observed in *D. madreporiformis* (Wulf.) Tuck. l. c., the apothecia of which are still unknown. The resemblance of *D. muricata* (Laur.) of the Carinthian alps, since found at Bormio (Anz. *Lich. Rar. Langobard.* n. 18) at once to this species, and to *D. ramulosa* (Hook.) Tuck., is however too great to permit us well to doubt that the three are congenerical; and the apothecia and spores of the latter associate it with *D. arctica* (Hook.) Nyl. And whether or not we regard the type of *Dufourea*, Ach., as sufficiently determined by his figure of *D. mollusca* (*Combea*, De Not.) it seems plainly impossible to supplant the well-defined *Dactylina* of Nylander by any reconstruction of *Dufourea* on the basis of *D. madreporiformis.*

Three of the four small, cæpitose, alpine or arctic earth-lichens, here brought together, are inhabitants of North America; and both of the species of which the apothecia are known, are confined to this continent. These apothecia often resemble young ones of *Cetraria cucullata*, but any final evolution like that of the *Cetraria*-fruit must be precluded by the cylindraceous thallus. They are still in some respects comparable with the shields of *C. aculeata*, in which, conditioned in the same way by the tubulose thallus, the obliquity of attachment more or less characteristical of *Cetraria*, is often obscure.

The 'more or less terete, within cottony and fistulous' type of thallus of *Dufourea*, Ach., which appeared sufficiently marked to induce him to arrange under his primary species (*D. mollusca*, L. U. p. 103, t. 11) several others (and among them *D. madreporiformis*) as '*species dubiæ*,' the

fructification of which was unknown, is in fact only of subordinate value
as respects the system, and of possible occurrence within the natural
limits of several genera. Thus *D. flammea*, Ach. (Cape of Good Hope,
Herb. Sonder) is inseparable from *Theloschistes; D. ryssolea*, Ach., is,
according to Nylander, a *Parmelia; and D. inanis*, Mont. (Gaudich. in
herb. Mont.!) clearly a *Ramalina;* its relation to the generical type being
not unlike that of *Cetraria aculeata* (the *Dufourea* of this group of *Cetrariæ*) to *C. odontella* and *C. Islandica.* And the very type of Acharius
(*D. mollusca*, C. B. S., Herb. Sonder) is almost (or, according to Stizenberger, quite) a *Roccella.* There remains only the little cluster of alpine
lichens here referred to *Dactylina*, Nyl.; differing from *Cetraria* proper
rather more than does *C. aculeata;* and possibly also distinguishable by
the spores.

IV.—CETRARIA, Ach., Fr.

Fr. L. E. p. 34. Schær. Spicil. (spp. excl.) p. 248. Tuckerm. Syn. N. Eng.
p. 13. Norm. Con. p. 12. Mass. Mem. (max. p.) p. 56. Stizenb. Beitr.
l. c. p. 175. Cetraria et Corniculariæ spp., Ach. L. U. pp. 96, 124;
Syn. pp. 226, 299. Eschw. Syst. pp. 20, 23. Koerb. Syst. pp. 7, 44.
Th. Fr. Lich. Arct. pp. 29, 35; Gen. pp. 49, 53. Cetraria et Cornicularia, Tul. Mém. pp. 22, 170, 175, t. 10, f. 5. Schwend. Untersuch. l. c. 2,
pp. 151, 177, t. 3, f. 30-33, t. 4, f. 1-12. Cetraria, max. p., et Parmeliæ f., Schær. Enum. pp. 12, 48. Cetraria et Platysma max. p., Nyl.
Syn. 1, p. 298, t. 8, f. 32-5, 43. Cetraria, et Imbricariæ sp., Anz. Catal.
pp. 20, 29. Parmeliæ sect., Mey. Wallr. Eschw. Bras.

Apothecia scutellæformia, subinde dilatata peltæformia, thalli
marginibus apicibusve oblique affixa, disco thallo discolore. Sporæ
subellipsoideæ, simplices, incolores. Spermatia oblonga, apice altero
l. sæpius utroque incrassata vel cylindrica; sterigmatibus pauci-
articulatis. Thallus adscendens, aut fruticulosus lobis l. subteretibus
l. canaliculato-foliaceis, aut expansus; subcartilagineus.

It cannot well be questioned, in view of *Cetraria*, that *Usneei* is immediately contiguous to *Parmeliei.* And universally accepted as is the separation of the bulk of the present genus from *Parmelia*, the limits of the
two groups remain still uncertain. Schærer steadily insisted on even a
conspecific relation between *Cetraria tristis* and *Parmelia lanata, stygia,*
and *Fahlunensis;* referring the cluster to the former genus in his earlier,
and to the latter in his latest work; and he is by no means alone in recognizing the evident points of relationship between all these lichens. But
the first of them (*Cetraria tristis*) is at any rate sufficiently alien in habit
to *Parmelia;* and we cannot wonder therefore that its systematic position
should be still further perplexed. In referring this to his *Cornicularia,*
Acharius took it for congenerical not only with *Cetraria aculeata*, Fr., the

place of which in *Cetraria* may be considered to be determined by *C. Islandica* and *C. odontella*, but no less with *Alectoria divergens*, Nyl. : and it is worthy of note that, after an exhaustive analysis of the little-known apothecia of the last, Nylander (in *Prodr. Fl. N. Gran.* p. 14, n.) goes far to confirm, from this point of view, its otherwise observable resemblance to the first; while Schwendener's remarks on the thalline structure of both, if not conclusive, may be said to point in the same direction. The last-named author, who has no hesitation in accepting the anatomical correctness of Fries's reference of *Cornicularia aculeata*, Ach., to *Cetraria*, and whose results indicate the position of *C. tristis* to be in some sort intermediate between *Cetraria* proper and *Alectoria*, is however once more with Fries, and wholly without doubt, as to the generical distinctness of *A. divergens*. In this uncertainty as to the true place of *Lichen tristis*, it is open to us to fall back upon *Cetraria ;* and declining to recognize the sufficiency, in so loose a genus, of the observed amount of anatomical discrepance, to find, rather, with the author of the *Lichenographia Europæa*, that, whether in thallus or apothecia, *C. tristis* is in fact not illcomparable with *C. odontella*. Nylander has sought to reconstruct the whole group in accordance simply with the characters afforded by the spermogones and spermatia; and he thus separates the two lichens we have just compared: it is important then to notice that no special indication is made by him of the observation of spermogones in *C. odontella ;* and that *C. tristis* is equally included in his *Cetrariei* (our *Cetraria*) a reference the more difficult that the spermogones of the species last named are admitted to point in other directions.——*C. Californica*, Tuckerm. Suppl. 2 (Amer. Journ. Sci., 28) p. 203, a tree-lichen, discovered by Menzies, and looking often rather like a discoloured, small form of *Ramalina calicaris*,[1] but in fact comparable, as respects the thallus, with *Cetraria aculeata*, and, especially as respects the apothecia, with *C. tristis*, proves also to agree with the latter in its spermogones and spermatia ; and constitutes therefore a very interesting addition to our scanty material for the final determination of the place of *C. tristis*.

It is quite impossible summarily to reject the evidence, confirmed now by the spermogones, that *Cetraria aculeata* is inseparable generically from

---

[1] Tulasne (l. c. p. 170) remarks on *C. tristis*, that its whole organization is closely comparable with that of *Ramalina scopulorum ;* with which may be compared Schwendener's observations on *R. calicaris*, &c. (*Untersuch.* l. c. 2, p. 155) and *C. tristis* (p. 150). There is no doubt much to be said against regarding *Lichen tristis* as an exceptionally ascendant *Parmelia*, and the question of its true position might rather be supposed to hang between *Cetraria* and *Alectoria ;* the plant being either united, as an extreme member, to one of these groups, or set up itself as the type of an intermediate one (*Cornicularia*, Hoffm.). But the difficulty remains (as compare Nylander, l. c. p. 307, and Anzi p. 29) of its apparent natural associableness with *Lichen lanatus ;* and this, however Alectoriiform, is yet, with common consent, reduced to *Parmelia*.

C. Islandica; or, notwithstanding the difference in the spermatia, that *C. Islandica* is congenerical with *C. cucullata:* and the bridge is in fact an old and well-accepted one which unites together these parts of one natural whole. We do not then leave the fruticulose *Cetrariæ* without finding them inseparably related to foliaceous forms; and these latter pass insensibly into that Parmelioid type, the varied expressions of which make up the great bulk of the genus. The relations of the plants before us to *Parmelia* are yet, for the most part, practically without difficulty; but the remark seems certainly less true of the relations of certain *Parmeliæ* to *Cetraria.* Here however, not to refer again to Schærer's sweeping judgment, corrected later by himself, the question may be raised if too much has not been made of the alleged distinction in the spermogones. It is difficult, in a full view of the lichen, to appreciate the real difference in this respect which, according to Nylander, should refer *Parmelia Fendleri,* Tuckerm., to *Platysma* of the former writer. And the case is perhaps only less clear as respects *Parmelia Fahlunensis.* So closely related is this plant to *P. stygia,* and so considerable is the amount of variation, as in all other respects so also in the spermogones of each, that, practical and useful as the asserted distinction undoubtedly is for the most part, there is perhaps some reason for the suspicion that it does not always hold good, and that even this criterion is insufficient to separate the species.——*Cetraria chrysantha,* Tuckerm. Suppl. 1 (Amer. Journ. Sci. 25) p. 423 (*Platysma septentrionale,* Nyl. Syn. 1, p. 315) an arctic lichen which Mr. Wright first found fertile in Japan, has the habit and size of the wide-lobed condition of *C. glauca,* but differs conspicuously in colour.

The European *Cetrariæ* are almost all known to be also North American, and a considerable part extends into Northern Asia; but we possess several unknown to Europe, and a larger proportion, including some of the most remarkable forms, is peculiar to Asia.——*C. tristis* is supposed by Dr. Th. Fries *(Lich.·Arct.)* to be scarcely known beyond the European arctic regions, and he cites J. Vahl to the effect that he never saw it in Greenland. It is however reckoned by Hooker (Append. Frankl. Narr. p. 762) among the lichens collected by Richardson in the 'Barren Grounds' of Arctic America.——*C. odontella* was reckoned by R. Brown an inhabitant of Melville Island (Parry's 1st Voy.) but what Mr. Babington has sent me as *C. odontella* of Melville Island, is, I think (the specimen is in fragments) *C. Islandica v. Deliscæi.* Bory sent out Newfoundland specimens of the same lichen (Herb. Kunth) as *C. odontella;* and these led, in the absence of the true plant, to the reference to it (in Syn. Lich. N. Eng. p. 14) of other arctic American specimens (Herb. Hook. Herb. Grev.) of the cited variety of *C. Islandica,* which is very distinct.——*C. lacunosa,* Ach., a very common North American lichen, known to me however only as growing on trees and dead wood, has lately been recognized (Th. Fr. l. c. Nyl. *Lich. Scand.* p. 289) in *rock*-specimens, which were also infertile, of the coasts of Norway.——*C. ciliaris,* Ach., a widely diffused and abundant North American lichen, which Nylander attributes also to Peru, is, to trust to a single fragment in the collection made by Mr. Wright, a native as well of Japan.——*C. chrysantha*, Tuckerm., is another species, common to North America (where it is only known in the western arctic regions) and arctic Asia; but first found in fruit in Japan.——And if the writer (*Obs. Lich.* in Proceed. Amer. Acad. 5, p. 398) has not erred in his recognition of *Dill. Musc.* t. 82, f. 4, the curious *C. Richardsonii*, Hook., is yet another Asiatic lichen, having been collected in Siberia, and sent to Dillenius by J. Ammann.

V.—EVERNIA, Ach., Mann.

Mann. Lich. Bohem. Mass. Mem. p. 60. Koerb. Syst. p. 41. Anz. Catal. p. 19. Th. Fr. Gen. p. 52. Stizenb. Beitr. l. c. p. 176. Evernia et Borreræ sp., Ach. L. U. pp. 84, 93; Syn. pp. 220, 244. Everniæ spp., Eschw. Syst. p. 23. Everniæ spp., Fr. L. E. p. 19. Tuckerm. Syn. N. Eng. p. 9. Parmeliæ sect., Mey. Entwick. p. 335. Wallr. Germ. pp. 490, 526. Schær. Spicil. p. 485. Corniculariæ sp., et Physciæ spp., Schær. Enum. pp. 4, 9. Evernia et Chloreæ spp., Nyl. Syn. 1, pp. 274, 283, t. 8, f. 13, 22. Evernia (max. p.) Schwend. Untersuch. l. c. 2, p. 157, t. 4, f. 13–15, t. 5, f. 1–6.

Apothecia scutellæformia concava subinde dilatata cyathiformia, disco thallo discolore. Sporæ subellipsoideæ, simplices, incolores. Spermatia oblonga l. bacillaria, apicem versus alterum l. utrumque fusiformi-incrassata, vel cylindrica; sterigmatibus pauci-articulatis. Thallus fruticulosus dein pendulus, angulatus vel foliaceo-compressus, mollis, medulla stuppea, rarissime (quoad nostras) passim indurata.

However closely approached by some aberrant Parmelieine types, as *Parmelia Camtschadalis* (Ach.) Eschw., and *Everniopsis*, Nyl., the position of the former of which, at least, is put quite beyond doubt by the similar lobation observable in our *P. perforata*, v. *cetrata*, Nyl., there can be no question that the four lichens which make up *Evernia*, as now generally understood, are genuine members of the *Usneei;* and in closest relation to *Cetraria, Dactylina,* and *Ramalina,* on the one hand, as to *Usnea,* on the other. *Platysma everniellum,* Nyl. (Hook. et Thoms. *Herb. Ind. Or.* n. 2062. *Evernia Stracheyi,* Babingt.) may be said perhaps to be still in question between *Cetraria* and *Evernia.* And *E. vulpina* must be admitted to mediate, as well in general habit as in an important detail of thalline structure, between the other northern species and *Usnea.*

The induration of the *medulla,* upon which character, first fully indicated by Tulasne (*Mém.* p. 27) Nylander separates *E. vulpina* as the type of his *Chlorea,* is yet sufficiently imperfect and irregular in that species; but assumes a much greater regularity in some of the lichens associated by him with it. These lichens are for the most part only imperfectly known; but may be said, as respects at least four out of five of them, to offer what may well appear the structure of *Usnea* with much the habit of *Evernia;* the Everniine habit being however, in two of the species (*E. Canariensis*, and *E. Poeppigii*) confined to the apothecia; and the thallus, in these species, being externally also best comparable with that of certain *Usneæ*. With all which, looking doubtless towards the separation of *Chlorea*, the rank of the new group is by no means as clear as its difference. And it is worth considering that another first step in the transition of *Evernia* into *Usnea* is taken within what is universally accepted as *Evernia* itself; in the strikingly Usneoid *E. divaricata* (*Usnea flaccida*, Hoffm.) the string-like *medulla* of which differs only in the degree of coherence of the filaments that make it up from that of *Usnea*.

In view of the structural modification just considered, it cannot surprise us to find *Evernia* losing at length that softness which has always been taken for one of its characteristical features. The change is sufficiently evident in older as compared with younger portions of *E. vulpina;* and in a not altogether dissimilar lichen of the Himalaya (Hook. et Thoms. *Herb. Ind. Or.* n. 1731. *Chlorea cladonioides*, Nyl.) the horn-like *medulla* of which makes up almost the whole of the thallus, this is in fact rigid.

All four of the well-known northern species are found within our territory. *E. divaricata* is confined to the Rocky Mountains, where it was first detected by Mr. E. Hall. *E. vulpina* is also confined to North-western America, where it is exceedingly luxuriant on the coast, and extends eastward, though here only infertile, as far as the Black Hills, Nebraska (Dr. Hayden).

VI.—USNEA (Dill.) Ach.

Ach. L. U. p. 127; Syn. p. 303. Eschw. Syst. p. 24. Fr. S. O. V. p. 234, sp. excl.; L. E. p. 17. De Not. Framm. p. 26. Tuckerm. Syn. N. Eng. p. 7, sp. excl. Schær. Enum. p. 3. Tulasne Mém. sur les Lich. p. 27. Norm. Con. p. 11. Mass. Mem. p. 72. Speerschneid. in Bot. Zeit. 1854, pp. 193, 209, 233, t. 7. Koerb. Syst. p. 2. Schwend. Untersuch. l. c. 2, p. 110, t. 1, 2. Th. Fr. Gen. p. 47. Stizenb. Beitr. l. c. p. 177. Parmeliæ sect., Mey. Entwick. p. 335. Wallr. Naturgesch. 2, p. 355; Fl. Crypt. Germ. 1, p. 541. Eschw. Bras. p. 226. Schær. Spicil. p. 499. Usnea et Neuropogon, Nyl. Syn. 1, p. 266, t. 8, f. 7–12.

Apothecia orbicularia, peltata, disco thallo subconcolore, l. rarissime discolore. Sporæ subellipsoideæ, simplices, incolores. Spermatia bacillaria, apicem versus alterum fusiformi-incrassata, vel cylindrica; sterigmatibus subsimplicibus. Thallus fruticulosus dein pendulus filamentosusve, teres, undique similaris, medulla duplici, interiori indurata axem sistente lignosum, exteriori stuppea.

The modification of thalline structure upon which, taken in connection with the colour of the apothecia, Nees and Flotow distinguished their

Neuropogon Poeppigii (*Linnæa*, 1834, p. 495) at once from *Evernia* and *Usnea*, remains good; and we may either accept the development of the generic conception, embarrassed though it may be by much that is still uncertain, in *Chlorea*, Nyl.; or, the rather, associating with the South American lichen (Poeppig. *in herb.* Kunz.!) the far from dissimilar *Evernia Canariensis*, Mont. (*Chlorea*, Nyl.) prefer to refer both to an emended *Evernia*. But the other constituent of *Neuropogon* (*N. antennarius*, Nees et Flot.) still retained by Nylander, is, however agreeing in the selected characters with the first, really alien to it; and must remain, with whatever marked difference, in fact an *Usnea* (*U. aurantiaco-atra* (Jacq.) *U. melaxantha*, Ach.). The plant reaches its perfection only in the austral regions of the earth; and the arctic form (found here at Melville Island, and in Greenland) is unknown in a fertile state.

The species of *Usnea* are very widely diffused. Of the nine recognized by Nylander (*Syn.*) as well under *Neuropogon* as *Usnea*, three only of which are European, we possess six. Half of these were first described from North American specimens, but have proved since to have a much wider range.——*U. barbata, a, florida* (the var. *campestris, a,* of Schær. *Spicil.* p. 504) passes into a pendulous condition (v. *campestris, γ,* Schær. l. c.) often sufficiently distinct, and recognizable as the var. *ceratina;* which the Swiss lichenographer has perhaps well restricted to regions *below* those occupied by the other pendulous varieties.——*U. trichodea,* Ach. *Meth.* p. 312, t. 8, f. 1, was described from a Nova Scotia specimen, but has been extended by Acharius and Nylander to cover plants from various regions. The lichen of our northern mountains which seems referable here, appears tolerably distinct, though the '*naked* margin' of the apothecium is not to be depended on; but southward (from New Jersey to Texas) we have another, and often larger, allied form, similar enough in some of its states to the northern plant, but in others approaching closely to *U. longissima;* to which species indeed Nylander now (in *Prodr. Fl. N. Gran.* p. 14, *not.*) refers Acharius's own *U. trichodea* (*L. U.* p. 626) from the Cape of Good Hope. Both the species last-named are distinguishable from filamentous forms of *U. barbata* by their always epapillate thallus.——*U. cavernosa,* Tuckerm. in Agass. L. Sup., Append. (since published as *U. lacunosa,* a ms. designation of Willdenow's, by Nylander, *Syn.*) proves to extend throughout North America, and has also occurred at the straits of Magellan (Commerson!) as well as in Polynesia (Pickering! in Wilkes Exped.) and in the East Indies (Herb. Hook.! Herb. Hook. et Thoms. n. 1718, b!). It is readily recognized by its pitted thallus.

Radiate apothecia are probably common to all *species* of *Usnea;* and the character must be allowed then to possess some value. *U. trichodea* and *U. aurantiaco-atra* are neither of them exceptions, as has been supposed; and the close resemblance of *U. Jamaicensis* to the former of these, and of *U. Taylori,* Hook. f. (the only two *Usneæ* recognized by Nylander in which I have not myself observed the feature) to the latter, makes any important difference in this respect certainly unlikely. Herein also *Evernia vulpina*, as exhibited especially in its finest known condition, on our Pacific coast, conspicuously illustrates the transition of its own generic type into *Usnea*.

VII.—ALECTORIA (Ach.) Nyl.

Nyl. Syn. 1, p. 277, t. 8, f. 16–18, 20–21. Anz. Catal. p. 9. Tuckerm. Lich.
Calif. p. 13. Corniculariæ spp., et Alectoriæ spp., Ach. L. U. pp. 120,
124; Syn. pp. 291, 299. Corniculariæ spp., et Everniæ spp., Eschw.
Syst. pp. 20, 23. Everniæ spp., Fr. S. O. V. p. 236; L. E. p. 20. Tuckerm. Syn. Lich. N. Eng. p. 10. Parmeliæ spp., Mey. Entwick. p. 335.
Wallr. Fl. Crypt. Germ. pp. 530, 540. Schær. Spicil. p. 499. Corniculariæ spp., Schær. Enum. p. 5. Bryopogon, Koerb. Syst., p. 5. Schwend.
Untersuch. 1. c. 2, p. 144, t. 3, f. 1–29. Bryopogon, Alectoriæ sp., et Corniculariæ sp., Koerb. Parerg. p. 4. Bryopogon, Alectoria, Corniculariæ
sp., et Oropogon, Th. Fr. Gen. p. 48. Alectoria et Oropogon, Stizenb.
Beitr. 1. c. p. 176.

Apothecia scutellæformia, innato-sessilia, disco thallo discolore.
Sporæ ellipsoideæ, simplices l. rarissime muriformi-multiloculares,
fuscescentes l. sæpius decolores. Spermatia bacillaria, apicem versus utrumque fusiformi-incrassata; sterigmatibus pauci-articulatis.
Thallus fruticulosus filamentosusve, teres, undique similaris, intus
stuppeus l. subinanis.

The lichens brought together in *Alectoria*, Nyl., though sufficiently
congruous in habit, and recognized as congenerical by Fries and by
Schærer, and, in the important respect of the anatomy of the thallus, by
Schwendener, appear yet to be representative of distinct spore-types, and
have thus come to be considered as constituting, in the opinion of some
recent lichenists, no less than three genera:—*Bryopogon*, Mass., Koerb.,
emended as respects the limitation of the spores in size by Th. Fries,
including the species with colourless spores, or of the type of *A. jubata;*
Alectoria, De Not., those with brown spores of the type of *A. ochroleuca;*
and finally *Oropogon*, Th. Fr., represented only by the South American
A. Loxensis, in which the brown spore attains to its final organization.
It appears however scarcely open to question, with those who recognize
(as we must here) that *Acolium* includes species with [a] simple, [b] biloc-
lar, [c] if we accept *A. Javanicum*, quadrilocular, and lastly, in Europe at
least, muriform-plurilocular spores, or who recognize simple, bilocular, and
quadrilocular spores in *Calicium*, that the spores of *Oropogon* offer no
greater difference from those of *Alectoria*, De Not., than those of *Acolium
Notarisii* from those of *A. Bolanderi;* it being understood that the last-
named lichen is in every respect as strictly congenerical with *A. Californicum*, as is *Calicium paroicum* with the analogously differenced *C. cory-*

nellum. Nor would it be surprising, in view especially of *Coniocybe*, should species of *Calicium* be yet found to occur, the spores of which should be describable as colourless; but it is far from necessary to suppose a case in order to explain, as probably only decolorate, the colourless spores of *Bryopogon;* facts sufficiently illustrative of this being by no means uncommon. And these facts, and others already touched, and to be touched upon hereafter, point not doubtfully, if we mistake not, to something like a rule,—that colour or the want of it being assumed to be, however important, an uncertain element in spore-history, and the ultimate or highest attainable condition of a type of spore being assumed to include, potentially, all the steps of the preceding process of evolution, such ultimate state may be expected to afford, in its total history, an index to the spore-modifications possible within the whole circuit of the natural group or genus to which the species furnishing the ultimate condition belongs. *Buellia petræa* and our *B. oidalea* are cases in point. Both offer the highest (muriform-multilocular) state of the brown type of spore, and, in the freely exhibited process of gradual evolution of this condition, both foreshadow or repeat every spore-modification conceivable within the limits of *Buellia;* and indicate as well the real, decolorate nature of some spores which, from a less comprehensive point of view, might well seem to be typically colourless. *Alectoria Loxensis* (Fée) Nyl. (Lindig *Herb. N. Gran.* n. 2571. *Oropogon,* Th. Fr.) should seem then to be to *A. ochroleuca* much as *Buellia petræa* to *B. coracina,* in which last the spores (Moug. et Nestl. n. 462) are commonly simple; and the apparently colourless spores of *Alectoria sulcata* (Lév.) Nyl. (*Syn.* 1, p. 281, t. 8, f. 20) should be as open perhaps to another explanation as the equally colourless but in fact decolorate ones of *Buellia atro-alba,* v. *chlorospora,* Nyl. (*Catillaria,* Koerb.). The general question thus opened, which is important in its bearing on the validity of many largely accepted genera of Massalongo and other more recent lichenographers, will be further considered in the progress of this work. Suffice it for the present to add that taking into account at once the spores of *Alectoria nigricans,* Nyl., as defined and figured by him (*Lich. Scand.* p. 71 ; *Syn.* t. 8, f. 17) and the exceedingly close (if not questionable) relation in which the lichen stands, in every other respect, to *A. ochroleuca,* it will be as difficult to refuse to make it congenerical with the last, as, in that case, to exclude *A. jubata,* &c., from similar relationship.

Of the eight species reckoned by Nylander (*Syn.*) four are common to the colder regions of the northern hemisphere, and one is peculiar as yet to North Western America. Of the other three, two are natives of the mountains of India; and the other of those of South America.——*A. divergens* (Wahl.) Nyl., is certainly far better comparable with *A. jubata, a, bicolor,* and *A. ochroleuca, a,* than with *Cetraria aculeata;* notwithstanding a degree of external resemblance to the latter. The apothecia of this arctic lichen are very little known, and have been fully described only by

Nylander (in *Prod. Fl. N. Gran.* p. 14, *not.*) who observes in connection with this full revision of the plant that it makes no slight approach to the still embarrassed *Cetraria tristis.*——*A. Fremontii,* Tuckerm. Suppl. 1, l. c. p. 422 (*Evernia Lich. Amer. exs.* n. 52) distinguished by its coarser, pitted thallus, and especially by its larger, yellow-pruinose apothecia (exceeding at length 3$^{mm.}$ in width) from filamentous conditions of *A. jubata,* passes yet into slender forms, which, if infertile, may readily be confounded with the older species.

Usnea has often been regarded, and with justice, as constituting an extreme, and the highest, of *Usneei;* themselves recognizable as the highest extreme of *Parmeliacei,* as of Lichens. And though *Alectoria* in fact brings up the rear in the present, linear arrangement, it is by no means to be taken for (so to say) a descendant of *Usnea.* Much rather would we regard both groups as parallel lines of ascent to *Evernia; Usnea* taking its departure from that modification of *Evernia* which begins in *E. vulpina;* and *Alectoria,* as represented by its principal type (*A. ochroleuca*) from *E. Prunastri.* But the centre of the family is shared with *Evernia* by *Cetraria;* and from the last we have in *Ramalina* a descending line, in another direction, strictly analogous to *Usnea;* as in *Roccella* a sufficient contrast and tolerable counterpart to *Alectoria.* Unlike however to *Alectoria* which we have supposed to constitute a distinct line of deviation from their common centre, parallel with *Usnea, Roccella* descends itself, it might seem, from *Ramalina,* and partakes with it, to at least a certain extent, in its peculiar analogy to *Usnea.*

————•————

Fam. 2.—PARMELIEI.

Thallus horizontalis, foliaceus, expansus (raro adscendus everniæformis, rarissime alectorioides) cartilagineo-membranaceus, subtus normaliter fibrillosus.

In nothing perhaps is the far too artificial character of the Method of Acharius more evident than in his attempted co-ordination of the genera. The remark is substantially Fée's (*Ess.* p. xxi.) but this author, though he led the way in a more natural arrangement, and gave effect to the real affinity of *Umbilicaria,* left yet (*Méth. Lich.* in *Ess.* 1824) the *Peltigerei* between the *Usneei* and *Parmeliei;* including also in the latter the genus *Sticta.* As Fries understood *Parmelia* (*S. O. V.* 1825. *Lich. Eur.* 1831) no other disposition of the *Peltigerei* remained open to him; and he also arranged the latter between the former and *Usneei.* When however the sections of *Parmelia,* Fr., gained gradually acceptance as genera, some reconstruction of the relations of all these groups might well have been looked for; and had been in a measure anticipated by Fries himself, as well as respects the true place of *Umbilicaria* (*L. E.* p. 348) as especially in his consideration, some years later (*Fl. Scan.* 1835) of the transition of *Cetraria* into *Parmelia*. But important as were these suggestions, they remained without fruit; and it was thus left to the writer of this (Lich. Calif. 1866) first to give full expression to the view that the *Parmeliei* are, in every respect, immediately contiguous to the *Usneei*.

Some of the more obvious points of contact of the two families have been noticed already; and all are well known. *Borrera*, Ach., was made up of members of both : and the difficulty which the father of Lichenography found in distinguishing really alien types remained, after Eschweiler had emended, and Fries had finally (*L. E.* pp. 75–8) reduced the genus; recurring in the emended *Evernia* as well of Fries as of Eschweiler; and perpetuated to this day in *Tornabenia*, Trev., and *Blasteniospora*, Trev. (*Theloschistes* Th. Fr.) both of which are still recognized by some as *Usneei*. The even more striking fact that so marked a fruticulose lichen as *Cetraria tristis* is yet in question between *Usneei* and *Parmelia*, has been considered in its place. And against all this, and the general evidence from structure, pointing at once to the superior affinity of *Sticta* to *Peltigerei*, and to the more central and higher place, in the tribe, of the latter, as compared with the *Parmeliei*, there is possibly nothing to set, beyond a certain superficial resemblance in certain *Cetrariæ*, to *Nephroma*. There is no doubt of this resemblance ; especially marked in *C. Stracheyi*, Bab. (Hook. et Thoms. *Herb. Ind. Or.* n. 2074, 2080. *Platysma nephromoides*, Nyl. Enum.) and accompanied in this species also,as in *C. leucostigma*, Lév. (*Sticta Wallichiana*, Tayl. Herb. Hook.) and, if I mistake not, in *C. citrina* Tayl. (*C. Teysmanni*, M. et V. de B. Herb. V. d. Bosch) by the surprising anomaly of what appear to be *cyphellæ ;* but it sinks into insignificance before the generical, and higher differences.

The centre of the *Parmeliei* is seen to be *Parmelia*, of the colourless series; filling here the place which is occupied by four genera in the *Usneei*, and offering analogues, we had almost said, to each. From *Parmelia* deviates *Theloschistes*, of the same series, the analogue of *Ramalina;* while a still greater divergence in the same direction is exemplified in *Speerschneidera*, which it seems possible to consider as in like relation to *Roccella*. In the brown series, on the other hand, the place corresponding to *Theloschistes* is taken by *Physcia*, the analogue here of *Alectoria* in the *Usneei;* and finally by *Pyxine*, an extreme and aberrant type, anticipating, as. respects the fruit, the similarly exceptional, next succeeding family.

VIII.—SPEERSCHNEIDERA, Trev.

Trev., cit. Stizenb., infra. Physcia sect. 2, Tuckerm. Obs. Lich., I. c. 4, p. 388. Nyl. Syn. 1, p. 413. Physcia sect. 3, Stizenb. Beitr. 1. c. p. 173·

Apothecia scutellæformia. Sporæ ex ellipsoideo oblongæ l. dac-

3

tyloideæ bi- rarius quadriloculares incolores. Spermatia oblonga; sterigmatibus pauci-articulatis. Thallus tereti-compressus, dichotomo-ramosissimus, implexus, appressus, cartilagineo-coriaceus, fibrillis obsoletis.

An ambiguous lichen from rocks in western Texas, where it was discovered by Mr. Wright. The appressed-orbicular habit, comparable with that often exhibited by *Parmelia lanata*, but more regular, associates it with the *Parmeliei;* and it possesses, in fact, some general, but superficial resemblance to narrow-lobed states of *Physcia aquila*, v. *detonsa*. Taking *Physcia*, as arranged by Nylander, to include the variously contrasted groups distinguished here as *Theloschistes* and *Physcia*, the plant before us may not appear ill-placed between these groups, though their real point of transition may be rather to be sought in *P. intricata* (Desf.) Schær. The almost terete, or at length compressed-terete, somewhat two-edged thallus of the Texas lichen is neither, however, foliaceous, nor much better comparable with the constricted types of *Physcia* (*P. intricata; P. ciliaris, v. angustata*) from association with which moreover the structurally distinct spores (as we must here regard them) at once separate it; as they do also, the want of any other features of resemblance being taken into consideration, from *Theloschistes*. As it is here placed, a certain analogy with *Roccella* is suggested ; and, at the tips of the thallus at least the plant, though much more delicate, is really comparable in habit with some slender, much-branched forms of *R. phycopsis;* while the spores, though rarely exceeding the bilocular stage, occur in a more developed one, also suggesting *Roccella :* with which genus it yet sharply contrasts in the anatomical features of the thallus. Spores 0.009–0.014 millim., long, by 0.0035–0.0055 millim., wide.

IX.—THELOSCHISTES, Norm., emend.

Tuckerm. Lich. Calif. p. 8. Theloschistes sectt. A, B, Norm. Con. p. 16. Borreræ, Corniculariæ, Dufoureæ, Parmeliæ, et Lecanoræ spp., Ach. L. U.; Syn. Everniæ spp., et Parmelia sect. D (Xanthoria) Fr. S. O. V. pp. 236, 243. Everniæ spp., et Parmeliæ sect. 1, spp., Fr. L. E. pp. 27, 72. Corniculariæ sp., Physciæ spp., et Parmeliæ sp., Schær. Enum. Blasteniospora. Trev., cit. Mass. Tornabenia, Physciæ spp., et Candelariæ sp., Mass. Mem. pp. 41, 146. Koerb. Parerg., pp. 20, 37, 62. Physcia sectt. A, a, B, b, Nyl. Prodr. Gall. p. 59; Syn. 1, p. 406, t. 8, f. 49, 51–2. Physcia sect. 1, Tuckerm. Obs. Lich. l. c. 4, p. 384. Theloschistes et Xanthoria sect. A, Th. Fr. (Lich. Arct. p. 66) Gen. pp. 51, 60. Physcia, Mudd Man. Brit. Lich. p. 111. Xanthoria, Stizenb. Beitr. l. c. p. 173.——Structuram exposuerunt Tulasne, Mém. pp. 16, 43, 60, 144, t. 1, f. 1–7 ; Schwendener, Untersuch. l. c. 2, pp. 158, 162, t. 5, f. 16, 17 et 3, pp. 154, 160, t. 8, f. 10–13.

Apothecia scutellæformia, disco luteo-aurantiaco. Sporæ polari-biloculares [rarissime, in sp. exot., quadriloculares] incolores. Spermatia ellipsoidea l. oblonga; sterigmatibus multi-articulatis. Thallus foliaceus squamulosusve appressus, aut adscendens erverniæformis, cartilagineo-membranaceus; plerumque flavicans.

Ideally considered, the polar-bilocular spore may be said possibly to mediate between the brown type, and the less highly organized, colorless one : in nature however, the first is, on the whole, as distinct as either of the others; and the groups characterized by it are also curiously marked by external features of difference. We cannot but adopt the oldest name for the group now before us, which, as here limited, becomes exactly equivalent to *Xanthoria*, Stizenb.; and brings together the species represented by *Lichen parietinus*, whether octosporous or polysporous (*Xanthoria*, A, Th. Fr.) and those of which *Lichen chrysophthalmus* is taken for the type (*Theloschistes*, Th. Fr.). Widely as authors have differed with respect to its constituents, the genus, so taken, is, notwithstanding, in several respects, a natural one; distinguishable readily from the other members of the present family, and, by its typically subfoliaceous thallus, separable as well from *Placodium*, of the *Lecanorei*. It is indeed at once seen that the squamulose conditions of *T. parietinus* (from some of which conditions *T. candelarius* widely differs only in its polysporous thekes) cannot be far separated from their foliaceous type; nor do the ascendant species (*T. chrysophthalmus*, the key to *T. cymbaliferus* (Eschw.) and *T. villosus*) diverge from this, other than were beforehand conceivable in a group so near to *Usneei*, and especially to *Ramalina ;* or other than (exactly) analogously to the ascendant varieties of *Physcia speciosa* and *P. ciliaris : —* but the case is possibly less clear as regards the relation of *Placodium*. There is yet no doubt that *Placodium elegans*, whatever resemblance may be found between its finest conditions and *Theloschistes parietinus*, is yet a member of another group; or that this other group is related to *Theloschistes*, precisely as *Lecanora*, as here taken, is related to *Parmelia*.[1]

Of the eight species, referable here, reckoned by Nylander (*Syn.*) the two foliaceous ones (*T. parietinus, T. candelarius*) are widely diffused, and belong at once to tropical and boreal, as well as austral latitudes : the remainder are natives of the warmer regions of the earth; only one (*T. chrysophthalmus*) extending far beyond them. But it is certainly probable that the number of species, as given, and generally received, is in fact too large. It would not indeed be practical to attempt to revive (*except. excip.*) the criticism of Wallroth (*Naturgesch.* 2, 333) and Meyer,

---

[1] This did not escape Norman; who, as he combined *Placodium* (DC.) Naeg. and Hepp, with his *Theloschistes*, consistently also reduced *Lecanora* (including *Squamaria*, DC.) to his *Parmelia*. (*Con.* p. 14.

and to reduce the group to modifications of but two specific types; *T. pa-rietinus* reclaiming *T. candelarius*, and *T. chrysophthalmus* being forced to include the whole of the ascendant cluster; — but no doubt this criticism has its rights. It appears impossible, in any large view, to extricate " *Physcia flavicans* " from the web of recognized varieties of *T. chrysoph-thalmus;* or clearly to distinguish *Physcia hypoglauca*, Nyl. (Lindig *Herb. N. Gran.* n. 22, 2595) however interesting in its spores, from the same. And *Dufourea flammea*, Ach. (*Physcia*, Nyl.) as exhibited in the instructive specimens of Drège, and interpreted by Laurer (*Herb.* Sonder) is only an instance in the present genus, and in *T. parietinus*, of a thalline anomaly, of which both the next succeeding genera exhibit marked and yet satisfactorily determinable examples. Nor is this the only proof that the foliaceous centre of *Theloschistes* is itself conditioned by the same *nisus* to ascend which marks the whole group; and relates it so intimately to the *Usneei*.

The species, etc., reckoned in the author's Synopsis, were revised in *Obs. Lich.* (l. c.) and those added which are found only southward of the limits of the earlier enumeration. Among these are the elongated conditions of *T. chrysophthalmus* (*Borrera pubera*, and *B. flavicans*, Ach.) which, as respects the pubescent state, and the wholly smooth and esorediate one, are confined to our extreme southern States and California; where only, with us, the lichen is fertile. Sorediate (sterile) forms, which are not deficient at the south (Galveston Bay, Texas, Mr. Ravenel) occur, however, also far northward (Nantucket, myself; and even Newfoundland, Nyl. *Syn.*) but without doubt only in maritime districts.——*T. parietinus*, v. *lychneus*, occurring with us precisely as in Europe (*Physcia controversa*, Mass., Koerb. p. 38) is a well-marked and elegant lichen, almost as deserving of specific distinction, one should say, as *T. candelarius;* but yet running very close, in its narrower and smoother state, to the v. *polycarpus* of the species first named. —— *T. parietinus* v. *Finmarkicus*. Ach., (*Borrera pygmæa*, Bory) commonly associated, as, an ascendant form, with the variety just considered, has occurred in Alaska (Dr. Kellogg) and proves to be common on the coast of California (Bolander. —— *T. parietinus* v. *ramulosus*, Tuckerm. Lich. Calif. (*Physcia pariet.* v. *ramulosa, Obs. Lich.* l. c.) is a curious and easily distinguishable Californian lichen, combining, with semi-terete lobes, much of the aspect of *T. candelarius* with the thekes and spores (and chemical reaction, with potash) of *T. parietinus*.

X.—PARMELIA, Ach., De Not.

Parmelia, De Not., cit. Mass. Mem. p. 48. Th. Fr. Lich. Arct. p. 51; Gen. p. 58. Mudd. Man. Brit. Lich. p, 92. Parmeliæ spp., et Borreræ, Dufoureæ, et Corniculariæ spp., Ach. L. U., Syn. Parmelia sect. Imbricaria (spp. citrin. excl.) Fr. L. E. p. 57. Tuckerm. Syn. N. Eng.

p. 23. Parmelia et Menegazzia, Mass. Neag. p. 3. Parmelia, Platysmatis spp., et Squamariæ spp., Nyl. Prodr.; Syn. 1, pp. 375, 309. Imbricaria et Menegazzia, Koerb. Parerg. p. 28. Imbricaria (I. tristi excl.) Anz. Catal. p. 25. Parmelia (Everniopsi excl.) et Anzia, Stizenb. Beitr. l. c. p. 174.

Structuram descripserunt Tulasne, Mém. p. 139, t. 2, f. 18–23; Speerschneider, in Bot. Zeit. 1854, pp. 481, 499, t. 12; Schwendener, Untersuch. l. c. 3, p. 157, t. 8. f. 3–6.

Apothecia scutellæformia, subpodicellata. Sporæ ex ovoideo ellipsoideæ oblongæve, simplices, incolores. Spermatia oblonga medio constricta apicibus plerumque acutis, raro acicularia; sterigmatibus pauci-articulatis l. subsimplicibus. Thallus foliaceus, lobatolaciniatus, appressus, raro adscendens everniæformis, rarissime constrictus filiformis, submembranaceus.

Of the (fifty, more or less) conspicuous forms belonging to this genus, nearly two-thirds occur within our territory. The central, typical character of the group is indicated by the marked predominance of horizontal forms; but its near relation to the preceding family is also evident, not only in the depressed *Cetrariæ*, but in its own tendency, observable in every well-developed subdivision, to pass into ascendant, evernioid states. Considered in its full extent, the subdivision represented by *P. lævigata* may be taken as exhibiting most fully the generical type. This species touches, on the one hand, an American lichen (*P. cetrata*, Ach., itself a state of *P. perforata*) and through this is immediately connected with *P. perlata*, which, though looking rather away from the present genus towards *Cetraria*, is yet of all others most remarkable for size ; while, on the other, and in its own line of differentiation (analogous to the specific evolution of *Physcia speciosa* as here taken) we have an elegantly diversified series of Parmeliine forms, passing at length into Physcioid (*P. physcioides*, Nyl., the same it should seem with *P. pinnatifida*, *Herb. Berol.*) and finally, in *P. Camtschadalis* and its variety *Americana*, Nyl., now simulating *Evernia furfuracea*, and now even *Physcia speciosa*, v. *leucomela*. And it adds still further to the interest of this subdivision, that, though normally glaucescent, it often oversteps its series, and appears in ochroleucous forms. Such are *P. (perlata) latissima*, v. *flavida*, Nyl. (Lindig *Herb. N. Gran.* n. 740) as also a similarly marked condition (*P. perlata* v. *flavicans*, Lich. Calif.) from California (Bolander) the last comparable rather with common states of *P. perlata* except in the larger spores ; and one also (occurring from Harper's Ferry in Virginia to Louisiana) with the other peculiar features of *P. crinita*, Ach. Nor is this tendency to an intenser coloration confined to the cetrarioid wing of the group of species before us; being also marked in *P. lævigata* v. sinuosa, Nyl., and in other varying, tropical forms, as *P. reducens*, Nyl.

(Lindig *Herb. N. Gran.* n. 799) as well as in a corresponding condition of *P. tiliacea* (v. *flavicans*, Tuckerm. in Wright *Lich. Cub.* n. 74). And what is possibly quite as remarkable is the similar change of color of the medullary tissue in *P. sulphurata*, Nees and Flot., *P. aurulenta*, Tuckerm., and P. *isidiocera*, Nyl. —— The evernioid *revergence* of this subdivision is observable also in *P. perforata ;* which, in the var. *cetrata*, Nyl., passes, more or less, into narrowed, many-cleft, channelled lobes, comparable often, apart from their type, with nothing but *P. Camtschadalis.*—— And it is with the same extreme type of *Parmelia* that one is tempted to compare the elongated, lax forms of *P. physodes*. That this species is near akin to *P. colpodes (Anzia*, Stizenb.) cannot well be denied ; but the anomalies and contradictions of the cluster, so constituted, are unexampled in the genus.

But the accumulation of marked features which distinguishes the group here typified by *P. lævigata* is not yet complete. *P. saxatilis* and its nearest allies belong to the group: and, in a well-known, alpine condition of the former (v. *omphalodes*, Hoffm.) it passes also into the brown series ; now very briefly to be considered. We have here, not to more than allude to the everniæform *P. ryssolea*, Nyl. *(Dufourea*, Ach.) or the still more anomalous *P. lanata*, Nyl. *(Cornicularia*, Ach.) so distinct an approach in *P. Fahlunensis*, as respects at least the spermogones, to *Cetraria*, that the predominantly Parmeliine character of the plant, and its admitted, close affinity to *P, stygia*, have proved insufficient, with the most learned lichenographer of the day, to retain it in *Parmelia*. It must, however, be admitted that the systematic value of the spermogones and spermatia is extremely uncertain ; and an illustration of this is afforded by the little cluster of species made up of *P. aleurites*, *P. placorodia*, and *P. ambigua*. Judged by the spermogones and their contents, these species, as Nylander has shown, might almost seem in difficult proximity to *Lecanora* § *Squamaria;* but the real stress of their affinities keeps them, without doubt, in *Parmelia*.

P. sulphurata, Nees and Flot., occurs fertile in Louisiana (Hale.) —— *P. aurulenta*, Tuckerm. Suppl. 1, l. c. p. 424; Nyl. *Syn.* p. 382, distinguished, like the last, by its pale-yellow medullary tissue, occurred originally on rocks in Virginia, but has been sent to me from most parts of the south, and from Illinois (E. Hall.) —— *P. Texana*, of the same memoir, is sorediiferous, and especially comparable with small, smoothish, southern states of *P. Borreri;* the lobes, in my numerous specimens, showing scarcely any trace of that tendency to elongation˜so characteristical of the American *P. tiliacea* (*P. scortea* '*lobis longiusculis*,' Ach. Syn.) though the lichen sufficiently agrees with the latter in the spores, and is referred to it by Nylander *(Syn.* p. 383.) —— *P. aleurites*, Ach., Sommerf., Nyl., (*P. hyperopta*, Ach., *Imbricaria*, Koerb.) is the *fertile* plant so named in Syn, Lich. N. Eng. p. 27, and is common in the higher forest (black growth) of the White Mountains, very often in company with *P. ambigua*.

With it has often been confounded, and by Acharius as well, a state of the next.——In *P. placorodia* (Ach., Nyl.) the latter author has satisfactorily united (*Lich. Scand.* p. 106) the North American lichen described as *P. placorodia* by Acharius (Tuckerm. *exs.* n. 71) with the European *P. aleurites*, v. *diffusa*, Ach. The first of these plants belongs evidently to the cetrariæform wing of *Parmelia*, and was described as *Cetraria* in Syn. Lich. N. Eng., being well comparable (except in the spermogones) with *C. ciliaris*, on rails, its constant companion, and *C. aurescens*. The other, more unmistakably Parmeliine, and always scurfy, so as to resemble a good deal *P. Borreri*, v. *rudecta*, is a common rail-lichen of New England, not rarely fertile, at least in the interior. The spores, as Koerber (*Syst.* p. 73) first pointed out, well distinguish this species from the immediately preceding. The two, together with *P. ambigua*, are remarkable (Nyl. l. c.) for their elongated, cylindrical spermatia. ——*P. Fendleri* (Tuckerm. in Nyl. *Enum. Gén.* Lich. Calif. p. 14. *Platysma*, Nyl. Syn. 1, p. 309) discovered on coniferous trees in New Mexico by Fendler, occurred to me abundantly on pines, and rails adjoining in Maryland, and has been found by Mr. Ravenel (also on pines) in South Carolina, and by Dr. Michener in New Jersey; the tree specimens being more lax and diffuse, and the rail-lichen with more of the habit of similar conditions of *Cetraria ciliaris*, with which it grows. The plant compares exactly in these respects with the original *P. placorodia*, Ach. (Tuckerm. *exs.*) and equally with that, belongs, as it appears to me, quite without doubt, to *Parmelia*. Spermogones never marginal in the strict sense in which this is true of *Cetraria;* nor in fact differing in any important respect from those of *Parmelia stygia.* ——*P. olivacea*, Ach., here as elsewhere is much modified in its saxicoline states (v. *prolixa*, Ach., Nyl.) becoming at length narrowly divided, and passing often into densely imbricated small lobes (f. *panniformis*), or besprinkled with rounded soredia (f. *dendritica*, Nyl. *Imb. Sprengelii*, Floerk., Koerb.) The last has only occurred to me (on granite rocks in the White Mountains, and near Boston) sterile, but the smooth form has been found fertile in Vermont (C. C. Frost). ——*P. molliuscula*, Ach., as interpreted by Nylander (*P. chlorochroa*, Tuckerm. *Obs. Lich.* l. c. 4, p. 383) which represents, in the ochroleucous, that evernioid tendency which we have found in both the other series, is found here abundantly in the lower regions of the Rocky Mountains; as also at the Cape of Good Hope and in Peru (Nyl.) I also possess it from the Asiatic deserts of Soongaria (*Herb.* Spreng). —— What is *P. congruens*, Ach., Nyl.? The lichen was originally described from specimens collected by Swartz, and he says of it (*Lich. Amer.* p. 5) that it inhabits *trees* in North America, and, more particularly, in New England. *P. congruens* of *Herb.* Floerk. (Camtschatka, Tilesius) is possibly the same with *P. molliuscula* v. *vagans*, Nyl., now referred by him *(Lich. Scand.)* to a form of *P. conspersa;* and is, at any rate, a rock-lichen. *P. congruens*, Spreng. *Syst.* 4, 1, p. 286, is, to judge by his own specimen (*Herb.* Spreng in *Herb.* V. d. Bosch) the smooth, North American form of *Sticta glomerulifera* (Tuckerm. *exs.* n. 105).

XI.—PHYSCIA (DC., Fr.) Th. Fr.

Th. Fr. Lich. Arct. p. 60. Stizenb. Beitr. l. c. p. 173 (P. euploca excl.) Physciæ spp., et Imbricariæ spp., DC. Fl. Fr. Borreræ spp., et Parmeliæ spp., Ach. L. U.; Syn. Hageniæ spp., et Parmeliæ spp., Eschw. Syst. p. 20. Parmelia sect. Physcia max. p., Fr. S. O. V. p. 243; L. E. p. 76. Eschw. Bras. p. 194. Tuckerm. Syn. N. Eng. p. 32. Hagenia, De Not. Framm. p. 7. Dimelæna sect. A, et B max. p., Norm. Con. p. 19. Physcia et Lobaria, Naeg. et Hepp. in Hepp Abbild. t. 1. Anaptychia, Koerb., Mass. Mem. p. 33. Anaptychia et Parmelia, Koerb. Syst. p. 49, 84. Anaptychia et Squamaria, Mass. Symm. p. 74. Physcia sect. A, b, et B, b, Nyl. Prodr. Gall. p. 59. Physcia sect. A, b, et B, c, Nyl. Syn. 1, p. 406, t. 8, f. 50, 53. Tuckerm. Physc. in Obs. Lich. l. c. 4, p. 384. Parmelia, Anz. Catal. Sondr. p. 29. Borrera, Mudd Man. Brit. Lich. p. 103. Physcia et Tornabenia, Th. Fr. Gen. pp. 51, 59.

Structuram expos. Tulasne, Mém. pp. 43, 63, 161, t. 1, f. 8–16, t. 2, f. 16–17; Speerschneider, in Bot. Zeit. 1854, pp. 593, 609, 625, t. 14; Schwendener, Untersuch., l. c. 2, p. 161, t. 5, f. 12–13, et 3, p. 154, t. 8, f. 1–2, 14.

Apothecia scutellæformia. Sporæ ellipsoideæ, biloculares [rarissime, in spp. exot., quadri-pluriloculares] fuscæ. Spermatia ellipsoidea vel oblonga; sterigmatibus multi-articulatis. Thallus foliaceus, ramoso-laciniatus, stellatus, aut adscendens erverniæformis, subcartilagineus.

Differing from *Parmelia* in general habit no less than in essential characters, as Fries first pointed out, *Physcia* is, in the same way though less decidedly, separable also from *Theloschistes.* Schwendener has largely shown the contrast between the confused tissue which constitutes the cortical layer in *Parmelia*, and the well-defined parenchyma of the more strictly foliaceous *Physciæ*, and the foliaceous forms of *Theloschistes;* while in his exposition of the relative thickness of the same layer, this writer has also explained what is no doubt the principal cause of the palpable difference between the more membranaceous thallus of *Parmelia*, and the more cartilagineous one of *Physcia*. It is, however, in its relations to *Theloschistes* that the group before us, typically indeed Parmeliine, but exhibiting a more evident tendency to pass into ascendant states than *Parmelia*, is especially interesting. *Physcia ciliaris* and *speciosa* are to *P. stellaris* exactly as *Theloschistes chrysophthalmus* to *T. parietinus;* and this is the same as to say that the modifications of thalline structure (Schwend. l. c. 3, p. 155) which should confirm the generical separation of the ascendant forms *(Anaptychia*, Koerb. *Syst. Tornabenia*, Mass.) penetrate really, in *Physcia*, within the circuit of the horizontal ones; — these last (or the horizontal *Physciæ* agreeing anatomically with *P. ciliaris)* being themselves reconcilable, as Nylander has shown *(Syn.)* with the cluster represented by *P. stellaris*, through the mediation of other states, associable together in every other respect, in *P. pulverulenta.*

It was not within the proposed scope of the skilful vegetable anatomist first cited to compare generally the apothecia of *Physcia* and *Parmelia*, but Fries had already done this: and it was only left to De Notaris *(Framm. Lich.* 1844) to show the uncertainty of the supposed distinction between the presence or absence of gonidia in the portion of thallus immediately under the hypothecium;[1] and fully to describe the spores. By this description the spore-character of the genus was shown to possess a remarkable precision and uniformity, and no exceptional facts offered, to disturb the estimate. That another estimate was however possible, might well have been inferred from the spore-phenomena of other groups; and such amended valuation has now become necessary. If then we look at the bilocular modification exhibited by the spores of most *Physciæ* as only one of a series of changes accomplished, in the process of its differentiation, by the brown spore, the value of this modification, in the system, is at once qualified; and there will be no presumption, but the contrary, against the possible occurrence of any or all the other gradal differences of the same spore-type, within the circuit of the same natural genus. And Nylander has described, within the small cluster represented by *P. obscura*, quadrilocular spores (*P. obscurascens*, Nyl. *Syn.* 1, p. 429) and 6-8-locular, verging on sub-muriform (*P. plinthiza*, Nyl. Lich. N. Zeal. in Linn. Soc. Lond. Journ. 9, p. 249).[2]

About two-thirds of the more conspicuous forms of the genus are known to occur within our territory. As compared with *Parmelia*, in which species extending northward are largely predominant, *Physcia* has a

[1] See the cited memoir under *Hagenia obscura* and *H. stellaris* (p. 11) and also under *Ricasolia* (p. 5) and *Ramalina* (p. 33). The variableness of the point in question might also be illustrated from *Parmelia*, and *Usnea;* but the character has kept its place in the books, with few exceptions. On a full review of the forms of *Lecanora subfusca*, Stizenberger (*Bot. Zeit.* 1868, n. 52) has found it impossible, — in which conclusion, the present writer, having repeated his analysis with some care, cannot but accord — to allow this feature even specifical weight; *L. Parisiensis,* Nyl. (*Lich. Jard. Luxemb.* in *Bull. Soc. Bot. Fr.)* proving to be quite inseparable from the older species.

[2] The modification of spore-structure exhibited in *P. obscurascens* is foreshadowed indeed in the spore-history of the ascendant conditions of *P. speciosa* (Tuck. in Wright Lich. Cub. n. 82, 83) as Nylander (*Syn.* p. 415) has fully indicated; but it is easy to see that the spores of this noble species, taken in its full extent, are typically bilocular.

4

southern range ; and the recent additions to our North American Flora have been almost wholly southern. *P. speciosa* passes with us also, as within the tropics, into its ascendant forms (v. *podocarpa;* v. *galactophylla*) and the last becomes also elongated (v. *leucomela*, Eschw.) but has not yet been found in the extremest, decumbent state.——In like manner *P. stellaris*, though its centre is not so clearly tropical as that of the last mentioned species (*P. speciosa*, v. *hypoleuca*, Ach.) yet reappears, if I am not mistaken, in the warmer regions of the earth, in many elegant forms ; of which two, — the var. *astroidea*, especially as characterized and diversified in the form *obsessa* (*Parm. obsessa*, Mont.) and the var. *Domingensis* (*Parm. Domingensis*, Mont., *Ph. crispa*, Nyl.) are found from Carolina to the Gulf of Mexico; and the former extends also northward.—— *P. picta* (Sw.) Nyl. (*Parmelia applanata*, Fée) is a very distinct, tropical species, occurring throughout the country south of Carolina, and especially interesting on account of its general resemblance to the next genus; which in one of its species even simulates the apothecia of the *Physcia*.

XII. PYXINE, Fr.

Fr. S. O. V. p. 267. Mont. Pl. Cell. Cuba, p. 187. Nyl. Lich. exot. in Ann. Sci. Nat. 4, 11, p. 255, not. ; Syn. Lich. N. Caled. p. 20. Tuckerm. Obs. Lich. l. c. 4, p. 400. Stizenb. Beitr. l. c. p. 157. Lecideæ spp., Ach. L. U. p. 216 ; Syn. p. 54. Circinariæ spp. Fée Ess. p. 127. Lecidea sect. Pyxine, Eschw. Bras. p. 245, 256. Parmelia sect. Pyxine, Tuckerm. Syn. N. Eng. p. 35.

Apothecia sub-scutellæformia, mox nigricantia. Sporæ oblongo-ellipsoideæ, biloculares, fuscæ. Spermatia oblonga; sterigmatibus pauci-articulatis. Thallus foliaceus, imbricatim lineari-laciniatus, subcartilagineus.

With a thallus and spermogones comparable in most respects with those of *Physcia picta*, itself extraordinarily differenced by its black hypothecium, we have in *Pyxine* (which thus anticipates in the present, the immediately succeeding family) the Parmeliaceous apothecium transformed into what is, to all appearance, the Lecideine ; even the modifications of this altered state repeating those of *Lecidea*. The development of the young fruit is however strictly Parmelieine ; and, carefully observed, this fruit is seen also, even in *P. Cocoes*, to be sometimes pale, or even white (Tuckerm. Syn. N. Eng. p. 24) at the base. And in *P. Meissneri* (*Obs. Lich.* l. c. 4, p. 400) the dealbation (for it is the denigration which is typical here) extends finally to the whole exciple ; then undistinguishable from that of *Physcia*.

The few known species are most closely akin, and confined to the warmer regions of the earth, excepting only *P. Cocoes* v. *sorediata* (*Obs. Lich.*, l. c. *Pyxine sorediata*, Fr.) which, hardly distinguishable, in the tropics, from the species to which it is here referred, extends far north-ward, occurring throughout the extent of the United States, as of Canada (A. T. Drummond) and presenting the maximum of development, as well as of typical distinctness attained by the genus.——*P. Cocoes, a,* is represented in Louisiana (Hale).

———•———

Fam. 3.—UMBILICARIEI.

Thallus horizontalis, foliaceus, coriaceo-cartilagineus, submon-ophyllus, substrato per gomphum affixus.

XIII.—UMBILICARIA, Hoffm.

Hoffm. Pl. Lich. 1, 1, p. 9, et Fl. Germ. p. 109. Fr. S. O. V. p. 266 ; L. E. p. 347. Tuckerm. Syn. N. Eng. p. 69. Schær. Enum. p. 23. Norm. Con. p. 25, t. 2, f. 19, a, b. c. Nyl. Lich. exot. in Ann. 4, 11, p. 217 ; Lich. And. Boliv. in Ann. 4, 15, p. 375; Lich. Scand. p. 113. Gy-rophora et Lecideæ spp., Ach. Meth. pp. 85, 100. Gyrophora, Ach. L. U. p. 36; Syn. p. 63. Turn. et Borr. Lich. Brit. p. 211. Eschw. Syst. p. 21. Gyromium, Wahl. Lapp. p. 481. Umbilicaria et Gy-rophora, Fée Ess. p. 68; Suppl. p. 8. Flot. in Bot. Zeit. 1850, p. 364. Naeg. et Hepp. in Hepp. Abbild. t. 1. Koerb. Syst. p. 93. Th. Fr. Lich. Arct. p. 163; Gen. p. 78; Lich. Spitzenb. p. 31. Mudd Man. Brit. Lich. p. 115. Stizenb. Beitr. l. c. p. 156. Lecideæ spp., Mey. Entwick. Umbilicaria et Lecideæ spp., Schær. Spicil. pp. 80, 104. Graphidis spp., Wallr. Umbilicaria et Macrodictya dein Lasallia, Mass. Ric. pp. 59, 60; Mem. p. 118.

Structuram exposuerunt Tulasne, Mém. p. 21, 181, t. 5, f. 5–20 ; Schwendener, Untersuch. l. c. 3, pp. 150, 179, t. 8, f. 15–17, t. 10, f. 10–13.

Apothecia subscutellæformia, denigrata, plerumque demum lirel-loso-prolifera. Sporæ subellipsoideæ, e simplici mox granulosæ, rarius dein muriformi-multiloculares, fuscescentes. Spermatia ob-longa; sterigmatibus multi-articulatis. Thallus ut supra.

It was long before the strangely modified apothecia of this genus were understood. Associated by Acharius with his *Idiothalami,* Umbilicaria came thus into a forced connection at once with *Lecidea,* and *Opegrapha;* and was reckoned as nearest now to the one and now to the other of these groups. Fries indeed remarked (*L. E.* p. 348) the ' many approxi-mations to the present genus among the *Stictæ* . . . and *Parmeliæ,* especially the exotic, umbilicate species of the latter, as compared with

U. atropruinosa,' and suggested that it might hereafter appear that the natural position of *Umbilicaria* were between the other two genera named. '*Est omnino,*' he adds, four years later (*Fl. Scan.* p. 280) '*ex hac grege*' (*Graphideis*) '*removendum, et inter Stictas et Parmelias inserendum.*' But Flotow (l. c.) first gave definite expression to this conception. He declared the apothecia of the *Umbilicariei* to be '*imperfect scutellæ*' (*unvollständige Scutellen*) and by adding to it the exotic, '*umbilicate Parmeliæ*' (*Omphalodium*, M. and Flot., Koerb.) left no longer any ground to question its position. Koerber (Syst. p. 92) maintains the same view, restricting however *Omphalodium* to the exotic species; and Nylander, who does not admit the latter genus as distinct from *Parmelia*, agrees in the Parmeliaceous character of *Umbilicaria*. There seems to be no reason to doubt that the two remarkable lichens brought together in *Omphalodium* (*Sticta hottentotta*, Ach., and *Parmelia Pisacomensis* (M. and Flot.,) Nyl.) satisfactorily mediate between the *Parmeliei* and *Umbilicaria*, to whichever family we refer them; but it is perhaps less easy, on the whole (nothwithstanding the evidence of the spermogones, Nyl. *Syn.* p. 399) to reconcile them with the former than with the latter, from which (*Umbilicariei*) indeed, *P. Pisacomensis* might be regarded as chiefly differing in being a less abnormal member of the family. *P. hottentotta* is at first sight more difficult, exhibiting as it does the habit as well as the coloration of many *Stictæ;* the spores however are in fact by no means alien to certain conditions of those of *Umbilicaria*, and the plant may be conceived as occupying a place in the *Umbilicariei* immediately analogous with *Parmelia* in the *Parmeliei*. In this view stress is of course laid on the (often stalk-like) disk, by which these plants are attached to the rock-surface on which they grow, as affording the by far most important of their thalline characters. The curious fringe of greenish-glaucescent, at length whitish, laciniate, *physcioid* lobules which (scarcely described perhaps except by Turner and Borrer, *Lich. Brit.* p. 217, 225, etc.) borders the disk of attachment in *Umbilicaria* is observable also, as respects its general features (though not as respects colour) in the fragment before me of *Omphalodium Pisacomense;* but in the herein as otherwise discrepant *O. hottentottum*, this fringe is made up of crowded, teretish branchlets, to be compared rather with the similar outgrowth ('*fibrillæ,*' Hoffm.) in *Sticta filix*, and explained doubtless by the root-like fibres ('*rhizinæ fasciculatæ,*' Nyl.) of other *Stictæ*. It is also noteworthy that the disk of the at length blackening apothecia of *O. Pisacomense* is not seldom papillated, much as occurs also in the otherwise not always dissimilar shields of *Umbilicaria Pennsylvanica*, and exactly as in *U. pustulata*, v. *papillata*, Hampe, from the Cape of Good Hope, as if the first-named might itself in time become proliferous; and that Delise (Hist. Stict. p. 136) has described a variety of *O. hottentottum*, '*disco umbilicato nigricante,*' (*Stict.* p. 135).

But it is not, as has already appeared, with *Parmelia* alone that the family before us betrays affinity. It is yet nearer, whether we consider external habit or important structural details, to *Sticta*. *Umbilicaria flocculosa*, Hoffm., reminds us at once of *Sticta fuliginosa;* and many other forms of the latter genus, as, for instance, dark conditions of *S. quercizans* v. *macrophylla*, T. herb. (*S. macrophylla*, Delis.!) *S. tomentella*, Nyl. (Lindig. *Herb. N. Gran.* n. **707**) *S. hirsuta*, Mont., and others of the same group, as well as *S. orygmœa*, might be cited in the same connection with *Umbilicaria:* which is also comparable with the tropical genus, as Fries has noted, in the apothecia. The latter resemblance is observable in both species of *Omphalodium:* and no less in the curious form of *Umbilicaria pustulata* from the Cape of Good Hope, already above cited, the thalline exciple of which being quite commonly undistinguishable in colour from the pale-brownish thallus, is, so far, unmistakedly Parmeliaceous ; in *U. Pennsylvanica*, &c.

The now generally received distinction of *Umbilicaria* and *Gyrophora* goes back to an early date. But Acharius soon gave up his attempt to separate generically, by the external fruit-characters, *U. pustulata* and *Pennsylvanica* (*Lecideæ*, Ach. *Meth.*) from the other species ; and neither Wahlenberg, Turner and Borrer, Eschweiler, or Fries recognized more than one genus. The species named, however, and especially the first of them, offer certain differences in the characterization of the thallus ; and, supported by these, Fée set up once more the old distinction in the apothecia, and sought later (*Suppl.* 1837) to confirm it by his interpretation of the spores. Flotow next, and much more satisfactorily, defined the latter organs ; and his improved statement of Fée's arrangement — separating from *Umbilicaria* the species with sub-simple spores, and retaining for the latter the name *Gyrophora*, — has been accepted by almost all later writers, and has found favour, on anatomical grounds, with Schwendener. We need not indeed delay long over the question whether the thallus of Gyrophora be structurally distinguishable from that of *Umbilicaria*, for the insufficiency of the argument, illustrated most instructively by the same author's exposition of the contradictions of *Sticta* (l. c. p. 166) is, in fact, admitted (p. 179) by himself. But it is not so easy to dispose of the spore-differences. There is no question that the group of alpine lichens represented by *U. proboscidea* and *U. hyperborea*, to which, as a low-country form, our *U. Muhlenbergii* (with its originally sublirelliform, at length strangely aberrant fruit) is to be referred, appears, at first sight, sufficiently distinguishable from *U. pustulata* and its allies, by the alleged microscopical characters. It is yet none the less true that, taken together, the spores of the former group are not typically colourless ; but that on the contrary, and as explained by the microscopical character of its best-developed species (*U. vellea*, &c.) Gyrophora, Fée, must be considered as referable to the coloured series, of which series the spores of *U. pustulata*, &c. (*Umbilicaria*, Fée) express the perfect type. And this type is reached indeed, beyond any question, in the group (of *Gyrophoræ*, Fée, and later authors) represented by *U. vellea*. The brown, granulose spores of the Swedish *U. spodochroa*, Hoffm., Nyl. (*U. vellea*, Fr. *pro p.*) in specimens collected by the writer near Gottenburg, present at length ('*quasi obsoletissime loculosæ*,' Norm. l. c., and Dr. Nylander puts it more strongly yet in *Lich. Scand.* p. 115) an almost muriform configuration, which is also expressed in the spores of *U. Dillenii;* and the probability of error in this conception of the spore (the whole history of which it is, in this very abnormal genus, by no means easy to trace) seems reduced to a *minimum* by another lichen of the same group, *U. haplocarpa*, Nyl. (*Lich. exot.* in. *Ann.* 4, 11, p. 217. *Lich. Boliv.* l. c. 4, 15, p. 377) of Peru, in which (and compare also *U. calvescens*, Nyl., at the last-cited place) the earlier differentiation at length quite muriform spores is distinctly described. Nor need we go so far for an illustration. A Californian lichen (*U. Semitensis*, Tuckerm. msc.) is before me, scarcely distinguishable in general aspect from *U. angulata* of the present writer, and like the latter a member of the same cluster with *U. spodochroa*, which is differenced in the spores precisely as *U. haplocarpa;* these organs (fortunately occurring in eights in the thekes) offering, in the fullest and most instructive manner, every known modification in the history of the muriform spore. There scarcely remains then a satisfactory difference to distinguish the *Gyrophoræ* from *Umbilicaria;* and this natural genus may be taken as affording pertinent evidence of the truth of the proposition — that the highest type of spore-structure exhibited in any natural group is not to be expected necessarily to appear in every, or even in most of the species subsumed (in the general concurrence of characters) under it ; these species offering, it may be, only subordinate stages of the typical differentiation.

In contrast with the genus next following (*Sticta*) the present has a decidedly northern range; and a third at least of its species are among the most characteristic inhabitants of alpine and arctic rocks throughout the northern hemisphere. Others appear to be excluded from or at least less at home in alpine districts; and the noble forms first described from North American specimens reach their perfection in the warmer regions of the southern Appalachians, and of the Atlantic slope. Of the thirty more or less distinct species known, all but two or three European, and the South American, and Indian ones, described by Nylander, are found within the limits of this work.——*U. phæa*, Tuckerm. Lich. Calif. p. 15, is only known to me from the rocks of the coast of California (alt. 1—3000 ft.) Mr. Bolander. Spores $\frac{11-14}{7-8}$ micromill.——*U. rugifera*, Nyl. *Scand.* p. 117, a new species from 'Eastern Siberia,' is represented, with scarcely a doubt, here, by a lichen from the Rocky Mountains (Prof. Shepard; Dr. Lapham) and the Yosemite Valley, California (Mr. Bolander) which agreeing generally in aspect with states of *U. proboscidea* is distinguished by its always regular (not gyrose, or proliferous) fruit, as by smaller size, lighter colour of the under side, &c. Spores of our plant

simple, a little brownish, 0.007—12ᵐᵐ· long, and 0.005—7ᵐᵐ· wide.——
U. murina, DC., is perhaps represented by a lichen of Alpine county,
California (Dr. Lapham) but the specimens are infertile.——The spores
of *U. angulata*, Tuck. Syn. N. Eng. (Coast of California, Menzies; Ob-
servatory Inlet, Northwest coast, Herb. Hook.) are, so far as I have seen
them, simple, scarcely a little blackening, and measuring, in the first-
named specimens, 0.012—20ᵐᵐ· long, and 0.007—10ᵐᵐ· wide; and, in
the others, 0.016—23ᵐᵐ· long, and 0.007—11ᵐᵐ· wide. In a lichen (*U.
Semitensis*, Tuckerm. in *litt.*) from rocks (of from 7 to 8000 ft. elevation)
in the Yosemite Valley (Mr. Bolander) which scarcely differs externally
but in its smaller size from *U. angulata*, the spores are however typically
muriform, offering at length seven to eight transverse series of spore-cells,
and measuring 0.023—30ᵐᵐ· long, and 0.011—16ᵐᵐ· wide. These spores
have only been seen colourless. The younger ones occur simple, and
bi-tri-quadrilocular; or in all the stages of evolution of this kind of
spore, which precede the last.——*U. Pennsylvanica*, Hoffm., proves to be
also an inhabitant of the Ural Mountains (Nyl. *Scand.* p. 113) and was
collected on 'mountain tops' in Japan, by Mr. Wright. And the same
lichen, in inferior condition, without perfect fruit, is given, if I do not
mistake, in Hooker and Thomson's Himalaya collection (n. 2099).

———•———

Fam. 4.—PELTIGEREI.

Thallus plano-adscendens, frondoso-foliaceus, coriaceo-membranaceus, subtus villosus, venis cyphellisve sæpius variegatus. Stratum gonimicum indolis variæ: e gonidiis aut viridibus (solitis) aut
cærulescentibus (collogonidiis) constans.

That *Sticta* is properly referable to the family before us was assumed
by the writer (Lich. Calif. p. 16) from the general concurrence of characters; the second paper of Professor Schwendener (*Laub- und Gallertflechten*) being then unknown to him. But the argument of this paper,
from the here especially significant structure of the thallus, leaves it
quite beyond question that the affinity of *Sticta* to *Parmelia* (and the
Parmeliei) is really remote, compared with its affinity to *Nephroma*.
Almost the whole of the lichens referable here is grouped at one of
the extremes; the analogical centre of the tribe being only represented,
if at all, in this family, by the small cluster of tropical forms (looking not
doubtfully towards *Pannaria*) which constitutes *Erioderma*. Nor is this
the only curious feature of the *Peltigerei*. Though the close affinity of
Sticta to *Nephroma* is scarcely to be questioned, or of the latter to *Peltigera*, and the at length plainly acicular and colourless spores of the last

should seem to refer it, unmistakably, to the colourless series, there is never entirely wanting some slight evidence of coloration; which becomes marked in *Nephroma* and *Sticta*, and is at least observable in *Erioderma*. There seems however to be no doubt entertained by authors that in all these cases the spores differ in type from those of *Solorina;* and the same view is, with some hesitation, accepted in this place. The family, as we understand it, is, in fact, — to give a wider, but not perhaps too wide a sweep to an observation of Professor Schwendener upon *Sticta*, — especially remarkable for the number and importance of the structural contrasts which find their reconciliation in it; and it is then the less surprising that a certain ambiguity of type must be admitted even in the spore-characters. But, however often it embarrass the systematist, this exuberance of differentiation, — whether exhibited in the *veins* or *cyphellæ* which diversify the under side, or the elsewhere almost unexampled prolifications of the upper; in the two-fold nature of the gonidial cells; in the extraordinary modification of the apothecia in their relations to the thallus; in the spores, reaching, for the most part the higher and often the highest stages of the colourless type, and yet obscured more or less by what suggests the coloration of the other; and, no less, in the spermogones and sterigmas, so far as these are known; — may well be allowed to indicate to him, not doubtfully, the position of the group, as the true centre of *Parmeliaceous* lichens. In his disposition of 1821 (*Vet. Ac. Handl.*) Fries makes his *Peltigera* (equivalent to our *Peltigerei*, excluding *Sticta*) the summit of foliaceous lichens, as *Usnea* of fruticulose; and Meyer (*Entwick.* p. 335) who gives to *Sticta* the second place, accords to *Peltigera* (in the same sense in which Fries understood it) the first;[1] as does Nylander (*Syn.*) to *Sticta*.

XIV.—STICTA (Schreb.) Delis., Fr.

Delis. Hist. Stict. 1822, spp. excl. Fr. L. E. pp. 49, 348. Mont. Pl. Cell. in. Ann.; M. et V. d. Bosch Lich. Jav. p. 8. Tul. Mém. pp. 20, 145, t. 1, f. 17–21, t. 2, f. 1–5. Norm. Con. p. 14, t. 1, f. 7, c, d. Mass. Mem. p. 27, t. 3–5. Koerb. Syst. p. 65. Th. Fr. Gen. p. 57. Mudd Man. Brit. Lich. p. 86. Stizenb. Beitr. l. c. p. 174. Schwend. Untersuch. l. c. 3, p. 166, t. 9, f. 2–7. Sticta max. p., et Parmeliæ spp., Ach. L. U. pp. 87–9; Syn. pp. 230, 195. Parmeliæ spp., Wallr. Eschw. Bras. Schær. Spicil. Sticta et Ricasolia, De Not. Framm. Lich. p. 5.

---

[1] "*Thallus . . . in Peltigereis foliaceus vix non perfectissimus evadit structura formaque.* Eschw. *Lich. Bras.* l. c. p. 171, where there seems to be no doubt that *Nephroma* (whether or not taken to be a member of the next following genus) *Peltigera* and *Solorina* were in view; *Sticta* being here relegated to *Parmelia*. In his earlier work (*Syst.* p. 24) this author had by no means a clear conception of *Nephroma*.

Ricasolia, Sticta, et Stictina, Nyl. Syn. 1, p. 332, t. 8, f. 44–6; Lich. Scand. p. 92; in Prodr. Fl. N. Gran. p. 17.

Apothecia scutellæformia, submarginalia, elevata, subinde nigricantia. Sporæ e fusiformi aciculares, bi-quadri-pluriloculares, fuscescentes l. incolores. Spermatia oblonga, apice utroque incrassata; sterigmatibus multi-articulatis. Thallus frondoso-foliaceus, varie lobatus, orbiculatus l. dein protensus, coriaceo-cartilagineus, subtus villosus cyphellis maculisve sæpius interspersis. Stratum gonimicum e gonidiis solitis aut collogonidiis constitutum.

The spores of *Sticta* are often at length colourless, and so described, as in a large part of *Sticta*, Nyl. *Syn.*, and in the second section of *Stictina* of the same author, contrasting in this way with the first, but the distinction is evidently only a relative one; and the genus must be admitted to show throughout, though doubtless here more and here less, the same evident tendency to coloration.[1]

As respects its position in the tribe, the genus is generally placed as if mediating between the frondose lichens (*Peltigerei* proper) and the foliaceous ones (*Parmeliei*) but the texture and other features of the thallus refer it to the former rather than the latter; not to speak of the (atypical) divergence in colour, of the spores, which seems best explainable in connection with those of *Peltigera*. And *Sticta*, for its part, as will hereafter be seen, assists us in explaining the often puzzling structural anomalies of the properly frondose genera. Not to delay here over an extended comparison of species, it may at least be said that the veiny variegation of the under side of *Peltigera* (as of *P. horizontalis*) is elegantly simulated in *Sticta dissecta* (*S. Peltigera*, Del.) and *S. Fendleri*, Mont., as also in *S. scrobiculata* and *pulmonaria;* and the prominent nerves of *Solorina crocea* and *Peltigera venosa* by the similar, though otherwise conditioned processes of *Sticta Filix.* And the resemblance indeed, as to upper surface, apothecia and their place of attachment, and even spores of *S. peltigerella*, Nyl., (Lindig *Herb. N. Gran.* n. 2533) to *Peltigera venosa* is too striking wholly to escape even casual attention. Tulasne (*Mém. Lich.* p. 20) has given several illustrations of the anatomical congruity of the members of the family, as here taken; and Schwendener (l. c.) has, later, conclusively shown that *Sticta*, from the same point of view, confined to the thallus, possesses absolutely no characters to distin-

---

[1] I observe this in *S. Lenormandii, tomentosa, quercizans, Boschiana, Filix, retigera, pulmonaria, laciniata, damæcornis, Urvillei,* and *orygmæa,* as also in *S. amplissima* and *pallida;* in many of which notwithstanding, perfect spores occur, perhaps more commonly, colourless, affording to that extent a diagnostic difference, and a suggestion of what I have ventured here to regard their typical character.

5

guish it from *Nephroma*. A conclusion scarcely indeed surprising in view of such *Stictæ* as *S. hirsuta*, Mont. !

The different structure of the gonidia (upon which Schwendener, l. c. p. 133, and *passim*, and De Bary, *Morph. u. Phys. d. Pilze*, etc., p. 257, are especially instructive) in the large group of species represented by *S. quercizans* (*Stictina*, Nyl.) from that in the group of which *S. damæcornis* may be considered a prominent type (*Sticta*, Nyl.) — first indicated indeed in a remark of Tulasne,[1] but only given full expression to by Nylander (*Flora*, 1860, p. 65. *Syn.* l. c.) is perhaps the most important observation that has been made upon *Sticta* since the genus was first distinguished by the *cyphellæ;* and has proved an invaluable guide in the study of the species. But it appears none the less true that the two vast species named belong without doubt to one and the same *natural* genus ; and the difference relied on to distinguish them sinks in fact fairly out of sight, in the preponderance of affinities which unite them. *Ricasolia* De Not., Nyl. l. c., agreeing with *Sticta*, Nyl., in the gonimous layer, embraces the elegant group of species represented by *S. amplissima* and *S. dissecta*, and is distinguishable if not by habit at least by the general absence of *cyphellæ;* but the latter are well-marked in *S. Wrightii* (Tuckerm. Suppl. 2, l. c. p. 204) which offers other points of resemblance to the wider conditions of *S. damæcornis;* — and nothing else appears to separate it.

It has already been suggested, and is perhaps sufficiently evident that *Sticta* occupies an extreme position in the present family, whether we regard its relations to the two families next immediately preceding it, or to the type of Peltigereine structure with which its own is most closely associated. And its range contrasts also with that of the *Peltigerei* proper. *Sticta* is mainly tropical, a large proportion of the species (as compare Nyl. Syn. 1, p. 333) occurring also in, or confined to austral regions, but scarcely a fifth known in the northern temperate ones, where about half the prominent forms occur only sterile. Rather more forms have been observed in Europe than have yet been detected here. I have seen no American specimens of *S. limbata, S. Dufourii,* or *S. herbacea;* nor has the tropical *S. damæcornis* found a home with us, as in the south of Ireland. But another species of the warmer regions of the earth (*S. quercizans*) not remote from *S. sylvatica*, is frequent, though infertile, in almost every part of the United States; and the place of *S. herbacea* may be said to be taken in all the extreme southern portion of the country (from South Carolina to Louisiana) by the also tropical *S. Ravenelii* (T. Suppl. 2, l. c. p. 203, and in Wright *Lich. Cub.* n. 66. *Ricasolia.* Nyl. *Prodr. N. Gran.* p. 24).[1] But little else has been added to our list. *S. fuliginosa*, Ach., was found by me, on rocks, near Boston, in 1848 ; and

---

"*Ses gonidies*," he says of *Sticta sylvatica*, "*resemblent plus à celles des Peltigera qu'aux gonidies du Lichen ci-dessus décrit*" (*S. herbacea*).—*Mém. sur les Lich.* p. 21.

has since occurred, also on rocks, at New Bedford, and on trunks in Mt. Desert (H. Willey) as well as in California (H. N. Bolander) and Vancouver's Island (Dr. Lyall) but the specimens are all infertile.——What really constituted *S. sylvatica* with Muhlenberg and Halsey is doubtful, neither of these writers having recognized the nearly akin *S. quercizans*, Ach.; but a lichen from the Catskill mountains (C. H. Peck) scarcely differs from the European species.——*S. linita*, Ach., was recognized as occurring in the United States by Delise (l. c.) and Dr. Nylander (Syn. p. 353) speaks of a state from Arctic America. Specimens are before me from Kotzebue's Sound (Herb. Church. Babingt.) and others from Behring's Straits (Mr. Wright) which may well be referable here, and I have also gathered a similar lichen (both on rocks and trunks) in the White Mountains, looking quite as distinct from *S. pulmonaria* as does Schærer's n. 385, but the species is a doubtful one, and my American specimens are without fruit.

XV.—NEPHROMA, Ach.

Ach. L. U. p. 101; Syn. p. 241. Fr. Fl. Scan. p. 258. Mont. Aperçu Morph. p. 11. Tuckerm. Syn. N. Eng. p. 18. Schær. Enum. p. 17. Norm. Con. p. 13. Tul. Mém. Lich. pp. 18, 177, t. 9, f. 18–23. Mass. Mem. p. 23, t. 2, f. 10–12. Koerb. Syst. p. 54. Th. Fr. Gen. p. 54. Stizenb. Beitr. l. c. p. 165. Schwend. Untersuch. l. c. 3, p. 173, t. 9, f. 8. Peltigeræ l. Peltideæ sect., Hoffm. Ach. Meth. DC. Mey. Entwick. p. 336. Fr. S. O. V. p. 240; L. E. p. 41. Schær. Spicil. p. 263. Nephroma et Nephromium, Nyl. Syn. 1, p. 316, t. 1, f. 18, t. 8, f. 36–7; Lich. Scand. p. 86.

Apothecia reniformia, thalli lobis productis postice innata, margine subintegro disparente. Sporæ subfusiformes, quadriloculares, fuscescentes. Spermatia oblonga, apice utroque incrassata; sterigmatibus multi-articulatis. Thallus frondosus, subtus villosus nec venosus. Stratum gonimicum e gonidiis solitis aut collogonidiis constitutum.

Margin of the apothecia commonly obscure, and the fruit is in fact described as immarginate by several recent writers. Eschweiler (*Lich. Bras.*) must also be cited as denying, and to the whole of the *Peltigerei*, as he understood the group (*Peltigera*, Fr.) any other than a proper exciple; and Stizenberger (l. c.) who follows him in this, goes so far as to reject even analogy with the Parmeliaceous apothecium. But the whole argument for analogy is not so easily disposed of. *Nephroma* is not only, as respects its thallus, immediately contiguous to *Sticta*, but its apothecia,

---

1 Now referred by Nylander, in the later edition of his Lichens of New Granada, and with reason, so far as appears, to the South American *S. erosa* (Eschw. *sub Parmelia*).

as interpreted by those of *Peltigera*, are also, through the latter, associable in a manner with those of *Sticta*. Nor is this all. Fries remarked of the fruit of *Sticta aurata* (*L. E.* p. 51) in itself not seldom comparable with that of *Nephroma*, that it agreed essentially with that of *Cetraria;* and it is with the genus last named that we may well compare the one before us. We do not indeed find in *Nephroma* the same satisfactory evidence of an originally closed thalline exciple, as is afforded by *Peltigera;* but the young, connivent apothecium is far from unlike that of *Cetraria*, which may also be taken to explain the mostly obscure margin. There is scarcely any difference apparent between apothecia of *Nephroma tomentosum* and others of *Cetraria lacunosa*, so closely approximated are the points of attachment in the two, though in the one case the fruit really adheres to the under side of the thallus, and in the other to the upper; and in the Himalayan *C. Stracheyi*, Babingt. (Hook. f. et Thoms. *Herb. Ind. Or.* n. 2080) even this distinction disappears, and the apothecium is quite like that of *Nephroma* in every important, external respect. *C. ciliaris* also is occasionally comparable with *Nephroma* in the same way as *C. lacunosa;* and Sprengel's *Peltigera* (*Nephroma*) *Americana* (*Syst. Veg.* 4, 1, p. 306) is only, as appears by his original specimen, a condition of the first-named. Indeed, we need look no further than the genus in hand to demonstrate its true affinity. In a fine specimen of *Nephroma antarcticum* before me, almost every one of the dozen and more apothecia is distinctly enclosed by a regular, entire margin, the Parmeliaceous character of which is quite beyond question.

It is another curious circumstance that *Cetraria*, though so well distinguished by its cartilagineous thallus, and other features pointing to a different affinity, yet agrees with *Nephroma* in offering indications of *cyphellæ;* these occurring both in *C. Stracheyi*, just mentioned, and in *C. leucostigma*, Lév. (*Sticta Wallichiana*, Tayl.) from the same region (Herb. Hook.) the scattered shields of which last well simulate those of *Sticta*. The *cyphellæ* (properly the modification known as *pseudo-cyphellæ*) of *Nephroma tomentosum* point, we need scarcely add, as obviously toward *Sticta*, as do other characters toward *Peltigera;* and the genus must continue to be regarded as mediating between the other two.

About twelve species are described, their range being northern (that of the finest, alpine and arctic) and austral. Of the European forms all but one occur here.——*N. lævigatum*, Ach., the smooth condition of what Acharius described as *N. parile* (Tuckerm. Syn. N. Eng. p. 18) and distinguishable from *N. tomentosum* (Hoffm.) Koerb., which is *N. resupinatum*, Ach. *a* (Tuckerm. l. c., & *Exs.* n. 13, *pr. parte*) by its smooth and naked under side, is common in the New-England mountains; and occurs also, rarely, with an at length bright-yellow medullary layer (California, Mr. Bolander) upon which compare Nylander l. c. p. 320, note.

XVI.—PELTIGERA (Willd., Hoffm.) Fée.

Fée Ess., suppl., p. 129. Mont. Aperçu Morph. p. 11. Tuckerm. Syn. N,
Eng. p. 19. Schær. Enum. p. 19. Norm. Con. p. 13, t. 1, f. 6, a, b. Tul.
Mém. Lich. pp. 17, 44, 64, t. 8. 'Mass. Mem. p. 19, t. 1, 2. Koerb. Syst.
p. 56. Nyl. Syn. 1, p. 322, t. 8, f. 38–9; Lich. Scand. p. 87. Speerschneid.
in Bot. Zeit. 1857. Th. Fr. Gen. p. 55; Lich. Spitzberg. p. 14. Stizenb.
Beitr. l. c. p. 166. Schwend. Untersuch. l. c. 3, p. 174, t. 9, f. 9. Pelti-
geræ sect., Hoffm. DC. Schær. Spicil. Fr. S. O. V. p. 240; L. E. p. 41.
Peltidea, Ach. L. U. p. 98; Syn. p. 237. Eschw. Syst. p. 22.

Apothecia peltæformia, thalli lobulis productis raro margini antice
adnata, margine lacero-crenato. Sporæ e fusiformi aciculares, quadri-
pluriloculares, demum incolores. Thallus frondosus, subtus villosus
venosusque, strato corticali ibidem nullo. Stratum gonimicum e
gonidiis viridibus, aut sæpius cærulescentibus (collogonidiis) constans.

The general distinction between the *Peltigera*-fruit and that of *Sticta*
lies in the fact that the former is at once peltiform, and originally innate;
whereby what in *Sticta* appears as the upper half of a closed, superficial
apothecium is reduced in the other to a depressed *veil*. The margin is
developed in both in the same way, and that of the present genus, though
in most of the forms far less regular, and often even obscure, is expressed
in *P. venosa* with all the definiteness of that of *Sticta;* some curious species of which (*S. Boschiana*, Mont., *S. peltigerella*, Nyl.) simulate, in their
turn, the habit of the *Peltigera*.

The genus offers the same fusiform-acicular spores which we find in
Sticta; but, in distinction from the latter, in which, as regards the great
mass of species, the spores are fusiform, and only rarely more elongated,
Peltigera presents, for the most part, the acicular type, and in only
two, otherwise receding species, do we find it varying to lanceolate, and
fusiform. As respects colour, in which *Sticta* and *Nephroma* are evidently (considered as members of the colourless series) aberrant, *Peltigera*
deviates far less. Its spores rarely shew indications of colour except
while still enclosed in the thekes; [1] and in fact are generally taken for
colourless. The genus is perhaps, in this respect also, a key to the
natural position of *Nephroma* and *Sticta*.

A striking feature of the group before us is its elongated, ascendant,
sometimes digitately divided fertile lobules; but this gradually disappears in the forms approaching *Sticta*, and in *P. venosa* the apothecia are
marginal. Mr. Wright detected, on islands of Behring's Straits, a dwarf,
arctic condition (f. *marginalis*) of *P. aphthosa*, in which the apothecia are

---

[1] " *Les spores des Peltidea canina et P. horizontalis semblent incolores vues
isolément; mais lorsqu'elles sont accumulées très abondamment sur une lame de
verre, elles y forment des taches fauves d'une couleur aussi intense que le disque
des scutelles dont elles sont sorties.*"—Tulasne *Mém. Lich.* p. 72.

also strictly marginal, and the whole plant indeed not a little resembles the species last named. A similarly, but much less dwarfed state of *P. canina*, with short fertile lobules, occurred at the same station; where *P. venosa*, perhaps always less impatient of cold, was particularly fine. The range of the genus is northern, and the eight or nine best-known species are common to Europe and North America. *P. canina*, *P. polydactyla* (as compare Nyl. l. c.) and probably others, extend also widely through the warmer regions of the earth, where the suitable conditions exist.

A thinner, glaucous form of *P. aphthosa*, in which the veins are peculiarly conspicuous beneath (v. *minor*, Tuckerm. *exs.* n. 102) is common and noteworthy in the New England mountains; and Mr. Wright collected it, on mountains, in Japan.——In a still more remarkable condition of *P. canina* (v. *spongiosa*, exhibited, but not satisfactorily at No. 103 of the just cited collection) the under side is at length most densely spongy-villous, the veins remaining visible only at the circumference of the thallus, and the thickness of the soft cushion of intertangled fibrils exceeding at length 2$^{mm.}$ This variety has only occurred in subalpine regions of the White Mountains. And the same regions furnish also, (on moist rocks) a reduced but fertile state (v. *sorediifera*) referable to *P. canina* by the under side and the pubescence and colour of the upper, but readily distinguished by its rounded, grey soredia; which are well comparable, though perhaps more often central, with those of *Sticta limbata*. The lichen approaches the v. *spongiosa* in its often dense *villus* beneath, but is always smallish. Mr. Wright found it on 'banks' in islands of Behring's Straits.——Southward a still smaller plant occurs (South Carolina, on moist rocks, Mr. Ravenel; California, Mr. Bolander) scarcely reaching two inches in diameter, but in other respects, unless it be the more naked under side, agreeing closely with small specimens of the other. To this last I cannot but refer *Peltidea erumpens*, Tayl. in Hook. Lond. Journ. Bot. 6, p. 184, from clay banks in Ireland; nor do Lindig's specimens of *Peltigera leptoderma*, Nyl. (Lindig *Herb. N. Gran.* n. 2559) appear to differ at all from the Carolina ones. The spores of both states of v. *sorediifera*, as well as those of v. *spongiosa*, accord satisfactorily with those of the type to which the lichens are here referred. To the southern condition of the first named of these varieties, another,—*P. canina*, v. *spuria*, Ach., excellent specimens of which have been sent to me by Mr. Ravenel and Mr. Bolander, approaches often near, and seems to offer indications (as also does my copy of Moug. & Nestl. n. 837, & Rabenh. *Lich. Eur.* n. 421, c) of soredia, but the thicker thallus is comparable rather with that of *P. rufescens*, to which Nylander refers the lichen. Very beautiful specimens of this variety, combining the habit and texture of v. *spuria* with the soredia of the other, were collected by Mr. Wright in Japan.——*P. canina* is typically tomentose above, but tropical specimens (Island of Juan Fernandez, Herb. Mont.; Venezuela, Fendler) are smoother and at length glabrous, and this condition, which is also thinner

(v. *membranacea*, Nyl.) occurs here in California (Mr. Bolander) and may be taken for *P. polydactyla.*——*P. polydactyla* v. *scutata*, Fr. (*Peltidea scutata*, Borr.! Grev.! *P. hymenina*, Floerk.! *P. horizontalis*, v. *hymenia*, Moug. et Nestl. n. 541, *pr. max. p.*) has occurred as yet rarely with me, and only barren. I possess, however, fertile specimens from trunks in Vancouver's Island (Dr. Lyall in Herb. Hook.) and the lichen is readily distinguished from the type by its crisped, at length densely-sorediate margins, and from *P. horizontalis* by the spores. To the species last named, and by the same criterion, must be referred the *P. polydactyla*, v. *scutata* of *Lich. Amer. exs.* n. 11 (and also of Nyl. *Syn.* 1. c. *pr. p.*) which has indeed, considered in its full extent, the whole habit of *P. horizontalis*; and is, according to Dr. Nylander (*Lich. Scand.*) Acharius's v. *lophyra* of that species.

Erioderma, Fée (*Ess.* p. 145. Suppl. p. 149. *Mont. Diagn. Phyc.* in *Ann.* 3, 18, p. 309) is a tropical genus of few species, referred, so far as then known, to *Sticta* by Acharius, and to *Peltigera* by Fries, and included in their *Peltigerei* by both Fée and Montagne, but associated with *Pannaria* by Nylander. The latter affinity will not indeed be questioned here, where *Pannaria* is viewed as immediately contiguous to the *Peltigerei;* but *Erioderma* possesses some features which should seem distinctively Peltigerine. The whole habit of the upper side of the thallus in the best developed form (*E. Wrightii*, Tuckerm. Suppl. 1, and in Wright *Lich. Cub.* n. 109) is quite that of *Peltigera*; nor do I know with what else to compare the under side of *E. unguigerum* (Bor.) Nyl. (*Peltidea glaucescens*, Tayl.). This side is less prominently veined or nerved in *E. Chilense*, Mont. (Valdiv., Lechler!) and, in the otherwise not dissimilar *E. polycarpum*, Fée (Cuba, Wright!) is besprinkled with tufts of black fibrils, passing, in *E. Wrightii*, into a dense, spongy cushion, well-comparable without doubt, to that of some *Pannariæ*, but yet not unexampled, as we have seen above, in *Peltigera*. The (marginal) apothecia are, as respects all external characters, similar to those of *Sticta;* but often terminate slightly produced lobules, one of the most characteristical notes of *Peltigera*. It is finally not perhaps without interest that the ovoid or ellipsoid, at length somewhat fusiform, simple spores, which shew the same indications of coloration noted already in the other Peltigerine genera, are often well comparable with young (simple) spores of *Solorina crocea*. And if I do not wholly mistake, there are not wanting other indications,—as in the breaking up of the spore-mass (sporoblast, Koerb.) when the spore becomes now distantly suggestive of that of *Lecanactis premnea*—of a still nearer relation to *Peltigera* and *Sticta*.

XVII.—SOLORINA, Ach.

Ach. L. U. p. 27; Syn. p. 8. Eschw. Syst. p. 21. Mont. Aperçu Morph. p. 11. Tuckerm. Syn. N. Eng. p. 20. Schær. Enum. p. 22. Norm. Con. p. 14, t. 1, f. 7, 6. Tul. Mém. Lich. p. 19. Mass. Mem. p. 25,

t. 3, f. 13–14. Koerb. Syst. p. 62. Nyl. Syn. 1, p. 329, t. 8, f. 40–42;
Lich. Scand. p. 91. Th. Fr. Gen. p. 56; Lich. Spitzb. p. 16. Stizenb.
Beitr. 1. c. p. 164. Schwend. Untersuch. 1. c. 3, p. 176, t. 9, f. 10–13.
Peltigeræ sect. Hoffm. DC. Schær. Spicil. Fr. S. O. V. p. 240; L.
E. p. 48. Mey. Entwick. Wallr. Germ.

Apothecia orbicularia thallo antice innata, margine evanido.
Sporæ ex ellipsoideo fusiformi-oblongæ, biloculares, fuscæ. Thallus
frondosus, subtus villosus venosusque, strato corticali ibidem inter-
rupto aut nullo. Stratum gonimicum collogonidiis aut viridibus
aut cærulescentibus constitutum.

Acharius misconceived the structure and affinities of this genus, as
did Eschweiler (*Syst.* p. 15, 21;) and the latter, though he restored it
finally (*Lich. Bras.*) to its place beside *Peltigera*, yet strangely, at the
same time attributed to the whole family the mistaken character by which
Acharius had sought to separate from it *Solorina*.[1] There was room for
the criticism of Fries (*S. O. V.*) and if lichenists followed the latter in
fully accepting the Parmeliaceous character of the *Peltigerei*, it was difficult to refuse to follow him in denying the distinctness of *Solorina* from
Peltigera. This distinction turns in fact now on the sharply defined spore-
differences.

The apothecia of *Solorina* become sometimes superficial, when a
regular, depressed, entire border, of the substance of the thallus, is occasionally to be made out. I observe this in American specimens of *S. saccata*, as well as in the very closely akin *S. Simensis*, Hochst., Flot. (Hook.
et Thoms. *Herb. Ind. Or.* n. 1765) and suppose it may be taken for the
rarely perfected true margin; only represented ordinarily by the soon
disappearing edges of the thin veil. A similar, entire border is sometimes to be seen in the apothecia of *Peltigera*, but much more frequently
the margin, in the latter, continues crenulate. ——Spermogones scarcely
known, either in *Solorina* or *Peltigera*.

This small group is represented in the alpine and arctic regions of the
earth by *S. crocea*, and in the temperate ones of Europe and America by
S. saccata. The former has heretofore only occurred in Arctic America,
but was found by Dr. Lyall of the Brit. Oregon Boundary Commission in
the Cascade Mountains (Herb. Hook.) and more lately by Mr. E. Hall in
the alpine regions of the Rocky Mountains. *S. saccata*, affecting with us
calcareous soils, has been found in New England (Mr. Russell) New York;
and northward to Behring's Straits (Mr. Wright). The curious variety
limbata, Schær., is an inhabitant of Greenland (Vahl in Th. Fr. *Lich.
Arct.* p. 49) and was found in islands of Behring's Straits, by Mr. Wright.

---

[1] "*E lamina proligera sola constant hujus Generis apothecia, fere ut in Artho-
niis.*" *Ach. in char. Solorinæ, obs., L. U.* p. 27. "*Apothecia . . substantia tantum medullari marginata. . . . . Peltigerinæ.*" Eschw. *Clav. trib. Lich.;
Lich. Bras. in calce.*

Fam. 5.—PANNARIEI.

Thallus horizontalis, frondoso-foliaceus dein multifidus l. squamulosus, coriaceo-membranaceus, hypothallo pannoso demum evanido.
Stratum gonimicum indolis variæ; e gonidiis viridibus (solitis) aut,
sæpius, cærulescentibus (collogonidiis) constans.

If we have really reached, in the *Peltigerei*, the summit of Parmeliaceous lichens, it cannot surprise us to meet next with another group, at
once approaching the former in essential structural characters, and yet
shewing marked evidence of degradation. And this is exactly what is
indicated by the *Pannariei;* or, to cite only, for the present, the chief
member of the group, *Pannaria.* In both alike of its principal sections,
determined significantly, as in most of the genera of the *Peltigerei*, by
the twofold structure exhibited by the gonidia, this genus displays the
foliaceous thallus, disappearing finally in what is only not the crustaceous.
One of the noble, austral forms of the section distinguished by green gonidia
(*Psoroma*, Nyl.) has much of the port at least of *Peltigera canina ;* but
the only northern representative of the group is the semi-crustaceous
P. hypnorum. Of the other section, in like manner, in which blue-
green gonidia (gonimous granules, Nyl. collogonidia, nob.) replace the
ordinary type of these cells (*Pannaria*, Nyl.) we have on the one hand species
(*P. molybdæa, plumbea, Gayana, fulvescens*) comparable with *Sticta*, and
yet on the other, and associable with the first by unquestioned affinities,
forms not only not foliaceous, but even, finally, in the opinion of almost
all lichenographers of the present day, not even lichenose. And this
brings us to the most interesting chapter in the history of *Pannaria*,—that
which concerns its relations to Collemaceous lichens.

It will hardly be doubted that even *Sticta* is brought into peculiarly
close relations with *Collema*, etc., by its blue-green gonidia; and Fries
was well able to compare with it (in *Mallotium*, Ach.) such Collemaceous
plants as *Leptogium Hildenbrandii* and *L. Menziesii.* But the affinity of
the latter to *Pannaria* is evidently far more intimate. The two groups
plainly touch at several well-ascertained points ; and there are not a few
forms now actually in question between *Lichenes* and *Collemaceæ:* thus
abundantly illustrating the justness of Koerber's remark that the dividing line between Collemaceous and true Lichens is by no means so sharply
drawn, in nature, as we have drawn it ('*dass die Scheidewand* . . ..
lange nicht so scharf gezogen sei, als wie wir sie gezogen haben.' *Parerg.*
p. 26). If, following the indications of habit, we compare, with the
microscope, the thalline structure of *Pannaria lurida*, Nyl. (*Collema*,
Mont. *Parmelia* (*Amphiloma*) *Russellii*, Tuckerm. Syn. N. Eng.) with
that of species of *Pannaria* externally not dissimilar, it seems impossible
to refer the former to any other genus: *P. fulvescens* (Mont.) Nyl. (*Herb.
Mus. Par.*) sufficiently mediating, in its perhaps rather lax medullary

6

tissue, and more distinctly concatenated gonidia, between it and *P. rubiginosa*, and the latter offering seemingly the first step of descent from the compacter, filamentous web of *P. molybdæa* and *P. plumbea*. And yet, if continuing the investigation, we compare the species first named, thus both by internal and external characters associated with *Pannaria*, with *Collema byrsæum* (*C. byrsinum*, Ach.) significantly agreeing with it, to a considerable degree, in habit, as in the important point of the nap of the under side of the thallus, and in the spores, it may well appear doubtful whether Montagne had not equal right ; and whether there be really, here, any distinction at all between *Pannaria* and *Collema*.

And the difficulty returns, under varied conditions, in the reduced forms, which make so large, and, in the north at least, so characteristical a part of *Pannaria*. It were indeed to be expected beforehand, in view of the evident approaches, — to say the least — in the higher types, towards Collemaceous structure, that such approaches, rendered yet more perplexing by the degradation of the thallus, should recur in the lower. *Lecothecium*, Trev., *Racoblenna* and *Collolechia*, Mass., *Pterygium*, Nyl., and *Wilmsia*, Koerb., are modern genera of *Collemaceæ*, every one of which may, notwithstanding, with fair show of reason be said, not merely to descend from, but even to be referable to *Pannariei*. Not by any means that a certain degree of structural change in the thallus is not recognizable in these groups, or this group, but that this change is, to a very great extent, — unless where chemical conditions may possibly have to come into account, as in *Collolechia* — inextricably involved in, and it should seem, in short, a corollary of, that *reduction* of the thallus,[1] which, confessedly, is not enough in itself to exclude any lichen from *Pannaria*. The modified structure follows the reduction, in fact, within the universally recognized limits of the genus. What is taken as sufficient to separate *Lecothecium nigrum*, Mass., (*Pannaria*, Nyl.) and *L. asperellum*, Th. Fr. (*Lich. Arct.*, and *herb. Auct.*, — the plant being comparable perhaps rather with *Pterygium pannariellum*, Nyl. *Scand.*, than with this author's *P. asperellum,* l. c.) from true Lichens, is not indistinctly traceable to an unquestioned lichen — *Pannaria tryptophylla ;* and even *Pterygium Petersii*, Nyl., analogous as are its structural details to those

---

[1] Compare Schwendener on the structure of the ' smaller squamules,' as contrasted with the larger, of *P. microphylla*, l. c. 3, p. 194, and on the thallus of *Racoblenna Tremniaca*, Mass., and *Lecothecium corallinoides*, Koerb. (*Pannaria nigra*, Nyl.) l. c. 4, pp. 162, 165. And his observation of the reduction of the thallus of *P. microphylla* into a ' through and through' parenchymatous tissue, holds good equally of *P. tryptophylla ;* which, though, on the one hand, compared by the German author with even *P. rubiginosa*, exhibits also, on the other, conditions, inseparable in thalline structure from *P. nigra*. But in reaching this merely parenchymatous thallus, *Pannaria* reaches ultimately *Pyrenopsis* and the *Collemei ;* all other distinction between the two families, as now understood, at last ceasing, except what may be made of the external habit.

of some *Collemaceæ*, is perhaps better explained by another American lichen (*Pannaria flabellosa*, Tuckerm. *Obs. Lich.* 1. c. 5, p. 401) not readily removable from the same family, or even the same genus with *P. trypto-phylla*. It is evident here that the writer is unable to adopt Nylander's estimate of the value, as a structural difference, of the indistinctness or even obsolescence of the hypothallus, in his *Pterygium*.

The indications afforded by the family last preceding of a disappear-ance of the thalline exciple, find their complement, in the present, in pseudo-biatorine forms, which considered apart from their obvious con-nections, should be referable to the *Lecideacei*. *Coccocarpia*, Pers., Mont., constituted, it is probable, by only the varying forms of a single species (Tuckerm. in Wright *Lich. Cub.* n. 104–107) is without doubt to be referred to the number of such pseudo-biatorine *Pannariæ ;* a conclusion suggested by if not involved in Nylander's reference of *P. plumbea* to *Coccocarpia*.

Psoroma, Nyl., only differs from *Pannaria* of the same author, in the structure of its gonidia ; but his more recent reference of the former to *Lecanora* (Lich. N. Zeal. in Journ. Linn. Soc. Lond. 9) hardly sufficiently takes into account its well-marked habit. The tropics furnish us, how-ever, with two other remarkable types, neither of them wholly alien to *Pannariei*, and both characterized by green gonidia. One of these (*Par-melia gossypina*, Mont. Wright *Lich. Cub.* n. 110. *Crocynia*, Mass. *Esam.*) is associated by Nylander with the still doubtful *Lichen lanugi-nosus*, Ach., in *Amphiloma*, Nyl.; but recedes remarkably in its byssus-like thallus, and in the habit of the apothecia is not ill-comparable with *Heterothecium Domingense*. The other, *Physcidia*, Tuckerm. *Obs. Lich.* 1. c. 5, p. 399 (Wright *Lich. Cub.* n. 92, 93) combines a thallus now like that of some *Physcia*, and now resembling rather a squamulose *Lecanora*, with a byssoid hypothallus, comparable with the thallus of *Parmelia gossypina*, composite (zeorine) apothecia with much of the aspect of those of *Pannaria sphinctrina*, Mont., and acicular, quadrilocular spores.

Heppia, Naeg., referred to the present family by Nylander, appears finally to agree with it in some particulars of habit, as it does also in internal characters. The proximity of the *Pannariei* to the *Peltigerei* is illustrated by this little lichen, referred by other authors, without excep-tion, to the near neighborhood of *Solorina ;* and perhaps even more evi-dently by *Erioderma*, Fée, here placed with *Peltigerei*, but by Nylander with *Pannaria*.

It has been stated elsewhere that the whole manuScript of this arrangement of Parmeliaceous lichens was completed, essentially as it now stands, before the researches of Professor Schwendener on the anatomy of the thallus had, in any form, become known to the writer. The passages cited below of a portion of the German author's general observations on the family now before us, and on its close relations to that next to follow, are therefore pertinent; and I add here a rough outline,

accommodated to the nomenclature of this book of what is said. The
author had already (l. c. 3, p. 146) delineated the 'unbroken series' of
Parmeliaceous types, which, connected with the *Usneei* through the
ascendant conditions of *Theloschistes* and *Physcia*, continues to develope
itself in the foliaceous forms of these genera, and *Parmelia*, and reaches
the summit of such development in *Sticta* and *Nephroma*. From these
last 'branch off' (differenced by the disappearance of the cortical layer
on the under side of the thallus) *Peltigera*, and *Solorina*. And, related
more closely to *Sticta* by the continuousness (not, however, without
important exceptions) of its cortical layer, next follows *Pannaria*, constituting with *Lecothecium* and *Pterygium* but a single family. From
Lecothecium, etc., 'the transition to the *Collemaceæ*, is, whether we regard
the medullary tissue or the gonidia, plainly a gradual one.' And, in like
manner, the *Collemaceæ*, for their part, connect themselves, immediately,
with the just referred to representatives of the *Pannaria* group. And
the author continues, still more particularly, in introducing his discussion
of the structure of *Pannaria*, as follows (p. 190) — The few species of
this remarkable genus mediate the transition of the so-called heteromerous Lichens into the homæomerous. While some (*P. plumbea, hypnorum*
etc.,) remind us in habit as well as anatomical characters of the *Parmeliaceæ*, others (*P. rubiginosa* and *tryptophylla*) display a decided relationship to the *Collemaceæ ;* without at the same time any room being left
to doubt that all are alike referable to the same natural group. In
P. rubiginosa and *tryptophylla*, and sometimes also in *P. microphylla*, the
gonidia possess, namely, thickened, gelatinous membranes, which often
completely fill up the interspaces of the filamentous tissue, and appear
even not seldom dissolved into a homogeneous pulp; in which, as in the
Collemaceæ, filaments and gonidia are imbedded. It follows from this,
he goes on finally to say, that the whole gonidium-bearing, or much the
larger part of the thallus, in these instances, assumes the character of a
gelatinous tissue, not essentially differenced from that of typical *Collemaceæ ;* and that only the smaller part, reduced sometimes, here and
there, almost to nothing, retains the normal features of the heteromerous
frond.[1]——For further illustrations of the pregnant fact just stated,

---

[1] " *Die grössere Zahl der aufgeführten Gattungen lässt sich in eine ununter-
brochene Reihe bringen, in welcher jede folgende sich ungezwungen an die vor-
hergehenden anschliesst. Geht man von Anaptychia aus, welche den Uebergang
zu den strauchartigen Formen vermittelt, so folgen nacheinander die übrigen
Gattungen der Parmelieen ; Parmelia, Physcia, Imbricaria. An diese reihen sich
durch Vermittlung von Sticta herbacca, pallida, dissecta und der übrigen Arten,
die zu den Nylander'schen Gattungen Ricasolia und Sticta gehören, die Genera
Sticta und Nephroma, beide zum Theil mit typisch blaugrünen Gonidien und unter
sich vollkommen übereinstimmend. Folgen nun, um die Reihe der allseitig um-
rindeten Flechten nicht zu unterbrechen, zunächst die Pannarien, an welche die
übrigen als Pannariaceen aufgeführten Gattungen sich anschliessen. Zwischen*

reference may be had to the cited memoir. It will scarcely be questioned that the observations of Prof. Schwendener, just set down, have an important bearing on some obscure points of lichenose structure. And it is impossible not to add that the argument from these results, supporting, it should certainly seem, the view taken, from a distinct standpoint, in the present treatise, of the Parmeliaceous nature of the *Collemei*, is sustained by the most thorough anatomical analysis of the plants in question ever yet made.

XVIII.—HEPPIA, Naeg.

Naeg. in Hepp Flecht. Eur. n. 49. Mass. Geneac. p. 7. Nyl. Énum. Gén. Lich. in Mém. Cherb. 5, p. 110. Koerb. Parerg. p. 25. Th. Fr. Gen. p. 56. Stizenb. Beitr. l. c. p. 164. Schwend. Untersuch. l. c. 3, pp. 152, 178, t. 9, f. 1. Solorinæ sp., Mont. Pl. Cell. Canar. in Webb et

Sticta und Pannaria fehlt allerdings ein vermittelndes Glied; doch stehen P. plumbea und einige ausländische Arten z. b. Coccocarpia aurantiaca, den Sticten nicht sehr ferne, während andererseits P. hypnorum durch die gelb-grüne Farbe der Gonidien auf die Parmeliecn zurückdeutet. Von den Gattungen Lecothecium, Racoblenna, Micarœa und Pterygium ist die Uebergang zu den Gallertflechten, was das Gewebe und die Anordnung der Gonidien betrifft, ein allmähliger zu nennen. Sowohl die Collemaceen . . . als die Omphalariaceen . . . schliessen sich unmittelbar an diese Repräsentanten der Pannariaceen an (wie mir scheint leichter oder doch eben so leicht, als die eine Abtheilung an die andere). . . . Von dieser Reihe zweigen sich an mehreren Punkten kleinere ab, deren Endglieder nach keiner Seite hin nähere Beziehungen verrathen. So von den Sticteen die Peltideaceen," u. s. w. Schwendener Untersuch., ubi supra.

"*Die wenigen Arten dieser ausgezeichneten Gattung vermitteln den Uebergang von den sogenannten heteromerischen Flechten zu den homöomerischen. Während die einen (P. plumbea, hypnorum u. a.) in ihren habituellen und anatomischen Merkmalen an die Parmeliaccen erinnern, zeigen die andern (P. rubiginosa, tryptophylla) eine ganz entschiedene Verwandtschaft mit den Collemaceen, ohne dass desswegen die Zusammengehörigkeit der ersteren und letzteren zu bezweifeln wäre. Bei P. rubiginosa und tryptophylla, zuweilen auch bei P. microphylla, besitzen nämlich die Gonidien gallertartig verdickte Membranen welche die Zwischenräume des Fasergeflechtes oft vollständig ausfüllen und in mänchen Fällen sogar zu einen homogenen Pulpa, in welcher wie bei den Gallertflechten Fasern und grüne Zellen eingebettet liegen, verschmolzen erscheinen. Demzufolge erscheint aldann der gonidienführende Theil des Lagers, welcher durchschnittlich ungefähr $\frac{2}{3}-\frac{3}{4}$ der ganzen Dicke einnimmt, stellenweise aber auch weiter nach unten vorspringt, als ein gallertartiges, fast durchweg interstitienloses Gewebe, dass von dem der typischen Collemaceen nicht wesentlich differirt, und nur der untere kleinere Theil, welche hie und da beinahe vollständig verdrangt ist, besteht aus einem lockern, lufthaltigen Fasergeflecht, wie man es bei den übrigen heteromerischen Flechten beobachtet.*" Schwendener, l. c Compare also, on the structure of the blue-green gonidia, De Bary, *Morph. u. Phys. d. Pilze, Flechten, etc.*, p. 257.

Berthel. Hist. Nat. Canar. p. 104, t. 6, f. 5. Lecanoræ sp., Krempelh. in Flora, 1851, n. 43.

Apothecia orbicularia, in thallo saccato-depressa, l. dein prominula margineque demisso subcincta. Sporæ ovoideo-oblongæ, simplices, incolores. Spermatia ellipsoidca; sterigmatibus simpliciusculis. Thallus frondoso-squamulosus, monophyllus, matrici arete adnatus, hypothallo obsolescente. Stratum gonimicum e collogonidiis constitutum.

The American lichen is either throughout closely applied to the earth on which it grows, or often, from the first, elevated at the margins; when these turn blackish beneath. Fronds, especially of the latter sort, reaching now 3$^{mm.}$ in the longest diameter, exhibit finally a well-marked lobation. Apothecia either sunken, when a thalline rim constitutes a spurious margin, or quite flat and wholly immarginate, or finally superficial, with, if I mistake not, a thin, depressed entire, true margin, of the substance of the thallus. Such were certainly to be expected, as in *Solorina*, in the case of sufficiently elevated fruit. More rarely also I find, in repeated instances, such superficial apothecia becoming turgid and thus immarginate in the sense, and with the whole look of cephaloid *Biatora* fruit. Spermogones (not heretofore described) have been observed by me, only on otherwise sterile fronds (with the whole structure, as well as the exact habit of fertile ones from the same region) collected in Texas (Wright). They are scarcely other than solitary, and mostly central, in the fronds, and appear as rather conspicuous, minute tubercles, of the colour of the thallus; clothed within with slender, sub-simple (that is, simple, or at length, if I do not mistake, very sparingly branched) sterigmas, bearing exceedingly minute, ovoid-ellipsoid spermatia.

It is impossible to deny the evident points of agreement between this little lichen and *Solorina saccata* v. *spongiosa*, Nyl.; but the former is not referable to *Solorina*, nor easily to *Peltigerei*. The family last named approaches indeed very closely, in the anatomical structure of the thallus, to *Pannariei*; but Schwendener appears to incline, on the whole, to recognize a predominant Pannarieine affinity in *Heppia*; as had already been done by Nylander. It needs in fact nothing but a sufficient reduction of the thallus, (of which reduction some of my American specimens appear to afford indications) to endue the finally superficial, or cephaloid apothecia with all the aspect of a *Pannaria*; akin, one might perhaps well venture to say, to *P. byssina*.

H. Despreauxii (Mont. l. c. *sub Solorina*) first detected in the Canaries, and afterwards recognized by Montagne in Ohio specimens (Lea) is found, not rarely, growing on the earth, from New England to Texas, as on calcareous pebbles in Kansas (E. Hall) and is the only known expression of this generical type: the European *H. adglutinata* (Krempelh.!) Mass. Lich. Ital. n. 157! Koerb.! *Parerg.* l. c., affording no differences.

XIX.—PANNARIA, Delis., emend.

Delis. in Dict. Class., cit. Dub. Bot. Gall. pp. 606, 655, et Endocarpi sp., p. 594. Parmelia sect. 2, Fr. L. E. p. 86 (spp. excl., et addita P. elæina, et Endocarpi sp.). Tuckerm. Syn. N. Eng. p. 35. Parmeliæ, Collematis, Lecanoræ et Lecideæ spp., Ach. L. U.; et Syn. Pannaria, et Parmeliæ, Collematis, Lecanoræ, Patellariæ spp., et Endocarpi sp., Dub. Bot. Gall. Parmeliæ sect., Collematis sp., Coccocarpia, et Endocarpi sp., Mont. in Ann.; Syll. Trachyderma, Norm. Con. p. 17. Pannaria, Coccocarpia, Racoblenna, Lecothecium, Collolechia, Toniniæ sp., et Endocarpi sp., Mass. Ric. pp. 109, 139; Mem. p. 54; Geneac, p. 7; Symm. pp. 55, 75. Psoroma, Amphilomatis sp., Pannaria, Coccocarpia, Pterygium, et Endocarpi sp., Nyl. Enum. Gén.; Syn. 1, p. 92, t. 2, f. 11–15; Lich. Scand. pp. 25, 121; et in Ann. Pannaria, Massalongia, Lecothecium, Collolechia, Pterygium, Wilmsia, et Endocarpi sp., Koerb. Syst. pp. 101, 105, 397; Parerg. pp. 45, 403. Pannaria, Coccocarpia, Massalongia, Racoblenna, et Pterygium, Stizenb. Beitr. pp. 142, 172. Structuram exposuerunt Tulasne, Mém. Lich. pp. 22, 148; Schwendener, Untersuch. l. c. 3, pp. 186, 190, t. 10, f. 7, 11, et 4, p. 161, t. 23, f. 10–13.

Apothecia sub-scutellæformia, l. lecanorina, l. zeorina, l. dein pseudo-biatorina. Sporæ ovoideo-ellipsoideæ vel oblongæ, l. simplices l. rarius bi-quadriloculares l. rarissime muriformi-pluriloculares, fuscescentes aut sæpius decolores. Spermatia (qu. cogn.) oblonga; sterigmatibus multi-articulatis. Thallus subfoliaceus e monophyllo laciniato-multifidus squamulosusve, subinde crustaceo-compactus. Stratum gopimicum e gonidiis, aut sæpius collogonidiis constans.

It is the secret of all systematic study, says Fries, adequately to apprehend the distinction between close affinity and superficial, or subtile differences.[1] The latter are to be worked out, and their secret extorted; but the interest of the investigation should not be permitted to blind us to the probably greater weight of the former. To Delise is due the credit of first indicating, in *Pannaria plumbea*, etc., *P. muscorum*, and *P. microphylla* (including, it should seem, *P. tryptophylla*) the outlines of the group before us; and to Fries (*L. E. exc. excip.*) for a clearer conception of its idea. But this idea could only come to its rights by the explication of all that was, in fact, involved in it; and, through such process

---

[1] *" Possunt sane v. c. asci . . vel unicam aut plures includere sporas in ceterum maxime affinibus, quos morphosi et metamorphosi congruis e tam subtilibus differentiis in diversas familias haud transferamus. Mysterium vero omnis systematici studii est rite percipere, magnam esse differentiam inter intimam affinitatem et externos vel subtilissimos characteres . . . Divinum . . effatum Linnæanum : genus dabit characterem, nec character genus, adhuc magis valet de familiis plantarum," etc. Fr. Summ. Veg. Scand. p. 264.*

of differentiation, the original group has passed now into near a dozen ; representing *Pannaria* analyzed. It is impossible, however, that this should be the end ; and the grave differences of opinion among lichenologists as to the value and limitation of these clusters, — what is *Pannaria* with one becoming *Coccocarpia* with another, what is *Pterygium* with one, *Lecothecium* with another, and what is *Lecothecium* with one, *Pannaria* with another, — point not uncertainly to a future reunion of the sundered types ; when the long lost idea, ennobled by the rich results of study, shall once more be recognized in its integrity.

The preliminary observations sufficiently shew that the present writer is, for his part, unable to adopt the opinions of those lichenographers who have elevated the anomalies of *Pannaria* into generical, and even ordinal distinctions. To do this is to disregard the natural connection and even continuity of most intimately related clusters of forms ; a fact tacitly admitted indeed by the most experienced of modern lichenologists, as well in his observations on the relations of his *Psoroma* and of *Coccocarpia* to *Pannaria* proper, as in those on the affinity of *P. nigra* (*Lecothecium & Collolechia,* of authors) to *Pterygium ;* and if he has recognized as sufficient the unsatisfactory difference which should separate the latter, this cannot destroy the value of his testimony as to all the former.

Psoroma, Nyl. (*Disp. Psorom. & Pannar.*) embraces almost the whole of the *Pannariæ,* of other authors, the gonimous system of which exhibits the normal structure of the *Parmeliacei.* Represented at the north only by the squamulose *P. hypnorum,* — the apothecia of which none the less interestingly exhibit the genuine Parmeliaceous type, so soon to disappear in the succeeding sections, accompanied also, in the var. *paleacea,* with other features of resemblance to *Sticta,* recurring there, — this group developes, at its centre, in the austral regions of the earth, into conspicuous, at length *frondose*-foliaceous forms, well worthy of its position as the highest extreme of *Pannaria ;* looking towards *Sticta,* and the *Parmeliei.* —— *P. lanuginosa* (Ach.) Koerb., the fruit of which is, at present, quite unknown, offers little to connect it with *Psoroma* beyond similar gonidia.

From these recedes *Pannaria* proper, conditioned, sometimes most perplexingly and in a manner unknown to the similarly receding groups of *Peltigerei,* by the seemingly abnormal structure of its gonimous system ; and no less by its frequently pseudo-biatorine fruit. It is observable however, that the section before us is mainly lecanorine, as respects its best developed species ; and that it is the reduced forms which in this, as in other respects, anticipate the various irregularities of the next. The highest cluster, or that more immediately represented by *P. rubiginosa,* is best exhibited in the tropical *P. pannosa,* and, especially, in the Polynesian *P. fulvescens* (Mont.) Nyl. The latter is unknown to North America ; but *P. pannosa* reaches, seen as yet only infertile, the low country of South Carolina (Ravenel) and Louisiana (Hale) and, in the tropics at least, is very evidently, not to say more, to *P. nigro-cincta*

(Mont.) Nyl., as *P. rubiginosa* (known only in lecanorine forms) to *P. tryptophylla*. And, as an extreme member of the same assemblage, associable perhaps structurally with *P. rubiginosa* through *P. fulvescens*, must be reckoned, if referred at all to the present genus, the remarkably retrograde *P. lurida*, Nyl. (*Collema*, Mont.) a not uncommon North American lichen, extending also to Japan (Wright) and the tropics; and combining, with often the exact habit of *P. rubiginosa*, an amount of deviation in thalline structure, from the latter, which can only be fully characterized as Collemaceous. The view to be here taken of the position of the *Collemei*, as in fact immediately contiguous to the *Pannariei*, removes the difficulty of attempting to conceive of such intimate relationship in plants of different orders, but it may still be questioned whether *P. lurida* should not follow *P. sub-lurida*, Nyl. (in *Ann.; Syn. Lich. N. Caled.* p. 5) into a still closer association with the group represented by *Collema byrsæum* (*Physma*, Mass. *Neag.* p. 6; *Dichodium*, Nyl. l. c.) the group being understood as properly intermediate between *Pannariei* and *Collemei*, but referable rather to the latter.——*P. rubiginosa* is found, not very uncommonly, throughout New England, and extends southward to South Carolina (Ravenel). In this species the degradation of the foliaceous thallus into the squamulose is at length most obvious; and if there were any doubt of its close relation to *P. tryptophylla*, none can well be entertained of the analogous affinity of *P. pannosa* to *P. nigro-cincta*.—— The species last named (*P. nigro-cincta* (Mont.) Nyl.) has occurred, on trunks, in the low country of South Carolina (Ravenel) and Louisiana (Hale); the specimens agreeing generally with one of the New Granada ones (Nyl. in Lindig. n. 818) but by no means so well marked as the others, or as one received from Montagne; and might almost be referred to the next. Even the Cuban Lichen (Wright *Lich. Cub.* n. 103) in some of its states at least, is ambiguous; and suggests readily the finest forms (as Fellm. *Lich. Arct.* n. 98) of the northern plant (*P. tryptophylla*). But the best forms of *P. nigro-cincta* suggest unmistakably *P. pannosa*.——*P. tryptophylla* (Ach.) Mass., occurs on trunks, and also, growing over mosses, on stones, in the mountains of New England, and in New York. Massachusetts (H. Willey). Vermont (C. C. Frost). The near affinity of this species to those immediately preceding, will hardly be disputed; but it stands also, in some of its states (and similar difficulties are not unknown elsewhere in *Pannaria*) in apparently close relations to another group (*Lecothecium*, etc., *Auctt.*) which we find ourselves compelled, in the present arrangement, to remove far from it.——*P. Hookeri* (Sm.) Th. Fr., of the Scottish and Scandinavian mountains, has occurred in Greenland, Vahl. (Th. Fr. *Lich. Arct.*) but the still more interesting *P. elæina* (Wahl.) Nyl., which Dr. Fries takes for intermediate between *P. rubiginosa* and *P. Hookeri*, is unknown as North American.——*P. microphylla* (Sw.) Del. (e Dub. l. c.) is as frequent probably in the northern States as *P. leucosticta;* and I possess it also from Ohio (Lesquereux) California (Bolander) and New

7

Mexico (Fendler). Both the lecanorine and pseudo-biatorine conditions are well marked.——*P. crossophylla,* Tuckerm. (*Obs. Lich.* l. c. 4, p. 404) an elegantly branch-lobed, minute rock-lichen, with bright-reddish, pseudo-biatorine apothecia, has only occurred at its original station in Vermont (Russell).——*P. granatina* (Sommerf.) Th. Fr. (*Lecanora,* Sommerf., Nyl. *Scand. Parmelia* § *Patellaria,* Fr. *Pyrenopsis,* Nyl. *Lich. Fellm.* Th. Fr. *Lich. Spitzb.*). Granite rocks; Notch of the White Mountains (myself) and in Gorham, N. H., (H. Willey). Thallus heretofore described as a chinky crust, made up of small, sometimes crenulate granules (Sommerf., Fries, Nyl.) or of cartilagineous squamules (Mass., Th. Fr.) but really, and in the European specimens (Herb. Th. Fr. Fellm. *Lich. Arct.* n. 4) equally with the American, peltate! and to be compared especially with *Omphalaria botryosa.* From this the plant before us appears at once and certainly to differ in its Lecanoreine and not Collemeine habit; and the details of structure, if they exclude it from the *Lecanorei,* as here understood, permit of its association with *Pannaria.* I am at any rate unable, in a full comparison, under the microscope, of the thalline structure both of this, and of *Collema hæmaleum,* Sommerf., referred here as a variety by Th. Fries, with the more reduced conditions of *P. microphylla,* etc., to discriminate any sufficient difference. The plant fills in this genus, if our view be not a mistaken one, a strictly analogous place to that occupied by *L. rubina* in *Lecanora.*——So closely related, in every respect, to the lichen just noticed is *Pyrenopsis hæmatopis,* Th. Fr. (*Collema* v. *hæmatopis,* Sommerf. *Pyr. rufescens,* Nyl.) found in Greenland (Vahl, e Th. Fr. *Lich. Arct.*) that its place must undoubtedly be determined by that of the former. I have only seen the specimens in Fellm. *Lich. Arct.* (n. 5) which are hardly satisfactory as respects condition, but appear to agree generally, in important external features, with *P. granatina.* It is to be hoped that the plant may be found in New England.——*P. brunnea* (Sw.) Mass., known only as an United States lichen, on the coast of Massachusetts (Oakes; H. Willey) is doubtless more common northward, and is found in Greenland (Vahl, e Th. Fr. *Lich. Arct.*) occurring also in the islands of Behring's Straits (Wright).——*P. cyanolepra,* Tuckerm. (Lich. Calif. p. 17). On the earth, California (Bolander). Closely resembles *P. nebulosa* (Hoffm.) Nyl., and the alleged difference may prove to be insufficient.——*P. leucosticta,* Tuckerm. (*Obs. Lich.* l. c. 4, p. 404) is found throughout the Atlantic and Gulf States; and in Ohio (Lesquereux). From this species, first described by me in Darlingt. *Fl. Cestr.* 1853, I am scarcely able to distinguish such specimens as I have seen of the European *P. craspedia,* Koerb., *Parerg.* p. 45 (Anz. *Lich. Langob.* n. 429) of Istria and Lombardy.——*P. lepidiota,* Th. Fr. (*Lich. Arct.* p. 74. *Lecid. muscorum var.,* Sommerf. *P. prætermissa,* Nyl. *Lich. Scand.* p. 124, *teste ipso,* p. 290) was referred by Sommerfelt, and Fries to *P. muscorum,* (Ach.) Del., but differs in its spores, and in other respects, and is perhaps nearest to *P. leucosticta ;* which is

not, however, known to occur with pseudo-biatorine fruit. *P. lepidiota*
has been found in Greenland (Vahl, in Th. Fr. l. c.) and in California
(Bolander). The spores in this, as in *P. muscorum*, *P. cyanolepra*, and
some other species (Koerb. *Syst.* p. 107) offer some indications of colour;
not unlike those observable in the similar spores of *Erioderma*.——*P.
Bolanderi*, Tuckerm. (*infra descr.*[1] Rocks, Ukiah, California (Bolander).
Perhaps rather associable, as respects the thallus, with the species immediately preceding, but very strongly differenced, as well by the polysporous thekes, —a new character in the present genus, —as by the Collemeine
habit of the apothecia, which recede in this direction much as those of
P. elæina (Wahl.) Nyl., are described as doing in another; and are really
not very much unlike the most mature ones of Mass. *Lich. Ital.* n. 174
(*Thyrea Notarisii*, Mass.).——With the Californian *Pannaria* just reckoned, before us, it is impossible, in the light afforded by Baglietto's recent
determination of *Endocarpon Guepini* as a Parmeliaceous lichen,[2] not to
see that the latter is really the nearest relative of the former; and, with
all who do not allow other than subordinate weight to the polysporous
anomaly, must fall also into *Pannaria*. As respects the thallus, *P.
Guepini* (Delis.) (occurring as yet, here, only at Needham, Mass., and on
the Maryland shore opposite Harper's Ferry, Virginia, Myself; and on the
coast of California, Mr. Bolander) differs from *P. Bolanderi* as a monophyllous from a polyphyllous, imbricate species—or somewhat as *P.
elæina* (as described) from *P. Hookeri*. In the fruit, however, as perhaps
much the most commonly exhibited, this difference is more marked. It
was always difficult, in the large number of specimens of our *P. Guepini*
before me, to trace any external indications of apothecia. Nor were
certain minute but regular cavities occurring now and then in the upper
surface of the thallus, supposed to relate at all to the fructification. But,
seen in section, under the guidance of the Italian lichenologist, these
cavities prove to contain, each a sunken *Parmeliaceous* hymenium; and

---

[1] *Pannaria Bolanderi (sp. nov.) thallo squamoso imbricato coriaceo-membra-
naceo olivaceo-fusco, lobis crenatis margine dein elevatis cæsio-pulverulentis, subtus
carneis nudis; apotheciis innato-sessilibus lecanorinis, disco rufo margine erecto
tumidulo integerrimo. Sporæ in thecis polysporis numerosæ* (35–60) *simplices,
incolores, longit.* 0,004$^{mm.}$—0,007$^{mm.}$ *crassit. circa* 0,003$^{mm.}$ Rocks (metamorphic
sandstone) coast of California (Bolander). Squamules of the specimens 3—4$^{mm.}$
in the longest diameter, and smaller; forming smallish, now closely, and now more
loosely imbricated clumps. There is something in the aspect of the squamules
which reminds one of the most developed portions of the thallus of *P. lepidiota;*
and the anatomical structure is not dissimilar in the two lichens, except that the
collogonidia, occurring in clusters of two to four, and these clusters measuring at
length 0,027$^{mm.}$ by 0,023$^{mm.}$ are larger in the present. Texture of *P. Bolanderi,*
like that of *P. Guepini,* largely parenchymatous. With iodine the hymenium
assumes a dull bluish tint, passing into a dirty brownish yellow.

[2] Baglietto in *Nuov. Giorn. Bot. Ital.* 2, p. 171, cit. Leighton, *Not. Lich.* n. 33,
in Ann. Nat. Hist., Sept. 1870.

to constitute therefore, the 'urceolate' stage of the fruit, as described by him. So much being gained, it were readily conceivable that the sunken hymenium should become finally superficial, and acquire therewith a thalline border: and this stage, which completes the history, though not observed as yet in the American plant, and probably always rare, is fully described in the European. Considered as a section of *Pannaria*, *Endocarpiscum*, Nyl., offers the earliest, allowable designation of these polysporous species, and is singularly appropriate; the other names proposed (*Guepinia*, Hepp; *Guepinella*, Bagl.) being, moreover, at once seen to conflict (in making it, so to say, necessary to provide a new specific name for the oldest species) with one of the best settled rules of nomenclature. With this section, or sub-section, we conclude our present list of North American lichens referable to what might altogether or with some few possible exceptions, be called *Pannaria* proper. It may yet be added that *P. pholidota* (Mont.) Nyl., an elegant, *Lecanora*-like, squamulose species of the island of Juan Fernandez, is also an inhabitant of Mexico (Nyl.).

Though scarcely well distinguishable in structure from the preceding section, the much smaller one now to be considered (*Coccocarpia*, Nyl.) is yet marked to a certain extent, by habit; and by its constantly pseudo-biatorine fruit. Of this section, the Chilian *P. Gayana* (Mont.) is unknown as yet as North American; and even *P. plumbea* (Lightf.) Del., though found throughout the extent of Europe, from the Lofoden Islands to Portugal, is deficient here. But the lichen last named passes, especially southward, as was first observed by Nylander, into states (Delis. *Lich. de Fr.* n. 4. Welwitsch *Crypt. Lusit.*) very closely comparable with *P. molybdœa* (*Coccocarpia*, Pers., & Auctt. *C. parmelioides* (Hook.) Tuckerm. in *Lich. Cub.* n. 104–107) and the latter, unknown in Europe, occurs, in one or other of its forms, throughout the United States. The apothecia of this species, though otherwise interpreted by even such observers as Montagne, and Tulasne, offer in fact, in their earlier recognizable conditions, no appreciable differences from similarly immature ones of *P. plumbea ;* and the symphicarpeous state into which they finally pass, is of course nothing against their relation to *Pannaria*. The (proper) margin, however commonly excluded, is not structurally deficient; it is often to be detected in tropical forms of the species, and occurs in North American specimens of the v. *cronia*, Nyl. (Alabama, T. M. Peters) with all the regularity, and indeed all the features of that of the analogous European lichen. I am inclined, after an examination of some extent, to regard the spores of *P. molybdœa* as typically bilocular, and as affording therefore another difference to separate the present group (*Coccocarpia*) from the preceding; but authors are by no means agreed upon this minute point of structure.[1]——*P. stel-*

---

[1] " *Costantemente omogenei, uniloculari, e solo per accidente vidi qualche sporidio con una linea irregolare trasversale, piuttosto dovuta alla non completa*

lata (Tuckerm. *sub Coccocarpia Obs. Lich.* l. c. 5, p. 402) Nyl. On *Ilex opaca*, South Carolina (Ravenel). Except in its minuteness well comparable with small forms of *P. molybdœa*, v. *incisa* (*Coccocarpia incisa*, Pers. Lindig. *Lich. N. Gran.* coll. 2, n. 68) and the fruit entirely similar to the younger ones of New Granada lichen cited ; with which our plant also agrees in its ' bilocular or binucleolate' spores. Its lobation is, at the same time, not unlike that of *P. tryptophylla*, etc. ; and Nylander (*Disp. Psorom. & Pann.*) has removed the lichen to *Pannaria* proper. But a resemblance to *P. tryptophylla* may be said to imply also no great dissimilarity to our next succeeding section (*Lecothecium*) and here we must remark not only that *P. stellata* is comparable with *P. flabellosa* and *P. Petersii*, but that the section *Coccocarpia*, as a whole, recedes, in an important detail of anatomical structure (the compacter medullary tissue) from *Pannaria* proper, in the exact direction of *Lecothecium*, as interpreted by *Pterygium*. *P. molybdœa*, etc., agree in the features of their medullary layer with *P. plumbea*, described already by Tulasne ; and the structure in question of these lichens suggests that of *Pterygium*, Nyl. ; here not distinguished from *Lecothecium*.

We have found *Coccocarpia*, while at one end represented by distinguished forms, passing yet, at the other, like *Pannaria* proper, into diminished conditions, comparable even with some of the lowest of Pannariine types. And we have also suggested, that, in addition to the argument from the always pseudo-biatorine apothecia of the group just reviewed, and its finally (it should seem) bilocular spores, there were not wanting indications of other structural agreement with the section now to be considered. But *Lecothecium* has an interest of its own independent of any supposed associableness with *Coccocarpia*. The former group, as we here understand it, exhibits structure which unquestionably anticipates that of *Collemei ;* and one or other of its members is now all but universally accepted as Collemaceous. If however the modification of structure referred to, first in fact shew itself within the undisputed limits of *Pannaria* (in *P. tryptophylla*)[1] it is impossible to avail ourselves of it for the generical separation of *Lecothecium nigrum*, Mass. And if we

organizzazione del l'endosporio di quello, che alla sua speciale morfologia." Mass. *Mem.* p. 54. Montagne, on the other hand, has no hesitation in calling the spores " *biloculares seu binucleolatas.*" Syll. p. 343.

[1] The observations upon which this remark rests were made in 1865, and some expression given to my view of their importance in a note to the description of *Pannaria cyanolepra*, in Lich. Calif. p. 17, the following year. But it now appears that far more important results, looking in the same direction, were reached by Schwendener in 1863. By the passage, already cited at the conclusion of the preliminary remarks on this family, it is evident that marked Collemaceous features are traceable, not only in *P. tryptophylla*, where they might perhaps have been beforehand reckoned possible, but in *P. microphylla*, and even *P. rubiginosa*. (Schwend. l. c.)

cannot separate the latter, surely the obsolescence of the hypothallus will not alone serve to distinguish generically the, in every other respect, similar *L. asperellum*, Th. Fr., which, according to Nylander (*Lich. Scand.* p. 25) is a *Pterygium*. From this species, *Pterygium Petersii* and *P. centrifugum*, Nyl., chiefly differ, as respects the thallus, in being more evidently foliaceous, and (as a consequence of this?) in exhibiting more distinctly the very regular, elongated cells which constitute the marked medullary tissue.——*P. nigra* (Huds.) Nyl. (*Collema*, Ach., *Lecothecium*, Mass., & Auctt.). Calcareous rocks, and sandstones, throughout the United States. Canada (A. T. Drummond). Virginia (Curtis). Alabama (Peters). Thallus parenchymatous throughout. Apothecia now reddish-brown (Trenton Falls, N. Y.) but more commonly black. Spores (of the Trenton lichen) ellipsoid, bilocular, or at length more oblong and 3-4-locular, $0,011–16^{mm.}$ long, and $0,0045–0,006^{mm.}$ wide. In the same Trenton lichen the approach appears to be a gradual one to var. *cæsia*, Nyl. (*Collolechia*, Mass., & *Auctt.*) wherein, through what seems a chemical change, the external colour alike and the normal structure of the thallus are modified. The extent of this degradation is, however, various in the European specimens, as is seen in comparing Nyl. *Herb. Par.* n. 115 with Anz. *Lich. Ital. Sup.* n. 10; and in the latter at least there is no difficulty in observing the parenchyma of the thallus. Spores of this variety, from Trenton, ellipsoid, or biscoctiform, bilocular, $0,011–14^{mm.}$ long. and $0,007–8^{mm.}$ wide. The external resemblance of *P. nigra* to *P. tryptophylla* is no doubt corroborated, to a certain extent, by the anatomical structure of these lichens; but we cannot well separate the former from the group with which it is here associated, and this group diverges from that which includes *P. tryptophylla*, in its spore-character; to say nothing of other differences.——*P. flabellosa*, Tuckerm. (*Obs. Lich.* l. c. 5, p. 401) Granitic rocks, Vermont (C. C. Frost). Sufficiently distinguishable externally from the last, especially by its marginal lobes, and indistinct hypothallus. As regards internal structure the two plants are generally alike. In a more luxuriant but infertile, similar lichen collected by me, on granite, in the White Mountains, the lobes of the circumference exhibit however, under the microscope, a compact medulla comparable only with that of *P. Petersii;* and the plant before us may be said to be, in several respects, intermediate between that species and *P. nigra*. Spores oblong-ellipsoid, 4-locular, $0,016–18^{mm.}$ long, and $0,0055–7^{mm.}$ wide. *Lecothecium adglutinatum*, Anz. (*Manip.* n. 12, *Lich. Langob.* n. 268) from granitic rocks in Upper Italy, seems to be well comparable with our plant.——*P. Petersii*,[1] Tuckerm., is only known to me from its

---

[1] *Pannaria Petersii: thallo parvulo membranaceo stellato-expanso e lividoglauco olivaceo-nigrescente, laciniis appressis plano-convexis centro squamulosodispersis delabentibus ambitu radiantibus laciniato-multifidis, hypothallo obsolescente; apotheciis minutis pseudo-biatorinis nigris, margine tenui demum subex-*

original locality. It is best compared with *P. flabellosa;* from which it differs in its regularly radiant, much darker thallus, almost obsolete hypothallus, etc. Traces of the hypothallus are distinctly observable however, in the plant before us, under the microscope; as in all the species of the present group, including *Lecothecium asperellum*, Th. Fr. The medullary layer is far better defined in *P. Petersii* than in the squamulose forms of *Lecothecium;* and is moreover modified in a marked way, (precisely as in *P. centrifugum*, Nyl. Syn. t. 2, f. 11) contrasting especially with what we find in *P. lurida.* But if the latter, Collemaceous as it is, approaches too closely to unquestionable *Pannariæ* to be readily separated from them, the present may be said to be, in like manner, associable with *P. flabellosa*, and through that with *P. tryptophylla.*—— The spores of the little group we have been examining sufficiently shew that *Pannaria*, if not advancing beyond the unilocular grade in its best-developed forms, shows an evident *nisus* in the direction of such advance, in its inferior members. And there is also some evidence, once more in the present group (*Lecothecium radiosum*, Anz., *e* Koerb. *Parcrg., sub Wilmsia*, p. 406) but by no means confined to it, that *Pannaria* offers really a decolorate exhibition of the modifications of the brown spore; and belongs therefore, not to the series in which *Lecanora* follows *Parmelia*, but rather to that which includes at once *Umbilicaria*, *Solorina*, and the equally decolorate *Collemei.* From this point of view it cannot of course surprise us should lichens otherwise sufficiently Pannarieine, be found to exhibit the highest, or muriform modification of the coloured spore. And it is certainly no more surprising than that this should be the case in *Collema*, as understood by Nylander.——*P. byssina* (Hoffm. *sub Collemate.* Koerb. *Parerg.* p. 410. *Leptogium*, Zw. *exs.* n. 174! Nyl. *Syn.* 1, p. 120). On the earth, Illinois (E. Hall). Massachusetts, at the tops of walls (H. Willey). Thallus of minute, imbricated or somewhat ascendant, ash-coloured or whitish squamules; reduced in most of the Massachusetts specimens to mealy granules; with the aspect now of *P. brunnea*, and now of *P. nebulosa* (Hoffm.) Nyl.; composed (as

cluso. Sporæ octonæ, ellipsoideæ simplices l. rarius biloculares, dein magis oblongæ sporoblasto variabili, incolores, longit. 0,011–0,023^{mm.}, *crassit.* 0,005–0,006^{mm.} *Lecidea*, Tuckerm. *in litt., et in* Nyl. *Syn.* 1, p. 93. *Pterygium*, Nyl. l. c. Lime-rocks, Alabama, T. M. Peters. The finally blackened apothecia of this and the other members of the present group, growing upon rocks, are by no means carbonaceous, or properly lecideine. In the excellent specimens before me of *Lecothecium asperellum*, Th. Fr. (*e herb. auct.*) and in *P. flabellosa*, it is easy to see that the young fruit is pale, and in no respect typically diverse from that of pseudo-biatorine states of other *Pannariæ;* and I observe young apothecia of precisely the same character in *P. nigra*, which occurs moreover, as noted above, and also by Nylander (*Lich. Scand.*) with brown fruit. And there can scarcely be a doubt that further enquiry would shew that the other forms agree in this respect also with these.

in *P. nebulosa*, Nyl. *Lich. Par.* n. 114) throughout of rounded cells (diam. 0,007–0,011$^{mm.}$) and collogonidia which are commonly solitary, and only rarely concatenate in threes and fours. Apothecia (reaching at length 1$^{mm.}$ in width, but more often smaller) innate-sessile, reddish-brown, darker perhaps, but otherwise very similar in aspect to those of the cited German specimen, except that in the Illinois lichen, in which the thallus is especially well-developed, this more evidently conditions the here almost lecanorine fruit. Spores in eights, ovoid-ellipsoid, muriform-plurilocular (long. ser. 4–6, more rarely 8; transv. ser. 2, rarely 3) pale-brownish while in the thekes, and now also when free, 0,018–0,30$^{mm.}$ long, and 0,007–0,014$^{mm.}$ wide. Often exactly resembling, in the spores, *Leptogium lacerum* and *L. subtile* (or as in Arn. *Lich. Fragm.* in *Flora*, 1867, t. 1, f. 6) but our plants are easily distinguishable by the differences of the thallus. I can entertain no doubt (and compare also the remarks of Koerber, l, c.[1]) that the German plant cited is a true *Pannaria ;* and the Illinois lichen here above described appears properly referable to it. The Massachusetts specimens are inferior in the thallus but similar in the apothecia and the spores. Hymenial gelatine becoming intensely blue with iodine.

Excluding the first section (*Psoroma*, Nyl.) of nine species, as reckoned by Nylander, which attains to its perfection only in the austral regions of the earth, the great bulk of *Pannaria*, of something less than forty species, appears certainly to be northern; but this is due to the number of reduced forms occurring northward; and, looked at in the light of its best-developed conditions, the genus is in fact largely southern, and analogous in this to *Sticta*. Rather less than half of the whole number of species has been detected in North America; and the European ratio is much the same ; but no doubt forms remain to be observed on this continent.

———•———

Fam. 6.—COLLEMEI.

Thallus frondoso-foliaceus l. dein crustaceo-diminutus, rarius fruticuloso-adscendens l. alectoriiformis, cartilagineo-l. coriaceo-membranaceus, humidus in plerisque subgelatinosus, hypothallo fere semper obsoleto. Stratum gonimicum plerumque inordinatum dis-

[1] " *Sie ist unter allen Collema-arten diejenige, welche am wenigsten dem Gattungstypus entspricht, da sie die für Collema (und verwandte Gattungen) so characteristische wasserhelle Pulpa mit den darin vertheilten Faserelementen durchaus nicht besitzt, auch die Microgonidien der Thallus etwas grösser sind, und sich seltener zu den bekannten Gonidien-schnüren verbinden.*" Koerb. *Pererg.* p. 410.

solutumve, e collogonidiis l. varie dein aggregatis l. sæpissime monil-iformi-concatenatis et in pulpa mucilaginosa nidulantibus, constans.

As respects the fructification there is no question that the great bulk of the groups before us is Parmeliaceous; and their anomalies of thalline structure have also, it should seem, not to be questioned Parmeliaceous points of departure. Careful comparison of the whole structure of such a series of lichens as *Pannaria rubiginosa, P. fulvescens,* and *P. lurida, Collema byrsæum,* and *Leptogium myochroum (L. saturninum,* Dicks., & *Auctt. pl.*) and its allies, or of such a series as *Pannaria tryptophylla,* and *P. flabellosa,* and the species brought together in *Lecothecium, Ptery-gium,* and *Collolechia* of authors, indicates, if I mistake not, far from doubtfully, that these are series, not of plants of mixed classes, or of lichens of mixed orders, but of types variously modified of what is most readily conceivable as the same tribe. *Pannaria lurida,* Nyl. (*Collema,* Mont.) is assumed, on very high authority, to be, on the whole, congener-ical with *P. rubiginosa;* and *Collema byrsæum* (*C. byrsinum,* Ach., *Physma,* Mass.) belongs, with as little doubt, to the higher groups of *Col-lemei:* but the congruity of structure in the first-and last-mentioned of these lichens is significant; and precludes, here, any distant separation of them.

It is the more or less gelatinous nature of the larger proportion of the *Collemei,* when wet, that has always attracted the attention of observers, from Micheli (*Gen.* p. 87) and Dillenius (*Hist. Musc.* p. 137–147) to the present day (Koerb. *Syst.* p. 394) and this, in itself however useful yet certainly subordinate distinction, suggested without doubt the long prevalent views of an essential diversity of structure in these plants (*Lichenes thallo extus intusque homogeneo,* Ach. *L. U.* p. 129, t. 14, f. 8. *Lichenes homœomerici,* Wallr. *Naturgesch. d. Flecht.* 1, p. 225) which later and more thorough investigation has by no means confirmed. This asserted difference in structure was yet far, at first, from being regarded as sufficient to exclude *Collema* from that place (among Lichens) to which the sum of its affinities referred it. Acharius grouped the genus with Parmeliaceous types, as did Floerke, Wahlenberg, Sommerfelt, and Fée; and Eschweiler vindicated for it the same position : while Meyer, Wallroth, and Schærer (*Spicil.*) refused to recognize in it anything higher than marked sections of their *Parmelia* and *Patellaria.*

Nor did Fries, in his earlier expositions of the Lichen-system (in *Vet. Ak. Handl.* 1821, & *Sched. crit.*) depart from the view that *Collema* is Parmeliaceous. We find here *Biatora, Collema, Parmelia* (in its largest sense) and *Peltidea* (in the same) making the first series of the highest division (*Hymenothalami*) as later (*Syst. Orb. Veg.* 1825) *Collemacei,* in-cluding *Ephebe,* make the last tribe of the same division. [1] In the work

[1] In the imperfect but often instructive sketch of the system as conceived by Prof. Naegeli (Hepp Flecht. Eur. Taf. 1.) *Collemeæ* take a similar place, as the last

8

last-named the relations of these plants to some of the lower and obscurer Algæ are however expressly noted, and the thought is carried a step further in the actual removal of *Synalissa, Thermutis,* and *Lichina* to a new section (*Byssaceæ*) intermediate between *Lichens* and Algæ proper. Still later this section (*Byssaceæ*) was extended by Fries (*Fl. Scan.* p. 291. *S. V. S.* p. 121) to include also his *Collemaceæ ;* and though burthened with ambiguous, and it has since proved, incongruous elements, the removal of which by Montagne (*Pl. Cell. Cub.* p. 106) may be said to have done away with much of the vitality of the section as it certainly invalidated its name,—furnishes the historical foundation of the arrangement which, under various names (*Collemaceæ,* Mont. *Aperc. Morph.* Schær. *Enum.* Mass. *Mem.* Nyl. *Lichenes homæomerici,* Koerb. Anz. *Phycolichenes,* Mass. *Sched.* Stizenb. *Homolichenes,* Th. Fr.) has since generally obtained.

It is notwithstanding difficult to get at the supposed value and systematic significance of this arrangement, as apprehended by the authors who have, since Fries, adopted it ;—and the difficulty is, we presume, an intrinsic one. Leaving out of sight the more or less gelatinous nature, when wet, of the *Collemei,* which, in this way and to this extent, approach some of the lower Algæ, and the strict affinity of the *Ephebei* to *Stigonema* and other groups, still, but perhaps not always to be reckoned among Algæ, the distinction of the family before us turns wholly on 1) a 'similarity' of thalline structure resulting from a certain, more or less marked confusion of the elementary parts, and 2) a general dissolution of the gonimous layer ;[1] and great stress cannot easily be laid on either of these

family of *Parmeliaceæ;* the *Lichineæ* being separated, as by Fries, but appended to *Sphærophoraceæ.*

[1] " *Ob gonidia thallo similari inspersa, strato scilicet corticali s. gonimo cum medullari confuso.*" Mont. *Pl. Cell. Cub.* p. 105. " *E cellularum stratis plerumque indistinctis in pulpam similarem confusis*" . . . . *gonidiis* " *stratum discretum nullum* " *informantibus.* Koerb. *Syst.* p. 393. " *Les grains gonidiaux sont disposés d'une maniere tout a fait spéciale* . . . . *le cortex n'est représenté le plus souvent que par un épithalle;* . . . . *d'autres fois par une couche de cellules anguleuses, distinctes. Le reste du thalle appartient au système médullaire et se compose d'une substance très avide d'eau (sorte de lichenine) parcourue par des filaments tubuleux, ou creusée, dans quelques Collémacés, de cavités arrondies contenant des grains gonidiaux; chez d'autres enfin tout le thalle est formé d'un tissu celluleux. Dans les formes fruticuleuses de ce meme groupe on observe parfois une axe central constitué par des éléments filamenteux articulés, disposés longitudinalement en une faisceau blanchâtre. . . rappelant en quelque sorte le cordon médullaire des Usnées. . . . Les espèces dont le thalle est formé de tissu celluleux different à peine, par leur structure intérieure, de quelques Lichénacés, mais elles se rapprochent par d'autres caractères des Collémacés; ces derniers se laissent d'ailleurs facilement reconnaitre par leur port tout spécial, par leur coloration foncée et mate, par leur coupe luisant sous le scalpel (conséquence de leur constitution gélatineuse) par leur grande distensibilité dans l'eau,*

anomalies, so long as both find evident analogies, and shall we not say again their point of departure, in the *Pannariei*.[1] *Pannaria* contains not merely, as Dr. Stizenberger (*Beitr.*, l. c. p. 172, *not.*) has observed, Collemaceous elements, but it does not appear to be conceivable without them. And these elements are traceable yet further back. It is in the *Peltigerei*, the centre of *Parmeliacei*, — in *Sticta* and *Peltigera* — that that modification of the gonidial system[2] begins which finds its explication in the family before us; and well-known habit as much favours these indications of affinity in the higher *Collemei* to *Sticta* and other *Peltigerei*, as, in both higher and lower, to *Pannaria*. Nor are 'true Lichens' without other instructive evidences, in the humbler groups, of not dissimilar confusion and disintegration of thalline structure.

These views, suggested by the observations on *Pannaria lurida* and *P. tryptophylla*, above indicated, find no uncertain support in Tulasne's summing up of the results of his examination of the Collemaceous thallus. The details show, says this eminent botanist, whose remarks are largely illustrated by his exquisite figures, "that the fronds of most simple structure are yet very complex, both as respects the number and the varied form of their elements; which deprives of much of its value the proposed division of the thalli of Lichens into homogeneous and heterogeneous. For the Collemas, which, according to Wallroth, should form alone the first class, are far from offering really homogeneous or similar fronds; and are by no means deprived absolutely, as Martius contends, of the gonimous layer." Even the *Lichinæ*, to which Schærer (*Enum.*) refused a place among either Lichens or *Collemaceæ*, "possess on the contrary, in an elevated degree, all the characters which distinguish the Lichens."[3]

---

en un mot, par une série de caractéres bien différents de ceux qui sont offerts par le thalle des Lichénacés." Nyl. *Syn. Lich.* p. 12. *" E stratis non distinctis . . . intus e gonidiis sparsis l. varie concatenatis et filamentis hyalinis compositus."* Th. Fr. *Lich. Arct.* p. 276. *" Thallo gelatinoso, homœomerico, substantiæ viridis Chlorophyll dictæ egeno."* Stizenb. *Beitr.* l. c. p. 139.

[1] Of the varied conditions of the gonimous system exhibited in *Collemei* none has so generally been accepted as characteristical, as the necklace-like strings, or chaplets of gonidia; but these are well marked in *Pannaria lurida* (Mont. *sub Collemate*) and are traceable no less in *Pannaria fulvescens* (Mont., *sub Parmelia*) the specimen (*Herb. Mus. Par.*) having been determined by Nylander; as in other species, here referred to *Pannaria*.

[2] Compare the passage from Schwendener, already cited at p. 44. And see also De Bary (*Morph. & Phys. d. Pilze*, etc.) p. 259. In view of these observations, unknown to the writer at the time of the preparation of his text, as given above, it is impossible to question the close structural affinity of *Peltigera*, etc. with *Collemei*.

[3] *" Les details dans lesquels nous venons d'entrer montrent que les frondes de la structure la plus simple sont encore assez complexes, quant au nombre et à la forme variée de leurs éléments, ce qui enléve beaucoup de valeur à la division proposée, des thalles des Lichens, en thalles homogénes (homœomerische oder gleich·*

There is no doubt, as respects the great bulk of *Usneei, Parmeliei,* and *Lecanorei,* that these groups are most readily conceivable as contiguous sections of a single series (Fr. *L. E.* p. 15) whether we regard external characters or those derivable from the spores ; but the case is scarcely as clear with respect to the *frondose*-foliaceous *Parmeliacei,* the (typical) differences of which in form might be taken to be corroborated, to some extent, by the spore-characters, as they are at length also by important ones in thalline structure. Thus regarded, *Umbilicariei,* — the spore type of which, no less than its abnormally conditioned apothecia, separate it from *Parmeliei,* notwithstanding the close affinity of the two groups as expressed in *Omphalodium Pisacomense,* Mey. & Flot., — would appear as the first marked member of another series, continued by *Sticta* and the other *Peltigerei,* passing through important changes in *Pannariei,* and finding its extreme point in *Collemei. Umbilicaria,* comparable in structure with the highest *Collemei* in everything except the gonidia, would thus begin a line including (as we understand it) all its most evident analogues ; and suggest as well the real position of *Sticta.* Nor should the fronds of *Paulia* and *Omphalaria* seem less significant, in this connection, than the *quasi*-Collemaceous fruit of the cited *Omphalodium.* The difficulties in the spore-character of the *Peltigerei,* which might well seem, as we have taken them, despite the everywhere traceable indications of colour, becoming at length distinct, to be rather referable to the colourless series, would thus, in like manner, be possibly lessened ; and, — those of the certainly contiguous *Pannariei* being explained by *Collemei,* much as *Sticta* by *Umbilicaria,* — *Pannaria,* etc., would be removed from a place (the colourless series, represented by the bulk of *Usneei, Parmeliei* and *Lecanorei*) less really related to them, to one not unsatisfactory. The distinction in the spore-characters of *Pannaria,* as here understood, and *Eucollemei,* is mainly that that of the latter is, —

schichtige Thalle, Wallr., Martius, etc.) et en thalles hétérogènes (ungleichschichtige oder heteromerische Thalle). Car les Collema qui, suivant M. Wallroth, devraient former à eux seuls la première classe, sont loin d'offrir des frondes vraiment homogènes ou similaires, et ne sont point davantage privés absolument, comme la prétendait M. Martius de couche grenue verte ou gonimique (grüne Kœrnerschicht;) si, en effet, ainsi que nous l'avons vu, la matière verte est chez quelques unes dissoute dans le mucilage de la fronde, chez un plus grand nombre elle est concentrée en globules, qui pour être réunis en chapelets, ou quelquefois dispersés, sans ordre apparent dans toute l'épaisseur du thalle, n'ent semblent pas moins des organes analogues aux gonidies des autres Lichens." Tul. *sur les Lichens,* p. 30, *tab.* 6, 7, 9. *" On peut faire remarquer ici que les Lichina, qui ont été souvent mis au nombre des Algues marines, et auxquels M. Fries et plus récemment M. Schœrer ont refusé une place parmi les Lichens d'Europe, en décrivant ou énumérant ces végétaux, que les Lichina, dis-je, possèdent au contraire, dans un degré élevé, tous les caractères qui distinguent les Lichens; il suffit pour s'en convaincre de rapprocher des détails qui précèdent ce que nous avons dit plus haut de leurs apothécies et de la structure de leur thalle."* Ibid. p. 188.

like the group itself generally, as compared with the other, — more richly differenced, and though the spores are, even more decidedly, without colour, soon and largely displays its real (muriform) type; a type however, as we have seen, not entirely without representation even in the genus first named. Allusion has been made to the scarcely questionable analogies connecting *Umbilicaria* as well with *Sticta*, as with the Collemaceous lichens ; but the relation in which these last stand to *Pannaria* is one, from whatever point of view we regard it, of close affinity.——It is not uninteresting here to add that the modifications, whether of external colour, or of conditioning internal structure, which beginning in *Sticta*, and instructively exhibited in *Pannaria*, find their explication in *Leptogium*, recur again, in " true Lichens," in the cephalodia (as explained by Nylander) of *Stereocaulon*.

Pannaria is conceivable then as a decolorate member of the series characterized by muriform (typically coloured) spores, and as contiguous therefore with *Umbilicaria*, and, to some extent at least if not with the bulk of, *Peltigerei* on the one hand, as especially with *Collemei*, on the other. There is yet an obvious contrast between the *Collemei* and *Pannaria*, in that while in the latter the greater proportion of the forms, and all the more typical ones, have simple spores, — the higher features of spore-modification showing themselves only in the receding sections, the confused and at length aberrant structure of which assimilates them to *Eucollemei*, it is the bulk and most typical portion of the former which displays the higher spore-characterization, and only, in general, the reduced and receding clusters in which the spores are simple. But *Colema byrsæum* approaches the highest *Pannariæ* as closely in its spores as in everything else; and *Pannaria lurida* makes equally significant advances from the other direction. And so manifestly do the two groups run together in their inferior types, that lichenologists are unable at present to indicate any satisfactory characters of discrimination.

There is some significant evidence that the simplification of internal structure corresponds in *Pannaria*, as elsewhere, with the reduction of the thallus. And, looked at in this light, the ill-definable generic differences of the higher, central portions of the family before us, which forms, as we venture to regard it, a parallel series contiguous to *Pannaria*, should possibly seem of no higher value than the to some extent corresponding sectional diversities of the latter. Nor does there at least appear to be any doubt that the greater number of these central Collemaceous types coalesce most readily into a single group, or sub-family (*Eucollemei*) distinguished sharply from the still embarrassed, and, as now made up, at once higher and lower cluster of fruticulose and filamentous types, which we associate in *Lichinei*.

According to the estimate of Dr. Nylander (*Syn.* p. 75) the whole number of known species of Lichens was 1361, and of Collemaceous Lichens 112; the proportion of the latter then being about one-twelfth.

Sub-Fam. 1. — LICHINEI.

Thallus fruticulosus filamentosusve, collogonidiis aut axem, demum dissolutum, sistentibus, aut in stratum sub-stipatis. Medulla plus minus parenchymatica. Apothecia globosa varie deformatave l. pseudo biatorina.

It might perhaps be beforehand conceivable that constriction should so modify Collemeine structure as to give, in at least extreme types, a peculiar prominence to the everywhere sufficiently marked gonimous system; — and we find, in the younger portions of *Ephebe* (Hepp. *Abbild.* t. 81, n. 712) and its nearest associates (*Ibid.* t. 82, n. 713) the collogonidia constituting the axis, and almost the plant. *Cænogonium,* Ehrenb., as Nylander has explained it, is perhaps a still more simple, gonidial thallus : but here chlorophyll, conditioning true gonidia, appears ; and the type is thus excluded from the *Collemei;* as it is also by the *ensemble* of its fructification. There are analogous instances in the present and other tribes of a marked predominance of the medullary layer ; and yet again of the disappearance of this layer in a general parenchymatous tissue ; and if neither of these extremes of reduction or simplification should be taken to be enough to exclude the plants exhibiting them from that place in the system to which the sum of their characters points, it will be difficult to adopt another rule in the case of those which are extraordinarily conditioned by the gonidial element.

External habit proved an uncertain guide to the real affinity of the plants now immediately before us, so long as their fruit-characters were unknown or undetermined ; and structure itself was long looked to in vain — the significance of the fructification being disputed — to distinguish some of them from (inferior) *Algæ,* which seem scarcely to differ but in failing always to ascend above an inferior stage of life. It is however the ennobled *Stigonema* (*Ephebe*) that should throw light on the rest of its group ; and though the probability (Koerb. *Parerg.* p. 448) remain, that, taken as a whole, these humble types may continue *in bivio,* — a part being always referable, from the point of view of system, to *Algæ,* this cannot embarrass those whose place is otherwise determined ; or the argument from them to the undetermined remainder. And keeping in view the essentially mediate character of the class we are here studying (*Lichenes quoad vegetationem ad Algas relatos, quoad fructum Fungos esse,* Fr. *S. O. V.* p. 60) it may well appear possible to accept all the evidence indicative of points of contact between Parmeliaceous Lichens and *Algæ,* without greater embarrassment or need of modification of the higher divisions of *Thallophyta,* than are offered or suggested by the close and often difficult relations between Graphidaceous and Verrucariaceous types and *Fungi.*

Nor has habit wholly failed to indicate or corroborate the received results of analysis. Notwithstanding the *Fucus*-like aspect and maritime habitat of *Lichina*, there is no longer any question, with lichenists, of its place; and one or other of its species has always been associated with Lichens. It should seem almost as difficult to recognize any other affinity in *Ephebe solida*, as in *Synalissa symphorea*. And though *Ephebe pubescens*, Fr. (*Scytonema dein Stigonema atrovirens*, Ag.) offers difficulties in its ill-developed fructification, and was regarded by phycologists as — from their point of view — closely resembling *Scytonema ocellatum*, Harv., I suppose few would deny that the former is more lichenose than the latter (*Herb. Grev.*) and fairly enough suggests the long-accepted comparison with forms of *Alectoria jubata*, and with *Parmelia lanata*, under which (in his *Cornicularia*) it was grouped by Acharius. The two remaining are reduced types, receding from the tribe, as in other instances of the present and immediately preceding families, in their pseudo-biatorine fructification; but the more important structural characters of one of them (*Spilonema*, Born., Nyl. *Syn.* 1, p. 89) confirm its external resemblance to *Ephebe*, and the slenderer thallus of the other (*Thermutis*, Fr. *Gonionema*, Nyl. l. c. *Stigonema pannosum*, Hepp *Abbild.* n. 713) offers, it should seem, but little to distinguish it.

The structural extreme indicated by the younger portions of the thallus of *Ephebe*, &c., an extreme especially emphasized by Nylander in his character of *Thermutis* (*Gonionema*, Nyl. l. c.) tends however, from the first, to modification indicative of greater complexity; and the constituents of the axial column to pass (as Harvey suggested in noting the relation of *Scytonema* to *Stigonema*, and Flotow in comparing *Thermutis* and *Ephebe*) into transverse series of collogonidia; a type primarily illustrated by *Spilonema*, Born. We are next carried a step further by the mature structure of *Ephebe*, Fr., wherein a medullary centre is represented by more elongated cells, and a true gonimous layer is even suggested. And the latter becomes finally distinct, and the whole lichenose thallus tolerably evident in *Lichina*, Ag.

It is this greater regularity of the gonidial system, first observed in *Lichina* by Tulasne (*l. supra cit.* & t. 9) and instructively exhibited both in this genus and *Ephebe*, as compared with his *Pterygium*, by Nylander (*Syn. p.* 90, t. 2) which distinguishing, and in the obvious direction of higher systematic position, the group before us from the *Eucollemei*, mediates as well between the strongly marked divergence of the latter, and the more regular exhibition of Parmeliaceous structure in the family here immediately preceding (*Pannariei*). Nor can such estimate be readily questioned, if we follow the learned lichenographer last cited in regarding *Pterygium*, notwithstanding its manifest discrepancies, all looking towards *Pannaria*, as still structurally associable with *Lichina;* whether the former be taken for Collemaceous or Pannariine. The point turns on the above alleged indications of structure, and if these are correctly understood, *Lichina* should be comparable with *Umbilicaria!;* and still more so with *Pannaria*, especially in those sections (*Lecothecium* & *Pterygium, Auctt.*) most nearly related to the *Collemei*.

But the agreement with higher sections thus obscurely suggested by nature in some of the best-developed representatives of the *Lichinei* must not be permitted to conceal the more obvious fact that these extreme and inferior expressions of lichenose vegetation are, by common consent, closely akin to the *Eucollemei*. Fries remarked (*S. O. V.* p. 300) the near affinity of *Lichina* to *Synalissa*. *Ephebe solida*, Born., may be said to combine the fructification of the genus last-named with the structure of its own. And Nylander has well indicated (*Syn.* p. 13) other approximations between the two groups.

XX.—EPHEBE, Fr., Born.

Fr. S. O. V. p. 266 ; Lich. Suec. n. 211 ; Fl. Scan. p. 294 ; Summ. Veg. Scand. p. 122. Tuck. Syn. N. Eng. p. 93. Flot. in Bot. Zeit. 1850, p. 73. Born., in Ann. Sci. Nat. 3, 18, p. 170, t. 7. Nyl. Lich. Par. n. 1 ; Syn. 1, p. 89, t. 2 ; Lich. Scand. p. 24. Hepp Abbild. n. 712. Th. Fr. Lich. Arct. p. 289. Stizenb. Beitr. l. c. p. 139. Schwend. in Flora, 1863, p. 241 ; Untersuch. l. c. 4, p. 167, t. 23, f. 14–17. Leight. in Ann. et Mag. Nat. Hist. 3, 16, p. 8. Koerb. Parerg. p. 446. De Bary Morph. u. Phys. d. Pilze., Flecht., u. s. w. p. 268. Lichenis sp., Ehrh. Crypt. Ach. Prodr. p. 217. Wahl. Lapp. p. 441. Usneæ sp., Hoffm. D. Fl. 2, p. 136, p. p. Corniculariæ sp., Ach. Meth. p. 305 ; Lich. Univ. p. 616 ; Syn. p. 302. Moug. & Nestl. Cr. Vog. n. 358. Schær. Spicil. p. 515. Confervæ sp., Dillw. Conf. Brit. Scytonematis, sp., dein Stigonematis sp., Ag. Syst. Alg. p. 42. Harv. Man. Brit. Alg. p. 12, 153. Kütz. Spec. Alg. p. 318, et tab. Phycol. t. 37, f. 3. Bangiæ sp., Lyngb. Hydroph. Collematis sp., Schær. Enum. p. 248.

Apothecia sub-lateralia, globosa, disco coarctato punctiformi-impresso. Sporæ oblongo - ellipsoideæ, simplices, incolores. Spermatia oblonga ; sterigmatibus sub-simplicibus. Thallus filamento-sus, decumbens, ramosus, nigricans ; collogonidiis majusculis axem primitus sistentibus, dein plus minus strati instar inter corticem et cellulas confusas medullares dispositis.

From the point of view of *Ephebe solida*, Born., the described apothecia of *E. pubescens* (Born. l. c. Nyl. l. c. Koerb. l. c.) are so manifestly irregular that, — having myself wholly failed in detecting them, — I have preferred to confine the generic character to the here well-known fruit of the species first named, which accords in its other structure with the older one. Stizenberger (in an earlier memoir than the one cited above) and Hepp, have indeed already disallowed the supposed fructification of the latter as parasitical ; but the plant upon which this is found remains still structurally diverse from *Nostoc*-like *Algæ*, and associable with the better-characterized, and still more evidently lichenose, American species.

And it is not enough that we touch here plants of another Class ; or that even the difference in thalline structure which distinguishes *E. pubescens* from these might, at least conceivably, be accounted for by mycelial cells of a parasitical fungus infesting the intercellular spaces of a *Sirosiphon*, Kütz. (De Bary, l. c. p. 269). It still remains true that *E. solida* exhibits commonly and abundantly that well-defined modification of the Parmeliine apothecium which characterizes *Synalissa* and other Collemeine lichens ; while in structure, however this be simplified, it recedes from the latter in a direction indicating affinity to higher (*Lichina — Pterygium — Pannaria*) rather than lower types ; and that *E. pubescens* is substantially, in everything except its abnormal fruit, congenerical.

The observations of Bornet (l. c., & in *Mém. Cherb.*) upon *Ephebe* and the closely related *Spilonema*, Born., were followed by those of Nylander, who has illustrated also (*Syn.*) the common relations of both to *Thermutis*, Fr. (*Gonionema*, Nyl.) and even, by associating with these, in his *Lichinei*, not merely *Lichina* but his *Pterygium*, to what must be regarded, from the point of view of the present treatise, as a higher than Collemeine type. But we find here (Nyl. l. c.) the structure of *Thermutis* (*Gonionema*, Nyl.) less perfectly characterized : and it was left to Schwendener (*Flora*, 1863, l. c.) to shew that as respects as well the gonidia (instructively exhibited already by Hepp's figure, above-cited) as the filamentous elements, *Thermutis* is really no less lichenose, or more 'Scytonematoid,' than *Ephebe*. " Dillwyn well remarks," says Harvey of his *Scytonema ocellatum* (Man. Brit. Alg. p. 154) " that it is most nearly allied to *Stigonema atrovirens;* and it seems indeed to be intermediate between *Stigonema* and *Scytonema*, the division of the sporidia " (gonidia) "in old filaments, assimilating it to the former genus." And Flotow, comparing (l. c.) in like manner, the young extremities of *Ephebe* and the thallus, as he understood it, of *Thermutis*, and these with the older portions of the first-named type, could regard both, — the apothecia of the last only being then known, — as referable to states of but a single species. Alike in both lichens, and in *Spilonema*, Born., as well (Schwend. l. c.) the tips of the thallus exhibit, under the microscope, a simple, axial row of collogonidia, exactly as in *Scytonema;* and this gonidial column breaking up then into 'transverse rings,' the older portions assume, in like manner, the internal structure of *Stigonema*. Not however without a very important difference. As Nylander expounded *Ephebe*, it was scarcely to be questioned that we had before us a true lichen. And Schwendener has shown that that irregular parenchyma which comes at length to occupy the centre of the oldest thallus as a medullary, and in this way to give character to the gonidial elements as now in some sort

9

gonimous, layer, is in fact traceable, in the form of slender filaments, to the youngest extremities; and that all this is characteristical generally, not of *Ephebe* alone, but of every member of the little group we have been considering.

Authors have reckoned three species of *Ephebe;* two of them peculiar to North America, and the other common to us and Europe. The last (*E. pubescens*) is very frequent in New England, ascending to alpine districts, and offering there, on moist rocks, its best-developed conditions; and it follows the mountains southward to Alabama (Mr. Peters). According to Bornet, the 'siliquose swellings, marked by tubercles, to each of which corresponds an immersed exciple,' and of which swellings 'there are never more than one or two in a tuft,' are not produced where the plant grows in very wet places; they have not occurred to me at all. Spermogones less rare, and though smaller, these are not unlike the apothecia of the next species.——*E. solida*, Born, described from specimens collected in the Blue Ridge (Lesquereux) and contrasting with the former in its less-developed thallus, and no less in its common and abundant fructification, has also been found in Vermont (Mr. Frost) and Massachusetts (Mr. Willey).——The third, *E. Lesquereuxii*, Born., named from sterile specimens collected by the eminent bryologist whose name it bears, in the mountains of Alabama, no longer exists in his herbarium; and is quite unknown in this country.

NOTE. — In his latest researches (*Untersuch.* l. c. 4, p. 161) published since the manuscript of this work was prepared, Schwendener separates *Lecothecium* etc., and *Lichina*, which he had earlier (l. c. 3, p. 152) included in his *Pannariaceæ*, and constitutes of them a new group (*Raccoblennaceæ*) intermediate, together with the next following (*Ephebaceæ*) between *Pannariaceæ* and *Collemaceæ*. It illustrates the difficulties of an arrangement from an exclusively anatomical point of view,—difficulties sufficiently observable in *Hagenia*, in the author's first part, and, especially in *Anaptychia,* in his second, — that *Ephebaceæ*, as here taken, is made to include as well the too discrepant *Cœnogonium*. In habit however, as well as in ultimate structure *Ephebe* has some apparent claims to an association with *Lichina;* and if the higher thalline constitution of the latter look away from *Collemei*, it is hazarding little to say that its whole habit favours, not a Pannarieine but a Collemeine affinity.

XXI.—LICHINA, Ag., Mont.

Agardh Syst. Alg. p. 274. Fr. S. O. V. p. 300; Summ. Veg. Scand. p. 121. Grev. Alg. Brit. p. 21, t. 6. Hook. Brit. Fl. 2, p. 270. Mont. in Ann. 2, 15, p. 150, t. 15. Tul. Mém. sur les Lich. p. 83, 187, t. 9, f. 1–6, t. 10, f. 12–18. Koerb. Syst. p. 429; Parerg. p. 444. Nyl. Syn. I, p. 91, t. 2, f. 16; Lich. Scand. p. 24. Schwend. Untersuch. l. c. 2, p. 175, t. 7, f. 12–14; 3, p. 152. Th. Fr. Lich. Arct. p. 288. Stizenb. Beitr. l. c. p. 140. De Bary Morph. et Phys. d. Pilze, etc., p. 267. Lichenis sp., Mich. Nov. Pl. Gen. p. 103. Ach. Prodr. p. 208. Sm. E. Bot. t. 2575.

Fuci sp., Lightf. Fl. Scot. 2. p. 964, t. 32. Sm. E. Bot. t. 1332. Turn. Fuci, 4, p. 16, t. 204. Stereocaulon? Ach. Meth. p. 317. Chondri sp., Lamx., cit. Nyl. Gelidii sp., Lyngb., cit. Mont.

Apothecia terminalia, globosa, disco coarctato punctiformi-impresso. Sporæ ellipsoideæ, simplices, incolores. Spermatia ellipsoidea, sterigmatibus simplicibus. Thallus fruticulosus, cartilagineo-corneus, fusco-ater; collogonidiis moniliformi-concatenatis, stratum inter corticalem sub-distinctum et medullarem sistentibus.

If the lichen last described and its immediate allies are readily comparable with some inferior types of *Algæ*, the present cluster has been regarded by the majority of authors, to a very recent period, as closely akin even to *Fucoideæ;* with which it also agrees in its marine, or at any rate maritime habitat. But *L. confinis* had passed for a lichen from Micheli's time, and was accepted as such by Fries (*S. O. V.*) when he still looked upon *L. pygmæa* as foreign to the class. And the two species correspond, it is no longer doubted, most closely; the whole structure of the larger one being repeated, if possibly with less stress and clearness, in the smaller. It appears indeed to have been habit alone which determined the recognition by phycologists of this type; its fructification being either unexplored by them, or admitted, as by Greville, to have in fact "no affinity with that of" fucoid Algæ. Montagne, and especially Tulasne, have now fully exhibited this fructification; and the latter author, and, more recently, Schwendener, have made clear the distinctly lichenose constitution of the thallus.[1]

The persistently undeveloped, or globular apothecium of *Lichina* admits easily of misconstruction; which it has by no means escaped, even among writers upon Lichens. Of this sort must be considered, —not to refer further to the unsatisfactory attempts to associate the plant with Verrucariaceous types, —the often repeated comparison of the type before us with *Sphærophorus;* carried so far, in one instance, that it is even proposed to bring both together as divergent members of the same tribe (*Sphærophoraceæ*, Naeg. in Hepp *Abbild.* t. 2). There is yet no real weight in the alleged resemblance of these lichens[2] as respects the excipular relation of the thallus to the hypothecium, however it suggested their comparison, and however, in both alike, the hypothecium fails to develope

[1] That the difference between the compact cellular tissue of the medullary layer of Lichina and the medullary filaments of *Collema* is only one of degree is sufficiently shewn by a comparison of the variations of this layer in *Pannaria;* which descends, in this respect towards *Collemei* much as, in the latter, *Lichina* ascends towards *Pannariei*, especially *Pannaria § Pterygium.* And the 'hyaline filaments' of *Collema* are not so much wanting (Koerb. *Parerg.* p. 445) as peculiarly modified in *Lichinei*, as here taken.

[2] "*Notez bien que je dis analogues, et non pas voisins.*" Mont. *sur la struct. du nucleus des genres Sphærophoron* . . *et Lichina*, in *Ann. Sci. Nat.* l. *supra c*:

into a proper exciple. This defect notwithstanding, it is still the rudimentary proper exciple which is primary in *Sphærophorus*, as in scarcely to be questioned relations of closest intimacy with *Caliciacei;* and the marked way in which the thallus of the former officiates as a partial receptacle, must be explained from the point of view of the latter. In *Lichina*, on the contrary, the thalline exciple is what is essential; and there is nothing in this to separate it from known modifications of the Parmeliaceous type.

Reference has already been made, in the preliminary remarks, to the important change in the systematic estimate of *Lichina*, which has followed the full explication of its structure; and Tulasne's cited observation in this direction, followed as it was by Nylander's exposition of the close relations of the plants before us to his *Pterygium* (not easily to be deprived of its affinity to *Pannaria*) is now corroborated by the latest writer who has concerned himself with the question. "In view of all these facts," says Prof. De Bary, "*Lichina* holds, in many respects, the middle between fruticulose heteromerous and Collemaceous lichens." [1] And the significance of these certainly not superficial judgments, as respects both Ephebe, and its equally retrograde allies, as finally the whole question of an ordinal separation of "*Lichenes Byssacei*," will scarcely be doubted. If the highest structure of these "byssaceous lichens" be best comparable with that of *Lichina*, and if the structure of the latter associate it with types (*Pterygium*) only fully explainable from a Parmeliaceous point of view, the latter is then indicated as the true position from which to survey the whole group; and its retrograde members must follow those which determine it. In one series of Parmeliaceous genera (*Cetraria*, etc.,—*Parmelia*,—*Lecanora*, etc.,) there is indeed a marked structural diversity from *Collemei* in the gonimous system; but in another (*Peltigera*, etc.,—*Pannaria*) this diversity at length disappears, and all the conditions which make *Collema* an ultimate possibility, find, if we mistake not, their sufficient exemplification.

There are two, now generally accepted species of this genus. The larger one, *L. pygmæa* (Lightf.) Ag., is found on maritime rocks 'which are exposed and almost dry at high water' (Hook.) through nearly all Europe, and as far north as the Southern provinces of Sweden and Norway. It is stated by Greville (*Alg. Brit.*) on the authority of Bory, that D'urville met with this on the coast of Chili; but no other American station has been indicated. The other, *L. confinis* (Müll.) Ag., occurring on rocks 'partially covered only at high tides' (Hook.; ' *ubi a summo fluxu maris haud inundatur, sed tantum sub procellis ab undis marinis irrigatur*,' Wahl. *Lapp.*) extends throughout the same European countries,

---

[1] "*Nach allen diesen Thatsachen hält Lichina in vieler Beziehung die Mitte zwischen den strauchartigen heteromeren und den Gallertflechten.*" De Bary *Morphol. u. Physiol. der Pilze, Flechten, u. Myxomyceten*, p. 268.

but, though its range reaches northward as far as the shores of the Icy Sea, has equally failed, hitherto, of detection in North America. *L. confinis* is readily distinguishable by its cylindrical thallus, and much smaller size; it was not however considered to differ in species by Turner (*Hist. Fuc.*) and Hooker remarks that his observations have led him to regard it 'as a mere variety of the preceding, whose different appearance is due to a more frequent exposure to a dry atmosphere' (Brit. Fl.) a view the probability of which is certainly not weakened by the failure of Nylander (*Syn.*) to indicate any other than the named points of diversity.——I refer here, provisionally, a New England lichen, found by me on rocks beyond the tides, but within reach of the spray in storms, at Cape Ann in Massachusetts, and since, by Mr. Willey, on rocks at least five miles from the sea, at New Bedford, which, agreeing in other respects generally with *L. confinis* is yet differenced constantly, and most remarkably, by what seems an intrusive, microscopical *alga*, supplanting almost wholly the proper gonimous system of the plant, and, as it were, substituting itself for it. These curious facts will be fully exhibited elsewhere.

Sub - Fam. 2. — EUCOLLEMEI.

Thallus foliaceus macro- l. microphyllinus, aut dein crustaceo-diminutus, rarissime fruticulosus, collogonidiis l. glomeratis l. in plerisque moniliformi-concatenatis in pulpam homogeneam filamentis medullaribus percursam sæpius confluentibus. Medulla in infimis parenchymatica. Apothecia normaliter lecanorina, nonnunquam persistenter globosa.

The extraordinary modification of thalline structure, which, commencing in *Peltigerei*, compels us to recognize two distinct lines of otherwise congenerical forms in each of the larger genera of that family, is further conditioned in *Pannaria* by a precipitate and at length extreme degeneration of the foliaceous type. Starting, we may say, like the other genera just named, as a normal, frondose group of *Parmeliacei*, and passing like them, into conditions in which the gonimous system is peculiarly modified, *Pannaria* ends in semi-crustaceous states the explication of which has proved exceedingly uncertain. From just such crustaceous conditions, the real relations of which to degenerant Pannariine forms are not seldom doubtful, ascends now another series (*Eucollemei*) at once contrasting with Parmeliaceous Lichens, and yet inextricably bound up with them. This new series, in which the structural changes suggested in *Peltigerei*, and begun in *Pannaria*, reach their full development, and the gonimous system an ascendency becoming almost inordinate, is made up however, not of well-defined but of most intricately correlated groups;

and modern science, with all its decided advantage as respects both extent and minuteness of knowledge, has still, it is admitted, to solve the problem of a satisfactory arrangement of it.

It is in his section *Mallotium* that we find the centre of the typical *Collema*, Ach., and the highest expression of Collemeine vegetation ("*quasi Stictæ hujus generis.*" Fr., *sub Leptogio, S. O. V.* p. 255). From this centre the more pulpy Collemas diverge in one direction, and the submembranaceous ones (*C. nigrescens, C. thysanæum*) meet finally the membranaceous ones (§ *Leptogium*) in the other. Scarcely anything was then known of crustaceous types referable here, but *Synalissa*, Fr. *S. O. V.*, is included among pulpy *Collemas*, while several more or less degenerate forms, in question between *Pannariei* and *Collemei*, are thrown together at the beginning of the enumeration; as what is now *Thermutis*, Fr., is appended to it. Leaving out of sight the last, it is easy to admit the simplicity and elegance, from his own point of view, of the conception of Acharius: and this shall perhaps excuse now an attempt to glance at the principal members of the whole sub-family, enriched with the discoveries of fifty years, from a still not dissimilar standpoint; or as constituents of but a single, most closely associable group.

The embarrassing relations of certain types and groups of Lichens at once to *Pannariei* and *Collemei* have been already considered; and the results are before the reader. It has appeared impossible to escape the conclusion that *Pterygium pannariellum*, Nyl., if, as should appear, it be identical with *Lecothecium asperellum*, Th. Fr., is other than congenerical with the type of *Lecothecium*; or that this type is other than correctly referred by Nylander to *Pannaria*. The *plus minusve*, say even the final obsolescence, of the hypothallus in these plants, is far from enough to obscure their admitted resemblances; and if the cited *Pterygium* exhibit, in all other respects, a sufficient congruity with *Pannaria nigra*, the microscope reveals to us no important structural difference between the latter and *P. tryptophylla*. [1] But it is perhaps not alone in *Pterygium*, *Lecothecium*, and *Collolechia* of authors that Pannariine structure has proved at length indistinguishable from Collemaceous. Not to

[1] "*Die Gattungen dieser Familie*" (*Lecotheciæ*, Koerb.) "*vermitteln sowohl hinsichtlich des äussern wie des inneren Lagerbaues die heteromerischen Flechten mit den homæomerischen und zeigen sich namentlich der Gattung Pannaria in hohem Grade verähnelt.*" Koerb. *Syst.* p. 397; and *vide Parerg.* p. 405.——"*Vix specie differt*" *Pannaria nigra* "*a tryptophylla. . . Accedere quoque videtur versus Pterygia, at apud hæc nullum adest stratum hypothallinum.*" Nyl. *Lich. Scand.* p. 126. What we cannot but call indications of such hypothalline layer are however to be seen in the figure of *Pterygium centrifugum* given in Nyl. *Syn.* t. 2, and are observable, under the microscope, in *P. Petersii;* while, in the latter, and perhaps even more evidently in *P. pannariellum* (*Lecoth. asperellum*, Th. Fr.) descending (hypothalline) cells, that is to say an imperfectly developed, true hypothallus is now to be made out.

refer again, at this place, to higher types which have been elsewhere considered, it appears probable that several semi-crustaceous forms, mostly of recent discovery, whether referred to *Collema* or *Leptogium*, have, to say the least, equal claims to rank as *Pannariæ;* and owe indeed the position they now hold mainly to the circumstance that the spore-history of *Pannaria*, though not without illustrations of development beyond the unilocular or simple stage has not yet been conceived as embracing the multilocular or muriform one.

And we are far from leaving *Pannaria* in the remote distance even when reaching what are now generally taken for true Collemeine types. It is perhaps scarcely to be doubted, from the point of view at least of the present treatise, that the small group of crustaceous lichens relegated by Acharius to one end of his *Collema* (sect. *Placynthium*, Ach.) is in fact mostly Pannariine. But the corresponding groups in the arrangement of Nylander, those namely which constitute for him the lowest exhibitions of Collemeine structure (SYNALISSA *max. p.* Nyl., & PYRENOPSIS, Nyl.) are themselves, with all the advance of knowledge, not wholly free from ambiguous elements; — the reference of such forms as *Pannaria Schæreri*, Mass., to *Pyrenopsis* rather than to *Pannaria*, appearing to be determined by habit more than by any clear criteria of structure, and even habit being much at fault in such as *Pyrenopsis Flotoviana*, Nyl. (*Pannaria* Nyl., *olim. Biatora*, Th. Fr. *Verrucaria*, Hepp). If however, comparing with *Pyrenopsis* the scarcely discrepant structure of *Synalissa polycocca*, Nyl. (*Syn.* p. 96) we follow this author's plain indications, and subsume *Pyrenopsis* under *Synalissa*, there is no doubt that the type of the last (*S. symphorea*) is sufficiently Collemeine. Too much so possibly for a satisfactory association with the inferior lichens thus brought into connection with it!

At this point it becomes then evident, if it were not before in *Enchylium* (Mass.) Koerb.,[1] that we are approaching so closely to a new section

---

[1] *Enchylium*, Mass. *Mem.* p. 93, is constituted of *E. synalissum* (*Synalissa symphorea* (DC.) Nyl.) and a crustaceous *E. affine*, Mass., for which last the genus is retained by Koerber. The medullary elements very sparing and imperfect in the specimens examined by me of *E. affine* (Mass. *Ital.* n. 312. Koerb. *herb.* Rabenh. *Lich. Eur.* n. 259) and according to Koerber the plant *"unterscheidet sich von"* *Psorotichia* (*Pyrenopsis*) *" eigentlich nur durch die vielsporigen Schläuche."* *Parerg.* p. 433. The reddish tinge so commonly characterizing the outer cells of *Pyrenopsis* is yet wanting here; and Nylander has given expression to a different view. *" Observetur obiter"* he says (*Bot. Zeit.* 1861, p. 337) *"Enchylium affine esse Omphalariam."* And it adds to the evidence of the mutual approaches of these ill-defined groups, that while Massalongo referred to *Omphalarieæ* both *Synalissa* (*symphorea*) and *Enchylium*, Koerb., Nylander places the latter and Koerber the former in closest proximity to *Pyrenopsis.* —— *Omphalaria decipiens*, Mass., is referred to *Pyrenopsis*, at the place last cited, by Nylander: but very perfect specimens (Arnold *in herb.* Krempelh.) suggest perhaps a higher position; as Koerber has indicated. (*Parerg.* p. 431).

of *Eucollemei*, that it may well be questioned whether *Synalissa sym-phorea* be really dissociable from OMPHALARIA, DR. & Mont. Typically indeed, as its name implies, this last group is an assemblage—almost wholly the result of enquiries since Acharius, and confined mainly to cal-careous rocks of the warmer regions of the northern hemisphere, and of intertropical countries—of frondose lichens, attached like *Umbilicaria* at a single point; and though looking, in some reduced, and otherwise dis-crepant states (*O. coralloides* (Mass., Nyl.) towards the similarly reduced European condition of *Synalissa symphorea*, it scarcely appeared to offer any type comparable externally to the unmistakably fruticulose American lichen (*S. sphærospora*, Nyl.) It is interesting then that one of the five remarkable species of *Omphalaria* which the calcareous rocks of the island of Cuba have yielded to the research of Mr. Wright, is perhaps the most elegant, fruticulose Collemeine lichen known as yet to science ; [1] and that the habit and texture of this associate it with *Omphalaria*. [2] As defined by Nylander (*Syn.*) the structural difference of the Collema-ceous group before us turns on 1, the immersed or innate, urceolate or even endocarpeine, or now tuberculiform apothecia, and 2, the solitary, or only at length glomerulate collogonidia; both features (as respects the Collemeine type) of degradation, which refer the group, notwithstanding its foliaceous thallus, to the next neighbourhood of *Synalissa* and *Pyren-opsis*: but neither of these characters is without exceptions, and there is no doubt that *Omphalaria* ascends finally towards, if it does not lose itself in *Collema*. It is here the place to notice the remarkably recedent *Phylliscum*, [3] Nyl. A globular, or persistently more or less closed, often

---

[1] *Omphalaria Wrightii (sp. nova) thallo centro affixo fruticuloso sub-dicho-tomo-ramosissimo olivaceo-viridi, subtus pallidiore, ramis teretibus implexis; apotheciis terminalibus globosis sub-clausis. Sporæ in thecis cylindraceis octonæ, ellipsoideæ, simplices, incolores, longit.* 0.016-23mm., *crassit.* 0.009-16mm.; *para-physibus filiformibus.* Shaded places on limestone cliffs, Island of Cuba; Mr. Wright. Texture of thallus that of *Omphalaria* as limited by Nylander; the mostly solitary collogonidia interspersed among conspicuous filaments. As seen in a cross-section, the filaments appear to be rather grouped at the centre, with but few gonidia; and the principal mass of the latter is collected at the circum-ference. Other instances of such return to structural regularity in fructiculose *Collemei* are indicated in Nyl. *Syn.* p. 13. Fronds at length one inch in diameter.

[2] It may be observed here that Fries has anticipated the at least possible refer-ence of his *Synalissa* to the later *Omphalaria*, DR. & Mont., by himself referring *Omphalaria phyllisca* to the type first named. (*Summ. Veg. Scand.* (1849) p. 563).

[3] It is a generally recognized rule that the historical connection of the original describer of a species with his plant shall be preserved by the retention of the specific name (unless quite inadmissible) first given to it; and the injustice of wholly supplanting *Endocarpon phylliscum*, Wahl., by *Phylliscum endocarpoides*, Nyl., is clear. The accurate author of the *Flora Lapponica* left little for systematic science to add to the history of the plant which he discovered and

also immersed apothecium is largely characteristical of the lowest Collemaceous Lichens, and has often been understood by lichenographers as in fact pyrenocarpous (Verrucariaceous). From our point of view indeed, this explanation is, *a priori*, most improbable; and the very learned writer last cited, has not hesitated to recognize, even in endocarpeine anamorphosis, the proper lecanorine apothecium, throughout his *Collemacei*, except in two instances; one of them the plant just referred to. This (*Phylliscum*) is readily associable in habit with Omphalarieine types, from which Montagne did not separate it, and one of which types (*O. leptophylla*, Tuck. Wright *Lich. Cub.* n. 1) was in fact pronounced a *Phylliscum* by a lichenist of the largest experience; but it contrasts with *Omphalaria* in range and habitat; and differs, as in some other respects, in its still more sunken or endocarpeine fruit. There is nothing however, to distinguish, externally, this apothecium from that of an *Omphalaria*[1] of Cuba, and the internal features may be said to offer only an extreme of the structure in other *Omphalariæ ;* the 'ostiolar filaments' noted by Nylander, affording, if we do not mistake, scarcely a decisive criterium, and the hypothecium possessing certainly no better claims to rank as an amphithecium.[2] Except as respects the size of the granules, the gonimous system

illustrated, but the fact that the internal structure of its 'subgelatinous' thallus really carries *Endocarpon phylliscum* into *Collemei;* in spite of its ' endocarpeine' fruit.

[1] *Omphalaria deusta (sp. nova) thallo membranaceo-cartilagineo atroviridi rotundato-lobato basi umbilicato-affixo, lobis integris undulatis; apotheciis sparsis depresso-globosis sub-clausis, apertura poroidea. Sporæ octonæ, ellipsoideæ, simplices, incolores, longit.* 0.011–16^{mm}·, *crassit.* 0.005-7^{mm}·; *paraphysibus capillaribus flexuosis.* Shaded rocks, Guajuybon, Island of Cuba, in company with *O. Wrightii ;* Mr. Wright.——Collogonidia solitary, or in twos and threes, interspersed among anastomosing filaments. Apothecia verrucarioid, resembling those of *O. phyllisca* (*Phylliscum*, Nyl.) and but little larger, but the orifice rather more ample. They are not well comparable with those of either of the other described Cuban species. Thallus half an inch to an inch in diameter; contrasting in its rounded lobes, and black colour, with the other species, and not a little suggestive of conditions of *Umbilicaria flocculosa*, Hoffm. (*Gyroph. deusta*, Ach.).

[2] The spermatia of *Phylliscum* might certainly appear to corroborate the other evidences of the marked distinctness of this type; but the value, in the system, of the differences in the spermatia is as yet wholly uncertain. In a minute, Collemeine lichen (*Synalissa Texana*, Tuckerm. herb.) from the calcareous rocks of Texas (C. Wright) the nodulose habit of which is so much that of *S. symphorea* (as given in Anz. *Lich. Ital.*) that I supposed it, before analysis, without doubt the same, and the interior structure scarcely differing unless in rather larger collogonidia and less distinct medullary elements (both differences looking towards *Phylliscum*) I find yet filiform, at length bowed spermatia, much as in the type last named; and there is no doubt that the organs in question belong to the thallus (unfortunately without apothecia) described. And quite similar spermatia recur in a crustaceous species with greatly reduced thallus, of the same genus as it is

10

of *Phylliscum* is also conformable to that of the typical *Omphalariæ*, as understood by Nylander; who does not recognize as belonging to the group any member of the *Omphalarieæ* of other authors, in which the collogonidia pass into chaplets. But the little cluster which exhibits this structure (concatenate collogonidia) and which includes as well *Omphalaria botryosa* (Mass.) Nyl., as the North American *O. umbella* (*Collema*, Nyl.) is in every other respect distinctly Omphalarieine.

COLLEMA, Ach., Fr., is thus reached, in the view of Nylander, before we have left the marked group which other lichenographers, relying on the *ensemble*, are agreed in associating as *Omphalariei*. *Collema nummularium*, Nyl. *Syn.* p. 103, as described by the eminent author cited, and as compared, in his figure, (t. 4, f. 9) with *Omphalaria Girardi* (f. 8) furnishes possibly other proof that anatomical structure may undergo marked modification, before the indications of habit, and these confirmed by the testimony of the microscopical fruit-characters, become at all obscure.

But the question thus opened between keeping up natural groups by extending the limits of their definitions and thus subordinating modifications of structure to evident conformity in habit, and the disregard of habit in view of conformity in anatomical details, is too wide for the occasion; and perhaps for the present condition of knowledge as to the real value, in the system, of such structural differences as separate *Omphalaria*, Nyl., from *Plectopsora*, Mass.[1] Suffice it to say that it is habit alone, in the last resort, which distinguishes *Omphalaria*, in the largest sense, from *Collema*, whether we look at the final advance in character of the former, or compare the most nearly related retrograde type of the latter. This type is *Lempholemma*, Koerb., which though comparable in part at least, in its reduced apothecia, with *Omphalariei*, and referred there by Stizenberger (*Beitr.*) differs yet in no important respect, either of *ensemble* or detailed structure from *Collema*, save only in its simple spores: the higher assemblage being largely characterized by a higher spore-structure.

here understood (*S. phylliscina*, Msc.) found in Massachusetts (Mr. Willey). These are possibly new facts in the history as well of *Synalissa* as of *Pyrenopsis*, Nyl., to which latter group the species last named may rather be referable; but they will scarcely be considered as unsettling the systematic position of the lichens in question, as indicated by habit, and determined by other structure.

[1] It is interesting that the same question arises, probably, in *Pyrenopsis*, Nyl. There is, at any rate, nothing in the detailed description of *Collema furfurellum*, Nyl. (*Lich. Scand.* p. 28) to separate the plant from *P̌yrenopsis*, except that '*granula ejus gonima sunt moniliformi-disposita;*' or, more explicitly, occur '*sæpius 2—4 cohærentia.*' Nor is this all. In the thallus of an original specimen of *Pyrenopsis fuliginea* (Wahl.) Nyl., collected at Refsbotten, Finmark, by Wahlenberg, in 1802 (*Herb. Fr.*) I find no difficulty in observing gonidial chains of 4—5—6 members; and the plant scarcely differs in any other respect from the descriptions But neither of these lichens can be regarded as quite at home in·*Collema!*

The spore-history of *Collema*, as the genus is here taken, makes indeed one of the chief points of interest and question in this otherwise closely associable group. Exhibiting, in the majority of species, what we cannot but regard as the muriform type, this type, in *Collema*, is notwithstanding constantly decolorate, and passes imperceptibly (earlier conditions of differentiation, occurring in the same species which exhibits finally the muriform, as in Arn. *Lich. Fragm.*, in *Flora*, 1867, t. 2, f. 26, 31, becoming fixed, as in Arn. l. c. f. 69–76, 93) into its opposite, the acicular. The passage is imperceptible, and the cluster in which elongated spores are typical (*Synechoblastus, Auctt.*) is thus as untenable as it is (in its type) well characterized. Nor does this extraordinary exhibition of what, looked at from the point of view of perhaps the best understood lichengroups, must be called anomalous development end, without showing pretty clearly that if *Collema* proper and *Synechoblastus* pass mutually into each other, and the latter may in fact be called only a marked, finally inordinate presentation of the earlier stages of spore-differentiation of the former, even the earliest stage is implied in it also; in such forms as *Collema pycnocarpum*, Nyl., (*Syn.* p. 115) as compared with its next of kin, *C. cyrtaspis* (*Obs. Lich.* l. c. 5, p. 387). Thus viewed, *Collema* may well appear a natural assemblage, of whatever rank ; and the anomalies of its spore-history, as of its thalline structure, as only the outcome of modifications which first meet us, if not in *Peltigerei*, at least in *Pannariei;* and recur, in part, so far as the spore-anomalies are concerned, in large groups (as *Thelotrema*) otherwise most widely separated from it.

We may be unable to claim for LEPTOGIUM, Fr., any better limits than have been found for other generical groups, and its distinctness has been called in question even by recent writers;[1] but, leaving out of view confessedly ambiguous forms, looking perhaps equally towards *Collema*, or even *Pannaria*, there will still remain the large, richly differenced, and yet congruous assemblage, which Fries separated, and almost all writers since him have accepted; and this it is doubtless difficult to arrange satisfactorily otherwise than by itself. As respects the great bulk of *Leptogium*, it may be said to be characterized by muriform-multilocular spores which are always, as in *Collema*, entirely without colour. The irregular differentiation of the spore-type remarked in the latter genus recurs however again here, where species with fusiform-acicular spores represent, more sparingly, *Synechoblastus;* and the earlier stages of the regular

[1] " *Leptogium et Collema inter se omnino confluunt.*" Nyl. *Animadv. (Bot. Zeit.* 1861, p. 337). " *Die Gattung Leptogium, von Collema nur durch das Vorhandensein einer zelligen Corticalschicht unterschieden, wird jedenfalls in Zukunft fallen müssen, da einerseits Leptogien-Arten vorkommen, denen diese Corticalschicht fehlt, andererseits dieselbe bei gewissen Gallertflechten vorkommt, die nicht in die bisherige Familie der Leptogieen gezogen werden.*" Koerb. *Parcrg.* p. 422, & *conf.* p. 420.

differentiation find interesting examples (contrasting curiously in other respects with *Lempholemma*, Koerb., as with *Collema pycnocarpum*, Nyl.) in *L. dendriscum*, Nyl., and *L. muscicola*. The group reaches its highest development in the large cluster of species of which *L. Tremelloides* is the most widely diffused type. But *Mallotium*, Flot., however now contrasting in habit, and always in the tomentose nap of its under side, is, on the whole, ill enough removable from the nearest neighbourhood to the cluster just named. And almost the same may be said of *Hydrothyria*, Russ.; which, if *Mallotium* be the *Sticta*, may be called the *Peltigera* of the *Eucollemei*.

NOTE. — The structure of the plants before us has been illustrated by Schwendener in the last part of his Researches (*Untersuch.* l. c. 4 (1868) p. 174). According to him, *Pannariaceæ* (from which he finally distinguishes *Lecothecium*, *Pterygium*, *Lichina*, &c., to constitute his *Raccoblennaceæ*) *Ephebaceæ*, *Collemaceæ*, and *Omphalariaceæ* are groups of equal rank, and naturally associable in this order; but only the last two are entitled to be especially distinguished as Jelly-lichens. The peculiarities of the Jelly-lichens may be reduced essentially to 1, the dissolution of the thickened, gelatinous membranes (principally of the gonidia, but in part also of the medullary filaments) into a structureless pulp, and 2, the modes of division, and hence of the grouping of the gonidia. Other features, as, for instance, the equal distribution of the gonidia throughout the tissue of the thallus, (*thallus homœomericus*) are not properly characteristical, since they are not unknown elsewhere, and in families remote, systematically, from the present. Save in the two points just noted, *Leptogium*, in its highest expressions (*Mallotium*, Flot.) must therefore (the inference is fully justified by our author's remarks) be generally comparable with *Sticta* and *Nephroma;* and there is no doubt of the strict anatomical resemblance of all these types, as respects as well the constitution and habit of the cortical layer, and of the fibrillose nap of the under side, as even the on the whole predominant, symmetrically divergent (or orthogonal-trajectory) disposition of the medullary filaments. Schwend. l. c. *passim.* The observations of the same author on the gelatinous thickening of the membranes of the gonidia in certain *Pannariæ* has been cited elsewhere; but this change in the constitution of the cells in question is not confined to *Collemei*, and its next of kin, *Pannariei*, but characterizes, more or less, the blue-green gonidia[1] (Schwend. l. c. 3, p. 133. De Bary *Morph. u. Phys. d. Pilze*, &c., p. 259) wherever these occur; or, at least, to copy Schwendener's instructive list, at the place last cited, of the genera which are structurally thus associable, in " *Sticta* (pr. p.) *Nephroma*, *Peltigera*, *Solorina*, *Pannaria*, *Micarœa*, *Lecothecium*, *Raccoblenna*, *Pterygium*, and *Lichina*." Is it questionable, then, from the purely anatomical point of view, that the *Collemei* are the outcome of modifications of Parmeliaceous structure?

XXII.—SYNALISSA, Fr., Nyl., emend.

Fr. S. O. V. p. 297. Collematis sp., et Pyrenulæ sp., Ach. Syn. p. 121,

[1] *Granula gonima*, Nyl., for which, as it is not questioned that these are really gonidial cells, the perhaps better-descriptive term, *collogonidia*, has been preferred in these pages.

317. Synalissa, Enchylium, Psorotichia, Thelygnia, et Pannariæ sp.,
Mass. Ric.; Mem.; Framm.; et in Flora Ratisb., in locis. Synalissa,
Enchylium, Psorotichia, et Porocyphus, Koerb. Syst. p. 422, 425; Parerg. p. 428, 433, 439. Schwend. Untersuch. l. c. 4, p. 166, 192, t. 23,
f. 23-24. Synalissa max. p., et Pyrenopsis, Nyl. Prodr. p. 18; Syn.
1, p. 93, t. 2, f. 2, 4, 5, t. 3, f. 2, 4; Lich. Scand. p. 25; Add. Nov. ad·
Lich. Eur. in Flora Ratisb., 1867, p. 370, 1863, p. 342, 1869, p. 82;
additis, teste auct., Collematis spp., Nyl. Syn., et Pannariæ, Psoroti-
chiæ, Stenhammariæ, et Verrucariæ Auct., spp., Animadv. in Bot.
Zeit. 19, p. 337. Synalissa, Enchylium, Psorotichia, et Pyrenopsis,
Stizenb. Beitr. l. c. p. 141, 143. Synalissa, Enchylium, et Psorotichia,
Krempelh. Lich. Bay. p. 99.

Apothecia depresso-globosa, disco urceolato l. dein aperto. Sporæ
ovoideo-ellipsoideæ, simplices, incolores. Spermatia ellipsoidea
oblongave, aut filiformia arcuata; sterigmatibus simplicibus. Thallus
corallino-granulosus rarius fruticulosus; textura in plerisque tota
parenchymatica; collogonidiis l. glomeratis l. dein moniliformi-concatenatis.

In arranging this group, made up on the one hand of lichens which it
is almost as easy to refer to *Pannariei*, and on the other of types unquestionably Collemeine, no better course has suggested itself than to follow
the outlines of Nylander's disposition, as emended in conformity with his
own suggestions. By associating *Synalissa conferta*, Born., with *S.
symphorea*, and recognizing *S. polycocca*, Nyl., as a member of the same
genus, this author (*Syn.* 1, p. 94) has, if we mistake not, fully broken
down the distinction between *Synalissa*, as understood by him, and his
Pyrenopsis (*Thelygnia*, Mass.) and the latter must be taken as properly
no more—to cite indeed his own words—than a 'sub-division' of the
former (*Syn.* p. 97). *Synalissa conferta* is structurally, as described, and
as fully appears in a specimen (Eastern Pyrenees, Montagne) without
doubt referable here, almost as much a fruticulose *Pyrenopsis* as a reduced *Synalissa* (Mass.). And however distinct in species be *S. polycocca*
from *Pyrenopsis fuliginea* (Wahl.) Nyl., it is very far from easy to regard
these lichens as other than congenerical. I know in fact, of no attempt
made as yet to distinguish the two groups referred to, by diagnostic
characters.

Apart indeed from *Synalissa conferta* as interpreted by the eminent
authority cited, another arrangement might suggest itself. *S. symphorea*
(*Synalissa*, Mass.) is in every respect a Collemeine lichen; but *Pyrenopsis* a group precluded by its parenchymatous tissue from the chief
structural peculiarities of *Collemei*, and, in the last resort, perhaps reconcilable with these only by a certain accordance in habit. How plausible
then to keep this low and even equivocal group together, and to assign to

Synalissa, Mass., a separate and higher place. It is yet to be remarked, for what it may be worth, that this would be to make much more here of the confusion of *cortex* and *medulla* in a general cellulose texture (parenchyma) than we are at all able to do either in *Pannaria* or *Leptogium;* and that *Synalissa* (Mass.) if we remove it from the place assigned to it by Nylander, must, in the end, fall into *Omphalaria*, or *vice versa*. Nor is this all. Should *Enchylium affine*, scarcely seeming to differ, as Koerber has remarked, from *Psorotichia*, (or *Pyrenopsis*) save in its polysporous thekes, prove yet, as plainly intimated by Nylander (*Bot. Zeit.* l. c.) to be rather associable with *Omphalaria*, we may anticipate a still greater reduction of genera, and our three groups of inferior *Collemei* disappear in one; itself nó less resolvable into *Collema*.

So long as Collemaceous Lichens were regarded as distinct in order, it was easy to overestimate the value of the persistently undeveloped apothecium not seldom exhibited by the lower types, as if this afforded evidence of a division analogous to *Angiocarpi*, in true Lichens. But the ordinal separation once given up, the great bulk of the groups included falls back, at once, into *Parmeliacei ;* and retrograde or inexplicate members must be considered from the new point of view. Only the presupposition of an ordinal difference, it is likely, has made it possible for lichenographers to accept at all of such constructions as *Obryzum*, Wallr.;[1] and Nylander, the latest writer who has reviewed all that is known of Collemeine vegetation, appears (*Syn.*) nowhere else to recognize Verrucariaceous structure, excepting only in his *Phylliscum*. And even this type,—whatever indications of fabric approaching that of the family before us may prove to occur in lichens undoubtedly Verrucariaceous, and the modification of the gonidia which should seem to be at the bottom of Collemaceous anomalies is not confined to the tribe in which it has its fullest development,—is, it will scarcely be denied, really Collemeine; and to be judged therefore from this, that is from a Parmeliaceous standpoint. Nor, as respects the crustaceous groups of *Collemei*, immediately in hand, the often inexplicate apothecia of which assume now the port of

---

[1] We have here (Massal. *Ital.* n. 138. Rabenh. *Lich. Eur.* n. 128) in point of fact, the thallus of a *Leptogium*, not to be distinguished from *L. palmatum* (Huds.) Mont. (Moug. & Nestl. *Cr. Vog.* n. 1058) at least in an infertile condition, except that in place of the normal apothecia are found, (it is important to observe, rarely) certain ' angiocarpous' or ' endocarpeine' ones, not reconcilable with those of the species, and shewing no reaction with iodine. " You might almost say," remarks Nylander, " that the apothecia and spermogones of some foreign species, dwelling parasitically in the thallus of this *Leptogium*, constituted *Obryzum*." (*Syn.* p. 136). According to Tulasne, who has especially illustrated *Obryzum corniculatum* (*Mém. sur les Lich.* p. 46, t. 6) a minute *Sphæria* infests the thallus of *Collema melænum;* and he suggests that such parasite, occurring on the thallus of *Collema*, may not impossibly explain *Thrombium bacillare*, Wallr., now referred by Koerber (*Parerg.* p. 444) doubtfully, to *Obryzum*. (Tul. l. c. p. 178).

those of *Verrucaria*, or failing to emerge, simulate in this way those of *Endocarpon*, is it too much to say that their affinity to lower clusters of *Pannariei* is even more evident than that of the frondose *Leptogia* to the higher.

The very humble, granulose, frequently somewhat coralloid, or at length fruticulose lichens, thus provisionally brought together here, possess, as respects the mass of them, as already remarked, a parenchymatous thallus; and only ascend to a distinctly Collemeine structure in one or two of the highest forms. With the exception of these last it is thus easy to compare the group with similarly reduced types of *Pannaria;* [1] and possible even, in the last resort, that very little of a distinctive character should offer, to separate supposed species of *Synalissa* (as here taken) from the former genus, beyond a degree of diversity in habit. Nylander has indeed illustrated the similarity of gonidial structure, which should appear to associate the rest of the group before us as well with *Synalissa*, Mass., as with *Omphalaria;* but he declines, in both groups, to recognize species in which the collogonidia become finally concatenate. If these species ought really to be recognized as in fact belonging to *Synalissa* and *Omphalaria*, as natural assemblages, the question assumes a new phase. In one of Wahlenberg's original specimens (*Herb. Fr.*) of *Pyrenopsis fuliginea* (Wahl.) Nyl., a specimen in other respects closely accordant with the descriptions, the gonidia (collogonidia) are commonly grouped in short chains of three to even five members; a similar structure appears in *Porocyphus areolatus*, Koerb. (*Herb. cel. Auct.*) and is indeed one of the characters of that genus, in other respects, once more, sufficiently agreeing in thalline features with *Pyrenopsis;* and finally there is nothing in the full description of *Collema furfurellum*, Nyl., (*Lich. Scand.* p. 28) which should forbid our citing it in the same connection. But lichens of this sort, with a parenchymatous thallus, little or no evidence of the Collemeine gelatinousness, and gonidia disposed in chains, may, habit apart, as well be referred to *Pannariei.*——As respects the apothecia, with a few exceptions which are sufficiently regular, more or less inexplicate conditions prevail: in the reduction however of even the most extreme of these to the tribal type, we follow Sommerfelt's explanation of the assumed Verrucariine fruit of *S. fuliginea;* and with equal confidence in the results.

For the most part easily overlooked, it is probable that but a small proportion of the existing representatives of *Synalissa*, as it is taken in this place, is as yet known, or at least fully understood; and the group demands especial attention in North America. The whole number of published species is not far from forty, of which all but five are European;

---

[1] The affinity is recognized by Anzi, with whom (*Catal. Sondr. consp. Syst.*) *Psorotichia* finds a place with *Lecothecium;* and by Koerber (*Parerg.*) in his observations on the position of *Pannaria Schœreri*, Mass.

one species having been recognized from Van Diemen's Land, and four in the United States. The plants occur equally on granitic and calcareous rocks.——*Atichia*, Flot., a very little known corticoline lichen of Germany, is added to his *Synalissa* by Nylander. *Pyrenopsis granatina* (Sommerf.) Nyl., and *P. hœmatopis*, Th. Fr., have already been considered, as perhaps better associable with our *Pannaria*. And the future may possibly witness other transfers in the same direction.

S. Schœreri (Mass., *sub Pannaria. Pyrenopsis*, Nyl.). Lime-rocks, Illinois, (E. Hall). Looking evidently towards *Pannaria ;* and perhaps not in fact differing except in a certain Collemeine habit.——*S. polycocca*, Nyl. Syn. (*S. fuliginea*, Tuckerm. *in litt.*). Granitic rocks, New Hampshire (Mr. Frost).—— *S. phœococca*, Tuckerm. [1] Upon similar rocks. North Carolina (Rev. Dr. Curtis). Massachusetts (Mr. Willey).—— *S. phylliscina*, Tuckerm. [2] Upon similar rocks, Massachusetts (Mr. Willey). ——*S. symphorea* (DC.) Nyl. (*S. sphœrospora*, Nyl. *Syn.*, '*forte non differt;*' Nyl. *Lich. Scand.*). Calcareous rocks, Alabama (Mr. Peters).——*S. Texana*, Tuckerm. [3] Calcareous rocks, Texas (Mr. Wright). And I have also scarcely sufficient specimens of another species (Mica-schist, Vermont, Mr. Russell) which greatly resembles *Psorotichia riparia*, Arn. (*Pyrenopsis*, Nyl. *Porocyphus*, Koerb.).

It is far from easy to determine, or rather find, spores in such North American specimens of *Synalissa* § *Pyrenopsis*, as have come before me. And, at the best, the type of such spores cannot but be obscure. Nylander's observation of something like bilocular spores in two species of his *Pyrenopsis* (*Lich. Scand.* p. 26, 283) is therefore interesting; and the further remark that in one of these instances the organs in question were

---

[1] Will be elsewhere described. Thallus dark brown, at length broken into areole-like masses, and the granules finally more or less coralloid; cellular tissue coarser than in *S. polycocca*, the reddish, exterior cells about 0,007–11$^{mm.}$ in diameter, and the interior, 0,018–25$^{mm.}$, or now 0,033$^{mm.}$ by 0,023$^{mm.}$; one to three collogonidia in the cells. Spores very imperfectly seen, ovoid-ellipsoid, simple, nebulous, without colour, 0.009–11$^{mm.}$ long, and 0,006$^{mm.}$ wide; but probably occurring larger. Paraphyses indistinct. Filaments not wholly deficient in the thallus. Spermatia ellipsoid; sterigmas simple.

[2] *Synalissa phylliscina (sp. nova) thallo granuloso tenui fusco-nigro; apotheciis globosis sub-clausis. Sporœ in thecis lato-fusiformibus octonœ, ovoideo-ellipsoideœ, simplices, fere incolores, longit.* 0,009–15$^{mm.}$ *crassit.* 0,005–7$^{mm.}$; *paraphysibus parcis brevibus.*—— External (reddish) cells 0,006–9$^{mm.}$ in diameter; the internal ones reaching 0,020–27$^{mm.}$ Collogonidia with the general features of those of *Omphalaria phyllisca* (*Phylliscum*, Nyl.) but smaller. Spermatia acicular, bowed; on simple sterigmas. Reaction of hymenial gelatine with iodine vinous-red.

[3] Thallus with the aspect of *S. symphorea*, at least in the European specimens, attached at the centre, nodose-lobulate, made up of mostly solitary collogonidia which are scattered amidst conspicuous filaments. Apothecia unknown. Spermogones situated similarly to apothecia, containing filiform, bowed spermatia, upon simple sterigmas. Collogonidia 0.006–11$^{mm.}$ in diameter.

constricted also at the middle, points to the every way probable inference that we have to do here with decolorate, and otherwise imperfect, exhibitions of the brown spore-type. —— Instead of the very minute, oblong spermatia indicated by Dr. Nylander as characteristical, so far as known, of the species of this genus, two of those above reckoned (*S. Texana*, & *S. phylliscina*) exhibit filiform and bowed ones, quite similar to those of *Phylliscum*, Nyl.; the only instance that I am aware of, in *Collemei*, in which such spermatia have been described. It is also observable that the large gonidia, and other structural features beside the peculiar coloration under the microscope, of *Phylliscum*, associate it with species of *ynalissa;* one of which (*S. phylliscina*) might almost be called a crustaceous *Phylliscum*, as the last type has been recognized by Fries as a foliaceous *Synalissa*.

XXIII.—OMPHALARIA, Dur. & Mont.

Dur. & Mont. in Fl. Alg. Mont. Cent. de Pl. cell. in Ann. 3, 12, n. 76, bis; Syll. p. 379. Endocarpi sp., Wahl. in Ach. Meth. Suppl. p. 25; Fl. Lapp. p. 463, t. 29, f. 2. Ach. L. U. p. 300; Syn. p. 100. Parmeliæ dein Collematis sp., et Endocarpi sp., Schær. Spicil. p. 544; Enum. p. 233, 260. Synalissæ sp., Fr. Summ. Veg. Scand. p. 563. Phylliscum, Omphalaria, et Collematis spp., Nyl. Prodr. p. 19, 27; Syn. p. 98, 103, 105, 136, t. 3, f. 5; Lich. Scand. p. 36. Tuck. in Nyl. Syn., & Obs. Lich. l. c. 5, p. 383. Phylliscum, Omphalaria, Thyrea, Arnoldia dein Plectopsora, et Corinophorus dein Peccania, Mass. Neag. p. 7; Symm. p. 59; & Opp. var. Koerb. Parerg. p. 429, 443. Krempelh. Lich. Bay. p. 99. Omphalaria, et Phylliscum, Anz. Catal. Sondr. p. 2; Manip. p. 2; Neosymb. p. 2. Phylliscum, Omphalaria, et Plectopsora, Stizenb. Beitr. l. c. pp. 140, 143. Schwend. Untersuch. l. c. 4, pp. 189, 194, t. 23, f. 3–9.

Apothecia sub-globosa, thallo plus minus immersa, l. verrucarioideo-prominula, rarius dein explicata scutellæformia. Sporæ ellipsoideæ, simplices, incolores. Spermatia ellipsoidea, aut nunc filiformia arcuata; sterigmatibus simplicibus. Thallus foliaceus l. rarissime fruticuloso-ascendens, umbilicato-affixus; collogonidiis plerumque solitariis glomeratisve, nunc moniliformi-concatenatis; filamentis medullaribus sæpius conspicuis.

This section of *Eucollemei* (*Collema, sensu latiori*) is adopted here in the signification in which Montagne understood it; as embracing the Collemas which are attached to the substrate at a single point. Adding the anatomically similar *Synalissa symphorea*, the section accords with *Omphalariei*, Koerb.; and leaving out the *Synalissa* named, as a separate generical type, it answers exactly to *Omphalaria*, Anz. (*ll. cc.*) excepting only, as regards both authors, in the case of *O. phyllisca* (*Endocarpon,*

Wahl. *Synalissa*, Fr. *Phylliscum*, Nyl.) the supposed Verrucariaceous structure of the fruit of which, re-asserted by Nylander, has procured general agreement to his distinction of this otherwise certainly marked lichen. As thus taken, the *Omphalariæ*, with very few exceptions, are most readily recognizable in habit, but offer some discrepancies in their thalline structure, illustrating the intermediate and ill-definable position of the group, between *Synalissa* (itself, as here understood, not without similar discrepancies) and *Collema*. In the larger number of species, the gonimous system, represented by solitary or only clustered collogonidia, reverts in fact towards *Synalissa ;* and the assemblage thus indicated, as differenced from the inferior one preceding it by better developed medullary elements, and a foliaceous thallus, constitutes *Omphalaria*, Nyl. (*Syn.*): the few forms exhibiting concatenate collogonidia being by this author referred to *Collema*.[1] These discrepant types (*Plectopsora*, Mass.) are however, none the less evidently Omphalarieine, and essential therefore to the completeness of our conception of the natural group of which they are members; in view of which, and of the little that is known of the value of the anatomical difference which distinguishes them, we may well follow Anzi in declining to keep them apart. But there is still no doubt that, in placing *Omphalaria cyathodes* in close neighbourhood to *Collema micrococcum*, the learned author of the latest *Synopsis Lichenum* has but given expression to a genuine affinity. As on the one hand, within the boundaries of the group before us, we all but touch *Synalissa*, so, on the other, the same group passes imperceptibly into *Collema ;* every point of structural diversity at length failing, in the first direction, except the foliaceous thallus, and, in the second, except the peculiar attachment. These differences serve notwithstanding to define the assemblage. As *Synalissa* finds its nearest analogues in the reduced types of *Pannaria*, and the great mass of *Collema* and *Leptogium* in the frondose *Pannariæ*, and, more remotely, in *Sticta* and *Nephroma*, *Ompha-*

---

[1] To judge by the description and figure, *Collema nummularium*, Duf. (Nyl. *Syn.* p. 103, t. 4, f. 9) should be far more at home in *Omphalaria;* notwithstanding the structural reduction. Nor can I see sufficient reason for questioning the place of *O. decipiens*, Mass., which, alien in its gonimous elements to *Collema,* possesses much to make it comparable with *Omphalaria pyrenoides*, Nyl., and differs from all types of *Pyrenopsis* in its originally frondose thallus (*specim. Arnold. in herb. Krempelh.!* Koerb. *Parerg.* p. 431). Medullary filaments by no means wholly deficient in this lichen, as asserted by Nylander (*Syn.* p. 103) and by Koerber (*l. c.*). Compare, as to this, De Bary, *Morph. & Phys. d. Pilze, Flechten, &c.*, p. 266. A frondose type once admitted into *Synalissa § Pyrenopsis*, it might well appear less difficult, in view of *Synalissa phylliscina*, to restore *Omphalaria phyllisca* to the position assigned to it by Fries, — a position to which it is not without intrinsic claims; — but this would be in effect to relegate, as a whole, *Omphalaria* to *Synalissa*, and doubtless the first step only to the re-establishment of *Collema* (*exc. excip.*) Ach.

laria, as respects no less its higher thalline structure, viewed in relation to *Synalissa,* and from the point of view of the structural type of *Collemei,* as its atypical fruit, stands, plainly enough, for *Umbilicaria.* [1]

Inexplicate apothecia, that is to say, gymnocarpous fruits in which the normal evolution has been prematurely concluded, and the organ assumes more or less of an angiocarpous aspect, are sufficiently common in the genus immediately preceding, and owing perhaps in part, as already suggested, to the prevalent presupposition of an ordinal difference in Collemaceous lichens, authors are not yet agreed as to the typically gymnocarpous character of the whole of them; though we scarcely find traces of the recognition of other structure in the learned lichenographer, who alone, since Acharius, has elaborated the whole family. [2] If indeed *Synalissa* and *Omphalaria* belong to *Collemei,* they belong to an assemblage, the great majority and all the highest types of which are undistinguishable in their general fruit-characters from Parmeliaceous families; and the presumption is thus an exceedingly strong one that exceptional forms of fructification, however looking in a different direction shall yet prove to be reducible to the same. But the fact of this reducibleness is perhaps not questioned by any author, as regards the larger part of the variously anomalous apothecia occurring in *Collemei,* and especially in *Omphalaria.* Though embarrassed, and to at least the same extent with *Synalissa,* with inexplicate receptacles, now sunken (endocarpoid) and now more prominent or verrucarioid, no doubt seems to be entertained that the group is really, and, as a whole, associable with *Collema,*

[1] This resemblance is marked in the Cuban *O. deusta,* described in a former note. In another interesting illustration of the present group of Lichens, found by Mr. Wright in company with *O. deusta,* and *O. Wrightii,* we have however the habit rather of a *Pannaria,* not remote from *P. plumbea.* —— *Omphalaria Cubana (sp. nova) thallo orbiculari incrassato viridi-olivaceo sub-imbricato basi umbilicato-affixo, lobis squamiformibus appressis, periphericis latioribus, omnibus crenatis, subtus rugoso-verrucosis; apotheciis lecanorinis, paraphysibus distinctis.* Shaded limestone cliffs, Guajuybon, Island of Cuba, Mr. Wright. Thallus (in the two specimens gathered) not quite half an inch in diameter, made up of crenate, closely appressed and coalescent lobes, which attain at length the thickness of 1mm. Collogonidia solitary, or in small clusters, amidst anastomosing filaments, which are most to be observed at the centre, as the collogonidia are most abundant at the circumference. A single, innate, lecanorine apothecium afforded no mature spores.

[2] It is true that the term 'perithecium' is employed by Nylander in describing the fruit of *Synalissa micrococca (Syn.* p. 95) as the section including this species is defined as possessing 'endocarpeine' apothecia; but both these terms must without doubt be used in a large sense, as, not to refer to the note on page 98 of the same work, or the difficulty of admitting Parmeliaceous and Verrucariaceous receptacles in one and the same genus, the section includes also our *S. polycocca,* Nyl., the apothecia of which are as distinctly undeveloped-lecanorine, as the same organ is admitted to be in *S. lignyota.*

save only in the extreme case, already repeatedly referred to, of *O. phyllisca* (*Phylliscum*, Nyl.).

But this plant, if well-comparable as respects its collogonidia with species of *Synalissa*, is yet in no other respect than the size of these organs separable from recognized types of *Omphalaria*, with which group it obviously better agrees in its foliaceous thallus; and being thus and to this extent clearly Collemeine, the presumption that its fruit shall be explicable from the same standpoint is as strong, as in any other case in which this explicableness is admitted. Nor in fact is the fruit really in the way. A certain form of anamorphosis being given, we should expect this modification of structure to reach at length its full exemplification. If all the other conditions of inexplicate apothecia before us are admissible as abnormal gymnocarpous types, the present can hardly be refused admission into the same category because simply the anamorphosis is here complete, and the wholly immersed disk becomes, as of course it must, no longer imperfectly, but perfectly nucleiform. *O. phyllisca* (Nyl. *Syn.* t. 3, f. 5) diverges no further from *O. phylliscoides*, Nyl., (*l. c.* f. 3) in this regard, than it were beforehand presumable, from the point of view of the latter, that another species should possibly diverge; and there is in short no other appreciable difference than what depends on this final completion of the process of reduction; of which we need not go beyond the present genus to find every other step. We cannot then speak, with Massalongo (*Neag.* p. 7) of a double exciple in *O. phyllisca*, without admitting the applicability of the same term in the case of other species, the understood character of the anomalies of which makes it impossible; nor of an amphithecium without the same consequence. *O. leptophylla*, Tuck. (Wright *Lich. Cub.* n. 1) is, I take it, admissibly an *Omphalaria;* and yet it is not without interest that this lichen has also been referred, and by authority so high that its citation is an element of value in this discussion, to *Phylliscum*. Even more similar, as well in colour as especially in the depressed apothecia opening equally by a pore-like aperture, is the Cuban *O. deusta*, already elsewhere described. And there is yet another new lichen, the significant relation of which to *O. phyllisca* can hardly be passed over. To refer the crustaceous *Synalissa phylliscina* to *Phylliscum*, Nyl., we must disregard that important distinction in the thallus upon which the very existence of *Synalissa* and *Omphalaria*, as separate groups, depends; and it is certainly no easier to elevate it to the rank of a genus. If then the *Synalissa* belong where we have placed it, why should not the type of *Phylliscum* be referable to *Omphalaria?*

Like *Synalissa*, *Omphalaria* has always been taken to be characterized by simple spores. Evidence of probable exceptions to this rule has however been given by Nylander, in the case of the former genus; and may well yet appear, as respects the latter. *Collema elveloideum*, Ach. (Nyl. *Syn.* p. 116. *C. phylliscinum*, Nyl. *Prodr., fide auct.*) in which the spores are described as bilocular, cannot but approach very closely to *Omphalaria*, as here understood.

Of the group as here taken, about twenty-five species have been indicated; all but seven of them European. About one half inhabit the south of Germany, and Italy, two only of these reaching northward as far as Westphalia, and one, the neighbourhoods of Paris and Jena; four the south of France, of which two are also found in Algeria, and one in Algeria and Alabama; one is known only as Algerian; and one ranges from the middle of Europe to the Icy Sea, and, in America, from Rhode Island to Lake Superior, and doubtless northward. Beside the two, common to North America and Europe, there is one American species peculiar as yet to Texas, and one to Alabama. Five tropical, American species are known, all of them from the island of Cuba. With the exception of *O. phyllisca*, the genus is almost wholly, though the rule is not quite without other exception, confined to calcareous rocks.

O. Girardi, Dur. & Mont., *e* Nyl. (*Coll. plutonium*, Tuck. *in litt.*). Lime-rocks in Northern Alabama (Mr. Peters). —— *O. pyrenoides*, Nyl. On similar rocks in Texas (Mr. Wright). —— *O. umbella*, Tuck. in Nyl. *Syn.* (*Collema*, Nyl.). Lime-rocks in Northern Alabama (Mr. Peters). I find no important difference in thalline structure between this and *O. botryosa*, Nyl. (*Plectopsora*, Mass. Herb. Koerb.) and the two plants are most closely akin; the apothecia of the latter being by no means always so inconspicuous or 'endocarpeine' as they are described. —— *O. phyllisca* (*Endocarpon* , Wahl., Ach. *Synalissa* Fr. *Omphalaria Demangeonii*, Mont. *O. Silesiaca*, Koerb. *Phylliscum*, Nyl.). Granitic rocks, White Mountains, (Mr. Russell). Vermont (Mr. Frost). Massachusetts (Mr. Willey). Rhode Island, (Mr. Bennett). Lake Superior (Prof. Agassiz).

XXIV.—COLLEMA, (Hoffm.) Fr., Flot.

Collema, Fr. S. O. V. p. 255. Flot. Collem. in Linnæa, 1850. Mont. Aperç. Morph. p. 12. Collema (C. saturn. excl.) Fr. Fl. Scan. p. 292; Summ. Veg. Scand. p. 121. Tuckerm. Syn. N. E. p. 89; Suppl. 2, l. c. p. 201; Obs. Lich. l. c. 5, p. 385, et 6, p. 263. Collema max. p., Nyl. Prodr. p. 19; Syn. p. 101, t. 2, f. 3, t. 3, f. 1–6, t. 4, f. 6, 19–21; Lich. Scand. p. 28; in Prodr. Fl. N. Gran. p. 1; Syn. Lich. N. Caled. p. 4. Collematis spp., Schreb., Hoffm. D. Fl. 2, p. 98. Ach. L. U. p. 129, 628; Syn. p. 308. Eschw. Syst. p. 20; in Fl. Bras. p. 231. Fée Ess. p. 66; Suppl. p. 127. Schær. Enum. p. 247. Parmeliæ spp., Ach. Meth. p. 221. Mey. Entwick. Schær. Spicil. p. 511. Parmeliæ spp., et Patellariæ spp., Wallr. Fl. Crypt. Germ. 1, p. 434, 545. Collema, Blennothallia, et Synechoblastus, Trevis. Lethagrium et Collema pr. p., Mass. Mem. p. 80, t. 13–17. Lempholemma, Synechoblastus, et Collema, Koerb. Syst. p. 400. Th. Fr. Lich. Arct. p. 276. Physma, Synechoblastus et Collema, Anz. Catal. Sondr. p. 2; Manip. l. c. p. 131. Stizenb. Beitr. l. c. p. 134. Physma, Lethagrium, et Collema, Krempelh. Lich. Bay. p. 90. Physma, Lethagrium, Synecho-

blastus, et Collema, Arn. Lich. Fragm. in Flora Ratisb. 1867, n. 8–9, t. 1–4.
    Structuram exposuerunt Tulasne, Mém. pp. 28, 45, 64, 178, t. 6, 7; Schwendener, Untersuch. l. c, 3, p. 153, 4, p. 185, t. 22.

Apothecia scutellæformia. Sporæ ovoideo-ellipsoideæ, l. simplices, l. dein fusiformi-elongatæ bi-pluriloculares, l. muriformi-pluriloculares, sub-incolores. Spermatia ellipsoidea oblongave; sterigmatibus, in plerisque, articulatis. Thallus foliaceus aut rarissime fruticulosus; strato corticali plerumque nullo l. indistincto; collogonidiis fere semper moniliformi-concatenatis; filamentis medullaribus conspicuis, laxis.

We reach, in Collema, not indeed the highest expressions of lichenose vegetation afforded by *Eucollemei*, but certainly the central and most typical representatives of the group. Here all the peculiarities of Collemeine structure find their best exhibition; and so marked at length is the development of mucilage and its conditioning influence upon the thallus, that even the unquestioned Parmeliaceous affinity indicated in the apothecia has proved insufficient, in the opinion of a majority of authors, to assure to these plants a place among " true Lichens." It is not however too much to say that instead of confirming the judgments of those writers who make of *Collemei* a separate Order, the best later research has in fact tended to invalidate these judgments; and if there now remain any clearly sufficient ground for the exclusion of the jelly-lichens and what go with them from that place in the system to which they should be referred by their fruit-characters, it is at least unknown to the present writer.

    The well-marked difference of these lichens was still not one to escape attention; and when Dillenius (*Hist. Musc.* p. 137, t. 19, f. 19–35) had contributed, as he did, above all others who had preceded and many who followed him, to their elucidation, it was not long in finding expression in a generical name (*Collema*, Hill, 1751) which, taken up, long after, by Schreber (in *Linn. Gen. Pl.* 1791) and provided with a character, prepared thus a way for the special labors of Hoffmann (*D. Fl.* 2, p. 98, 1795) and finally of Acharius. Some writers indeed among those who succeeded the latter, as Wahlenberg, Meyer, Wallroth, and Schærer, in his principal work (*Spicil.* p. 511) declined to recognize in *Collema* anything higher than a section of *Parmelia;* but Eschweiler's careful review (*Syst. Lich.* 1824. *Lich. Bras.* l. c. p. 231) and justification of the distinctions of the group, undoubtedly better expressed the opinion of the time. This was in fact now ready for a more searching analysis; and Fries's limitation of *Collema* by the exclusion from it of *Thermutis, Synalissa,* and *Leptogium* (S. O. V. 1825, p. 255, where the *Mallotia* appear also to be within the author's view) determined at length the course of subsequent study, and the point of departure of Flotow (1. c.) Koerber (*Syst.* 1. c. *Parerg.*) and Nylander.

But the advance of knowledge, since Fries wrote, leaves the *Eucollemei* by no means where they were when he reconstructed the group. *Omphalaria*, most clearly touching *Collema* (as seen in the comparison of *C. chalazanum*, &c., with *O. cyathodes*) on the one hand, brings it next into no questionable relation with the once distant *Synalissa*, on the other. Indeed this latter relationship is fully implied in Fries's final reference (*Summ. Veg. Scand.*, *suppl.*) of *Omphalaria phyllisca* (*Endocarpon*, Wahl., Fr. *L. E.*) to *Synalissa*. Nor has the connection of the assemblage now immediately before us proved in fact much less intimate with *Leptogium*. Here however the for the most part sufficiently striking difference in habit effectively intervenes; and has proved enough to countervail even Anzi's demonstration of a cellular cortical layer in *Collema aggregatum*. And the parallel spore-history of these two groups, (*Collema* and *Leptogium*) as here taken, looks perhaps in the same direction; that is to their continued separation.

This spore-history is especially interesting; and cannot be passed without some brief consideration. In a general view of the spores of 'true Lichens,' as these are distinguished by most authors from Collemaceous Lichens, it will perhaps be admitted to be easy to reach the inference already presented by the writer in print (Lich. Calif. p. 6) that all known modifications of spore-structure, to whatever extent distinguishable among themselves, are yet reducible to variations of but two clearly defined types; and that it is less feasible at present to subsume them under one. Led by such instances as *Parmelia, Lecanora, Biatora,* and *Lecidea*, on the one hand, and *Physcia, Rinodina, Heterothecium,* and *Buellia*, on the other,—by so large and important a proportion of the class, — we have seemed then to discern two series (1. c. p. 9) and really to be able, for the most part, to distinguish these series, notwithstanding decoloration and other exceptions, in a manner as satisfactory as were at all to be expected. Much of the argument of the present book proceeds from this assumption, and will now be left 'for what it shall prove to be worth' (1. c. p. 10) satisfied as I am that the results reached are not without value. But the difficulties remain. It is possible, I believe, by a sufficiently extensive investigation of the whole spore-development of such natural groups as *Thelotrema* and *Pyrenula*, as here understood, and a careful appreciation of the varied details, to explain most apparent anomalies as decolorate exhibitions of stages of evolution of the muriform or (normally) coloured spore ; and these large and analogous genera, the extraordinary exuberance of variation in the apothecia of the one of which exhibits so curious a contrast with the poverty of the other, appear thus to be more readily interprètable than some smaller ones. This is not however at present the case with *Gyalecta*, Anz.; as evidenced especially in this writer's striking comparison of his *G. acicularis* (*Catal.*

Sondr. p. 62. *Lich. Langob.* n. 81) with the at once similar and yet dissimilar *G. cupularis.* And *Collema* affords a still better example of the same sort. We have here, in one series of, in the last analysis, mutually explanatory forms, all the most important modifications of spore-structure known to Lichens. What is evidently a decolorate example of the muriform spore is traceable backward to regularly quadrilocular — bilocular — simple conditions, which then, again, narrowing and lengthening, pass finally into the perfect acicular type. There is no question of the extremes of evolution reached, or of the completed mediation of these extremes, within the limits of a single process of differentiation, and of a single group. [1]

In attempting next, on the basis of the latest universal *rèsumè,* that of Nylander (*Syn.*) some reckoning of the number of probable species of *Collema* known, it appears desirable to view the group apart from the discrepant forms, provisionally only, for the most part, associated with it; and, in this view, to exclude therefore all plainly crustaceous, as certainly doubtful, species; all forms which are associable, by their attachment, with *Omphalaria;* and, as well, the confessedly ambiguous *C. byrsæum* (Afzel) (*Physma,* Mass.) and *C. opulentum* (Mont.) (*Homothecium,* Mass.). As to the remainder there is no controversy, beyond what hinges on the value of the spore-differences, already immediately above, as elsewhere considered; and the always uncertain estimates of what constitutes species. Of typical *Collema,* as thus understood, something over forty species have then been reckoned. These are largely northern, and especially European; but the number common to America with Europe will probably be increased. The number of forms running into or peculiar to the warmer and intertropical regions of the earth is small; and the group contrasts with *Leptogium* in this respect. Much, we can hardly doubt, remains to be discovered, as certainly to be fully determined, here ; especially in our calcareous districts. And if the large, long known, and important cluster represented by *C. pulposum* is still so uncertain in Europe, as the varying opinions of lichenographers, with regard not only to the inner circle of more evidently related forms, but no less to the to these strictly akin *C. limosum, C. crispum, C. plicatile* of authors — not to speak of still other more recent discriminations — demonstrate it to be, we may well hesitate in positively determining the little we have yet learned of the group, in North America.

We are at once embarrassed, in attempting to arrange our species according to the method of this book, by the ambiguity of the spore-

---

[1] The spores of *Collema* are commonly defined as colourless; Th. Fries *(Lich. Arct.)* denoting however these organs in several species as ' *luteolo-hyalinæ* ' or ' *luteolæ,*' and Mudd (Man. Brit. Lich.) describing them, in nearly half of his species, as more or less ' pale yellow.' In about the same proportion of my American Collemas, similar indications of colour are often, or more or less observable; or the spores at least seen to be brownish, while still included in the thekes.

characters. The evolution of the spores indicates plainly a two-fold *nisus*, observable not merely in *Collema* as a whole, as here taken, but even within the narrow limits of a single species; — *C. flaccidum* offering, in a word, as will be seen below, unmistakable exhibitions of both the acicular and the muriform spore-types. Nor are the, here important, thalline characters always clear as yet; though we venture, to some extent, to rely on our interpretation of these, in bringing together some hitherto widely separated clusters.

Sect. 1. — COLLEMELLA.

1. *C. cladodes*, Tuckerm. [1] Lime-rocks, Trenton Falls, New York. Analogous here to *Leptogium dendriscum* in the genus immediately following.

Sect. 2. — LATHAGRIUM.

2. *C. myriococcum*, Ach., Nyl., Arn. Growing over mosses, on lime-rocks, Rockland county, New York (Mr. Austin). A similar plant occurs at Trenton Falls, but infertile. Spores simple, from roundish becoming ovoid or even ellipsoid, disposed, in a single series, in narrowed, or more rarely otherwise, in ventricose thekes. *C. chalazanum*, Ach., is kept separate (not without hesitation) by Nylander, and, more decidedly, by Arnold; but the distinction appears to be difficult. Of the two names, *myriococcum* was the first published. The fully developed thallus of this species looks evidently in the same direction with that of *C. omphalarioides*, Anz. (*L. Etr.* n. 46) and the latter plainly corresponds, not only, as its author suggests, with *C. aggregatum*, but no less with *C. pycnocarpum*.

——3. *C. pycnocarpum*, Nyl. Trunks, common in New England and the northern states. Ohio (Lesquereux). Illinois (E. Hall). South Carolina (Mr. Ravenel). Alabama (Mr. Peters). This lichen and the next are representatives here of the much less conspicuous *C. conglomeratum*, Hoffm., and, recently separated *C. verruculosum*, Hepp, of Europe; and all together make one natural cluster, or species *sensu latiori*. *C. conglomeratum*, and the two American members of the cluster, belong to *Synechoblastus*, as understood by those who receive that group as a genus; but *C. verruculosum*, however closely akin to the rest, and associated with *C. conglomeratum* by Arnold *l. c.*, is none the less, and in the same restricted sense, a *Collema*. Compare the still more striking instance of

---

[1] *Collema cladodes (sp. nova) thallo pumilo cartilagineo fruticuloso pulvinato atroviridi, ramis teretibus longitudinaliter tenuissime striatis fastigiato-subramosis, periphericis stellato-radiantibus; apotheciis minutis terminalibus lateralibusve depresso-globosis. Thecæ confertæ clavatæ; paraphysibus parcis irregularibus.*
—— Trenton, N. Y. Thallus not much exceeding a quarter of an inch in diameter, with the texture and colour of *Collema;* the concatenate collogonidia interspersed among anastomosing filaments. Perfect apothecia scarcely seen.

this confusion of spore-types in *C. flaccidum.*——4. *C. cyrtaspis*, Tuck. *Obs. Lich.* l. c. 5, p. 387. Trunks, apparently rare at the North, but found in Massachusetts (Mr. Willey). It becomes common in the middle states and southward; where, as westward, it has the same range with the last. The present still appears to me a distinct link in the chain which connects *C. conglomeratum* and *C. pycnocarpum.* Spores quadrilocular, longer than those of *C. pycnocarpum;* averaging from 16 to almost 23^{mmm} in length, and 4 to 7^{mmm} in breadth.——5. *C. laciniatum*, Nyl. Lime-rocks, Alabama (Mr. Peters). On calcareous rocks, Kansas (Mr. E. Hall). Spores scarcely exceeding the bilocular stage in the Alabama lichen; but becoming quadrilocular in that from the island of Cuba (Wright *Lich. Cub.* n. 4). Habit of the plant entirely congruous with that of *C. pycnocarpum*, and *C. cyrtaspis;* and the spores appear to confirm the affinity.——6. *C. microphyllum*, Ach. Elm bark, Weymouth, Massachusetts, (Mr. Willey). Illinois (Mr. Hall). The minuteness of the thallus makes its real type less easily discoverable; I incline however to regard this as closely approximating, in both European and American specimens, to the type exhibited in *C. callibotrys*, especially as shown in *C. verruciforme.* The plant is thus also brought into near relation (as indicated by Schærer) to *C. conglomeratum;* while its distinctly muriform spores suggest at once the not wholly dissimilar ones of *C. verruculosum*, above noticed.——7. *C. callibotrys*, Tuck. *in litt. ad cel.* Nyl., & *Obs. Lich. l. c.* 5, p. 386. *Fere C. coccophylloides*, Nyl. Prodr. Nov. Gran. p. 1? Trunks, South Carolina (Mr. Ravenel). I have noted in the description of this species that the at first curiously squared spores become at length ellipsoid or even oblong-ellipsoid, and either regularly quadrilocular, or the spore-cells finally divided (sub-muriform). Together with *C. coccophyllum* and *C. verruciforme*, Nyl., and *C. quadratum*, Lahm, the present constitutes a natural cluster, or species *sens. lat.*, the evolution of the thallus in the best-developed members of which connects it with *C. pycnocarpum*, and no less with *C. aggregatum*, &c.——8. *C. verruciforme*, Nyl. On Red Cedar, Weymouth, and New Bedford, Massachusetts (Mr. Willey). Quite inferior, in its almost crustaceous thallus, to Schær. n. 416, which is the type of *C. verruciforme*, and approaching rather to *C. quadratum*, Lahm, as that is described; but the distinctness of the latter is scarcely yet made out. According to Mr. Willey's observations, the squared spores become finally ellipsoid, and regularly quadrilocular, as in the last species.——9. *C. leptaleum*, Tuck. *Obs. Lich.* l. c. 6, p. 263. Trunks; New England to Virginia. New York (Mr. Russell). South Carolina (Mr. Ravenel). Alabama (Mr. Peters). Louisiana (Hale). And collected also, by Mr. Wright, in the island of Cuba, and in Japan. The cluster to which this belongs is represented in Europe by *C. aggregatum*, Nyl., and in intertropical America by *C. implicatum*, Nyl. (*Herb.* v. d. Bosch. *Coll.* Lindig. n. 749. Orizaba, Mexico, Dr. Mohr) and *C. glaucophthalmum*, Nyl. (*Coll.* Lindig. n. 813) and is associable, by its peculiar habit of thallus, as exemplified especially in *C. aggregatum*, with *C. callibotrys*, Tuck., and *C. coccophylloides*, Nyl.; however marked may well, at first, appear the difference in the spores. The real significance of the group represented by *C. callibotrys* is not however to be got from depauperate exhibitions of it (*C. quadratum*, Lahm) or from anything less than a complete view of its spore-history. Nor is it, we will venture to say, other than likely that the elongation of the spore in *C. aggregatum*, &c., represents only an extreme, to be explained hereafter, in the course of discovery, by the mediation of forms with much shorter spores; exactly as in *C. flaccidum*. In that case it is possible that the present cluster shall prove in fact too near to the one immediately preceding.——10. *C. microptychium*, Tuck. Lich. Calif. p. 35. Trunks of Elm, Chestnut, and other trees; New England. Related by the spores to *C. leptaleum*, but the thallus is widely diverse, and looks rather towards the next.——11. *C. flaccidum*, Ach. Granitic rocks, and also on trunks, common in the north, and in the mountains southward, to Virginia. In the Carolinas, infertile (Mr. Ravenel). The spores, in European specimens of this species (as in Schær. 413, 414, and Moug. & Nestl. 1059, and as figured by Hepp, 651) are very commonly ovoid, and offer little to distinguish them from conditions of the typo in *Collema* proper; especially when, as I observe in Zw. exs. 166, this ovoid spore clearly betrays a *nisus* to become muriform-plurilocular. And this sufficiently explains Nylander's relegation of *C. flaccidum* (*Syn.*) to the neighbourhood of *C. furvum;* and his more recent denial (*Lich. Scand.*) of any appreciable diversity between the spores of these two lichens. But if the lichen-group before us be indeed so far determinable as a " *Collema*," it is none the less certain that its ulterior development is that of " *Synechoblastus;* " or that the alleged spore-difference, upon which it has been sought to construct even a generical distinction, disappears thus entirely within the circuit of modifications of a single species. The gradual evolution of the ovoid into long fusiform spores is sufficiently exhibited even by the European specimens, and the contrast between Hepp's figure already cited and that of Massalongo (*Mem.* n. 109) seems in fact greater than the measurements express: in our lichen however the elongation of the spore is commonly much more pronounced than in Massalongo's; and we cease finally to find any criterion of distinction, in this regard, from *C. nigrescens*. The latter is indeed closely approached, in all respects, by some of our tree-forms of the present; and the two species belong clearly to one and the same cluster.——Of the plants referred to *C. abbreviatum*, Arn., l. c., the writer possesses only Schær. 413, 414, which have not afforded to him any sufficient differences from Zw. 166, or from *C. flaccidum*. But even the perplexing spores figured by Arnold (l. c. t. 4, n. 77–80) are no more difficult to admit (compare the same writer's n. 74) as an element of *C. flaccidum*, than that lichens so generally similar as those just cited, of Schærer and v. Zwackh, should not at any rate be members of one and

the same specific group. In the absence of most of the cited specimens of *C. abbreviatum*, no further remark can here be ventured on the asserted structural discrepancy between it and *C. flaccidum*, than that there seems to be a considerable diversity, in those species of the section before us in which the cortical layer has been observed to be cellular, in the distinctness with which this is exhibited. It is possible then that in this respect as well, the present small but in all respects distinguished cluster, shall prove to illustrate the entire resolution of " *Synechoblastus*."
——12. *C. nigrescens* (Huds.) Ach. Trunks. Northern and middle states to Virginia. South Carolina (Mr. Ravenel). Illinois (E. Hall). California (Bolander). Var. *leucopepla* is a smaller lichen, with white pruinose apothecia, and rather longer spores, in which last respect only it differs from v. *leucocarpa*, Babingt., of Tasmania; and both may well be compared with the Spanish v. *cæsia*, Ach. It (v. *leucopepla*) is common at the South, from South Carolina, (Mr. Ravenel) to Lousiana (Hale) and Texas (Mr. Wright) and has even occurred on the south shore of Massachusetts (Mr. Willey).——More distinct from the type of the species is the rupicoline sub-sp., *C. ryssoleum*, Tuck. Lich. Calif. p. 34, growing on granitic rocks from New England to Virginia (Tuckerman) in New York and New Jersey (Mr. Austin) and in the mountains of North Carolina (Mr. Curtis) the ovoid or at length cymbiform spores of which (18–27$^{mmm.}$, but reaching 32$^{mmm.}$ long) contrast with the long-fusiform ones (46–57$^{mmm.}$, but reaching 70$^{mmm.}$ long) of the bark-lichen, exactly as we have seen above in the analogous spore-history of *C. flaccidum*.

Sect. 3.—Eucollema.

13. *C. coccophorum*, Tuck. *Obs. Lich.* l. c. 5, p. 385. On the earth; Valley of the *Rio Grande*, Texas (Mr. Wright). Oakland, California (Mr. Bolander). Spores (now biscoctiform, and constricted at the middle) never exceeding the bilocular stage ; 11–18$^{mmm.}$ long, and 7–9$^{mmm.}$ broad. The habit is quite that of species associable with *C. pulposum;* and the spores (now comparable, except in size, with those of *Buellia atroalba*) offer nothing to distinguish them from decolorate expressions of the coloured type.——14. *C. Texanum*, Tuck. Suppl. 2, l. c. 28, p. 200. Bark of trees in the valley of the *Rio Grande*, and on the earth in the prairies of the *Blanco*, Texas (Mr. Wright). On calcareous earth, Alabama (Mr. Peters). Spores ovoid-ellipsoid, rarely constricted at the middle, not exceeding the bilocular stage; 9–15$^{mmm.}$ long, and 5–8$^{mmm.}$ broad. Close to *C. pulposum*, and it may be too close; but the narrowed, radiant lobes of the described lichen are rather comparable with those of *C. laciniatum*, Nyl., and *C. cyrtaspis;* and suggest as well the Irish *C. multipartitum*, Sm. The relation of the little group of European lichens (*C. stygium* (Schær. pr. p.) *C. Laureri*, Flot., *Synechobl. Mülleri*, Hepp) now associated, with the species last named, under *Synechoblastus*, by authors, to *Eucollema* and *C. multifidum*, is not unlike that of the present

to *C. pulposum.*——15. *C. pulposum* (Bernh.). On the earth. Including here a variety of forms, more or less clearly associable together, but the limits of which are uncertain. One of these, distinguishable by its commonly concave apothecia, the margin of which is more or less granulate-irregular, seems hardly diverse from *C. crispum*, Nyl. (Fellm. *Lich. Arct.* n. 7) and has occurred in Canada (Mr. Drummond) Massachusetts (Mr. Willey) Vermont (Mr. Frost) and New York (Dr. Sartwell). ——But, here at least, this lichen approaches very closely to another,—*C. tenax* (Sw.) Ach., especially notable for the marked development of the thallus; occurring, in calcareous soils, in Pennsylvania (Muhl.), Ohio (Lesquereux) and New York.——And there is still another, ill-comparable with either of the two preceding, and differenced by the disappearance of the thallus, the attenuated margins of the rather large apothecia, and the more numerous longitudinal series of cells in the spores, which agrees so well both with the character and with Swedish specimens (*Herb.* Torssell) of *C. limosum*, Ach., Nyl., that it may perhaps be referred to it. It has been found as yet only on the prairie-lands of Illinois (Mr. Hall). ——16. *C. melænum*, Ach. On calcareous rocks. Greenland, J. Vahl. (Th. Fr. *Lich. Arct.* p. 277.)——17. *C. cristatellum*, Tuck. Lich. Calif. p. 29. On the earth, in gravelly soils, New Mexico (Mr. Fendler). California (Mr. Bolander). ——18. *C. furvum*, Ach., Nyl. On calcareous rocks, New York, and Maryland. And the same, probably, from Vermont (Mr. Russell) and Canada East. With the aspect of *C. flaccidum*, and very near to it. I have seen but one fertile specimen (Trenton Falls) the ellipsoid, muriform spores of which agreed exactly with those of European specimens (*Herb.* Floerk. *Herb.* Fr.) and with the description of Nylander. ——19. *C. granosum* (Wulf.) Schær. Ohio? A single specimen, unfortunately infertile, of this well-marked lichen, occurred to me in the herbarium of Mr. Lesquereux, where it was associated with lichens of Ohio; and similar, also infertile specimens were found on rocks, in Illinois, by Mr. Hall. The plant is found in Europe on rocks, especially calcareous; and very rarely also on trees. It is closely akin to *C. furvum.*——20. *C. pustulatum*, Ach. On mosses; Pennsylvania (Muhl.). On calcareous rocks; Alabama (Mr. Peters). Well-marked by the minute apothecia, and no less in habit. In the latter respect however it is not impossible to detect some points of agreement, especially in the lobation, with states of the last.——21. *C. stenophyllum*, Nyl. (North America, Drummond) is compared with *C. pustulatum*, with which it is described as agreeing in its ' sufficiently small ' and concave apothecia; but is unknown to me.

XXV.—LEPTOGIUM, Fr., Nyl.

Leptogium, Fr. S. O. V. p. 255. Nyl. Prodr. p. 24, max. p.; Syn. p. 118. max. p., t. 2, f. 6–7, t. 4, f. 10–17; Lich. Scand. p. 32, max. p. Colle-

matis spp., Hoffm. D. Fl. 2, p. 98. Ach. L. U.; Syn. p. 308. Eschw.
Syst.; et in Fl. Bras. p. 231. Fée Essai et Suppl. Schær. Enum.
Parmeliæ spp., Ach. Meth. Mey. Entwick. Schær. Spicil, p. 511.
Parmeliæ spp., et Patellariæ spp., Wallr. Fl. Crypt. Germ. Leptogium, et Collematis sp., Fr. Fl. Scan. p. 293; Summ. Veg. Scand. p.
122. Tuck. Syn. N. Eng. Leptogium, Mallotium, et Stephanophorus,
Flot. Mont. Aperç. Morph. Collematis spp., Leptogium, Polyschidium, et Mallotium, Mass. Mem. pp. 83–5, 86. Mallotium, Leptogium,
et Polyschidium, Koerb. Syst. p. 417. Mudd. Man. Brit. Lich. p. 44.
Krempelh. Lich. Bay. p. 97. Müll. Principes de Classif. p. 82. Leptogium et Polyschidium, Anz. Catal. Sondr. p. 5. Th. Fr. Lich. Arct.
p. 282. Stizenb. Beitr. l. c. p. 144.

Structuram descripserunt Tulasne, Mém. pp. 30, 46, 178, t. 6, f.
10–12; Schwendener, Untersuch. l. c. 3, p. 153, 4, p. 183, t. 23, f. 1, 2.

Apothecia subscutellæformia, lecanorina 1. pseudo-biatorina.
Sporæ ovoideo-ellipsoideæ, 1. simplices, 1. dein fusiformi-elongatæ
bi-pluriloculares, l. sæpissime muriformi-pluriloculares, subincolores.
Spermatia oblonga; sterigmatibus articulatis. Thallus foliaceus aut
rarius fruticulosus; strato corticali distincto; collogonidiis sæpissime
moniliformi-concatenatis; filamentis medullaribus conspicuis laxis.
Medulla nunc parenchymatica.

If the *Eucollemei* may be considered as ascending from certain crustaceous types, in themselves not always distinguishable without difficulty
from others which descend from *Pannaria*, it is scarcely less clear that
the extreme of development of Collemeine vegetation now before us
reverts also to the same higher group; and displays thus the same affinity which was recognizable in its beginnings. The approaches are indeed
mutual; nor does it appear to be necessary, at this place, to more than
refer again to the significant examples already elsewhere cited. *Pannaria lurida*, outcome only of a series of structural modifications all looking
the same way, may be said, in short, to exhibit a satisfactory transition
to Collemeine structure in a plant still inseparable from *Parmeliacei;*
and *Collema byrsæum*, whether we take it for an imperfect *Leptogium*, or
rather, with Massalongo, for a sufficiently characterized intermediate
type (*Physma*, Mass.) approaches *Pannaria* similarly from the other
direction.

The whole probable number of species of *Leptogium* known, is less
than that of *Collema*, and will not perhaps, if we leave out of account
several little known, inferior types, looking towards the next preceding
family, much exceed thirty. Although the larger part of what has been
described belongs to the colder regions of the earth, almost all the finest
examples of the genus are intertropical. We possess, here, as yet about
one half of the whole, and the number will not improbably be increased,

as well by the determination of some minute forms which have so far escaped attention, at the north, as by the addition of some most interesting ones, known to occur in Mexico, to our southern Flora. Adding these last indeed, the North American list which follows, would embrace not far from two thirds of the best settled types of *Leptogium*.

Sect. 1.—POLYSCHIDIUM.

1. *L. intricatulum*, Nyl. *Syn.* p. 135. Beech trunks in the White Mountains (Herb. Oakes). Apothecia unknown; but the plant appears to be associable with the next. Collogonidia finally occurring in strings of three or four.——2. *L. dendriscum*, Nyl. *Syn.* p. 135. Branches of shrubs, Florida (Herb. E. Michener). Agrees generally with the lichen found in the island of Cuba (Mr. Wright) but the specimen is without fruit.——3. *L. muscicola* (Sw.) Fr. Rocks, among mosses, in mountainous and alpine districts. White Mountains. Brattleborough, Vermont (Mr. Frost). Coast of California, and in the Yo Semite valley (Mr. Bolander). Islands of Behring's Straits (Mr. Wright).

Sect. 2.—LATHAGRIUM.

4. *L. albociliatum*, Desmaz., Nyl. *Lich. Scand.* p. 35. *Polyschidium cetrarioides*, Anz. *Catal. Sondr.* p. 7, & *Lich. Langobard.* n. 13. *L. leucothrix*, Tuck. *in litt.* Rocks, among mosses, Mendocino county, and in the Yo Semite valley, California, (Mr. Bolander.) The regular, appressed fronds, one and a half to two inches in diameter, are not well comparable with the reduced, muscicoline condition described and published by Anzi; but the agreement of the two plants in anatomical structure, as in all observed, essential features, is perfect. Apothecia of the European lichen not seen; those of the American are very commonly more or less ciliate, like the thallus; especially when young. Though growing here, as in Europe, in society with *L. muscicola*, the species has little enough, in either form, to associate it with that plant, beside its oblong-ellipsoid, or cymbiform, bilocular spores. As compared with the only published measurement of the foreign lichen (Anz. *l. c.*) the spores of ours are rather larger; measuring $\frac{18\text{-}25}{6\text{-}9}$mmm. —— We have found the distinction of a section *Lathagrium* (*Synechoblastus*, Auct.) sufficiently difficult in *Collema*; it is interesting however that the spore-anomaly upon which the distinction turns, recurs in *Leptogium*. *L. Brebissonii*, Mont. (*Synechoblastus ruginosus*, Hepp) with 'fusiform-acicular, 8–12-locular' spores, though an inhabitant of Europe, of the Canary Islands, and of Tahiti, is unknown as North American; but *L. adpressum*, Nyl. (*Syn.* p. 131) with fusiform, plurilocular spores, is a Mexican lichen (Orizaba, F. Müller in Nyl. l. c. Dr. Mohr!).

Sect. 3.—EULEPTOGIUM.

5. *L. subtile*, Nyl. On the earth. New England (C. Wright, H.

Willey). New Jersey (C. F. Austin). Ohio (Lea). Illinois (E. Hall). Islands of Behring's Straits (C. Wright). Much more rarely on trunks; Massachusetts (H. Willey). All our plants, the longitudinal series of cells in the spores of which are commonly six to eight, though sometimes scarcely exceeding four, appear to be strictly associable in a single species, and not to differ from Zw. *exs.* n. 175, both specimens of which are cited by Nylander; and Nyl. *Lich. Paris.* n. 2.——*L. pusillum*, Nyl., and *L. spongiosum*, Nyl., are other minute species, as yet unknown here. ——6. *L. minutissimum*, Floerk.; Moug. & Nestl. n. 1239; Anz. *Lich. Langobard.* n. 411; Arn. *Fragm.* in *Flora*, 1867, p. 121, t. 1, f. 10–16. On the earth, Illinois, E. Hall. I cannot but keep this apart. Spores $\frac{20\text{-}30}{9\text{-}11}$mmm.; the longitudinal series of spore-cells four to five. Thallus much more developed than in *L. subtile*, and rather approaching that of the next species, with which Nylander has united *L. minutissimum*.—— 7. *L. lacerum* (Sw.) Fr. Rocks, common. Canada (A. T. Drummond). New England (J. L. Russell). New York to Maryland. Ohio (Lea). A much dissected form (v. *lophæum*) is not rare, and one with terete branchlets (v. *bolacinum*, Schær.? but the same with *Lich. Helv.* n. 407, *dextr.*, in my copy) occurs.——8. *L. scotinum* (Ach.) Fr. On rocks, Auburn, and in the Yo Semite valley, California (H. N. Bolander). The group of lichens referred here is readily distinguished from *L. lacerum* by the darker coloration, and in part also by entire, or only notched lobes. The range of variation, though to a considerable extent similar to that indicated by my European specimens, is however greater, and ends in narrowed forms comparable only with the var. *lophæum* of the next preceding species. But even these forms are at least suggested by some European ones (*Coll. scotinum*, Sauter *in herb.* Krempelh.) and the widest state of our plant (v. *platynum*) may be said to differ from such conditions as Nyl. *Lich. Paris.* n. 101, much as the Californian *L. albociliatum* from the cited European; or as *L. tremelloides* v. *azureum* from the v. *cyanescens*, and v. *minus*. Spores of the Californian lichen $\frac{27\text{-}50}{9\text{-}13}$mmm., agreeing in all respects with those of the foreign plant; which, like *L. albociliatum*, and the species immediately following, is not known to be elsewhere exhibited in North America.——9. *L. palmatum* (Huds.) Mont. Rocks; coast of California (Menzies; H. N. Bolander). North West coast, 49° N. lat. (Dr. Lyall). Spores $\frac{25\text{-}46}{11\text{-}18}$mmm.; the longitudinal series of spore-cells oftener ten. The species is evidently akin to the next preceding.——10. *L. Apalachense* (Tuck.) Nyl. *Syn.* p. 133. *Collema*, Tuck. Suppl. 2, l. c. 200. Calcareous rocks, Alabama (T. M. Peters). On similar rocks in Missouri (E. Hall). Cortex ill-developed; and the lichen is in all respects quite isolated as respects American species, but is well compared by Nylander with the European *L. Schraderi*.——11. *L. dactylinum*, Tuckerm. *Obs. Lich.* l. c. 4, p. 383. Nyl. *Syn.* 1, p. 123. Rocks (calcareous schist) Brattleborough, Vermont

(C. C. Frost). Lime-rocks in Missouri (E. Hall). Sufficiently remote from typical conditions of *L. Tremelloides;* but its characters are much the same with those of plants perhaps not easily to be kept apart from *L. Tremelloides,* v. *microphyllum.* Collogonidia mostly solitary and scattered without order in *L. dactylinum;* but they also occur in short strings of three to six.——12. *L. crenatellum,* Tuckerm. Suppl. 2, l. c. p. 200. Trunks, Vermont (C. C. Frost). Spores $\frac{16\text{-}20}{7\text{-}9}$mmm., always in fours in the thekes; the longitudinal series of spore-cells four.——13. *L. pulchellum* (Ach.) Nyl. *Syn.* p. 123. *Collema corticola,* Tayl. *Leptogium,* Tuck. in Lea Catal. Ohio. Trunks, and rocks. New England, and southward to Virginia, common. Ohio, (Lea). Mountains of Carolina and Georgia (H. W. Ravenel). Alabama (T. M. Peters). Texas (C. Wright). Ill-described, and surprisingly compared with *Collema pustulatum* and *C. nigrescens,* with the latter of which it is placed, in his sect. *Lathagrium,* by Acharius. *L. cimiciodorum,* Mass. (Anz. *Lich. Venet.* n. 14. *Herb.* Krempelh. Rabenh. *Lich. Eur.* n. 762) scarcely differs in any respect from the American lichen; which is certainly close also to the next species. Spores of *L. pulchellum* $\frac{20\text{-}30}{7\text{-}12}$mmm.; the longitudinal series of spore-cells oftener six.——14. *L. Tremelloides* (L. fil.) Fr. Rocks and Trunks. With the species last preceding we enter the at length extraordinarily modified group which has its centre in the tropics. The present is however by no means confined to the warmer regions of the earth ; extending, in less perfect forms, very far northward, and reduced at length, here, to conditions scarcely at all recognizable. At the extreme south (Alabama, J. F. Beaumont; Mississippi, Veitch) smooth, wider-lobed forms occur, best comparable with v. *azureum* (Sw.) though rather inferior in size and colour; and even, as we come north, at length (South Carolina, H. W. Ravenel) sparingly isidiophorous. In Lousiana (Hale) the passage of v. *azureum* into v. *foveolatum* (*Leptogium,* Nyl.) appears also to be represented. At the north (New England and middle states, as in Europe) a smaller and less regularly-lobed, often complicate form, beset more or less, or at length quite covered with isidioid branchlets — v. *cyanescens,* Ach., prevails; and this occurs also at the south (Louisiana, Hale). Much more difficult are the reduced forms — v. *microphyllum* (*L· juniperinum,* Tuck. Suppl. 2, l. c. p. 200) occurring on rocks and upon the earth, in New England and New York ; in Tennessee (H. W. Ravenel) and in Texas (C. Wright) the very near relation of which even to *L. minutissimum* becomes finally (Illinois, E. Hall) almost conceivable, and to *L. dactylinum,* Tuck., certainly probable. In the larger, tropical forms of this species (v. *azureum*) the spores are often also larger than in the northern lichen, and reach in the v. *foveolatum* (Venezuela, Fendler) even $\frac{34\text{-}46}{16\text{-}18}$mmm., as the longitudinal series of spore-cells are increased to eight and ten ; but these figures, like the thalline characters of the plant, illustrate only an extreme of evolution, and differences not to be depended

13

on. Spores of the lichen of the United States rarely exceeding $\frac{18\text{-}27}{7\text{-}9}$ mmm.; the longitudinal series of spore-cells more commonly four, but reaching six. In the var. *microphyllum* the spores are perhaps a little smaller.——
15. *L. marginellum* (Sw.) Mont. Trunks; Louisiana (Hale) Alabama (J. F. Beaumont) Texas (H. W. Ravenel). A Cuban specimen of this lichen is before me, which, if we except the minute wrinkling of the thallus ('*rides excessivement petites,*' Mont.) presents little to distinguish it from *L. Tremelloides* beside the minute, marginal apothecia; and three of the four careful figures (Hoffm. *Pl. Lich.* t. 37, f. 1. Sw. *Lich. Amer.* t. 18. Mont. *Pl. Cell. Cub.* t. 6, f. 2) may be said to look the same way, and thus to confirm Nylander's reduction of the plant to a variety of the older species. But this reduction is less easy in view of other specimens (Wright *Lich. Cub.* n. 7) the lobation of which — as suggested perhaps in the '*lobis longiusculis* of Acharius, and exhibited, if I mistake not, plainly enough by Dillenius, t. 19, f. 32, — is irreconcilable with *L. Tremelloides*, and points, not obscurely, towards *L. chloromelum*. And, from this new point of view, we have not only a possible explanation of the narrowed, elongated lobes with crisped margins of the cited form of *L. marginellum* — a form which is in fact exactly repeated, in every important respect except the apothecia, in a North American condition of *L. chloromelum* — but can scarcely avoid associating with the former, as only a further development of the same lichen, the wider, scarcely crisped, and much more strongly wrinkled *L. corrugatulum*, Nyl. (*Lich. Cub.* n. 6. Lindig *Herb. N. Gran.* n. 2659). As thus understood, *L. marginellum* partakes at once of the characters of, and stands between the species last preceding and the one next following; differing however, for the most part, from the latter, scarcely otherwise than in its extraordinary fruit-characters. The Louisiana specimens are rather intermediate between the smoother, crisped form, and that exhibited in *L. corrugatulum.*——
16. *L. chloromelum* (Sw.) Nyl. Trunks and rocks. Canada (A. T. Drummond). New England (Porter, &c.) common, and southward to Virginia. South Carolina (H. W. Ravenel). Alabama (T. M. Peters). Louisiana (Hale). Texas (C. Wright). The specimen figured by Swartz (*Lich. Amer.* t. 18) may be taken to explain the imperfectness of Acharius's description of this lichen, which first found full appreciation in the hands of Montagne (*Pl. Cell. Cuba,* p. 109, t. 6, f. 1) though the latter afterwards confused it, in part, with his *L. Brebissonii*. It is well exhibited in Wright *Lich. Cub.* n. 8; and the same plant is most widely diffused in North America, and reaches even Canada. To trust indeed the evidence of my own herbarium alone, the species should rather appear a northern one, penetrating tropical regions, than the contrary. It is at any rate more difficult to discriminate the intertropical plant, lost as it soon is in perplexing relations to *L. phyllocarpum*, (comp. Lindig *Herb. N. Gran.* n. 2660, & n. 43, *Coll.* 2^{dæ}) *L. Javanicum*, &c. This apparent confusion with what are assumed to be distinct species extends also to

the North American lichen; both *L. phyllocarpum* and *L. bullatum* being Mexican plants (Nyl.) and the former at least most closely approached by some of the Texan specimens of the present; as others exhibit a thallus not appreciably distinguishable from that of the original *L. Javanicum.* ——17. *L. Burgessii* (Lightf.) Mont. Trunks, White Mountains, rare. Also in Maine (Herb. Oakes). Spores apiculate, irregularly muriform-multilocular, more or less fuscescent, $\frac{32-46}{16-18}$mmm. Cortex very coarsely cellu-lose.—*L. inflexum*, Nyl., inhabiting South America from Venezuela! to Bolivia! was originally observed in Mexico, and approaches so near 'arcte accedit,' Nyl. *Syn.*) to *L. Burgessii*, that one might prefer to char-acterize the fine northern lichen as extending southward, not without modification, into the tropics.——18. *L. myochroum* (Ehrh., Schær.). Trunks, throughout the United States, except the Pacific coast, infertile. Rocky Mountains, fertile; and Arctic America (Herb. Hook.) Greenland (Vahl in Th. Fr. *Lich. Arct.*) Islands of Behring's Straits (C. Wright). By uniting, as constituents of the same section (*Mallotium*) *L. Burgessii* with the species now immediately before us, Acharius may be said to have brought together what are on several accounts the most remarkable members of the present genus, and to have precluded as well the later elevation of the section to generical rank: the lichen first named being at once associable with *L. myochroum*, and yet not dissociable from *L. Tremelloides*. It is impossible not to recognize the affinity of *L. resupinans*, Nyl. (Mandon *Pl. Boliv.* n. 1715) on the one hand to *L. Menziesii* of the same collec-tion, and so to *L. myochroum;* as on the other to *L. inflexum*, Nyl. (Man-don *l. c.* n. 1721) and so to *L. Burgessii*. [1]

The difficulties found in the way of a satisfactory determination of *L. myochroum* (Ehrh. 1785) as occurring throughout the North American continent, led to an examination of all the material at hand, immediately illustrative of this species; and the results of this examination will now be set down, with only the preliminary remark, that as I have accepted Schærer's view, so far as it extended, of the limitation of the species, I follow him also in adopting for it what is without doubt the oldest name. Nylander's exhaustive characterization (*Syn.* p. 127) of *L. saturninum*

[1] In this view it will not be surprising if the South American *Mallotia* should illustrate each other. It is the extraordinary difference of *L. resupinans*, in other respects closely resembling *L. Menziesii*, that the apothecia are produced (so far as appears, only) on the under side of the thallus, and conditioned therefore by the nap which covers that side; and the Bolivian specimens of *L. inflexum* shew that in this noble, southern exhibition of an extreme northern type, the nap is not rarely visible on both surfaces, and that apothecia in their normal position may exhibit a similar conditioning by a so to say foreign element, as if they were below; there being in fact, so far, no difference in the sides. This extension of the cortical cells into fibrils, above, is observable also in other specimens of *L. inflexum* (Venezuela, Fendler) and is sometimes rather conspicuous in the North American *L. myochroum*, as it is not wholly wanting in the European.

(Dicks. 1790) and *L. Hildenbrandii*—the latter of which, it is now said, is really entitled, as the original *Lichen saturninus*, Sm., 1788, to the name of the former—is, carefully examined, enough perhaps of itself to open anew the question of the distinctness of these lichens; and no unimportant light is thrown upon its solution by a similar consideration of his *L. Menziesii*. This last, a name only ('*Smith msc.*') as respects Acharius, who expressly notes it as otherwise unknown to him, was recognized much later, upon what authority does not appear, in a Chilian lichen, by Montagne, and is now cited (Nyl. l. c.) as a native of various regions of South America (Mandon *Pl. Boliv.* n. 1715, *pro p!* Lindig *Herb. N. Gran.* n. 2546!) of the Cape of Good Hope (*Herb. Kunz.!*) of the Himalaya (Hook. & Thoms. *Herb. Ind. Or.!*) and of China (Nyl. l. c.). It will be safe probably to add to these Japan (C. Wright!) and Hawaii (H. Mann!) from which the common lichen of the United States is scarcely separable; and *L. Menziesii* will come thus to stand for *L. myochroum* or *saturninum* of authors, as it occurs in regions exotic to Europe: neither of the other two plants named above being recognized by Nylander except as European. But taking into account only the South American lichens, of the determination of which we are tolerably certain, it is still beforehand likely that a plant generally so similar as the New Granada lichen above cited, to the European, and with so wide a range, should vary into forms even nearer to, if in fact separable from the latter; and such seems, if I may rely on my material, to be the fact. If the plant now exhibits, in tropical regions, a somewhat similar exuberance to that which characterizes *L. Tremelloides* similarly conditioned, even these states are well comparable with more northern ones; and fade out, as the atmospherical conditions change (in the Himalaya, in Japan, &c.,) into others quite undistinguishable: and the 'species' comes thus at last to rest, so far at least as the fertile forms go, on no other definable character than rather larger spores; exactly as with the largest tropical states of *L. Tremelloides* as compared with inferior, especially northern ones.

Our more common, lead-coloured North American lichen has thus been referred to *L. Menziesii*, only to pass, with it, into too near affinity with the European *L. myochroum*. The latter occurs however in two marked forms, now generally reputed species. One of these (*L. saturninum* (Dicks.) Nyl., is admitted (Th. Fr. *Lich. Arct.*) to be common to Arctic America and Europe; and it is interesting that Schærer (*Spicil.*) referred the lead-coloured American state, which he had from the Carolina mountains, to the other—his var. *saturnina*—which is *L. Hildenbrandii* (Garov.) Nyl. What then, we have next to ask, is the probable value of this discrimination? The question might hardly suggest itself to North American lichenists, who, if they followed Schærer in recognizing a southern form of the species, would probably not differ from him in assigning to it a merely subordinate rank. But such judgment is worth little without revision from a point of view which shall also include

Europe; and there the enquiry is less simple. At first view indeed the contrast between 1) the northern, characteristically black-greenish state, only velvety beneath, and commonly sterile (Moug. & Nestl. *Vog.* n. 454, a, b. Fr. *Suec.* n. 299. Schær. *Helv.* n. 424,500. Anz. *Langobard.* n. 292) which represents *L. saturninum*, and 2) the southern, rufous-glaucous condition, rugulose above, and fleecy beneath, and commonly fertile (Moug. & Nestl. n. 454, c, d. Schleich. *exs.* Schær. n. 423. Mass. *Ital.* n. 28. Herb. Krempelh. Anz. *Ital. Sup.* n. 2) which stands for *L. Hildenbrandii*, is so considerable, that we cannot wonder that modern writers have agreed in elevating what served only as a subordinate difference in the older lichenographers into specific diversity: yet a closer examination shall not improbably result in invalidating every character upon which this diversity is predicated. As respects colour, though the difference noted is clearly appreciable, finding recognition in Koerber, as possibly also, to some extent, conditioning judgments where it is not expressly recognized, little stress is laid upon it by most authors, and neither Acharius, Schærer, nor Nylander, take it at all into account. The fact undoubtedly is that in each form, and in *L. Menziesii* as well, we have a paler, more or less lead-coloured condition, becoming darker, and ultimately blackening: something however of the difference between brownish and reddish is certainly suggested by what is perhaps the best coloration of the two European lichens, and is to be traced also in that of the Himalaya, passing there, before blackening, into a fine purplish. I observe it here, only in specimens from New Mexico (Fendler). Conceding then, for what it may be worth, such degree of variation in this respect between the northern and the southern lichens, we pass to the conspicuous corrugation of the upper side in *L. Hildenbrandii*, of which also there is no trace in *L. saturninum;* and here too the same high authorities agree in an adverse opinion. The distinction, unnoticed by Acharius, is given up by Nylander, in his *L. Menziesii,* — the Bolivian specimens determined by him having a wrinkled surface and the New Granada ones being smooth, — and in this he only concurs with Schærer's judgment of the corresponding European states; a judgment since corroborated by that of Arnold, to be cited below. It is, as the case is conditioned, quite unlikely that the character should really be worth more in Europe, than out of Europe. As respects my North American specimens, traces of wrinkling only appear in an Alabama lichen (T. M. Peters) and in the cited one from New Mexico; both might possibly be referred, as ill-conditioned states, to *L. Hildenbrandii;* the latter of them is yet, at the same time, scarcely to be distinguished from one of the Himalaya plants, referable, it should seem, to *L. Menziesii.* It only remains to consider the various development of the nap of the under side, which enables us to discriminate a velvety (*brevissime tomentosa*) condition from a fleecy one (*'fibrillose rhizinosa'*) and this difference again is well taken. As however the *tomentum* tends always to pass into *rhizinæ* at the base of the lobes (*'lanugine tenuissima subtomentosi et versus basin fibrillis parvis obsiti,'* Ach. *L. U.*) and the part which remains velvety as compared with that which has become fleecy is now greatly reduced, it is evident that the distinction may well be expected ultimately to disappear in transitional forms; and such I regard a specimen before me, from Floerke's herbarium, of his *Coll. saturninum β tomentosum;* and, no less, *L. saturninum,* A, *sterile* of Anz. *Lich. Langobard.* n. 9. Neither of these has the wrinkled upper surface of *L. Hildenbrandii,* but Arnold (*Lich. Fragm.* l. c.) has referred the Italian lichen to the latter. The common plant of the United States belongs without doubt to this intermediate state, associated by Schærer and Arnold with what has been called *L. Hildenbrandii,* and by Anzi with *L. saturninum* (Dicks.) and I refer to it also the cited lichens from Hawaii, and Japan, as, in part, those of the Himalaya. Only the specimens from the Rocky Mountains, and those from Arctic America, exhibit, with entire satisfactoriness, the velvety nap of the more northern plant; it is still not improbable that this condition of the under side may recur here in southern, and otherwise modified specimens; as it certainly does, in great perfection, in an elegantly lead-coloured, fertile lichen from Sardinia (Herb. Duby).

These notes will perhaps afford some satisfactory justification of the enlarged view of this species which I have been led to prefer. There are certainly reasons why even attempts at such larger judgments are most desirable.

XXVI.—HYDROTHYRIA, Russell.

Russell in Proceed. Essex Inst. 1, p. 188 (1856). Nyl. Syn. 1, p. 135. Stizenb. Beitr. l. c. p. 144. Leptogii sp., Russ. in litt., olim. Tuckerm. Lich. exs. n. 150.

Apothecia pseudo-biatorina. Sporæ fusiformes, quadriloculares, incolores. Thallus foliaceus, strato corticali distincto; gonimo e collogonidiis moniliformi-subconcatenatis; filamentis medullaribus compactis; subtus venosus.

In this type, remarkable alike in its characters and its habitat, *Collema,* Ach., which we found to reach its extreme of development in the *Leptogia* of more recent authors, may be said now to revert evidently towards *Pannaria,* and even *Peltigera.* With the general aspect of *Leptogium* proper, and so far less separable therefore, it should seem, than the *Sticta*-like *Mallotia, Hydrothyria* offers, at last, what is unquestionably a heteromerous thallus; and may thus be regarded as completing the evidence that Collemeine structure is, in the final analysis, inseparable widely from Pannarieine. The lax filaments, intermingled with gonidial chains, which represent the much confused gonimous and medullary layers in *Leptogium myochroum,* give place here to a compact medullary tissue, comparable, except in the size of the filaments, to that of *Pannaria molybdæa*, and *Peltigera;* and the gonidia, less prone to the moniliform development, are rather crowded back into a true gonimous layer. But unlike *Peltigera,* with which the nerves or veins of the under side, — bundles, in both cases, of the medullary filaments, — so curiously associate it, the cortical stratum of *Hydrothyria* is for the most part continuous; and, in this respect, as in the not uncommon extension of this *cortex,* below, into a delicate pubescence, the plant may obviously be compared also with *Nephroma.* It is at the same time to be observed that there is nothing in the structure above described to exclude our plant from *Leptogium* beyond the veins of the under side; and it is in fact, in most other structural features, well-comparable with *L. albo-ciliatum,* Desmaz., to the neighbourhood of which, it should, as a *Leptogium,* be referable.

H. venosa, Russ. l. c. (*Leptogium fontanum,* Russ. *in litt. olim.* Tuckerm. *Lich. exs.* n. 150 (1857). *Hydrothyria,* Nyl. l. c.) grows upon stones, under water, and fruiting in this situation, in mountain brooks of Vermont and New Hampshire (Russell) in Connecticut (Prof. D. C. Eaton) in New Jersey (C. F. Austin) and "in great abundance, on small pebbles, at the bottom of a clear brook," at Big Trees, Mariposa, California (alt. 6500 ft.) (H. N. Bolander) .——— Spermogones have not been observed.

———◆———

Fam. 6.—LECANOREI.

Thallus crustaceus, aut effiguratus aut rarissime papilloso-ramulosus aut uniformis, matrici adnatus, hypothallo diminuto l. minus conspicuo.

Indications of an atypical dissolution of the foliaceous into a more or less crust-like thallus have met us already in *Theloschistes,* and *Physcia,* and have proved as instructive as remarkable in *Pannaria,* but the present family is typically crustaceous; and, however now rivalling, or even approaching foliaceous types in its highest expressions, the difference of texture is not easily mistakable, and is evident also in the few fruticulose forms. So conspicuous indeed is, on the whole, the contrast between the effigurate *Squamariæ* and *Placodia* of authors, and *Lecanora* proper, that the former, though differing in nothing but their lobation from the nearest allied granulose forms, have been separated generically by most recent writers — only Stizenberger returning here to the simpler conception of Acharius.

But marked as is the exhibition, in *Lecanorei,* of the reduction — carried finally to the utmost possible degree — of the Parmeliaceous thallus, the loss is more than made up by the variety and complexity of the fruit. This complexity has perhaps its typical maximum in *Pertusaria ;* which passes yet, on the one hand, with scarcely a break into *Lecanora,* while serving, on the other, to render clearer the connexion of still more widely aberrant members of the tribe and family.

Thus viewed, the *Lecanorei* fall easily into three sub-families, distinguished by well-marked differences in the fruit. In the first of these, or *Eulecanorei*, the tribal type is more or less exactly expressed by the apothecia, and the thallus also often reverts towards that of the *Parmeliei*, so that questions may arise as to the dominant affinity of certain of its forms, conceivable even as descending from certain other foliaceous ones (as *Placodium* from *Theloschistes ;*) and, taken by itself, the group is not without its difficulties. But these are only varied, and far enough from wanting, in our second sub-family — *Pertusariei* — to which might even, at first sight, be refused a place in the tribe. The 'naked nuclei' of *Pertusaria* are yet certainly conceivable as nucleiform hymenia, imbedded in the typically compound, wart-like but Parmeliaceous apothecium of the genus; and such explanation of this extraordinary fruit is supported by the tendency of various forms to revert to lecanorine types, and finds what appears its complement in *P. bryontha* (a *Lecanora* in fact in all but the spores) and even (as compare the lucid description of *L. tartarea* v. *pertusarioides*, Th. Fr. *Lich. Arct.* p. 100) in *Lecanora* itself. The instance last-cited is by no means the only one in which the typical Parmeliaceous apothecium, at one stage or other of its development, anticipates or illustrates that of *Pertusaria ;* but it is perhaps the most interesting, as occurring in a group which is approached equally by recedent forms of the other. *Pertusariei* then, in whatever respects inferior to the sub-family here immediately preceding, is superior in interest in the fruit; this affording the extremest modification conceivable of the *Lecanora*-fruit, within the clear limits of the tribal type. The spores of *Pertusaria* afford possibly another criterion of the affinity of the genus to *Lecanora ;* and serve also to distinguish it from otherwise now nearly related forms, which are presented, in a wonderfully varied series of even more difficult modifications, passing finally, one might almost say, into *Biatora* and *Pyrenula*, in our last sub-family — the *Urceolariei*.

The number of distinct forms included in the *Lecanorei*, as here taken, is very large; embracing possibly not far from half of all comprehended in the present tribe, which approaches more distantly to a not very dissimilar numerical relation to the whole Class.

———

Sub-Fam. 1. — EULECANOREI.

Apothecia scutellæformia.

Adding the species of *Urceolaria*, Ach., with simple spores, the group represents exactly (*exceptis excipiendis*) the genus *Lecanora* of this author, and (similarly taken, and excluding in particular *Urceolaria scruposa*) the *Parmelia* sect. *Placothallæ* of Fries's latest revision of the Scandinavian Lichens. The more modern variations from this construction have been determined by the microscope; *Rinodina* being separated by its distinct type of spore from *Lecanora*, and *Placodium* from both the others, as well by its sporal structure (exhibiting the polar-bilocular subtype) as its multi-articulate sterigmas.——*Lecanora*, which is directly analogous, as respects the great mass of its species, with *Parmelia*, affords the type of the sub-family. From this centre, *Placodium* diverges, in the colourless series, exactly as *Theloschistes* in the *Parmeliei;* and *Rinodina*, in the coloured, as *Physcia*. Though strictly crustaceous, and indeed as regards the by far greater number of forms, granulose, the group offers many marked instances of a tendency to revert to a higher (thalline) structure; but such intermediate conditions (as *Squamaria* & *Placodium* of authors) are here less typical, and, in accordance with the Acharian conception, as anew presented by Stizenberger, subordinated.

XXVII.—PLACODIUM (DC.) Naeg. and Hepp.

Naeg. & Hepp in Hepp Flecht. Eur., t. 2, et passim. Tuckerm. Obs. Lich. l. c. 6, p. 265; Lich. Calif. p. 18; Lich. Hawai. p. 4. Anz. Catal. Lich. Sondr. p. 39, addita Gyalolechia, p. 38. Nyl. Lich. Scand. p. 135, addita Lecanora sect. A, p. 140. Stizenb. Beitr. l. c. p. 171, addita Lecaniæ sect. ult. saltem pro p., ibid. Lecanora sect. Rinodina pr. p., et sect. Placodium, pr. p., Ach. L. U. p. 77. Parmelia sect. 3, pr. p., et sect. 4, pr. p., Fr. L. E. p. 114, 161, 123. Theloschistes pr. p., Norm. Con. p. 16. Physcia pr. p., Ricasolia, Fulgensia, Gyalolechia, Solenopsora, Pyrenodesmia, Callopisma, Candelaria pr. p., Blastenia, Xanthocarpia, Biatoræ sp., et Biatorinæ sp., Mass. Opp. varr. in locis. Amphiloma, Psoromatis sp., Candelaria pr. p., Callopisma, Blastenia, Biatoræ sp., et Biatorinæ sp., Koerb. Syst. Amphiloma, Gyalolechia, Ricasolia, Psoromatis sp., Candelaria pr. p., Callopisma, Pyrenodesmia, Xanthocarpia, Blastenia, Biatoræ sp., et Biatorinæ sp., Koerb. Parerg. Xanthoria pr. p., Gyalolechia, Caloplaca, Blastenia, Biatorinæ sp., et Biatoræ sp., Th. Fr. Lich. Arct.; Gen.; & Lich. Spitzberg.; in locis. Placodium, Callopisma, Biatorinæ sp., et Lecideæ sp., Mudd Man. Brit. Lich. Placodii sp., Amphiloma, Thalloidimatis sp., Caloplaca, Biatoræ sp., Patellariæ sp., et Blastenia, Müll. Principes de Classif.

Structuram exposuerunt Tulasne, Mém. sur les Lich. p. 61, 150, 153, 161; Fuisting, de nonnull. apoth. p. 22, 27.

Apothecia subscutellæformia, lecanorina, l. pseudo-biatorina margine l. proprio l. composito, disco plerumque luteo-aurantiaco. Sporæ ellipsoideæ, polari-biloculares (rarius normaliter biloculares, rarissime simplices) incolores. Spermatia oblonga l. bacillaria;

14

sterigmatibus fere semper multi-articulatis. Thallus crustaceus, aut effiguratus aut rarissime suffruticulosus aut uniformis, sæpius flavescens.

The lemon-coloured *Placodia* make part, as Fries remarked (*L. E.* p. 114) of but a single series, which, beginning with *Theloschistes* (the lemon-coloured group of *Parmelia-Imbricaria*, Fr.) ends with the analogous section of the (granulose) *Patellariæ*. But notwithstanding the many difficulties, noted also by Koerber (Syst. p. 110) — who, it is observable, distributes, at the place cited, the *Gyalolechiæ* also among the two groups to which he refers almost the whole of our *Placodium* — most lichenographers have agreed in recognizing a sufficiently marked distinctness of texture, which, taken in connexion with the whole history of the development of its nearest allies, refers *Lichen elegans* to the crustaceous, and *L. parietinus* to the foliaceous families. And the difference is certainly less between the two extremes of the crustaceous thallus, than between the highest forms of this and the foliaceous. Taken as a whole, *Placodium*, as here understood, is well-marked by the predominant coloration of both thallus and apothecia; as by the tun-shaped, polar-bilocular spores. To the character first named there are yet some exceptions, which assume the rank of genera in many works. But *Pyrenodesmia*, Massal., differs, as Koerber remarked, in nothing but colour from his *Callopisma;* and the distinction is still more obviously inadequate to separate the American, arboricoline *P. camptidium* and *P. Floridanum* from the same group with the otherwise closely related *P. ferrugineum.* And we are thus not without plain indications, that however distinguished by the predominance of species of the lemon-colored series, the genus is by no means confined to it. The thalline exciple is often distinct enough, and predicable of all the species; but it disappears, sometimes almost from the first in the granulose section, when the often marginate disk assumes the whole aspect of *Biatora.* Yet we find positively no real difference of structure between the at length pseudo-biatorine apothecia of *P. aurantiacum* (*Callopisma*, Auctt.) and the so-called biatorine ones of *P. ferrugineum* and *P. sinapispermum* (*Blastenia*, Auctt.).——There is in general no safer criterion in the present group than that afforded by the spores. We find these varying however even in *P. vitellinum* to obsoletely bilocular, and even simple; and the difference is only one of degree between such spores and those of other species, referable to *Gyalolechia* of authors. And if *P. fulgens*, DC. (*Fulgensia*, Massal.) be found, as Anzi (*Catal. Sondr.* p. 46, with which compare also Th. Fr. *Lich. Arct.* p. 81) describes it, with all the characters of *Gyalolechia bracteata*, excepting only that the spores are simple, one might well incline to assume that those of the *Gyalolechia* are as properly describable as sometimes simple, and to restore both these most closely allied lichens, as more or less aberrant forms, to their ancient and natural associations.

Placodium differs from the other genera of this sub-family in its multi-articulate sterigmas (*arthrosterigmata*, Nyl.) the most complex form which this structure assumes; pointing also, as do so many other features of the genus, towards *Theloschistes*.

The range of the group is decidedly northern : but not a few forms recur, under the suitable atmospherical conditions, in the warmer regions of the earth ; and others, described principally by Nylander (in *Prodr. Fl. N. Gran.* p. 28) are confined to tropical countries. Of the forty odd best known species, not quite half have been found as yet to occur in North America; and the relative proportion of the North American to the European is about the same.

The fruticulose exaltation of the crustaceous thallus, though perhaps more remarkable than the sub-foliaceous one, has received much less attention. *Lecanora fruticulosa*, Eversm., from the Kirguis deserts, has indeed long been known in the memoir in which it was illustrated, but specimens are rare; and no other instance of the kind (if we except *Lecidea conglomerata* and *L. vesicularis*) had occurred till the discovery of the Californian *Lecanora Bolanderi*. The little group is now increased by the addition, from the same region of North-western America, of two fruticulose *Placodia*. The terete and solid thallus of these is as properly crustaceous as that of the fruticulose *Lecanoræ*, and so far diverse from all fruticulose expressions of *Theloschistes;* but the two lichens differ from each other more than do the analogous Californian conditions of *Lecanora*, though perhaps equally conceivable as illustrations of a single type (*Thamnoma*). *P.* (*Thamnoma*) *coralloides*, Tuckerm. *Obs. Lich.* l. c. 6, p. 287, though distantly comparable (so far as the few specimens go) in its decumbent habit, as well as in colour, with *Theloschistes chrysophthalmus* v. *flavicans*, is yet a crustaceous lichen; and the simply bilocular spores, showing no indications of an isthmus, rather resemble, except that they occur only in eights, those of *P. vitellinum.* ——And the affinity of the other species to the present genus is still more unmistakable. The erect, fastigiately-branched trunks of *P. cladodes*, described at the place just cited, are densely crowded together, and their papillæform tips constitute a warted crust, with much the habit of that of some granulose *Lecanora*, or *Placodium*, and the colour of *P. elegans.*

P. fulgens, DC., has occurred, in its perfect, subfoliaceous condition, on calcareous earth, in the bad lands of Judith, Nebraska ; as also on the North Platte, nearer to the Rocky Mountains (Dr. Hayden) and in Montana (Mr. M. A. Brown) accompanied by the granulose v. *bracteatum* of authors. The spores (of the variety) though often simple, occur also in variously imperfect bilocular conditions ; but I observe not wholly dissimilar spores in some of my foreign specimens of *a;* and both forms may perhaps well be kept together as varying states of a single, so far aberrant, *Placodium.* A granulose condition of this species (v. *alpinum*, Th. Fr.) exceedingly near, as described, to the other, has occurred in Greenland

(J. Vahl in Th. Fr. l. c.).——*P. murorum* (Hoffm.) DC., is by no means so common with us as *P. elegans ;* and its range of variation is far less known. Of calcareous states I possess only a granulose, lemon-coloured lichen (Neosho river, Kansas, E. Hall) which scarcely differs from the very reduced var. *citrinum*, Nyl. (Moug. & Nestl. *Crypt.* n. 742) perhaps hereafter to be given a separate place. Spores of this $\frac{8-14}{3-4\frac{1}{2}}$mmm.——
P. teicholytum, DC., is wholly unknown as North American. We have yet an unquestionable member of the same stock from the lime-rocks of Kansas (Mr. Hall) which combines a white, areolate, finally lob-ulate thallus, with the habit of that of *Lecanora muralis* v. *albo-pulver-ulenta*, Schær. (Lich. Helv. n. 334) and scarcely middling-sized, zeorine apothecia (0mm. 5–0mm. 9 in width) with small spores ($\frac{9-14}{3.7}$mmm.) and may take the name, with whatever ultimate rank, of *P. galactophyllum*.——
P. eugyrum, Tuckerm. Suppl. 1, l. c. p. 425, from lime-rocks in Texas (Mr. Wright) is a crustaceous, effigurate lichen, not wholly unlike in habit to *Lecanora circinata*, and comparable also with some conditions of *P. callo-pismum* (Ach.) Merat, from which it differs in its rusty-brown colour, &c.
——We have indications of two interesting species of the group of effig-urate *Placodia* with ash-coloured thallus, from Western America. One of these, *P. peliophyllum*,[1] is an inhabitant of the precipices of the Yosem-ite valley, California. The other, referable perhaps, as a depauperate form, to *P. variabile* (Pers.) Nyl., was detected on rock-specimens from the Rocky Mountains (Dr. Hayden).

To the cluster which includes *P. cinnabarrinum* (Ach.) Anz., so familiar throughout the United States, is to be referred also the more conspicuous *P. bolacinum*, Tuck. (Lich. Calif. p. 18).——*P. vitellinum* is, in fact, in its best expressions, subsquamulose; and this indication of a higher than the granulose type of thallus finds its complement in the nearly akin but lobulate and radious *P. crenulatum* (*Xanthoria*, Th. Fr. *Lich. Arct.* p. 70. *Lecanora*, Nyl. Scand. p. 140) 'intermediate in habit,' says Th. Fries, 'between' *P. murorum* and *P. vitellinum*, which has been found in Greenland by J. Vahl (Th. Fr. l. c.) and also in Labrador (*Herb.* Krempelh.).——*P. luteo-minium*, Tuck. (Lich. Calif. p. 18) is a granulose lichen of the west coast, belonging to the same cluster. The other species to be added to our list are all of the granulose section (*Cal-lopisma*, corresponding with *Eulecanora* in the next succeeding genus).
——*P. fusco-luteum* (Sommerf., Th. Fr.) is, according to the latter author, found in Greenland (J. Vahl) and some scattered apothecia grow-ing with Mr. Wright's specimens of the next species may belong to it. It

---

[1] *Placodium peliophyllum (sp. nova) thallo crustaceo verrucoso cinereo-glauco, ambitu laciniato lineari-multifido; apotheciis (lat. 1–2*mm.*) sessilibus disco casta-neo, margine thallino integro demum flexuoso. Sporæ octonæ ellipsoideæ polari-biloculares, incolores, longit.* 0,014–21mm., *crassit.* 0,005–9mm. Not well comparable with any described species: but the specimens scanty.

is described as similar in size and aspect to *Lichen fusco-luteus*, Dicks.; and, if found in Scotland, may possibly have been included in his species by the British author; but an original specimen from the herbarium of the latter, in my possession, has the solitary, muriform spores of *Hetero-thecium* (*Lopadium*) and is the *Lopadium fuscoluteum* of Mudd (Man. Brit. Lich. p. 190) who first made the correction.——*P. fulvo-luteum* (Nyl.) is a smaller lichen, with the habit of *P. sinapispermum*, and is referred by Th. Fries, from whom I have excellent specimens, to the rather uncertain *Lichen Jungermanniæ*, Vahl. It occurs in Greenland (J. Vahl in Th. Fr. *Lich. Arct.* p. 121) and also in islands of Behring's Straits (Mr. Wright).——*P. sinapispermum* (DC.) Hepp, resembling the last in the size of its darker, soon convex apothecia, has also been found in Greenland by Vahl, and in the alpine region of the Rocky Mountains by E. Hall.——*P. rupestre* (*Lichen*, Scop. *Biatora*, Koerb. *Syst. L. calvus* Dicks. *Lecanora*, Nyl. *Scand.* p. 447) the whole aspect of which, not to speak of the spermogones, refers it here, where both Fries, and Nylander have given it a place, differs yet, like *P. fulgens*, in its simple spores; and has not, like that species, afforded tolerably clear evidence of a more normal spore-structure. It is yet scarcely to be said that all indications looking towards the bilocular stage are wanting to the spores of this lichen, as compare Hepp. *Abbild.* t. 3, n. 7; more than sustained by what I observe in the spores of the American plant. This has occurred, on lime-rocks, in Vermont (Messrs. Russell and Frost) in the Helderberg mountains, N. Y. (Mr. C. H. Peck) and at Trenton Falls, N. Y.—— *P. camptidium*, Tuck. *Obs. Lich.* l. c. 5, p. 403, & 6, p. 287, is most commonly pseudo-biatorine, when specimens often resemble states of *Biatora rubella* v. *spadicea*, or may be passed over at length as convex conditions of *Lecanora subfusca;* and its range is southern, extending southward even to Cuba; but it is not uncommon in Southern Pennsylvania, and has recently turned up about New Bedford in Massachusetts (Mr. Willey).——From the last, *P. diphasium*, Tuckerm. Suppl. 1, l. c., p. 426, occurring as yet only in Texas (Mr. Wright) differs in being always zeorine, and conspicuously in the colours, resembling rather *Lecanora varia*. Both the species last named are associable with *P. ferrugineum*, though differing so strikingly from it; but *P. Floridanum*, Tuckerm. *Obs. Lich.* l. c. 5, p. 402, & 6, p. 287 (Florida, Mr. Beaumont; Texas, Mr. Wright) which extends also to Cuba (Wright *Lich. Cub.* n. 111) recedes farther from common types, and reminds us rather of small forms of *Rinodina sophodes*.

The present genus developes, as has already been seen, analogously with *Lecanora;* but its differentiation is less varied, and the subdivisions now far from as strongly expressed. I am still inclined to take *P. cinnabarrinum* (Ach.) Anz., which is common throughout the United States, as, equally with some rock-forms of *P. aurantiacum* (compare here Wright *Lich. Cub.* n. 114) representative of the Lecanorine section *Aspi-*

cilia; and the tri-quadrilocular spores of *P. Brebissonii* (Fée) and *P. spadiceum,* Tuckerm. Lich. Hawaii, as an anticipation and illustration of the analogous evolution of the spore-type of *Lecanora,* in the section *Lecania.* The polar sub-type becomes quadrilocular in *Theloschistes* also (in *Physcia hypoglauca,* Nyl.) : but with this stage our present knowledge of the evolution of this kind of spore ceases.

XXVIII.—LECANORA (Ach.).

Ach. L. U. p. 77, pro magna p., et Urceolariæ sp., p. 74.   Stizenb. Beitr.
l. c. p. 169, et Acarospora max. p., p. 168, et Lecania pr. p. 170.   Nyl.
Lich. Scand. p. 139, max. p., et Squamaria, p. 130.   Parmelia, b, Placothallæ p. magna p., Fr. Summ. p. 105.   Parmelia, sectt. 1, Placodium
max. p., 2, Psora, 3, Patellaria max p., et 4, Urceolaria pr. p., et Biatoræ sp., Tuckerm. Syn. N. Eng. p. 37, &c.   Parmelia pr. p., Amyg-
dalaria, et Ophioparma, Norm. Con. pp. 15, 18, t. 1, f. 8, 9, 11.
Squamaria, Lecania pr. p., Lecanora, Hæmatomma, Acarospora, et
Aspicilia, Mudd. Man. Brit. Lich. p. 127, &c.   Placodium, Lecanora,
Lecania pr. p., et Biatoræ spp., Müll. Principes de Classif. p. 37, &c.
Gussonea, Pleopsidium, Psoroma pr. p., Ochrolechia, Zeora, Polyozo-
sia, Pachyospora, Lecanidium, Dimerospora, et Sarcogyne, Auctt.

Structuram descripserunt Tulasne, Mém. sur les Lich. p. 150, 152,
158, 191, t. 3, 4, f. 15–22, 10, f. 19–23, 13, f. 18–23; Fuisting de nonnull.
apoth. pp. 10, 33.

Apothecia scutellæformia, margine nunc composito.   Sporæ ex
ellipsoideo oblongæ, simplices, rarissime bi-quadri-loculares, l. elon-
gato-fusiformes pluriloculares, incolores.   Spermatia l. oblonga l.
bacillaria, l. acicularia arcuata ; sterigmatibus sub-simplicibus.   Thallus crustaceus, aut effiguratus aut rarissime papilloso-fruticulosus
aut uniformis.

Excluding the immediately preceding group (*Placodium*) and the next
following one (*Rinodina*) the separation of which is determined by differences in the spore-type, *Lecanora,* as here taken, embraces (*exceptis
excipiendis*) the whole of the species referred to the genus by Acharius ;
and to his *Parmelia* sect. *Placothallæ* (*Summ.* l. c.) by Fries.   The
ground-idea of this construction has been best exhibited by Dr. Stizenberger ; but he (l. c.) distinguishes the polysporous, effigurate group
(*Acarospora,* Massal.) and separates also the species with bi-plurilocular
spores (*Ophioparma,* Norm.   *Lecania,* Mass., *Dimerospora,* Th. Fr.).
Nylander retains all these in *Lecanora ;* accepting however the generical
distinctness of the effigurate, true *Lecanoræ* (*Squamaria,* DC., Nyl.) he
is led, in like manner, to include in the present genus the granulose species of *Placodium.*   Other recent authors have assumed in their con-

structions both the generical validity of the effigurate type of thallus, and also that of each of the several gradations in the typical differentiation of the spores; and hence not a few subdivisions of the group, cited above. It remains thus, as here taken, a large one; but with that objection we are little concerned, provided the genus be also, approximately, a natural one. '*Malo . . . contra characteres, quam affinitatem naturalem peccare.*' (Fr. *Summ.* p. 428.) But is it certain that even the sharpest characters (those namely derivable from the spores) should not be subordinated to the whole *idea* of the plant? And, still further, is there nothing justifying a fair presumption that a natural group shall tend to exhibit, within its circuit, the entire differentiation of its spore-type? These questions have been already above touched upon; and the writer's solution of them will appear as well in the now proposed arrangements of the present, and other large groups.

Like the preceding genus, the present, as I understand it, passes then by quite imperceptible gradations from the subfoliaceous thalline type (sect. *Squamaria*, ascending also very rarely into fruticulose conditions, sect. *Cladodium*) into the granulose-crustaceous (sect. *Eulecanora*) which last embraces the great bulk of the species, and exhibits the whole differentiation of the spores. So far, the apothecia (though not without significant anticipations of possible variation) are for the most part regular : but this does not continue; and the slight indications of an urceolate depression of the fruit observable in *Placodium*, are expanded here into a group (not without effigurate and even fruticulose forms) of well-marked lichens (sect. *Aspicilia*) which paves the way for the extreme, variously aberrant, and polysporous section, *Acarospora*. The distinction of the higher modifications of thallus (in sect. *Squamaria* and *Cladodium*) from the granulose, is notwithstanding, from our point of view, scarcely a valid one; being determined mainly by the relatively considerable number of higher forms : and the genus may as easily be regarded as constituting a single large group — *Eulecanora sensu lat.* — supplemented by two smaller ones.

The already observed *nisus* of the crustaceous thallus to elevate itself to the foliaceous, and even the fruticulose, is repeated, often on a larger scale and with greater diversity of modification, in *Lecanora ;* but the fruticulose type is as rare here as in *Placodium*. It is yet represented in North America by no less than three lichens, confined, like the fruticulose species of *Placodium*, to the Pacific coast. ——*L. Bolanderi, Obs. Lich.* l. c. 6, p. 266, was discovered on the sandstone rocks of California by the friendly botanist after whom it is named. Terete as is the many-branched thallus of this lichen, it certainly suggests some conditions of the most perfect (monophyllous) state of *L. rubina ;* with which, as with the rest of the *Squamariæ*, it also agrees in its elongated, bowed spermatia. The comparison may remind us of the supposed development of the Asiatic *L. fruticulosa*, Eversm. (the shorter, staff-shaped spermatia of which, taken in connexion with other features, refer it to a different section) from *L. esculenta* (Pall.) Eversm. So closely indeed is the latter associable (through *L. affinis* of the same author) with *L. fruticulosa*, that it has even been doubted whether all three might not be states of a single species,[1] probably always, when *in situ*, peltate. There is yet no doubt, from specimens received since the publication of *L. Bolanderi*, that its fronds are developed from scattered, papillæform granules.——In *L. thamnitis* (Lich. Calif. p. 20) from the same region, where it was found by the same botanist, the short trunks are crowded together into a warted crust, contrasting indeed with *L. Bolanderi*, but scarcely otherwise than as complicate states of *L. rubina* with monophyllous ones.——And finally in *L. phryganitis* (Lich. Calif. p. 19) we have neither the peltate fronds of *L. Bolanderi*, nor the effuse crust of *L. thamnitis*, but dense patches, made up, at the centre, of crowded erectish trunks, which are elongated, at the circumference, into finally decumbent branches. All three are notwithstanding closely akin ; and as closely related, by their apothecia, to the otherwise sufficiently diverse *L. pinguis* and even *L. varia*. It is clear then that the fruticulose species of *Lecanora* are intimately associable at once with the sub-foliaceous, and the granulose ; and our first division (*Cladodium*) is but a modification of our second — *Squamaria*.

The sub-foliaceous conditions of *Lecanora* make, as a whole, but a small part of the very numerous *Eulecanorei ;* and less than twenty species are credited (Nyl. *Enum.* p. 111. *Lich. Scand.* p. 130) to *Squamaria*, almost all northern or austral lichens, rather inadequately represented as yet in North America. The fine terricoline species of the calcareous regions of Europe are indeed scarcely known here. But either *L. crassa* or *L. lentigera* (the single infertile specimen resembles both species) accompanies *Placodium fulgens* in the Bad Lands of Judith, Nebraska (Dr. Hayden) and is possibly significant of future accessions to our knowledge of this group from the same region.——*L. Frostii*, Tuck. Suppl. 1, l. c. p. 425. *Obs. Lich.* l. c. 6, p. 267, an inhabitant of granitic rocks from New England to Virginia, is commonly sorediiferous, and fertile specimens have as yet scarcely occurred, save to the excellent cryptogamist

---

[1] *" Die dritte art "* (*L. fruticulosa*) *" ist durch die bei'm Zerbrechen kenntlich werdende Structur der zweiten so mit der ersten verbunden, dass man nicht nur die Beziehung derselben auf eine und dieselbe Gattung, sondern geneigt ist, noch einen Schritt weiter zu gehen und die Frage aufzustellen : ob wir nicht hier nur drei verschiedene Entwickelungs — und Ausbildungsstufen der einen Lecanora esculenta vor Augen haben, wie dieses unser College, Herr* Eversmann, *in seiner Abhandlung zur Genüge angedeutet, wenn auch nicht ausgesprochen hat."* Fr. Nees r. Esenb. *Nachtrag üb. Lich. esc. in Act. Acad. C. L. C. Nat. Cur.* 15, 2. The thallus in the first is yet fruticulose, and not properly isidioid ; in whatever way we explain it. I possess original specimens of each of the forms described by Eversmann, through the kindness of the late Dr. Lucæ, of Berlin.

whose name it bears.——*L. gelida* (L.) Ach., of the north of Europe, was found in Greenland by J. Vahl. (Th. Fr. *Lich. Arct.* p. 83).——*L. thamnoplaca*, Tuckerm.[1] (a very marked representative of the olivaceous series) the adnate, lobulate thallus of which is in fact made up of short, closely crowded trunks, much as in *L. rubina*, v. *complicata* (Anz. *Lich. Ital.* n. 158) and should so far differ from *L. Montagnæi* (Fr.) Schær., with which it agrees in a certain resemblance of the fruit to *L. badia*, is one of Mr. Bolander's most recent discoveries, on the granitic rocks of Nevada. ——*L. rubina* (Vill.) Ach. (*L. chrysoleuca*, Auctt.) is the type of an elegantly varied group of rock-lichens of the alpine regions of Europe, which, finding its centre of evolution here in the Organ mountains of Texas (Wright) and the Rocky Mountains (Hayden; E. Hall) extends northward even to Arctic America (Herb. Hook.) and descends thence to the northern shore of Lake Superior (Agassiz). Beside the more widely diffused monophylline condition, Mr. Wright collected in Texas the pale-fruited, peltate form of the south of Europe (*Squamaria peltata*, DC., Nyl.!) the bluish-black under side of which (*hypothallus glaber*, Fr.) is not only powdery, as Schærer (*Spicil.* p. 436) observed, but even, if I mistake not, at length almost villous; and the still better marked and less ascendant, black-fruited v. *opaca* (*S. melanophthalma*, DC., Nyl.). Only an inferior (campestrian) state of this fine species, with short, erectish lobes crowded together so as to pass into gyrose plaits above, and always brown below, is known in New England and the adjacent regions. The related *L. cartilaginea* of the north of Europe, is quite unknown here. But its place is perhaps made up by *L. Haydeni*, Tuck. *Obs. Lich.* l. c. 6, p. 267, with a still more distinctly subfoliaceous, convoluted thallus, occurring free, and 'covering many square miles' in the Laramie plains, Nebraska, where the wind heaps it even into drifts (Dr. Hayden). The fronds of this species are almost Parmeliine, and comparable with those of *P. conspersa*, but the texture is crustaceous; and *L. rubina*, to which it is nearest, varies in the same direction, and in its hypothallus still more conspicuously, from the family type.——*L. muralis* (Schreb.) Schær. (*L. saxicola*, Auctt.) is common throughout the United States, and passes, westward, into several marked varieties. One of these, and undoubtedly the noblest condition of the species, is undistinguishable from the var. *Garovaglii*, Anz. (*Lich. Langob.* n. 270) and has occurred here, in Nevada (Bolander); and another, calcareous form, perhaps scarcely

---

[1] *Lecanora thamnoplaca (sp. nova) thallo ex areolis squamiformibus subinde crenatis turgidis, centro stipitatis, ambitu lobatis, pallide cervinis; apotheciis (1 — 1,5ᵐᵐ· lat.) innato-superficialibus, disco rufo-nigro, margine demisso. Sporæ octonæ, ovoideo-ellipsoideæ, simplices, incolores, longit. 0,009–16ᵐᵐ·, crassit. 0,005–8ᵐᵐ·* Nevada (Mr. Bolander). Thallus at length caulescent at the centre, the stout stipes, which are divided above, now exceeding 3ᵐᵐ· in height. I should compare this feature, generally, to the analogous modification of structure in *Lecidea vesicularis*. Spermogones not seen.

separable from the var. *versicolor*, Nyl. (*Lich. Scand.*) was found in Missouri (Prof. C. U. Shepard) and in Kansas (Mr. Hall).

It is acknowledged, even by those who accept the generical distinction of the squamulose-effigurate type of thallus (*Psoroma*, Auctt., *Placodium* l. *Squamaria*, Auctt.) of the *Lecanorei*, that there is no satisfactory *difference* between this and the granulose. The passage of the latter into scales, prolonged at length into lobes, which revert again to squamaceous, or even granulose conditions, takes place within one and the same circle of crustaceous decline. And the centre, embracing the great bulk of the forms included in this circle being granulose, we may claim to explain excentrical conditions by the seldom wanting links which connect them with the ordinary, crustaceous type. This centre of the *Eulecanorei* we have now reached, in the section *Eulecanora* proper. As here taken, the group includes by far the larger part of the granulose *Lecanoræ*, Ach.; and, with similar exceptions, determined for the most part by the microscope, the most of *Parmelia* sect. *Patellaria*, Fr. We remove however *L. cinerea* from this to the next following section, and add to the present those species of the section *Urceolaria* (Fr.) which only differ in their composite or zeorine margin. This latter overgrowth makes the only important exception to the general regularity of the scutellæform apothecium in *Eulecanora;* and it is one clearly of subordinate account. Not only are we put to it, as Dr. Th. Fries has remarked (*Lich. Arct.* p. 99) to distinguish *L. Cenisia* even specifically from *L. subfusca;* but admitting the zeorine group in its narrowest sense (*Zeora*, Koerb.) two genera must also be recognized in the cluster represented by *L. ventosa.*

As respects the spores, the present section, in the great majority of its species, is directly analogous with *Parmelia;* and exhibits the primary (simple) condition of the colourless type. But the complexity of sporal structure is apt (as often remarked) to increase with the degradation of the thalline; and *Eulecanora*, though sufficiently true for the most part to its analogical relations, yet offers exceptions of no little interest. These exceptions are still far from being dignified by other accompanying differences of structure; and they illustrate in fact only the typical differentiation of the same spore, of which the remaining species exhibit the earlier stage. *L. aipospila* (*Dimerospora*, Th. Fr. *Lich. Arct.* p. 97) scarcely differs in the character of its spores from the rock-lichens to which it is otherwise most nearly related, except as the bilocular state of *Placodium fulgens*, or the bilocular spores of *P. vitellinum*, from the simple ones. Nor is it easy to see, if the next following step in the differentiation, represented by *L. athroocarpa*, Dub., Nyl. (*Lecania fuscella*, Massal.) be separated generically, how we can avoid distinguishing, in the same way, the analogous stage of development of the polar spore; of which *Placodium Brebissonii*, and the *Physcia hypoglauca* of Nyl. *Syn.* (t. 8, f. 51) afford instances. And when the dactyloid spore, passing easily into the fusiform, becomes finally attenuated into the acicular, I know not how to regard this series of slight gradations, which no one reckons of other than subordinate account in the *Peltigerei*, as of any higher (representing as it does only the gradual completion of the type of spore) in *Lecanora* or *Biatora*. *Lecania* is, in fact, as respects the spore-type, to *Ophioparma*, Norm. (*Hæmatomma*, Mass., & Auctt.) precisely as *Biatora sphæroides* to *B. rubella;* and (taking into account the near relation of the fusiform peltigerine spore to the more dactyloid, as expressed into some *Nephromas*) scarcely otherwise than as *Peltigera venosa* to *P. horizontalis*, and *P. canina;* or again as *Sticta pulmonaria* to *S. amplissima*.

This group is very largely northern. Of the seventy odd best distinguished forms referable to it, less than a third is known as yet as North American; but we possess quite two thirds, and with little doubt more, of the European ones.

The right extreme of the section *Eulecanora*, as here taken, is occupied by the cluster represented by *L. pallescens* (*Ochrolechia* Massal.) distinguished by its large spores, and not without other features pointing towards *Pertusaria;* with which genus it is in the line of direct analogy. Following this is *L. atra*, and its few near allies, passing imperceptibly into the larger group typified by *L. subfusca;* which finds its complement in that distinguished by the elegant *L. ventosa* (*Ophioparma*, Norm.). The central cluster of species is with little doubt that represented by *L. subfusca;* and this universal lichen may perhaps well be taken for the centre of the whole section. Continuous as this cluster is (as compare Nyl. *Lich. Scand.* p. 157) with *Squamaria*, so that nothing in short but the overbearing predominance of higher thalline development excuses the separation of the latter from it, we can hardly wonder if it include approaches to squamariæform and even fruticulose overgrowths. Nor are such, as will be seen, wanting.

L. frustulosa (Dicks.) Ach., has occurred in Greenland (J. Vahl in Th. Fr. *Lich. Arct.* p. 108) and in Vermont (Mr. Frost).——*L. Cenisia*, Ach., was found by the same botanists, in the same regions ; and in California, by Mr. Bolander.——*L. Hageni*, Ach. (*L. subfusca*, v. *umbrina*, Nyl.) is generally taken for distinguishable from *L. subfusca;* and has occurred in Greenland (J. Vahl, *fide* Th. Fr. l. c.) and, rather sparingly, on dead wood, old brick, and rocks, from Canada (Mr. A. T. Drummond) to Pennsylvania (Dr. E. Michener) and the Rocky Mountains.——Very close to the last is *L. Sambuci* (Pers.) Nyl., detected, on Elm and Poplar bark, in Massachusetts, by Mr. Willey.——Of the brown series, *L. phæobola*, Tuckerm.,[1] a native of *Coniferæ* in California, offers an example

---

[1] *Lecanora phæobola* (*sp. nova*) *thallo crustaceo papillato-verrucoso olivaceofusco, verrucis minutis mox turbinatis lævigatis ; apotheciis* (1–1,5$^{mm.}$ *lat.*) *subsessilibus rufo-fuscis, disco nitido turgescente, margine thallino excluso. Hypothecium incolor. Sporæ fusiformi-ellipsoideæ, simplices, incolores, longit.* 0,009–15,$^{mm.}$,

in several respects curious; but two fine rock-lichens of the extreme north of Europe — *L. poliophœa* and *L. aipospila*, are as yet unknown to this continent. Each of these last named European species shews indications of thalline overgrowth, as well centripetal as centrifugal; the former or fruticulose luxuriance is marked however very much more strongly in the Californian lichens above separated to form our first section: and these, it is not to be doubted, relate really to *L. varia* not a little as *L. aipospila* to *L. subfusca*. —— The remarkably incrassated, areolate-plicate *L. pinguis*, Tuck. *Obs. Lich.* 1. c. 6, p. 268, another of Mr. Bolander's important Californian discoveries, belongs also to, and constitutes an all but effigurate exaltation of, the group represented by *L. varia;* which, in this, as other ways, may be said to touch at length, if not to include, the finally peltate *L. rubina*. ——*L. atrosulphurea* (Wahl.) Ach., was found in Greenland by Vahl (Th. Fr. 1. c.).

    L. Brunonis, Tuckerm.,[1] a rupicoline species, which has occurred only on the coast of California (Mr. Bolander) has, in its best forms, much the aspect of a *Pannaria*, not remote from *P. microphylla :* it appears yet to be referable, by internal, thalline structure, and by that of the spermogones, to the stock of *L. subfusca* in *Eulecanora*. Though otherwise sufficiently diverse from *L. aipospila*, this lichen agrees with the northern one in its bilocular spores. ——*L. athroocarpa*, Duby, Nyl. Prodr. p. 88, & Lich. Scand. p. 168 (*Lecania fuscella*, Massal.) resembling a minute state of *L. subfusca*, but differing in its finally quadrilocular spores in pleio-sporous sporesacks, has been found as yet only (on *Sarcobatus*, accompanied by *L. Hageni*) at Deer Creek on the North Platte (Dr. Hayden) at San Diego, California, on shrubs (Dr. J. G. Cooper) and, on Birch, at New Bedford, by Mr. Willey.

    Of the group represented by *L. ventosa* (*Ophioparma*, Norm. *Lepadolemma*, Trev. *Hœmatomma*, Mass.) *L. hœmatomma* is quite unknown to me as North American, but it occurs within the confines of the region of Norway embraced in the *Lichenes Arctoi* of Dr. Th. Fries; and '*Amer.*'

---

crassit. 0,003–5$^{mm.}$; *paraphysibus conglutinatis.* —— Bark of *Libocedrus* and *Abies*, California (H. N. Bolander). Spermogones black. Spermatia staff-shaped, on simple sterigmas. Thalline border of the apothecia soon disappearing; and the aspect of these (scanty) specimens is quite that of *Biatora*. Spores resembling those of *Lecanora badia*. The reaction with iodine is blue.

    [1] *Lecanora Brunonis (sp. nova) thallo ex areolis minutis glebulosis subinde confluentibus squamiformibus imbricatis cervino-fuscescentibus ; apotheciis (circa* 1$^{mm.}$ *lat.) sessilibus, disco rufo-fusco nigricante submarginato mox turgido marginemque thallinum integrum excludente. Sporæ octonæ, ellipsoideæ l. oblongoellipsoideæ, biloculares, incolores, longit.* 0,011–18$^{mm.}$, *crassit.* 0,004–7$^{mm.}$—— Sandstone, and serpentine rocks, San Bruno mountains, and Oakland hills, California (H. N. Bolander). Spermatia acicular, bowed; sterigmas simple. With the abundant, true gonidia, scattered collogonidia sometimes appear (under the microscope) which I take to be alien.

is appended to it in the General Enumeration of Nylander. We have throughout the southern country, from South Carolina (Mr. Ravenel) to Texas (Mr. Wright) upon bark, and also on rocks in New Mexico (Wright) the elegant, tropical *L. punicea*, Ach., which may serve to illustrate the proper affinity of the other more divergent members of the group, to *Eulecanora* proper. So closely does this species approach *L. subfusca*, that a form of the latter with similarly coloured disk, (comp. the v. *erythrocarpa*, Mont. *Cub*. p. 207) may well be undistinguishable from it, but by the spores, and spermatia. And the American representative of *L. elatina*, Ach., is most readily passed over, in some of its numerous forms, for *L. subfusca*, though in fact so well distinguished, as in other respects, by the composite exciple. The finer conditions of this lichen (*Biatora dein Parmelia ochrophœa*, Tuckerm. Syn. N. E. p. 61, & *Lich. Exs*. n. 91, 111) are but ill-comparable with the rarely fertile European state; but the smooth, glaucescent thallus becomes at length leprous and ochroleucous, when nothing remains to separate it but its better developed fruit. A possible form of this (Vermont, Mr. Frost) with thin smooth, dispersed thallus, and paler, minute apothecia which are more evidently pruinose than in the American state of *a*, is well comparable with published specimens of *Hæmatomma cismonicum*, Beltram. (Rabenh. *Lich. Eur*. n. 531).

Thus far *Lecanora* is marked, as a whole, by the regularity of its apothecia; and it is not difficult, in most cases, to explain aberrations. But this is far from being as easy in the two small, almost wholly *rupicoline* groups which follow. In the first of these the innate apothecium is finally so modified that the very genus becomes doubtful, if not the tribe; and even the most patient comparison of such modifications with the type to which they are referable, may fail (for want at least of sufficiently instructive specimens) of a satisfactory issue. Perplexing rock-forms occur however in other groups; nor is it necessary to go far to find an exact analogue of the one now before us, which is well known as *Aspicilia*. This analogue is furnished by the immediately preceding genus (*Placodium*), several species of which (as *P. chalybæum* and *P. variabile;* and also *P. cinnabarrinum*) differ from other species precisely as forms of *Aspicilia* differ from *Eulecanora;* and are quite as separable from their otherwise natural allies. The section is indeed, as are other sections, more largely developed in *Lecanora*, and has received proportionate attention; but the difference (depending on the more or less innate apothecium) upon which its distinction is based, is no less a subordinate one in this, than in the other.

L. cinerea is the well-known type of *Aspicilia*, and exhibits, or at least serves to explain, in mountainous countries, almost the whole circle of variations which distinguishes the group. From this, also effigurate in Arctic America, the radious *L. circinata* appears to me to differ much as *Placodium candicans* from *P. chalybæum*, or as *Lecanora muralis* from *L. varia*. Nor does *L. melanaspis* (Wahl.) Ach. (placed with *L. circinata* in his sect. *Psora* by Fries; and in similar relations both with the latter and with *Aspicilia* in Nyl. *Scand.* p. 162) diverge any more widely than in a better-developed thallus, and more superficial fruit; the last varying indeed from the more innate type much as *Urceolaria ocellata* from *U. scruposa*. But this sub-foliaceous overgrowth of *Aspicilia* (*Alphoplacium, si placet;* the analogue of *Squamaria*) passes also, in the curious free-lichens of the Siberian and other deserts, from a probably originally peltate, squamariæform condition (*L. esculenta; L. affinis*) into a perfectly fruticulose one (*L. fruticulosa*, Eversm.; *Sphærothallia*, Fr. Nees pr. p., the analogue of *Cladodium*) a luxuriance suggested also by the isidioid thallus of *L. oculata*.

About thirty forms referable to this section as here taken, have been described, but the number of species is possibly much less; the extent of the group constituting *L. cinerea* being quite differently apprehended by different writers. With the exception of two or perhaps three (Nyl. *Enum. Gén.* p. 113) the species are all northern, and nearly all common to Europe and America.——*L. melanaspis* (Wahl.) Ach., *a*, *alphoplaca*, Fr., has occurred in Greenland (J. Vahl, in Th. Fr. *Lich. Arct.* p. 82) but elsewhere, on this continent, only (on lime-rocks) in Kansas (E. Hall) and in the Yosemite Valley, California (H. N. Bolander). *L. circinata*, Ach., though a northern lichen, is yet quite unknown as North American. ——*L. cinerea* is by no means less diversified here than in Europe; and if *Gyalecta odora* (occurring with us on granitic rocks) be to be added, as by Koerber, and by Nylander, to the series of forms explainable by it, — fairly reaches over into the next succeeding sub-family.——Both the terricoline species of Europe — *L. verrucosa* (Ach.) Laur., and *L. oculata* (Dicks.) Ach., are natives of Arctic America; and the former has also occurred in the Yo Semite valley, California (Mr. Bolander). And it is observable in this connection, that *Pertusaria glomerata*, the companion, in other countries, of *L. verrucosa*, is far from rare in the alpine regions of New England.——*L. glaucomela*, Tuckerm.,[1] from California, is rather a sub-species, to be arranged under *L. oculata*.

The stress of difference in the last group (*Aspicilia*) is on the concav-

---

[1] *Lecanora glaucomela (subsp. nova) thallo crustaceo cartilagineo primitus contiguo lævigato glaucescente; apotheciis* (1—1,5$^{mm.}$ *lat.*) *sessilibus planis, margine thallino crenulato discum nigrum submarginatum vix superante. Sporæ in thecis lingulæformibus octonæ, ellipsoideæ, simplices, lato-limbatæ, longit.* 0,018 — 21$^{mm.}$, *crassit.* 0,009 — 14$^{mm.}$, *paraphysibus filiformibus.*——On the branches of *Abies muricata*, California (Mr. Bolander). Spermatia staff-shaped; sterigmas simple. Only the thekes shewing the blue reaction with iodine. The spores (rather smaller than those of *L. oculata*) always disposed in a single series in the strap-shaped thekes. The species of which I suppose this to be a form, and which is remarkable for its branched thallus, is unknown as yet in Western America south of the arctic zone.

ity of the innate, but otherwise, at least as represented in the best forms, sufficiently regular apothecium. But in that now to be considered — *Acarospora* — which constitutes our last section of *Lecanora*, though the species are equally all but confined to rupicoline and terricoline conditions, and the apothecia vary as much as, and similarly to those of the last, passing also at length into punctiform or pseudo-endocarpeine states, the stress of difference is on the exceedingly minute and innumerable spores. The question of the systematic value of deviations from the normal number of spores contained in the thekes may be said to be so far determined, that writers are generally agreed in subordinating lesser differences of the kind to the affinity indicated by the sum of other characters of the lichen. And perhaps none will deny that *Lecanora Sambuci*, Nyl., (*L. scrupulosa*, Auctt.) and *Rinodina sophodes*, Koerb., are clearly referable to the groups to which they are in every other respect naturally akin, notwithstanding the variation in the contents of the thekes. Nor are we at all able to allow that the case is otherwise with the polysporous *Parmelia colpodes*, Ach. (*Anzia*, Stizenb.) this lichen being quite too closely associable with octo-sporous species to be well separated generically from them. But why should we stop here? The more numerous such spores become, the less perfect (as seen abundantly in *Theloschistes candelarius* and *Placodium vitellinum*) they are; and when finally all attempt at estimation of difference of type has to be given up, and the spores are fairly inappreciable, should not this manifestly increase instead of diminishing the value of the other characters? That is surely an unsatisfactory evidence of affinity which brings together (as in *Acarospora*, Stizenb. *Beitr.* l. c. p. 169) lichens as incongruous as *Lecanora cervina* and *L. constans*, Nyl.; nor is it in fact certain, or even unlikely, that this aberration in the way of degradation may not recur in any genus or even group. The spores of *L. constans* (generally well comparable with *Rinodina sophodes*) are at length (as noted in the writer's *Obs. Lich.* l. c. 5, p. 404) bilocular, and resemble 'the younger conditions of the biscoctiform type; as if in fact the plant were a remarkable micro- and polysporous deviation from the type of *L. sophodes*, in which the final development of the spore peculiar to that type has been precluded.'

Tulasne (*Mém. sur les Lich.* p. 85) has touched but cursorily on the myriosporous[1] anomaly, but compares it, not without evident significance, to an irregularity of the same sort occurring in species of *Sphæria;* as in other Fungi.

---

[1] This term sufficiently denotes the extreme of polysporous deviation, as observable in *Acarospora, Biatorella,* and *Sporostatia* of authors. But indications of less irregularity, and even of return to a normal condition are not wanting within the limits of these myriosporous groups; as in *Lecanora oligospora*, Nyl. *Prodr.* p. 80, '*thecis sporis* 32 – 8,' upon which the author of the species further remarks that the plant is possibly only a variety of *L. cervina.* Compare here the remarks of Müller, *Principes de Classif.* p. 12.

As regards the thallus, *Acarospora* ranks with the other subfoliaceous divisions of *Lecanora ;* being yet distinguishable from them no less by the irregularity of the spores than (much as *Alphoplacium* from *Squamaria*) by the smaller spermatia. In all about twenty more or less marked forms have been described, but the limits of *L. cervina* are understood as differently as those of *L. cinerea* in the last group, and the number of probable species may be very much less. Almost all are northern, and European ; of which the more conspicuous ones have been recognized here. Nylander reckons (*Enum. Gén.* p. 112) three austral species, one of which, found also (Nyl. l. c.) in tropical America, extends within our limits.

L. molybdina (Wahl.) Schær., heretofore confined, on this continent, to the arctic zone, has recently been detected at Tadousac in Canada (Mr. Drummond).——*L. chlorophana* (Wahl.) Ach., is also an arctic lichen, occurring in Greenland (J. Vahl, *fide* Th. Fr. l. c.) but Mr. Wright collected it in the Organ mountains, Texas ; and it has since been found in Utah (Mr. S. Watson), in Alpine co., California (Dr. Lapham), and on the coast of California (Mr. Bolander).——The Chilian *L. xanthophana*, Nyl. *Enum. Gén.* (named by the present writer, the same year, *L. chrysops*, Suppl. 1, but previously described, under another name, by the eminent author first cited) collected in Texas and Mexico by Wright, has since occurred in Missouri and Kansas (E. Hall) in the Rocky Mountains (Dr. Hayden) in South Carolina (Mr. Ravenel) and recently, even in New Jersey (Mr. Austin).——Closely approximate to the last is the terricoline *L. Schleicheri* (Ach.) Nyl., found in the alpine districts of the Rocky Mountains (Dr. Hayden ; Mr. E. Hall) as on the coast of California (Mr. Bolander).——*L. cervina* (Pers.) Sommerf., is, in one form or other, all but everywhere diffused in North America ; its finer forms are however rare. I have *a, glaucocarpa*, Sommerf. (taken by Fries also for the type of the species) only from the lime-rocks of Vermont (Mr. Frost).——The var. *β, squamulosa*, Fr. (*L. cervina, a*, Nyl. *Scand.*) extends to other than calcareous rocks, and has occurred on granite in Vermont (Mr. Frost) as in Greenland (J. Vahl, in Th. Fr. l. c.) and in the finest luxuriance, on granitic rocks, in the Yosemite valley, California, and in Nevada (Mr. Bolander).——An infertile lichen (designable as *L. thamnina*) which I cannot but associate with the other Californian forms of *β*, proves yet to be really made up of crowded trunks (as in *L. thamnoplaca* of the same region, and *Lecidea conglomerata*) the longest of these trunks, which branch irregularly above, and are there flattened into the brown squamules constituting the outer crust, having a height of 7$^{mm.}$ This remarkable overgrowth has not been described by European writers, as occurring in their forms of the species before us ;[1] it looks at least possible however

---

[1] It is yet observable that Fries describes (*L. E.* p. 127) the squamules of *L. cervina* as sub-peltate ; and in this view the analogy of *L. thamnina* with *L. rubina*, v. *cómplicata*, Anz. (*Lich. Langob.*) is evident.

in a thick-crusted state of β, from Finmark, received from Dr. Th. Fries (*Acarospora peliscypha* (Wahl.) Th. Fr. *Lich. Arct.* p. 89) and may diminish the value of the distinction of *L. thamnoplaca.* The arctic *Acarospora peliscypha*, Th. Fr., to which I cannot but relate the equally granitic *A. rugulosa*, Koerb. *Parerg.* p. 59 (*e descr.*) if on the one hand not easily to be kept apart from our β *squamulosa*, is yet, on the other, most readily conceivable (Koerb. 1. c. p. 61) as only a better-developed condition of our third form, — γ, *discreta*, Fr. ; and, were it possible to distinguish specifically the granitic states of *L. cervina*, these last might perhaps be subsumed (as in the writer's Lich. Calif. p. 21) under an emended *L. peliscypha.* This v. *discreta*, long known only by the inappropriate designation of *Endocarpon smaragdulum*, Ach., is at once the most degraded, and the most common form of the species, and occurs everywhere on the granitic rocks of the northern states, and northward to Greenland ('*minime rara*,' Th. Fr. 1. c.). It is observable, rarely, in excellent condition, on dead wood (near Boston) and the oxydated state, f. *sinopica* (*Endocarpon*, Wahl.) is conspicuous on our alpine rocks (White Mountains).——It is only by the fewer and larger spores that Koerber distinguishes his *Acarospora glebosa, Syst.* p. 156, from his *A. smaragdula*, but the difference is an interesting one ; and the plant first-named having occurred (similar in all external respects, and exactly so in the dimensions of the spores to the European specimens, but the number of spores in the thekes, so far as seen, averaging only from 12 to 20) in California (Mr. Bolander) may be here indicated as f. *glebosa*.——Under the name *Sarcogyne*, Flotow first distinguished a little group of lecideoid apothecia, apparently and perhaps finally quite without thallus, which there seem to be sufficient reasons for regarding an anamorphosis of *L. cervina.* Borrer (Leight. Angioc. Lich. p. 17) referred at least the *Lecidea privigna*, Ach. (which he distinguished from *Lichen simplex*, Dav.) to the same species which should also include *Endocarpon smaragdulum* of authors, and is followed in this by Mr. Leighton, 1. c. ; while Dr. Nylander (*Prodr.* p. 79. *Lich. Scand.* p. 176) has explained the whole group as aberrations of *L. cervina.* I possess specimens of the graniticoline Vermont lichen above referred to *L. cervina* β *squamulosa*, in which the soon biatoroid apothecia occur not seldom quite free of the scales, when I cannot see that they differ appreciably from other, always ecrustaceous ones, referable to *Sarcogyne privigna.* Compare here *Acarospora glaucocarpa*, v. *depauperata*, Anz. *Lich. Lang.* n. 395 with *Sarcogyne platycarpoides* of the same author, Ibid. n. 359 ; and also Nyl. *Scand.* pp. 175–6. All the best known European forms are found here. The var. *privigna*, in various conditions, and including as well f. *simplex*, Koerb., as f. *Clavus*, Koerb. (v. *eucarpa*, Nyl.) are inhabitants of our granitic rocks ; and the v. *pruinosa*, Nyl., takes their place on our limestones.——In the anamorphosis under consideration Lecideine structure is so closely simulated that it is easy to compare *Sarcogyne platycarpoides*, Anz. (*Lich. Lang.*

16

n. 359) with *Lecidea zeoroides*, Anz. (n. 357) in company with which it grows; notwithstanding the distinctly black hypothecium, and normal spores, of the latter. And it is, at any rate, not clear, in view of North American specimens before me, the hypothecium of which passes from colourless to blackish-brown, that we can exclude any lichen from the present place on account merely of the finally blackening hypothecium. *Stereopeltis*, De Not. (Anz. *Lich. Lang.* n. 381. Rabenh. *Lich. Eur.* n. 682) only known to me indeed in these specimens, which represent *S. Carestiæ* of the author first cited, is so far scarcely to be distinguished from an American lichen (Massachusetts, Mr. Russell, 1848; Pennsylvania, Dr. Michener; Rhode Island, Mr. J. L. Bennett; California, Mr. Bolander) subsumable, it has certainly appeared, under *Sarcogyne privigna*, v. *Clavus*, Koerb., as sufficiently reconcilable with Flotow's conception of the structure of his genus (Koerb. *Syst.* p. 266) and in fact not differing otherwise, except in this interior denigration, from recognized forms of it. As respects the spore-character, these blackened states of the fruit of *L. cervina*, prove also to revert to normal conditions; and a *Sarcogyne* on sandstone from California (Mr. Bolander) is to *S. privigna* exactly as *Acarospora glebosa*, Koerb., to *A. smaragdula;* the spores being always few, and observed not seldom in eights, in the thekes.[1]

XXIX.—RINODINA, Mass., Stizenb.

Stizenb. Beitr. l. c. p. 169. Tuckerm. Lich. Calif. p. 20. Rinodina, Mass. Ric. p. 14; et Mischoblastia, Ibid. p. 40; addita Diploiciæ sp., Geneac. p. 20. Psora, Naeg. et Hepp in Hepp. Abbild. t. 2, et cætt. Lecanoræ spp., Ach. L. U. p. 77. Nyl. Lich. Scand. p. 147; in Prodr. Fl. N. Granat. p. 31. Parmelia sectt. Placodium pro p., Psora pr. p., et Patellaria pr. p., Fr. L. E. pp. 113,129,149. Dimelænæ spp., Norm. Con. p. 20, t. 1, f. 10, b. e. Amphilomatis sp., et Rinodina, Koerb. Syst. pp. 112,122. Dimelæna, et Rinodina, Th. Fr. Lich. Arct. pp. 94, 124; Gen. pp. 67, 71. Dimelæna, Rinodina, et Diploiciæ sp., Koerb. Parerg. pp. 52, 69, 117.

Apothecia scutellæformia, margine nunc composito, rarius biatorina. Sporæ ellipsoideæ, biloculares, rarius dein quadri-pluriloculares, fuscæ. Spermatia oblonga l. bacillaria; sterigmatibus subsimplicibus. Thallus crustaceus, effiguratus aut uniformis.

[1] In a considerable number of specimens from the sandstone, and in others from the Yosemite granite, the spores measure 0,008–0,011$^{mm.}$ by 0,003–0,005$^{mm.}$, and it would be easy to assume that the thekes were normally octosporous. In a specimen from Ukiah I find however still larger spores, measuring 0,012–0,018$^{mm.}$ by 0,004–0,007$^{mm.}$, thus corresponding closely with the spores of *Lecanora oligospora*, Nyl. *Prodr.* p. 80, which the author remarks is perhaps only a variety of *L. cervina*.

The typical difference in the spores separates this genus from the other groups of *Eulecanorei:* and its relation to the centre (*Lecanora* § *Eulecanora*) is much that of *Physcia* to *Parmelia ;* and to *Placodium,* much that of *Physcia* to *Theloschistes.* As presented in the great majority of species, the differentiation of the spore does not advance beyond the bilocular stage, which is commonly assumed to express the spore-character of the group : but *R. Conradi,* Koerb. *Syst.* p. 123, as well as *Lecan. pyreniospora,* Nyl. *Scand.* p. 151, f. 6, offer the quadrilocular ; and *L. diplinthia,* Nyl. (in *Prodr. Fl. Gran.* l. c. p. 31) as described (' *sp. fuscæ ellipsoideæ seriebus 4-loculosæ, scilicet loculis 2 apicalibus simplicibus, et seriebus 2 mediis singulis e loculis 2 constitutis, vel interdum e loculis 3'*) the sub-muriform-plurilocular gradation. This last modification characterizes also *R. sabulosa,* Tuckerm. Lich. Calif.; *R. Carestiæ,* Bagl., *cit.* Arn.; and *R. Lusitanica* of the latter author (*Flora,* 1868, p. 244) who calls the spores of his lichen '*fast parenchymatischen.*' It thus sufficiently appears that though far less fully exhibited than in *Buellia,* as here taken, the whole differentiation of the brown spore is indicated in *Rinodina;* which thus prefigures our conception of *Buellia.* The for the most part granulose thallus is modified here just as in *Placodium* and *Lecanora;* passing into squamulose, and finally into radious, and somewhat lobed conditions (sect. *Dimelæna,* Stizenb.).

Of the twenty odd best-marked forms described, more than two-thirds are northern, and nearly as large a proportion (due doubtless to fuller study) European ; but scarcely half have been recognized as yet in North America.

Of the effigurate section (*Dimelæna*) we possess all the northern species. *R. nimbosa* (Fr. *Diploicia,* Mass., Koerb.) is confined as yet to Greenland (Vahl, *e* Th. Fr. l. c. p. 95) but may well occur, in alpine districts, southward of this limit.——*R. oreina* (Ach.) Mass., which is common in the northern States, extends southward, along the mountains (North Carolina, Rev. M. A. Curtis; Tennessee, Mr. Ravenel) and is found also in the Rocky Mountains (Dr. Hayden) and in California (Mr. Bolander).——*R. chrysomelæna* (Ach.) has perhaps mainly a southern range, having only occurred once (on granite boulders, New Bedford, Mass., Mr. Willey) north of Pennsylvania (Hornblende rocks, Chester co., Dr. Michener) where Muhlenberg probably discovered it; but extending southward to Georgia (Mr. Ravenel).——Of the granulose section (*Eurinodina,* Stizenb.) *R. sophodes* is the familiar type, and may well embrace, as in Nylander's view, a considerable number of forms which pass for species with other writers. Several of these tend to squamulose luxuriance, as *R. Zwackhiana,* Krempelh., of the Bavarian alps ; and *Lecanora tephraspis,* Tuckerm. Suppl. 1, l. c. p. 425 (from rocks inundated most of the year, at Brattleboro', Vermont, Messrs. Russell and Frost) is another, exhibiting similar features. These are not however wholly wanting in the varied modifications of *R. sophodes,* v. *confragosa,* Nyl.; to which may

perhaps safely be referred the larger proportion of our rock-*Rinodinœ*.
——*R. Ascociscana* (*Lecanora*, Tuckerm. Suppl. 2, l. c. p. 204) is a common bark-lichen of the White Mountains; and is found also in Massachusetts; in Vermont (Mr. Frost) in Canada (Mr. Drummond) and in Illinois (Mr. Hall). Mr. Frost, and Mr. Willey observe it also on rocks. Thallus squamaceous. Apothecia lecanorine, with crenulate border; 0$^{mm.}$, 6–1$^{mm.}$ wide. Spores 0,025–40$^{mm.}$ long, and 0,011–18$^{mm.}$ wide.——*R. turfacea* (Wahl.) Koerb., and the closely akin *R. mniarœa* (Ach.) Th. Fr., are earth-lichens of Arctic America (J. Vahl, e Th. Fr. l. c. C. Wright) and the former is not uncommon in the alpine region of the White Mountains.
——*R. Bischoffii* (Hepp) Koerb. *Parerg.* p. 75, a lichen not without marked features, from the calcareous rocks of Germany and Italy, is represented here on lime-rocks, in Kansas (Mr. Hall) and in Texas (Mr. Wright). Apothecia soon blackening, and looking rather like those of some *Lecidea* or *Buellia*. Spores (characterized by the wide, dark interstice between the spore-cells, looking like a brown band, as noticed by Koerber) 0,014–20$^{mm.}$ long, and 0,011–14$^{mm.}$ wide, in the lichen from Texas; and a little smaller, or about 0,012–18$^{mm.}$ long, and 0,007–9$^{mm.}$ wide, in that from Kansas.——*R. sabulosa*, Tuckerm. *l. supra c.*, is a terricoline species from California (Mr. Bolander). Spores in eights, from regularly bilocular becoming soon, and most commonly quadrilocular; and the two (larger) middle cells not unfrequently but irregularly passing into four; 0,024–32$^{mm.}$ long, and 0,010–16$^{mm.}$ wide.

I add here as an appendix, with little hesitation, the myriosporous *R. constans* (Nyl.) described by Massalongo as a distinct generical type (*Maronea*) the minute but at length truly bilocular spores imitating sufficiently (much as the nucleiform hymenium of *Pertusaria* does the mature fruit of *Lecanora*) the younger (colourless) condition of the *Rinodina*-type, and the lichen agreeing with this genus generally. The American plant is described, under the more recent name of *Lecanora Berica*, in the writer's *Obs. Lich.* l. c. 5, p. 403,[1] and is common throughout the United States. Its spores are now constricted at the middle; one of the best indications perhaps of the coloured spore in its bilocular stage, when colour is wanting.

Sub-Fam. 2.—PERTUSARIEI, Nyl.

Apothecia composita, difformia.

The typically compound and closed receptacles of the crustaceous group before us may well appear abnormal as respects Parmeliaceous

---

[1] It is observed here that ' the spores are described as simple by all the authors who have remarked on them'; but Arnold (*Lich. Fränk. Jur.* in *Flora*, 1860, p. 71) had already noticed in specimens of *Maronea Kemmleri*, Koerb., that the spores were ' *meist mit je* 2 *Oeltröpfchen versehen.*'

lichens; but they are none the less explainable from our present point of view. An always included hymenium may be called nucleiform, but is not on that account necessarily Verrucariaceous; and there is nothing in the hymenium of *Pertusaria*, and the structure immediately conditioning it, to exclude it from Lecanorine affinity. Direct evidence to such affinity is afforded moreover by the fact that species slip back, not seldom, into scutellæform states; in one at least of which the normal apothecium of the sub-family last considered is so distinctly presented, that the lichen may almost pass, and is indeed claimed, at once, for a *Lecanora*, and a *Pertusaria*.

Scarcely less clear is it that if *Pertusaria* thus reverts to *Lecanora*, the latter, for its part, is not without anomalies anticipatory of *Pertusaria*. This is especially seen in the distinguished cluster of *Lecanoræ* which of all others most nearly approaches, in the spores, to the group now before us. The fruit of *L. tartarea*, v. *pertusarioides*, Th. Fr., is described (*Lich. Arct.* p. 100) as rounded and flattened warts, impressed above with now as many as ten, minute, yellowish-rosecoloured disks. And *L. pallescens*, v. *rosella*, Tuckerm. herb., is a similarly irregular, American lichen, in which what should be the disk of a simple apothecium is divided, by processes from the interior of the margin, meeting at the centre from which they appear to radiate, into from five to fourteen, small, at first ovate disks, passing at length into mere cracks between the very numerous processes; and these last becoming thus predominant at the expense of the hymenium, the Pertusarieine type is not seldom, or doubtfully suggested.

It is then, in this view, the lecanorine hypothecium — not rarely extended upwards into a margin in the *Eulecanorei*, as well as in *Gyalecta* — which explains the now evident inner border of lecanoroid *Pertusariæ;* and furnishes, in the compound species, at once the dissepiments which part, and the common tissue which envelopes, and even (in *P. Wulfenii*) finally encircles, with an elevated, blackening ring, the clustered hymenia.

But *Pertusaria* touches *Phlyctis* and *Thelotrema*, on the one hand, almost as clearly as *Lecanora*, on the other; and unites thus the now almost Parmeliine *Eulecanorei* and the sometimes too discrepant *Urceolariei* in one and the same natural family. It is yet hardly to be questioned that the group stands in nearest relations to *Eulecanorei;* and the spores, instead of at once removing it, as *Phlyctis*, &c., are removed, from the line of direct analogy with *Parmelia* and *Lecanora*, are in this line, and offer, though the ultimate differentiation be not reached, the most remarkable known expression of the Lecanorine spore-type; foreshadowed only in *L. tartarea*, &c. Nylander's recent discovery of a Pertusarieine type (*Varicellaria*, Nyl.) in which the second stage in the evolution of the colourless spore is exhibited, suggests indeed the possible occurrence of other types, displaying its further development. But *Pertusaria leuco-*

sticta, Mont. (*Syll.* p. 361) with annularly plurilocular spores, should be rather associable, as Nylander has associated it, with his *Phlyctis Boliviensis* (Lindig *herb. N. Gran.* n. 900) : and *Phlyctis*, whatever its affinity to *Pertusaria*, is without question much nearer to *Thelotrema;* if indeed, in the last resort, it prove well separable from the latter.

While the resemblances of *Pertusaria* to *Lecanora* have been recognized by authors, and illustrated especially by Fries (*L. E.* p. 419) the agreement has been general to consider these resemblances as relations rather of analogy than affinity, and, with scarcely an exception, the former genus has been placed among angiocarpous lichens. Nylander, on the contrary, assigns to his sub-tribe *Pertusariei* (*Lich. Scand.* p. 177) a place between his *Eulecanorei* (which includes *Urceolaria*) and his *Thelotremei*. Stizenberger (*Beitr.* l. c. p. 167) follows the author just cited in referring *Pertusaria* to *Parmeliacei;* but neither distinguishes *Urceolaria* from his *Lecanoreæ*, nor the genus before us from *Thelotremeæ*.

XXX. — PERTUSARIA, DC.

DC. Fl. Fr. 2, p. 319. Schær. Spicil. p. 64; Enum. p. 226. Fr. L. E. p. 418, addita Parmeliæ sp. pr. p., p. 186. Leight. Brit. Angioc. Lich. p. 26, t. 9, 10, 11. Norm. Con. p. 27. Mass. Ric. p. 186. Naeg. et Hepp in Hepp Abbild. t. 2, etc. Koerb. Syst. p. 381; Parerg. p. 310. Th. Fr. Lich. Arct. p. 258, addita Lecanoræ sp., p. 217; Gen. pp. 69, 105. Mudd Man. Brit. Lich. p. 271. Porina, et Variolariæ, Isidii et Lecanoræ spp., Ach. L. U.; Syn. Pertusaria, et Variolariæ, Isidii et Thelotrematis spp., Turn. et. Borr. Lich. Brit. p. 191, etc. Pertusaria et Varicellaria, Nyl. Enum. Gen. p. 117; Lich. Scand. p. 177; Lich. exot. l. c. pp. 220, 241; in Prodr. Fl. N. Gran. p. 35; Syn. Lich. N. Caled. p. 31. Stizenb. Beitr. l. c. p. 167. Th. Fr. Lich. Scand. p. 322.

Structuram exposuit Tulasne, Mém. sur les Lich. pp. 48, 59, 189, t. 11, f. 1–10.

Apothecia globulari-difformia, clausa porisque pertusa, hymenia (1–00) nucleiformia includentia; aut explanata, lecanoroidea. Sporæ magnæ, ellipsoideæ, simplices l. rarissime biloculares, incolores. Spermatia acicularia, recta; sterigmatibus simplicibus. Thallus crustaceus, uniformis.

The genus is remarkable, no less for its typically compound apothecia, than for the transformation of these into soredia (described at length by Turner and Borrer, under *Variolaria*, Pers.) and of the thallus into that coralloid overgrowth which the older writers distinguished as *Isidium*. '*Hæc Variolariæ et præcipue Isidii formatio,*' remarks Fries, '*reliquis plerisque Angiocarpis peregrina (nam ad omnes Lichenes hæc metamorphosis incaute extenditur) etiam affinitatem cum Parmeliis confirmat.*'

(*L. E.* p. 420.) But interesting as is the group, in several respects, the species are ill-defined; and their limits more than commonly uncertain. No clear difference has been indicated for *Varicellaria*, Nyl., beyond the subordinate one of bilocular spores.

Pertusaria is generally diffused; the fifty described species being divided pretty equally between northern, and southern (tropical and austral) regions, and the type (*P. pertusa*) together with *P. leioplaca*, reckoned cosmopolitan by Nylander (*Enum. Gén.*). Almost the whole of the northern forms are European; but only half of them are known as yet as North American. Accessions to this number may however be expected; though a satisfactory estimate of the variableness of known conditions has perhaps yet to be made.

P. bryontha (Ach.) Nyl., interesting as almost equally referable to *Lecanora* (in which the older writers placed it) and the present genus, is an alpine and arctic lichen, and has occurred here, in Greenland (J. Vahl, in Th. Fr. *Lich. Arct.* p. 117, where it is made a section of *Lecanora*) and in islands of Behring's Straits (Mr. Wright).——*P. dactylina* (Ach.) Nyl. in *Prodr. Fl. N. Gran.* p. 36, note (*Isidium*, Ach.) was also found by Mr. Wright in islands of Behring's Straits, and illustrates the fruticulose overgrowth of the Pertusariine thallus.[1]——*P. velata* (Turn.) Nyl. *Scand.* p. 179 (*Parmelia*, Turn. in Linn. Trans. 9, p. 143, t. 12, f. 1) with lecanoroid apothecia, has long been known to me, and is common throughout the United States; but has in great measure escaped the attention of authors. It is near to *P. multipuncta* (Sm.) Nyl. in *Prodr. N. Gran.* p. 35 (*P. faginea*, Tuck. Synops. N. E. p. 85) which is found everywhere. ——*P. lecanina*, described below,[2] is another lecanoroid species, peculiar to California.——*P. pustulata* (Ach.) Nyl. in *Prodr. N. Gran.* p. 35, and in *Herb.* Lindig n. 2877, is everywhere a common lichen here, and distinguishable by its bi-sporous thekes.——*P. glomerata* (Ach.) Schær. (*Parm. verrucosa*, b, Fr. Tuck. Syn. N. Eng. p. 42) occurs frequently in the alpine

[1] A similar *Pertusaria*, growing over mosses, in the alpine district of the Great Haystack, New Hampshire, differs (in my specimens) in having a less evidently, or not at all isidioid-elongated thallus; and I have found no spores.——*Isidium melanochlorum*, DC. (*I. stalactiticum*, Clement., Ach.) appears, as Acharius called it, 'distinct from *I. dactylinum*,' and to possess the aspect of *Pertusaria ;* but the specimens in my possession (Welwitsch *Cr. Lusit.* n. 22. Delise in *herb.* Duby.) have not afforded me hymenia.

[2] *Pertusaria lecanina (sp. nova) thallo tenui æquabili pallide lutescente ; apotheciis lecanoroideis* (0^{mm}·, 6–1^{mm}· *lat.*) *sessilibus monothalamis primitus albo-pulverulentis, margine thallino integro, disco carneo-pallescente submarginato. Sporæ binæ in thecis, ellipsoideæ, longit.* 0,092–142^{mm}·, *crassit.* 0,030–50^{mm}·——On bark of *Æsculus Californica* (growing in company with *Pertusaria leioplaca* and *P. pustulata*) and also on bark of *Pinus insignis*, in California (Mr. Bolander). Except in being larger, and in their pale-yellowish colour, the apothecia are not very dissimilar to those of a minute, finally often zeorine, southern and tropical variety of *Lecanora subfusca* (v. *duplicata*, of the present writer) given in Wright *Lich. Cub.* n. 119.

regions of the White Mountains; as also in islands of Behring's Straits (Mr. Wright).——*P. rhodocarpa,* Koerb. (*e* Th. Fr. *Varicellaria microsticta,* Nyl.) is an inhabitant of Arctic America (Nyl.).

Sub-Fam. 3.—URCEOLARIEI.

Apothecia plus minus urceolata.

Referred here *ex affinitate,* as *Hymenelia,* Krempelh., to *Aspicilia,* and that to *Lecanora;* however the characters should appear now to indicate other dispositions. But *Thelotrema* and *Gyalecta* are sometimes sufficiently lecanorine; and *Urceolaria,* which is but ill-separable from the rest, is placed with *Lecanorei* by almost common consent. The group affords by far the most evident points of passage of the scutellæform apothecium into the Lecideaceous; and plainly touches even the Verrucariaceous; genera and clusters referable to it having been commonly assigned by authors to each of the latter tribes. We have here in short the thallus of *Parmeliacei* reduced finally to a *minimum;* and as complement to this degeneration, a remarkable diversity in the always aberrant apothecia, and complexity in the spores.

Dirina, the carbonaceous hypothecium of which may be taken, as by Fries (*S. O. V.*) for an inchoate proper exciple, is representative of *Lecanora* in the present sub-family; and is placed indeed with *Eulecanorei* by both Koerber and Th. Fries. But *Gyalecta,* though, as typified by *G. rubra,* sufficiently lecanorine, appears, as a genus, to offer no uncertain indications of relationship to the coloured series; as if in fact it were a mainly northern, decolorate analogue of the mainly southern, and typically coloured *Thelotrema:* and its lecanorine significance should suggest therefore an analogy rather with *Rinodina.* The predominance of the coloured spore-type is indeed evident generally in this group of anomalous genera; and *Urceolaria* may perhaps properly be regarded as representing its real centre. While taking hold of *Lecanora,* on the one hand, this genus almost touches *Gyalecta,* on the other; and, not to speak of the obvious bearing, in the latter direction, of *Urceolaria actinostoma,* it is observable that *U. Valenzueliana,* Mont., is without doubt a *Gyalecta;* as *U. scruposa, bryophila* took finally the same position with Acharius. And, once more, *Urceolaria* comes exceedingly near to *Thelotrema;* and, with the latter, offers the same tendency to pass into compound conditions, which, anticipated by a pregnant instance, already cited, in *Lecanora,* has found its full expression in *Pertusaria.*

From *Urceolaria* diverges then, on this side, *Thelotrema,* in the same series; and, on that, *Gyalecta.* And at each extreme of the group, we find the similar and correspondent sub-types, — *Conotrema,* and *Gyrostomum;* wherein Parmeliaceous character all but disappears.

XXXI.—CONOTREMA, Tuckerm.

Tuckerm. Syn. N. Eng. p. 86. Koerb. Parerg. p. 105. Th. Fr. Gen. p. 75.
Stizenb. Beitr. l. c. p. 158. Lecideæ sp., Ach. L. U. p. 671 ; Syn. p. 27.
Lecideæ sect., Nyl. Enum. Gén. p. 127; Add. nov. ad Lich. Eur. in Flora,
1867, p. 329.

Apothecia urceolata, truncato-conoidea, subinde patellato-aperta,
excipulo proprio atro ; thallino tenui, evanido. Sporæ cylindraceæ,
pluriloculares, incolores. Spermatia haud visa. Thallus crustaceus,
uniformis.

C. urceolatum, originally found by Swartz, and by Muhlenberg in Pennsylvania, but equally common in New England and Virginia, extending
southward indeed (in the mountains) to South Carolina (Mr. Ravenel)
and ascertained recently to occur also in Germany (Koerber, l. c.) is the
only species known to me ; but Dr. Nylander describes his *Lecidea homalotropa* (Nyl. *Add. ad Lich. Eur. l. supra c.*) as of the same type with,
and yet specifically distinct from *C. urceolatum.* The apothecia of the
latter become finally somewhat explanate, and patellæform. Spores of
the American lichen long-cylindraceous, 30–40–locular, and reaching the
length of 0,160ᵐᵐ· Whatever the external resemblance of *Conotrema* to
Gyrostomum, Fr., — and the former was closely associated with the latter
by Acharius, and doubtfully by Fries (*S. O. V.*) their spores separate the
two plants obviously and widely.

It is only as an extreme member of the present sub-family, — itself, in
not a few other instances, on the verge of exclusion from the tribe — that
the type before us can be associated with *Parmeliacei.* There is yet a
certain degree of resemblance in *Conotrema* to Urceolareine types, as
perhaps especially to *Gyalecta ;* and, with one important exception, the
lichen has been placed, by the more recent writers who have considered
it, in proximity either to *Thelotrema*, or to *Gyalecta.* It is not so easy to
follow Nylander in making it an appendix to his *Lecidea ;* especially as
he does not hesitate to associate the very similarly aberrant *Gyrostomum*,
Fr., with *Thelotrema.* But *Gyrostomum* looks away from the present
family rather in the direction of certain *Graphidacei ;* it is interesting
therefore that the learned writer just cited has more recently suggested,
in view of the European lichen described by him as *Lecidea homalotropa*,
that this, together with *Conotrema urceolatum*, from which the first is
said to differ particularly in its flat apothecia ('*præcipue apotheciis
planis*') may possibly be better referable to *Melaspilea*, Nyl. The latter
was indeed first published nine years after the publication of *Conotrema ;*
but it appears certainly difficult to detect any especially noteworthy
resemblances between the lichens named which are not sufficiently coun-
terbalanced by the discrepancy in their spores.

17

XXXII.—DIRINA, Fr., Massal.

Fr. S. O. V. p. 244; L. E. p. 193, addita et Parm. sp., p. 177. Mass. Sui Gen. Dirin. &c. Koerb. Syst. p. 154. Nyl. Prodr. p. 97; Énum. Gén. p. 116. Th. Fr. Gen. p. 67. Lecanoræ sp., Ach. L. U. p. 361. Dirina, et Urceolariæ sp., Schær. Enum. p. 92. Secoligæ sp., Norm. Con. p. 18, t. 1, f. 9, b. Lecaniæ sect., Stizenb. Beitr. l. c. p. 170.

Apothecia scutellæformia, hypothecio corneo, nigro. Sporæ fusiformes, quadriloculares, incolores. Spermatia acicularia, arcuata; sterigmatibus simplicibus. Thallus crustaceus, uniformis.

Lecania, Massal., differs from *Lecanora* proper in nothing but the spores; which yet express only a different degree of evolution of the same type. But *Dirina* is remarkably distinguished by its black, horny hypothecium (*excip. proprium*, Fr. *S. O. V.*) not however extending upwards into a margin. It is true that in some tropical *Lecanoræ* (*L. granifera*, Ach., placed by him next to *L. Ceratoniæ; L. mesoxantha*, Nyl.; and *L. subfusca* v. *melanocardia*, Tuckerm. in *Lich. Cub.* n. 117, which perhaps is *L. endophæa*, Nyl.)—all referable to the *subfusca*-group, the spermatia of which accord with those of *Dirina*—we have also a similarly discoloured hypothecium; but there is something distinguishing in the habit of the type before us. It reminds us, as Fries has remarked, at once of *Pertusaria* and *Urceolaria;* and the place assigned to it by Nylander is exactly between these genera. Nor is *Dirina* without relations, sometimes proving difficult, to Graphidaceous types. A condition of *D. Ceratoniæ* is not a little suggestive of *Chiodecton myrticola;* and was referred to *Chiodecton* by Fée. And *Platygrapha*, Nyl., approaches even closely to the Lecanorine group before us. This is apparent in *P. dirinea*, Nyl., to which this author, above all others competent in the case, has referred *Dirina multiformis*, Mont. & V. d. Bosch (*Herb. Jungh.!*) and perhaps even more remarkably in *Platygrapha Californica*, Nyl., described as a *Dirina* by the present writer (Lich. Calif. p. 17).

Beside the two European forms or species, the genus is represented by a species from Chili; and another from the Cape of Good Hope (Nyl. *Enum. Gén.*). It has not yet occurred nearer to the North American continent than the Sandwich Islands, where a small form of *D. repanda* was found, on volcanic rocks, by H. Mann.

XXXIII.—GYALECTA (Ach.) Anz.

Anzi Catal. Lich. Sondr. p. 62, addita Biatorinæ sp., p. 73; Manip. p. 146; Symb. p. 11; Neosymb. p. 8. Gyalectæ sp., Lecanoræ sp., et Lecideæ spp., Ach. Syn. Gyalecta max. p., Parmeliæ sp., et Biatoræ spp., Fr. L. E. pp. 134, 194, 261, 264. Gyalecta, Phialopsis, Petractis, Secoliga,

Biatorinæ spp., et Sagiolechia, Mass. opp. varr. Koerb. Syst. ; Parerg.
Gyalecta, Patellaria pr. p., et Biatoræ spp., Naeg. et Hepp in Hepp
Flecht. Eur. t. 1, &c. Lecideæ sect. 1, A, B max. p., c. sp., et sect. 2,
k, sp., Nyl. Lich. Scand. pp. 108, 207, 240. Gyalecta, Petractis, Pachy-
phiale, Biatorinæ spp., Sagiolechia, et Rhexophiale, Th. Fr. Lich. Arct. ;
Gen. Gyalecta, Secoliga max p., Ramonia, et Lecaniæ sect., Stizenb.
Beitr. Gyalecta, Lecaniæ sect., et Patellariæ spp., Müll. Principes de
Classif.

Apothecia urceolato-biatorina, margine ·subcrenulato ; excipulo
proprio colorato (rarius nigro) connivente, l. dein explanato, a thallino lecanorino l. incompleto plus minus marginato. Sporæ ex
ovoideo-ellipsoideo fusiformes vel aciculares, bi-quadri-pluriloculares, loculis rarius irregulariter l. nunc muriformi-divisis. Thallus
crustaceus, uniformis.

G. rubra (Hoffm.) Mass., is an undoubted lecanorine lichen, the affinity of which to *G. carneo-lutea* was indicated by Turner (Linn. Trans. 9,
p. 145) and allowed by Fries, — and to *G. exanthematica* (which Turner
had also intimated) as well as to *G. foveolaris*, &c., by Massalongo (*Ric.*
p. 146). The last-named species has been especially illustrated by Dr.
Th. Fries (*Lich. Arct.* p. 138) and his excellent specimens leave little
reason to question the correctness of his conclusion that there is no real
difference in type between it and *G. rubra*. Neither of these well-marked
species has yet been detected in North America. Nor have any of the
interesting forms inhabiting calcareous rocks in Europe, excepting only
G. cupularis, occurred here, where the calcareous Lichen-flora has yet to
be explored : and we possess therefore no fully sufficient means of reaching an opinion on the position of *G. epulotica*, Ach., and *G. Prevostii*, Fr.,
which Nylander continues to refer to his (section) Gyalecta, but Koerber,
and others, to the Eulecanoreine *Aspicilia* and *Hymenelia ;* with the
former of which last-named groups the graniticoline *G. odora*, Ach., is
perhaps with less difficulty associable. It appears still likely that species
occur with constantly simple spores ; and such (as, for instance *G. epulotica* and *G. Prevostii*) may well approach conditions of *Lecanora* sect.
Aspicilia, or express better (as *Pinacisca similis*, Mass.) the Gyalectine
type.

The bilocular gradation is sufficiently well expressed in *G. Valenzueliana* (Mont.) Tuckerm. (*G. asteria*, Tuck. *Obs. Lich.*, and in Wright
Lich. Cub. n. 173) and less satisfactorily in the biatoroid *G. lutea* (Dicks.)
and *G. Pineti* (Schrad.). The remaining species, for the most part,
exhibit the oblong or fusiform type, becoming acicular in *G. acicularis*,
Anz., as in *G. cornea* (*Biat. carneola*, Fr.) and also appear fully referable
to the colourless series. From this however the ultimate internal structure of the (equally colourless) spores of *G. cupularis*, *G. abstrusa*, and

several others, distinctly diverges, exhibiting the characteristical differentiation of the brown spore; and *Gyalecta* must be admitted, and is admitted, and by authors elsewhere sufficiently disposed to insist on the value of such differences, to possess by no means a satisfactory spore-character. But *Thelotrema*, viewed in its whole extent, furnishes an instructive example of a similar confusion of types, on a much larger scale; and the manifest difficulties in the way of dividing this large genus from the point of view of the spores, may well influence our construction of the smaller assemblage before us.

The spores of *Gyalecta* tend now to an excess of number in the thekes, of which *G. Valenzueliana*, above noticed, *G. nana*, Tuckerm. *Obs. Lich.* l. c. 5, p. 415, and *G. corticola* (*Pachyphiale*, Lönnr.) are instances. But the last, in the European (Koerb. *Parerg.* p. 112) as well as the American specimens (*G. ceratina*, Tuckerm. l. c., *fide* Nyl. in *Bot. Zeit.*) reverts towards if it does not reach the normal number.

The thallus is well exhibited in *G. Valenzueliana ;* but in other corticoline species, as *G. abstrusa* (Wallr.) Arn., *G. cornea* (Sm.) *G. corticola* (Lönnr.) &c., it finally disappears, and nothing remains but general affinity to connect the at length biatorine apothecia with the present genus or family. With the just-named biatoroid expressions of *Gyalecta*, I follow Nylander in considering *G. lutea* (Dicks.) and *G. pineti* (Schrad.) as properly associable.

The denigration of the proper exciple appears an insufficient reason for excluding any lichen from the present sub-family which may otherwise be referable to it; and instances of the sort are far enough from uncommon. Among these we may reckon here the very curious *G. rhexoblephara* (*Lecidea*, Nyl. *Rhexophiale coronata*, Th. Fr. *Secoliga* sect. *Sagiolechia*, Stizenb.) appearing indeed, at first sight, to have little to do with *Gyalecta*, even in the largest view of the genus. Examined however more attentively, the peculiarities of the plant will be found possibly more explainable from the point of view of Gyalectine types, than from any other; if its position be not in fact determined by that of *G. protuberans* (Ach.) Anz. (Schær. *Helv.* n. 203. *Herb.* Krempelh.) in which the exciple is not originally, or truly carbonaceous. Young apothecia of *G. rhexoblephara* are often similar to those of *G. exanthematica*, except in colour. Those of *G. protuberans* are distantly comparable with *G. leucaspis*, Krempelh.!; but they rather resemble those of *G. lecideoides*, Massal. (*Herb.* Th. Fr.) as is remarked also by Koerber (*Parerg.* p. 109).

These blackened gyalectine types are especially interesting as illustrations of the near affinity of the present genus to *Urceolaria*, which approaches it in several recedent forms, as particularly in *U. actinostoma ;* while *Gyalecta* imperfectly anticipates, in like manner, in instances already considered, (of which *G. lecideoides* is one) the Urceolariine spore. And it is worth adding that the same radious wrinkling, observable so commonly in the margin of the gyalectine exciple, and deepening into clefts in *G. carneo-lutea*, *G. exanthematica*, and finally in *G. protuberans* and *G. rhexoblephara*, is far from strange to *Urceolaria ;* which exhibits a now deeply-cleft, though finally, as in other species, obtuse margin in *U. chloroleuca* of the present writer (Wright *Lich. Cub.* n. 123).

The range of *Gyalecta* is decidedly northern. Of the twenty-five described species, four-fifths are European. *G. lutea* extends into, and is common in the tropical countries, where *G. pineti* also occurs, at least in Cuba; and several species are peculiar to these regions. It is perhaps not surprising that Lichens generally so minute, should have in great measure escaped attention here; but a very considerable part of the European forms are but recent acquisitions.——*G. lutea* (Dicks.) Tuckerm. Lich. Hawai., is not rare in New England, and southward I have it from Alabama (Mr. Beaumont). It extends also to the tropics (Wright *Lich. Cub.* n. 177).——*G. pineti* (Schrad.) less observable, has occurred in Vermont (Mr. Frost) in Massachusetts (Mr. Willey) in New York (Herb. Ravenel) and in New Jersey (Mr. Austin).——*G. absconsa*, Tuckerm. *Obs. Lich.* l. c., is only known as yet from South Carolina (Mr. Ravenel).——*G. corticola* (Lönnr.) (*Secoliga fagicola*, Hepp in Koerb. *Parerg.*, *G. ceratina*, Tuckerm. l. c.) exceedingly like *G. cornea* (*Biat. carneola*, Auctt.) but at once distinguished by the spores, is probably not uncommon, but most easily escapes notice. It has occurred as yet only at Amherst, on Elm and Ash (Myself) and at Weymouth, on Red Cedar (Mr. Willey).——*G. Flotovii*, Koerb., also well distinguished by the spores, and found in Amherst, on Elm, is probably not rare, but overlooked.—— The arctic *G. rhexoblephara* (Nyl.) discovered, by J. Vahl, in Greenland (Th. Fr. *Lich. Arct.* p. 205) was found also, in islands of Behring's Straits, by Mr. Wright.

XXXIV.—URCEOLARIA, (Ach.) Flot.

Flot. Lich. Sil. cit. Th. Fr. Nyl. Prodr. p. 95; Lich. Scand. p. 176. Stizenb. Beitr. l. c. p. 168. Parmelia sect. Urceolaria (*P. lepad. excl.*) Fr. L. E. p. 190. Urceolariæ spp., Gyalectæ sp., et Verrucariæ sp., Ach. L. U. pp. 51, 74 ; Syn. p. 10. Diploschistes, Norm. Con. p. 20. Urceolaria max. p., et Limboria (saltem pr. p.) Mass. Ric. pp. 33, 155. Urceolaria, et Limboria (saltem p. p.) Koerb. Syst. pp. 168, 376.

Structuram exposuit Tulasne, Mèm. sur les Lich. p. 155, t. 4, f. 1–14, 5, f. 1–4.

Apothecia urceolato-scutellæformia; excipulo proprio atro connivente, dein sæpius explanato, discum nigrum margine, a thallino lecanorino (rarissime obsoleto) demum discreto, cingente. Sporæ ovoideo-ellipsoideæ, muriformi-pluriloculares, fuscæ. Spermatia oblonga l. bacillaria; sterigmatibus sub-simplicibus. Thallus crustaceus, uniformis.

The importance of this group is not to be measured by its size. While evidently Lecanorine, as respects the principal species, it may be said to take hold of both *Gyalecta* and *Thelotrema;* and thus to harmonize otherwise discordant, Biatoroid, and even Verrucariæform conditions with the Parmeliaceous type. Nor are its relations to *Pertusaria* entirely without significance; the fruit of *Urceolaria* tending readily to become compound, when it is not difficult to select samples (at least in the condition of *U. cinereo-cæsia* published in Wright *Lich. Cub.* n. 161) not distantly suggesting that of the genus first-named. If we consider the best known forms, we find the first (*U. ocellata*) receding towards *Lecanora,*—the finally inflexed, but more often obscure margin of the proper exciple being coloured like the thallus. The second (*U. scruposa*) offers at once the type of the group, and its point of nearest affinity to *Thelotrema;* and both thalline and proper exciple play an important part in its history. While in the third (*U. actinostoma*) the proper exciple constitutes the apothecium, and remaining closed (Koerber's remarks on his *U. clausa, Parerg.* p. 105, should be compared here) the lichen looks not unlike a *Gyalecta,* and differs in fact but little from some species of that genus, even in character. When the proper exciple of *Thelotrema* blackens, there may remain little but the often evanescent veil to distinguish it from *Urceolaria;* and *T. Santense,* Tuck. *Obs. Lich.* l. c. 5, p. 406, is a conspicuous example, of which *T. compunctum,* Nyl. (*Urceolaria,* Ach.) and with little doubt *Urceolaria thelotremoides,* Mass. *Ric.* p. 35, furnish others, of such Urceolariiform species. Massalongo says indeed of the last-named, that the species of *Urceolaria* proper differ from it in no single generical character; which may be true, without our being able to take a tropical bark-lichen out of its own series of affinities, and refer it to a northern, saxicoline group.

As the centre of a sub-family especially conditioned by the spores, it should not surprise us to find in *Urceolaria* something looking towards an explanation of the discrepancies from the prevailing spore-type, occurring in some more recedent members of the group. I venture to think that the development of the *Urceolaria*-spore, taken in its full extent (as from colourless, and bi-quadrilocular, it becomes muriform-plurilocular, and brown) is thus instructive, in the case of *Gyalecta.* And it is certainly suggestive, as respects *Thelotrema,* that the multiform differentiation of the spores of this genus is conceivable, at least in its larger features, as a varied exhibition, in detail, of the progressive changes in the evolution of the Urceolariine type.

The five or six described species are all saxicoline or terricoline, and mainly northern. *U. scruposa* passes indeed southward to Polynesia (Nyl. *Enum. Gén.*) and is very nearly akin to one of the two tropical forms (*U. cinereo-cæsia,* Ach.) if indeed the latter (as compare Nyl. in *Prodr. Fl. N. Gran.* p. 35) be really distinguishable from it. Of the best-determined, European conditions, all are found here except *U. ocel-*

lata. U. scruposa is common throughout the country, on granitic rocks and on the earth, from New England to New Mexico (Mr. Fendler) recurs in its calcareous conditions in Nebraska (Dr. Hayden) and is especially fine, in terricoline states, in California (Mr. Bolander). The curious form of the same species in which its apothecia occupy parasitically the thallus of *Cladoniæ* (v. *parasitica*, Sommerf. *Lapp.* p. 100. Nyl. *Scand.* p. 177) is also found here (Rhode Island, Mr. J. L. Bennett) and particularly fine specimens have been sent from California (Mr. Bolander).——*U. actinostoma*, Pers., is as yet very rare; having only occurred at Weathersfield, Connecticut (Mr. Wright) at Aiken, South Carolina (Mr. Ravenel) and (on lime-rocks) in Kansas (Mr. E. Hall).

XXXV.—THELOTREMA, (Ach.) Eschw.

Eschw. Syst. p. 15, et Lich. Brasil. 1. c. p. 172. Fr. S. O. V. p. 269, et L. E. p. 427. Nyl. Enum. Gén. 1. c. p. 117; Lich. exot. 1. c.; Prodr. Fl. N. Gran. p. 40; Syn. Lich. N. Caled. p. 32; et Ascidium, Ejusd., ll. cc. Tuckerm. Obs. Lich. 1. c. 5, p. 405; 6, p. 269; Lich. Hawai. 1. c. p. 227. Volvaria (Gyrostomo excl.) et Thelotrema, Stizenb. Beitr. 1. c. p. 168. Thelotrema pr. p., Ascidium, et Myriotrema, Fée Ess. pp. 41, 49; Suppl. p. 88. Thelotrema, Ascidium, et Leptotrema, Mont. Pl. Cell. Cub. p. 163, t. 8, f. 2; Crypt. Guy. p. 55, t. 16, f. 4; Syll. p. 362–4. Volvaria, Thelotrematis spp., Ascidium, Ectolechia, Myriotrema, Coscinedia, Brassia, Antrocarpon, & (?) Mass. Ric. p. 141; Alcun. gen. p. 10; Miscell. p. 38; Esam. comp. p. 12, &c.

Apothecia urceolata, e verrucæformi scutellato-aperta, disco velato; excipulo proprio varie colorato margine sublacero cum thallino concreto. Sporæ ex ellipsoideo oblongæ, bi-pluriloculares, l. demum muriformi-multiloculares, fuscæ l. decolores. Spermatia fere incognita. Thallus crustaceus, uniformis.

T. lepadinum, Ach., the species first indicated (Ach. *L. U.*) as distinct from *Pertusaria*, and attaining to its perfection in the northern hemisphere, may perhaps still be regarded as the type of the now widely expanded genus; and the character remain as it was conceived by Acharius (*Syn.*) Eschweiler, and Fries. In this species the excipular envelopes are in fact triple; and there is no doubt of its sufficient distinction from *Urceolaria*. But the innermost of these envelopes (*velum* Eschw.; *excipulum interius*, Fr.) tends manifestly to abortion; and little reliance can be put upon it, in its proper form at least, in the tropical groups. It recurs indeed here, and sometimes very elegantly expressed, as in *T. platycarpum, Obs. Lich.*; but this species is closely associable in every other respect with *T. leucastrum*, of the same memoir, in which it is deficient. The resemblance of such abortive conditions, in which moreover the proper exciple not seldom blackens, to the immediately preceding genus, is not however enough to obscure for a moment the natural distinctness of the two groups. If *Urceolaria* be in fact a modification of the Lecanorine form of the Parmeliaceous apothecium, *Thelotrema* is as clearly an anticipation of the Verrucariaceous; and though receding to dilated, and even scutellate conditions, these scarcely approach the perfection of the former, except as they depart from their own distinct centre. Imperfectly scutellæform states of *Thelotrema* are sufficiently numerous, and afford interesting indications of what is now generally acknowledged as its proper affinity; but the Verrucariaceous expression of the other line of divergence from *T. lepadinum*—marked especially in *Ascidium*, Fée (called by Montagne a monocarpous *Trypethelium*) as well as in the closely akin *T. depressum*, Mont., and disappearing at length in immersed forms (*Myriotrema*, Fée, *Leptotrema*, Mont.) now curiously suggestive of *Endocarpon*—is significant, and may well at first appear the more so.

The weight of the evidence appears yet to sustain the conclusion of Eschweiler, that notwithstanding the presence of an inner hypothecial layer, the value of which this author perhaps understates in the present genus, as he ignores its existence in the *Verrucariacei*, and, still further, the imperfectness and inconstancy of the proper exciple (*perithecium annulare*, Eschw.) it is indeed this last, explained from the point of view of the now blackening lecanorine hypothecium (called by Eschweiler, in *Urceolaria*, *perith. subcupulare*, *Syst.* f. 12, 17) and taken in connection with the structure of the thalamium, which determines, and as Lecanoreine, the position of *Thelotrema*.

But this Thelotrematous modification of the hypothecium of *Urceolaria* is often obscure, and at length obsolete; when the inner exciple, or accessory hypothecium, enclosed now in what appears a merely thalline receptacle (as in Leight. Brit. Ang. Lich. t. 12, f. 1, 2) may so simulate a really better exhibition of the Lecanoreine type than is predicable of the genus, that the whole structure shall appear at sight as referable to *Gyalecta* as *Thelotrema*; or, all excipular relation even of the thallus disappearing, may come at length (as in *T. compunctum*, *T. Wightii*, &c.) to constitute the apothecium. Such simple apothecia are readily taken (as by the present writer, in observations on *T. simplex*, *Obs. Lich.* l. c. 6, p. 271) for exhibitions of the proper exciple, and have probably elsewhere been described as such ('*margo proprius*') by authors; but this proper exciple, the representative of the lecanorine hypothecium, must be said, from our present point of view, to be in fact wanting in such forms.

The inner exciple, or veil, is itself, as has been remarked already, very often abortive, or obscure; but its place is taken, in numerous tropical species, by a remarkable crustaceous covering of the disk, saluted not seldom by the same name. This, which is well marked in *T. actinotum* (*Obs. Lich.* l. c. 5, p. 411) and *T. Wrightii* (of the same memoir) appears, if compared with *T. auratum* (described at the same place) to illustrate the *nisus* of the proper exciple (constituting here the inner wall of the exterior exciple) to become compound; and the processes which make it up are exactly comparable, if I do not mistake, with the similar ones in compound fruits of *Urceolaria scruposa* (Fr. *Lich. Suec.* n. 282) and in those tending to become compound of *U. ocellata* (Rabenh. *Lich. Eur.* n. 122). Other compound conditions looking rather towards *Pertusaria*, are described by Montagne (*Crypt. Cub.* p. 167. *Crypt. Guy.* p. 55) and in the present writer's *Obs. Lich.* l. c. 5, p. 408, 411.

Ascidium, Fée *Ess.* p. 42, 96, is distinguished by no generical difference from *Thelotrema depressum*, Mont. (Wright *Lich. Cub.* n. 165, *determ. Nyl.*) beyond the peculiar thickening of the often conspicuous but finally even obsolete thalline exciple, and the inferior *grade* of evolution of the spores; and I incline, with Dr. Stizenberger (*Beitr.* l. c.) and in agreement with Nylander's earlier judgment (*Enum. Gén.* l. c. p. 118) to consider it not well separable. Montagne's view of the thickened thalline exciple of *Ascidium*, as if constituting a *stroma*, and of the generical type, as if conceivable as a 'monocarpous *Trypethelium*' (*Crypt. Guy.* p. 57) was influenced, we cannot doubt, by what he regarded the predominant Verrucariaceous affinity of the former, as of *Thelotrema:* but Nylander also (in *Prodr. Fl. N. Gran.* p. 50, note) keeps the two types distinct, even though he at the same time refers *Thelotrema depressum* to *Ascidium.*

It has been remarked already of the spores of *Urceolaria*, that they suggest, in the successive changes of their evolution, the varied differentiation of the present genus. We find here, — in *T. lepadinum* — the perfect expression of the coloured type, and, associable with this species externally more or less, a variety of forms, the spores of which, though now, in themselves considered, referable to the colourless series, are yet also well comparable with the *earlier* conditions of the coloured, as abundantly exemplified in *Urceolaria*, *Graphis*, & *cætt.* And the possible inference is that lichens otherwise associable, are not to be dissociated because some of the species offer only earlier gradations of the perfect sporetype indicated by others; and that such natural genera as the present may still be kept together.

Nor are we without positive evidence looking in the same direction. Colour is indeed often deficient in what should be coloured spores; but instead we may find approximations, in the spore-cells, to parenchymatous complexity. And where the last clew is wanting, indications of colour often appear. The little group separated by Fée as *Myriotrema* seems at first possibly almost distinct; but it is interesting in this connexion, that *T. glauculum*, Nyl., though referred to the section expressed by *Myriotrema*, is yet compared by him, than whom no one has more extensively illustrated the genus, with the brown-spored *T. compunctum* (*Prodr. Fl. N. Gran.* p. 47, note). With this last the other curiously agrees in

18

its external characters; while *T. clandestinum*, Fée, and *T. catastictum* of the present writer (*Obs. Lich.* l. c. 6, p. 270) suggest not improbably a mediation of the difference in the spores. *Leptotrema*, Mont. & V. d. Bosch. in M. *Syll.* p. 363 (*Thelotr. Prevostianum*, M. in *Ann.*) is, in this view, far less remote from *Myriotrema*, Fée, than was supposed; and the passage from colourless spores with entire spore-cells, to brown spores with at length murally divided spore-cells, takes place imperceptibly in one and the same series of most intimately related forms.

In all from seventy-five to eighty species of *Thelotrema*, almost the whole from intertropical countries, have been indicated; the credit for by far the larger part being due to the labours of Nylander. A single well marked species (*T. lepadinum*) is common to Europe and North America, but extends also within the tropics, and appears again (Nyl. *Consp. Gen. Thelotr.*) in austral regions. Several are only known as yet in the southern parts of the United States; where another occurs (*T. subtile*) reaching northward to New England, and found also, according to Nylander, in tropical Australia.

T. lepadinum has only once occurred to me (on Birch) in the northern States, but is found in Arctic America (Hook. in Rich. Append. Frankl. Narr. p. 760) and in Oregon (*Herb.* Hook.). Southward it becomes more common (South Carolina, Mr. Ravenel; Louisiana, Hale; Texas, Mr. Wright) but the apothecia are smaller.——We have however another northern species in *T. subtile*, Tuck. Suppl. 1, l. c. p. 426, described later by Nylander (*Exp. Lich. N. Caled.*) under another name, which, found originally in Vermont (Mr. Frost) and the year after by myself in Virginia, has also since proved to extend far southward. It is to these southern and at length semi-tropical regions that we are yet to look for the full exhibition of *Thelotrema*, as a North American genus. From the neighbouring island of Cuba, Mr. Wright has sent from thirty-five to forty species, and the number will probably be increased. A few of these are already known to occur within our limits. *T. granulosum*, Tuckerm. Suppl. 1, l. c. p. 426, was found on Bald Cypress, in Louisiana (Hale). ——*T. cavatum* (Ach.) Nyl., a common tropical species, has recently been detected, on trunks, in Southern Texas (Mr. Ravenel).——*T. Domingense* (Fée *herb.*, *sub Ascidio.* Nyl.) occurs in Mississippi (Dr. Veitch) and has lately been found in South Carolina (Dr. Mellichamp). From this scarcely differs, except in the rose colour of the interior of the thalline exciple, *Ascidium rhodostroma*, Mont. *Guy.* l. c. (compare Nyl. in *Prodr. Fl. N. Gran.* l. c.) to which may be referred specimens, finally, it is to be remarked, shewing no trace of the coloration in question, from Louisiana (Hale).——*T. monosporum*, Nyl. (*N. Gran.* l. c., *Syn. N. Caled.* p. 38) as determined by himself, is another discovery, on Bald Cypress, in Louisiana, of the lamented Hale; and a form in which the apothecia are scarcely at all protuberant above the thallus, was collected in southern Texas by Mr. Ravenel.——That the great tropical assemblages, *Thelo-*

trema and *Graphis* should offer some, perhaps difficult, points of contact, will surprise no lichenist familiar with these exceedingly varied genera ; and such species as *Graphis reniformis*, Nyl. (Lindig *Herb. N. Gran.* n. 2651, &c.,) and *Thelotrema lirelliforme* and *T. leiostomum* of the present writer (Wright *Lich. Cub.* n. 149, 150) in some at least of their forms, may be said to suggest, if they are not examples of, such approximation. But I shall venture to go farther. *T. leucastrum*, Tuckerm. *Obs. Lich.* 1. c. 6, p. 269 (Wright *Lich. Cub.* n. 158) is not to be denied affinity of a very close kind to *T. platycarpoides* of the same memoir (*Lich. Cub.* n. 157) and to *T. platycarpum* (*Lich. Cub.* n. 139) of an earlier. And in this case, and in view especially of such forms as *T. leucastrum*, v. *difforme* (*Lich. Cub.* n. 159) not to speak of such as *T. schizostomum* of the same memoir (*Lich. Cub.* n. 138) and *T. chionostomum*, Nyl. (Cuba, Wright) it is for me impossible to exclude from the same generical affinity, several species now referred, and by very high authority, to *Graphis*. Among these, — which include also *T. syngraphizans* (Nyl. *sub Graphide, in litt.*) from the Bonin Islands (Wright) comparable at once with *T. lirelliforme* and *T. leucastrum*, but nearest to the former, and *T. albo-rosellum* (Nyl. *sub Graphide*, in *Prodr. N. Gran.* p. 87. Lindig Herb. n. 2694) suggesting, from every point of view, a comparison with *Thelotrema platycarpum* and its nearest allies, — is here to be named *T. leprocarpum* (Nyl. *sub Graphide*, in *Prodr. Fl. N. Gran.* p. 85, note) from Bald Cypress, Louisiana (Hale). This last has the habit of the *Graphis* above cited, and of the *Thelotrema*-group with which it was compared, as also of *T. schizostomum;* but differs from all these in its large, muriform spores.——
T. Auberianum, Mont., the centre of a group of varying conditions illustrated in part by the writer in Wright *Lich. Cub.* n. 145-148, has been sent to me from Florida.——*T. Santense*, Tuckerm. *Obs. Lich.* 1. c. 5; p. 406, remarkable as well for the isidioid branchlets, into which its thallus tends most readily to pass, as for its large, urceolariæform apothecia, was discovered, on Elm, in South Carolina (Mr. Ravenel) and has since occurred only in Alabama (Mr. Beaumont).——*T. glaucescens*, Nyl. in *Prodr. Fl. N. Gran.* p. 47, note) is a small species of the same near affinity with the last, and very close to *T. compunctum* (Ach.) Nyl. (Wright *Lich. Cub.* n. 152). It has been found in South Carolina (Mr. Ravenel) Southern Alabama (Mr. Beaumont) and Louisiana (Hale).——
T. Ravenelii, Tuckerm. emend. (Nyl. in *Prodr. Fl. N. Gran.* p. 50, note) occurring in South Carolina (Mr. Ravenel) and Alabama (Mr. Peters) is distinguishable from the next following species by the absence of the scattered, scarlet granules within the crust, as by the more open and better margined apothecia, but scarcely by the spores ; and its rank is uncertain.——*T. Wightii*, Nyl. *Endocarpon*, Tayl. *Thel. Ravenelii*, Tuckerm. Suppl. 1, 1. c. p. 426, *pro p.*) inhabits the whole low country of the South, from South Carolina (Mr. Ravenel) to Texas (Ravenel).

XXXVI.—GYROSTOMUM, Fr.

Fr. S. O. V. p. 268. Nyl. in Prodr. Fl. N. Gran. p. 51; Syn. Lich. N. Caled.
p. 39. Gymnotrema, Nyl. Enum. Gén. l. c. p. 119. Thelotrematis? sp.,
Fée Ess. p. 95. Mont. Guy. p. 55. Volvariæ sp., Stizenb. Beitr. l. c.
p. 168. Lecideæ sp., Ach. Syn. p. 27.

Apothecia ex urceolato explanata, orbicularia l. elongato-diffor-
mia; excipulo proprio atro, margine integro; thallino demum disparente. Sporæ ellipsoideæ, muriformi-pluriloculares, fuscescentes.
Spermatia haud visa. Thallus crustaceus, uniformis.

G. scyphuliferum (Ach.) Fr., the type of the genus, remains the only
species; and presents a (supposed) modification of the Urceolarieine pat-
tern approaching, perhaps too closely, to some modifications of *Graphis.*

With this singularly aberrant exhibition of the final degradation of
the Parmeliaceous apothecium, occurring here in the low country of
South Carolina (Mr. Ravenel) in Florida (Mr. Beaumont) in Louisiana
(Hale) and in southern Texas (Mr. Ravenel) the reckoning of the members
of the present tribe is completed.

APPENDIX.

MYRIANGIUM, Mont. & Berk.

Mont. & Berk. in Hook. Lond. Journ. Bot. 4, p. 72. Mont. Pl. Cell. cent.
6, in Ann. Sci. Nat. 3, 10, p. 245; Syll. p. 380. Mass. Symm. p. 97.
Nyl. Prodr. p. 27; Syn. 1, p. 139; in Prodr. Fl. N. Gran. p. 4. Stizenb.
Beitr. l. c. p. 142.

Apothecia lecanoroidea, multilocularia, loculo singulo thecam
singulam fovente, paraphysibus nullis. Sporæ oblongo-ovoideæ,
sub-muriformes, incolores. Thallus frondoso-orbiculatus, friabilis,
totus cellulosus, ambitu plicato-striatus effiguratusve, absque
gonidiis.

Not even as the most abnormal type (' *le genre le plus anormal* ') does
it appear possible to agree with Montagne in associating this plant with
the *Collemei.* Admitting, in certain specimens, a resemblance in habit to
some *Omphalariæ*, as perhaps to *Thyrea Notarisii*, Mass. *Lich. Ital.*
n. 174, what we have here before us is a cryptogam in which the very
element of structure upon which all the essential differences of *Collemei*
hang, is deficient. And the difficulties (Nyl. ll. cc.) are scarcely less in
finding a place for it among other Lichens. It is appended here there-

fore only because no more definite position, whether within, or, what is the rather to be anticipated, without the Class, has yet been determined. *M. Duriæi*, Mont. & Berk. in *Fl. Alg.*, the original species (Pyrenees, Montagne! Mass. *Lich. Ital.* n. 27! Rabenh. *Lich. Eur.* n. 635!) has been traced already to Algeria, to Australia, and South America (Brazil, Pabst! Lindig *Herb. N. Gran.* n. 2583, 2669, 2789!) and, reaching Cuba (Wright!) should be likely to appear also within our southern boundaries. And the plant (*M. Curtisii*, Mont. & Berk.) which does occur here, and extends northward along the coast (Carolina, Curtis, Ravenel; Alabama, T. M. Peters; Massachusetts, C. J. Sprague, H. Willey) though certainly noticeable, at least in its best conditions, for general luxuriance — the larger thallus becoming also effigurate, and the apothecia perhaps more perfectly lecanoroid — is by no means satisfactorily distinguished from the other. The 'striate-plicate' circumference found by Montagne in both his species, and re-affirmed by Massalongo of *M. Duriæi*, may in fact be considered as implying the at length certainly striking, but inconstant lobation of the North American *Myriangium;* and one of the New Granada forms of the older species (Lindig n. 2583) as determined by Nylander, is quite as distinctly effigurate as the Carolina plant.[1] The apothecia are similar in both, and similarly modified; and the supposed diversity in the thekes (Mont. *Syll.*) is far from characteristical. And this last remark applies also to the results obtained by Nylander (*Syn.*) from the specimens before him; neither the thekes of the Carolina plant, nor its spores differing, in a wide view, in any important respect, from those of *M. Duriæi*.[2]——The lobulate margin of the North American plant is at length quite free from the substrate, when the under side of the fringe is seen to be entirely similar in all respects, whether of configuration, colour, or smoothness, to the upper; an observation not perhaps wholly without bearing on the question of the affinity of *Myriangium*.

[1] It is, in this connection, observable, that both the species, as defined, are now recognized as European plants; — *M. Duriæi*, Millard, in *Mem. Soc. Sci. Nat. Strasb.*, being referred by Dr. Nylander (*Flora*, 1869, p. 298) to *M. Curtisii*.

[2] Very commonly roundish-ovoid, or 'ovate-ventricose' (Mass.) and not much exceeding 0,050mm. in their longest diameter, the thekes of *Myriangium* occur also oblong, or 'obovate-oblong'; and the latter condition was understood by Montagne to be characteristical of his *M. Curtisii*. But this exceptionally elongated state, which I have observed to measure 0,069–92mm. in length by 0,023–35mm. in width, is by no means confined to the North American specimens, or even more frequent in them. Spores of the Carolina plant averaging 0,025–35mm. in length by 0,007–11mm. in width.

Trib. II.—LECIDEACEI, Fr.

Apothecia libera, rotundata, patellæformia, aperta, dein et hemisphærica globosave cephaloidea; excipulo proprio; thallino normaliter nullo.

The important part filled by the thallus in the *Parmeliacei* is conspicuous also in the (at least ideally) always present thalline receptacle of the apothecium. But, in the present tribe — otherwise now sufficiently resembling *Lecanorei*, and now not ill comparable with *Usneei* — this thalline border is deficient; and the hymenium is bordered only by the proper exciple: a rule not invalidated by sundry exceptions (as *Bæomyces æruginosus, Buellia albo-atra,* &c.) in which the apothecium is conditioned also extraordinarily by the thallus. The two tribes differ then, to use an expression of Acharius (*Meth.* p. 32) ' *quantum patellulæ a scutellis discedant.*' And this originally patellæform type of fruit, characteristical of *Lecideei*, and often called *biatorine*, is predicable equally of *Stereocaulon* and *Cladonia;* which genera are scarcely in fact to be well separated from *Biatora*, but by the thallus.

There is really nothing to distinguish the crust of *Bæomycei* and *Lecideei* from that of *Lecanorei:* but the thalline evolution of *Cladoniei*, — combining as it does, especially in *Cladonia*, together with biatorine apothecia, both the horizontal and vertical types of thallus — is so remarkable, that we can hardly avoid allowing it an influence on our total estimate (as compare Fr. *S. O. V.* p. 247) of the tribal characters; whether or not, with Eschweiler (*Lich. Bras.* p. 240; followed herein by one or two others, as, according to Th. Fries, by Massalongo, and by the present writer in Syn. Lich. N. Eng.) we go so far as to regard it, in some sense, the highest expression of lichenose vegetation.

The position of *Cœnogonium* is uncertain: but the constitution of the thallus forbids its association with *Collemei;* while the apothecia are evidently biatorine. Is it possible then to conceive of it as occupying, in the present tribe, a position analogous to that of *Pannariei-Collemei* (to look at these for the moment as one) in *Parmeliacei?* *Cœnogonium* will in that case interrupt the natural contiguity of *Cladoniei* and *Lecideei;* but only as *Pannaria*, &c., interrupt that of *Parmelia* and *Lecanora.*

The tribe is a large one, and though much smaller, in the number of species, than the *Parmeliacei*, greatly exceeds this, in the colder and especially the arctic regions of the earth, in the number of individuals; *Cladonia* being as remarkable in this respect, as it is also for its variableness. "*Nulla certe vegetabilia*," Nylander remarks of this genus (*Syn.* 1, p. 188) "*copia majori et latius distributa inveniuntur.*"

Reckoning roughly those added since the publication of the estimates of Nylander (*Syn.*) the whole number of probable species of *Lecideacei*, as here taken, known to science, may be set down as not very far from about a third of the whole number of species of Lichens. In the spores the colourless type predominates, at least as largely as in *Parmeliacei*.

Fam. 1.—CLADONIEI (Zenk., Koerb.) Th. Fr.

Thallus duplex: horizontalis, squamulosus l. granulosus, nunc evanidus, et verticalis caulescens, dein suffruticulosus (podetia).

Considering, with Fries, the *Lecideacei* as a series of evolution running parallel with *Parmeliacei*, it is evident at once that the present family corresponds with the *Usneei* of the latter tribe. It is distinguished however by the remarkable character that the erect thallus of the *Cladoniei* springs from a horizontal one; which, whether with Koerber (*Syst.* p. 9) we attempt to distinguish it from the true thallus, as a certain development of the hypothallus (*protothallus*, Koerb.) or the rather assume that it corresponds, in all respects, with the thallus of the *Lecideei*, is equally interesting, in its relation to the other. This horizontal thallus, especially developed in *Cladonia*, is conspicuous also in *Pilophorus fibula*, and scarcely less so in *Stereocaulon condensatum*, and *S. cereolus ;* but disappears, or is even obsolete from the first, in the more fruticulose forms of all the genera.

In the line of analogy afforded by the spores, *Stereocaulon* answers more particularly to *Roccella*, of the *Usneei; Pilophorus* may be compared perhaps rather with *Usnea;* and *Cladonia,* with *Dactylina* and *Evernia.*

The *Cladoniei* constitute about one-fifth of the present Tribe.

XXXVII.—STEREOCAULON, Schreb.

Schreb. Gen. Pl. p. 768. Ach. L. U. p. 113. Fr. L. E. p. 200. Tuckerm. Syn. N. E. p. 44 (sect. 2 excl.) Mass. Mem. p. 74. Koerb. Syst. p. 10. Nyl. Prodr.; Syn. 1, p. 230, t. 7, f. 7–31. Th. Fr. Monogr. Ster. et Piloph. p. 9–67, & tabb. 1, f. 1–3, 2, 3, 4, f. 1 ; Beitr. z. Kenntn. der Cephalod., in Flora, 1866, p. 18. Stizenb. Beitr. l. c. p. 167. Patellariæ sect., Wallr. Fl. Crypt. Germ. 1, p. 438.

Structuram exposuerunt Tulasne, Mém. sur les Lich. pp. 26, 173 ; Schwendener, Untersuch. in Naeg. Beitr. 2, p. 173, t. 7, f. 10–11 ; Die Algentypen d. Flechtengonid. pp. 16, 27, 33.

Apothecia patellæformia, excipulo proprio, dein cephaloidea, solida. Sporæ fusiformes l. aciculares, 4-pluriloculares, incolores. Spermatia ex oblongo sæpius bacillaria l. acicularia; sterigmatibus

simplicibus. Thallus fruticulosus, erectus, solidus, squamulis gran-
ulisve, in ramulos corallinoideos nunc abeuntibus, plus minus
vestitus (podetia) horizontali granuloso 1. sæpius evanido.

This well marked natural genus might be supposed more distant from
Cladonia than it really is, were it not for the little group of curiously
intermediate lichens constituting *Pilophorus*, Th. Fr. The species of
Stereocaulon are especially mountain plants; and distributed, in such
situations, throughout the earth. About three quarters of the twenty
odd described species inhabit however the mountains of the intertropical
regions, and the centre of distribution may therefore well appear, as it
did to Fries (*S. O. V.* p. 248) whose remark is fully illustrated by the
monography of Dr. Th. Fries, as '*magis tropicum.*' All the well ascertained European species occur in North America, except, as yet, *S. nanum;*
and several others, found in Mexico, extend, it is possible, farther north.

Among those who have contributed to our knowledge of *Stereocaulon,*
Floerke, Fries, and Laurer should be especially named; these writers
having satisfactorily determined the important forms of the northern
hemisphere. The illustration of the less known, tropical species was left
for the more recent monography of Dr. Th. Fries; and the still later
revision of the genus given in the *Synopsis* of Dr. Nylander. This work
was the first to attempt a full exhibition of the still imperfectly understood ' *cephalodia* '; but most important additions have since been made
to our knowledge of these structures in the cited memoir (*Beitr. z. Kenntn.
d. Cephalodien*) of Dr. Fries.

S. ramulosum, Ach., the collective name of a group of tropical and
austral forms, which later writers have variously discriminated, is credited
by him to North America, as it is also by Muhlenberg (*Catal.* p. 106) and
may be what Dr. Fries (l. c. p. 30) has indicated, under his *S. argus,* as
sent to Swartz by Menzies. The group appears to be well represented
in Mexico, but no member of it is known to me as occurring within the
United States; nor was there any *Stereocaulon* in the collection of his
lichens with which the late Mr. Menzies favoured me.

S. sphærophoroides, Tuckerm. (Th. Fr. l. c. p. 44. Nyl. *Syn.* 1, p. 234)
an inhabitant of the Canary Islands, is cited by Nylander, l. c., on the
authority of the herbarium of Mr. Lenormand, as occurring also in
' Carolina'; a locality from which I have never received it.

S. nanodes, Tuckerm. Suppl. 2, l. c. p. 201 (Nyl. *Syn.* p. 251) is found
on rocks along water courses in the White Mountains. The granules in
this species become squamiform, and the tips of the branches assume
then an aspect often not a little suggestive of the extraordinary lichen
following.——*S.* (*sub-gen. Phyllocaulon*) *Wrightii,* Tuckerm. Suppl. 2, l.
c. p. 202, was found by Mr. Wright on an island of Behring's Straits; but
the apothecia are unknown. This plant is comparable also with the
equally sterile *S.? pulvinatum,* Ach., of the Cape of Good Hope (Drège

in *herb.* Sonder) which is placed by Nylander under *Siphula;* but is much more evidently related to the present genus.[1]

XXXVIII.—PILOPHORUS, Th. Fr.

Th. Fr. De Ster. et Piloph. Comment. (1857) p. 40; Monogr. Ster. & Piloph. p. 68, t. 4, f. 2–4. Cenomycis sp., Ach. L. U. p. 567; Syn. p. 275. Cladoniæ sp., Fr. L. E. p. 242. Stereocaulon sect. Pilophoron, Tuckerm. Syn. N. Eng. p. 46. Pilophoron, Tuckerm. Suppl. 1, l. c. p. 426 (May, 1858). Nyl. Syn. 1, p. 228, t. 7, f. 4, 5, 6. Stizenb. Beitr. l. c. p. 166.

Apothecia cephaloidea, solida. Sporæ ellipsoideæ, simplices, incolores. Spermatia bacillaria; sterigmatibus subsimplicibus. Thallus verticalis subsimplex, primitus solidus granulatus (podetia) horizontali granuloso-squamuloso.

The cephalodia associate this type with *Stereocaulon,* as does the whole aspect of the New England lichen (*P. fibula*) but the spores with *Cladonia;* and the form first observed (*P. acicularis* Ach.) is not ill-comparable with certain *Cladoniæ* of the scarlet-fruited section.

Three species have been described,—[1] *P. acicularis* (Ach.) Th. Fr., discovered by Menzies, his own ticket says, 'on stones and dead trees, frequent on the west coast of N. America, 1787–1788,' and since observed there by others; as according to Nylander, in Australia, and at the Cape of Good Hope;—[2] *P. fibula* (Tuck.) Th. Fr., on moist rocks, in the mountains of New England, and lately observed in the New York mountains (C. H. Peck) and —[3] *P. robustus,* Th. Fr. (*P. polycarpum,* Tuckerm. l. c.) from Norway (Th. Fr.) and islands of Behring's Straits (C. Wright).

According to recent observations of Dr. Fries (in *Flora,* 1865, p. 483) *P. fibula* is however to be reckoned also a Norwegian lichen; and *P. robustus* proves no longer distinguishable from it in species. Though now fully prepared to assent to this, it seems to me impossible not to carry the reduction further; and to admit that if *P. fibula* and *P. robustus* agree with one another, each of these extremes agrees also with *P. acicularis,* and may be subsumed under it. The specimens from Menzies, of the western lichen, do not indicate the substrate, but resemble in all respects other western ones (N. W. coast, Douglas in *Herb. Hook.;* Oregon, Scouler in *Herb. Hook.;* Rocky Mountains, *Herb. Hook.*) either undoubtedly or probably rupicoline. And recent specimens from maritime rocks in California (Mr. Bolander) leave it beyond question that the

---

[1] *Stereoc. chlorellum,* described, as respects the thallus, at the same place with the two species last named, is in fact, as indicated by Nylander (in *Prodr. Fl. N. Gran.* p. 11) only a very minute, starved, and sterile condition of a *Ramalina;* referable perhaps rather to *R. polymorpha.*

horizontal thallus of *P. acicularis* agrees generally with that of *P. fibula*, in which this feature was first observed. In other respects these two plants differ, externally, scarcely otherwise than in size; and the spores, in any large view, not appreciably. All which is equally true of the relations of the robuster, arctic condition (*P. robustus*) to the original type (*P. acicularis.*) [1]

XXXIX.—CLADONIA, Hoffm.

Hoffm. Pl. Lich. 2, p. 2; D. Fl. p, 114. Schær. Spicil. pp. 18, 278; Enum. p. 183. Floerk. de Clad. Comment. p. 5. Fr. L. E. p. 205. Eschw. Lich. Brasil. l. c. p. 260. Tuckerm. Syn. N. Eng. p. 47. Mass. Mem. p. 75. Koerb. Syst. p. 15. Nyl. Syn. 1, p. 187, t. 6, f. 24–30; Lich. Scand. p. 49. Th. Fr. Lich. Arct. p. 145; Lich. Spitzberg. p. 28. Stizenb. Beitr. l. c. p. 167. Cenomyce, Ach. L. U. p. 105; Syn. p. 248. Cladonia, Scyphophorus, and Pycnothelia, Fée Ess. p. 83. Patellariæ sect., Wallr. Naturgesch. d. Säulchen-Flecht. p. 5; Fl. Crypt. Germ. 1, p. 395. Heterodea, Cladonia, & Cladina, Nyl. Syn. Lich. N. Caled. p. 9.

Structuram expos. Tulasne, Mém. sur les Lich. pp. 24, 36, 171, t. 10, f. 6–11, t. 11, f. 11–7; Schwendener, Untersuch. l. c. 2, p. 168, t. 6, f. 23–27.

Apothecia patellæformia excipulo proprio, mox cephaloidea, subinania. Sporæ ovoideo-oblongæ, simplices, incolores. Spermatia bacillaria; sterigmatibus simpliusculis. Thallus horizontalis squamuloso-foliaceus aut crustaceus, verticalem fistulosum subsimplicem aut fruticuloso-ramosum subinde granuloso-squamulosum (podetia) proferens.

---

[1] In conformity with this view, the arrangement of the forms of *Pilophorus*, known to me, will be somewhat as follows:— *P. acicularis* (Ach.) (*Cenomyce*, Ach.) — West coast of North America, Menzies, &c.—*f. fibula* (*Stereocaulon*, Tuck. *Pilophorus*, Th. Fr.) — Moist rocks in the mountains of Eastern America, Tuckerman, &c.—*f. robustus* (*Piloph.* Th. Fr. *P. polycarpum*, Tuckerm.) — Moist rocks in Norway (Blytt) and Finmark (Th. Fr.) as in islands of Behring's Straits (C. Wright). Spores of the Western lichen, as seen in specimens from five collectors, from ellipsoid becoming more or less fusiform, and measuring from 0,018$^{mm.}$ to 0,024$^{mm.}$ in length, by 0,005$^{mm.}$ to 0,008$^{mm.}$ in thickness. Those of f. *fibula*, as seen in my own specimens, are less fusiform than the spores finally become in the Western lichen, and measure 0,018$^{mm.}$ to 0,023$^{mm.}$ in length, and 0,005$^{mm.}$ to 0,007$^{mm.}$ in thickness; in the New York specimens they vary however from ellipsoid to clubshaped and fusiform, measuring from 0,014$^{mm.}$ to 0,027$^{mm.}$ long, and from 0,005$^{mm.}$ to 0,008$^{mm.}$ thick. And those of f. *robustus*, in my Finmark specimens (*Herb.* Th. Fr., & *Lich. Scand. rar.* n. 11) are also rather ellipsoid, measuring from 0,160$^{mm.}$ to 0,023$^{mm.}$ in length, and from 0,005$^{mm.}$ to 0,008$^{mm.}$ in thickness; but become longer and fusiform in the plant from Behring's Straits, measuring now 0,023$^{mm.}$ to 0,025$^{mm.}$ in length, and 0,005$^{mm.}$ to 0,007$^{mm.}$ in thickness.

From fifty to sixty species are now known. Of these about a fifth appears to be distributed pretty equally throughout the earth, and (owing to the greater number of distinct natural regions embraced) the larger proportion occurs in intertropical and austral countries; but the genus makes nowhere so vast and important a part of the whole vegetation as in the arctic zone. All the European species, it is probable, occur within our limits, where *C. straminea* (Sommerf.) Fr., an inhabitant of northern Norway, is yet however to be detected; and we possess several unknown to Europe.

C. endiviæfolia (Ach.) Fr., is perhaps represented by a small specimen in my herbarium from Florida (Dr. Chapman) and I possess specimens ticketed 'Carthagena' from Gaudichaud.[1]——*C. mitrula*, Tuckerm. in Darlingt. *Fl. Cestr.* p. 444 (Nyl. l. c. p. 203) is common throughout the southern states, extending also to Mexico (Nyl. l. c.) and Cuba (Wright *Lich. Cub.* n. 40). Northward it has occurred in Ohio (Lea; Lesquereux) in New Jersey (Mr. Austin) and in Massachusetts (Mr. Willey).——The specimens published by the writer (*Lich. exs.* n. 124) as *C. decorticata*, Floerk., agree closely with excellent ones from Floerke's herbarium, and may be taken perhaps to constitute a slenderer state ('*fortasse forma gracilior*,' Th. Fr.) of what Dr. Th. Fries has described as *C. coralloidea*, Ach. (whose own descriptions are far enough from satisfactory) and Dr. Nylander as *C. decorticata*, Fr. To the last (*C. decorticata*, Fr., Nyl.) Dr. Fries (*Lich. Arct.* p. 148) well refers Fr. *Lich. Suec.* n. 81, and, as well as Nylander, the less instructive Schær. *Lich. Helv.* n. 279. The slender form (*C. decorticata*, Floerk.) passes, if I do not mistake, imperceptibly, in our mountains, into the stouter one (*C. decorticata*, Fr.) and Floerke's designation is much to be preferred to the doubtful one of Acharius.——*C. fimbriata*, v. *adspersa, podetiis mox elongatis inferne squamulosis superne furfuraceis l. decorticatis sæpe subulatis*, Tuckerm. in Wright. *Lich. Cub.* n. 32 (*Cladonia adspersa*, Mont. & V. de Bosch *Lich. Jav.* p. 330) which appears to extend through the warmer regions of the earth, is common also, in various conditions, throughout the United States. The epidermis is sometimes scurfy throughout, but it is more commonly squamulose, and this peculiar development of squamules is what especially marks the lichen, and tends to obscure what I conceive to be its real affinity. Specimens occur, at first sight comparable even with

---

[1] All these specimens exhibit the yellow reaction, on the under side, with potash; 'which is not the case,' according to Mr. Leighton (*Not. Lich.* in Ann. Nat· Hist. Nov. 1866) 'with *C. alcicornis*,' or *C. ceratophylla*.——*C. alcicornis* is also to be added to the number of South American *Cladoniæ* (St. Catharine, Brazil, Pabst *in herb.* V. d. Bosch, *sub nom. C. endiviæfol.*) but the specimens, though offering the whole aspect, and the characteristical, marginal fibres of the northern lichen, are tinged by potash rather as described in *C. endiviæfolia*. The writer has elsewhere (Amer. Naturalist, April, 1868) expressed an opinion on the value of such tests.

conditions of *C. furcata*, and others (with symphycarpeous apothecia) which
it is difficult not to refer to *C. squamosa* (and the plant of Montagne is so
referred by Nylander, l. c. p. 209) but it differs essentially in possessing
true scyphi, and seems to be connected, by various intermediate conditions (as, *e. g. Lich. Cub.* n. 31) with *C. fimbriata;* bearing to this last
perhaps a similar relation to that which *C. muscigena*, Eschw. (Wright
Lich. Cub. n. 42) bears to *C. macilenta.*——*C. Santensis*, Tuckerm. Suppl.
1, p. 427, discovered in the low country of South Carolina (Mr. Ravenel)
has since occurred in the upper country; but other localities, including
California (Lich. Calif. p. 23) are, for the present, uncertain. Nylander
has referred (in Leight. *Not. Lit.* l. c.) the ' *C. Santensis status imper-
fectus*' of the writer in *Lich. Cub.* n. 26, to the nearly akin *C. athelia*,
Nyl., first published, a little later, the same year with the species first
named, and he distinguishes it also by its showing no reaction with potash; but a *Cladonia* from Texas (Wright) is before me, which, agreeing in
all other respects with *C. Santensis*, and equally belonging to the *Cladoniæ
perviæ*, is yet so similar, as respects the podetia, to the Cuban lichen (with
which it also agrees in showing no reaction) as to suggest rather that the
supposed difference in the *apices* between these two species is of subordinate account; and that they differ only chemically.——*C. lepidota*, Fr.
herb., of the ochroleucous series, perhaps analogous, in this series, to
C. degenerans of the brown series, but reminding us a little, in the final
evolution of the podetia, of *C. Santensis*, was discovered in Essex, Massachusetts, by the late Mr. Oakes, and has since occurred only in Weymouth and New Bedford (Mr. Willey) in New Jersey (Mr. Austin) and in
South Carolina (Mr. Ravenel).——*C. cristatella*, Tuckerm. *Obs. Lich.* l. c.
4, p. 394 (*C. Floerkiana*, Tuckerm. Syn. N. Eng. p. 55, & *Lich. exs.* n. 133,
non Fr.) is our most common, low-country scarlet-fruited species, and, if
I mistake not, is related to *C. cornucopioides*, much as *C. Floerkiana* to
some conditions of *C. macilenta. C. cristatella* is a northern lichen, and
disappears southward in small forms approaching the next.——*C. muscigena*, Eschw. *Lich. Brasil.* l. c. p. 262, of which excellent specimens are
given in Wright *Lich. Cub.* n. 42, is a common South American sub-type,
comparable with *C. fimbriata*, v. *adspersa*, and with *C. decorticata*, of the
brown series, and represented here, in the Southern States, by *C. pulchella*, Schwein., differing only in size. The latter is described in the
writer's Suppl. 1, p. 427. *C. isidioclada*, Mont. & V. de Bosch *Lich. Jav.*
p. 31, appears hardly distinct from *C. muscigena;* to which *C. sphæru-
lifera*, Tayl. (sub *Cenom.*) may also well be referable. Dr. Nylander (l. c.
p. 224) refers this last to *C. macilenta;* from which he does not indeed
distinguish Eschweiler's plant, except as a variety.——*C. cetrarioides*,
Schwein. *herb.* (Tuck. Suppl. 1, l. c. p. 427) is still only known to me in
the original specimens (from North Carolina) of Schweinitz.——*C. lepo-
rina*, Fr. (Tuck. l. c. p. 428. Nyl. l. c. p. 227) occurs throughout the

Southern States, at least south of Virginia, and Mr. Wright found it in "stony pine woods" in Cuba (*Lich. Cub.* n. 44).

Thamnolia (Ach.) Schær. *Enum.* p. 243, (*Cladonia vermicularis*, Auctt.) is accepted as a distinct generical type by Nylander (*Syn.* p. 263, t. 8, f. 6) and its place in the system is, according to him, immediately after *Siphula*, in his series *Ramalodei.* It is yet impossible for me to regard this lichen as anything but Cladonieine, to say the least; and the f. *taurica* occurs in our mountains (as also in Sweden, as compare Th. Fr. *Lich. Arct.* p. 162, where the same view is maintained) so exactly similar to subulate podetia of *Cladonia gracilis*, intermingled with which it often grows, in everything but colour, that without ocular evidence of diversity, I must decline to separate it. The extreme infrequency of the described spermogones, which, so far as appears, only one lichenographer (Nyl. l. c.) has fully examined, detracts from the value of this note. The described apothecia have only been seen twice: in the first instance these differed 'neither in external nor internal structure' from those of *Cladonia* (Th. Fr. l. c.) and in the second (Mass. in *Flora*, 1856, n. 15) the internal parts were sufficiently Cladoniine, however irregular ('*abnormia*,' Mass.) the receptacles. Schwendener (*Untersuch.* l. c. 2, p. 167) finally, has compared at length the thalline structure of *Cladonia* with that of *Thamnolia*: but the whole of his argument for the separation of the latter may be said to turn on the continuity of its cortical layer; and the value of this fact in the system, is by no means determinable by its anatomical interest.

Fam. 2.—CŒNOGONIEI.

Thallus horizontalis, conferveo-filamentosus.

XL.—CŒNOGONIUM, Ehrenb.

Ehrenb. in Hor. Phys. Berol. Fée Ess. p. 78; Suppl. p. 134. Fr. S. O. V. p. 301. Mont. Pl. Cell. Cub. p. 107; Syll. p. 381. Nyl. Enum. Gén. l. c. p. 119; Obs. sur les Cœnog. in Ann. Sc. Nat. 4, 16, p. 89, t. 12. Karsten Geschlechtsl. d. Pflanz. p. 42. Schwend. in Flora, 1862, p. 225; Untersuch. in Naeg. Beitr. 4, p. 172, t. 23, f. 18–21. De Bary Morph. & Phys. d. Pilze, &c., p. 270.

Apothecia patellæformia, excipulo proprio pallido. Sporæ ex ellipsoideo subfusiformes, sæpius biloculares, incolores. Spermatia fusiformia; sterigmatibus simplicibus. Thallus e filamentis articulatis in telam subdeterminatam viridulam intertextis.

We do not leave *Cladonia*, without passing, in the variations of *C. squamosa*, into what is technically *Biatora;* and Fries has given expression to this instructive fact in his *Biat. Cladonia* (*L. E.* p. 256). It is indeed as easy and natural to regard *Cladonia*, *Bæomyces*, and *Biatora* as constituting one continuous series, as it is to conceive of *Parmelia* (upon which compare Norman *Con.* p. 14) and *Lecanora* as making such a series. The approximation of the two groups last named is yet interrupted by *Pannaria*, with all that its ultimate structure associates with it ; and *Cænogonium* is here provisionally regarded as occupying, in *Lecideacei*, a place analogous to *Pannariei*, &c., in *Parmeliacei.*

Montagne followed Fries in arranging the type before us with *Thermutis*, &c., but in whatever structural resemblances these plants agree, it is sufficiently evident that, in the present condition of knowledge, we are not entitled to class them together; and *Cænogonium* must be excluded from *Collemei*. Its exclusion is less obvious, it is true, from the very anomalous and ill-defined *Pannariei :* and here we have also to note, as not without bearing in the same direction, that its apothecia are, whether externally or internally, not a little similar to those of the biatoroid *Gyalecta lutea;* and that Nylander places it, in his *Lecideei*, next before *Gyalecta.*

The structure of the thallus of *Cænogonium* is not so simple, or *Conferva*-like, as was at first predicated of the genus. We find, and in all well-ascertained forms, that the filaments are made up of 1, a central series of cylindrical cells, with green content considered to be chlorophyll, and 2, of slenderer, colourless thread-cells which longitudinally band, or at length loosely surround, the first. The first may be taken to represent gonidia (Nyl. *Cænog.* l. c. Schwend. l. c.) and the second will then stand for the medullary filaments (Nyl. l. c. *Hyphen*, De Bary l. c.).

Ten species are reckoned by Nylander in his revision of the genus, all of them belonging to the warmer regions of the earth. Four of these occur in Cuba (Wright) and I possess *C. Linkii* also from Mexico. *C. interpositum*, Nyl. l. c., a native also of the island of Bourbon, was found, on trunks, in Louisiana (Hale) and is the only *Cænogonium* known as yet within the limits of the United States.

Cystocoleus, Thwaites (Ann. Nat. Hist. 2, 3) founded on *Racodium rupestre*, Pers., is associable in structure with *Cænogonium;* but is only known in a sterile condition. Fries observed that this plant was blackish-green when moist (*Summ. Veg. Scand.* p. 123) and it is the type of his emended *Racodium* (*genus persistit tantum in prima specie, quæ vero a Fungis excludenda,' Ibid.* p. 521) to which he gave a place next to *Ephebe;* but the peculiarities of its structure were first indicated by the English author cited. The axial part of a filament of *Cystocoleus* appears to offer nothing to distinguish it, in any marked way, from the same part in *Cænogonium;* and in the former equally with the latter, the pale-green hue of the content of these central cells is attributable to chlorophyll, as the cells therefore are describable as a kind of gonidia (De Bary l. c. p. 270. Schwend. l. c. p. 173). In *Cystocoleus* however the peripherical thread-cells with colourless content, answering to the 'medullary' filaments of *Cœnogonium*, are few (commonly five to six) in number, and blackish-brown; and they coalesce into a close integument, sheathing the central column.

Cystocoleus rupestris (Pers.) Thwaites l. c., has occurred, in this country, only in North Carolina (Rev. Dr. Curtis). These specimens, determined already by Dr. Curtis as the plant of Persoon, prove exactly similar, in the analysis, as above given, to the foreign ones.

———•———

Fam. 3.—LECIDEEI.

Thallus crustaceus, aut effiguratus aut rarissime papilloso-ramulosus suffruticulosusve aut uniformis, matrici adnatus.

It has been remarked already that *Cladonia* exhibits, within the circle of variations of a single species, what is now, so to say, *Bæomyces*, and what is now *Biatora;* the disappearance of the podetium explaining the latter case, and the to this superadded prolongation of the apothecium downwards into a stipe, the former. But if *Cladonia* may thus fairly be taken to include, from the point of view of the fruit, both the other genera, and the tribe itself even, as Fries understood it, with scarcely an exception, disappear, from the same stand-point, as it does with Wallroth, in a single genus,[1] we may leave further argument to those who deny or disregard the affinities in question, and assume here the sufficiency of Fries's demonstration of his *Lecideacei.*

With not a little of the aspect, in some species (as *B. imbricatus,* Hook.) of an epiphylline *Cladonia*, and in others (as *B. roseus*) of such forms as *Cladonia mitrula*, and comparable again (as in *B. byssoides*) with *Stereocaulon* (to which Schærer once referred the species last-named, as Eschweiler the whole genus) *Bæomyces* is perhaps nearer to *Biatora;* and with the exception of *B. roseus*, was united with it by Fries. Nor does it seem to be certain that the *nisus* to develope vertically, so characteristical of the preceding family, and exhibited in *Bæomyces* by the frequent extension of the hypothecium downwards into a stalk or stipe, is not properly predicable (as by Fries *S. O. V.* p. 247) of the whole tribe, and therefore also of *Biatora* and *Lecidea.* The often elevated fruit of

[1] *Patellaria*, Wallr. *Fl. Crypt, Germ. exc. excip.*, the sections of which, referable here, differ in fact only, as the author says, '*blastematis ratione, nec tamen cymatiorum natura,*' (l. c. 1, p. 348).

Biatora chlorosticta, Tuckerm. (*Obs. Lich.* l. c. 4, p. 419, *sub Lecid.,* & *Lich. exs.* n. 139) becomes at length (a fact first observed by my friend Mr. Willey) distinctly substipitate; and *Helocarpon,* Th. Fr. (*Lich. Arct.* p. 178) may possibly, in this view, well pass, (as it would have passed, in the Friesian System) for a stipitate *Lecidea.*

The central position, in the present tribe, of *Bæomyces,* is perhaps also indicated by its many-jointed šterigmas (*arthrosterigmata,* Nyl.) as compared with the simpler structure of the same parts in the *Cladoniei* and *Lecideei;* but the genus passes imperceptibly into forms only with difficulty distinguishable, at least in other respects, from *Biatora.*

Lecidea, Ach., *pro max. p.,* was shewn by Fries to constitute two distinct series, the one (*Lecidea,* Fr.) separated from the other (*Biatora,* Fr.) by its always black exciple, a marked and sufficiently constant modification (upon which compare Stizenb. *Beitr.* l. c. p. 137, not.) and these series, of which Dr. Nylander also avails himself (*Lich. Scand.,* p. 186) in arranging the Acharian genus, as adopted by him, are here received as genera.

The family includes, especially in the sub-families *Biatoreei* and *Eulecideei,* the great bulk of the tribe; and will doubtless continue long to afford, as it has afforded, a field of the most interesting enquiry.

Sub-Fam. 1. — BÆOMYCEI, Fée.

Apothecia substipitata.

XLI.—B Æ O M Y C E S, P e r s., D C., N y l.

Pers. in Ust. Ann. cit. Ach. DC. Fl. Fr. 2, p. 341. Duf. Rév. Clad., cit. Nyl. Nyl. Syn. 1, p. 175. Bæomyces, & Lecideæ sp., Ach. L. U., pp. 108, & 191. Bæomyces, et Biatoræ sect. 1, spp., et sect. 2, sp., Fr. L. E. pp. 246, 257, 258. Bæomyces, et Parmeliæ sp., Wallr. Fl. Crypt. Germ. 1, pp. 467, 561. Bæomyces, Sphyridium, et Zeoræ sp., Flot. Lich. Sil.; in Jahresbericht. d. Schles. Gesellsch. 1842. Bæomyces max. p., et Lecideæ sp., Schær. Enum. pp. 142, 182. Bæomyces, et Biatoræ sect. 2, Norm. Con. p. 21. Bæomyces et Icmadophila, Mass. Ric. pp. 26,138. Bæomyces, Sphyridium et Icmadophila, Koerb. Syst. pp. 151, 273. Anz. Catal. Sondr. pp. 17, &c. Th. Fr. Gen. pp. 68, 81. Bæomyces et Lecaniæ sect., Stizenb. Beitr. l. c. pp. 166, 171.

Apothecia patellæformia excipulo proprio l. cephaloidea margine obsoleto, sub-stipitata. Sporæ ex ellipsoideo subfusiformes, e simplici nunc bi-quadriloculares, incolores. Spermatia oblonga; sterigmatibus multi-articulatis. Thallus horizontalis, crustaceus, effiguratus aut uniformis.

The natural position of *B. roseus*, Pers., the type of *Bæomyces* with Fries, and Flotow, as a member of the same genus with *B. byssoides* (L.) Schær. (*Sphyridium*, Flot.) is indicated for me, with sufficient distinctness, by *B. absolutus* (Venezuela, Fendler; Wright *Lich. Cub.* n. 23, 24) and perhaps illustrated as well by a curiously suggestive condition of *Cladonia mitrula* (Alabama, Peters). Nor is *B. absolutus* without value, possibly, in determining the place of *B. æruginosus* (Scop.) DC. (*Biatora icmadophila*, Fr.) the generally admitted and significant resemblance of which to *B. roseus* is scarcely invalidated, either by the frequent presence of an accessory thalline border, or by the clearly patellæform type of its more normal, and yet sub-stipitate apothecia. [1]

Fifteen species of *Bæomyces*, as here taken, are reckoned by Nylander (*Syn.* l. c.) of which the four European ones are common to the United States. Two of these are also Australian, and a third occurs in Nepal (Nyl. l. c.). The remaining eleven species are either tropical or austral.

B. absolutus, Tuckerm. Suppl. 2, p. 201, a native of Venezuela and Cuba, has occurred also on wet rocks at Hillsborough, North Carolina (Rev. Dr. Curtis) and on the earth, in Alabama (Mr. Peters).——*B. fungoides* (Sw.) Ach., regarded by Fries (*S. O. V.* p. 250) as a condition of *B. roseus* ('*quo australius natus, eo longiora' exserens 'podetia'*) an opinion which later investigation has done little to invalidate, is a native of the West India islands; and also, according to Nylander, of Mexico.

Sub-Fam. 2. — BIATOREI.

Apothecia subsessilia, excipulo disco pallidiori.

XLII. — BIATORA, Fr.

Fr. in Vet. Ac. Handl. 1822, p. 263; S. O. V. p. 250; L. E. p. 247; max. p. Esch. Syst. p. 17. Mont. Pl. Cell. Cub. p. 195; Aperçu Morph. p. 11, max. p. Tuckerm. Syn. N. Eng. p. 57, pr. p.; Lich. Calif. p. 23. Lecideæ spp., Ach. L. U. p. 32. Fée Ess. p. 51. Schær. Spicil. p. 101; Enum. p. 94. Borr. in Hook. Br. Fl. 2, p. 173. Eschw. Lich. Bras. l. c. p. 241. Nyl. Enum. Gén. p. 119; Lich. Scand. p. 185; in Prodr. Fl. N. Gran. p. 53; Syn. Lich. N. Caled. p. 41; Addend. nov. ad Lich. Eur., in Flora Ratisb. Tuckerm. Obs. Lich. l. c. 5, p. 417; 6, p. 272. Patellariæ spp., Meyer. Wallroth. Psora, et Biatora, Flot in Koerb. Grundr.

---

[1] Montagne, at any rate (*Ann. Sci. Nat.* 4, 8, p. 298) subordinating the differences in the thallus, and in the spores, determined *B. absolutus*, in Fendler's specimens, as *Biat. icmadophila*, v. *stipitata*. The latter is indeed a peculiarly northern species, but putting out of sight the difference in the crust of the tropical lichen, its apothecia are well-comparable with naked (or normal) ones of *B. æruginosus*.

20

d. Cryptogamenk.; in Bot. Zeit. 1850, p. 382. Biatora max. p., et Secoligæ sp., Norm. Con. pp. 18–22. Psora, Biatora max. p., Pyrrhospora, Psilolechia, Biatorina max. p., Bilimbia, Tricholechia, Bacidia, Ropalospora, Sporacestra, Scoliciosporum, Biatorella, et Chiliospora, Mass. opp. varr. & Auctt. pl.

Structuram exposuerunt Tulasne, Mém. sur les Lich. p. 151, 167, t. 10, f. 28–31; Fuisting l. c. p. 30.

Apothecia patellæformia, excipulo proprio ceraceo colorato dein sæpius cephaloidea. Sporæ ex ellipsoideo simplici oblongæ bi-quadriloculares 1. fusiformes 1. aciculares dein pluriloculares, incolores. Spermatia (quantum observ.) ex oblongo bacillaria; sterigmatibus subsimplicibus. Thallus crustaceus, effiguratus aut uniformis.

The genus is accepted here, generally, in the sense of Fries; certain species, as those referable to *Bæomyces*, and *Heterothecium*, being however excluded. It is exactly analogous to *Lecanora*, and, like this, exhibits, but in greater fullness and detail, the whole differentiation of the colourless spore. All the steps of this process are displayed also in the central group of most closely allied forms (modifications in fact of but a single natural species according to Fries) of which *B. vernalis*, *B. sphæroides* and *B. rubella* are well-known northern representatives. It is impossible to sunder, generically, these species, and the groups which they represent, by any differences beyond those based on, and representing the successive steps in the process of development of what is, at the bottom, the same spore. And the more or less arbitrary assemblages of species which we thus gain, if available now as subordinate divisions, are perhaps as often undesirable breaks in the continuity of the larger natural group, or genus.

For the naturalness of this group, and the distinctness of the series of forms which constitutes it from that exhibited by *Lecidea* will scarcely be denied; however difficult the extrication of its real rank in the system.

The number of assumed species of *Biatora* and *Lecidea*, as here understood, taken together, is now as large as its reckoning is difficult. Not a few of these forms are, with little doubt, integrant parts of species the true limits of which are still undetermined. Even the groups best studied, as those of the northern hemisphere, and especially of Europe, are still, many of them, far from settled; and there is no question that many new forms are yet to be ascertained, some of which may well throw important light on the old. Most of the European *Biatoræ* are common to North America; which possesses some others unknown elsewhere, or at least to Europe. The genus has long occupied the attention of our lichenists; but the want of authentic foreign specimens has hindered some of these, otherwise best qualified, from satisfactory judgments: which only the long-continued, kind assistance of friends and correspondents abroad, emboldens the present writer to hope he has, in any degree, attained.

As understood then by many recent authors, *Biatora* (as here taken) falls apart into five distinct groups, received as genera, exhibiting the successive changes in the differentiation of the originally simple, colourless spore; the first two, in which the spore continues simple, differing only in the thallus being either effigurate (*Psora*, Mass.) or granulose (*Biatora*, Mass.). But the process of differentiation tends always to its completion, and the stage of this process exhibited in *Biatora*, as thus restricted, is not by any means without fore-shadowings of succeeding ones. These find distinct expression in, first, the bilocular modification, or in *Biatorina*, Mass.; and then in the 4–8–locular (*Bilimbia*, De Not.). And the last of all, into which *Bilimbia* imperceptibly passes, and the acicular spores of which exhibit the perfection of the colourless spore-type, is *Bacidia*, De Not. The polysporous, biatorine lichens (upon which the remarks already made under the polysporous section of *Lecanora* may be compared) are also separated, by the same authors, as *Biatorella*, De Not.; &c. From the point of view of the present treatise, neither of the just-named genera can be accepted as valid; and it is not always that we find satisfaction in availing ourselves of them even for the construction of sections. The effigurate group (*Psora*) which begins the list of biatorine lichens, and the polysporous group (*Biatorella*) which may end it, correspond indeed interestingly with the similar sections of *Lecanora*: with regard however to the whole remainder, or great bulk of the genus, as here taken, it is plain that we have but a single series of most closely related forms; inseparable, in fact, but as species, by any character, but the inadequate and now sufficiently arbitrary spore-character. The groups exhibiting the several stages in the evolution of the originally simple spore are smaller in *Lecanora*, and it is perhaps easier to restore *Dimerospora*, *Lecania*, and *Ophioparma* to their ancient places, than the corresponding, larger groups which have been separated from *Biatora*; but the principle is the same.

With present information, and it being understood, here as elsewhere, that Mexican species are but little known, I reckon the number of North American species of *Biatora*, as thus constituted, at about sixty; some brief review of which, in the order of the divisions just indicated, may now follow.

Of the elegant group of effigurate lichens, making the first section (*Psora*) only two,— *B. Russellii*, Tuckerm. (*Obs. Lich.* 1. c. 4, p. 417, *sub Lecid.*) an inhabitant of lime-rocks, and *B. rufo-nigra*, Tuck. Syn. Lich. N. Eng. p. 58, of granitic,— are as yet known to me to occur commonly throughout the United States; and *B. lurida* and *testacea*, of the calcareous rocks of Europe, as well as *B. albilabra*, are wanting.——*B. globifera* (Ach.) Fr., reckoned indeed as North American by Acharius, and an inhabitant of Greenland (J. Vahl) according to Dr. Th. Fries, has only been sent to me from California (Mr. Bolander).——*B. luridella* (*Lecidea*, Tuckerm. l. c. p. 418) a minute species (the scales passing indeed into glebous conditions) somewhere between the last species, with which it agrees in its subimmarginate apothecia, and *B. lurida*, which it rather resembles in colour, and the more appressed thallus, was found (on the earth) in the mountains of New Mexico (Mr. Fendler) and in the Rocky Mountains (Dr. Hayden).——More remarkable is the Californian *B. scotopholis* (Tuckerm. Lich. Calif. p. 24) comparable now with *B. rufo-nigra*, and now much rather with *Lecidea fusco-atra*.——*B. ostreata* (Hoffm.) Fr. *Summ.*, has only occurred (on charred pine stumps, in Vermont) to Mr. J. L. Russell.[1]——*B. decipiens* (Ehrh.) Fr., though known to Muhlenberg, and (through him probably) to Hoffmann (*D. Fl.* 2, p. 162) as North American, as long ago as 1796, and found in Arctic America by Richardson, is yet, — so small is the extent of our explored alpine districts, and perhaps also of a calcareous low country like what the plant often inhabits in Europe, — positively known to me from no other localities than the 'bad lands of Judith,' in Nebraska, accompanying *Placodium fulgens* and *Buellia epigæa* (Dr. Hayden) similar soils in Missouri and Kansas (Mr. Hall) and in Montana (M. A. Brown) and volcanic rocks in California (Mr. Bolander).——The last species is yet approached by *B. crenata* (*Endocarpon crenatum* Tayl. in Hook. Lond. Journ. Bot. 6, p. 156. *Lecanora chonion*, Tuckerm. Suppl. 1, l. c. p. 425) remarkable for its hollowed, or even funnel-shaped, larger and mostly entire, brown, or now white squamules; which is frequent on denudated spots in the prairies of Texas (Mr. Wright). The reference to the English botanist's description is due to Dr. Nylander; but the resemblance of the American lichen to Zeyher's Cape of Good Hope specimens, from which Taylor's description was drawn, had been before indicated. *Endocarpon spcireum*, Tayl. (l. c.) founded on other Cape specimens, can hardly be sufficiently differenced. The finally black apothecium of *B. crenata*, like that of *B. decipiens*, is originally biatorine, and may now be describable as lecanoroid; but the exciple offers no trace of gonidia.——And the same prairies furnish us with another elegant member of the present group in *B. icterica*,

---

[1] The small spores seldom observed in the European lichen (Koerb. *Syst.* p. 176. Th. Fr. *Lich. Arct.* p. 169. Nyl. *Lich. Scand.* p. 243) were detected, in his specimens (in 1851) by Mr. Russell; and I have myself since, more than once, succeeded in finding them. They become irregularly ellipsoid, the protoplasm dividing frequently into two rounded portions, as in *B. rufo-nigra*, and the length scarcely much exceeding, unless when the spore is misshapen, twice and a half the diameter. These dimensions are exceeded however in the European lichen, the spores of which are described by Nylander (l. c.) as '*long.* 0,011–12, *crass.* 0,0025–0,0035 *millim.*'; and also as described by Massalongo (*Ric.* p. 94). *B. rufo-nigra* offers possibly, in its blue-black apothecia, and even in its thallus, some other points of at least distant comparison with *B. ostreata;* the originally pale exciple of which appears ill-compatible with any other than its present place.

Mont. (*Lecidea endochlora*, Tayl. l. c. *Biatora Tuckermani*, Fr. *herb.*
Lecanora Wrightii, Tuck. l. c.) for the reference of which to the original
description, I am again indebted to Dr. Nylander. The greenish-yellow
thallus of this contrasts pleasingly with that of the preceding. Mon-
tagne's specimens of his species were from Valparaiso, and Taylor's from
Buenos Ayres. With us the lichen occurs from Texas (Mr. Wright) to
Kansas (Mr. Hall) and still further northward to lat. 46° in Minnesota
(Mr. Lapham).

The large group succeeding corresponds with *Eulecanora*, and may be
distinguished as *Eubiatora*. Characterized for the most part by the
granulose type of thallus, not seldom much reduced, this ascends also to
squamulose conditions, now but ill-separable from *Psora*. Among these
the most interesting and difficult is *B. coarctata* (Ach.) Th. Fr., probably
cosmopolitan, which occurs in this country in various forms, from Vermont (on calcareous rocks, Mr. Frost; on manganese ore, Rev. Dr.
Hitchcock) and Massachusetts (on granite, Mr. Willey) to South Carolina
(on sand-rock, Mr. Ravenel) and California (on the earth, Mr. Wright ;
Mr. Bolander). Distinctly biatorine conditions of this lichen were referred to his *Lecidea* by Acharius, as also by Borrer (*herb.*) but the whole
species (placed by Fries, as by Koerber, among the *Lecanorei*) Fr., was
first recognized as properly lecideine by Nylander (*Prodr.*).——Comparable with the last is yet the well-characterized *B. glebulosa*, Fr. (Zw. *exs.* n.
78. *B. Wallrothii*, Koerb.) observed, in this country, only (on the earth,
thinly covering rocks) in California (Mr. Bolander).——Much more common is *B. decolorans* (Hoffm.) Fr., of our mountains (Tuckerm. *exs.* n.
45) but its range is northern, and I am not acquainted with it south of
Pennsylvania (Dr. Michener).——The nearly akin *B. flexuosa*, Fr. *Summ.*,
occurred on charred surfaces of white pine logs in the White Mountains ;
and is perhaps common on rails ; I have observed it southward as far as
Maryland.——*B. viridescens* (Schrad.) Fr., may be considered as connecting this little assemblage with the one immediately following, and
occurs commonly (on rotting logs) in the lower forest of the White
Mountains, as also in swamps in western Massachusetts ; and Mr. Frost
has sent it from Vermont ; as Mr. Austin from New Jersey.

The northern forms of the group of which *B. vernalis* (as here understood) may be taken for a representative, have been especially studied,
but the group extends into the tropics, and reaches there indeed its
maximum of development. Among tropical representatives of *B. vernalis* may be named particularly *B. cinereo-rufescens*, *B.`lætior*, and
B. subvernalis (*Lecideæ*, Nyl.) and *B. luteo-rufula* (*Lecidea*, Tuck.) all
but the last of which are published in Wright's *Lichenes Cubæ ;* but the
head of the whole group is the elegantly various *B. parvifolia* (Pers.)
(Tuck. *Obs. Lich.* l. c. 5, p. 272) of which not a few forms (n. 179–186) are
also to be found in Wright's collection. This species often curiously
counterfeits *Pannaria*, and was referred to that affinity by Montagne

(*Pl. Cell. Cub.*). It occurs with us, in a well-marked squamulose state (*Pannaria Halei*, Tuck. *herb. Lecidea*, Nyl. *Enum.*, *Suppl.*) in Louisiana (Hale) but is much more common in reduced, often isidioid forms (*Lecidea Santensis*, Tuck. Suppl.) which are found throughout the Southern States, and have been observed by me as far north as Virginia; and by Mr. Austin even in New Jersey. It is not easy to regard this last, and the first-cited Louisiana lichen, as members of the same species; but the range of variation of *B. parvifolia*, as exhibited especially in Mr. Wright's rich Cuban collections, is, as I at least have understood these, undoubtedly very wide.——*B. russula* (Ach.) Mont. (not of Tuckerm. Syn. N. E.) is another tropical expression of the type of the present group, extending however not only through the southern country, but northward as far as Ohio (Lea) and New York (Halsey) just as in Europe it reaches Portugal and the extreme south of France (Nyl.).——*B. cinnabarina* (Sommerf.) Fr., is a similar lichen, belonging to the extreme north, and found here in Greenland (Fries) and at Pend Oreille river in North West America (Dr. Lyall in *herb. Hook.*).——*B. vernalis* (L.) Fr. *Lich. Suec. n.* 224, & *Summ.*, *a* is common in our mountains (Tuck. *exs.* n. 44) in muscicoline and corticoline conditions, and occurs also in Arctic America (Mr. Wright) and, more rarely, on the coast, in southern New England. The spores are very commonly, indeed mostly, simple, but bilocular ones occur occasionally in my specimens, as they do also in the cited plant of Fries, and in Stenh. *Lich. Suec. n.* 54, *a;* and indications are not wanting of still further possible modification. There is reason then for continuing to regard *B. sphæroides* (Sommerf.) as very closely akin to *B. vernalis.*——*B. sanguineo-atra* (Fr. *herb.*, *quoad exempl. meum Lich. Suec. n.* 223) Tuck. Syn. N. Eng. p. 60, is more common, and extends southward to the mountains of Georgia (Mr. Ravenel). In this the spores appear to be typically simple, but indications of a further evolution are by no means wanting.——*B. cuprea* (Sommerf.) Fr., of Arctic Europe, has occurred also in Greenland (J. Vahl, *e* Th. Fr. *Lich. Arct.* p. 194) and Mr. Wright collected it in an island of Behring's Straits.——Not wholly dissimilar to the last is *B. atrorufa* (Dicks.) Fr., of our alpine districts (White Mountains) though here the darker thallus is evidently squamulose. *B. castanea*, Hepp (Th. Fr.! *Lich. Arct.* p. 195) the apothecia of which are not without points of resemblance to *Leptogium muscicola*, has been found in Greenland (J. Vahl, *e* Th. Fr. *Lich. Arct.* p. 195) and in the alpine region of the Rocky Mountains by Mr. E. Hall.——*B. rufo-fusca*, Anz. (*Catal. Sondr.* p. 76; *Lich. Lang.* n. 178) is identical, according to Dr. Th. Fries, with *Lecid. aquilonia*, Krempelh., and has occurred in Greenland (Th. Fr. in *Flora* 1866, p. 452).

B. Tornoensis (Nyl.) Th. Fr. *Lich. Arct.* p. 196 (*Lecidea*, Nyl. *Lich. Scand.* p. 195, & in Fellm. *Lich. Arct. n.* 148) a minute species with scarcely any thallus, and dark reddish-brown, or blackish, convex apothecia, is distinguished by its large spores, and occurs (in Arctic Europe, and) in Greenland (J. Vahl, *e* Th. Fr. *l. c.*).——Comparable with the last in size at least, as respects all but the spores, is *B. fuscescens* (Sommerf.) Fr., the flat, blackening apothecia of which, and the blackening hypo-thallus, associate the lichen, at first sight, with minute forms of *Lecidea enteroleuca*, or *Buellia parasema*, for which it may possibly be passed over. This appertains also, primarily, to the arctic zone, growing especially on birch-bark, and has been found in North America only in Greenland (J. Vahl, *e* Th. Fr. *l. c.*)——*B. exigua* (Chaub.) Fr., is not unlike *B. fuscescens*, but its range is much wider, the lichen occurring commonly throughout the United States. The fruit of this also at length blackens, when it is sometimes difficult satisfactorily to distinguish it from minute conditions of *Lecidea enteroleuca*; to which species Nylan-der (*Prodr.*) referred the present.——*B. Nylanderi*, Anz. *Catal. Sondr.* p. 75 (*Lecidea fuscescens*, Nyl. *Prodr.*, *L. fuscescens*, v. *leprodea*, Nyl. *Lich. Scand.* p. 213) inhabiting pine bark in France and Italy, and occurring to me here (on Pitch-pine) in Cambridge, Massachusetts, as, on the same bark, at New Bedford, to Mr. Willey, appears certainly to be well distinguished. The plant is comparable, generally, with some small conditions of *B. rubella*, but has globular spores.——*B. uliginosa* (Schrad.) Fr., is very common, according to Fries, in Europe; and may prove so here, though easily overlooked. I have found it on the earth in the alpine regions, as well as on the charred surface of old pine stumps, in the White Mountains, and on the earth in Watertown; and Rev. Dr. Curtis has sent me excellent specimens (agreeing exactly with one of those, on a similar soil, in Moug. & Nestl. *Cr. Vog.* n. 747) from North Carolina; and Mr. Hall, from Illinois.——*B. rivulosa* (Ach.) Fr., is com-mon on granitic rocks in New England, but (the fruit soon blackening) it may easily be passed over for a *Lecidea*. Spores of the common low-country lichen oblong, at length a little curved, or bean-shaped. Alpine specimens however (White Mountains) which appear also to be at length distinguishable by a thickened, strongly chinky thallus, made up of large areoles, exhibit smaller, roundish-ovoid spores; and may well be referable to the var. *mollis*, Wahl. (*Fl. Lapp.* p. 472) which is *Lecidea mollis*, Nyl. *Lich. Scand.* p. 223. And there is also to be mentioned, as a member of the same cluster, a bark-lichen, according to Fries only a corticoline form of *B. rivulosa*, as it ranks also in Nyl. *Lich. Scand.*, but distinguished by others as *B. Lightfootii*, which has been detected, on Hemlock, in Massa-chusetts (the specimens agreeing pretty closely in most respects with the foreign ones) by Mr. Willey.——*B. quernea* (Dicks.) Fr., closely simu-lated by a condition of our form of *Lecanora elatina*, which form was indeed referred to it in Syn. Lich. N. Eng., proves to be one of that inter-esting group of European lichens which is confined, in North America, to the Pacific coast. Mr. Bolander's specimens agree entirely with the European. The exciple, in these specimens, is by no means originally immarginate, as asserted by several recent describers, especially Koerber

(*Syst.* p. 209, where the supposed structural deficiency is relied on as a character of the new genus *Pyrrhospora*) and the European lichen agrees in fact, in this respect, as elsewhere (*Obs. Lich.* l. c. 6, p. 275) indicated, with the American. Spores of our plant reddish-brown in the thekes, and more rarely when free ; the colourless ones appearing possibly most perfect.——*B. lucida* (Ach.) Fr., resembling rather a member of the lecanorine group represented by *Lecanora varia*, and occurring in fissures of rocks, and also on dead wood (Fr.) has been found, in the latter habitat, in Arctic America by Richardson (Hook. Append. Frankl. Narr.) and elsewhere, on rocks, and the roots of Cedars, in Southern Massachusetts (Mr. Willey) in Rhode Island (Mr. J. L. Bennett) and in New York (Mr. C. H. Peck). With this species we complete our list, as it now stands, of *Biatoræ* with simple spores. [1] There is an obvious convenience, in the present place, in considering it apart, and in permitting also the successive modifications of the originally simple spore, as this gradually accomplishes the evolution of its type, to determine the remaining groups : but the sundering of natural affinities which is thus made necessary, invalidates the arrangement ; and Nylander has refused to recognize it at all. *B. vernalis* (as here understood) *B. cyrtella*, *B. sphæroides*, and *B. rubella* are types of these structural differences, as of the genera of *Biatorei* supposed to be predicable upon them ; but the lichens named are members also of a single group of species, which, whether or not we sunder, Nature keeps together.

In the immediately following little cluster of *Biatoræ*, fuller expression is given to the indications afforded by the last of *bilocular* modification ; and — excluding some forms possibly referable elsewhere, as *Biatorina pyracea*, Massal., to *Placodium*, and *B. pineti* and *B. lutea*, Koerb., to *Gyalecta* — the group is identical with *Biatorina* of recent authors. *Biatora cyrtella* (Ach.) in its blackening, convex condition (Vermont, Messrs. Frost and Russell ; White Mountains) which is referred here by Dr. Nylander, is distinguishable, and the spores, though commonly simple, become at length bilocular and a little oblique ; but paler-fruited states (Vermont, Mr. Frost) even though often more frequently bilocular, are perhaps also conceivable as a corticoline expression of *B. vernalis.*—— *B. globulosa* (Floerk.) is determined by his *Exs. ;* the *B. anomala*, Fr.,

---

[1] Many interesting forms are doubtless yet to be added. *B. mutabilis* (Fée) is a native of Mexico (Nyl. *Enum.*) and is possibly represented by a Louisiana lichen (Hale) agreeing exactly with a Brazilian one (*Herb. Kunz.*) referred by the late Dr. Meissner to *B. mixta*, Fr. It is probable that what is now called *B. atropurpurea* was intended in this reference ; and both the Brazilian and Louisianian specimens are well-comparable with the first-named, except indeed that the similar spores appear always to be simple. Other tropical species probably extend farther north ; and the Cuban lichens of the present group, among which, beside others already named, are *B. oncodes*, *B. orphnæa*, *B. furfurosa*, *B. polycampia* (*Lecideæ*, Tuck. *Obs. Lich.*, & in Wright *Lich. Cub.*) may, some of them, be found in Florida.

which included it, being, ' *expressis verbis*,' a collective name, largely relating (at least in *Summ. Veg. Scand.*; as also in Ach. *Syn.*, *teste* Nyl.) to *B. cyrtella*. *B. globulosa* appears to be represented by a lichen occurring on dead wood in the White Mountains, well comparable externally, and in the rather elongated, bilocular spores, with the lower, right hand specimen of Moug. & Nestl. n. 1330. In another, also inhabiting dead wood, and hemlock bark in the same region, and finally resembling Zw. *exs.* n. 89, the apothecia are however originally paler than in any of my foreign specimens, and the spores, as in the last preceding species, more commonly simple. Compare as to this Nyl. *Lich. Scand.* p. 202.——
B. miliaris (Wallr.) (*Scutula Wallrothii*, Tul. *Lecid. anomala*, v. *Wallrothii*, Nyl.) a rare parasite of the thallus of *Peltigera canina*, has been detected, in this country, only (in southern Massachusetts) by Mr. Willey.
——*B. denigrata*, Fr., is peculiar to dead wood, and has occurred to me in Cambridge, with a darker thallus however than even that of Rabenh. *Lich. Eur.* n. 626. It is comparable with *B. uliginosa*, but the spores (exactly agreeing, in my specimens, with those of Fr. *Lich. Suec.* n. 98) are typically bilocular. *B. cumulata* (Sommerf.) a well-marked lichen of arctic Europe (Th. Fr. *Lich. Arct.* p. 187, & *Lich. exs.* n. 44) which most authors have referred to *Lecidea*, Fr., is also an inhabitant of Greenland (J. Vahl, *e* Th. Fr. l. c.).——*B. mixta*, Fr., is determined by the published lichen (*Lich. Suec.* n. 40) and can scarcely be supplanted by the indeterminable *Lichen Griffithii*, Sm., two out of three of Borrer's specimens of which, given to me in 1841, possess the spores of Rabenh. *Lich. Eur.* n. 627, representing the very similar small condition of *B. atropurpurea* which Schærer published. *B. mixta* is confined to trunks, occurring on Maple in Vermont (Mr. Frost) and on Firs, in the upper forest of the White Mountains (Myself) as in Lower Canada (Mr. A. T. Drummond) and, on various trees, in Massachusetts (Mr. Willey).——This lichen has been sent also, in fine condition, but offering some peculiarities, from California (Mr. Bolander).——
B. atropurpurea (Massal.) though sometimes closely resembling the last, with which it was often united by the elder lichenists, is a more conspicuous lichen, and easily distinguished by its larger, ellipsoid spores, which are at length regularly bilocular. The dark-brownish, flattish state (*Lecidea Griffithii*, Borr. *pr. p.*) has occurred, on Hemlock, in Vermont (Mr. Frost) and Massachusetts (Mr. Willey) as on other bark in Alabama (Mr. Beaumont). But the apothecia soon blacken; and such a condition, becoming also commonly convex (Vermont, on Maple, Mr. Frost; and not uncommon elsewhere in New England, and in New York, as also in California (Mr. Bolander) and Russian America (Dr. Kellogg) is sometimes far from unlike *Lecidea enteroleuca*.[1] I observe, very rarely, tri-

---

[1] *B. melaleuca*, Tuckerm. herb. (Nyl. in *Prodr. Fl. N. Gran.* p. 56, *not.*) collected, too scantily, in the island of Cuba by Mr. Wright, is comparable at once both with *B. atropurpurea*, to the neighbourhood of which Nylander has referred

21

locular spores in the black, convex form of *B. atro-purpurea.* In a lichen (*B. fusca,* Hepp) which is an exceedingly near relation ('*gehört jedenfalls in die nächste Nähe,*' Koerb. *l. inf. cit.*) of the present, the author last named (*Parerg.* p. 143) describes however ' *äusserst wandelbare* (*mono-, dy- bis tetrablastische*) *Sporen*'; an observation not without special interest from the point of view of the present memoir.

The group we have just considered exhibits the first modification of the originally simple, but finally plurilocular spore of *Biatora,* as here taken. It was not obscurely foreshadowed in the larger assemblage of species (with commonly simple spores) which preceded it, and it anticipates in the same way, by sufficient indications, that now to come before us. Here the spore ('*anfänglich meist dyblastisch,*' Koerb. *Syst.* p. 211) assumes a dactyloid, or at length fusiform shape, and becomes regularly quadri-plurilocular; — the type and only distinction of the genus *Bilimbia* of authors.

Biatora trachona, Flot. in Zw. *exs.* n. 117, occurs, and is probably common, on shaded, granitic rocks, in Hampshire, Massachusetts; and the oblong or dactyloid, quadrilocular spores agree with those of my specimen of the cited European lichen; to which Nylander also referred the American plant. In otherwise similar, Vermont specimens (Mr. Frost) the spores are mostly simple (only shewing at length irregular indications of division) and agree better with the description of Koerber (*Syst.* p. 197) who has referred the species to the group with simple spores. —— *B. tricholoma,* Mont. *Guy.* p. 35, appears to present no features of importance to separate it from a Cuban lichen, growing upon leaves and bark (Mr. Wright) which I cannot distinguish from the later *Lecidea leucoblephara,* Nyl. The latter was founded on specimens from the low country of South Carolina (Mr. Ravenel) and, according to Nylander (in *Prodr. Fl. N. Gran.* p. 52, *not.*) it has occurred also in the north of France. The minute apothecia are distinguishable by an accessory, white-fibrillose border, relieved by the dark-greenish crust. This accessory border becoming obsolete, the proper margin is finally less obscure. Spores oblong and subfusiform, quadrilocular. [1] —— *B. artyta* (*Lecidea,* Ach. *L. U.* p. 170) was from Schleicher, and Schærer pronounces the latter's specimens of

t, and *Heterothecium leptocheilum,* Tuckerm. (*Obs. Lich.* l. c. 5, p. 280; *Lich. Cub.* n. 227). And there is not wanting other evidence looking towards a possible connection of the northern lichen with the microsporous section of *Heterothecium.*

[1] Other tropical species referable to the present group, and possibly occurring within our southern limits, are *Biatora triseptata* (Hepp) M. & V. d. B., found by Mr. Wright in Cuba, and a more remarkable form of which (f. *artyloides,* Tuck.) is given in Wright *Lich. Cub.* n. 207; *B. leucocheila* (*Lecidea,* Tuck. *Obs. Lich.* l. c. 5, p. 278) also a Cuban lichen; as are *B. pusilla,* Mont., *B. palmicola* (*Lecidea,* Tuck. l. c.) *B. scitula* (*Lecidea,* Tuck. l. c.) *B. pellœa* (*Lecidea,* Tuck. l. c.) and *B. thysanota* (*Lecid.* l. c.). With the last is in some respects comparable *B. majorina* (*Lecidea,* l. c.) included in Lindig *Herb. N. Gran.,* n. 811.

his lichen to be identical with the *Lecidea sabaletorum v. muscorum* of his own *Spicilegium*, and *Lich. Helv.* n. 194. Two distinct lichens are confused indeed in the latter publication; but one of them, and the only one to which the excellent description of Acharius will apply, is the well-marked alpine and arctic species published by Massalongo as *Bilimbia sabulosa*, and by Dr. Th. Fries (*Lich. Arct.* p. 185) who adopts an older, but not a species name, of Floerke's, as *B. syncomista*. Instructive specimens from the friendly author of the latter designation, and others, approved by Massalongo, of his plant (*Herb. Krempelh.*) have afforded no satisfactory differences from Schærer's specimen, or indeed from the character of Acharius. Mr. Wright detected our American representative of the species in an island of Behring's Straits. The hypothecium finally blackens, as in Schærer's plant, and others from Dr. Sauter, as well as in the Swedish ones; and this is indicated also by Acharius. Spores subfusiform, 2–3–, but at length 4–locular.——*Biatora sphæroides* (*Lecidea*, Sommerf., *a*) is only known to me in specimens from the extreme north of Europe, and in entirely corresponding ones, collected in Franklin's first voyage (*Herb. Hook.*) in arctic America, and by Mr. Wright, in an island of Behring's Straits. The apothecia are generally paler than in *B. vernalis;* but the important difference is in the regularly quadrilocular spores. Sommerfelt described however a darker form (v. *obscurata*) with similar spores, but appearing constantly distinct according to Dr. Th. Fries, (*Lich. Arct.* p. 182) which occurs also in Greenland (J. Vahl, *e* Th. Fr. l. c.).——*B. hypnophila* (Turn.) is, so far as my information of the true limitation of the last species goes, a plant of more southern range, reaching as far south as Portugal (Welwitoch) in Europe, and the middle states, at least, in this country, and is sufficiently characterized by its minute, soon livid, or grayish, and blackening, subglobose apothecia, and pluri(5–8)locular spores. This, which is well described (as *Bilimbia hypnophila*, l. c.) by Dr. Th. Fries, is the *Biatora muscorum* of Leighton (*Exs.* n. 91) and the *Lecidea viridescens* of the British Flora (*Herb. Borr.*) under which latter name it was first pointed out to me by my friend Mr. Russell. It occurs commonly upon mosses and also on the earth, in New England and New York; in Ohio (Mr. Lesquereux) Illinois (Mr. Hall) and New Jersey (Mr. Austin). The same plant is found upon schist, in Vermont (Mr. Russell; Mr. Frost) and I have collected it, in the White Mountains, upon dead wood. The finally fusiform, and 5–6–locular spores of the lignicoline, tropical lichen published in Wright *Lich. Cub.* n. 204 (*B. rufella*, Tuck. *in litt. Lecid. sphæroides*, v. *vacillans*, Nyl. *Lich. Scand.*, & in *Prodr. Fl. N. Gran.* p. 58, *not.*) should seem to refer it rather to the present species (*L. sphæroides*, v. *sabuletorum*, Nyl. *Scand.*) than the preceding (*L. sphæroides*, *a*, Nyl. l. c.) and, in that view, it may perhaps be said to strengthen the evidence that *B. hypnophila* should be kept apart from *B. sphæroides.* But if we distinguish specifically the Cuban lichens already referred to, as coming very close to the northern *B. vernalis*

(*L. subvernalis*, &c., given in Wright *Lich. Cub.* n. 198, &c.,) it may be less easy to apply a different rule in the case of the Cuban lichen before us.——*B. milliaria* (Fr., sub *Lecidea, pro p.*, & *Lich. Suec.* n. 29. *Bilimbia*, Koerb. *Syst.*, Th. Fr. *Lich. Arct.*) distinguishable by its small, globular, *black* apothecia, occurs on mosses in the alpine regions of the White Mountains, the elongated, dactyloid or subfusiform spores varying from 5- to plurilocular ; and on dead wood (v. *ligniaria*, Fr.) — when the spores are smaller, and commonly quadrilocular — both in the mountains, on charred pine stumps, and at Cambridge, Massachusetts.——*B. cupreorosella* (Nyl.) *Bilimbia bacidioides*, Koerb. *Parerg.* p. 167) Lime-rocks, Orange County, New York (Mr. Austin). In this interesting addition to our species, which agrees sufficiently with the published specimen (Mass. *Ital.* n. 211, B) as with the descriptions of Koerber and Stizenberger (*L. sabulet.*, *monogr.* p. 9, t. 1, B) the distinction between the present section (*Bilimbia* of authors) and the next (*Bacidia*) must be said to disappear ; the lichen being fairly assignable to either.

And we have thus reached, once more almost insensibly, a new, and the ultimate modification of the spore of *Biatora*, — the acicular. The continuous series of structural variations which commences in *B. vernalis*, finds its apparent complement in *B. rubella*. There is no break in the continuity. And *B. sphæroides*, taken as representative of its stock (*stirps*) as clearly passes, on the one hand into *B. rubella*, so taken, as, on the other, into *B. vernalis*. The just-cited description of *Bilimbia bacidioides*, Koerb., to make no other references to northern lichens, is of itself sufficient to indicate that Nature does not recognize these distinctions (the distinction, that is, between fusiform and acicular) here, any more than in *Peltigera* and *Sticta*. And it is scarcely open to doubt that both this species, as already remarked, and the tropical *Biat. medialis* (*Obs. Lich.* l. c. 6, p. 280, and Wright *Lich. Cub.* n. 203, especially as compared with n. 204) are in fact equally referable to *Bilimbia* and *Bacidia*.

But, suggestive as is the Friesian construction of *B. vernalis* (*L. E.* p. 260) which may well prove to have anticipated the method of much future study, it can hardly be denied that this group, under the microscope at' least, falls readily into smaller ones ; and that the integrant members of these are not seldom recognizable as what we call species. With respect however to the members of the smaller group, brought together, in the spirit of the same science, under *B. rubella* (*Lecidea luteola*, *Prodr.* p. 114) by Nylander, the case is by no means as clear. The tropical lichens approaching *B. parvifolia*, and yet more closely akin to *B. vernalis*, appear to be more distinguishable from the northern lichen, and from each other, than the corresponding tropical conditions associable with *B. rubella*. (*Obs. Lich.* l. c. 5, p. 279.) And the remark is perhaps equally true of the northern members of these groups as compared with their types. It is easier, in short, to look at *B. rubella* as a protean species, than as a group of species. Nor will spore-measurements, even though these represent results of a good many observations, well avail, where there is nothing else to rely upon.

The *Biatoræ* with much elongated, or acicular spores, constitute the genus *Bacidia*, De Not. The group is represented by many fine, but closely related forms in the tropics, among which the squamulose *Biatora microphyllina* (*Lecidea*, Tuck. *Obs. Lich.* l. c., and in Wright *Lich. Cub.* n. 211–218) an interesting analogue of *B. parvifolia*, in the first section, *B. prasina*, Mont. & Tuck., with almost filiform spores, and several interesting species from New Granada, published by Nylander (in *Herb. Lindig*, & *Prodr. N. Gran.*) are especially noteworthy. But I cannot follow the author last named, in separating as species (*Prodr. N. Gran.* p. 62, *not.*) the varying conditions of *B. microphyllina ;* or in distinguishing *Lecidea millegrana* (Tayl.) Nyl. (Wright *Lich. Cub.* n. 219. Lindig *Herb. N. Gran.* n. 771, &c.,) from *B. rubella.*

The view now to be offered of the latter species, as represented in North America, has not been arrived at, without repeated attempts to reach other results. But, conspicuously characterized as the intermediate conditions, supposed to be peculiar to America, undoubtedly appear, these are, if I mistake not, inseparable, in any large view, from the states, common to us and Europe, which begin and end the series ; and the differences of the last from each other, however considerable, are thus, here at least, explained by the mediation of the first. The apothecia, which (typically) differ from those of *B. vernalis*, and *B. sphæroides*, in being larger and flatter, and, in their primary condition, in an often brighter tint, become finally darkened, and pass into states most readily referable to *Lecidea ;* the at first pale hypothecium passing also, through a not dissimilar series of gradations, into dark-brown, dark-claret-coloured, and black. In all this, no really satisfactory stopping-place offers ; and should we attempt to keep apart from the exotic our more important American forms, and seek in *Lecidea spadicea*, Ach., the point of union of *Biatora suffusa* and *B. Schweinitzii*, the first of the last-named will none the less be found running into *B. rubella*, as the last into *B. muscorum.*

Biatora rubella (Ehrh.) Rabenh. (*B. vernalis, a, luteola*, Fr. L. E. p. 260. *B. luteola*, Fr., *Summ., a*) has occurred to Mr. Russell, and myself, on Elms and on Red Cedar in New England, in a state exactly accordant with the European (Moug. & Nestl. n. 641). But the granulose crust of this form becomes at length compacted even in the European lichen (*Bilimbia rubella v. fallax*, Koerb.; Stenh. *Lich. Suec. n.* 53, *pro max. p.;* and *Biat. polychroa*, Th. Fr., is perhaps another example, resembling not a little one of our common American forms) and this condition, with still large but darker apothecia, is probably what Acharius described (from Muhlenberg's specimens) as *Lecidea spadicea* 'apoth. fusco-badiis demum nigricantibus ;' and may still be called v. *spadicea*. It is far more frequent here than the other; extending throughout the United States, and common also in tropical America (Wright *Lich. Cub. n.* 220) where it

passes into the elegantly lecanoroid v. *millegrana* (*Lich. Cub.* n. 219).——
In the last-named form (v. *millegrana*) the margin is now white-pruinose,
when it is not always easy to distinguish it from a similar European state
of *a* (v. *porriginosa*, Ach.; *Herb. Borr.;* Rabenh. *Lich. Eur.* n. 581) not
unknown here; but in a very frequent North American condition, the
margin of which is undistinguishable in colour from the soon dark disk,
the whole apothecium is often suffused with white (*Biat. suffusa*, Fr.;
Tuck. *exs.* n. 135) indicating the v. *suffusa*. This occurs on trunks
throughout the northern States, and southward to South Carolina (Mr.
Ravenel) and has also been found on schist in Vermont (Mr. Frost).——
But the *Lecidea spadicea* of Acharius, is defined by him as finally blackening, and this variation becomes remarkably conspicuous in another
North American lichen, which may be said to touch, on the one hand, the
last, and, on the other, the immediately succeeding variety. This (*Biat.
Schweinitzii*, Fr. *herb.* Tuck. *exs.* n. 136) with a thallus commonly granulose, but occurring also more compacted, offers apothecia passing at
length, from paler and biatorine conditions, into entirely black ones, the
opake disk and shining margin of which exceedingly resemble *Lecidea
premnea*, Fr. *Lich. Suec.* n. 26 (being the plant so-called in the writer's
Syn. N. E. p. 67) and may be designated v. *Schweinitzii.*——Very near to
the last, but distinguishable by its smaller size and shorter spores, is the
v. *incompta*, Nyl. (*Prodr.* p. 115. *Lecidea incompta*, Borr.! Schær. *Lich.
Helv.* n. 212) a trunk-lichen, occurring, sufficiently well-marked, in New
England, in New York (Dr. E. C. Howe) and in Texas (Mr. Wright).
But this bark-form is not easily to be separated, at least here, from a
more common terricoline state (f. *muscorum*, Nyl. *Herb.* Th. Fr. Rabenh.
Lich. Eur. n. 514) with longer spores, which is frequent in New England,
and extends westward to Minnesota (Mr. Lapham) and northward to
Behring's Straits (Mr. Wright). I possess at least a New England, terricoline lichen which scarcely differs appreciably from the cited European
specimens (or from Rabenh. *Lich. Eur.* n. 496) of the v. *incompta*, excepting only that the now short spores become finally rather elongated; thus
agreeing generally with those of the three next preceding states, which
are, in like manner, sufficiently congruous with those of *a*, and of Stenh.
Lich. Suec. n. 53. These conditions of *B. rubella* (as here understood)
are members of what appears a single series of mutually related forms.
It remains to notice some small varieties, sometimes less easily referable
to the type. Among those known to Europe, v. *fusco-rubella*, Nyl. (*Lecid.
laurocerasi*, Delis.! *in Herb. Dubis.*) approaches however (as compare
Nyl. in *Prod. N. Gran.* p. 64, *not.*) too closely to the American v. *spadicea*, to be readily distinguishable; and either of these names might perhaps be adopted for the American lichen.——Very close to the last is the
v. *atro-grisea* (*Biat. atro-grisea*, Delis. *Lecid. luteola* v. *endoleuca*, Nyl.)
combining a pale hypothecium with externally blackened apothecia, —
which I cannot but recognize in a Californian lichen (Mr. Bolander).——

More distinct certainly appears a form from moist rocks, with granulose crust, and small, finally convex and blackening fruit, and slender spores (Pennsylvania, Dr. Michener; Vermont, Mr. Frost; New Jersey, Mr. Austin; western New York, Mr. Willey) referable, it should fully seem, to the v. *inundata,* Fr. (*Bacidia,* Koerb. *Syst. Secoliga,* Stizenb. *Bemerk.* p. 33). This form also occurs on rotten wood in Europe (f. *gibberosa,* Fr. *S. V. S. ?*) and such specimens, with livid, irregularly tumid apothecia, have been found by me in our mountains. In concluding here this review of the large and varied group of lichens which I cannot but associate together as states of *B. rubella,* it is proper to say that the smaller forms, comparable especially with v. *arceutina,* Ach., Nyl. (Stizenb. *Bemerk.* p. 38) have not yet been sufficiently explored, in North America. So far however as the examination of such forms, known to me—and I am indebted to my friend Mr. Willey for a peculiarly instructive collection, made in southern Massachusetts—extends, there is nothing to justify the separation of any of these lichens from the specific type we have been considering.——*B. stigmatella,* Tuckerm.,[1] found on trunks in Louisiana (Hale) can also, it is probable, rank no higher than a sub-species of *B. rubella.*——*B. umbrina* (Ach.) (*Lecidea,* Ach. *L. U.* p. 183, *e* Nyl. *Lich. Scand.* p. 209. *L. holomelæna,* Floerk., Schær. *Lich. Helv.* n. 536) is distinguished by its curved (now hooked and now S shaped) spores, and occurs, probably very commonly, on stones in walls, and also on mortar, and rocks, throughout New England; as also in New Jersey (Mr. Austin) and Virginia (Rev. Dr. Curtis). A variety (v. *asserculorum,* Koerb. Rabenh. *Lich. Eur.* n. 500) is frequent on old rails and pales, on the coast.——*B. chlorosticta* (*Lecidea,* Tuck. exs. n. 139; *Obs. Lich.* 1. c. 4, p. 419) an inhabitant of White Cedar at Hingham, and found also by Mr. Ravenel on Pine and Cypress in South Carolina, has recently been observed by Mr. Willey to occur not uncommonly, on the southern shore of Massachusetts, with sub-stipitate apothecia; suggesting (in this regard only) a comparison with *Helocarpon crassipes,* Th. Fr. Indications of this condition (f. *sub-stipitata*) are afforded by my other specimens; and the fruit was described at first as 'at length a little elevated.'——*B. chlorantha,* Tuck. Syn. N. Eng. p. 60, often conspicuous in the contrast offered by its lecideoid apothecia to its greenish thallus, is comparable, at least in the colourless hypothecium if in no other respect, with the later-published *B. atrogrisea,* Delis., but differs in its much smaller and slenderer

---

[1] *Biatora stigmatella : thallo granuloso-farinoso ochroleuco; apotheciis minutis* (0,3–0,5mm. *lat.*) *sessilibus subplanis e luteolo nigricantibus intus albis, margine tenui evanescente. Sporæ octonæ, aciculares, graciles, quadriloculares, incolores, longit.* 0,022–32mm., *crassit.* 0,002–3mm. *paraphysibus conglutinatis.*—Louisiana (Hale). Thallus not unlike that of *B. guernea;* but the granules more minute, and paler. Approaches some tropical types (as *Lecidea ischnospora,* Nyl. Lindig Herb. N. Gran. n. 2773) but is scarcely referable to any one of the minuter European members of the stock of *B. rubella.* The reaction with iodine is blue.

spores (0,023–34$^{mm.}$ long, and about 0,003$^{mm.}$ wide) which are numerous in the thekes. That the thekes are polysporous was first distinctly observed by Dr. Stizenberger, who found the spores 'in forties and fifties' in some of my specimens (Stizenb. *in litt.*) which have since afforded me similar results ; in many others the state of the thalamium precluded enquiry. The species, originally found on Pines on the coast of Massachusetts, and on Fir and Birch in the White Mountains (Myself) has since occurred on Fir, in the New York mountains (Mr. C. H. Peck) and on granitic rocks, New Bedford, Mass., (Mr. Willey).

It only remains to consider, as an appendix to the more easily determinable groups of *Biatora*, those myriosporous species, the exceeding minuteness (if not imperfectness) of the spores of which impedes any fair appreciation of structure, and real affinity. These species are brought together in *Biatorella*, and other genera, of recent authors ; and are now united in *Biatorella*, Th. Fr. (*Gen.* p. 86). But whether or not the condition which distinguishes them is to be taken as indicative of structural decline, Tulasne's comparison, already cited, of the myriosporous lichens with similarly aberrant *Fungi*, loses none of its interest for us in view of the fact that our best-known polysporous *Biatora* is itself a *Fungus*, according to Fries.

B. campestris, Fr. (*Sarcosagium biatorellum*, Mass., *ex* Almquist in *Flora*, 1869, p. 439). On the earth ; Illinois (Mr. E. Hall). Agreeing with the foreign specimens (*Herb. Fr.* Anz. *Lich. Lang.* n. 307). Rabenh. n. 507). Thallus indistinct, but true gonidia were observed. The reaction of the hymenium with iodine is marked. What is perhaps the same lichen was collected, too sparingly, on 'rocky ground,' in New Jersey (Mr. Austin). *B. fossarum*, (Duf.) Mont. (*Lecidea*, Nyl. *Prodr.* p. 116). On the earth ; 'not rare on sterile clays,' Illinois (Mr. Hall). New Jersey (Mr. Austin). Exactly agreeing with the European plant, as this is described ; and the linear spores 0,007–11$^{mm.}$ long, and about 0,003$^{mm.}$ wide. —— *B. cyphalea, Sp. nov.*, is manifestly of the same stock as the last, but differs in a granulose, becoming compact and chinky, white thallus ; reddish-brown apothecia (0$^{mm.}$5,–0$^{mm.}$8, wide) which are often conglomerate ; short, cuneate, 50–80–spored thekes ; and ellipsoid spores measuring only 0,003–4$^{mm.}$ long, and 0,002$^{mm.}$ wide. It was detected on Elm-bark, in Illinois (Mr. Hall) and has not occurred elsewhere. —— *B.'Ilicis*, Willey *msc.* On Holly, New Bedford, Mass. (H. Willey). The very minute apothecia blackening and in this way observable on the white crust. Spores globular. —— *B. geophana* (Nyl. *sub Lecid., Scand.* p. 212). On the earth, upon flat rocks, New Jersey, Mr. Austin. Apothecia without apparent margin, black. Spores globular, 0,006$^{mm.}$ to 0,008$^{mm.}$ in diameter, and from fourteen to eighteen in the thekes ; paraphyses not distinguished ; but the blue reaction with iodine sufficiently evident. This very obscure plant has since been detected, at New Bedford, Mass., by Mr. Willey. It appears to agree, in all its features, with the cited description of Nylander.——*B. resinæ* (Fr.) (*Lecidea*, Fr. *Obs. Myc.* Nyl. *Prodr.* p. 117; *Scand.* p. 213. *Peziza*, Fr. *Syst. Myc.*, 2, p. 149) is probably not a lichen, notwithstanding its behaviour with iodine. It occurs here on the exposed and indurated resin of the White Pine, where it was first detected at New Bedford (Mr. Willey) and similarly on the Pitch Pine, in Vermont (Mr. Frost) as on Larch in New Jersey (Mr. Austin). Another plant, similar to this as respects paraphyses and spores, but with black apothecia, not unlike those of *Lecan. cervina*, v. *privigna*, f. *simplex*, occurs on the resin of White Pine, in Vermont (Mr. Frost) but has afforded no blue reaction with iodine.

XLIII.—HETEROTHECIUM, Flot., emend.

Flot. in Bot. Zeit., 1850, p. 369, 553, pro max. p. Heterothecium, Mont. & V. d. Bosch Lich. Jav. p. 36. Lecanoræ sp., et Lecideæ sp., Ach. Lecanoræ et Lecideæ spp., Fée Ess. p. 107, 114; Suppl. p. 103, 111. Biatoræ et Lecideæ spp., Fr. L. E. pp. 259, 335. Megalospora, Mey. & Flot. in Nov. Act. Nat. Cur. 19, Suppl. Mont. Aperçu Morph. p. 11. Heterothecium, Biatoræ spp., et Sporopodium, Mont. in Ann. Sci. Nat.; Guy. p. 36, t. 16, f. 1; Syll. p. 338; M. & V. d. Bosch Lich. Jav. p. 36. Lecideæ sect. A, * * * * * Nyl. Enum. Gén. l. c. p. 122; Lich. exot. in Ann. Sci. Nat. l. c. p. 224, 260; in Prodr. Fl. N. Gran. p. 65; Syn. Lich. N. Caled. p. 49. Tuckerm. Obs. Lich. l. c. 6, p. 280. Megalospora, Psorothecium, Bombyliospora, Lopadium, Heterothecium, et Sporopodium, Mass. Ric. pp. 105, 114; Alc. Gen. p. 9; Esam. p. 16. Megalospora, Bombyliospora et Lopadium, Koerb. Syst. p. 210, 256; Parerg. p. 174, 228. Mycoblastus, Bombyliospora, et Lopadium, Th. Fr. Gen. p. 83, 89. Lecideæ sp., Psorothecium, et Heterothecium, Stizenb. Beitr. l. c. pp. 160, 162.

Apothecia patellæformia, excipulo proprio margine sub-incrassato subinde lecanoroideo. Sporæ plerumque magnæ, ex ellipsoideo oblongæ, l. simplices l. bi-pluriloculares l. muriformi-multiloculares, subincolores l. fuscescentes. Spermatia (quantum observ.) ellipsoidea l. oblonga; sterigmatibus simplicibus. Thallus crustaceus, uniformis.

The monograph of *Heterothecium* promised by the author of the genus did not appear; and little remains to illustrate his conception of it,[1] but some cursory remarks in the cited letter to Fries (*Bot. Zeit.* l. c.). Together with much going to shew that the author's investigations were still far from complete, we find here, grouped around *H. tuberculosum*, as centre,

[1] The genus was named indeed, and the European lichens taken to belong to it, reckoned, in Koerber's *Grundriss d. Cryptogamenkunde*, 1848, two years before the publication in the *Bot. Zeitung ;* but without descriptions.

H. versicolor, H. endochroma, H. Domingense, and *H. leucoxanthum;* which is precisely *Heterothecium* as finally accepted by Montagne. Among the species originally brought together in *Megalospora*—the first conception of the genus, and, in some respects, possibly the purest—*Lecidea sanguinaria* was however included; and Flotow retained this, though '*mit unsicherheit,*' in his later revision. For reasons to be given below, I shall venture here to take the same view of this difficult lichen; and cannot hesitate also to consider *H. pezizoideum* as in fact congenerical with *H. leucoxanthum.*

Thus viewed, with the exception at least of the still doubtful *Lecidea sanguinaria,* and *L. grossa,* the group is a natural one, and is accepted as such by Nylander, who has largely illustrated it, and with whom it constitutes the last division of the first section of his *Lecidea;* or, as we should express it, the head of *Biatora.* From this last the present genus is distinguished (leaving out of account the mostly superficial, though often striking resemblance to *Lecanora*) by its spore-type: being really analogous in *Biatorei* to *Physcia,* in *Parmeliei, Rinodina,* in *Lecanorei,* and *Buellia* in *Lecideei;* though better comparable as a tropical group, and tending similarly to more varied modifications, and even anomalies of spore-structure, to the equally tropical *Thelotrema* and *Graphis.* In all these genera the spores belong (in great part manifestly) to that series, the ultimate modification of which is the muriform-multilocular; expressed here by the section *Lopadium,* and in *Buellia* by the section *Rhizocarpon.* And such is the general affinity of the lichens brought together in the last-named groups to those which express in their spores the next preceding stage of differentiation (*sectt. Bombyliospora,* & *Eubuellia*) that the question has been raised already (Th. Fr. *Lich. Arct.* p. 226, & *Gen.* p. 92) with respect to *Rhizocarpon,* Massal., whether there is really reason for keeping it apart from *Buellia.* Dr. Fries's striking illustration from acolium, 'the analogous genus of the *Caliciacei,*' where *A. Notarisii* appears scarcely otherwise to differ from *A. tigillare* than as *Rhizocarpon* from *Buellia,* and that also from *Rhizocarpon geographicum,* Massal., the variety *alpicolum* of which is in fact a *Buellia,* are much to the point; and so too, if I do not mistake, is an analogous example from *Arthonia,* where *A. cyrtodes,* Tuck. (*Obs. Lich.* l. c. 6, p. 285) presents in one form (Wright *Lich. Cub.* n. 245) otherwise specifically undistinguishable from the other, spores similar to those of *Bombyliospora,* and in the other (*Lich. Cub.* n. 246) the mural-multilocular ones typical of this section of *Arthonia* (*Arthothelium,* Massal.) and of *Lopadium.* These observations apply equally to the section of the present genus with bilocular spores (*Psorothecium,* Massal.).

Nor can the evidence of affinity afforded by general similarity of structure and habit be safely disregarded. This brings closely together *H. Taitense,* Mont. (*Psorothecium,* Massal.) and *H. tuberculosum* (*Bombyliospora,* Massal.) and is so decided in the case of *H. vulpinum* (which should belong to *Heterothecium*, Massal.) that there is possibly no other way to distinguish it from *H. Domingense* (and *Bombyliospora*) than by the mural spore-cells.

The *Buellia*-spore is at first colourless and simple; and if we conceive this primary condition as becoming (like other modifications) typical, and in a lichen otherwise referable to the present, large-spored group, we shall have perhaps the best, and in some points of view a far from uninteresting explanation of one of the anomalies of *H. sanguinarium*.

The position of myriosporous lichens in the system, must, it is evident, be determined, by those lichenists who allow to the anomaly referred to only a subordinate value, by whatever other evidence the plants afford. *Biatorella* becomes thus reducible to *Biatora ;* and *Sporastatia* to *Lecidea*. And Flotow exercised only a similar act of judgment in referring *Lecidea conspersa*, Fée, to *Heterothecium*. The very minute spores of this species shew indeed no trace of structural modification, like that which illuminates those of *Rinodina constans ;* but the whole habit of the lichen associates it, not with *Biatora* § *Biatorella*, but with the present genus. And the same must be said of the myriosporous *Lecidea Wrightii* (*Obs. Lich.* l. c. 6, p. 275; Wright *Lich. Cub.* n. 235) which, associable with *Biatorella* by nothing but the minuteness and number of the spores, offers a tartareous thallus ill to be compared with anything representing thallus in the group just-named, and apothecia with the exact aspect of those of *Heterothecium tuberculosum* v. *porphyritis*.

The genus is, as already remarked, mainly confined to the warmer regions of the earth. Of the conspicuous forms known (rather exceeding forty) four fifths are intertropical; five of which extend northward into our Southern States. Only five are decidedly northern ; two of which are common to Europe and the northern half of North America, one is peculiar to the latter, and two are found only in Europe.

The designation *Megalospora* is retained by Massalongo, and by Koerber, for *H. sanguinarium* (L.) Flot., with which species, in several respects apparently anomalous,[1] the view we have now to offer of the genus, as represented here, may not improperly commence. This well-known lichen, occurring commonly, on trunks, dead wood, rocks, and on the earth-incrusting mosses, in the mountains of New England, where it ascends to alpine districts, and also on the north-eastern coast, extends probably through arctic America, where Mr. Wright found it in islands of Behring's Straits, and descends the west coast to California (Mr. Bolander). Its apothecia are described by several recent writers as structurally im-

---

[1] Considered as a *Lecidea*, in the sense of Fries, the plant, or its stock (compare Nyl. in *Prodr. Fl. N. Gran.* p. 72) is in fact isolated; whether still kept within the larger group, as by Nylander, or made to rank as a separate generical type, as by most other recent lichenographers. But this isolation is at least less marked from Flotow's position.

marginate ('*propter excipuli defectum immarginata*,' Koerb.) and this is possibly not far from expressing the now common opinion of lichenists. But the presumption is against such anomaly ; and both Acharius (*Lichenogr.*) and Fries have described a proper exciple, coloured like the disk in its normal (black) state. Very few however, it is likely, have been able to repeat these observations, and I offer therefore the following, for what they shall prove to be worth. In their common, convex condition, the (mature) apothecia illustrate certainly Acharius's description of an immarginate, turgid disk, which has taken up with it in its turgescence, a portion (*apophysis*, Ach.) of the thallus upon which it grows ; and there is little in this case, even in section, to suggest an excipular margin. But flatter, which are also to be considered more normal examples, are often a little elevated, at *all* points, above the thallus, when there appears (quite frequently in our plant, but to be observed also in the European) a white, depressed, marginal ring, contrasting with the colour of the epithallus, and, in some of the specimens published by the writer (*Lich. exs.* n. 137) visible to the naked eye. Examined with a sufficient lens this ring is seen to be minutely filamentous, and comparable therefore (it is possible) with the filamentous border of *Biatora tricholoma*, Mont.; and similarly also to Montagne's lichen, as described by him, in which this border is said to be rufous (as it occurs in a Cuban specimen before me, referable here) the corresponding part in the northern plant is not rarely more or less tinged with the hue of the red layer, commonly taken for hypothecial ('*excipuli proprii sanguinei*,' Mass.). But the filamentous margin of the tropical *Biatora* becomes finally all but obsolete, and a proper, excipular border obscurely visible ; and, in like manner, in the oldest and largest, flat apothecia (measuring now, in undoubtedly single instances, from 2 to 3$^{mm.}$ in width) of the set of North American specimens of *H. sanguinarium* before me, the filamentous ring ceases to be observable, and there appears instead, not seldom, what in other lichens might easily be construed as a depressed, originally pale but blackening (or now, here and there reddening) proper margin. And whether the comparison have any real value or not, there is little in the appearance of this supposed, or simulated margin to distinguish it from the equally depressed and blackening, true border in old, turgid apothecia of *H. endochroma* (Fée) Flot. (Wright *Lich. Cub.* n. 226) ; and the whole habit of such apothecia, both in the cited species, and in *H. leptocheilum*, Tuck. (*Lich. Cub.* n. 227) is not a little suggestive of the northern lichen ; though young fruits offer nothing certainly of the strange convexity of those of the latter. But in *Biatora quernea*, another lichen of the present family which has been repeatedly described as structurally immarginate, the proper margin (as noted in *Obs. Lich.* l. c. p. 275) though not undiscoverable in young apothecia, becomes yet clearly evident only in the largest and most perfect ones.——The protoplasm of the large spore of *H. sanguinarium* acquires the same yellowish tinge which is observable in those of *H. versicolor*

(Fée) and other instances: but the value of this note is questionable; and the genus, as a whole, with only a few decided exceptions belonging to the last section, in which the ultimate, muriform configuration of the spore-type is reached (*Lopadium*) exhibits colourless spores. That these are not typically colourless, but rather decolorate, is yet as conceivable in the case of *Lecidea grossa* (Pers.) Nyl. (*Catillaria, Auctt. Psorothecium,* Mass. *Esam.*) and other lichens, which Massalongo has, not without reason, associated with it, as in the case of *Catillaria concreta,* Koerb., in its confessedly difficult relations to some recognized forms of *Buellia.*

It is here the place, in view of *Lecidea grossa*, to say again, with Fries, that even the most subtle characters must give place to undoubted affinity. To us it is impossible to question the continuity of the series of changes by which the pale hypothecium of *Biatora rubella, a,* is transformed into the finally black one which underlies the intensely black disk of a form, already above alluded to, of *B. rubella,* v. *Schweinitzii;* and the latter, however Lecideine, — and it simulates as well, very closely, *Lecidea grossa,* — is none the less a *Biatora.* In *B. atro-purpurea* (Mass. *Lecid. intermixta,* Nyl.) which, passing through a succession of changes, in both external and internal coloration, similar to that of *Biatora rubella,* reaches at length, in like manner, a blackened state most readily comparable with *Lecidea,* we have a yet more interesting example of the same sort; as this species agrees also with *L. grossa* in the structure of its spores. Nor is this denigration of the hypothecium any more strange to the genus before us; as, to take but a single instance, fully appears in "*Lecidea melanocarpa,* Nyl. (*Heterothecium sensu Flot.*) . . . apothecia atra intus fere nigra (vel hymenio solum sectione cinerascente) hypothecium denigratum,*" &c. (Nyl. *Lich. exot.* l. c. p. 260) which, as described, is scarcely less Lecideine, though, at the same time, without doubt associable with the same cluster of species which includes *Heteroth. tuberculosum,* than *Lecidea grossa.*

Of the section with bilocular spores (*Psorothecium,* Mass.) no example has been found within the limits of the United States. *H. versicolor* occurs in the island of Cuba (Wright *Lich. Cub.* n. 225) with *H. leptocheilum,* and *H. endochroma,* both also given in Wright's collection, and the last also in Mexico (Nyl.) *H. Simodense* (*Lecidea,* Tuck. *Obs. Lich.*) is a Japanese lichen. The last three of these species are distinguishable from the first by their much smaller spores, but they are closely related to each other and to that in every other respect. And the first is equally near to types of the next section (*Bombyliospora,* Massal.) which only differs from the present in the number of the spore-cells.

H. (*Bombyliospora*) *tuberculosum* is the earliest described of a group of similar lichens, which, occurring throughout the intertropical regions, affords also one example in the milder districts of western, and the mountains of central Europe; and another not known beyond New England in America. The last two are easily distinguishable from each other, but look like outlying representatives of the same type; of which the tropics offer us many more modifications. It is difficult not to follow Flotow in referring the European *Biatora pachycarpa* to a variety of *H. tuberculosum;* and if the American *B. porphyritis* is, at present, geographically considered, and hence possibly otherwise, more distinct, examples are not wanting of forms from the warmer regions of the earth which approach it so closely, that we may well doubt whether the remote ancestor of our New England lichen differed at all from the predecessor of the tropical ones. Nor is it safer here to rely upon the number of spores in the thekes, than in *Pertusaria;* upon the perplexities in this regard in which genus, and especially in the stock represented by *P. leioplaca,* Koerber (*Parerg.* p. 318) and especially Nylander (in *Prodr.* Fl. N. Gran. p. 37) furnish instructive observations. Thus viewed, the group of lichens now immediately before us, will be associable possibly in something like the following order.

Heterothecium tuberculosum (Fée) Flot.

a, porphyrites: apotheciis nigrescentibus, primitus albo-pruinosis, margine concolori; sporis solitariis, 3–6–locularibus. Biatora porphyritis, Tuck. Syn. N. E., p. 61, & *Lich. exs.* n. 96.—Trunks in the White Mountains; and in swamps in Western Massachusetts. New Bedford, Mass. (Mr. Willey). Vermont (Mr. Frost). Distinguishable, as compared with the next, by its dark, pruinose apothecia, and shorter spores; and remarkable for its northern range. In the finest condition of the lichen, which inhabits the original forest, at an elevation of not far from 3000 feet, in the White Mountains, the apothecia are very large, reaching from 2 to 3$^{mm.}$, and at length exceeding 4$^{mm.}$, in width. Spores also large, as in all the forms; which are scarcely to be well distinguished by differences in this regard.

β, pachycarpum: apotheciis rufo-fuscis (nigrescentibus) margine pallido dein denigrato; sporis solitariis, 6–12–locularibus. Lecidea tuberculosa, Fée *Ess.* p. 107, t. 27, f. 1, & Suppl. p. 103. *Biatora pachycarpa,* Fr. *L. E.* p. 259. *Heterothecium tuberculosum,* & *v. pachycarpum,* Flot. in *Bot. Zeit.* l. c. *Bombyliospora versicolor* & *B. pachycarpa,* Massal. *Ric.* p. 115.——Trunks in tropical countries (Wright *Lich. Cub.* n. 228. Lindig. *Herb. N. Gran.* n. 709, 723, 755, &c.) and occurring also, but rarely fertile, in western Europe, and in the Bavarian Alps, (*Herb. Borr.* Zw. *exs.* n. 80. *Herb. Krempelh. Herb. Th. Fr.*) Apothecia commonly lighter coloured than those of the last, and the spores longer; but the former difference will not hold; and in a Hong Kong specimen, with blackened apothecia (Mr. Wright) before me, the spores are quite the same with those of the American plant. Nylander remarks (*Prodr.* p. 118) that Fée's species is scarcely more than an exotic form of *Biatora pachycarpa;* and I am at a loss to indicate any distinction between them.

The tropical lichen owes its name to the often warted thallus; but this difference at length disappears. In the f. *chlorites* (*Lecidea*, Tuck. *in litt.* Nyl. in *Prodr. Fl. N. Gran.* p. 66) these warts are sulphur-coloured within, and the plant (Wright *Lich. Cub.* n. 229) is also distinguishable by smaller apothecia. It has been detected in southern Alabama (Mr. Beaumont).

γ, *pachycheilum* : *apotheciis rufo-fuscis* (*nigrescentibus*) *margine turgidulo pallido; sporis* 2–4^{nis}, 4–8–*locularibus, curvulis.* *Lecidea pachycheila,* Tuck. *Obs. Lich.* l. c. 6, p. 281, & in Wright *Lich. Cub.* n. 230. Nyl. l. c. p. 67. The pale exciple, and shorter, often sickle-shaped spores, occurring in 2s and 4s in the thekes, distinguish this lichen, which has been found on the seaboard of South Carolina (Mr. Ravenel) in southern Alabama (Mr. Beaumont) in Mississippi (Dr. Veitch) and in Louisiana (Hale). Dr. Nylander compares it with the f. *chlorites* of the preceding variety, but it also closely approaches the next.

δ, *amplificans* : *apotheciis 'pallide spadiceo-testaceis'* (*nigrescentibus*) *margine turgido pallido; sporis* 4–8^{nis}, 9–11–*locularibus.* *Lecidea amplificans,* Nyl. in *Prodr. Fl. N. Gran.* p. 67, & in *Herb.* Lindig, n. 2812. So far as my specimens go, this New Granada lichen appears probably the finest condition of the species. It is readily comparable with the last however, and through that with *L. tuberculosa*, Fée, with which it also agrees in its warted thallus.

H. Domingense (Pers.) (*Lecanora*, Ach., Fée. *Parmelia gyrosa*, Mont. *Heterothecium*, Flot.). — Trunks in the low country of South Carolina (Mr. Ravenel) and Louisiana (Hale). From this, *H. vulpinum*, Tuckerm. (*Obs. Lich.* l. c. 6, p. 281, *sub Lecid.* Wright *Lich. Cub.* n. 233) as respects all more obvious features, whether of thallus or apothecia (though the last are smaller) should scarcely be separable; but the larger spores are muriform-multilocular, as characteristical in the next section. Very different inferences may be drawn from this. One may well be that the weight of the evidence favours placing the lichen with *H. Domingense*, notwithstanding the great difference in the spores; its relation to the other being not dissimilar to that of *Arthonia cyrtodes* β, already cited, to *a* : and that thus we have a new instance in the argument against allowing more than subordinate value to the distinction of the muriform spore generally, from the antecedent plurilocular; not without interest, especially in such genera as *Thelotrema, Graphis,* and *Pyrenula*.——In *H. aureolum*, Tuckerm. (*Lecidea*, Tuck. l. c. Nyl. in *Prodr. Fl. N. Gran.* p. 68) we have, on the other hand, dissimilarity in general habit from *H. Domingense*, with similarity in the spores. These small-spored species of *Heterothecium* make less applicable the original name of the genus (*Megalospora*) but are by no means separable from it. But the final modification of the type of spore, of which *Bombyliospora* expresses a stage, is the muriform-multilocular: characterizing (in the present group of Lichens) *Heterothecium*, Mass., and *Lopadium*, Koerb.; and exactly corresponding to our section *Rhizocarpon* in *Buellia*. Of this convenient but artificial section we possess two species.——*H. leucoxanthum* (Spreng.) (*Lecidea*, Spreng. in *Act. Holm.*, 1820, p. 46. Nyl. in *Prodr. Fl. N. Gran.* p. 69. *Heterothecium tricolor*, Mont. *Syll.* p. 341. *H. bicolor*, Flot. in *Bot. Zeit.* l. c.). Swamps in the upper country of North Carolina (Rev. Dr. Curtis) South Carolina (Mr. Ravenel) Alabama (Mr. Peters) Mississippi (Dr. Veitch) Louisiana (Hale) Texas (Mr. Ravenel). Otherwise only intertropical. Spores solitary, large, oblong, more or less yellowish-brownish, the at first grumous protoplasm developing into many small spore-cells, crowded together in (15–25) somewhat regular (but soon irregular) annular series, like coarse mason-work; from three to four times longer than wide.——*H. pezizoideum* (Ach.) Flot. in *Bot. Zeit.* l. c. (*Lecidea*, Ach. Nyl. *Scand.* p. 212. *Lopadium*, Koerb. *Syst.* p. 210. Th. Fr. *Lich. Arct.* p. 201. *Biatora vernalis* β, f., Fr. *L. E.* p. 264. *Trachylia phæomelana*, Tuck. *Lich. exs.* n. 98).— On fir bark in the White Mountains; and in Maine (Myself) and on cedars, New Bedford (Mr. Willey). On the earth, growing over mosses, Greenland (J. Vahl, *e* Th. Fr. l. c.) and in islands of Behring's Straits (Mr. Wright). A northern lichen which the turbinate (substipitate) apothecia well distinguish from all but the Cuban *H. turbinatum* (*Lecidea*, Tuck. *Obs. Lich.* l. c.). Another northern species of the present section is *H. fusco-luteum* (Dicks.) of alpine districts in Scotland (*Herb. Dicks. Herb. Hook.*) first referred to its true affinity by Mudd (Man. Brit. Lich. p. 190) which may well occur, at least in arctic America.

It has been remarked above that the obvious affinity of two or three myriosporous lichens of the present family is with *Heterothecium ;* and that there is nothing to associate them with *Biatora* § *Biatorella* but the abnormal character of their spore-evolution; an irregularity by no means confined to *Biatora*. One of these lichens was referred here by Flotow; and another resembles this. The third, though associable only with a very different cluster, is yet equally at home here.——*H. conspersum* (Fée) Flot. in *Bot. Zeit.* l. c. (Wright *Lich. Cub.* n. 224). A tropical species, which has occurred in southern Alabama (Mr. Beaumont). Spores exceedingly minute, and numerous; globular.——*H. nannarium*, Tuckerm.,[1] a dwarf indeed in this large-fruited genus — the apothecia scarcely reaching 0,3$^{mm.}$ in width — is otherwise generally comparable with the last; but the disk of the fruit is not powdery (*conspersus*) and the thekes, instead of being long-club-shaped, are ovoid. I have it only from Texas (Mr. Wright).——*H. Wrightii*, Tuckerm. (*Lich. Cub.* n. 235) a Cuban myriosporous species, with the aspect of a state of *H. tuberculosum*, may possibly prove to occur within our southern limits.

---

[1] *Heterothecium nannarium* (*sp. nova*) *thallo granuloso-farinoso citrino; apotheciis valde minutis* (0,15–0,25$^{mm.}$ *lat.*) *sessilibus sub-planis, disco ferrugineo-fusco, margine flavicante. Sporæ in thecis ovoideis numerosissimæ, minutissimæ, globulares, incolores, paraphysibus parcis.*—On bark, near the Blanco, Texas (C. Wright). The reaction with iodine is blue.

Sub - Fam. 3. — EULECIDEEI.

Apothecia subsessilia, excipulo atro.

XLIV. — LECIDEA (Ach.) Fr., emend.

Fr. Vet. Ac. Handl. 1822, et S. O. V. p. 252, max. p. ; L. E., p. 281, spp. excl. Eschw. Syst. p. 17. Flot. Lich. Sil. ; in Koerb. Grundr. d. Crypt. ; in Bot. Zeit. 1850, p. 382. Mont. Aperçu Morph. 1. c. p. 11. Tuckerm. Syn. N. E. p. 63 ; Lich. Calif. p. 24. Lecidea, Ach. L. U. p. 32, Syn. p. 11, pr. p. Schær. Spicil. p. 101, Enum. p. 94, pr. p. Eschw. Lich. Bras. l. c. p. 241, pr. p. Nyl. Enum. Gén. l. c. p. 123, Lich. Scand. p. 185, Lich. And. Boliv. l. c. p. 381, Addend. nov. ad Lich. Eur. in Flora Ratisb. ; pr. p. Patellariæ spp., Mey., Wallr. Lecidea et Scolecites, Norm. Con. p. 22. Thalloidima, Psoræ sp., Lecidea, Arthrosporum, Toninia, Rhaphiospora, pr. p., et Sporastatia, Mass. Ric., et opp. varr. Astroplaca, Thalloidima, Schæreria, Porpidia, Stenhammera, Lecidella, Lecidea, Arthrosporum, Toninia, Rhaphiospora, pr. p. ; et Sporastatia, Koerb. Syst. ; Parerg. Lecidea max. p., Stenhammera, Scolecites max. p., Biatoræ sp., et Sporostatia, Stizenb. Beitr. l. c.

Structuram exposuerunt Tulasne, Mém. sur les Lich. pp. 15, 165, t. 13, f. 14–17; Fuisting l. c. p. 23.

Apothecia patellæformia, excipulo proprio carbonaceo, atro. Sporæ ex ellipsoideo fusiformes l. dein aciculares, e simplici, rarius bi-quadri-pluriloculares, incolores. Spermatia ex oblongo bacillaria l. filiformia; sterigmatibus subsimplicibus. Thallus crustaceus, effiguratus aut uniformis.

" *Servavi hoc loco genus eodem sensu, quo primitus proposui, utpote habitui et practicæ Lichenum cognitioni optime inserviente. Recentiores ad species disco strato carbonaceo imposito tantum restrinxerunt, et, licet hi limites magis Systematici videantur, in natura facile evanescunt et simillima removent.*" Fr. L. E. p. 282. In accordance with the method of the present treatise, the species with brown spores are however excluded; and the systematic value of the several structural modifications of the colourless spore is estimated as in *Lecanora* and *Biatora*.

Almost all the *Lecideæ*, as here understood, were first made known as European; it is yet every way probable that a very large part of these will prove to be common to the northern hemisphere. And Nylander has shewn (*Lich. And. Boliv.*) that the group of familiar, saxicoline species typified by *L. contigua* is well represented in the Andes of South America; which thus afford, he says (*l. c.*, in *Ann.* 4, 15, p. 366) additional evidence of the truth of what he has elsewhere affirmed — that the saxicoline lichens, generally, have of all others the widest distribution.

But what with the abundance and variableness of the rock-*Lecideæ*,.

23

the determination of *species* (compare Fr. *L. E.* p. 282) is especially difficult; and the labour which has been given to this in Europe has yet to be
attempted here. Estimates of European lichenographers of the present
day differ indeed so widely as to the rank of the forms described, that it
is hardly to be questioned that the confusion which Fries (*Lich. Eur.*)
did so much, here as elsewhere, to remove, threatens now, with the
increasing depreciation of other standards of judgment in view of a merely
microscopical one, to return; and the species to become as uncertain as
they were before Fries. The vast extent of our territory is less then in
the way of an early determination of our *Lecideæ*, than the paucity of
enquirers, and the perplexities of the enquiry. Of the thirty species now
known to me as North American, but two are properly or mainly calcareous; while the proportion of calcareous forms in the rupicoline groups
of Europe is nearly one quarter of the whole number of forms: a fact
which indicates sufficiently an interesting field for exploration. Another
is, without doubt, afforded by the maritime rocks of California, the
lichenose Flora of which has been so largely exhibited by Mr. H. N.
Bolander; and yet another, and perhaps the most promising of any, by
the alpine rocks of the Rocky Mountains. And there is no reason to
suppose that the desultory studies of the very few lichenists who have
collected in the ranges of the Appalachian chain, though this has yielded
us almost all we know, have exhausted its treasures.

We find the true centre of *Lecidea* in the large group of lichens,
inhabiting mostly granitic rocks, of which *L. contigua*, Fr., is the well-
known type (*Lecidea*, Koerb.). But the black hypothecium of this
species passes gradually, in forms otherwise closely allied to it, into a
colourless (*Lecidella*, Koerb.) looking not seldom, and in other respects
(especially in the little cluster typified by *L. arctica*) towards *Biatora*.
With the arctic cluster is most readily associable *L. enteroleuca ;* and the
needle-shaped, bowed spermatia of the latter species relate it to the
effigurate section (*Psoræ* sp., *Thallædema*, Auctt.) much as the same
organs in *Lecanora subfusca* connect this with the effigurate section of
Lecanora. With this sketch of the outlines of the genus, conceived strictly
in the sense of Nylander, as respects that portion of his *Lecidea* to which
the name is here confined, we proceed to indicate briefly such species as
have been added recently to our list.

Of the first section (*Thallædema*) consisting of effigurate species,
almost all calcareous, analogous to *Squamaria* in *Lecanora*, and to *Psora*
in *Biatora*, though differing from the last in a much more evident tendency
in the spores (a tendency not however quite unknown to the biatorine
group) to pass into bilocular conditions, we possess only the long-ascer-
tained *L. candida* (Web.) Ach., and *L. vesicularis* (Hoffm.) Ach., indicated
as occurring in Arctic America by Hooker, and the former also by Th.
Fries. *L. vesicularis* is only known to me, as an United States lichen, in
specimens recently collected in the Uintah mountains, Utah (S. Watson)

and in Ogden, Utah (Dr. Lapham) but there exists also a specimen in Schweinitz's herbarium which may possibly have been collected in the United States. The 'bad lands' of Nebraska, where *Placodium fulgens*, and *Buellia epigœa* were found by Professor Hayden, may possibly yet increase our knowledge of the present group.

To the far less conspicuous assemblage of forms represented by *L. enteroleuca*, Ach., we have to add *L. vitellinaria*, Nyl., a parasite of the thallus of *Placodium vitellinum*, which has been found in Greenland specimens of the *Placodium* by Dr. Th. Fries (*Lich. Arct.* p. 222) and has occurred to me in Rocky Mountain ones (Prof. Hayden).——Rock-forms of *L. enteroleuca* are not uncommon throughout the country, from Nebraska (Dr. Hayden) to Pennsylvania (*determ. Nyl.*, Dr. Michener) and North Carolina (Rev. Dr. Curtis) and sometimes (Vermont, Mr. Frost) sufficiently resemble specimens of his *L. sabuletorum* f. *arenaria* (*L. sabuletorum*, Koerb., Th. Fr.) determined by Flotow. But the minutely granulate thallus of the last is at length more distinctly areolate-verrucose, and such a condition (v. *theioplaca, areolis verruculosis in crustam pallide stramineam congestis*) occurring on serpentine rocks in California (Mr. Bolander) might easily be taken for distinct, yet agrees with the present species in its spores, and spermatia, and only differs in colour (though this is interesting in its bearings on the true rank of the cited *L. sabuletorum*) conformably to the variations of the bark-lichen. From some of these saxicoline states appears scarcely to differ otherwise than in habitat the v. *muscorum* (*L. sabuletorum*, v. *muscorum*, Th. Fr. *Biat. Wulfenii*, Hepp) occurring in Greenland (J. Vahl, *e* Th. Fr. *l. c.*) and in islands of Behring's Straits (Mr. Wright).——Other muscicoline and terricoline *Lecideœ* accompany the last in arctic and alpine districts, of which *L. arctica*, Sommerf., is not uncommon in the alpine region of the White Mountains; and has been found also in Greenland (Th. Fr. *l. c.*) and, with the last, by Mr. Wright.——*L. pallida*, Th. Fr., readily distinguished from *L. arctica* by its pale thallus, has also occurred in Greenland (J. Vahl, *l. c.*).——And *L. borealis*, Koerb., was collected by Mr. Wright in islands of Behring's Straits, the specimens agreeing with Schær. *Helv.* n. 195, as also with authentic ones of *L. alpestris*, Th. Fr.[1]——*L. turgidula*, Fr.

---

[1] The latter name is given, as in many similar cases by recent writers, in what I must consider mistaken deference to the *L. sabuletorum β, syncomista,* b, *alpestris* of Sommerfelt. But the author of the Supplement to the *Flora Lapponica* did not refer his lichen to any "*Lecidea alpestris*," but to *L. sabuletorum,*—that is to an old species; and the writer who first proposed for it the rank of a new one, should seem to have a right to the credit of it. And I shall venture here to express anew the opinion,—for correction at least, if it require it,—'that the name which may happen to be given to a variety has no precedence; but may be adopted or not, if the plant be taken up as a species.' The case is the same with sections of genera. The other method has at least the objection that it makes the earlier writer whose variety-name it is sought to elevate into a species-name

(*Lich. Suec.* n. 25) inhabiting the bark and dead wood of Pines, &c., was detected in Greenland by J. Vahl (Th. Fr. *l. c.* p. 217) and I have observed it accompanying other lichens (on *Libocedrus*) from California (Mr. Bolander).——*L. melancheima*, Tuck. Syn. N. Eng. p. 68, & *Lich. exs.* n. 138 (*L. sabuletorum* v. *euphorea*, Fr. L. E. p. 340, & *Lich. Suec.* n. 154; *non* Floerk. *L. euphoroides*, Nyl. *Lich. Scand.* p. 244) is common throughout New England, but not known to me from any locality southward.—— *L. Diapensiæ*, Th. Fr. l. c., is also to be credited to our alpine districts; but the White Mountain lichen, which is frequent on dead sods of *Diapensia*, differs from the description, and from my European specimens, in having often larger, at length flexuous, and not rarely *brownish* apothecia; agreeing however with the others internally.——*L. myrmecina*, Fr., has occurred, rarely, on rails, at Ipswich, Mass. (Oakes) and, on White Cedar, at New Bedford (Mr. Willey).

The central group of saxicoline, mostly graniticoline *Lecideæ* is well represented throughout the Appalachian chain, and was here first studied, in North Carolina, by Schweinitz. But his herbarium is the only evidence of this; and a vast deal remains to be done before the limits even of our better known forms can be other than obscure.——*L. spilota*, Fr. (*Lich. Suec.* n. 409) is not rare on trap and other rocks on the coast of New England, and has also occurred (on schist) in Vermont (Mr. Frost) at Lake Superior (Prof. Agassiz) and in California (Mr. Bolander).—— *L. polycarpa*, Floerk. (Nyl. in Fellm. *Lich. Arct.* n. 189) is only known to me in specimens from alpine rocks in the White Mountains, which agree with the cited ones, and in habit with *L. confluens ;* and from Labrador (*Herb. Krempelh.*).——*L. auriculata*, Th. Fr. *Lich. Arct.* p. 213, inhabiting Arctic Europe, and also Greenland, is unknown to me.——*L. amylacea*, Ach., Nyl. (*L. elata*, Schær.) is another inhabitant of Greenland (J. Vahl *e* Th. Fr. l. c.) which is as yet undetected elsewhere within our limits. ——*L. aglæa*, Sommerf. (*Herb. Krempelh.*) occurs in the alpine region of the White Mountains.——*L. Armeniaca* (DC.) Fr., is only as yet known as North American, from Greenland (J. Vahl *e* Th. Fr. *l. c.*) but there seems to be no reason why this fine species should not reach (in alpine districts) much more southern latitudes.——*L. atro-brunnea* (DC.) Schær. (*Lich. Helv.* 144. *Herb. Th. Fr.*) an inhabitant of Greenland (J. Vahl, *e* Th. Fr. *l. c.*) and of the alpine region of the Rocky Mountains (Dr. Parry) as of the Pacific coast (H. Mann; Bolander) is also to be looked for on the alpine rocks of New England. The nearly akin *L. fusco-atra*,

---

responsible for an opinion which he has expressly disclaimed. Acharius determined *Gyalecta abstrusa* (Wallr.) Arn., as merely a bark-form (*β truncigena*) of *G. foveolaris*, and it was indifferent whether he distinguished by name such form or not; but Wallroth, if the synonymy (Koerb. *Syst.*) be right, was first to say that this lichen was *not* a member of *G. foveolaris*, but a distinct species, and the responsibility or credit of the judgment belongs to him.

Ach., Fr., known already as occurring in New England, as in Arctic America, proves to be common in California (Mr. Bolander). ——*L. insularis*, Nyl. (*Lich. Par.* n. 58. *Herb. Th. Fr. Lecidella*, Koerb.) a well-marked lichen, with brown, warted thallus, and very minute fruit, has occurred, growing, in little patches, with *Buellia geographica* on the Oakland hills in California (Mr. Bolander) and with little doubt is to be detected elsewhere. ——*L. tenebrosa*, Flot. (Zw. *exs.* n. 134. Fr. *Lich. Suec.* n. 406, c.) interesting as a lecideine *Aspicilia* (*conf.* Koerb, *Parerg.* p. 99) accompanies *Buellia geographica* in the alpine region of the White Mountains; and probably descends. ——*L. lugubris*, Sommerf., Nyl. (Fr. *Lich. Suec.* n. 351) occurs in the same region with the last; and is well marked by its lobulate scales, and globular spores in strap-shaped thekes. (Koerb. *Syst.* t. 1, f. 5).

Thus far, if we except the effigurate section (*Thallædema*) in which the spores exhibit an evident tendency to become bilocular ('*obsolete dyblastæ*,' Koerb.) these are reckoned unilocular, and the group (*Eulecidea*) corresponds with the major part of *Eulecanora* and *Eubiatora ;* in both of which the 'simple' spore predominates. But the line of distinction between 'obsoletely bilocular' or 'pseudo-bilocular' and bilocular spores is sometimes a difficult one to trace; and *Eulecidea*, in as far as we have examined it, may well be said to express, in perhaps a different degree, the same *nisus* to pass into bilocular forms that we find in *Thallædema*. This is sometimes (as in *L. enteroleuca*, v. *theioplaca*, indicated above, and in the v. *lutosa*, Nyl. (Schær. *Helv.* n. 579) which last has no claims to generical distinction superior to those of the first) so marked indeed, that we may well hesitate to call such spores unilocular ; and the form last named of the just-cited species is in fact referred, by both Koerber and Massalongo, to their *Catillaria ;* the division, in their arrangements, corresponding, in the group before us, to *Biatorina* in their *Biatorei*. Natural affinity, as indicated generally, and in particular by the spermatia, appears however, as observed by Nylander (*Prodr.* p. 125) to forbid the separation of such forms from the cluster typified by *L. enteroleuca ;* [1] and, judged in the same way, another *Catillaria* (*C. concreta*) in which there is no doubt of typically bilocular spores, can scarcely be relieved from Nylander's relegation of it (l. c. p. 129) to a colourless condition of *Buellia atro-alba*. The bilocular stage in the evolution of the spore, so fully exhibited in the second section of *Hetherothecium*, is in fact suggested, rather than exem-

---

[1] Schærer's specimen (*Lich. Helv.* n. 579) of his ' *Lecidea lutosa,* Montagne! *in litt.*,' affords me pseudo-bilocular spores exactly similar to those of the rock-forms of *L. enteroleuca*, to which species Nylander has reduced the former ; and I have obtained only similar results from *Buellia* (*Catillaria*) *lutosa*, Anz. (*Lich. Lang.* n. 360). Hepp's figure of the spores of his *Biat. lutosa* (Montgn.) *vera* (*Flecht. Eur.* n. 506) under which Schærer's *Lecid. lutosa* is only cited *pro p.*, represents however what appear to be colourless *Buellia*-spores. Two lichens are then, it should appear, currently known under these cited names.

plified, in *Lecidea.*——*L. acclinis*, Flot. (*Arthrosporum*, Mass., Koerb.)
detected here as yet only upon Poplar (Weymouth, Mr. Willey) combines
the habit of small conditions of *L. enteroleuca*, with which it also agrees in
its spermatia, with irregularly crooked, 4–locular spores (0,009–18$^{mm.}$ long,
and 0,003–6$^{mm.}$ wide) of the type of *Bilimbia*. Very close to this but constantly distinguishable by its still more minute fruit (scarcely exceeding
0$^{mm.}$, 2–0$^{mm.}$, 3, in width) and always straight spores of half the size
(0,005–9$^{mm.}$ long, and 0,0025–35$^{mm.}$ wide) is another little lichen which we
owe to the same acute lichenist (New Bedford, and Weymouth, on very
various barks, Mr. Willey) and may distinguish as *L. declinis.* ——But the
present genus affords us, in *L. caudata*, Nyl. (Fellm. *Lich. Arct.* n. 192)—
occurring not uncommonly, from the base to the alpine region of the White
Mountains, in company with externally similar states of *Biatora rivulosa*
— a very interesting example of typically plurilocular spores in a lichen
otherwise clearly associable with the central, graniticoline group of true
Lecideæ.

It is not without difficulty that Dr. Th. Fries (*Lich. Arct.* p. 173) refers
L. caudata to the *Toniniæ* of Massalongo ; but we possess some genuine
species of the latter group which correspond with *Bilimbia-Bacidia* in
Biatora ; the scope of the differentiation being here quite inexpressible
by *Bilimbia* alone. Several *Toniniæ* are squamaceous; but the little
cluster of forms represented by *L. aromatica*, includes the humblest
modifications of the granulose type.——One of these is the minute
L. granosa, Tuckerm. (*Obs. Lich. l. c.* 5, p. 420) inhabiting mortar, and
old bricks, in South Carolina (Mr. Ravenel) and Louisiana (Hale).
Apothecia minute (about 0$^{mm.}$, 2–0$^{mm.}$, 5, in width). Spores dactyloid,
becoming staff-shaped, 2–4–locular, 0,009–18^{mm} long, and 0,0025–30$^{mm.}$
wide. Spermatia needle-shaped, bowed. The same lichen from tiles, in
shady places, in the island of Cuba (Mr. Wright) was published in *Lich.
Cub.* n. 236. It has also been detected on lime-rocks, in western New
York (Mr. Willey) and in Missouri (Mr. Hall).——*L. massata*, Tuckerm.
(Lich. Calif. p. 25) is another, with glebous thallus, and flat, middling-
sized apothecia (0$^{mm.}$, 6–1$^{mm.}$, 5, in width) not unlike those of *L. aromatica*
(Sm.) Ach., but small, cymbiform, constantly bilocular spores (0,009–16$^{mm.}$
long, and 0,003–5$^{mm.}$ wide) and has only occurred, on earth, on the coast
of California (Mr. Bolander). The spores of *L. aromatica*, now (Herb.
Borr.) not ill expressing the type of *Bilimbia*, pass at length into elongated,
plurilocular forms (Herb. Krempelh.) almost better associable with that
of *Bacidia.* ——The same remark is applicable to the spores of *L. squalida*
(Schleich.) Ach., a lichen found as yet, on this continent, only in Greenland (J. Vahl, in Th. Fr. l. c.).——Most closely related to *L. squalida*,
but yet very remarkably distinguished (it should appear) from it by the
regular extension of the squamules downward into slender, branched
stems, which penetrate the earth, like roots, is *L. caulescens* (Anz. *Catal.
Sondr.* p. 67. *Lich. Lang.* n. 139) to which may be referred another

earth-lichen of California (Mr. Bolander) which also differs, like the Italian, in the colours, from *L. squalida.* Thallus of our plant undistinguishable generally, above, from that of *L. squalida,* except that the range of coloration is from glaucescent to livid-fuscescent, passing finally into black; but extending, below the surface of the earth, into irregularly dividing stems which reach but scarcely exceed half an inch in length. Apothecia also generally comparable with those of *L. squalida,* and often conglomerate. Spores from dactyloid becoming clavate, and staff-shaped; plurilocular; sometimes not exceeding $0,016-30^{mm.}$ in length, and then $0,0035-60^{mm.}$ in width, but more often longer and narrower, or $0,024-48^{mm.}$ long, and $0,003-50^{mm.}$ in width. In one specimen I find the younger apothecia commonly bordered below by white fibrils, of which there is no trace in the mature ones, or, generally, in the other specimens. —— *L. ruginosa,* Tuckerm. (Lich. Calif. 1. c.) from serpentine rocks of California (Mr. Bolander) is another member of the present section, the slenderer spores of which are quite as perfectly acicular ($0,025-41^{mm.}$ long, and $0,0025-30^{mm.}$ wide) as those of our alpine *L. flavovirescens* (Dicks.) Borr.

Eulecidea is thus sufficiently analogous with the corresponding central groups both of *Biatora,* and *Lecanora.* And, like these genera, it affords an example of the myriosporous anomaly (*Sporastatia,* Mass., to be compared with *Biatorella* and *Acarospora*) in the, in all respects, well distinguished *L. morio* (DC.) Schær., inhabiting Arctic America (Dr. Kane) as well as the alpine region of the Rocky Mountains (Dr. Parry) and the White Mountains.

XLV.—BUELLIA, De Not., emend.

Buellia, Tuckerm. Lich. Calif. p. 25. Lecidea, Naeg. in Hepp Flecht. Eur. t. 1. Buellia et Lecideæ sect., De Not. Framm. Lich. l. c. p. 22. Lecideæ spp., Ach. Fr. L. E. Patellariæ spp., Mey. Wallr. Catolechia pr. p., Diplotomma, et Lecideæ spp., Flot. in Koerb. Grundr.; in Linnæa, 1849; in Bot. Zeit. 1850, pp. 367, 380. Dimaura pr. p., et Abacina pr. p., Norm. Con. p. 23. Catolechia, Diploicia, Diplotomma, Buellia, Leciographa, et Rhizocarpon, Mass. Ric. in locc., Geneac. p. 14. Koerb. Syst.; Parerg. Lecidea, sect. B, a, spp., et d, spp., Nyl. Enum. Gén. l. c. p. 123; Prodr. p. 119; Lich. Scand. p. 232; Lich. And. Boliv. l. c. p. 381; in Prodr. Fl. N. Gran. p. 69. Catolechia, Buellia, Leciographa, et Rhizocarpon, Anz. Catal. Sondr. pp. 63, 87; Manip.; Symb. p. 19; Neosymb. p. 12. Catolechia, Buellia, et Rhizocarpon, Th. Fr. Lich. Arct. pp. 175, 225; Gen. pp. 80, 91; Lich. Spitzb. p. 43. Buellia, et Rhizocarpon, Stizenb. Beitr. l. c. p. 160.

Apothecia patellæformia excipulo proprio atro. Sporæ ex ellipsoideo oblongæ, e simplici bi-quadri-loculares, l. demum muriformimulti-loculares, fuscescentes. Spermatia oblonga l. bacillaria; sterigmatibus simplicibus. Thallus crustaceus, effiguratus aut uniformis.

This group is strictly analogous to *Rinodina* in *Lecanorei*, as that represents *Physcia;* it is however, in one respect, more interesting than either of the others named, as expressing most fully the differentiation of the brown spore. As indicated by De Notaris, *Buellia* embraced both effigurate and uniform types, but was expressly confined to bilocular species. Massalongo next, availing himself of the distinction by Flotow, on certain peculiarities of the exciple, of two marked *Lecideæ* allied to *Buellia* (*Catolechia* and *Diplotomma*) separated from the latter its effigurate species (*Diploicia*) and having elevated the quadrilocular *Lecidea parasitica* to the rank of a separate genus (*Leciographa*) finally gave effect to a suggestion of De Notaris by distinguishing *Rhizocarpon;* thus constituting what might have been called the *Buelliei*. The criticism which followed found especial expression in the nearly contemporary emendations of Anzi, and Th. Fries. These writers both united the effigurate members of the group in a single genus (*Catolechia*) and the latter, taking advantage of the fact that the bilocular spore, here as elsewhere, varies now to quadrilocular, availed himself of it to refer *Leciographa* to *Buellia;* as Anzi, equally with Fries (*Lich. Arct.*) reduced *Diplotomma* to *Rhizocarpon*. It was left then to Stizenberger to subordinate the distinction of the effigurate species; and nothing remained, at last, of the *Buelliei*, but *Buellia* and *Rhizocarpon*. But *Rhizocarpon*, Mass.,[1] expresses only the completion of a process of differentiation of the spore, the earlier stages of which are expressed by *Buellia;* and the difficulties in which the attempt to keep the two apart is entangled, obvious enough already in critical instances in both, and as well in the very uncertain *Catallariæ* of authors, find at last their full manifestation in the final arrangement of Dr. Fries (*Gen.*). Another solution of the problem had not indeed escaped the attention of the accurate writer cited. "*Negari quoque non potest*," he says, "*haud parvam inter Buelliam atro-albam et Rhizocarpon petræum, inter B. scabrosam et Rh. geographicum, etc., adesse affinitatem, quare forsan haud immerito possint hæc genera in unum redigi*" (*Lich. Arct.* p. 226) which had indeed already been done, in *Lecidea*, Naeg. It might well appear then far from difficult to conceive, with Naegeli, and Nylander, that the saxicoline *Buelliæ* and *Rhizocarpa* constitute parts of but a single series of most intimately related lichens; a series explained still further by known forms of the one group which yet scarcely advance beyond stages of evolution characteristical only of the other; but it was left to the Californian *B. oidalea* to complete the history, and shew that the corticoline *Buelliæ veræ* culminate, no less than the *Diplotommata*, in corticoline *Rhizocarpa*. This were indeed plainly presumable from the point of view of the present memoir; and is in strict analogy with what is now known of *Rinodina:* but the exhibition of the muriform spore in

---

[1] This name (Massal. *Ric.* p. 100) is later than *Buellia;* and can hardly derive any precedence from having been used, *in another sense*, by Decandolle.

Buellia oidalea is far more perfect than anything described in the Lecanoreine genus.

There are sixty odd described forms of *Buellia ;* differing however no little in probable rank. Of these, three fourths are European, and comparatively few, except the almost cosmopolitan *B. parasema, lactea,* and *geographica,* have been recognized beyond Europe and North America. It is yet to be presumed that a much wider extension awaits the saxicoline groups. Scarcely half of the European forms (reckoning here, as above, not a few which we cannot regard as species) have been detected within our limits ; but we possess several peculiar to the country.

The effigurate section of *Buellia,* as known in the northern hemisphere (*Catolechia,* Flot., Anz.) consists of species with bilocular spores, which are connected most readily, and, as in the corresponding sections of *Lecanora, Biatora,* and *Lecidea,* by the spermatia as well, with the group (*Buellia, Auct. pl.*) with uniform thallus. But we have to interpose here a yellow, areolate, but marginally lobulate lichen from the Cape of Good Hope, — *B. Africana* (*Lecidea,* Tuck. *Obs. Lich.* l. c. 4, p. 406) — the spores of which are thrice septate. The crustaceous species with uniform thallus (*Eubuellia*) run through, on the other hand, the whole series of modifications of the coloured spore : culminating, in the corticoline group, in *B. albo-atra* and *B. oidalea ;* and, in the saxicoline, in *B. geographica.*

Of the effigurate section (*Catolechia*) we possess four of the six species. *B. epigæa* (Pers.) (Schær. *Lich. Helv.* n. 299. Rabenh. *Lich. Eur.* n. 343) has occurred, on the earth, in company with *Placodium fulgens,* in the 'bad lands of Judith,' Nebraska, and on the North Platte (Miss. and Yellowstone Exp.) Prof. Hayden. —— *B. radiata,* Tuck. (Lich. Calif. p. 25) is an areolate species — the areoles either passing into a lobulate margin, or the margin, in another form, reduced to a black, hypothalline fringe. Apothecia of *Diplotomma,* as Flotow understood it, and often strikingly lecanoroid, but the finally convex and pruinose disk rests on a black hypothecium. Spores small, bilocular, 0,007–0,012$^{mm.}$ long, and 0,005–0,007$^{mm.}$ wide. —— *B. badia* (Fr.) Koerb., must include, I think, an earthlichen from the Yosemite valley, California (Mr. Bolander) which adds then another to the number of European species confined here to the west coast. Thallus of our plant made up of turgid or glebous, mostly irregular, and now somewhat stalked, brown squamules, with something of the make of those of the much nobler species next following. Apothecia (0,$^{mm.}$ 5–1$^{mm.}$ wide) sessile, flat, opake, with a thin, at length scarcely flexuous margin, and a brown hypothecium. Spores small, 0,007–16$^{mm.}$ long, and 0,005–7$^{mm.}$ wide. The lichen is comparable also with the (exclusively lignicoline) *B. turgescens* (Nyl.) of New England, scarcely indeed differing at all in the spores ; and *B. turgescens,* it is further observable, resembles still more closely *Lecidea insularis,* Nyl., which Flotow was inclined (Koerb. *Syst.* p. 239) — without, it is evident, microscopical investigation — to regard as a variety of *B. badia.* —— *B. pulchella* (Schrad.)

24

(*Lecidea Wahlenbergii*, Ach.) is a native of arctic America (Hook.). The plant of the White Mountains referred here, seems possibly a depauperate state, but has never occurred fertile.——*B. scabrosa* (Ach.) Koerb., growing very commonly in Europe on the thallus of *Bæomyces byssoides*, has escaped me, if it occur, in our mountains; but is found in Greenland (*J.* Vahl, *e* Th. Fr. l. c.). Fries associated this lichen with the species next preceding; and Nylander has recognized the same affinity; but the evidence of lobation, now obscure enough in that, quite disappears here.

Of *Eubuellia*, as here constituted, and reckoning the species according to Nylander's limitation of them, which differs very considerably from that of other writers of whose estimates I have availed myself above, two-thirds are known as North American.——*B. lactea* (Mass.) Koerb., well marked by its many-angled, white areoles, imposed upon, and the whole often bordered by a conspicuous, blackish hypothallus, is common on granitic and other rocks, throughout the Appalachian mountain-system, reaching to Tennessee and Georgia (Mr. Ravenel) and is common also in California (Bolander). *Lecid. lepidastra*, Tuck. (Suppl. l. c. p. 429) offers flat, dilated, crenulate and squamaceous areoles, and no trace of the dark hypothallus of *B. lactea;* but the microscopical characters of the two scarcely differ; and, in view of the instructive series of forms of the European lichen published by Massalongo and Anzi, it is certainly less easy to keep our plant apart.——*B. stellulata* (Tayl. in Mack. *Fl. Hib.* Nyl. *Lich. And. Boliv. Herb.* Borr. *Herb.* Lindig, 2, n. 156) looks like a very minute form of the last species. It has occurred on sandstone in California (Mr. Bolander) and on trap rocks in New Jersey (Mr. Austin). Spores 0,007–0,013$^{mm.}$ long, and 0,004–0,007$^{mm.}$ wide.—— *B. atro-alba* (Flot.) Th. Fr. (Fr. *Lich. Suec.* n. 382) has probably the same range with *B. lactea*, but is more easily passed over. It is common in New England; and I have it from Pennsylvania (Dr. Michener) and the mountains of Virginia (Rev. Dr. Curtis). In the var. *chlorospora*, Nyl. (*determ. ipso*) which is common in our mountains, the spores are colourless and thus constitute *Catillaria*, at least of Anzi, with whom this name designates only a section of *Buellia.*——*B. pullata,* Tuck. (Lich. Calif. p. 26). Sandstone rocks, California (Mr. Bolander). Areoles squamaceous. Spores 0,012–0,018$^{mm.}$ long, and 0,005–0,009$^{mm.}$ wide.——*B. coracina* (Moug.) Th. Fr. (*Lecidea*, Moug. & Nestl. n. 462. Nyl. in Fellm. *Lich. Arct.* n. 193) remarkably conditioned by the predominant, black hypothallus, and interesting also as affording an example of very commonly simple (mature) spores—a condition as rare in the coloured as it is common in the colourless series—is abundant in the alpine region of the White Mountains; and was brought from arctic America by Dr. Kane. ——*B. halonia* (Ach.) a Cape of Good Hope rock-lichen, with an areolate, greenish-yellow thallus, of which excellent specimens were collected by Mr. Wright (N. Pacif. Expl. Exp.) has occurred also on the coast of California (Mr. Bolander).——*B. papillata* (Sommerf.) (*B. insignis*, Th.

Fr. *Lecid. insignis*, β, Hepp Fl. Eur. n. 40) occurs, in the v. *geophila*, Th.
Fr., in Greenland (J. Vahl *e* Th. Fr. l. c.) and in the var. *albo-cincta*, Th.
Fr., in islands of Behring's Straits (Mr. Wright). The spores of the first-
named variety are quadrilocular, according to Dr. Fries; and I observe,
rarely, traces of three dissepiments (which Hepp found also in his cited
lichen) in the v. *albo-cincta ;* as much more evidently in another plant,
clearly referable to the present species, from the Rocky Mountains (Dr.
Parry).——*B. parasema* (Ach.) Koerb., is found, according to Nylander,
throughout the earth. It is a native of arctic America (Hook. Th. Fr.)
and occurs commonly throughout the United States. Spores bilocular;
but they pass, rarely, in several specimens (near Chester, Pa., Myself;
Ohio, Lea; Texas, Mr. Wright) into tri-quadrilocular conditions, sufficiently
explaining the typically quadrilocular v. *triphragmia*, Th. Fr., which
probably occurs here. In a state of the last from Nicaragua (f. *sorediata*)
I observe also 6–locular spores. A thin, white bloom is sometimes
observable in the apothecia of Texas specimens, to be referred to the
v. *cæsio-pruinosa*, Nyl. (Wright *Lich. Cub.* n. 240).——*B. dialyta* (Nyl.
sub *Lecid.* in *Flora Ratisb.* 1869, p. 123. *Buellia parasema* var. *micro-
carpa*, Tuckerm. *in litt.*) differs from the last species in its minute,
immarginate, scabrous apothecia; and the spores are 0,019–26$^{mm.}$ long,
and 0,006–10$^{mm.}$ wide. The lichen occurred on *Pinus contorta*, in California (Mr. Bolander). But I cannot distinguish from it a New England
plant, found upon Hemlock, in Vermont (Mr. Russell) and in Massachusetts
(Mr. Willey) the general features, and all the characters of which are in
fact quite the same.——*B. myriocarpa* (DC.) (*Lecidea*, Nyl., *Lich. Par.*
n. 61) occurs not uncommonly on the scaly bark of Pines, and on old rails
and planks in New England; as in Greenland (J. Vahl in Th. Fr. l. c.)
New Jersey (Mr. Austin) and Illinois (Mr. Hall). It is found also on
granitic rocks in New Hampshire (Mr. Frost) and Massachusetts.——
B. Schæreri, De Not. (*Lecid. nigritula*, Nyl.) similar to small conditions of
the last, but with very minute spores, like those of some *Calicium*, is
perhaps not rare, but I have only met with it on dead wood, in the White
Mountains; and received it from New Bedford (Mr. Willey) and New
Jersey (Mr. Austin).——*B. turgescens* (*Lecidea*, Nyl. *in litt.*) a common
inhabitant of old rails and poles in Massachusetts, is distinguished from
B. myriocarpa, by its well-developed, plicate-verrucose thallus, often
closely resembling that of *Lecidea insularis*, Nyl. Spores small, 0,009–
14$^{mm.}$ long, and 0,005–7$^{mm.}$ wide.——*B. Elizæ* (*Lecidea*, Tuckerm. Suppl.
1, l. c. p. 428) remarkable for its blood-red disk, has been found on the
bark of Pines,—Tower Hill, County Sussex, Virginia, Mrs. Tuckerman,
and in Vermont (Mr. Frost)—and of White Cedar, New Bedford, Mass.
(Mr. Willey). Spores bilocular, measuring 0,009–0,015$^{mm.}$ in length, and
0,004–0,007$^{mm.}$ in width.——*B. vernicoma* (*Lecid.* Tuck. Suppl. 1, l. c. p.
429) a minute lichen of granitic rocks, in Massachusetts (Oakes) in Pennsylvania (Dr. Michener) in New Jersey (Mr. Austin) and at Aiken, South

Carolina (Mr. Ravenel) and occurring also, rarely, on Beech trunks at New Bedford (Mr. Willey) is readily distinguishable by its straw-coloured, granulose thallus, and no less by its quadrilocular spores; measuring 0,012-0,016$^{mm.}$ in length, and 0,004-0,005$^{mm.}$ in width.——We may conveniently here notice, together, some species, either certainly or possibly parasitical on other lichens. Such plants have been little looked for in this country; and it is likely that there remain others to be detected, even in the present genus.——*B. saxatilis* (Schær.) Kb. (Zw. *exs.* n. 140, Schær. *Helv.* n. 240) has been found on talcose schist and on limestone in Vermont (Mr. Frost). Thallus less developed, but not unlike that of the cited lichen of v. Zwackh; with which the American specimens appear to agree entirely in the apothecia, and spores. Nylander regards the plant '*quasi myriocarpa ecrustacea*' (*Scand.* p. 237) inhabiting the thallus of other lichens ; in which case, the separation of the next species becomes questionable.——*B. inquilina*, Tuck. (Lich. Calif. p. 32) is an inhabitant of the thallus and apothecia of normal conditions of *Pertusaria*, occurring in Pennsylvania, in North Carolina (Rev. Dr. Curtis) South Carolina (Mr. Ravenel) and Texas (Mr. Wright). Spores biscoctiform, bilocular, 0,009-0,015$^{mm.}$ long, and 0,009-0,007$^{mm.}$ wide.——*B. parasitica* (Floerk.) Th. Fr. (Nyl. *Lich. Par.* n. 68) has been found, within our limits, on *Pilophorus acicularis*, f. *robustus*, in islands of Behring's Straits (Mr. Wright) and on the apothecia of *Lecanora pallescens*, v. *corticola* in California (Mr. Bolander).——A new, polysporous species, allied to the last, as to *Lecid. glaucomaria*, Nyl., but the spores from 35 to 50 in the thekes, has been detected by Mr. Willey on *Pertusaria pertusa, saxicola*, and will be described elsewhere. And the same lichenist finds on the crust of the *Pertusaria*, as on that of *Lecanora tartarea*, a parasitical *Buellia* still nearer to *Lecid. glaucomaria;* but I find no spores measuring more than $\frac{12\text{-}16}{5\text{-}7}$ micromill.——*Abrothallus Smithii*, Tul. (*Herb. Borr.*) with soleiform, bilocular spores, and found here on *Parmelia saxatilis* and *P. Borreri*, is now excluded from Lichens.

Thus far *Eubuellia* has afforded no other light on the process of differentiation of the brown spore, than the passage of the more common bilocular into quadrilocular (or, very rarely and exceptionally, plurilocular) conditions. But we should not expect the evolution to stop here; and the next species may fairly be said to complete the history, and to mediate satisfactorily between the bi-quadrilocular *B. parasema*, and *papillata*, and the distinctly muriform-multilocular *B. oidalea*.—— *B. albo-atra* (Hoffm., Nyl.) Th. Fr. *Gen.* (Zw. *exs.* n. 123. Fr. *Lich. Suec.* n. 413) the regularly quadrilocular spores of which soon exhibit plain indications of the next or muriform modification, is not uncommon, especially on Elm, in New England; as in New York (Mr. Willey) and Canada (Mr. Drummond) and was found by Mr. Wright, on *Æsculus*, in California. The rupicoline state (v. *saxicola*, Fr.) occurs on lime-rocks, Kansas (Mr. Hall) and on the sandstone of the Connecticut valley, in

Mass.——The last species, presenting perhaps the ideal centre of *Buellia*, is well distinguished, not only by the spores, but by the lecanoroid features of its apothecia; in the next however, there is nothing externally, to separate the plant from ordinary states of the cluster represented by *B. parasema.*——*B. oidalea*, Tuck. (*Lecidea, Obs. Lich.* l. c. 4, p. 405) in which the spores are perfectly muriform-multilocular, exhibiting eight to twelve closely approximated, transverse series, each of three to four cells, was found, on Oaks, in California (Mr. Wright) and occurs there also on Pines and Firs, and on dead wood (Mr. Bolander) as in Oregon (Prof. Newberry). The spores of this species are either solitary, or in twos, threes, fours, fives, or sixes in the thekes, and vary therefore no little in size; the largest observed measuring 0,046–0,088$^{mm.}$ in length, and 0,018–0,024$^{mm.}$ in width; but the average of more common measurements perhaps not ill-expressed by $\frac{30}{16}$ micromill. Most intimately associable with this, and scarcely to be distinguished but as a sub-species, is *B. penichra*, an inhabitant of the living trunks, and found also on the dead wood of *Abies Douglasii*, in the Yosemite valley, California, (Mr. Bolander) the difference of which consists in a white thallus, and much-reduced apothecia, and especially in the spores (which occur, so far as observed, in fives and eights in the thekes) shewing no more than four transverse series of cells; nor exceeding 0,018–0,023$^{mm.}$ in length by 0,010–0,013$^{mm.}$ in width.

The few remaining, rupicoline species (*Rhizocarpon*, Massal.) also exhibit the muriform structure (fully described in Koerb. *Syst.* p. 258) and are related to the bilocular rock-*Buelliæ*, much as *B. oidalea* to *B. parasema.* The most remarkable of these, as respects at least thalline development, is *B. Bolanderi*, Tuckerm.,[1] discovered by the unwearied botanist whose name it bears, in company, and often intermingled, with the curiously similar *Biatora scotopholis* (Lich. Calif. p. 24) on the maritime rocks of California. Thallus of minute, chestnut-coloured squamules, the darker colour, and always raised margins of which serve sufficiently to distinguish it from that of the cited *Biatora.* Spores either solitary, or in twos, or in fours, in the thekes.——With the evidence before him of two North American lichens allied to the species

---

[1] *Buellia Bolanderi* (*sp. nova*) *thallo areolato-squamuloso castaneo, areolis minutis cartilagineis primitus rotundatis concavis dein lobatis in ambitu elevatis subtus nigris; apotheciis* (0$^{mm.}$, 5–1$^{mm.}$ *lat.*) *sessilibus plano-convexis, margine tenui evanido. Hypothecium fusco-nigrum. Sporæ in thecis saccatis l. solitariæ l.* 2^{næ} *l.* 4^{næ}, *ellipsoideæ, muriformi-multiloculares* (*ser. transv.* 8–12, *long.* 4–5) *nigro-fuscæ, longit.* 0,030–50$^{mm.}$, *crassit.* 0,021–25$^{mm.}$.——Sandstone rocks, Oakland Hills, California (H. N. Bolander) Alpine co., California, alt. 7000 ft. (Dr. Lapham). Almost a squamulose lichen; but the key to its thalline evolution is without doubt to be found in that of *Lecidea fusco-atra.* The reaction of the hymenial gelatine with iodine is blue.

now to be set down, as to the real value of the distinction derived from the number of spores contained in the thekes, the writer cannot hesitate to subordinate the differences based upon that distinction by Flotow, and to return to the conception, viewed now indeed in the light of more recent knowledge, of Fries. And here it is also to be added, that, as those forms which recede from the rest in their much larger and fewer spores, are in fact forms of the most perfect condition of the species, and might be subsumed under that condition with only an extension of its spore-character, their place in the arrangement is rather before than after the more common, and, as respects the spores only, more normal states.——
B. petræa (Flot. *emend.*).   (*Lecid. atro-alba* (Ach.) Fr. *L. E.* p. 310, *max. p.*) *a, Montagnei* (*Lecid. Montagnei* & *L. geminata*, Flot. Koerb. *Syst.*, *sub Rhizoc. L. geminata*, Nyl. *Prodr. Rhizocarpon Montagnei*, Koerb. *Parerg.* p. 229. *Buellia*, Tuck. Lich. Calif.). Spores solitary, or in twos, in the thekes. Granitic rocks, Greenland (J. Vahl *e* Th. Fr. l. c.) and elsewhere, on the same rocks, in arctic America (Dr. Kane). Massachusetts, on similar rocks, best comparable with Fr. *Lich. Suec.* n. 406, A, and with Anz. *Lich. Ital. Sup.* n. 306 ; as are most of our specimens. Vermont, on similar rocks, Mr. Frost; the spores commonly solitary. New Jersey (Mr. Austin). Rocky Mountains (Prof. Hayden). California, on mica slate (Mr. Bolander).——*β, vulgaris* (*Lecid. petræa*, Flot. Koerb. *Syst.* p. 260, *sub Rhizoc. L. petræa*, Nyl. *Prodr.; Lich. Scand.* p. 233). Spores normally in fours, or in eights. A very common and variable lichen, occurring on granitic, and other rocks, especially northward; in Greenland (J. Vahl, *e* Th. Fr. l. c.) Canada (Mr. Drummond) and New England; following the mountains southward to Virginia and North Carolina (Rev. Dr. Curtis) and appearing also on the Pacific coast (Mr. Bolander). On often inundated rocks in our mountains, the areoles disappear in a thin, contiguous thallus (v. *lavata*, Fr.) or, both areoles and apothecia being greatly reduced in size, and the crust oxydated, we have, commonly in the mountains and on the north coast of New England, the conspicuous v. *Oederi*, Koerb.——*B. geographica* (L., Schær.) occurring, probably everywhere, on the rocks of arctic America (Hook.; Th. Fr.) abounds also in alpine and subalpine districts in Canada and New England, and descends far below, in the mountains. It has been found southward in the mountains of North Carolina (Mr. Buckley) and is common on the sandstones of the coast of California (Mr. Bolander).
——*B. alpicola* (Nyl.) Anz., is less distinctly characterized, in such European specimens as I have seen (*Herb. Torssell.* Schær. Helv. n. 173. Anz. *Lang.* n. 199. Rabenh. *Eur.* n. 618) except by the spores, which offer the instructive anomaly of not advancing beyond the bilocular stage. In the White Mountains however, the corresponding condition with bilocular spores (which is confined to the alpine region) is recognizable not merely by the brighter colour of its smaller fronds, contrasting often pleasingly with the greener expansions of *a*, and its larger areoles, but is

distinguished by apothecia (always at length exceeding the crust) of twice the size. It is difficult not to consider our two plants distinct : but Koerber (*Parerg.* p. 234) and Th. Fries (*Lich. Arct.* p. 236) are of a different opinion as to the European; the latter remarking also that Wahlenberg's specimens of his (original) v. *alpicola* offer no differences in the spores from *a*.

Trib. III.—GRAPHIDACEI, Eschw., Nyl.

Apothecia difformia, sæpius elongata (lirellæformia) excipulo proprio, aliquando indistincto.

At first sight, *Graphis*, as exhibited in the tropics (and we might add *Pyrenula*, as here taken) appears well comparable with *Thelotrema;* and even in the feature which compels us to refer the latter (as compared both with *Pertusaria* and *Urceolaria*) to an extreme type of *Parmeliacei*. But, viewed more attentively, the large tribe before us is seen to be far less conditioned by the thallus; and to present unmistakable evidences of a quite inferior position in the scale of lichenose vegetation. Eschweiler indeed (*Syst.* p. 13) degraded the *Graphidacei* ('*forma nimirum apotheciorum elongata, hinc minus perfecta quam concentrica, quæ vegetationis summa est,*' &c., *Lich. Bras.* p. 65) to the very bottom of the Lichen-system; but Fries (*L. E.* p. 359) has vindicated for the tribe its now generally accepted place, as a deformation of the *Lecidea*-type; which, here as elsewhere, ascends, exceptionally, into lecanoroid expressions: *Graphis* being, in this view, to *Heterothecium* perhaps much as *Opegrapha* to *Buellia*.

At one extreme, represented by *Lecanactis* and *Platygrapha* (Fam. *Lecanactidei*, Stizenb.) the Graphidaceous type reverts, even in form, to those of the two preceding tribes, and has, in this condition, been sometimes associated with them: but the passage from such outlying groups into the true center of the tribe before us (Fam. *Opegraphei*, Stizenb.) is imperceptible; as is also that by which the compound *Glyphidei*, Fr., and the abnormal *Arthoniei*, Koerb., depart in the other direction.

Of one of the two principal groups (both of the colourless series) constituting the *Lecanactidei*, almost a fifth inhabits extra-tropical regions, and, of the other, almost the whole. The *Opegraphei*, on the other hand, though represented, at one extreme, by some, mostly small, genera, a large proportion, and, in one case, two-thirds of the members of which are also northern, find their type in the great tropical group *Graphis*, of which only one-ninth reaches beyond the tropics. The proportion varies a little in the *Glyphidei;* for though *Glyphis* be almost confined to tropical countries, a quarter of *Chiodecton* (of the colourless series) extends beyond. It is probably far from time to estimate *Arthonia;* but, according to Nylander's enumerations, while the genus is distributed more equally than others, the preponderance of forms is still in favour of the tropics.

The elucidation of the spore-types is sometimes sufficiently embarrassing in the present tribe, but I incline to consider four-fifths of the species as, in one way or other, referable to, or at least as exceptional forms associable with, the coloured series. *Graphis* itself affords much such a diversified exhibition of modifications of spore-structure referable, it should seem, to the normally brown type, as the variously analogous *Thelotrema*, and *Pyrenula;* and like these genera, it offers not seldom apparent, though perhaps not in fact irreducible anomalies, as well in the spores, as in the apothecia.

The tribe is, as yet, far from fully represented here, even as respects northern forms. No *Enterographa*, nor *Lithographa* is known; and *Platygrapha periclea* has been observed but by a single lichenist. The larger part of the forms of *Lecanactis*, all but one of the exclusively saxicoline *Opegraphæ*, and even *Graphis Lyellii*, are strangers to us. It is possible that some of these are really wanting, but the most, as especially *Lithographa* (inhabiting granitic rocks in Sweden) and the calcareous *Opegraphæ* may well be looked for. The number of tropical *Graphidacei* reckoned as known to occur within our limits, is also smaller than should be expected, but will doubtless be enlarged when the lichens of the extreme south are more fully explored. Few herbariums are sufficiently rich in material for the profitable determination of these tropical species; and it is only quite recently that the Cuban collections of Mr. Wright, and the admirable ones of Lindig have put me in a position for attempting it. Most fortunately however, I have been able to avail myself, in almost all the more obscure southern forms, and in many of the northern, of the great knowledge of Dr. Nylander; whose illustrations of Graphidaceous types surpass in extent and importance those of any other lichenographer.

Fam. 1.—LECANACTIDEI, Stizenb., salt. pr. p.

Apothecia subrotundo-difformia, rarius elongata; marginata.

XLVI.—LECANACTIS (Eschw.) Koerb., emend.

Lecanactis, Koerb. Syst. p. 275 (additis Opegr. plocina, & Pragmopora premnea). Th. Fr. Gen. p. 93. Tuck. Obs. Lich. l. c. 6, p. 283. Opegraphæ sp., & Lecideæ spp., Ach. L. U. pp. 32, 43. Schær. Spicil. p. 51, 204. Borr. in Hook. Br. Fl. 2, p. 144, 176, 179. Nyl. Prodr. p. 137, 151 ; Lich. Scand. p. 240 ; in Prodr. Fl. N. Gran. p. 70. Lecanactis pro p., Eschw. Syst, p. 14. Lecanactis, Pyrenotheæ sp., & Parmeliæ sp., pro p., Fr. L. E. p. 374, 450, 183. Lecanactis, Schismatommatis spp., & Coniangii sp., Massal. Ric. p. 53, 55; Alc. Gen. p. 13. Schismatomma, Mudd Man. Brit. Lich. p. 222, non Flot. & Koerb. Lecanactis sect. 3, Stizenb. Beitr. l. c. p. 156.

Apothecia rotundata rarius oblonga, excipulo proprio integre

25

nigro. Sporæ e dactyloideo fusiformi-oblongæ, quadri-pluriloculares, incolores. Spermatia oblonga l. bacillaria; sterigmatibus simplicibus. Thallus crustaceus uniformis.

All but one (*L. Leprieurii* (Mont.) of tropical America) of the seven or eight species are northern. Another (*L. premnea* (Ach.) Tuck. *l. c.*) extends however, perhaps throughout the warmer regions of the earth; and offers, in these regions, some often notable varieties. The relation of the lecideoid species to the present tribe is mediated by the closely akin *L. illecebrosa* (a *Lecidea*, according to Acharius, Schærer, and Nylander) and *L. lyncea*, which Borrer, Schærer, and Nylander have referred to *Opegrapha*.

With the exception of *L. Leprieurii*, all the species are European; but only two have as yet been observed here. *L. abietina* (Ach.) Koerb., is, according to Hooker (in Richards. Append. to Frankl. Narr.) a native of arctic America (Richardson) but has not been found elsewhere in North America, except on *Abies grandis*, in California (Mr. Bolander) where it is accompanied by its remarkable spermogones, the spermatia of which measure $\frac{11\text{-}16}{3\text{-}4}$ micromill.——*L. premnea* (Ach.) Tuck. *Obs. Lich.*, a widely diffused, tropical lichen, reaching also into the northern hemisphere,—where it had yet so passed out of knowledge, before the publication of the *Prodromus* of Nylander, that Montagne could describe the Java plant as a new species (*Lecid. coniochlora*)—has occurred, on Cypress, in Louisiana (Hale) the specimens agreeing, externally, with tropical ones (Hong Kong, Mr. Wright) and the spores, (measuring 0,019–0,023ᵐᵐ· in length, and 0,003–0,005ᵐᵐ· in width) sufficiently with those of Nyl. *Lich. Par.* n. 67. From this cannot be separated a generally similar lichen, from Pine, and Oak bark in California (Mr. Bolander) the spores of which measure 0,015–0,021ᵐᵐ· in length, and 0,003–0,005ᵐᵐ· in width. Nor, in that case, is our New England plant (*L. chloroconia*, Tuck. l. c.) found, on various trunks, in Massachusetts, and New Hampshire (Myself) as in Vermont (Mr. Frost) and western New York (Mr. Willey) and the spores of which scarcely exceed 0,011–0,017ᵐᵐ· in length, by 0,003–0,005ᵐᵐ· in width, any longer to be kept apart, except (presenting, as it does, much the smallest spores known in the rather large group of forms which I have ventured, at the above-cited place, to bring together under *L. premnea*) we admit it to the rank of a variety,—v. *chloroconia*.

XLVII.—PLATYGRAPHA, Nyl.

Nyl. Classif. 2, p. 188; Prodr. p. 161; Lich. exot. l. c.; in Prodr. Fl. N. Gran. p. 93. Anz. Catal. Sondr. p. 93. Mudd Man. Brit. Lich. p. 244. Lecanoræ sp., Ach. Lecideæ sp., Fr. L. E. p. 337. Schismatomma, Flot. & Koerb. in Koerb. Grundr. d. Cryptogamenk. Koerb. Syst.

p. 271. Th. Fr. Gen. p. 92. Schismatommatis sp., Mass. Ric. p. 57. Lecanactidis sect., Stizenb. Beitr. 1. c. p. 156. Mull. Principes de Classif. p. 67.

Apothecia rotundata oblongaque, excipulo proprio margine plerumque occulto 1. obsoleto, accessorio thallode coronato. Sporæ ex oblongo fusiformes, quadri-pluriloculares, incolores. Spermatia oblonga 1. bacillaria; sterigmatibus simplicibus. Thallus crustaceus, uniformis.

That a mere name, based on a lichen far from representative of the group before us, as developed at its proper centre (*Schismatomma*, Flot. & Koerb. 1. c. 1848) extended next to cover almost the whole of *Lecanactis* (*Schismatomma*, Mass. 1. c. 1852) as more lately substituted for *Lecanactis* (*Schismatomma*, Mudd, 1. c. 1861) and characterized only in 1855 (*Schismatomma*, Koerb. 1. c. & *Parerg.*) when it is referred to *Lecideacei*, should invalidate the definite *Platygrapha*, Nyl., of the same year, is certainly a difficult conclusion for those who have learned from the writer last named to estimate the real extent and significance of the group. The elucidation of *Platygrapha* is in fact due to Nylander; who, alone of lichenographers, has pursued, and defined it, in its tropical home. Represented, at the extreme north, by but a single lichen, only two others of the twenty-five species extend beyond the tropics, in the eastern hemisphere; one reaching from the Canaries and Portugal to Shropshire in England, and the other occurring in Algiers. And our own *P. ocellata* is in like manner, properly, a tropical species.

P. periclea (Ach.) Nyl. (*Schismatomma dolosum*, Flot. & Koerb.). On Hemlock bark, New Bedford, Mass. (Mr. Willey; the fortunate finder of a long-desired plant).——*P. Californica* (Tuck.) Nyl. in *Syn. Lich. N. Caled.* p. 58, not. (*Dirina*, Tuck. Lich. Calif. p. 17). On the bark of Oaks and Pines, California (Mr. Bolander). With the whole habit, and, it may be added, structure, of a Lecanoreine lichen, and resembling not a little a common Californian condition of *Lecanora glaucoma*, this might well seem referable, and by the evidence at once of the hypothecium, the spores, and the spermatia, to *Dirina*; but I can have no hesitation in accepting the emendation of Dr. Nylander, and referring it to the present genus. The series of affinities which enables us to connect the lichen —in spite of its alien habit, not qualified by any details of structure looking definitely in the present direction—with *Graphidacei*, takes its start however, it is evident enough, from the tropical centre of the group; from such types as *P. dilatata*, and *P. leucopsara*, Nyl. (Lindig *Herb. N. Gran.* n. 2887) and by no means from the outlying and depauperate *P. periclea.* Spores of *P. Californica* 0,016–0,018mm· long, and 0,003–0,004mm· wide.——*P. ocellata*, Nyl. (*Lecanactis punctillum*, Tuck. *in litt.*). On Beech trunks, and on *Berchemia*, in the low country of South

Carolina (Mr. Ravenel). Also a Lecanoroid species, comparable now (as in Lindig n. 788) in general aspect, with conditions of the equally minute *Lecanora subfusca*, v. *duplicata*, Tuck. (Wright *Lich. Cub.* n. 119) and now (as in Mr. Ravenel's specimens) rather with similarly reduced forms of *L. atra.*——*P. Ravenelii*, Tuckerm.[1] Trunks, on the southern coast of Texas (Mr. Ravenel). There can be no question of the Graphidaceous character of this species, which yet, together with more commonly, and perfectly lirellæform apothecia, offers also the irregularly rounded ones indicating the Lecanactidean type; and the fusiform spores of *Platy-grapha*.

XLVIII.—MELASPILEA, Nyl.

Nyl. Prodr. p. 170; Lich. Scand. p. 263; in Prodr. Fl. N. Gran. p. 111. Th. Fr. Gen. p. 98. Lecideæ sp., Fée Ess. p. 107, t. 26, f. 6; Suppl. p. 103. Nyl. Lich. Par. n. 99. Lecanactidis sp., Fr. S. O. V. p. 288; L. E. p. 377. Opegraphæ f., Schær. Spicil. p. 331; Enum. p. 158. Abrothalli, dein Catillariæ, dein Buelliæ sp., Mass. Ric. p. 89, & opp. varr. Buelliæ sp., & Hazslinszkya, Koerb. Parerg. pp. 189, 257.

Apothecia rotundata, l. oblonga opegraphoidea, excipulo proprio nigro. Sporæ obtuse ellipsoideæ l. solæformes, biloculares, fuscescentes l. subincolores. Spermatia oblonga; sterigmatibus simplicibus. Thallus crustaceus, uniformis, aut sæpius obsoletus.

This little group, founded upon two closely allied European lichens, has been extended by Nylander to include several South American species, one of which is found also in Texas. The type (*M. arthonioides*) is not ill-comparable, as respects the present tribe, with *Graphis patellula* (Meissn.) Nyl., nor do the oblong, plurilocular spores of the latter express (as we look at them) anything more diverse from those of the former than a higher *grade* of evolution of the same type. There are however other differences; and the cited *Graphis*, compared as it must be with *G. pezi-*

---

[1] *Platygrapha Ravenelii (sp. nova) thallo effuso tenui leproso l. granulato cinereo-glaucescente; apotheciis lirellæformibus* (1$^{mm.}$, 5–2$^{mm.}$ long.) *rarius rotundatis flexuoso-lobatis (circ.* 1$^{mm.}$ *lat.) sessilibus, nigris, albo plus minus suffusis, margine dein denudato tenui erecto. Hypothecium nigrum. Sporæ octonæ, fusiformes, quadriloculares, incolores, longit.* 0,025–41$^{mm.}$, *crassit.* 0,005-6$^{mm.}$. On various barks, Corpus Christi, Texas, Mr. Ravenel; to whom I take pleasure in dedicating the lichen. The rare, rounded or lecanoroid apothecia have the aspect of those of *P. leucopsara*, Nyl., (Lindig *Herb. N. Gran.* n. 2887) to which however our plant is by no means so near as to *P. dirinea*, Nyl. (*Dirina multiformis*, Mont. & V. d. B. Herb. V. d. Bosch.) the spores of which ('*long.* 0$^{mm.}$ 025, *lat.* 0$^{mm.}$ 0025,' M. & V. d. B. *Lich. Jav.*) I regret to have been unable to discover in my specimen. Reaction of the hymenial gelatine, in our Texan lichen, with iodine, vinous red.

zoidea, Ach., is seen to be referable (as by Nyl. in *Prodr. Fl. N. Gran.*) to the group typified by *G. dendritica.* Several members of this last group have passed for *Lecanactis* of authors; and it is not without interest possibly that two species of *Melaspilea* have suggested to lichenists the same relationship. The exciple of the latter separates it from the *Arthoniei.*

Two species are known to occur within our limits. *M. arthonioides* (Fée) Nyl., has been found by me, on trunks, in swamps, in Hadley, Mass., and presents the aspect, as compared with our northern lichens, of a *Lecidea*, or *Buellia;* or,—the crust being mostly obsolete—of a similar Fungus.——*M. angulosa*, Nyl. (*Lecanactidis sp. nov.*, Tuck. *in litt.*) resembles on the contrary a *Graphis* of the *dendritica*-group; and has occurred in Texas (Mr. Wright) as also in Brazil (Nyl.).

———•———

Fam. 2.—OPEGRAPHEI, Stizenb.

Apothecia lirellæformia, rarissime rotundato-difformia.

Two interesting types of this well-characterized and (in the tropics) most largely developed centre of the tribe are, as above indicated, wanting with us. One of these,—*Enterographa*, Fée (*Stigmatidium*, Mey., *pro p.* Nyl.)—belonging it should seem to the, in this tribe, sparingly represented colourless series, and resembling now *Chiodecton*, and now some lirellate *Arthonia*, not remote from *A. rubella*, may well have been overlooked; as several species occur in Europe, and others in the West Indies, and in Japan.——The other,—*Lithographa*, Nyl. *Prodr.* p. 195—is entirely extra-tropical, and distinguished not only by its simple spores, and the areolate thallus of some of its forms (*Placographa*, Th. Fr. *Haplographa*, Anz.) but as affording also the only examples that we have (Nyl. *l. c.* p. 147. Anz. *Catal. Sondr.* p. 97) of myriosporous *Graphidacei.*

XLIX.—OPEGRAPHA, (Humb.) Ach., Nyl.

Opegrapha, Humb. Fl. Frib. Pers. in Ust. Ann. Bot. Ach. L. U. p. 43, pro max. p.; Syn. p. 70, pro p. Schær. Spicil. p. 45, pr. p. Fée Ess. p. 24, pr. p.; Suppl. p. 18, pr. p. Fr. S. O. V. p. 273, pr. p.; L. E. p. 361, pr. p. Borr. in Hook. Br. Fl. 2, p. 143, pr. p. Mônt. Pl. Cell. Cub. p. 180, pr. p.; Crypt. Guy. p. 38, pr. p.; Syll. p. 348, pr. p. Nyl. Enum. Gen. l. c. p. 131, pro max. p.; Prodr. Gall. p. 151, pro max. p.; Lich. exot. l. c.; Prodr. Fl. N. Gran. p. 90; Syn. Lich. N. Caled. p. 54. Opegrapha pr. p., Oxystoma, & Scaphis, Eschw. Syst. p. 14. Graphis pr. p., Mey. Nebenst. p. 330. Eschw. Lich. Bras. p. 81. Opegrapha, Norm. Con. p. 25, t. 2, f. 18, l. c. Opegrapha pr. p., &

Encephalographa, Massal. Mem. p. 101; Geneac. p. 13. Anz. Catal.
Sondr. p. 94. Th. Fr. Gen. p. 95. Opegrapha, Zwackhia, & Ence-
phalographa, Koerb. Parerg. p. 248, &c. Opegrapha, Melanospora,
& Stictographa, Mudd Man. Brit. Lich. p. 226. Opegraphæ sect., &
Encephalographa, Stizenb. Beitr. l. c. p. 153.

Apothecia lirellæformia (rarius rotundata) subsimplicia, plerumque
superficialia, excipulo proprio fere semper integre nigro. Sporæ
parvulæ, ex ellipsoideo dactyloideæ l. sæpius fusiformes, bi-quadri-
pluriloculares, fuscescentes l. decolores. Spermatia oblonga l. bacillaria; sterigmatibus simplicibus. Thallus crustaceus, uniformis l.
sæpe hypophlæodes.

The indications of natural habit which suggested the discrimination
of *Graphis* from *Opegrapha*, are still instructive ; and in the tropical
species of the group before us (as this group is recognized by Nylander,
following here, it should seem, the conception of Acharius, as best expressed
in the *Lichenographia*) no less than in those of the northern hemisphere.
The present genus is, for the most part, readily distinguished from *Graphis*
by its superficial, subsimple, always black apothecia, deprived wholly of
thalline or thalloid margin; but the value of even the last of these differences
has been variously estimated by authors,—neither Fries, nor Eschweiler, in
his latest work, according it more than subordinate importance—and the
rest are clearly of small account. It might indeed at first appear that
the smaller, dactyloid, or at length slenderly fusiform spores (leaning,
says Koerber, towards the *Lecanactis*-type) differed also from those of
Graphis in being referable—as were perhaps the less surprising in a
group so largely northern—to the colourless spore-series ; and it is certainly true that, in the greater proportion of forms, perfect spores are
commonly colourless, and in some possibly always so. There is yet
another presumption, looking the other way. In those tribes of Lichens
which approach nearest to Fungi the proportional exhibition of the
coloured type is vastly increased; and in *Graphidacei* this is as more than
four to one. Nor are indications of colour wanting in several forms (as
O. varia, *O. involuta*, *O. microsema*, Nyl.) while in the little group of
species (Nyl. in. *Prodr. Fl. N. Gran.* p.92) represented by *O. lentiginosa*,
and *O. diplasiospora*, Nyl.,—certainly *Opegraphæ*, in spite of the vacil-
lating characters of the hypothecium, in everything else—as well as in
that represented by *O. cerebrina*, we find typically brown spores, well
assumable as the key to the position of the whole genus; the anomalies
of which, in this respect, are paralleled, not only in *Graphis*, but other
natural groups (as *Thelotrema*, and *Heterothecium*) of the coloured series.

According to the views maintained here, unilocular spores, which might
also, and even probably, so far as analogy appears, be colourless, should
be by no means impossible within the limits of the present natural group ;

and in this case it may be difficult to keep *Lithographa*, Nyl., separate from it.

There is no instance as yet of an *Opegrapha*, exhibiting the final, mural-multilocular stage of differentiation of the coloured spore. *O. Ruiziana*, Fée, offers indeed decolorate spores of this structure, and looks generally, as presented in Lindig's collection, — and the same remark may be made of the externally not dissimilar *O. ovata*, Fée (*Herb. Meissn.*) —almost as much like *Opegrapha* as *Graphis ;* but both these lichens belong really, as indicated by Nylander, to the latter genus.

Of the thirty species, more or less, now known, (Nyl. *ll. cc.*) the larger part is extra-tropical. Some northern species extend into tropical regions, and tend thus to equalize the proportional distribution; but the genus contrasts evidently, in this respect, with *Graphis*. Seven or eight are known to me as North American; but the number is doubtless to be increased, both at the north, and, especially, at the south. Not one of the *Opegraphæ* of calcareous rocks in Europe has yet been observed here.

The stock of *O. lentiginosa*, Lyell (Nyl. in *Prodr. N. Gran.* p. 92, *obs.*) is represented here by two lichens. One of these — *O. tribulodes* [1]— described below, is scarcely perhaps to be distinguished from the European species but by the colourless hypothecium, and rather larger spores. It has occurred, only parasitical on *Trypethelium cruentum*, in Texas (Mr. Ravenel) and Alabama (Dr. Curtis). The other — *O. demissa* — a description of which is for the present reserved, is marked by larger, rather sunken fruit, scattered over an indistinct pale spot on the bark of Holly, Witch Hazel, and Poison Dogwood in southern Massachusetts (Mr. Willey) and yet larger spores.—— *O. oulocheila*, Tuckerm. (Lich. Calif. p. 32) was found by Schweinitz, on granitic rocks at Salem, North Carolina ; and is best comparable, as respects both habit, and spores, with *O. cerebrina* of European lime-rocks.—— *O. microcyclia*, Tuck. *Obs. Lich.* l. c. 6, p. 285 (*O. myriocarpa*, Suppl. 1, l. c. p. 429 non Mont.) inhabits Yellow Birch and other trees in New Hampshire, and Massachusetts, and is readily distinguished by its granulose thallus, and very minute, roundish apothecia. Spores in eights, in short, ellipsoid thekes ; dactyloid or sub-dacryoid ;

---

[1] *Opegrapha tribulodes, thallo nullo ; apotheciis in Trypethelio cruento parasiticis, minutis ellipticis oblongisve simplicibus l. dein 3-4-cuspidatis nigris, disco rimæformi dein sub-dilatato. Hypothecium incolor. Sporæ in thecis abbreviatis (ovalibus l. saccato-clavatis) octonæ, ellipsoideæ, biloculares medioque sæpe constrictæ, nigro-fuscæ, longit.* 0,016–21mm., *crassit.* 0,006–9mm., *paraphysibus subdistinctis.*——Southern parts of Texas (Mr. Ravenel). Alabama (Dr. Curtis). —— Thalline features of *O. demissa* as yet very obscure ; but the plant is not parasitical. Apothecia commonly 1mm. in length, scattered and simple, white within. Spores in eights (in clavate thekes) bilocular, and constricted at the middle, brown, 0,016–23mm. long, 0,006–9mm. wide. Paraphyses not always indistinct. With iodine, in some specimens, only the tips of gravid thekes shew a slight bluish tinge ; but in others, the blue reaction is more marked.

quadrilocular; fuscescent; $0{,}012$–$0{,}018^{mm.}$ long, and $0{,}004$–$0{,}006^{mm.}$ wide.
—— *O. varia* (Pers.) Fr., is common on trunks, throughout the United States, and has occurred (f. *diaphora*) on sandstone in California (Mr. Bolander). Spores dactyloid; 4–5–6–locular; often coloured, but perhaps the most perfect ones colourless; in eights, in obovate-clavate thekes.
—— *O. atra* (Pers.) Nyl., is perhaps also not uncommon, but I have met with it (in the fine var. *hapalea*, Ach.) only at Chelsea, Mass.; and received it only from New Bedford (Mr. Willey). Spores short-dactyloid, quadri-locular, in short, often pyriform thekes.—— *O. vulgata*, Ach., Nyl., is found on trunks throughout the country, and is especially common southward. It passes also to shaded rocks (f. *lithyrga*) in Weymouth, Mass. (Mr. Willey). Spores fusiform; 3–6–locular; colourless; in clavate thekes.
—— *O. Bonplandi*, Fée (*Ess.* p. 25; *Suppl.* p. 19, *pr. p.* Nyl. *Lich. exot.* l. c. p. 229, & in *Herb. Lindig* n. 2613) appears to be represented by a lichen from the low country of South Carolina (Mr. Ravenel) the blunt-fusiform, not rarely fuscescent spores of which, becoming 7–9–locular, remind one a little, at least in their colourless state, of the spores of certain forms of *Lecanactis premnea.* In the reference of our lichen to *O. Bonplandi*, I include in my view of the latter, *O. abbreviata*, Fée, as scarcely other than a variety (Nyl. *Lich. exot.* Lindig Herb. n. 2719). The plant before us is closely akin to another tropical lichen, — *O. prosodea*, Ach. (Nyl. *Lich. exot.*, *l. c.*, p. 229) with coarse, thick, prominent fruit, which, occurring in Cuba, should not improbably also come within our limits.
—— *O. viridis*, Pers. (Nyl. *Lich. Scand.* p. 256. *O. rubella*, Moug. & Nestl. n. 648) often resembles, and was referred to *O. herpetica* by Acharius, but differs essentially in the internal characters. I have found it in Massachusetts, on the bark of *Coniferæ ;* and Mr. Willey (New Bedford) on Beech; and it may also be represented by some southern lichens (North Carolina, Rev. Dr. Curtis; South Carolina, Mr. Ravenel; Florida, Dr. Chapman) which differ sufficiently in their minuteness at least, from *O. prosodea.* Should this last however occur with us, and, as is possible, in small forms, it may well include the southern plants here cited under *O. viridis.* Spores of *O. viridis* broad-elongated-fusiform; 10–14–locular; in short, clavate-oblong thekes. *O. herpetica*, Ach., Koerb., is yet unknown here; the lichen so named in Halsey's catalogue of New York lichens (1823) not having been determined by the spores, and being referable, by the synonymy, to *O. viridis ;* as is also the *O. herpetica* of the present writer's Syn. Lich. N. Eng. p. 75.—— *O. astræa*, Tuck. (Lich. Calif. p. 33). Upon Holly, Elm, Maple and Bald Cypress, in the low country of South Carolina; and in southern Texas (Mr. Ravenel). It occurs also in the island of Cuba (Mr. Wright) and is very remarkable for the white vesture of its apothecia, which have the aspect rather of *Graphis.* Spores in eights, in clavate thekes; dactyloid; 4–6–8–locular (the cells squared) fuscescent, or decolorate; $0{,}016$–$0{,}025^{mm.}$ long, and $0{,}005$–$0{,}007^{mm.}$ wide.

L.—XYLOGRAPHA, Fr., Nyl.

Fr. Syst. Myc. 2, p. 197. Nyl. Classif. 2, p. 187; Enum. Gén. 1. c. p. 128; Prodr. p. 147; Lich. Scand. p. 249. Mass. Miscell. Lich. Coemans Not. sur quelques Crypt. p. 14. Th. Fr. Gen. p. 99. Koerb. Parerg. p. 275. Stizenb. Beitr. 1. c. p. 153. Lichenis, dein Opegraphæ sp., Ach. Prodr.; L. U. p. 253. Hysterii sp., Wahl. Pers. Limboriæ sp., Ach. Opegraphæ sp., Fr. & Tuck. in Lich. Amer. exs. n. 97.

Apothecia ex angulato-patellæformi sæpius lirellæformia, excipulo proprio ceraceo. Sporæ ellipsoideæ, simplices, decolores. Spermatia acicularia; sterigmatibus simplicibus. Thallus crustaceus, uniformis; aut obsoletus.

Opegrapha parallela, Ach., was referred by Fries (l. c.) to Fungi as a distinct type (*Xylographa*) closely allied to the genus *Stictis ;* and the same botanist, at one time, distinguished from Lichens, '*crustæ defectu et loco natali,' Calicium turbinatum,* Pers. (*Sphinctrina,* Fr. *S. O. V.*). In restoring afterwards the latter to Lichens (*L. E.*) Fries restored it also to *Calicium ;* and it is difficult to see how he could have done anything else, or how we can call the now general distinction of *Sphinctrina* (as a lichen-group) from *Calicium,* other than arbitrary. The case of *Xylographa* is without doubt less clear. The North American *X. opegraphella* is obviously a lichen; akin too, generally, we can scarcely deny, to *Opegrapha* and *Graphis ;* and congenerical with the less distinctly lichenose European species; in which case analogy requires that the apothecia of all the forms should be taken for equivalent to the same organs in the *Opegraphei* proper. But there remains still, to separate this little group, at least from *Opegrapha,* the softer texture of the biatorine exciple, and the unilocular spores.[1] In view of analogies in other tribes, we cannot lay great stress on the latter of these differences, either here, or in *Lithographa,* Nyl.; but the former is less open to question, and looks evidently away from *Opegrapha,* and in the direction rather of *Graphis.* It is this last genus which furnishes us with all the most remarkable exhibitions of what may be called biatorine exciples to be found in *Opegraphei ;* and this affords, in its, in one sense, extremest section (*Fissurina*) conditions of the exciple perhaps not wholly without reason to be compared with states of the fruit of *Xylographa opegraphella.*

---

[1] Perhaps not always unilocular. The '*goutelletes claires, souvent au nombre de deux, placées a chaque extrémité de la spore*' (Coemans, l. c.) are characteristical in other forms as well as in *X. parallela,* and suggest now a bilocular spore not unlike those of several *Biatoræ,* as comparable also with decolorate *Pyrenula*-types. And Dr. Nylander has just described a *Xylographa* (*X. platytropa,* Nyl. in *Flora,* 1868, p. 163) with 'colourless or pale brown spores, which are 6-10-locular, and the cells oftener bilocular.' In view of this, the spores of the other species should be taken for decolorate rather than typically colourless.

26

Three species have been recognized in Europe, by Nylander, of which one is found here; and a fourth is peculiar to this country. *X. opegraphella*, Nyl. (*Opegrapha stictica, Lich. Amer. exs.* l. c., *non* Nyl.) comparable as respects the shape of its apothecia, which are now rounded and now lirelliform, with both *X. flexella*, Nyl. *Prodr.* (Moug. & Nestl. n. 1094) and *X. parallela* (*Herb. Floerk.* Fellm. *Lich. Arct.* n. 205) is yet commonly lighter-coloured, and especially distinguished by its conspicuous, rather turgid, warted thallus; which is now however almost obsolete. This thallus is comparable with that of a similarly turgid state of the crust of *Lecanora pallida* v. *cancriformis* (Hoffm. *L. cæsio-rubella*, Ach.) as this occurs, upon dead wood, on the coast of Massachusetts, as with that of *L. cinerea*, and other lichens, with the same habitat; and it is no doubt peculiarly conditioned by the substrate. Spores of *X. opegraphella* oblong-ellipsoid, 0,011-0,015$^{mm.}$ long, and 0,0035-0,0050$^{mm.}$ wide.——*X. parallela*, Fr., has rewarded the search only of Mr. Willey, who obtained it from dead Firs, at Dixville Notch, New Hampshire. Spores ellipsoid, 0,008-0,016$^{mm.}$ long, and 0,005-0,007$^{mm.}$ wide.

LI.—GRAPHIS, Ach., Nyl.

Nyl. Enum. Gén. l. c. p. 128; Prodr. p. 148; Lich. exot. l. c. pp. 226, 244, 260; in Prodr. Fl. N. Gran. pp. 73, 131, & t. 1, 2; Syn. Lich. N. Caled. p. 69. Graphis, Ach. L. U. pp. 46, 264, 674, max. p. Graphis max. p., Opegraphæ spp., & Glyphidis sp., Ach. Syn. pp. 70, 80, 107. Graphis max. p., Opegraphæ spp., Sarcographæ sp., Fissurina, & Arthoniæ spp., Fée Ess. p. 33, &c.; Suppl. p. 26, &c. Graphis, Leiorreuma, Sclerophyton, Medusula, Pyrrhochroa p. p., & Diorygma, Eschw. Syst. p. 13. Graphis, Opegraphæ spp., Sclerophyton, & Ustalia p. p., Fr. S. O. V. p. 272. Graphis pr. p., Asterisca pr. p., Leucogramma & Platygramma, Mey. Entwick. p. 330. Graphis pr. p., Leiogramma pr. p., Sclerophyton, & Ustalia pr. p., Eschw. Bras. p. 65, &c. Graphis, Opegrapha pr. p., Lecanactis p. p., Sclerophyton, Medusula, Fissurina, & Arthonia p. p., Mont. Pl. Cell. Cub. p. 170; Crypt. Guy. p. 39, &c.; Syll. p. 344. Graphis, Opegrapha pr. p., & Ustalia, Stizenb. Beitr. l. c. p. 153.

Apothecia lirellæformia, sub-ramosa, l. rarissime rotundato-difformia, plerumque innata, excipulo proprio l. colorato l. nigro, basi sæpius incolore, a thallino thallodeve fere semper coronato. Sporæ ex ellipsoideo oblongæ l. erucæformes, quadri-pluriloculares, l. muriformi-multiloculares, fuscescentes l. decolores. Spermatia (quantum cogn.) oblonga l. bacillaria; sterigmatibus simplicibus. Thallus crustaceus, uniformis.

The northern representatives of *Graphis*, as here taken, are so few, and express so imperfectly the richly diversified tropical type, that I have cited above only those writers the scope of whose observations embraces the whole genus. It will be readily seen how various have been the judgments upon it. The acuteness of Eschweiler led him indeed into discriminations in the present tribe, especially in *Graphis*, and *Opegrapha*, which have not been followed; and some of which he abandoned himself. Others, as Fries, have questioned the validity of distinctions, which yet, with the insufficient material before them, they did not wholly reject. But it was left to Nylander to revert to the simplicity of Acharius's conception; and, in fact, to found *Graphis*, enriched now with a vast accession of forms, anew.

The lecanoroid character of the large group before us, becomes at length marked in many tropical conditions, and easily influences its separation from *Opegrapha*, though the feature is finally indistinct; but there can be no doubt that *Graphis* touches *Thelotrema*, and is illustrated by the latter at least equally multiform natural genus; as also by the lecanoroid group of *Biatorei* (*Heterothecium*). The variations in colour of the very commonly concealed proper exciple of *Thelotrema* have scarcely received the attention that has been given to those of *Graphis*, but there is no doubt of their occurrence; and the generical inseparableness of such varying conditions of the former genus from each other, may well influence our judgment of the exceptionally coloured or entirely colourless exciple (as, for example, in the clusters once separated as *Ustalia*, and *Fissurina*, by authors) in the latter. In neither of these genera, nor in *Arthonia*, does it appear that we can (*ceteris paribus*) separate generically biatorine from lecideine types; however natural and convenient such discrimination be in the *Lecideei*.

The large group of species represented by *G. scripta* and *G. elegans*, approaches so closely to *Opegrapha* as at length to be only distinguishable by the spores; and the group is referred to *Opegrapha* by Fries and Montagne; as it was also united with *Opegrapha*, under *Graphis*, by Meyer; and, latterly, by Eschweiler. It recedes, however, from the other type, not merely in the more or less conspicuous thalline margin, but further in what must be called a tendency to modification of the proper exciple; this being, largely, colourless below (*perith. mere laterale*, Eschw. *Excip. propr. incompletum*, Fr.). The latter distinction is, notwithstanding, to say nothing more, an uncertain one; and the clusters of forms exhibiting it afford also, not seldom, complete evidence of a return to the wholly black exciple (*perith. integrum*, Eschw.) thus leaving little but habit, and the internal characters, to connect the group with *Graphis*, as here taken. Every stage, if I mistake not, in the gradual transformation of the 'merely lateral' into the 'entire' exciple may be observed in the universally distributed *G. scripta*; and notwithstanding the great authority of Nylander in the present tribe, it is no more easy to follow him in elevating the difference in question into a specific distinction, than Acharius, in taking it for generical. The state of *G. scripta* in which the exciple is wholly black, or 'entire,' (*G. assimilis*, Nyl.) if less common than the other, occurs, at least, in so many of the marked varieties of the species, that it may perhaps be presumed to occur in all; and *G. analoga*, Nyl. (*Lich. exot.* l. c. p. 244) as described, should seem to be scarcely more than an analogous condition of one of the similarly variant, and otherwise undistinguishable forms of *G. scripta*, with spores now finally muriform (*G. sophistica*, Nyl.).

Of the next succeeding group in Nylander's disposition of the genus, the typical species is *G. dendritica*. The exciple of this is, more commonly, wholly black, or 'entire'; but forms, in all other respects similar, and exhibited in a precisely similar series of variations, frequently occur, in which the hypothecium is colourless below (*G. inusta*, Ach., Nyl., *G. Smithii*, Leight.) as in the ordinary states of *G. scripta ;* which thus illustrates, in this phase of variation, and is illustrated by, the present. But the peculiar line of development of *G. dendritica* is sufficiently marked ; its dilated exciples now offering rounded conditions, comparable rather with *Lecanactis* (to which such conditions have in fact been referred) and the *Lecideei ;* and now passing into confluent ones (*Medusula*, Auctt.) reckoned at first even alien to the tribe. It does not at least appear to me to be questionable that the North American *G. dendritica* passes directly, in both its 'entire' and 'dimidiate' states, into genuine *Medusulæ* of authors. *Ustalia*, Fr., Eschw., *pro p.*, a remarkable tropical cluster of species, with flat, reddish disks, is not only near to the group represented by *G. dendritica* (as compare Fr. *L. E.* p. 373) but perhaps not easily, in any wide view, if we deny stress to biatorine analogy, to be separated from it. There seems to be no more reason for distinguishing the *Ustaliæ*, properly so called, from the *Graphides dendriticæ*, than for separating, generically, the coloured or colourless species of the next succeeding group from those with black exciples; as, for instance, *G. chrysenteron*, Mont. (*Leucogramma*, Mass. *Esam.*) or *G. hololeuca*, Mont. (*Glaucinaria*, Mass.) from *G. Afzelii*, Ach. (*Diplolabia*, Mass.).

Fries, at first (*S. O. V.*, with which compare *L. E.* p. 373) referred *G. Lyellii*, of our last section, to his *Graphis ;* the type of which was *G. Afzelii*. But interesting as is this indication of apparent affinity in the two sections, we have only to look at the species last named when denuded of its white vesture, to incline to place it, with Eschweiler, not in his *Leiorreuma*, with *G. Lyellii*, but rather with *G. comma* and *G. intricata*, in his *Graphis*. And there is no doubt that the great, central group of *Graphis*, now before us, of which *G. Afzelii* has been regarded by some writers as representative, as is *G. frumentaria*, Fée, by Nylander, takes hold at once of both of the preceding groups, and exhibits the summit of development to which the genus attains. It is here too that lecanoroid features become especially marked, and that *Thelotrema* is so plainly touched, that it appears doubtful to which genus certain species shall be referred. Like the *Ustaliæ*, the group is a wholly tropical one, though extending here and there into conterminous, or sub-tropical regions. Following Fée, Nylander places here the sometimes differently understood *G. grammitis* (*Diorygma*, Eschw. *Fissurina*, Mont.) which may be said, possibly, to look in one direction towards the coloured *Medusulæ* or *Ustaliæ*, and in the other towards forms closely associable with *G. frumentaria.*

The aspect of the best developed conditions of the remaining small group (*Fissurina*, Fée, *Diorygma*, Eschw.) as *G. Babingtonii* (Mont.) and *G. nitida*, is that of the last ; and there is certainly no important difference in structure between the species named and *G. grammitis ;* which, as already cited, has been reckoned congenerical with them by most eminent lichenographers. But *G. grammitis* is not so easily removable from the neighbourhood of *G. chlorocarpa ;* and though the walls of the exciple be less easily discernible in the *Fissurinæ* proper, an exciple is never, so far as the writer's observation has gone, (and compare here Fée *Ess.* t. 1, f. 7, *β*) in any absolute sense, deficient. *Fissurina* is then undistinguishable from *Graphis ;* of the central type of which it may easily be regarded a colourless degeneration. Indeed in certain low forms common in the tropics, and referable here, *Graphis* may be said, perhaps, to reach its extremest degradation ; nothing appearing to the naked eye, or even to an ordinary lens, but certain paler cracks in the bark upon which these humble lichens grow.

Graphis differs generally from *Opegrapha* in its larger spores, some features in the differentiation of which are also distinguishable ; the ellipsoid spore becoming now elongated and cylindraceous (*erucæform*, Koerb.) especially in the first group ; and this elongated, or the ellipsoid state (with entire sporoblasts) passing readily and frequently into the muriform. And the natural assemblage before us affords, if I mistake not, no little evidence looking to shew not merely that the different gradations in the differentiation of the same spore-type may be exhibited within the limits of a single genus, but even within the circle of forms of one and the same *natural* species. There does not appear to be any important diversity between the two forms of *Arthonia cyrtodes*, Tuck. (*Obs. Lich. l. c.*, 6, p. 285) except that in *a*, the spores (of the same type with, and when young undistinguishable from those of *β*) have not yet reached the perfection indicated in the latter. So *Graphis sophistica*, Nyl. (*Stenographa anguina*, Mudd Man. Brit. Lich. p. 235) repeats the forms of, and differs in no known respect from *G. scripta*, save that the now less elongated spore (when young quite similar to young conditions of *G. elegans* and *G. scripta*) exhibits finally the completion, as does *G. scripta* a less advanced stage, of the muriform type. Compare further, as to this interesting point, *G. anguilliformis*, Tayl., Nyl. (in *Prodr. Fl. N. Gran.* p. 76, fig. 31, & in *Herb. Lindig* n. 2634) with *G. vernicosa*, Fée, as exhibited in the same publications ; *G. striatula* (Ach.) Nyl., with *G. elegans ; G. hæmographa*, Nyl. (*l. c.* p. 88, & in *Herb. Lindig* n. 878) with *G. cinnabarrina*, Fée, of the same publications ; and *G. instabilis*, Nyl., with

G. Babingtonii (Mont.). And the argument from *Graphis* is, at any rate, sufficiently direct against the distinction of *Volvaria* (Massal. *Ric.* p. 141. Stizenb. *Beitr.* l. c. p. 168) from *Thelotrema ;* and equally against the separation of *Bombyliospora* from *Heterothecium.* Otherwise, indeed, if a specific difference be to be admitted between the two forms of *Arthonia cyrtodes*, and the latter of them referred to *Arthothelium*, Mass., the former should not lack plausible claims to stand for a new genus.

It might seem possible to regard *Opegrapha*,—if we omitted to consider the little group (Nyl. in *Prodr. N. Gran.* p. 92) with bilocular, brown spores, represented at the north by *O. lentiginosa*, and by several, better developed forms in the tropics,—as belonging to the colourless series ; perfect spores being, in most species, more commonly colourless, and coloration being possibly quite unknown in some, and the differentiation generally resembling that of this series, the acicular type of which is indeed almost reached :—but the difficulties in the way of excluding the brown-spored group are far from slight ; while *Thelotrema* offers numerous instances of analogous discrepancies in a genus, the spores of which may be taken, and by an induction perhaps sufficiently general, to be typically coloured. Might we not, in short, beforehand expect that large, natural genera, developed mainly in the tropics, and abounding in external variations from their types, should exhibit similar ones in their internal features ? *Opegrapha* is after all but a wing of *Graphis ;* distinguishable perhaps, but, strictly speaking, scarcely distinct. The eminent writers who have carried out this view, and regarded the whole of the first section of *Graphis*, as here taken, or even the first two sections, excluding tropical subsections of the last, as generically inseparable from *Opegrapha*, have yet excepted (Fries however, in *S. O. V.*, only with hesitation) *Graphis* proper (our third section) as, at any rate, distinct. But it proves, if I am not greatly mistaken, quite impossible, in the present state of knowledge of the genus, to maintain this exception; and the third section must follow, therefore, the fortunes of the other two. If then we are content, here, to leave *Opegrapha* apart from *Graphis*, it is only as next to it; and as, at all events, a member of the same spore-series.

Taking, as it seems to be safe to do, the whole number of clearly distinguishable, and for the most part reckoned specific forms of *Graphis*, as here understood, described by authors, as a hundred and fifty, one eighth is known to occur beyond intertropical regions. But of this eighth the larger part is also properly tropical ; and the proportion is seen then to be very small which belongs to the temperate zones. No species penetrates the polar regions. Of the six forms inhabiting Europe, five occur within our limits, or all except *G. Lyellii ;* and we possess also one other northern *Graphis*, unknown elsewhere. Southward, thirteen tropical or sub-tropical *Graphides*, one of them not indeed here confined to the southern states, have thus far been detected.

Of the first division (family, or stock of *G. scripta*) five species (as I am best able to reckon them) are known as North American.—— *G. eulectra*, Tuckerm. (Lich. Calif. p. 34) is distinguished by a stroma-like accessory exciple; and has only occurred in New England (Myself) and Illinois (Mr. E. Hall). Spores in eights; erucæform; 12–15–locular; the length six to eight times exceeding the diameter; colourless, or pale brownish. —— *G. scripta* (L.) Ach., occurs everywhere, at the North and South alike, in the common European forms, and passes into some states, especially southward, unknown to Europe.—Among these is the v. *tenella* (*Graphis*, Ach., Nyl. in *Prodr. Fl. N. Gran.* p. 73, & *Herb. Lindig* n. 864) a readily observable, tropical lichen, which has been found in Texas (Mr. Wright) and appears ill-separable from the species. — The condition of *G. scripta* with wholly black, or entire exciple (*G. assimilis*, Nyl.) is perhaps less common than the dimidiate form, but occurs in New England, and at the South. Spores, in these forms, in eights, from ellipsoid becoming oblong, and erucæform, 6–10–locular, the length thrice to five times exceeding the diameter; colourless, or at length scarcely brownish. In the southern lichen the spores are now abbreviated and ellipsoid, and the flattened, approximated spore-cells need only to commence the next succeeding process, of division vertically, to introduce the v. *analoga* (*G. analoga*, Nyl.) which is to the form now immediately to follow exactly as *G. assimilis*, Nyl., to his *G. scripta*.—The v. *sophistica* (*G. sophistica*, Nyl.) is then the condition of the ordinary, dimidiate state of *G. scripta*, in which the spores reach the muriform stage; but though found in Europe, and tropical America, this has only very recently been observed here (southern Texas, Mr. Ravenel). The form differs from *a* (*G. scripta*) in nothing but the grade of evolution of the spores; and in the now diminished number of spores contained in the thekes (as to which compare *Buellia oidalea*, &c.,) and can be detected only by the microscope. Spores of our plant observed only in twos and fours; offering eight to twelve transverse series of spore-cells; 0,023–0,053$^{mm.}$ long, and 0,011–0,023$^{mm.}$ wide.—— *G. elegans* (Sm.) Ach., is distinguished from the last species by the thicker, furrowed margins of the exciple, and longer, often broader spores, and is almost confined, here, to the South (North Carolina, Rev. Dr. Curtis; South Carolina, Mr. Ravenel; Florida, Dr. Chapman; Alabama, Mr. Beaumont; Louisiana, Hale; Texas, Mr. Ravenel) but has turned up also, like *Biatora parvifolia*, in New Jersey (Mr. Austin). The North American lichen (as also the tropical, as exhibited in Cuba) is commonly smaller and often slenderer than the European, but like that (Fr. *L. E.* p. 370) varies much as *G. scripta*. Spores in eights; erucæform; 8–11–locular; the length five to seven times exceeding the diameter; colourless, or scarcely brownish. —The thalline margin is finally obscure in the European plant, and sometimes quite disappears in certain forms of the tropical (*Opegrapha striatula*, Ach., *e* Nyl. *Graphis*, Nyl. *O. rimulosa*, Mont.) but these forms, though now greatly narrowed, and also elongated, so as to look rather like *G. scripta*, do not appear to be clearly distinguishable, in any wide view, by the

external characters. The spores vary indeed, occasionally, in these sub-
tropical representatives of *G. elegans*, so far as to present a larger number (12–16) of spore-cells (such spores measuring, in specimens from
South Carolina, and Texas, 0,039–0,069$^{mm.}$ in length, and 0,009–0,011$^{mm.}$ in
width) but I have found no reason to reckon this difference as expressing
any more than an occasional exuberance. — Much more important however is the fact that it was among these tropical forms, now approaching
so closely to *G. elegans*, if now again, as might perhaps be expected,
receding from it, that the muriform modification of the spore was first
observed (*G. substriatula*, Nyl.) in the species-group before us. No reason
appears for estimating the value of this difference any higher here than
in G. *scripta ;* and the lichens exhibiting it must, in this view, be brought
together as a variety (*substriatula*) either of *G. elegans*, or, if the sub-
tropical lichen really prove, in the end, to be distinguishable in species,
of *G. striatula ;* and will, in either case, correspond, as does the plant
sometimes, most closely in other respects, to *G. scripta*, v. *sophistica*. It
is observable, as illustrating the intimate relation of the lichens we have
been considering, that while some forms of the tropical *G. elegans*, v. *striatula* (*G. striatula* (Ach.) Nyl.) as, for instance, *Opegr. rimulosa*, Mont.
Guy. (*Herb. Mont.*) offer exactly the spores of *G. elegans*, a specimen of
the *Opegr. elegans* of the same work (*Herb. Mont.*) most readily comparable, externally, with the European lichen (as in Moug. & Nestl. n. 360)
and almost equally so with *Herb.* Lindig n. 862 (*G. striatula*, Nyl.) which
last is assimilated by the spores also to *G. elegans*, proves yet to be differenced, internally, by muriform spores. I have not yet met with muriform
spores in my North American specimens referable to the stock of *G. elegans*, and the hymenium is but imperfectly developed in many of these
specimens; but Dr. Nylander recognized a South Carolina lichen as
belonging to his *G. striatula*. To judge by the Cuban lichens of the
affinity we are now considering, in the collections of Mr. Wright, the
elongated spore with entire spore-cells is far more common than the more
advanced, muriform one. And there is, if I mistake not, some evidence
in these collections, that the condition of the v. *striatula* above-noticed,
which is distinguishable from other conditions, as from *G. elegans*, *a*, only
by an increase in the number of (entire) spore-cells, is finally further
differenced by apothecia not a little like those of *G. tumidula* (Fée) Nyl.
(Lindig *Herb. N. Gran.* n. 2723) towards which — separated by its very
large spores — the specimens we refer to may then be said to look.——
G. rigida (Fée) Nyl., is another tropical lichen, to a form of which (v. *enteroleuca*, Nyl.) specimens from Texas (Mr. Wright) were referred by Dr.
Nylander. Spores solitary, and in fours; oblong-ellipsoid ; muriform-
multilocular ; the length twice to thrice exceeding the diameter; colourless, or at length brownish. —— *G. Pavoniana*, Fée, one of the lichens
found on Cinchona bark, and with a little of the aspect of some *Ustaliæ*,
has occurred in Texas (Mr. Wright) as determined by Dr. Nylander. The

spores, as described by Fée *Suppl.* p. 29) for I have scarcely seen good ones, are erucæform, 10–12–locular, and colourless.

Of the second division (stock of *G. dendritica*) five species have been detected within our limits. —— *G. dendritica*, Ach., occurs rather sparingly on the coasts of New England, and in New Jersey (Mr. Austin) but becomes very common and much varied at the South (South Carolina, Mr. Ravenel ; Florida and Alabama, Mr. Beaumont; Louisiana, Hale ; Texas, Mr. Ravenel). The thin, dark-brown hypothecium sometimes blackens.—But again, the hypothecium becomes pale, or even colourless (*G. inusta*, Ach., Nyl., founded on a Canadian lichen ; *G. Smithii*, Leight.) this state exhibiting all the modifications of the species, and being otherwise undistinguishable. It occurs throughout the same region with the other. — The apothecia of *G. dendritica*, in both conditions of the hypothecium, become finally often confluent, forming rounded or irregular, variously divided patches (*Medusulæ* sp., Auctt.) which constitute the v. *medusula*, Nyl. ; occurring commonly at the South, and found at New Bedford, Mass., (Mr. Willey). Spores of *G. dendritica* in eights ; broad-oblong ; commonly four– but reaching six– to eight–locular ; the length twice and a half to four times exceeding the diameter; fuscescent. The spores are scarcely erucæform, being less elongated than in most of my specimens of the European, and of the tropical lichen, though more like those of such states as Rabenh. *Lich. Eur.* n. 606. The southern plant is also curiously marked by the irregular division (of sometimes all, but more commonly part) of the spore-cells into two ; an anticipation at least of the muriform stage. —— *G. scalpturata*, Ach., inhabiting tropical America, is a rather larger, finer lichen than the last, but closely akin to it. It has occurred here in Louisiana (Herb. Austin). Spores, so far as observed, solitary, muriform-multilocular, brown, reaching at length $0^{mm\cdot},083$ in length by $0^{mm\cdot},019$ in width. But spores occur of half these dimensions; and the lichen is otherwise strictly comparable with one from southern Alabama (Mr. Beaumont) the brown, muriform spores of which measure $0^{mm\cdot},041–69$ in length by $0^{mm\cdot},017–23$ in width, and occur in twos, threes, fives, and eights, in the thekes. The young spores, in both these lichens, resemble those of the last species. The material in hand appeared to be sufficient, in the case of *G. scripta*, to fully authorize an expression of the opinion that the conditions of that lichen with muriform spores are not properly separable in species from the remainder, with which, in other respects, they undoubtedly agree ; and the argument could not but have its bearing on the strictly analogous case of *G. elegans*. It does not follow indeed that *G. dendritica* can be shown to be another example of the same sort; but there is at least no doubt of the very close relationship of *G. scalpturata* to the former (in its forms with colourless hypothecium) and such specimens of the latter as Lindig *Herb. N. Gran.* n. 750, as compared with n. 729, and Lindig, 2, n. 139, as compared with n. 2637, reduce perhaps the question of a specific distinction between the two lichens solely to the spore-difference; and bring them therefore under the same category with *G. scripta* and *G. elegans*, as here understood. It must be taken for additional evidence that the spores of *G. scalpturata* are not always solitary and exceptionally large, but vary in number and size, as in analogous cases in this and other genera, that Nylander finds *Lecanactis pruinosa*, Mont. *Guy.*, to differ, in no other respect from conditions recognized by him of the *Graphis* last cited, than in being octosporous.——*G. tricosa*, Ach. I refer here a lichen from southern Texas, (Mr. Ravenel) which, while at once a very marked expression of the *Medusula*-type, differs from *G. dendritica* in smaller spores (0,011–0,016^{mm} long, and 0,005–0,007$^{mm.}$ wide) but no clear line of separation is apparent between it and certain Texan and other southern lichens, which, with spores similarly reduced, are otherwise perhaps too near to *G. dendritica*, v. *medusula*, Nyl. Acharius finally referred *G. tricosa* to *Glyphis;* and the difficult relations of the latter group to the extreme members of the great cluster of lichens represented by *G. dendritica*, become apparent in view of the matchless series of Graphidaceous types illustrated by Nylander. ——*G. erumpens*, Nyl., at first not unlike a *Fissurina*, but assuming finally much the look of *G. pezizoidea*, Ach., as given in Lindig n. 2723, has been found in South Carolina (Mr. Ravenel) and in southern Alabama (Mr. Beaumont). Spores in eights; oblong; 4–8-locular; the length thrice to five times exceeding the diameter; fuscescent.——*G. patellula* (Meissn.) Nyl. *in litt.* (*Opegrapha*, Meissn.; *Arthonia*, Fée; *Lecanactis*, Nyl. Enum.; *L. paterella*, Tuck. *in litt.*) is a curious, rounded form, well-comparable with *Melaspilea arthonioides*, as respects general habit, but really near akin to the last, and of the present group; in which rounded forms are not uncommon. It has been found, on Holly, in the low country of South Carolina (Mr. Ravenel) and in Florida (Mr. Beaumont). Spores in sixes (and, probably, eights) oblong and erucæform; 6–10-locular; the length thrice to six times exceeding the diameter; fuscescent. In specimens from Cuba (Mr. Wright) the spores vary to 11- and 12-locular, but I have seen none with '*quinze à dix-huit sporidies*,' as described by Fée (*Suppl.* p. 41).

Of the third group (stock of *G. frumentaria*) two North American species have been observed.——*G. scolecitis*, Tuckerm.,[1] has occurred

---

[1] *Graphis scolecitis* (*sp. nova*) *thallo tenuissimo lævigato viridi-cinerascente nigro-limitato ; apotheciis innato-prominulis elongatis gracilibus acutis flexuosis simplicibus l. rarius furcatim subramosis, excipulo rufo discum rimæformem pallidum tenuiter marginante. Hypothecium incolor. Sporæ octonæ, lato-ellipsoideæ' 6-loculares loculis integris, l. 1, l. 2, sæpius divisis, incolores, longit.* 0,018–23$^{mm.}$ *crassit.* 0,007–9$^{mm.}$——Trunks, southern Alabama (Mr. Beaumont). Best comparable perhaps with forms of *Graphis* not remote from the stock (*stirps*) of *G. grammitis;* but probably new. The spores, which are surrounded by a halo, are neither well distinguishable from the muriform sort, as often presented, nor from that with typically entire spore-cells; and exhibit the unsatisfactoriness

only in southern Alabama (Mr. Beaumont).——*G. Afzelii*, Ach., a conspicuous lichen, has been found as far north as Wilmington, North Carolina (Mr. Buckley) and occurs in South Carolina (Mr. Ravenel) Florida (Dr. Chapman) Alabama (Mr. Beaumont) Mississippi (Dr. Veatch) and Texas (Mr. Ravenel). Spores in eights; ellipsoid; quadrilocular; the length twice to twice and a half exceeding the diameter; not coloured.

There remains only to notice a single, small group (*Fissurinæ*) confined to the southern States, of which two species have been determined. ——*G. Babingtonii* (Mont. *sub Fissurina*) as exhibited here (South Carolina, Mr. Ravenel; Alabama, Mr. Beaumont) differs from *G. instabilis*, Nyl. (*Prodr. Fl. N. Gran.* p. 86) in the thallus and thalline exciple being thicker, and in possessing the internal characters of Montagne's lichen. Spores cocciform, or rounded, quadrilocular (the spore-cells being regular) colourless.——*G. nitida* (Eschw.) Nyl., occurs in specimens resembling the foreign ones in South Carolina (Mr. Ravenel) and Alabama (Mr. Beaumont) but no spores have been detected. One or two other lichens belonging to this group, and from the same districts, are undeterminable for the same reason.

———•———

Fam. 3.—GLYPHIDEI (Fr.) Mont.

Apothecia plura in stromate thallode verrucæformi collecta.

We have noticed already a tendency, in this lower tribe, to revert towards the crustaceous representatives (*Lecanorei*) of the highest; and have found this tendency especially marked in species of *Graphis*, of the stock of *G. frumentaria*. It is then the less surprising that we are now to see *Pertusaria* repeated, in Graphidaceous types of equally extraordinary character; which yet revert to *Graphis*, just as the genus first-named does to *Lecanora*. It was however with the compound *Verrucariacei* that the two groups now to be noticed were associated by Acharius; by Eschweiler, in both his works; and even by Fée; whose illustrations, especially of *Chiodecton*, are surpassed in importance by few that have appeared. Fries, at first (*S. O. V.* p. 270) rejecting, for both genera, any closer relation than that of analogy with *Trypethelium*, placed them, together with *Medusula*, Eschw., and *Conioloma*, Floerk., in his *Glyphidei*, which was next to his *Graphidei ;* and has been followed in this, as regards the types now before us, by Montagne; but he finally (*L. E.*) restored *Chiodecton* to the other affinity, where Fée also left it, when (*Suppl.* p. 48) following Fries, he recognized *Glyphis* as a Graphidaceous type.

of this distinction when looked at without regard to the real type of the spore. There is no reaction of the hymenial gelatine with iodine.

Well distinguished as they appear, for the most part, in habit, *Glyphis* and *Chiodecton* make no uncertain approaches to each other (as *G. labyrinthica* to *C. seriale*) and their distinction may be said to be largely determined by the spores; *Chiodecton* being comparable in this respect with *Opegrapha*, as *Glyphis*, most evidently with *Graphis*.

With the genus last named the connection of both groups must, in view of what is now known of them, be called intimate. *Medusula* of Eschweiler and others—based upon a demonstrable aberration of the stellate groups of apothecia in *Graphis dendritica*, &c., in which, finally, by the confluence of the crowded proper exciples, an irregular, maculæform apothecium, as, often, by that of the thalline exciples, a stroma[1] is produced,—is, at first sight, scarcely less distinct than *Glyphis ;* and certain lichens may be said to be still in question between the two. Perhaps no one, familiar, in a measure, with these groups, can attentively examine the fine set of specimens given in Lindig *Herb. Nov. Gran.*, to illustrate *Graphis tricosa*, Ach., and *G. intricans*, Nyl., and *Glyphis medusulina* and *G. actinobola*, Nyl., without the decided impression that we have here, at one end of a most intimately related series of forms, a *Graphis*, of the group represented by *G. dendritica*, and at the other so close an approximation to *Glyphis labyrinthica* that we may well incline, with the learned lichenographer to whom we owe the elucidation of these lichens, to regard it as *touching* the last-cited *Glyphis*. But *Glyphis actinobola* (as in Lindig n. 2656) appears inseparable from *Graphis intricans* (as in n. 2579 of the same collection) by any difference beside the unsatisfactory one assumable from the blackening hypothecium ; and the lichen last named (as in Lindig n. 2610) differs scarcely at all from *G. tricosa* (Lindig, 2, n. 148) except only in the rather smaller spores. And *Chiodecton*, though so marked in type (*C. sphærale* and *C. myrticola*) as scarcely to be comparable with other groups of *Graphidacei*, beside *Glyphis*, unless with some forms of *Platygrapha* and *Enterographa*, passes notwithstanding into extreme states (as compare the large series of specimens of *C. perplexum*, Nyl., in Lindig *Herb. N. Gran.*, especially n. 2577) not distantly suggesting similarly extreme conditions of *Graphis dendritica* v. *medusula*. With the last indeed—the type of *Medusula*, Eschw.,—Fries, as we have seen above, though far from implicitly accepting its generical separation, significantly associated both *Chiodecton* and *Glyphis*, in his *Glyphidei*.

LII.—CHIODECTON, Ach.

Ach. Syn. p. 108 ; in Linn. Trans. 12, p. 43. Eschw. Syst. p. 19 ; Lich. Bras. l. c. p. 168. Fée Ess. p. 38, 62, t. 1, f. 17, & tt. 17, 18 ; Monogr. Gen. Chiod. in Ann. Sci. 17 ; Suppl. p. 49, t. 40. Fr. S. O. V. p. 271 ;

---

[1] '*Hoc enim, typice ut loquar, tantum ex apotheciis confertioribus oritur.*' Fr. *S. O. V.* p. 270.

L. E. p. 417. Mey. Entwick. p. 325. Mont. Pl. Cell. Cub. p. 160 ; Crypt. Guy. p. 58 ; Syll. p. 356. Schær. Enum. p. 226, t. 8, f. 6. Leight. Brit. Anz. Lich. p. 24, t. 8, 9. Norm. Con. p. 27. Tul. Mém. Lich. p. 184, t. 10, f. 24-27. Nyl. Enum. Gén. l. c. p. 134 ; Lich. exot. l. c.; in Prodr. N. Gran. p. 109, t. 2, f. 51 ; Syn. Lich. N. Caled. p. 66. Th. Fr. Gen. p. 96. Stizenb. Beitr. l. c. p. 152. Trypethelii sp., Ach. in Act. Gorenk., cit. ipso. Chiodecton, Melanodecton, & Leucodecton pr. p., Mass. Ric. p. 149 ; Esam. p. 43.

Apothecia rotundato-difformia oblongave, plano-convexa, immarginata, hypothecio nigricante suffulta, in stromate albo immersa. Sporæ fusiformes 1. nunc oblongo-ovoideæ, quadri-pluriloculares, rarissime muriformi-multiloculares, fere semper incolores. Spermatia acicularia; sterigmatibus simplicibus. Thallus crustaceus, uniformis.

The systematic perplexities involved in the natural relation of *Graphis tricosa* to *Glyphis* remain now as great as they were when Acharius considered them ; being by no means removed by Nylander's acute distribution, between *Graphis* and *Glyphis*, of what were once certainly reckoned varied forms of the lichen first named. It appears to be out of the question to frame a character for *Glyphidei* which shall exclude *Medusula ;* and equally impossible to exclude the Medusuline type from the circuit of variation of *Graphis dendritica*. But whatever the difficulties of *Glyphis*, *Chiodecton* is too closely akin wholly to escape them ; and is itself, whether simulating *Platygrapha*, or developing into Medusuline forms, or now almost suggesting (as to Acharius) Trypetheliine ones, one of the best-marked types of Graphidaceous lichens.

Acharius did not recognize any proper exciple in *Chiodecton* or in *Glyphis*, but his description of the apothecia (*Monogr. l. c.*, pp. 37, 44) at least opens the way to such inference, and it is perhaps too much to say, with Eschweiler, that he 'wholly overlooked the structure.' The latter author was yet first to indicate (*Syst.* p. 19) that *Glyphis* agrees with all typically developed *Graphidacei* in the possession of a distinct exciple ; though he considered this to be only represented by a hypothecium in *Chiodecton*. But the microscope scarcely confirms the asserted structural diversity of the latter ; and it may be said to be, in this respect, chiefly distinguishable by its almost always plano-convex thalamia being immarginate ; while the concave or channelled exciples of *Glyphis* may be said to be margined. And when *Chiodecton* offers, as in *C. seriale*, perfectly flat, or even impressed hymenia, it is not always easy to distinguish it from *Glyphis labyrinthica* by any prominent, external difference in the excipular envelope.

In the great majority of species of *Chiodecton* we find fusiform spores, with the spore-cells of such spores, as they occur in the colourless series ; and, with one exception (in *C. Feei*, Meissn.) Fée describes no other type. '*A peine peut on découvrir,*' says this writer, '*dans ces organes de légèrez différences, dont les plus importantes se rapportent à la dimension et au nombre.' (Suppl.* p. 50). But Nylander's description of the spores of *C. seriale,* from Acharius's specimen (Nyl. in *Prodr. Fl. N. Gran.* p. 110, n.) varies in important respects from that given by Fée (*Suppl.* p. 50, t. 40) and adds another to the already noted interesting features of this lichen. [1] Cuban specimens, collected by Mr. Wright, and agreeing entirely with Nylander's plant in Lindig's collection (*Herb. N. Gran.* coll. 2, n. 33) offer oblong-ovoid, or more rarely oblong, quadrilocular spores, without the colour, but with the spore-cells of *Glyphis labyrinthica,* and of the erucæform type ; of which the spores of the species last named are a reduced expression. Nor is this apparent divergence in the direction of the coloured series, the only one. In Montagne's description of his *C. lacteum* (*Pl. Cell. Cub.* p. 161) we find '*asci breves obovati sporidia* 5–6 *oblonga intus granulosa* (*immatura ?*) *continentes,*' which readily suggests the doubt whether riper specimens might not offer the muriform structure. And, in fact, in original specimens of his lichen given to me by the friendly author, I find, in obovate or saccate thekes, oblong-ovoid or also oblong, colourless or scarcely coloured, muriform-multilocular spores ; very commonly resembling the similarly smallish spores of *C. seriale,* except that here, instead of four sporoblasts, we have six to ten transverse series, and two to four longitudinal ones. It is evident then that if *Chiodecton* is comparable with *Opegrapha,* as regards the predominant type expressed in its spores, it is comparable with it also in its anomalies. [2]

Twenty-three species of this genus are reckoned in the various publications of Dr. Nylander; and, adding *C. umbratum,* Fée, and *C. Montagnæi,* the number of distinguishable forms may be called twenty-five. Two of these belong to the European Flora ; one of them being found on rocks at Cherbourg in Normandy, and the other on shrubs in the islands of Hyères (near Toulon) and on rocks in the Channel Islands, and Ireland ; and three are natives of Chili. All the rest are inter-tropical ; two of them reaching however within our southern limits.

[1] Massalongo (*Ric.* p. 149) had already made the same observation on the spores of this species, which he inclined then to refer to *Arthonia.*

[2] These anomalies have been excluded, in the case of *Opegrapha,* by many writers (*Encephalographa,* Massal. *Lecidæe* sp., Nyl. *Stictographa,* Mudd) and this is one of the possible solutions of the question in which spore-series to place the genus. But the distinction of the divergent *Opegraphæ,* by colour alone, is by no means so easy as that of *Rinodina* from *Lecanora,* or *Buellia* from *Lecidea ;* and the present writer has preferred, in view of similar but scarcely irreducible anomalies in *Thelotrema,* &c., to retain this natural genus in its entirety ; and, in like manner, not to separate *Chiodecton seriale* and *C. lacteum,* Mont., from the group with which each has so much in common. The last-cited lichen of Montagne was but doubtfully referred by him to the *C. lacteum* of Fée ; and it seems now impossible, in view of this author's description and figure of the spores of his species (*Suppl. t.* 40, *Chiod.* 4 *bis*) to consider the Cuban plant as associable with it. This may therefore appropriately take the name of its first describer (*C. Montagnæi*).

C. rubro-cinctum, Nyl., is found here, but as yet only in the sterile condition (*Hypochnus rubro-cinctus*, Ehrenb.) upon Bald Cypress (*Taxodium distichum*) in Louisiana (Hale). Spores (Lindig *Herb. N. Gran.* n. 2569) fusiform; quadrilocular; colourless.

C. Montagnæi (*C. lacteum*, Mont. *Pl. Cell. Cub.* p. 161, *e specim. ccl. auct.*, non Fée) has occurred fertile, but without perfect spores, on trunks in Louisiana (Hale). Spores (of the original Cuban lichen, since found also by Mr. Wright) in eights, in obovate thekes; oblong-ovoid; muriform-multilocular; the length twice to twice and a half exceeding the diameter; scarcely a little brownish.

LIII.—GLYPHIS, Ach., Mont., Nyl.

Mont. Crypt. Guy. p. 59. Nyl. Enum. Gén. l. c. p. 134; in Prodr. Fl. N. Gran. p. 107 ; Syn. Lich. Nov. Cal. p. 82. Glyphis pro. p. (excl. G. tricosa) Ach. Syn. p. 106; in Linn. Trans. 12, p. 36. Eschw. Syst. p. 19 ; Lich. Bras. p. 164. Fr. S. O. V. p. 271. Graphidis sp., Ach. L. U. p. 674. Trypethelii spp., Ach. in Schrad. Journ. Bot. Sarcographæ sp., & Glyphis, Fée Ess. pp. 58, 61, & Suppl. pp. 43, 47, t. 40. Massal. Mem. p. 113. Asteriscæ sp., & Glyphis, Mey. Entwick. pp. 331, 332. Actinoglyphis & Glyphis, Mont. Syll. p. 355. Mass. Esam. p. 42. Stizenb. Beitr., l. c. p. 152.

Apothecia rotundata l. oblonga, concava, nigra, in stromate albo conferta. Sporæ ex ellipsoideo oblongæ erucæformesque, e quadri-pluriloculares, fuscescentes l. incolores. Spermatia haud visa. Thallus crustaceus, uniformis.

The affinities of the small group before us have been already touched upon. So closely is it akin to *Graphis*, that *G. tricosa*, a species of the group represented by *G. dendritica*, may be said to constitute one extreme of a continuous series of forms, the other extreme of which is a *Glyphis*, intimately associable with *G. labyrinthica*. The latter makes no uncertain approaches, on the one hand towards *G. heteroclita*, and, on the other, towards the cluster represented by *G. favulosa*, and its place in the genus appears tolerably assured ; but Acharius referred it here in significant connection with his *Graphis*,—finally *Glyphis tricosa ;* while Fée, and Meyer rejected both lichens to the *Medusula*-group. Nor did it escape Eschweiler (*Lich. Bras.* pp. 93, 102, 150) whose observations on the systematic value of the colour of the hypothecium, in the present tribe, are especially important, that the whole of *Glyphis*, as he knew it, might hereafter prove referable to *Medusula*, and thereby to *Graphidacei ;* or Fries (*L. E.* p. 360) that this relegation might well be, so far at least as theory is concerned, to *Graphis*.

The at length elongated patches (compound apothecia) of *Glyphis labyrinthica* are narrowed sometimes (Cuba, Mr. Wright) into lirellæform states suggesting, and indeed resembling *G. heteroclita*, Mont. (*Actino-glyphis*, Mont.). But remarkable as is the development of lirellæ in this species—fully comparable now with simple forms of *Graphis scalpturata*—there is little else to separate it generically from the *Glyphis* first named, and its lirellæ disappear finally in rounded patches which it is easy to associate with those of *G. labyrinthica*, or even, more distantly, with those of *G. favulosa*.

The little cluster of remaining forms of *Glyphis* embraces *G. cicatricosa* and *G. favulosa*, Ach., and *G. confluens*, Mont., Nyl., which were some years since united by the writer as *G. Achariana* (Suppl. 1, *l. c.* p. 429) neither of the names before given to the members of the new species appearing to have any special appropriateness to it, as a whole. In his Lichens of New Granada (*Prodr. Fl. N. Gran.* p. 108) Dr. Nylander consents to the reduction of *G. favulosa* to *G. cicatricosa*, and only admits *G. confluens* with the remark that it is scarcely more than a variety ; and the species thus sketched wants but little of being equivalent to the earlier one first cited. The differences between his species, indicated by Acharius, certainly disappear in large collections of specimens ; and both forms pass into confluent states, inseparable from the others by any distinctions derivable from the spores. A comparison indeed of Eschweiler's descriptions of *G. cicatricosa* and *G. favulosa* (*Lich. Bras.* pp. 166, 167) with those given by Acharius, will sufficiently shew the difficulty of determining these forms ; which appears also in the fact that the Portuguese lichen (Welwitsch *Cr. Lusit.* n. 56) was referred to *G. cicatricosa* by Montagne, and to *G. favulosa* by Nylander.—Thus understood, the species before us is sufficiently well marked, and though making evident approaches to the others, the group composing it has had the good fortune never to be disturbed in the place which Acharius assigned to it ; and may pass therefore for the generally accepted expression, or idea, of *Glyphis*. It may still be observed that though the typically compound apothecia are remote enough in aspect from most Graphideine types, they are still intimately associable with forms as intimately associable with *Graphis tricosa ;* and further that simpler conditions of the fruit scarcely differ in external appearance but in being smaller from similarly rounded or short-oblong apothecia of *G. scalpturata*, and other species of the stock of *G. dendritica*.

Beside his *G. actinobola* and *G. medusulina* (*Prodr. Fl. N. Gran.* p. 108) the very difficult relations of which both to *Graphis tricosa* and *Glyphis labyrinthica* have already been touched upon, Nylander reckons, in his latest publications, four species of the present genus ; from which excluding *G. confluens*, above otherwise explained, we have left three, tolerably definite, and well understood forms. All are tropical, but one (*G. Achariana*) has occurred on the coast of Portugal ; and inhabits also our southern States.

G. Achariana, Tuckerm. *l. c.*, 1858, occurs on various trees and shrubs, in the upper country of North Carolina (Rev. Dr. Curtis) in the low country of South Carolina (Mr. Ravenel) throughout Alabama (Mr. Peters; Mr. Beaumont) in Mississippi (Dr. Veitch) Louisiana (Hale) and southern Texas (Mr. Ravenel). The more common condition presents the features of *G. cicatricosa*, and becomes readily confluent (*G. confluens*, Auctt.) but the state with larger apothecia, and more numerous rounded exciples (*G. favulosa*) also at length confluent, is not wanting. Spores in eights; erucæform; 7–10–locular; the length from three to five or more rarely six times exceeding the diameter; without colour.

———•———

Fam. 4.—ARTHONIEI, Koerb.

Apothecia difformia, immarginata, stromatoideo-subconfluentia.

LIV.—ARTHONIA, Ach., Nyl.

Nyl. Syn. Arth. 1856; & in Prodr. Lich. Gall. p. 163; Enum. Gén. l. c; p. 132; Lich. exot. l. c.; Lich. Scand. p. 257; Lich. N. Gran. in Prodr. Fl. N. Gran. pp. 97,136; Syn. Lich. N. Caled. p. 60. Arthonia, Spilomatis spp., Graphidis sp., & Lecideæ sp., Ach. L. U. pp. 25, 135, 178, 272; Arthonia, Coniocarpon, Spilomatis sp., & Opegraphæ f., Schær. Spicil. pp. 8, 219, 223, 244, 323; Enum. pp. 154, 241. Arthonia, Conioloma, & Pyrrhochroæ sp., Eschw. Syst. p. 17, &c., & Lich. Bras. pp. 109, 105. Arthonia pro p., Coniocarpon, & Graphidis spp., Fée Ess. p. 30, &c., e Nyl. Coniangium, Conioloma, Trachylia, Ustaliæ sp., & Opegraphæ ff. deformatæ, Fr. S. O. V. pp. 271, 275, &c.; L. E. pp. LXXVII, 377, 402. Graphid., Lecid., & Verruc. ff. deform., Mey. Entwick. p. 194. Arthonia, Graphidis f., & Patellariæ ff., Wallr. Fl. Crypt. Germ. 1, p. 320, &c. Arthonia, Coniocarpon, Coniangium, & Ustaliæ sp., Mont. Pl. Cell. Cub. p.173; & Aperçu Morph. p. 11. Arthonia, Arthothelium, Coniocarpon, Trachylia, Nævia, Coniangium, & Pachnolepia, Massal. Mem. p. 117, & Framm. Arthonia & Coniocarpon, Leight. Brit. Graph. pp. 51, 58. Arthothelium, Arthonia, Coniangium, Pachnolepia, & Trachylia, Koerb. Parerg. p. 260. Arthonia, Coniangium, & Arthothelium, Th. Fr. Gen. p. 96. Arthothelium & Arthonia, Stizenb. Beitr. l. c. p. 152.

Apothecia rotundata oblongave, margine accessorio thallode nunc instructa, proprio destituta, plus minus aggregata l. dein in pseudostroma difforme l. rotundatum l. stellatum confluentia. Sporæ (in thecis plerumque abbreviatis pyriformibus) oblongo-ovoideæ (nymphæformes) l. oblongæ l. rarissime fusiformes, 2–4–pluriloculares,

28

demum et muriformi-multiloculares, fuscescentes l. decolores. Spermatia oblonga l. bacillaria l. acicularia; sterigmatibus simplicibus. Thallus crustaceus, uniformis, aut hypophlæodes.

The history of *Arthonia*, as above sketched, sufficiently displays the uncertainties which have always embarrassed the group. One marked type, exhibited in *A. cinnabarrina* (*Coniocarpon*, DC. *Conioloma*, Floerk.) has yet found general acceptance with lichenists; and has lost none of its instructiveness by its explanation (Schær. *Spicil.* p. 244; Koerb. *Parerg.* p. 264) through *A. ochracea.* It was indeed with *Chiodecton* and *Glyphis* that Eschweiler (*Syst.; Lich. Bras.*) and Fries (*S. O. V.*) placed *Coniocarpon ;* which both (in the works named) recognized as a compound type, conditioned, like *Chiodecton*, by a genuine stroma. Nor was even this inference, as we may well suppose, without reason. *A. cinnabarrina* and *A. ochracea*, taken together, are well comparable externally with *Chiodecton perplexum*, Nyl. (elegantly exhibited in Lindig's New Granada Lichens) no less in the earlier and simpler conditions (crowded at length into irregular patches) wherein a common margin, or stroma, is clearly discernible, than in the confluent, now stellate and now irregular clusters, deprived finally of any trace of excipular conditioning by the thallus, into which the apothecia of all these lichens finally collect themselves. Other examples of an often conspicuous thalloid margin are afforded by *A. chiodectella*, Nyl., and *A. glaucescens*, Nyl., as by our American specimens of *A. impolita ;* and it is scarcely doubtful that analogy should require us to assign the same (theoretical) value to the thalline conditions of the apothecia of *Arthonia*, as thus exhibited, that we assign to those of species of properly stromatous genera; or that *Chiodecton* is most closely akin (as compare also Massalongo's observation, *Ric.* p. 149, already cited) to the *Arthonia*-group represented by *A. cinnabarrina.*

But the lichen last named is an exceptional expression of *Arthonia ;* and, taken as a whole, the genus is rather marked by a general obsolescence of any marginal relation of the thallus, and in place of such margin (or presumable stroma) by that confluence of originally or theoretically proper exciples into an undistinguishable, and here almost structureless mass, which we have above called *pseudo-stroma.* This deformation appears to be analogous to, and explicable in the same way with extreme conditions of the *Glyphidei*, as of medusuline states of *Graphis.* [1] But the accompanying confusion of structure,—leaving only the thekes and their contents to redeem *Arthonia* from an internal obscurity as perplexing as its external,— though greater than in *Chiodecton* is yet in the same direction; as if to afford yet another indication that the genus before us

---

[1] " *Sic quoque Lecideæ nonnullæ in formas simillimas abeunt apotheciis diminutis pluribus confluentibus.*" Eschw. *Bras.* l. c. p. 109. And this author fully distinguishes such symphycarpeous fruits, to be compared with those of *Cladonia*, from the proliferous ones so common in tropical *Lecideei* (*Ibid.* pp. 251, 257).

is, *as a whole*, to be taken for an abnormal exhibition of what was, in inception, a compound type.

Eschweiler (*Syst.* pp. 17, 19, fig. 28) was the first to indicate those peculiarities of spore-structure which have done so much to lighten the determination of *Arthoniæ ;* and his cited descriptions and figures of 1824 (to be compared with the fuller account in his Lichens of Brazil) differ in no important respect from the latest definitions. It was long however before lichenists availed themselves of this invaluable clew ; and when the spores were at length studied, their general features of agreement in the several groups into which the natural genus had fallen apart, failed at first to incite a reunion of its members. Massalongo's writings represent thus, here as elsewhere, the period of greatest discrimination or dismemberment; since which the tendency has been clearly the other way. This is evident in Koerber's successive elaborations of the group, as in its treatment by Dr. Th. Fries. Stizenberger, finally (1862) leaves only *Arthothelium* apart from *Arthonia ;* and even this distinction failed to find recognition in the *Arthonia* of Anzi (1860).

The spore-type here, though more often peculiarly modified, when it stands sometimes in rather difficult relations to that of *Opegrapha*, reverts notwithstanding to, and, thus explained, is in fact the same with that generally expressed by *Thelotrema, Heterothecium*, and *Graphis ;* and its history is available therefore in the explication of those genera. Several interesting illustrations are afforded by *Arthoniæ*, of which the already cited *A. cyrtodes*, Tuck. (*Obs. Lich. l. c.* 6, p. 285, & in Wright *Lich. Cub.* n. 245–6) is one, that this type has really an extent not unlike that attributed to it in the present treatise; and that the systematic value of the muriform modification of the plurilocular spore is by no means so great as has often been supposed.

Chrysothrix, Mont. (*Syll.* p. 382. *Cilicia noli-tangere*, Mont.! in *Ann.*, 2, 2, p. 275, t. 16, f. 2) a byssaceous, tropical lichen, appearing to be properly analogous to *Cænogonium*, is excluded here from *Arthonia*, Nyl.

The contributions of Dr. Nylander to the illustration of *Arthonia*, so much exceed those of any other writer, that the genus, as here taken, may be said largely to rest on his determinations. '*Jam* 72 *species*,' said this author, in 1861 (*Lich. Scand.* p. 257, n.) '*hujus generis naturalis cognitas habeo* ;' and so considerably has the number been augmented in his recent publications, that it may be now reckoned at close on a hundred ; of which, as might be expected, the larger part ('*longe maximus numerus*') is tropical. Other estimates of European *Arthoniæ* shew however that the specific limits of even these are by no means yet agreed upon ; and it cannot be doubted that the group, as a whole, whether we regard the probable number of so-called specific forms to be embraced in it, or their distribution, is still more than ordinarily uncertain. This is at any rate the case here, where these lichens have attracted as yet, except in a few districts, only casual attention. Fortunately, the writer of this contributed, some years since, almost the whole of the North American *Arthoniæ* known to him, to the learned monographer of the group; and is now able therefore to cite his determinations, in the list subjoined, of by far the larger part.

North American species with pale (not black) fruit.

A. cinnabarrina (DC.) Wallr. (*Coniocarpon*, Fr. *L. E.* p. 379. *Conioloma coccineum*, Eschw. *Bras.* p. 170). On various barks, western New York (Mr. Willey). South Carolina (Mr. Ravenel). Alabama (Mr. Beaumont). Louisiana (Hale). Texas (Mr. Ravenel). This fine species varies greatly in the colours, as shewn especially, in our plants, by Mr. Ravenel's specimens from Texas. One set of these, differing in its brown, often white-pruinose, or at least white-edged clusters, without a trace of the characteristical colour to which the species owes its name, is further marked by elongated, clavate thekes, and rather smaller spores (0,015–23$^{mm.}$ long, and 0,005–7$^{mm.}$ wide) but I observe such thekes in European specimens of *A. cinnabarrina ;* and they occur as well in the near akin but much smaller lichen next to be set down.——*A. chiodectella*, Nyl. in *Flora*, 1869, p. 125. On Bald Cypress (*Taxodium*) Louisiana (Hale). Thekes from pyriform at length clavate. Spores 0,017–23$^{mm.}$ long, and 0,007–8$^{mm.}$ wide. A plant from Texas (Mr. Ravenel) probably referable here, offers rather smaller spores.——*A. pyrrhula*, Nyl. (*A. medusæa*, Tuckerm. *in litt.*). Trunks, frequent in New England, and I have observed it in Virginia. North Carolina (Rev. Dr. Curtis).——*A. rubella* (Fée) Nyl. (*Graphis*, Fée). On various barks, at the South. South Carolina (Mr. Ravenel). Alabama (Mr. Beaumont). Louisiana (Hale). Texas (Mr. Wright). As respects our other species sufficiently distinguishable, but its relations with the older *A. caribæa* (Ach.) Nyl., are perhaps less clear. Both are *Ustaliæ* of authors.——*A. conturbata*, Nyl. (*Prodr. Fl. N. Gran.* p. 98, *n.*). On bark, Tampico, Mexico, Nyl. l. c.——*A. platyspilea*, Nyl. (l. c. p. 99, n.). On Mangrove, Tampico, Mexico, Nyl. l. c.——*A. leucastræa*, Tuckerm. [1] Trunks, Texas (Mr. Wright).——*A. impolita* (Ehrh.) Borr. (*Parmelia*, Ach. *Meth.* Fr. *L. E. Arth.* pruinosa, Ach. *L. U.* Nyl.). Bark of Oaks, California (Mr. Bolander). Enumerated by Muhlenberg in his list of North American lichens, but is unknown in the Atlantic

[1] *Arthonia leucastræa (sp. nova) thallo effuso farinoso lacteo; apotheciis innatis oblongis elongatisque planis rufo-fuscis albo-pruinosis in pseudo-stroma radiato-stellatum demum confluentibus. Hypothecium fuscescens. Sporæ in thecis pyriformibus* 6–8^{næ}, *ovoideæ, quadriloculares, loculis extremis amplioribus, mediis subinde divisis, incolores, longit.* 0,012–16$^{mm.}$, *crassit.* 0,005–7$^{mm.}$. The hymenial gelatine finally reddens with iodine. Distinct from *A. polygramma*, Nyl. (in *Prodr. Fl. N. Gran.* p. 99, & in *Herb.* Lindig n. 817) which has smaller, darker, more irregular fruit, and oblong-ovoid spores, with entire spore-cells. The spores of *A. impolita* are similarly diverse, as is also the whole habit; unless indeed in the remarkable form called by Nylander v. *medusula* (*Lich. Par.* n. 84).

states, and I was unprepared therefore to recognize it in the often perfectly lecanoroid, Californian lichen (*Lecanora fecunda*, Tuckerm. Lich. Calif. p. 20) referred here by Nylander (*Syn. Lich. N. Caled.* p. 60, *not*.).——*A. glaucescens*, Nyl. *in litt.* Trunks, North and South Carolina (Mr. Ravenel). Also remarkable for its lecanoroid aspect. The lichen is near to *A. velata*. A northern form (New Jersey, Mr. Austin. New Bedford, Mass., Mr. Willey) comparable with both these species, differs yet in its larger spores, measuring $\frac{20-25}{5-7}$ micromill.——*A. velata*, Nyl. (*Prodr.* p. 165. *Zw. exs.* n. 48, *exempli mei*) f. *develata*, Nyl. Trunks in Hampshire, Mass. (Myself). New Bedford (Mr. Willey).——*A. cinereo-pruinosa*, Schær. (*Enum.* p. 243, & *Lich.* Helv. n. 251). On Yellow Birch, in the White Mountains.——*A. cupressina*, Tuckerm.,[1] observed only on White Cedar, Mass. (Mr. Willey) is readily distinguished from the in some respects similar species next following, by the colours ; and differs also in its smaller spores.——*A. lecideella*, Nyl. (*A. glaucina*, Tuck. *in litt.*). On various trees and shrubs, and also on dead wood, common in New England. Ohio (Lea). Illinois (Mr. E. Hall). North Carolina (Rev. Dr. Curtis). Texas (Mr. Wright).

North American species with black fruit.

1. Spores bilocular.

A. glebosa, Tuckerm.,[2] remarkable for its thallus, made up of turgid, glebous or irregular squamules, which are finally nodulose or somewhat plicate, much as in *Buellia badia*, has occurred in the Yosemite valley, California (Mr. Bolander).——*A. lurida*, Ach. (*Coniangium vulgare*, Fr. *L. E.* p. 378; *Lich. Suec.* n. 1). Dead wood in the White Mountains. Apothecia brownish-black.——*A. patellulata*, Nyl. (*Lich. Scand.* p. 262, & in Fellm. *Lich. Arct.* n. 209). Trunks in the White Mountains (Myself). New Bedford (Mr. Willey).——*A. dispersa*, Nyl. (*Lich. Scand.* p. 261. Moug. & Nestl. *Cr.* n. 359). On shrubs, and trees, New Bedford, and Weymouth (Mr. Willey).

---

[1] *Arthonia cupressina (sp. nova) thallo effuso tenuissimo leproso albido ; apotheciis minutis (0mm., 2–0mm., 4 lat.) rotundatis convexis e pallido-fuscescente dein obscuratis viridulo-suffusis. Hypothecium pallidum. Sporæ in thecis pyriformibus oblongo-ovatisve ovoideo-oblongæ, quadriloculares (loculis subæqualibus) incolores, longit.* 0,011–16mm., *crassit.* 0,003–5mm.—On White Cedar, New Bedford, Mass. (Mr. Willey). Reaction with iodine, blue.

[2] *Arthonia glebosa (sp. nova) thallo e squamulis bullatis lævigatis dein plicatis fuscescentibus ; apotheciis rotundatis convexis (circ.* 0mm., 5 *lat.) mox confertis confluentibusque nigris. Hypothecium fusco-nigrum. Sporæ in thecis pyriformibus octonæ, ovoideæ l. oblongo-ovoideæ, biloculares medio constrictæ, dilute fuscescentes l. incolores, longit.* 0,010–16mm., *crassit.* 0,005–6mm. Upon mosses on rocks, California (H. N. Bolander). The reaction of the hymenial gelatine with iodine is vinous-red.

2. Spores 4–pluri–locular.

A. diffusa, Nyl. *in litt.* Trunks in the White Mountains (Oakes).——
A. lurido-alba, Nyl. *in litt.* On dead wood in the White Mountains
(Oakes).——*A. astroidea*, Ach., Nyl. (*Opegr. atra* v. *macularis*, Fr. *L. E.*
p. 367; Lich. Suec. n. 24). On bark, very common at the north, and
found also in North Carolina (Rev. Dr. Curtis). Now curiously suggestive
of *Opegrapha* atra. A Texan lichen scarcely otherwise discernible offers
6–locular spores, measuring 0,018–19$^{mm.}$ long, and 0,003-5$^{mm.}$ wide.——
A. mediella, Nyl. (*Lich. Scand.* p. 259. *A. trabinella*, Th. Fr. *Lich. Arct.*
p. 240 *e* Nyl.). On dead wood, Greenland (J. Vahl *e* Th. Fr. l. c.)——
A. ramosula, Nyl. (*Prodr. Gall.* p. 167). North America, Nyl. *Enum.
Gén. suppl.*).——*A. oxytera*, Nyl. (in *Prodr. Fl. N. Gran.* p. 105, *n.*). On
bark, Tampico, Mexico, Nyl. l. c.——*A. atrata* (Fée) Nyl. *Exp. N. Caled.*
(*A. substellata*, Nyl. *N. Gran.* p. 106, *fide ipsius*). On bark, southern
Texas (Mr. Ravenel).——*A. polymorpha*, Ach. (Nyl. in *Prodr. Fl. N. Gran.*
p. 105, & in *Herb. Lindig* n. 2603). On Bald Cypress; South Carolina
(Mr. Ravenel). Not unlike specimens of *A. spectabilis* (the *A. polymorpha*,
with scarcely any doubt, of Muhl. *Catal.* ; as it is also the *Opegr. polymorpha* of the present writer's Syn. N. Eng. p. 76) but with small, oblong-
ovoid, quadrilocular spores. ——*A. complanata*, Fée (Nyl. *N. Gran.* p. 106,
& in *herb. Lindig* n. 760). Trunks, South Carolina (Mr. Ravenel) and
Alabama (Mr. Peters).——*A. pinguis*, H. Willey *msc.* On the young bark
of White Pine, and observed also on other bark, Weymouth, and New
Bedford, Mass. (Mr. Willey). Spores fusiform, 8-locular.——*A. platy-
graphidea*, Nyl. (in *Prodr. Fl. N. Gran.* p. 104, *n.*). On bark, Tampico,
Mexico, Nyl. l. c.

3. Spores muriform-multilocular.

A. interveniens, Nyl. (l. c. p. 104, n.). On *Tilia*, &c., South Carolina
(Mr. Ravenel).——*A. tædiosa*, Nyl. (l. c. p. 136). On Holly, and Wax-
myrtle, South Carolina (Mr. Ravenel). On Red Maple, New Bedford
(Mr. Willey).——*A. macrotheca*, Fée (*Suppl.* p. 42, t. 40). Trunks, southern Texas (Mr. Ravenel). Spores in sixes and eights, fuscescent or
decolorate, ovoid-ellipsoid, 0,050-0,069$^{mm.}$ long, and 0,018-0,023$^{mm.}$ wide.
Better comparable with *A. mesoleuca*, Nyl. (*N. Gran.* p. 104, n.) a Mexican
lichen, as this is described, than with Lindig's specimen of the present
(*herb. N. Gran.* n. 732) except in the larger spores. My plant is very
near to the species next following. ——*A. spectabilis*, Flot. (*Arthothelium*,
Mass. Rabenh. *Lich. Eur.* n. 418). On various barks, not unfrequent
from New England to Virginia. Ohio (Lea). South Carolina (Mr. Ravenel).
Spores fuscescent or more often decolorate, ovoid-ellipsoid, 0,024-0,037$^{mm.}$
long, and 0,011-0,018$^{mm.}$ wide.

LV.—MYCOPORUM, (Flot.) Nyl.

Mycoporum, Flot. in Koerb. Grundr. Nyl. Prodr. Gall. p. 171; Lich. Scand. p. 291 ; & in Prodr. Fl. N. Gran. p. 111. Th. Fr. Gen. p. 98. Lecideæ sp., Schær. Spicil. p. 199 ; Lich. Helv. n. 232; & Enum. p. 131. Rhizocarpi? sp., Massal. Ric. p. 103. Arthothelii sp., Koerb. Parerg. p. 261.

Apothecia subcomposita, pseudo-stromate difformi nigro hymenia (1-plura) fovente. Sporæ (in thecis abbreviatis, subpyriformibus) oblongo-ovoideæ 1. oblongæ, bi-quadri-loculares, 1. dein muriformi-multiloculares, fuscescentes 1. decolores. Spermatia haud visa. Thallus crustaceus, uniformis 1. hypophlœodes.

The compound character assumed finally by *Arthonia* has been re-marked under that genus. Eschweiler was first to indicate this, referring the group, as he limited it, together with *Coniocarpon*, to his *Trypethel-iaceæ*, (*Syst.* p. 17) which included the compound types of both *Graphi-dacei* and *Verrucariacei ;* and when, later (*Lich. Bras. l. c.* p. 110) he places *Arthonia* at the end of his *Graphideæ*, it is not without the sug-gestive remark, that '*ob verrucas discolores pro stromate habendas nucle-orum rudimenta fovente*,' it should still seem to be properly associable with that section of the *Trypethelinæ* represented by *Porothelium*, Eschw. But interesting as is the appropriateness of the hypothetical character just cited to the present little cluster of arthonioid lichens, as understood by Nylander, we may notwithstanding doubt if Eschweiler would not rather have referred *Mycoporum pycnocarpum*, Nyl. (as compare *Poroth. arthonioides, Lich. Bras.* p. 153; & *Syst.* fig. 21) to his *Porothelium ;* as Flotow acutely suspected the same type in his *M. elabens.*

It is indeed impossible quite to deny the existence of something like mutual approaches between the compound groups of *Graphidacei* and those of *Verrucariacei ;* and equivocal types, if we do not possess them already, might well be expected to occur. The reference of *Mycoporum* (Flot.) Nyl., to a different tribe from *Mycoporum*, Mey. (*Porothelium*, Eschw. pro p., *Melanotheca*, Fée pro p., Nyl. *Tomasellia*, Massal., Koerb.) does not affect the remarkable congruity of these types ; and states of *Mycoporum pycnocarpum*, Nyl., are none the less better comparable with *Melanotheca*, Nyl., or, in aspect at least, with Verrucariaceous expressions like *Trypethelium nigritulum* of the same author (Lindig *herb. N. Gran.* n. 2794) than with anything Graphidaceous, because the latter affinity is in fact mediated by *Chiodecton.*

From the genus last named, and the family represented by it, the present little group is, as in other respects, sufficiently distinguished by the want of a stroma; and its real interest and significance appear rather to lie in its relations to *Arthonia.* In place of the stromatous modification of a thalline exciple, we have, in our representative of *Mycoporum*, Nyl., in which the confluence of parts is carried further than in *Chiodecton*, a similarly difform, compound apothecium, resulting wholly from the confusion of proper exciples (pseudo-stroma[1]) and this differs possibly in no respect from the warts of *Arthonia*, except that while in the latter the hymenium, or synhymenium, is assumed to be simple, and undistinguishable into hymenia, the distinctness of these may more or less be made out in species of the former. This is all; and it may well hereafter prove that Eschweiler's cited observation was in fact a vaticination; and that *Mycoporum*, as here taken, is only *Arthonia* finally understood. And with due respect to the learned monographer of the latter genus, I shall venture to add that *A. ambiguella*, Nyl. (Lindig *Herb. N. Gran.* n. 827) appears almost as referable to the one group as the other.

As respects the spores, *Mycoporum*, Nyl., is well associable with that group of *Arthoniæ* which finds its complete expression in *A. spectabilis*, Flot. (*Arthothelium*, Massal.) and Koerber's reference of *M. elabens* to this group (*Parerg.* p. 261) though certainly disputable from the standpoint of present views of *Arthonia*-structure, as compared with *M. pycnocarpum*, may yet prove an anticipation of the ultimate verdict.

Beside *M. elabens* of Flotow, Nylander has indicated three European species, the minuteness of which will probably long obscure their real distribution; and two better developed tropical ones. Of these, one of the latter only is known as yet as North American; but either, or all the others, may prove also to occur.

M. pycnocarpum, Nyl. (in *Prodr. Fl. N. Gran.* p. 111; & in *Herb.* Lindig, n. 891) an inhabitant of Mexico (Nyl. *Enum. Gén.*) as of other parts of tropical America, is common, on various barks in the northern states (*determ.* Nyl.) and was found in North Carolina by Schweinitz (*Herb. Fries*). It offers very commonly the aspect of a minute (as if collapsed, or at length confluent compound) *Verrucaria*, but passes finally into variously difform, trypethelioid warts, the minute, rounded disks of which simulate ostioles. Spores in eights, in pyriform, or now oblong thekes; oblong-ovoid or oblong (constricted at the middle) from quadrilocular with entire cells becoming muriform-multilocular (transverse series of cells 8–12, longitudinal 2–3) fuscescent or decolorate; 0,023-0,043$^{mm.}$ long, and 0,009-0,016$^{mm.}$ wide. The spore-character of the genus, based in part upon species unknown here, is yet, it will be seen, far from imperfectly represented by the differentiation of the spore of our *Mycoporum*.

---

[1] *Sarcothecium*, Massal. *Mem.*, is equivalent to Stroma. *Pseudo-sarcothecium*, Koerb. *Parerg.* p. 394, which ' *entsteht erst durch das Zusammenfliessen der einander eng genäherten Fruchtgehäuse in Verlaufe des Wachsthums derselben* ' is on the other hand practically equivalent to *Pseudo-stroma*. The concluding part of Dr. Koerber's work had not reached the writer, at the time the latter term suggested itself, and was introduced, as above, into his text.

AGYRIUM, (Fr.) Nyl.

Nyl. Prodr. Lich. Gall. p. 148; Lich. Scand. p. 250. Coem. Notice sur quelques Crypt. p. 19. Th. Fr. Lich. Arct. p. 242; Gen. p. 100. Stizenb. Beitr. l. c. p. 152. Anz. Symb. p. 20. Stictis, dein Tremellæ sp., Pers. Obs. Myc. ; Syn. Agyrii sp., Fr. Syst. Myc. 2, p. 231.

Apothecia rotundata l. oblonga, homogenea, ceracea, immarginata. Sporæ (in thecis clavatis) ellipsoideæ, simplices, sub-incolores. Sper matia haud cognita. Thallus 'parum vel vix visibilis.'

A Fungus, according to Persoon, and Fries, but referred to Lichens by Nylander, who associates it with *Xylographa*, in his tribe *Xylographidei*, placed next before *Graphidei*. Dr. Th. Fries has accepted this construction of the plant, but reduces *Xylographidei* to a sub-family (that is, family, in our arrangement) of *Graphidei*. Dr. Stizenberger equally accepts the assumed lichenose character of both types, but puts *Xylographa* in *Opegraphei*, and *Agyrium*, Nyl., in *Arthoniei*. A significant approach to the latter view may be found in the *Prodromus* of Nylander, where the rock-*Opegraphæ* with simple spores (*Lithographa*, Nyl.) make one of the members of his *Xylographidei*.

If we admit *Xylographa* as a Graphidaceous type, explained and primarily represented by X. *opegraphella*, Nyl., there seems to be no reason for excluding it from its natural association with the *Opegraphei*. With regard however to *Agyrium*, Nyl., sufficient grounds for disposing it with, or even near either of the other groups named, scarcely appear. It is associable even with *Arthonia* by little more than superficial habit. And the evidence of lichenose affinity is confined to the (only occasional?) presence of gonidia in the now, but not always, whitened patches of woody fibre upon which the apothecia grow; and the, in itself alone scarcely conclusive, reaction of the latter with iodine. These apothecia are finally immarginate, and are deprived in fact, according to Mr. Coemans, of any true exciple. He yet remarks '*autour des jeunes* apothèces . . . *un mince anneau, formè de cellules brunâtres, vestige d'un conceptacle partiel et fugace,*' which, if it be what I think I observe in some of the specimens before me (Moug. & Nestl. n. 1096. Anz. *Lich. Lang.* n. 466) deserves perhaps further consideration; and suggests rather a biatoroid fruit, than an Arthoniine.

A. rufum (Pers.) Fr., is the only species of *Agyrium*, as here understood, and is a native of the middle and north of Europe. Specimens from dead wood at New Bedford, collected by M⁻ᵗ Willey, who alone, of American botanists, has observed the plant, agree with the European (Nyl. in Fellm. *Lich. Arct.* n. 206) and behave similarly (the hymenium

29

shewing a blue reaction) with iodine.   Spores ellipsoid; simple; often limbate or at length nebulose ; colourless; 0,011-0,013$^{mm.}$ long, and 0,006-0,007$^{mm.}$ wide.   Smaller, reddish spores also occur; as in the European plant.

Trib. IV.—CALICIACEI.

Apothecia turbinato-lentiformia (crateriformia) globosave, excipulo proprio l. nudo, sæpius stipitato, l. a thallino accessorio recepto, capitulum discoideum e sporis nudis coacervatis compactum submarginante.

The distinction between *Acolium Bolanderi* (Lich. Calif. p. 27) and *Sphærophorus globiferus* may certainly appear, at first sight, to be greater than that between *Dirina* and *Roccella*. As the two latter are yet associable by their (typically) thalline exciples, the former obviously agree in the original dissolution of the disk into a naked spore-mass. It is in this sense that Nylander (*Syn.* p. 141) has associated the groups here regarded as constituting the Tribe before us as his ' *Series Epiconioidei* '; and the common character is so extraordinary that we may well suspect a greater congruity of structure than has possibly yet been shown.

If, to take two eminent types of the *Series* just named, we compare sections of the apothecia of *Acroscyphus*, Lév. (Hook. & Thoms. *Herb. Ind. Or.* n. 2188, 2190) and *Acolium tigillare*, immersed as commonly in its thalline wart, we scarcely find other (essential) difference of structure beyond a more distinct conditioning of the proper exciple of the former by the thallus; in which respect it is almost rivalled by Californian species of the latter genus. And the argument is then direct, as the close affinity of *Acroscyphus* to *Sphærophorus* has never been disputed, to the proper Caliciaceous character of this last; the question of thallus, otherwise than as in peculiar relations to the apothecia, not here entering into the discussion. But the structure of *Acroscyphus* is in fact, as may be inferred from the opinions of authors upon *Sphærophorus*, much clearer than in the latter; and notwithstanding the significant agreement in the spores and spermatia, it is by no means so easy to refer this to the type of *Caliciacei*. The affinity did not however escape Turner and Borrer (*Lich. Brit.* p. 105, 119) nor Fries; though the latter finally rejected it. It was indeed, in the case of the authors first named, only that larger affinity, expressed also by the *Epiconioidei* of Nylander, which was intended; and though other relationship was confessedly most obscure, no attempt was made, or has perhaps ever been made, distinctly to reconcile the *Sphærophorus*-fruit with that of the *Caliciei*.

The interest lies in the so-called ' nucleus,' representing at once, in *Sphærophorus*, both proper exciple and hymenium. This nucleus, as clearly described by the English authors just cited (*Lich. Brit.* p. 113) who left very little for others to add to their observations, is found, when dissected, " to consist internally of a thickish outer stratum, purplish, and of a metallic lustre, then a narrow white line, encompassing a brownish less solid core." [1] The description is from *S. globiferus*, but applies as well to *S. fragilis* and *S. compressus*, and is the typical structure of the genus. Montagne (*Recherch., sur la struct. du nucl. des Sphæroph., &c.,* in *Ann.* 2, 15, p. 146, t. 15, f. 1) has quite omitted to notice the 'brown core'; which might well have qualified his explanation of the shape of the outer layer of the 'nucleus' by "*une saillie hémisphérique de la couche medullaire ou centrale du thalle, représentant une sorte de torus.*" For, passing the question of origin, this globular, brown core is at least a part of the apothecium, and in fact the base of it; and may therefore prove properly comparable, as, if I do not greatly mistake, it is comparable, with the hypothecium of the *Caliciei.* We find in *Acolium*, which, as here taken, includes all the highest Calicieine types, and bridges in fact the at first startling interval between at length athalline *Calicium* and fruticulose *Acroscyphus*, no little diversity in the proportions as well as in the differentiation of the envelopes and internal parts of the fruit. Even the proper exciple is in this way reduced, in those species in which the apothecium is directly conditioned by the thallus, and becomes (in *A. tigillare, A. ocellatum*, Koerb., *A. Californicum*, &c.) a thin, and finally disappearing line; while its similarly varying hypothecium is sometimes peculiarly incrassated. In an apothecium of the Californian *A. Bolanderi* now before me, the hypothecium, instead of exhibiting, as commonly, a more or less lunate outline, is hemispherical, and, being bordered by the narrow line of the white layer, and conditioning similarly to *Sphærophorus* the shape of the spore-mass, fairly counterfeits, if it does not also explain, the peculiarities of the latter.[2] Under the microscope, the hymenium of this last is seen moreover to take its departure from the white layer, precisely as in *Acolium ;* and the relations of the same layer to the 'brown core' or hypothecium, offer no appreciable differences.

But, if we admit that the extraordinary apothecium of *Sphærophorus* is determined by its nucleiform hypothecium, and that, this being assumed to be explainable from the point of view of *Acolium*, there is nothing left to exclude the former from *Caliciacei*, it is still to be remarked that such abnormal reduction of the exciple is here normal; and that it is only as an extreme deformation of the tribal type, and because there is, from our standpoint, in which the fruit is primary, no other place for the genus, that it can be accepted as a member of the Tribe before us.

Very much less questionable is *Acroscyphus*, where the whole struc-

[1] Compare the figures in Leighton's Brit. Angiocarpous Lichens (1, f. 1–3) and Tulasne l. c. (t. 15, f. 2, 3).

[2] Compare Nylander's figure of the *Pilophorus*-fruit (*Syn.* t. 7, f. 6). We have here, as in *Sphærophorus*, and the case noted in *Acolium*, a certain extreme of anamorphosis. Is it entirely without bearing on the question of anamorphosis in *Omphalaria*, considered above, especially at p. 84?

ture of the apothecium is really the same with that of members of the *Acolium*-group with accessory thalline exciple ; and nothing is left to distinguish the type but its fruticulose thallus. As respects this thallus, the step from it is possibly longer than it might be to the distinctly lobed though still crustaceous fronds of *Acolium Californicum :* but the congruity of the fruit of these lichens is clear; and disposes, for us, of the question of their relationship.

But if *Acolium* tends, in one direction, to illustrate a modification of structure which finds its highest expression in *Acroscyphus*, no less evident, in another, is its exceedingly close relation to *Calicium*. This genus, as constituted by Persoon, and accepted in the separate publications of Acharius, as in those of Turner and Borrer, and of Schærer (*Spicil.*) included all the generic Calicieine types (as represented in Europe) here considered. Later however, in a final review of these plants, printed in the Stockholm transactions (1815–1817) the Swedish lichenographer distinguished a remarkable biatoroid group (*Coniocybe*) from the other, more commonly lecideoid, stipitate species; and sought also to separate those with ' sessile apothecia' (*Cyphelium*, Ach.) but the latter construction, in which normally sessile *Calicia* were not a little confused with subsessile conditions of stipitate species, failed of recognition.

Fries, who accepted *Coniocybe*, had relegated *Calicium turbinatum* to the *Fungi* (*Sphinctrina, S. O. V.*) but restored it, as an appendix to *Calicium*, in his *Lichenographia ;* where the truly sessile species were presented, though not wholly without admixture of foreign elements, as a separate section; equivalent, or nearly so, to *Calicium*, sect. *Acolium*, Ach. *Syn.* Further advancement might well be anticipated for the latter section, especially as represented by *C. tigillare ;* and this species was the type of the very confused *Acolium*, Fée (*Ess.* p. 28, t. 3, f. 15). In his *Flora Scanica* (1835) Fries also fully recognized the distinctness of the sessile from the stipitate *Calicia*, but appended the former to his *Trachylia ;* the type of which (*L. E.* p. 402) had been the (arthoniine) *T. arthonioides*, and the final construction of which (*Summ. Veg. Scand.* p. 118, 1846) was still embarrassed. De Notaris, the next year (*Giorn. Bot. Ital.* 1847) first gave definite position to the group in his *Acolium ;* adopted since by the majority of lichenists.

Near as is *Coniocybe* to *Calicium* (§ *Cyphelium*) *Sphinctrina* is perhaps still nearer; being scarcely separable indeed, — if we decline to recognize any absolute distinction in the originally closed exciple,— except by the parasitical nature and consequent, athalline character of most of these plants : a difference which disappears in *S. microcephala* (Sm.) (*S. Anglica*, Nyl.) and is admitted to be insufficient in *Acolium stigonellum*. But the other extreme of *Caliciei* becomes more distinct from the center. In *Acolium* the stipe is absolutely deficient, and this evidence of degeneration disappearing, unmistakable indications of a higher tone of structure, significant even of Lecanoreine analogies, supervene ; and the family, reverting thus towards higher groups, connects itself fairly with them, and with the Class.

The family *Sphærophorei* includes, according to Nylander (*Syn.* p. 169) five species, in two genera. One of these genera (*Acroscyphus*) is common to Mexico and the Himalaya. The other (*Sphærophorus*) is northern and austral; two of its forms extending however within the tropics. We possess the three northern species.——*Siphula*, Fr., is not without points of approach to *Sphærophorus*, and is here, provisionally, prefixed to the latter; but its fructification is unknown.——Of the *Caliciei*, as here taken, about sixty marked, or specific forms, are reckoned by recent authors; the whole, and including also in this the *Sphærophorei*, being referable to the coloured spore-series. The *Caliciei* are mainly northern; but the number of forms inhabiting intertropical and austral regions (at present about one sixth of the whole) will probably hereafter be increased.

Fam. I.—SPHÆROPHOREI.

Thallus verticalis, fruticulosus.

*SIPHULA, Fr.

Fr. L. E. p. 406. Nyl. Syn. p. 261; Lich. Scand. p. 67. Th. Fr. Lich. Arct. p. 31; Gen. p. 113. Stizenb. Beitr. l. c. p. 175.

Apothecia (ignota). Spermatia 'linearia.' Thallus fruticulosus, teretiusculus, parce ramosus, basi quasi radicatus, intus stuppeus.

S. ceratites (Wahl.) Fr., upon which the genus was constituted, is an alpine and arctic lichen, compared by Wahlenberg, and Acharius, with *Cladonia gracilis*, v. *taurica;* but decisively distinguished by its solid thallus. It occurs in islands of Behring's Straits (Mr. Wright).—— *S. simplex* (Tayl.) Nyl. (*Dufourea*, Tayl. New Lich. l. c. p. 185) from the west coast of North America (Menzies) is scarcely to be distinguished, by the description, from *S. ceratites ;* and is admitted by Nylander (*Syn.*) to be 'perhaps only a more simple variety' of the latter. The place of the genus, which Nylander has increased by the addition of five other, more or less related, but likewise sterile lichens, is uncertain; but *S. Pickeringii,* Tuck. in Bot. Wilkes exp. p. 124, t. 4, from the Sandwich islands, appeared, in a single specimen not now within reach but sufficiently exhibited in the cited figure, to offer something not at all unlike the thalline conceptacles of *Sphærophorus.* And though no trace of a proper exciple, or its equivalent, which should illuminate further the curious conformation of the thallus referred to, was detected in this specimen, there is no doubt that *S. ceratites* is comparable, as well anatomically as in respect to habit, with the genus next following.

LVI.—SPHÆROPHORUS, Pers.

Pers. in Ust. Ann. d. Bot.   Ach. L. U. p. 116; Syn. p. 286. Turn. & Borr.
Lich. Brit. p. 105.   Fr. in Vet. Ak. Handl. 1821; S. O. V. p. 258; L.
E. pp. 404. Schær. Spicil. p. 7, 242; Enum. p. 176. Eschw. Syst. p. 23;
Lich. Bras. p. 60.   Fée Ess. p. 80. Mey. Entwick. pp. 86, 324. Mont.
Recherches in Ann., Mars, 1841; Aperçu Morph. in Dict. Univ. d'Hist.
Nat. 1846. Tuck. Syn. N. Eng. p. 81. Leight. Brit. Ang. Lich. p. 5,
t. 1, f. 1–3. Tul. Mem. sur les Lich. pp. 77, 185, t. 15, f. 1–9. Norm.
Con. p. 27. Mass. Mem. p. 71. Koerb. Syst. p. 51. Nyl. Syn. p. 169,
t. 5, f. 45–47; Lich. Scand. p. 46. Schwend. Untersuch. in Naeg. Beitr.
2, p. 163, t. 5, f. 14–16, t. 6, f. 1. Th. Fr. Lich. Arct. p. 243; Gen. p. 100;
Lich. Spitzb. p. 47. Mudd Man. Brit. Lich. p. 263. Stizenb. Beitr.
l. c. p. 151.

Apothecia globosa, excipulo proprio (hypothecio) mere infero
thallino ex apicibus ramorum intumescentibus formato incluso.
Sporæ e thecis cylindraceis mox ejectæ, sphericæ, simplices, violaceo-
nigricantes. Spermatia ellipsoideæ oblongave; sterigmatibus simplicibus. Thallus fruticulosus, erectus, intus stuppeus.

Sphærophorus and *Calicium* are, at any rate, brought close together
by the remarkable deformation of the disk; and it is further significant
that these lichens accord also in their thekes, and spores, and are not discordant in their spermatia. No other place then, in the system, having
been satisfactorily indicated for *Sphærophorus*, there is beforehand ground
for presuming that the structure of its fruit shall prove to be reconcilable
with the same structure in the *Caliciei*. The point has been considered in
a preceding page; and I have not hesitated to embody above the results
of my observations in the generical character.

This well-characterized type is found in all cold, northern and austral
climates; but especially in the austral, where (Nyl., l. c.) every form is
represented. *S. compressus* becomes also tropical; and occurs on the
wooded hills of Cuba (Mr. Wright). In the United States, one of the
species but little transcends alpine districts ; the other has a rather wider
distribution.

S. compressus, Ach. Rocks, and on the earth. Canada, *Herb. Hook.*
Arctic America, *Hook.* Flattened conditions of the other species are not
to be confounded with this.——*S. globiferus* (L.) DC. On the earth in
alpine districts, and descending. Arctic America, *Herb. Hook.* White
Mountains. Dennysville, Maine (infertile) *Russell.* North West coast,
Herb. Hook. Coast of California (Mr. Bolander).——*S. fragilis* (L.) Pers.
Alpine rocks. Arctic America, *Hook.* White Mountains.

LVII.—ACROSCYPHUS, Lév., Mont.

Léveillé in Ann. 3, 5, p. 262. Mont. in Dict. Univ. d'Hist. Nat. art. Sphæroph.; & in Ann. 3, 11, p. 243.   Tul. Mém. sur les Lich. pp. 81, 186, t. 15, f. 10, 12.   Nyl. Syn. p. 173.

Apothecia crateriformia, excipulo proprio nigro thallino clavato, ex apicibus ramorum intumescentibus formato, recepto.   Sporæ e thecis cylindraceis mox ejectæ, obtusissime ellipsoideæ medio constrictæ, biloculares, fuscæ.   Spermatia oblonga; sterigmatibus articulatis.   Thallus fruticulosus, erectus, solidus, medulla primitus flavescente, dein chondroideo-cartilaginea.

The final evolution of the medullary layer, which I have not found noticed by authors, sufficiently distinguishes the thallus of this type from that of the preceding.   The apothecia, it has been above remarked, agree in all essential points of structure with those of *Acolium ;* of which *Acroscyphus* may be taken for a fruticulose exhibition.   In this view it is interesting as clearly lessening the perhaps too sharp contrast between *Sphærophorus* and the *Caliciei.*

The oblong spermatia of the present genus (Tul. *l. c.* t. 15, f. 12) differ, like the spores, but little from those of *Acolium tympanellum* (Nyl. *l. c.* t. 5, f. 32) but the jointed sterigmas (*arthrosterigmata*, Nyl.) afford a marked distinction in this tribe.

Originally collected (growing upon the earth, and dead wood) by Humboldt and Bonpland, at Perote, in the State of Vera Cruz, Mexico (Tul. *l. c.*, Nyl.) this lichen has since been found, upon trunks, in Peru (Mont. *l. c.*) and in the Himalaya mountains by Hooker.   It is not improbable that it may occur within the southern boundary of the United States.

Tholurna, Norm. (*Bot. Zeit.* 1863, p. 225) a corticoline lichen of the Norwegian alps, is the latest addition to fruticulose *Caliciacei*, and is regarded by Nylander (in *Prodr. Fl. N. Gran.* p. 144, n.) as the type of a distinct family, to be placed next after the *Sphærophorei ;* and inclining, on the one hand, towards these and the *Caliciei*, and, on the other, towards *Pilophorus* and *Cladonia papillaria.*   The last comparison is indeed directly suggested by the podetiiform, fistulous thallus of the new lichen ; but its fruit, however differently conditioned, refers the plant to the near neighbourhood of *Acroscyphus*, with which it appears also to well agree in its spermogones and their contents, as first described by Nylander.   As seen in section (or, at least, so far as seen by me) the apothecium of *Tholurna* offers a hypothecium differing from that of *Acroscyphus* in being much less crescent-shaped, or even straight ; as if it were a black band, relieved, on the one hand, by the white base of the thalline receptacle, and, on the other, by the equally straight, white, interior layer of the exciple.   But there is nothing in this, apart from the thallus, which is not observable in species, as well of *Calicium*, as of *Acolium ;* and the thallus, if, in spite of obvious analogues, in other tribes, beside the cited one from *Cladonia*, we are to regard it as excluding the new type from the *Sphærophorei*, is perhaps no more distinguishable from the thallus of *Sphærophorus*, than is already that of *Acroscyphus*. The plant should be sought for, on the branches of firs, in arctic America ; and may not impossibly prove also to occur in alpine districts further southward. I owe my excellent Norwegian specimen to my friend Mr. C. F. Austin, who received it from a correspondent at Christiana.

———◆———

Fam. 2.—CALICIEI.

Thallus crustaceus, aut effiguratus, aut uniformis.

LVIII.—ACOLIUM, (Fée) De Not.

De Not. in Giorn. Bot. Ital. (1847) cit. Mass. Mass. Mem. p. 149 (excl. A. saxatili). Koerb. Syst. p. 302 ; Parerg. p. 283. Arn. Lich. Frank. Jur. in Flora, 1860, p. 80. Anz. Cat. Sondr. p. 98. Mudd Brit. Lich. p. 253. Stizenb. Boitr. l. c. p. 158. Tuckerm. Lich. Calif. p. 27 ; Lich. Hawai. in Proceed. Amer. Acad. 7, p. 232. Calicii spp., Ach. L. U. pp. 39, 232, t. 3, f. 1. ; Syn. p. 55. Turn. & Borr. Lich. Brit. p. 132. Fr. S. O. V. p. 276 ; L. E. p. 400. Schær. Spicil, p. 226 ; Enum. p. 163. Mont. Aperçu Morph. p. 11 ; M. & V. d. Bosch Lich. Jav. p. 55. Cyphelium pro min. p., Ach. in Act. Holm. 1815, p. 261. Th. Fr. in Vet. Ak. Förhandl. 1856, p. 128 ; Lich. Arct. p. 244 ; Gen. p. 101. Acolium pr. min. p., Fée Ess. p. 28, t. 3, f. 15 ; Suppl. p. 145. Trachyliæ spp., Fr. Fl. Scan. p. 282 ; Summ. Veg. Scand. p. 118. Tuckerm. Syn. N. Eng. p. 77 ; Obs. Lich. l. c. 5, p. 390 ; 6, p. 263. Norm. Con. p. 26. Nyl. Monogr. Calic. p. 28 ; Prodr. p. 27. Trachylia, Pyrgillus, & Tylophoron, Nyl. Syn. p. 164, t. 5, f. 29–36 ; in Prodr. Fl. N. Gran. p. 6 ; Syn. Lich. N. Caled. p. 8.

Structuram exposuit Tulasne Mém. sur les Lich. p. 80.

Apothecia crateriformia, rarius urceoliformia, sessilia, excipulo proprio nigro l. nudo l. a thallino accessorio marginato. Sporæ e thecis cylindraceis mox ejectæ, sphericæ ellipsoideæve, l. simplices l. bi-quadriloculares, l. dein muriformi-pluriloculares, fuscescentes. Spermatia ellipsoidea oblongave, rarius bacillaria l. acicularia ; sterigmatibus simpliciusculis. Thallus crustaceus, uniformis l. subsquamulosus l. rarissime effiguratus l. in parasiticis nullus.

The general view here taken of the position and significance of this genus has been already intimated. It furnishes the highest types of Calicieine structure ; and rises into forms with which even *Acroscyphus*, of the immediately preceding family, is comparable, in everything but the fruticulose thallus. The following brief exposition of the peculiar relations of the apothecia to the thallus in a very important part of the group before us will illustrate this; and explain as well why I am unable to follow an eminent lichenographer—to whose vast knowledge of Lichens this work has been much indebted—in his estimate of these relations in a tropical type. As viewed by Nylander (in *Prodr. Fl. N. Gran.* p. 6) the way in which the apothecia of his *Tylophoron* (Lindig *Herb. N. Gran.* n. 2633, 2653, & Coll. 2, n. 1, 33) are conditioned by the thallus, not only excludes it from the present genus, but constitutes it the type of a new tribe of his Ser. *Epiconioidei*, equivalent at once to *Caliciei*, and to *Sphærophorei*; between which groups he considers it to belong. It is possible indeed, as these tropical lichens (*Tylophoron protrudens*, and a closely related *T. moderatum*, Nyl. *l. c.*) offer no internal, structural differences of account from *Acolium*, as represented by *A. tympanellum*, &c., that such value would not have been attached to their lecanoroid features, however striking, had the remarkable Californian species been then known to science. In view of these however, it is perhaps not venturesome to say that the distinction of *Tylophoron* is questionable also from the point of view of *A. tigillare*. From this centre of the group a series of forms departs, in one direction, towards *Calicium*; and this series being the only one heretofore (if we except the new *Acolium ocellatum*, Koerb. *Parerg.*) represented in Europe, the lecanoroid features of the principal, central species have been commonly subordinated. There is notwithstanding no doubt that in perhaps the finest conditions of *A. tigillare*, the apothecia occupy regular, more or less hemispherical or conoidal, thalline warts (compare Laurer in Sturm D. Fl. 2, t. 32) and the question arises, if, in the absence of any series of forms explaining and extending this peculiar feature of the cited species, lichenographers had reason for subordinating the difference, they have not now much more for insisting upon it, and giving it even place in the generical character, in the presence of such series. Irrespective of the discoid spore-mass, the apothecia of *A. ocellatum* (Flot.) Koerb., as of *A. Californicum* and *A. Bolanderi*, are suggestive even of some *Thelotrema*; but these pronounced lecanoroid features, which unavoidably condition the descriptions of the lichens named, are yet plainly analogous to, and only more marked exhibitions of those of *A. tigillare*. Nor does there appear to be ground for a different explanation of *Tylophoron*, Nyl.; nor in fact for supposing generally, that, other structural conditions being equal, the more constant presence of an accessory thalline envelope is any less significant or characteristical, in the group now before us, than its more constant absence: both modifications of structure being already and undeniably represented. It is scarcely necessary to add that the former, or lecanoroid exhibition of *Acolium*, is, for us, especially significant of the group, and its rank; and that the latter represents rather its deterioration. And these views are not obscurely sustained by analogous discrepancies in other tribes; as, for a single example, the *Graphidacei.* The instructiveness of *A. tigillare* is not however confined to the explanation possibly afforded by it of the lecanoroid wing of *Acolium ;* nor are we wholly without evidence of a tendency in the same direction, in the other wing. In New England specimens of the lichen just named, now before me, the thickness of the thallus being much reduced, the (full-sized) apothecia are largely denuded; and these, not expanding, as normally, into a patellæform shape, present rather a persistently conical one (observable also in young *A. tympanellum*) as if in anticipation of *A. Javanicum* (M. & V. d. Bosch) Stizenb. (*Trachylia*, Nyl., Tuck. *Pyrgillus*, Nyl. *Syn.*) while in others of the latter, commonly quite naked species, the larger part of the mature cone is covered, at times, and even conspicuously, by the thallus.

The more or less crateriform apothecium of *Calicium* is anticipated in those species of *Acolium* (as *A. tympanellum*, &c.) which most nearly approach the genus first named. But in *A. tigillare* the proper exciple (well exhibited in Laur. Lich. in Sturm *D. Fl.* t. 32) is rather urn-shaped, and will possibly once more explain the extraordinary urn of *A. Javanicum ;* the external difference of this last not being corroborated by any sufficient internal. In the remaining species, or at least the American ones, the proper exciple may also be described as crateriform. From this, *A. leucampyx* (*Trachylia*, Tuck. *Obs. Lich. l. c.* 5, p. 390; and in Wright *Lich. Cub.* n. 21) is yet to be excepted, the apothecia of this curious lichen, though in fact not ill-comparable with certain states of *A. Javanicum*, passing yet into oblong, now aggregated, and compound conditions, distantly suggestive even of *Graphidacei ;* and, in particular, of *Chiodecton.*

In some observations by the present writer on the genus before us (*Obs. Lich. l. c.* 6, p. 264) prominence was given to the pale apothecial layer, which originating on the one hand in a modification of the proper exciple, passes on the other into the thalamium. It was remarked that this layer exhibits itself externally, being traceable into the powdery inner margin of *A. tympanellum* and *A. leucampyx ;* and that it might deserve to be considered by itself. Further examination has tended to confirm this view, and even to suggest a stronger expression of it; that we have, namely, here, something analogous to the more or less distinct *veil* of *Thelotrema.* It is perhaps not clear how much this term, taken as it is to include as well the 'interior exciple' of the last-named genus, should properly cover; but there is no doubt that authors have applied it to what appears commonly, and may be described, as a kind of bloom, and—in this extent— it is equally applicable in the *Caliciacei ;* assuming the character even of an accessory margin in several species, of *Calicium* as of *Acolium*, and being further the remains, in these, of what has been a continuous external covering. And states may well occur in which greater compactness shall give this covering a fair title to be called membranaceous; if indeed the two forms of *Tylophoron*, Nyl., do not sometimes furnish such indica-

tions. The two noble Californian species already cited, though neither is remarkable for any peculiar consolidation of the powdery vesture concealing at first the disk of the young apothecium, furnish yet some interesting features, the examination of which is favoured by the large size of the fruit. In both of these, as seen in section, while the thick, brownish-black hypothecium of the proper exciple disappears, or at least loses its colour more or less completely above, enough is at times visible to exhibit, by contrast, the equally ascendant, interior, pale layer, which is in fact the only one (obscurely) reaching, or at least conditioning the thalline edge of the apothecium. We have here then, distinguishable by colour, if in no other way, something like a double envelope; and the structure is identical with what has elsewhere been noticed (*Obs. Lich.* l. c.) in other types. The white layer in the mature, turbinate fruit of *A. tympanellum* is, seen in section, not far from straight, as in many *Calicia*, or only a little lunate; but in the young conical state, which strikingly resembles *A. Javanicum*, it offers a distinctly ellipsoid outline, as in the latter, and resembles a delicate sack, enveloping the spore-mass.
——Very little has occurred to me in authors, upon the point just considered. Turner and Borrer (*Lich. Brit.* p. 122) describe the apothecium of *Calicium* as "in its earliest state closed with a very thin membrane (most conspicuous in *C. tympanellum*)" and cite also a passage of Acharius (*L. U.* p. 10) in which such a "membrane, so extremely thin that it readily dissolves," is attributed as well to "certain *Arthoniæ* and *Calicia*," as to *Solorina*, *Peltigera*, and *Nephroma*. This last observation was vague; but the hinted structure in *Calicium* was recognized by Fries, who gave it at first (*S. O. V.* p. 276) generical value; but passed it over, finally, in his *Lichenographia*. Montagne, however (*Aperçu Morph. de la Fam. des Lich. in Dict. Univ. d'Hist. Nat.*, 1846) not only retained but extended it to the whole tribe, the apothecium of which is, according to him, "*d'abord recouvert d'une membranule (velum) puis pulverulent;*" and is the latest authority in the matter with which I am acquainted.

The variations in proportion, and shape (as seen in section) of the black and white excipular layers in different Calicieine types, have been already touched upon, and the attempt made to shew that even the extraordinary divergence (from our point of view) of *Sphærophorus*, is counterfeited at least, by *Acolium*. But the normally nucleiform hypothecium of *Sphærophorus*, by which the saccate outline of the white layer, as seen in *Acolium Javanicum*, is reversed, precludes at once any proper excipular features; and the veil is deficient. In *A. leucampyx*, on the other hand, so predominant does the white margin become, as wholly to overlay at length, and conceal the black one. *Calicium* also furnishes some interesting illustrations of this kind of diversity. In many species, the blackish hypothecium (at least in mature apothecia) almost excludes the white layer, which is observable (in section) only as a narrow, not far from straight line above. But in *C. turbinatum* the white layer, as seen in section, appears much in excess; and the same is true of *C. triste*, Koerb. (Hamp. *in herb*. Th. Fr.) and *C. Ravenelii ;* and possibly also in other species, especially of an inferior lichenose grade.

In the spores, *Acolium* exhibits the whole differentiation of the brown type. Dr. Th. Fries, in his observations on the insufficient distinction of *Rhizocarpon*, Massal., from *Buellia* (*Lich. Arct.* p. 226) has well drawn attention to the significant fact that the spore-forms of both these groups occur in *Acolium ;* and indeed in otherwise most closely related species. *A. Bolanderi* has first added simple and spherical spores to the history of the genus. But this species belongs none the less to the same section, or natural cluster, which shall include *A. Californicum*. The remarkable modification of the coloured type exhibited in *A. leucampyx* has been considered in the description of that lichen (*Obs. Lich.* l. c. 5, p. 390).

Twenty species, or marked forms of *Acolium*, as above taken, are reckoned by authors; of which fourteen are northern, and the rest tropical. Only three of the ten European forms have as yet occurred here; but we possess four peculiar to the country, and one tropical species. The important group represented by *A. tympanellum*, and including as well the related saxicoline forms described by Nylander, as the parasitical *A. stigonellum*, is, quite remarkably, deficient east of the Rocky Mountains ; although the species first named is said to agree generally, in its geographical distribution, with *A. tigillare*, and to be found, in the mountainous regions of Europe, in the same places (Nyl. *Syn.*). Muhlenberg reckons indeed (*Catal. pl. Amer. Sept.*) *A. stigonellum*, but I have seen nothing nearer to this species than an externally not dissimilar, parasitical *Buellia* (*B. inquilina*, Lich. Calif., append.) inhabiting Pertusariæ, in the southern states.

A. Bolanderi, Tuckerm. (Lich. Calif. p. 27) from sandstone rocks exposed to the sea-fog, Oakland hills, California (Mr. Bolander) is remarkable as well for its spherical, simple spores (0,008–16$^{mm.}$ diam.) as for its conspicuous, accessory thalline exciple (measuring, in the best conditions, 1$^{mm.}$ –2$^{mm.}$ 5, in width, but also occurring, in reduced states of the lichen, considerably smaller) in which last feature it agrees with the next two following species.——*A. Californicum*, Tuckerm. (*Trachylia, Obs. Lich.* l. c. 6, p. 263) from the same rocks with the last (Mr. Bolander) is distinguished by its lobulate thallus. Apothecia 2–3$^{mm.}$ wide. Spores bilocular, 0,018–25$^{mm.}$ long, and 0,010–18$^{mm.}$ wide. The general agreement, in all the most important structural details, of these two lichens, taken in connection with the difference in their spores, furnishes evidently a new argument against the generical separation of the round-spored *Calicia* (*Cyphelium*, Koerb. Anzi. *Chænotheca*, Th. Fr.).——*A. Carolinianum*, Tuckerm.,[1] a recent discovery in the low country of South

---

[1] *Acolium Carolinianum (sp. nova) thallo tartareo æquabili l. dein ruguloso rimoso e glaucescente pallide lutescente ; apotheciis in verrucis thallinis mastoideis* (1–2$^{mm.}$ *lat.*) *innatis, disco plano-convexo nigro, margine nullo. Sporæ octonæ,*

Carolina, resembles not a little, in its apothecia, *A. Bolanderi ;* and adds another member to this interesting section of *Acolium.* The American plant is closely related to *A. ocellatum* (Flot.) Koerb. (Anz. *Lich. Lang.* n. 211) as is that to *A. tympanellum ;* but surely no lichenist would venture to dispute the distinctness of the first-named from the last. *A. tympanellum* is here confined to the Pacific coast.——*A. tympanellum* (Ach.) De Not. On dead wood, Yosemite valley, California (H. Mann). One of a few lichens of the eastern hemisphere which are unknown in North America except at the extreme west.——*A. chloroconium,* Tuckerm. (Lich. Calif. p. 28). On living *Quercus agrifolia ;* coast of California (Mr. Bolander). Apothecia small, measuring $0^{mm\cdot}$, $5-0^{mm\cdot}$, 6, in diameter. Spores bilocular, $0,007-12^{mm\cdot}$ long, and $0,005-6^{mm\cdot}$ wide. There is some evidence of an imperfect, blue reaction of the hymenial gelatine with iodine.——*A. viridulum* (Schær.) De Not. On Red Pine, Vermont (Mr. Russell). On Hemlock Spruce, New Hampshire (Mr. Willey).——*A. tigillare* (Ach.) De Not. On dead wood, common in New England. Arctic America (Richardson). New York (Halsey). New Jersey (Mr. Austin). Illinois (Mr. Hall).——*A. Javanicum* (Mont & V. d. B.) Stizenb. On logs of Bald Cypress (*Taxodium*) Louisiana (Hale).

LIX.—CALICIUM, Pers., Ach., Fr.

Calicium, Fr. Fl. Scan. p. 283; Summ. Veg. Scand. p. 118. Norm. Con. p. 26. Calicii spp., Pers. in Ust. Ann. Bot. Ach. L. U. p. 39, t. 3, f. 2 ; Syn. p. 55. Turn. & Borr. Lich. Brit. p. 119. Schær. Spicil. p. 224. Fr. L. E. p. 334. Calicium & Cyphelii spp. pl., Ach. in Act. Holm. l. c. Calicium, Cyphelium, & Sphinctrina, De Not. in Giorn. Bot. It., cit. Massal. Massal. Mem. p. 151. Stenocybe, &c., Nyl. in Bot. Notis., 1854, cit. ipso. Calicium, Cyphelium, Stenocybe, & Sphinctrina, Koerb. Syst. p. 304 ; Parerg. p. 287. Calicium & Sphinctrina, Nyl. Mon. Cal. p. 5; Syn. p. 142, t. 5, f. 1–28 ; Lich. Scand. p. 37; Syn. Lich. N. Caled. p. 7 ; Addend. Nov. ad Lich. Eur. in Flora Ratisb. Calicium, Chænotheca, & Sphinctrina, Th. Fr. Gen. p. 102. Calicium, Chænothecæ sect., & Sphinctrina, Stizenb. Beitr. l. c. p. 157.

Structuram exposuit Tulasne, Mém. sur les Lich. pp. 77, 185, t. 15, f. 13–17, 20.

ellipsoideæ, biloculares, fuscæ, longit. $0,012-18^{mm\cdot}$, *crassit.* $0,007-9^{mm\cdot}$ On old logs of Cedar, Bluffton, South Carolina (Dr. J. H. Mellichamp). There is no trace of a margin externally, and the brownish-black walls of the proper exciple often do not extend upward beyond the white layer. This white layer — for the most part more or less straight, or a little concave — is now and then indeed (as seen in section) distinctly convex, precluding any regular extension of the exciple upwards, and giving to the thick hypothecium (as also noticed above in a similar deformation of *A. Bolanderi*) something of the peculiar outline of that of *Sphærophorus.* In this new *Acolium* some slight blue reaction of the hymenial gelatine with iodine is sufficiently evident.

Apothecia turbinato-lentiformia, stipitata, excipulo proprio fusco-nigro l. atro marginata. Sporæ e thecis cylindraceis mox ejectæ, sphericæ ellipsoideæ oblongæve, simplices l. bi- rarissime quadriloculares, fuscescentes. Spermatia ellipsoidea oblongave, rarius acicularia; sterigmatibus sub simplicibus. Thallus crustaceus, uniformis rarius subsquamulosus, obsoletusve, l. in parasiticis nullus.

In restoring his *Sphinctrina turbinata* (*S. O. V.* p. 120) to Lichens, Fries replaced it in *Calicium ;* and later authors have scarcely succeeded in indicating distinguishing characters for their *Sphinctrina* (the ' originally closed exciple' being, as we take it, equally predicable of *Calicium*) beyond the much elongated and bowed spermatia. To judge of this difference in the only way we can — by analogy — it seems certainly insufficient ; while the remaining assumption that these lichens are separable from *Calicium* as exclusively parasitical is embarrassed by *C. microcephalum* (*Sphinctrina Anglica*, Nyl.) ' so exactly similar to *C. sessile*' (*C. turbinatum*, Pers.) ' that we should certainly regard the two plants as the same, did not the thallus in *C. microcephalum* appear really to belong to the pilidia' (Turn. & Borr. *Lich. Brit.* p. 131) a remark equally applicable to the American plant.

But whether or not we subsume *Sphinctrina*, De Not., under *Calicium*, the spore-history of the former group, as exhibited by Nylander (*Syn.* p. 142, t. 5) may well serve to explain that of the latter, as here taken ; the species brought together in *Sphinctrina* at the place cited offering, at once, spherical, ellipsoid, and finally oblong and bilocular spores. As *Acolium* must be allowed to include a species (*A. Bolanderi*) with spherical spores, and ellipsoid ones are not wholly wanting in species of *Cyphelium*, De Not. (as in *C. chrysocephalum* and *C. melanophæum*) no sufficient reason appears for the generical distinction of the group last named ; and however significant its relations to *Coniocybe* (*Chænotheca*, sect. 1, Stizenb. l. c.) it is even nearer to *Calicium*.

Lichens of the present family are distinguishable by the typical deformation of the disk from elevated, or stipitate conditions (as *Biatora chlorosticta*, Tuck.; *Heterothecium pezizoideum* (Ach.) Flot., *Lecidea flavovirescens* (Dicks.) Borr., *Helocarpon*, Th. Fr.) of the *Lecideei*. But the evolution of the stipe is sometimes imperfect in genuine *Calicia*, and such subsessile states are to be discriminated from the always sessile apothecium of *Acolium*.

About forty species, or distinct forms of *Calicium* are reckoned by authors, of which six or seven are only known from tropical or subtropical regions, where one or two European ones have also been detected ; the rest are northern. Not half of the European *Calicia* have yet been recognized here ; but we possess several peculiar to the country.

Sect. 1.—CYPHELIUM, De Not.

C. trichiale, Ach. On Hemlock trunks, and on decaying wood; Mountains of New England. Also on the coast (Mr. Russell, Mr. Willey). *C. melanophæum*, Ach., has not yet occurred here; the lichen rather doubtfully referred to an ecrustaceous state of it in Syn. Lich. N. Eng., being, elsewhere referable by the spores.——*C. brunneolum*, Ach. On decaying wood, in the mountains, with the last.——*C. phæocephalum* (Turn.) Turn. & Borr. Decaying wood, with the last. Sent also from Canada (Mr. Drummond) and New Bedford (Mr. Willey).——*C. chrysocephalum* (Turn.) Ach. Hemlock trunks in the mountains of New England. Found also, on trunks, New Bedford (Mr. Willey). On *Pinus*, California (Mr. Bolander).

Sect. 2.—CALICIUM, De Not.

C. lenticulare (Hoffm.) Ach. (Tuck. *Lich. exs.* n. 145. *C. quercinum*, Pers., Nyl.). Decaying wood in the mountains of New England; and occurring also in the v. *subcinereum*, Nyl. (*C. viride*, Syn. N. Eng., *non Auctt.*).——*C. curtum*, Turn. & Borr. Old wooden fences, Manchester, Mass. (Oakes) and elsewhere on the coast. White Mountains.——*C. subtile*, Fr. (*Lich. Suec.* n. 14). On dead wood. Arctic America (Hook.). Common in the mountains of New England; where it also occurs on the trunks of Hemlock and other trees, with a distinct, white thallus. Such a form is *C. parietinum* v. *albonigrum*, Nyl. *Syn.*, from Oak trunks, Hadley, Mass. (Myself). New York, on dead wood, (Mr. Peck). New Jersey, on the same (Mr. Austin). Illinois, on the same (Mr. Hall). Alabama, on the same (Mr. Beaumont). Texas, on the same (Mr. Ravenel). California, on the same (Dr. J. G. Cooper) and on *Pinus muricata* (Mr. Bolander). The small spores (averaging 0,005–8$^{mm.}$ in length, and 0,0025–0,0045$^{mm.}$ in width) of my plants are, so far as observed, always simple; and they should therefore be referable to *C. parietinum*, Nyl. *Syn.* But this differs in nothing beside the unilocular spores from *C. pusillum*, Nyl. *Syn.;* and both conditions were brought together in the same author's earlier *C. subtile* (Nyl. *Prodr. Gall.*).——*C. fuscipes*, Tuckerm.,[1] distinguished by its pale stipes and larger spores from the species just reckoned, as by the spores from *C. pallescens*, Nyl. *Scand.*, has no doubt a much wider extension than that given below.——*C. trachelinum*, Ach. On

---

[1] *Calicium fuscipes (sp. nova) thallo obsoleto ; apothecis turbinato-lentiformibus subtus albidis, disco convexo nigro, stipite firmo fusco. Sporæ in thecis cylindraceis octonæ, ellipsoideæ l. oblongo-ellipsoideæ, semper simplices, fuscescentes, longit.* 0,009–16$^{mm.}$, *crassit.* 0,004–7$^{mm.}$.——On dead wood (Oak rails) New Jersey (Mr. Austin). Canada (Mr. Drummond). Larger and stouter than *C. subtile*, with larger spores. Apothecia exactly turbinate-lentiform, the under side, as well as the upper portion of the brown stipe, as if thinly white-varnished. The hymenial gelatine offers a feeble blue reaction with iodine.

dead wood, common in the New England mountains. Missouri and Illinois (Mr. Hall). North Carolina, on Oak trunks (Rev. Dr. Curtis). South Carolina (Mr. Ravenel). Occurs, in the White Mountains, with the apothecia and curiously flattened stipes of *C. hyperellum* v. *baliolum*, Ach., and was, in this condition, formerly taken by me (Syn. Lich. N. Eng. p. 79) for an athalline state of the latter species, which scarcely differs indeed but in its crust.——*C. hyperellum*, Ach., Wahl. Trunks of *Abies Douglasii*, Yosemite valley; and, with *Acolium tympanellum*, Big Tree grove, California (Mr. Bolander). Unknown east of the Rocky Mountains, at least in states clearly distinguishable from the last species.——*C. roscidum*, Floerk., Nyl., v. *trabinellum*, Nyl. On dead wood. Arctic America (*C. chlorellum*, β *trabinellum*, Hook.! *C. phæocephalum* β, Fr. *L. E.*; Tuck. Syn. N. E., *non* Turn. & Borr.) Hooker herb. Western Massachusetts, and White Mountains. Also New Bedford (Mr. Willey). Missouri (Mr. Hall) and a similar lichen sent from South Carolina (Dr. J. H. Mellichamp).——*C. disseminatum*, Fr. (*Lich. Suec.* n. 16). On dead wood in the White Mountains.——*C. citrinum* (Leight.) Nyl. On the thallus of *Biatora lucida*, White Mountains (Mr. Willey).——*C. Ravenelii*, Tuckerm. (*Obs. Lich.* l. c. 5, p. 389). Old pine palings, South Carolina (Mr. Ravenel).——*C. Curtisii*, Tuckerm. (Suppl. 2, l. c. p. 201.) On *Rhus typhina*, in Berkshire, Mass. (Rev. Dr. Curtis) and near Salem (Mr. Russell). Also near Albany, N. Y. (Mr. Peck) and near Buffalo (Miss M. L. Wilson). What appears the same lichen has occurred also on Alders, in the White Mountains (Mr. Willey) and on *Robinia pseudacacia* in Virginia (Rev. Dr. Curtis). Belongs to the same cluster with the next species, and exhibits similar internal features (Koerb. *Syst.* p. 306) but the originally colourless stipes, turbinate-*lentiform* apothecia, and simple, or only rarely bilocular, never quadrilocular spores (11–17 micromill. long, and 4–7ᵐᵐᵐ· wide) appear to distinguish it.——*C. byssaceum*, Fr. (Th. Fr. Lich. Scand. Rar. n. 48). On *Alnus serrulata*, New Jersey (Mr. Austin). The most minute of our *Calicia*, and not easily to be detected at all, the specimens being even slenderer than the European, which last occurs on *Alnus glutinosa*, but also on other trees. Stipes always black. Spore-development feeble. Spores obsoletely bi-quadrilocular (11–21ᵐᵐᵐ· long, and 5–6ᵐᵐᵐ· wide). A rather larger plant, from *Rhus venenata*, New Bedford (Mr. Willey) offers regularly 4-locular spores, 16–23ᵐᵐᵐ· long, and 5–9ᵐᵐᵐ· wide.

Sect. 3.—SPHINCTRINA, De Not.

C. microcephalum (Sm.) Turn. & Borr. (*Lich. Brit.* p. 130. *Sphinctrina Anglica*, Nyl. *Syn.*). On old fences, Ipswich (Oakes). New Bedford (Mr. Willey). Thallus well agreeing with the description of Turner and Borrer, as with the later one of Mr. Mudd (Man. Brit. Lich. p. 255) and the lichen is referred here by Nylander, *l. c.*——*C. tubæforme* (Massal. *sub Sphinctrina, Mem.* p. 155. *S. microcephala*, Nyl. *l. c., non* Turn. &

31

Borr.). Parasitical on *Pertusaria pustulata*, at Chelsea, and Milford, Massachusetts; and on *Pertusaria*-thallus in Henrico county, Virginia (Myself). New Bedford (Mr. Willey). South Carolina, on *Pertusaria* (perhaps *leioplaca*) Mr. Ravenel. —— *C. leucopodum* (Nyl. *sub Sphinctrina*, *Syn.* p. 144). Parasitical on *Pertusaria*-thallus, Henrico county, Virginia. —— *C. turbinatum*, Pers. Parasitical on *Pertusaria pertusa*. Pennsylvania, *Muhlenberg*. Canada (Mr. Drummond). Very common at the North, and probably extending southward.

LX.—CONIOCYBE, Ach.

Ach. in Act. Holm. 1816, p. 283. Fr. S. O. V. p. 276; L. E. p. 382; Fl. Scan. p. 286; Summa Veg. Scand. p. 119 (excl. C. nigricante). Schær. Enum. p. 174. De Not. in Giorn. Bot. It., cit. Massal. Norm. Con. p. 27. Massal. Mem. p. 159. Koerb. Syst. p. 318. Nyl. Monogr. Calic. p. 24; Prodr. Gall. p. 33; Syn. Lich. p. 16, t. 5, f. 37–43; Lich. Scand. p. 43. Th. Fr. Lich. Arct. p. 251; Gen. p. 102. Calicii spp., Pers. in Ust. Ann. Bot. Ach. L. U. p. 39; Syn. p. 61. Turn. & Borr. Lich. Brit. p. 119. Schær. Spicil. p. 224. Chænothecæ sect., Stizenb. Beitr. l. c. p. 157.

Apothecia globosa, stipitata, excipuli proprii colorati margine subevanido. Sporæ e thecis cylindraceis mox ejectæ, sphericæ, simplices, subincolores. Spermatia haud observata. Thallus crustaceus, uniformis, leprosus, l. obsoletus.

Calicium has been taken by some authors to have an originally open exciple, and *C. turbinatum* (*Sphinctrina*, De Not.) to be distinguishable by its exciple being originally closed. Any excipular envelope beside the veil, has sometimes been denied altogether to *Coniocybe*. Both distinctions are however, analogically, improbable. Nor am I able to find any difference, in the originally closed condition of the apothecium, between *C. turbinatum*, and *CC. phæocephalum*, *hyperellum*, and *trachelinum ;* or to suspect for a moment the genuine exciple of *Coniocybe*. It is not so easy to examine satisfactorily the youngest, often minute conditions of the latter; but *C. pallida* and *C. furfuracea* v. *sulphurella* throw some real light upon the ultimate evolution of the genus, and permit perhaps the (more probable) supposition that the apparent, original difference in structure here, is not, at least, an absolute one.

Beside this uncertainty as to the original condition of the proper exciple, and whether this, as well as the veil, at first entirely encloses the spore-mass, we have left, to distinguish the present group from *Calicium*, the more marked biatoroid habit, and more nearly colourless, globular spores; or, as neither of these characters has much weight when viewed from the stand-point of *Calicium* § *Cyphelium*, only, at last, the globular outline and, by this determined, at length obscure margin of the fruit, — a difference which, as Schærer said (*Spicil.* p. 225) is far from satisfactory.

Four species, all of them European, are reckoned by Nylander; of which two occur within our limits.

C. furfuracea (L.) Ach., on the roots of trees, and on decaying wood, in shade; New England (Mr. Russell). New York (Mr. Peck).——
C. pallida (Pers.) Fr., on trunks; New England (Messrs. Russell and Frost).

Trib. V.—VERRUCARIACEI (Fr. 1821. Fée) Stizenb.

Apothecia globosa, apice poro pertusa; excipulo exteriori proprio (perithecio) nucleum gelatinosum interiori plus minus distincto (amphithecio) inclusum, tegente.

Acharius associated *Pertusaria* and *Thelotrema* with his *Pyrenula ;* and *Glyphis* and *Chiodecton* with *Trypethelium.* Turner and Borrer wrote before the appearance of the latest writings of the Swedish lichenographer, and make no mention of *Chiodecton* and *Glyphis;* but they regard *Pertusaria* as coming between *Thelotrema* and *Bathelium* (*Trypethelium*) and 'nearest to' the latter, while the *Thelotremata,* 'in what seems their perfection, approach the *Parmeliæ,* or still more nearly the *Urceolariæ.*' (*Lich. Brit.* pp. 166, 192). Fries (*S. O. V.*, 1825) removed both *Glyphis* and *Chiodecton* from this association to the place which they now occupy, as did Meyer, the same year, the former ; retaining however the latter in its Acharian affinity, to which Fries also, later (*Lich. Eur.*) restored it ; and it was left to Montagne to correct the error. Not so easy was the correction of the position of the other two genera. The nearness of *Thelotrema* to *Phlyctis* and *Gyrostomum* was indeed indicated by Fries (*S. O. V.*) and he finally (*Summ. Veg. Scand.*) as Eschweiler (*Lich. Bras.*) had already done, referred the first-named to the *Lecanorei ;* but was not followed in this by Montagne, who, with the great majority of lichenists, still looked at the genus as Verrucariaceous. Even more general has been the indisposition of authors to allow determining weight to the lecanorine features of *Pertusaria ;* and Nylander was perhaps the first to assign to the type, without hesitation, what we must here regard its natural rank.

Acharius's explanation of the Verrucariaceous apothecium, which I follow almost all recent lichenographers in adopting here, may well suggest the clearer exhibition of not dissimilar features in *Thelotrema.* Eschweiler indeed (*Lich. Bras.*) has denied the analogy ; and neither he nor Fries recognize any interior tunic in *Verrucaria.* This inner exciple is certainly obscure enough in the great majority of species of *Thelotrema ;* and it is perhaps therefore the less surprising that we find it, in general, no better marked in the humbler groups before us. It is still difficult to avoid wholly the recognition of such interior, excipular layer in the *Verrucariacei* (as compare Nyl. *Syn.* p. 21) as in the *Caliciacei;* [1] while yet we can hardly question the removal of *Thelotrema* from the tribe to which it is perhaps, none the less, the key.

---

[1] And compare the analogous structure in the Pyrenomycetes; as, in particular, De Bary, Morph. & Phys. d. Pilze, &c., p. 98, fig. 37, c.

No such complexity of excipular structure appears however to be predicable of *Pertusaria ;* the type of which, as already suggested in another place, may be considered as simply a peculiar modification of the lecanoreine hypothecium, conditioned by the here dominant *nisus* to become compound.

Conformably with the view that the Verrucariaceous fruit is in fact analogous to that of *Thelotrema*, it is the exterior covering of the former, however diminished, that is equivalent to the proper (exterior) exciple of the latter, and still to be called *perithecium ;* while the interior envelope (*tunic*, Leight.) assuming especial importance in the types with included fruit, may be distinguished as *amphithecium*, the term used by Koerber, and sufficiently explained by him [1] (*Syst.* p. 320). Such use of the terms appears, on several accounts, preferable to their transposition; upon which compare Th. Fr. *Lich. Arct.* p. 252.

But though reduced by the signal losses to which we have above referred to what is, for the most part, a heap of obscure forms, of a type so low that the larger part perhaps is on the verge of exclusion from the class, the present tribe is still dignified by a foliaceous family, and needs therefore but a (possible) fruticulose expression, to exhibit all the series of thalline development which distinguish *Parmeliacei*, *Lecideacei*, and *Caliciacei*. And in this view, *Graphidacei*, which with all its surprising variety of modification, and mostly well-marked lichenose character, is still confined to the lowest type of thallus, might certainly seem as inferior, as, according to Eschweiler, it should be regarded, in the elongation (as compared with the concentrical figure which is characteristical in all the other tribes) of its fruit.

Considered in the way of analogy, the foliaceous *Verrucariacei* (*Endo-carpei*) may be said to represent *Umbilicaria* and *Pannaria ;* passing, like both of these, into microphylline, and, like the last, into finally almost crustaceous forms. These foliaceous expressions excepted, it is so easy and natural to refer the whole remainder of the tribe to a single family (*Verrucariei*) that the bulk is, without hesitation, subsumed by Nylander under a single genus. This family affords however some apparently available grounds of further specification. We here distinguish, following most lichenographers, the types with coloured perithecia (sub-fam. *Segestriei*) regarding these as offering some other marked indications of superiority, and as analogous at once to *Eulecanorei* and to *Biatorei*. Compound apothecia and a peculiar thalloid receptacle (stroma) finding

---

[1] It is yet obvious, from the above, that we cannot adopt the expression that the amphithecium is to be called, without qualification, the analogue of the hypo-thecium in higher lichens ('*das Analogon des Keimbodens* (hypothecium) *bei den gymnokarpischen Flechten,*' Koerb. l. c.) this place belonging rather to the perithe-cium, as representing the most important hypothecial layer; while the amphithecium stands for a layer, everywhere of inferior value, and, in higher lichens, for the most part, unknown.

however a significant representative in the *Sphæriacei*, in Fungi, give marked distinction to our next sub-family (*Trypetheliei*) notwithstanding its often difficult relations to *Pyrenula ;* and *Trypethelium* has been universally accepted as an analogue of *Pertusaria.* And the final, varied deformation of the lecanorine type (*Urceolariei*, finding its centre in *Thelotrema*) is fitly represented here by our last sub-family — the *Pyrenulei.*

Estimates of the limitation of species vary so much in this tribe, that while one European author reckons not far from two hundred specific forms in Germany alone, another scarcely allows two hundred and fifty to be known to science. The tribe is remarkable for the very small proportion of types referable to the colourless spore-series.

Fam. I. — ENDOCARPEI, Th. Fr.

Thallus foliaceus l. squamæformis.

As in immersed types of *Thelotrema*, it is the interior exciple (amphithecium) which plays the largest part in the family before us, almost indeed constituting the fructification in its principal group ; and the perithecium, which alone is equivalent to the at length marginant hypothecium of the higher tribes, is proportionally diminished. Extreme then as is the position of *Endocarpon*, as exhibited in its best-developed forms (comparable only with *Umbilicaria*) it is not to these, but far humbler representatives of the generic type, and indeed to the analogies afforded by the next family that we are to look for the full explication of its fruit-character.

And this remark may possibly prove as applicable to the difficulties of the spores, as to those of the excipular envelopes. The now largely accepted separation of *Dermatocarpon*, Eschw., from *Endocarpon*, rests on not dissimilar grounds to those which are as generally taken to distinguish *Pannaria* from *Lecothecium*, Trev.; the differences in the thallus being corroborated, in both cases, by modifications of the spore. In the latter however this modification is only a gradal difference of the same spore-type, assuming here the same direction of *ascent* which so often accompanies the degradation of the thallus. Two Italian lichens not otherwise distinguishable from *Dermatocarpon* (*Placidiopsis*, Beitr., Koerb.) differ from the foliaceous species in precisely the same way. And the only distinction in the case of *Endocarpon*, Hedw., lies in the fact that the spore here is muriform ; requiring us to consider that this last little group belongs to a different spore-series, and therefore genus, from *Dermatocarpon*, or else that the latter is to be taken as offering a decolorate exhibition of a stage in the differentiation of the same, coloured spore. The last view has already commended itself in *Umbilicaria*, and finds present support in the great predominance of the coloured spore-series in the *Verrucariacei*. The commonly decolorate exhibition of this spore-type in *Verrucaria*, as here taken, is a case seemingly in point;. and even *Segestria*, if we are not much in error, may furnish another.

Beside *Endocarpon*, as thus understood, only *Normandina* is referable to the present family.

LXI.—ENDOCARPON, Hedw., Fr.

Endocarpon, Hedw. Stirp. Crypt. Endocarpon, Fr. (L. E. p. 407) S. V. S. pp. 119, 563. Endocarpon (excl. E. lætevirente) Tuck. Syn. N. Eng. p. 82. Endocarpon pro max. p., Ach. L. U. p. 55; Syn. p. 97. Fée Ess. p. 87. Schær. Spicil. p. 58. Leight. Brit. Ang. Lich. p. 10, t. 1, &c. Verrucariæ spp., Turn. & Borr. Lich. Brit. p. 203. Borr. in E. Bot. Suppl. Endocarpon, et Dermatocarpon pro max. p., Eschw. Syst. p. 16. Fr. S. O. V. p. 259. Endocarpon max. p., Placidium, Catopyrenium, et Dermatocarpon, Mass. opp. Endocarpon max. p., Endopyrenium, Placidiopsis, Catopyrenium, et Dermatocarpon, Koerb. Syst.; Parerg. p. 307. Endocarpon max. p., et Verrucariæ spp., Nyl. Prodr. pp. 174, 178; Pyrenoc. p. 11; Lich. Scand. p. 264. Endocarpon pro p., et Rhodocarpon, Lönnr, in Flora, 1858. Endocarpon max. p., et Dermatocarpon, Anz. Catal. Sondr. p. 102. Mudd Man. Brit. Lich. p. 265. Dermatocarpon, Placidiopsis, et Endocarpon Th. Fr. Gen. p. 103. Dermatocarpon, Placidiopsis, et Endocarpon pro p., Stizenb. Beitr. l. c. p. 150.

Structuram exposuerunt Tulasne, Mém. sur les Lich. pp. 22, 90, 189, t. 12; Schwendener, Untersuch. l. c. 3, p. 184–189, t. 10, f. 1–9.

Apothecia thallo immersa, perithecio diminuto, amphithecio pallido l. demum nigricante, paraphysibus mucilaginoso-diffluxis. Sporæ ovoideæ, ellipsoideæ, l. oblongæ, simplices l. nunc bi-quadriloculares l. muriformi-multiloculares, fuscescentes l. decolores. Spermatia ellipsoidea oblongave; sterigmatibus aut simplicibus aut multiarticulatis. Thallus foliaceus squamulosusve, dein crustoso-diminutus.

The relations of the foliaceous *Verrucariacei* to those typically crustaceous are exceedingly close. Acharius distinguished *Verrucaria* by its 'double perithecium,' the simple one of *Endocarpon* being so described that it is not clear that he did not regard it as representing both the envelopes of the former. Turner and Borrer (whose observations were unfortunately left unfinished) saw rather that it is the amphithecium or inner envelope of *Verrucaria* that is equivalent to the included exciple of Endocarpon (*Lich. Brit.* p. 207) and though they do not say that it is in the 'ostiole' of the foliaceous group that we are to look for the representative of the outer envelope (perithecium) of *Verrucaria*, these most careful lichenographers united the two genera. Borrer reaffirmed this view, later, in the Supplement to English Botany. And Dr. Nylander, though he separates, but by no firmer character than the many-jointed sterigmas, the truly foliaceous, and a part of the squamulose *Endocarpa* (*Endocarpon*, Nyl.) refers all the rest to his *Verrucaria*. Habit however, the aggregate expression of the idea embodied in an organism, lends value to differences which might not otherwise attract special attention; and may enable us to reach constructions at least less complex than either of those cited. As here taken the genus before us is equivalent to the Acharian conception of the group, as finally reformed by Fries; and to *Endocarpon* and *Dermatocarpon* of Anzi.

Starting, like *Pannaria*, with truly foliaceous lichens, so well marked indeed as to be better comparable with *Umbilicaria*, *Endocarpon* runs as readily as the former into squamulose conditions. *E. Moulinsii*, in its best forms perhaps the finest of *Endocarpa*, is scarcely more diverse from the humblest of the squamulose species, than *Pannaria molybdæa* and *P. plumbea* from *P. tryptophylla* and *P. nigra*. In both genera modifications of the spore-structure lend now apparent weight to the differences resulting from the deterioration of the thallus; while yet in neither are these changes in the internal configuration of the spore confined to the lowest forms, but occur also in species referable fairly to the foliaceous type. *Endocarpon pusillum*, Hedw., is, on the one hand, far from unlike in most respects, externally, to *E.* (*Dermatocarpon*) *arboreum*, while, on the other, it is scarcely distinguishable from a lichen (*End. Garovaglii* (Mont.) Schær.) so similar often to the crustaceous *Staurothele umbrina*, that the latter might even be taken, says Nylander (*Pyrenoc.* p. 20) for a saxicoline state of the same species. [1]

In one respect the parallel with *Pannaria*, so far at least as present knowledge extends, is less close. The sterigmas of the genus just named are assumed to be always jointed. This is indeed the case also in the higher forms of *Endocarpon*, and the character holds good of such diminished ones as *E. hepaticum* and *E. compactum* (Mass.) Nyl. ; but in *E. cinereum*, *E. monstrosum*, Mass., and *E. pusillum*, we have (Nyl. l. c.) simple sterigmas. The distinction in question, as presented in other groups of Lichens, is yet clearly of but subordinate value; and no good reason appears for laying greater stress upon it in the family before us.

Even as here understood, *Endocarpon* is a small group, but twenty-four species referable to it, not a few of them more or less doubtful, being reckoned by Nylander (*Pyrenoc.*) and the number having been but little increased since. The group is northern and austral ; but extends to the mountains of tropical regions. Of the conspicuously foliaceous species

---

[1] Compare Dr. Th. Fries's apposite remarks on his *E. pulvinatum*,—'*Lichen maximopere insignis, melius evolutus quam Dermat. rufescens et Endoc. pusillum, Hedw. (Dermat. Schæreri, Koerb.) sed habitu, colore, apotheciis magis cum Stigmatommate, Koerb. congruens; est enim omnino ut St. clopimum thallo foliaceo, pulvinato-imbricato præditum.*' (*Lich. Arct.* p. 257).

we possess all the better known ones; of the squamulose, several are wanting.

E. miniatum (L.) Schær., *a* (embracing as well *E. glaucum*, Ach. *Syn.*, as respects at least its North American habitat; as without doubt also *E. Muhlenbergii* of the same work) occurs on various rocks (lime rocks not excepted) from Greenland (Vahl in Th. Fr. *l. c.*) throughout the United States, to the mountains of New Mexico (Mr. Fendler). Acharius (*l. c.* p. 103) suggested the possibility that his two species last named might be only forms of his *E. miniatum ;* and it is in fact improbable that they can be well distinguished even as varieties. —— Certain forms of *a* (Vermont, Mr. Frost) agree in the reticulate wrinkling of the under surface with the var. *fulvo-fuscum* (*E. fluviatile* v. *fulvo-fuscum*, Tuck. Syn. N. Eng. p. 83) which is however an aquatic condition, and confined as yet to the alpine lake in which it was discovered. —— The polyphyllous state of the species, growing on dry rocks, — v. *complicatum*, Schær., has the same range with *a*, but is more common at the north. —— From this the var. *Manitense*, Nyl. (*E. Manitense*, Tuck. in Agass. Journ. of a Tour, &c. *E. gyrophoroides*, Schwein. *in herb. Fr.*) differs, as Montagne observed (*in litt.*) and Nylander has since stated, much as a polyphylline state of the f. *Muhlenbergii ;* and is remarkable for its very dark (brown) colour. The lichen has occurred in North Carolina (Schweinitz) in Georgia (Mr. Ravenel) and in islands of Lake Superior (Prof. Agassiz). It is far from difficult to mistake for it conditions of *Umbilicaria flocculosa.* —— But the aquatic state of the polyphylline condition of the species, as I here follow Schærer in regarding it, — v. *aquaticum*, Schær. (*E. fluviatile*, DC., Fr.) which is not uncommon in New England, and occurs in New Jersey (Mr. Austin) and in North Carolina (Mr. Ravenel) varies also to dark forms (Fr. *Lich. Suec.* n. 37. Stenh. Lich. Suec. n. 29) now easily suggesting that if *E. Muhlenbergii* (including the varr. *fulvo-fuscum* and *Manitense*, above indicated) could be taken for a species, with a range of variation similar to that of *E. miniatum*, it might possibly be said to be in fact European, as well as American, and even (Nyl. *Pyrenoc.* p. 12, and *specim. c herb. Sond.*) African.

Acharius described a state of his *E. miniatum* (v. *cirsodes*, Syn. p. 102) with a 'granulate-scabrous,' or papillose under surface ; and I find the same feature well marked, and the minute warts passing now and then into fibres, in a lichen from New Mexico (Mr. Fendler) and the Rocky Mountains (Mr. E. Hall) otherwise well comparable, except that it blackens beneath, with fine, sub-simple specimens of *E. miniatum* v. *complicatum*, from the same region. But the former is perhaps more properly to be referred to *E. Moulinsii*, Mont., recognized also by its friendly author in specimens from Texas (Mr. Wright). These latter specimens are yet far from characteristical, and but ill-represent the noble lichen of the Himalaya (Jacquemont *in herb. Mus. Par.* Hook. & Thoms. *Herb. Ind. Or.* n. 2218) which, in size, and in the aspect of both surfaces, but especially in the hirsute under side, compares at length closely with *Umbilicaria hirsuta.*

In other species which agree with the preceding in the gonidia, and the spores, and, so far as these are known, in the spermogones and their contents, the thallus is reduced, and becomes at length squamulose, and finally semi-crustaceous. But this reduction is less marked in *E. arboreum*, Schwein. (*E. Tuckermani*, Mont., Raven.) which though agreeing with the others following in being attached generally by a (here conspicuous) blackening hypothallus, is yet truly foliaceous and compared by Fries (*L. E.* p. 407) with a '*Sticta haud rite evoluta.*' The species was first detected at the South (Schweinitz) where Mr. Ravenel has especially elucidated its variations; but is common also, and equally fine, on old trees at the North.——The last species is closely related to *E. rufescens*, Ach., growing on the earth, in Texas (Mr. Wright) New Mexico (Mr. Fendler) and in the Rocky Mountains (Dr. Hayden).——And *E. rufescens* is itself so near to *E. hepaticum*, Ach., occurring in similar habitats to the other, and from Greenland (Vahl, in Th. Fr. l. c.) to New England; New Jersey (Mr. Austin) Illinois and Kansas (Mr. Hall) and New Mexico (Mr. Fendler) that authors only distinguish the last by its smaller, darker, and commonly thinner fronds; and rather smaller spores.

More distinct is *E. cinereum*, Pers., differing also from the other species preceding in its simple (not jointed) sterigmas; by which character Nylander excludes as well this as the next from *Endocarpon*, and associates them with his *Verrucaria*. *E. cinereum*, v. *cartilagineum*, Nyl. (*E. dædaleum*, Krempelh.) is an earth lichen, which has occurred in Greenland (Vahl, *e* Th. Fr. l. c.) and, in a state scarcely distinguishable, in the Yosemite valley, California (Mr. Bolander). We have here another example of the peculiarly limited distribution of certain common European lichens, in this continent.——*E. ochroleucum*, Tuckerm.,[1] a rupicoline lichen, which admits of some comparison, as respects general habit apart from colour, with *E. Schæreri* (Fr.) (*E. miniatum* v. *monstrosum*, Schær.). The latter is however made up of peltate squamules; and our plant, which has occurred only on the coast of California (Mr. Bolander) consists rather of stipitate areoles. The bearing of the nigrescent spores of this species on the question, above touched upon, of the distinction by its

---

[1] *Endocarpon ochroleucum (sp. nova) thallo areolato-diffracto crasso flavo-virescente, areolis confertis turgescentibus lævigatis, centralibus substipitatis, periphericis lobulatis; apotheciis immersis, perithecio atro, amphithecio nigricante. Sporæ in thecis lanceolatis 6–8næ, cymbiformes, biloculares loculis approximatis, dilute nigro-fuscéscentes, longit. 0,018–26*mm* crassit. 0,0035–55*mm*.*——On serpentine, Mendocino county, California (Mr. Bolander). Areoles small, the central ones not much exceeding, at the summits, 1*mm* in diameter; but these, or several of them together, are prolonged downwards into thick stipes reaching 2*mm* in height. Spores sub-fusiform, longer and narrower than those of *E. Custnani*, Mass. (Hepp. n. 669) but of similar structure. Spermogones not observed.

spore-character of *Dermatocarpon*, Eschw., from *Endocarpon*, will be observed.——The difference in the sterigmas which serves to separate *E. cinereum* from the species immediately preceding it, recurs in the only one we have now left to notice, but is quite insufficient in either to over-weigh the affinities which, by the almost general consent of lichenographers, unite all these lichens in a single, natural group. In *E. pusillum*, Hedw. (*Verrucaria pallida*, Nyl.) the lichen upon which the genus *Endocarpon* was originally founded, and occurring here, upon the earth, in Texas (Mr. Wright) on calcareous rocks in Vermont (Mr. Frost) and in Illinois, Missouri, and Kansas (Mr. Hall) the spores are larger, fewer, and muri-form-multilocular; and it relates therefore, in this respect, to the other species, much as *Umbilicaria pustulata* to the majority of forms (with simple, decolorate spores) of the latter group: or still more nearly as *Pannaria byssina* (Hoffm.) to the rest of the genus with which we have associated it. *E. pusillum* is doubtless vastly more common here than our few stations should seem to indicate, and may well be found also in the reduced state which is *E. Garovaglii* (Mont.) Schær. Beside this last, and the far from well-defined *Dermatocarpon glomeruliferum*, Mass. (Anz. Venet. n. 118) the only other known *Endocarpa* with muriform spores are *Dermatoc. arenarium*, Hamp. in Koerb. *Parerg.* p. 309, characterized by a return of the spores to more normal conditions as respects number and size, in which respects *Buellia petræa*, as here taken, furnishes some important analogies; and the externally well-marked *E. pulvinatum*, Th. Fr. It should yet be said that Lönnroth, and Stizenberger, have united the crustaceous *Staurothele*, Norm., with their *Endocarpon* (*Dermatocarpon*, Mass., not of Eschw.) and that Nylander (*Pyrenoc.* l. c.) and Th. Fries (the place is quoted above) have indicated points of contact in the two groups; which differ, none the less, as *Physcia* from *Rinodina*.

LXII.—NORMANDINA, Nyl.

Nyl. Classif. 2, p. 191, cit. ipso; Prodr. Gall. p. 173 ; Exp. Syn. Pyrenoc. p. 10. Th. Fr. Lich. Arct. p. 256; Gen. p. 104. Mudd Man. Brit. Lich. p. 268. Stizenb. Beitr. l. c. p. 149. Lenormandia, Delis. in Desmaz. Cr. Fr. Nyl. Lich. Par. n. 89. Koerb. Parerg. p. 43. Massal. Sched. Crit. cit. Th. Fr. Verrucariæ sp., Borr. in E. Bot. Suppl. t. 2602, f. 1, & t. 2658. Mont. Syll. p. 366. Endocarpi sp., Hook. Br. Fl. 2, p. 158. Leight. Brit. Ang. Lich. p. 13, t. 3, f. 1. Coccocarpiæ ? sp., Babingt. Lich. N. Zeal. p. 9.

Apothecia verrucis thallinis immersa, perithecio diminuto, amphi-thecio nigro, paraphysibus obsoletis. Sporæ oblongo-cylindraceæ, 8–loculares, incolores. Spermatia haud visa. Thallus squamæ-formis, monophyllus.

The type and only ascertained species is *N. Jungermanniæ* (Delis.)

Nyl., discovered (growing upon mosses, and also upon other lichens) in Europe, where Leighton first elegantly exhibited the fructification; but since found in New Zealand (Babingt. l. c.) in Mexico, Bolivia, and New Granada (Nyl.) as well as in Cuba (Mr. Wright) and Venezuela (Mr. Fendler). I have observed it here on *Pannaria rubiginosa* from the mountains of South Carolina (Mr. Ravenel) on *P. molybdæa*, from Louisana (Hale) and on mosses from the Yosemite valley, California (Mr. Bolander). The apothecia have been rarely seen, and nothing has been added to Leighton's description except by Nylander; who first indicated that the interior envelope is 'immersed in thalline tubercles.' (*Prodr.* p. 173). The six fruits which I have had the good fortune to discover in the scanty Carolina specimens, certainly tend to confirm this character, and are well comparable with younger conditions of *Porina mastoidea* (Ach.) Fée; but it is perhaps a variable one, and is passed over by Nylander in his later *Expositio Pyrenocarpeorum*. Spore-cells, in the most perfect spores, eight.

With this is most readily associated (as by Borrer, Leighton, and Nylander) *N. lætevirens* (Turn.) (*Endocarpon viride*, Ach. *Normandina viridis*, Nyl.) the fructification of which, if we except a single, imperfect, and as yet scarcely available observation recorded by Mr. Leighton (l. c.) is entirely unknown. It occurs not uncommonly on moist earth in the alpine region of the White Mountains.

Fam. 2.—VERRUCARIEI.

Thallus crustaceus.

Sub-fam. 1.—SEGESTRIEI.

Apothecia solitaria, perithecio colorato.

Segestria, indicated by Fries in 1825 (*S. O. V.* p. 263) as differing from *Verrucaria* as *Biatora* from *Lecidea* (*L. E.* p. 429) is the original type of the principal assemblage before us, and was understood by its author to embrace three of the six or seven distinct clusters recognized by later writers, in the *Verrucariei* with coloured perithecia; and bark as well as rock-lichens. And we append to it here another group (*Staurothele*, Norm.) which while agreeing in some important respects with the first, differs from it in its always blackening perithecia; and from *Verrucaria* in the perithecium not being originally black. If then we compare (as we have already the *Endocarpei* to the foliaceous *Parmeliacei*) the *Verrucariei* to the *Lecanorei*, *Segestriei* will represent, in some sort, *Eulecanorei*, *Segestria* — *Lecanora*, and *Staurothele* — *Rinodina*. *Staurothele* is only known in rock forms, but *Segestria*, as here taken, is also corticoline. The argument for the separation of *Pyrenula* from *Verrucaria* is based however on a difference of lichenose rank scarcely predicable of the *Segestriei*, in almost half of the species referable to which, the most of them corticoline, authors have recognized what we may call lecanorine analogies; and it is difficult not to admit that we have to do, in the latter, with a higher, and as respects at least the principal assemblage, a not indistinctly marked, natural group.

LXIII.—SEGESTRIA, Fr. S. O. V., p. 263.

Segestrella, Fr. L. E. pp. 429, 460 (excl. S. rubra). Sphæromphale exparte, Porina max. p., Thelocarpon, Thelochroa, Segestrella, Thelopsis, Microglæna, Thelenella, Verrucariæ spp.; Geisleria, & Weitenwebera, Auctt. recent.

Apothecia in verrucis thallinis immersa, perithecio colorato, amphithecio pallido 1. dein nigricante, paraphysibus capillaribus. Sporæ ex ellipsoideo oblongæ 1. fusiformes, e simplici bi-quadri-pluriloculares 1. dein muriformi-multiloculares, incolores. Spermatia (quantum obs.) oblonga 1. acicularia; sterigmatibus simplicibus. Thallus crustaceus, effiguratus aut uniformis.

After much consideration and many revisions of results, I shall venture here to set down what I believe to be a conceivable, and in several respects desirable interpretation of a group of lichens, the larger part of which has not yet been detected in North America; leaving it to others to give effect, so far as this ought to be done, to what is suggested. These lichens are certainly brought together by much agreement as well in habit as in the details of structure; but the application of all standards of judgment is especially uncertain in the *Verrucariacei*. It is however, if I do not mistake, the spore-characters upon which later arrangements of the types that make up the group largely rest; and the view to be taken in this place of the value of the arrangements in question, must depend therefore so far on our estimate of these characters.

When first looked at, the group should appear to embrace types referable to the colourless, as others referable to the coloured spore-series, as here taken; but the presumption is much against the exhibition of the former series in the present tribe; and there is no lack of instances, here as elsewhere, of decolorate conditions of the coloured spore. We may possibly find then, that, congruity in habit and general structure leading the way, the apparent diversities in the spore-structure shall explain one another, and what seemed typical distinctions prove only subordinate ones; gradal modifications of one and the same spore-type. The polysporous anomaly has elsewhere been touched upon, and I shall add only now that its rather remarkable presentation in the group before us is far from sufficient to affect our estimate of the value of the anomaly derivable from the higher tribes.

Thelocarpon coccophorum (Mont.) Nyl., to which the former writer attributed a foliaceous thallus, associating the plant with *Physcia*, and quadrilocular spores, is defined by Nylander (*Pyrenoc.* p. 10) who at first took it for a *Lecanora*, as crustaceous, and the spores as simple. If really associable with the present tribe, and with the other *Thelocarpa*, the Segestriine character of the lichen cannot well be doubted; in which case its 'lobulate, radiant' thallus will distinguish it as the analogue here of the effigurate groups in the *Eulecanorei*. In the other known species of *Thelocarpon*, Nyl. (*Sphæropsis*, Flot. in Bot. Zeit. 1847, p. 65. *Thelomphale*, Koerb. *Parerg.* p. 321) the instructive descriptions appear to indicate a close affinity to *Segestria* ; as Fries, as above taken, understood it. Should this be made out (and Dr. Stizenberger, *l. c.*, has already united *Thelocarpon* and *Thelopsis*) the spore-character of *Segestria* will only require a similar modification to that which *E. Guepini* makes necessary in the character of *Endocarpon*. The spores of these species are defined as 'for the most part uni-septate' (Nyl.) or 'obsoletely bilocular' (Koerb.) and are contained in polysporous thekes.

Of the two rock-lichens referred to *Segestria* by Fries, one (*S. thelostoma* —the type of *Thelochroa*, Mass.? Koerb.?) has since proved (Leight. Brit. Ang. Lich. p. 34, t. 15, f. 2) to be sharply distinguished from the other by its simple spores. According to the views maintained in the present work, simple spores may characterize species of any genus ; and they afford thus no ground for rejecting the other evidence of affinity connecting *S. thelostoma* with *S. lectissima*. It is interesting, taken in connexion with the described lecanoroid features of *Thelocarpon coccophorum*, Nyl., and with the well-marked, tartareous thallus of *S. thelostoma*, that both Smith and Hooker regarded the latter as better associable with *Lecanora* ; while even Leighton suggests (*l. c.*) that 'it may be improperly placed among the *Angiocarpi*.'

Segestrella, Koerb. *Syst.*, the type of which is *S. lectissima*, Fr., is also dignified, in *Segestria mammillosa*, Th. Fr., by a 'thick, intricately ramulose-torulose' thallus ; and the quadrilocular spores become finally, in *S. Ahlesiana*, Koerb., plurilocular.

Geisleria, Nitschke (Rabenh. *Lich. Eur.* n. 574. Koerb. *Parerg.* p. 326) an earth-lichen found as yet only in Westphalia, and regarded by its discoverer and by Koerber as especially distinguishable from *Sychnogonia* (*Thelopsis*, Nyl.) by its octosporous spore sacks, is perhaps as readily associable with *Segestrella* ; and is in this connexion interesting, as its spores, though very commonly quadrilocular ('*normaliter tetrablastæ*,' Koerb. *l. c.*) tend at length (Nitschke *l. c.*, and I have made the same observation) to a sub-muriform interior configuration ; suggesting that the lichen, and the group to which it shall prove to belong, is possibly, after all, as regards its spore-character, a decolorate exhibition of the differentiation of the (normally) coloured type. And the same remark holds good of *Thelopsis*; *T. inordinata*, Nyl. (*Lich. Kurz.* in *Flora Ratisb.* 1867, p. 9) differing mainly, it should appear, from *T. rubella*, in the spores being 'not regularly 3-septate, but exhibiting also oblique or longitudinal dissepiments'; or as *Geisleria* with submuriform spores from the same type with regularly 4-locular ones.

Thus far the Lichen-clusters considered, with the exception of the muscicoline *Thelocarpon coccophorum*, and *Thelopsis*, are confined to inorganic substrates, or, at least, known only as parasitical; and, taken in connexion with a specific type yet to be noticed, might be considered as bearing a similar relation to *Verrucaria*, as, in that case, the remaining corticoline members of *Segestria* would bear to *Pyrenula*, in the *Pyrenulei*. The European *Thelocarpa* would then be to *Thelopsis*, much as *Segestrella*, Koerb., to *Porina*, Mass. But the difficulty in distinguishing generically the saxicoline and corticoline series in the *Pyrenulei* is greatly increased, as already suggested, in the higher group before us; and there certainly seem to be no characters, or no sufficient ones, for the purpose. *Thelopsis*, Nyl. (*Segestrellæ* sp., Zw. *Sychnogonia*, Koerb.) is in fact a corticoline *Segestrella*, further differenced by polysporous thekes; and the argument here from general structure will not readily yield to any yet drawn from the structural anomaly noticed.

Scarcely more distinct in aspect and less so in details is the tropical, corticoline group represented by *Segestria nucula*, Fr. (*Porinæ* sp., Ach.). The marked lichenose features of this group have been recognized by almost all lichenographers who have considered it; but differences sufficient for its separation from the section *Segestrella* do not appear.

We found the habit of the last-named, saxicoline section exhibited, as well in the corticoline *Thelopsis*, as combined with entire agreement in structural details in *Porina*; and it now remains to recognize in a lichen from the lime-rocks of the island of Cuba (Mr. Wright) what might well be taken for a saxicoline *Porina*, did not the spores (the differentiation of which has here at length fully reached the muriform stage) denote it rather a rock-*Thelenella*. The description of the manifestly Segestriine *Verrucaria thelostomoides*, Nyl. *Pyrenoc.* p. 41, from which the learned author himself says that his *V. luridella*, from Bolivia, 'scarcely differs,' leaves nothing to be desired in its application to this Cuban lichen, and I cannot therefore venture to distinguish the latter; which mediates, it should seem, on the one hand, between *Porina* and *Segestrella*, and completes, on the other, the evidence of *Geisleria* as to the true spore-type of the whole group.

The noticed specimens from Cuba of what is probably to be called *Segestria thelostomoides* agree still further with the corticoline *Thelenella*, Nyl. (*Microglæna*, Koerb.) of Europe, in the contents of the spermogones; the spermatia of the former being needle-shaped and bowed, and borne on simple sterigmas. *Thelenella* then will also appear to be fully associable with *Segestria*.[1]

It is not at once easy to follow those recent writers who have united what Koerber has distinguished as *Weitenwebera* (*Parerg.* p. 327) to his *Microglæna* (*Thelenella*, Nyl.) the two muscicoline lichens being rather remarkably distinguished from the other ; and only in fact related to the present group (*Segestria*) from which they afford an evident passage into *Verrucaria*, by the originally more or less coloured and softish perithecia. The elegant *Verr. leucothelia*, Nyl. (Fellm. *Lich. Arct.* n. 219) belongs however to the same cluster with his *V. sphinctrinoides ;* and sheds important light on the true affinity of the last.

But two lichens referable to *Segestria* have been observed as yet in North America. *S. lectissima*, Fr., so far at least as all the other characters go, but with the longer 7–10–locular spores ascribed by Koerber to his *S. Ahlesiana* (*Parerg.* p. 324) has occurred to me once on granitic rocks near water in the White Mountains.——*S. nucula*, Fr. (*Porina*, Ach.) is found on various barks in South Carolina (Mr. Ravenel) and in southern Alabama (Mr. Beaumont).

LXIV.—STAUROTHELE, Norm.

Staurothele, Norm. Con. p. 28, t. 23, b, c. Th. Fr. Lich. Arct. p. 263 ; Gen. p. 107. Verrucariæ sp., & Pyrenulæ sp., Ach. L. U. pp. 51, 64 ; Syn. p. 120. Verrucariæ sp., & Sagediæ sp., Fr. L. E. pp. 415, 441. Verrucariæ sp. Wallr. Fl. Crypt. Germ. 1, p. 308. Nyl. Pyrenoc. p. 21 ; Lich. Scand. p. 269. Verrucariæ & Lecanoræ spp., Schær. Spicil. pp. 336, 429. Endocarpi sp., Leight. Brit. Ang. Lich. p. 19, t. 6, f. 1, 2. Lönnr. in Flora, 1858. Stizenb. Beitr. l. c. p. 150. Paraphysorma, Mass. Ric. p. 116. Thelotrematis sp., Næg. & Hepp in Hepp Flecht. Eur. t. 2. Anz. Catal. Sondr. p. 104. Sphæromphale pro p., & Stigmatomma, Koerb. Syst. p. 335 ; Parerg. p. 329.

Apothecia verrucis thallinis immersa, perithecio nigricante, amphithecio pallido, paraphysibus diffluxis. Sporæ ellipsoideæ, muriformi-multiloculares, fuscescentes. Spermatia haud visa.[2] Thallus crustaceus, effiguratus l. uniformis.

[1] *Thelenella eminentior*, Nyl. *Exp. Lich. Nov. Caled.*, a bark-lichen, of which the author says '*faciem proxime habet Verrucariæ nuculæ*' (*Segestria nucula*, Fr.) should seem to confirm this ; and as well the reference to *Segestria* of the tropical species of *Porina*, Mass. ; the published character of the New Caledonian lichen offering no differences from the latter type, except that the 'fusiform-oblong' spores exhibit the muriform configuration.—In a later work (*Syn. Lich. N. Caled.* p. 86) received since the above was written, Dr. Nylander refers the cited *Thelenella* to the neighbourhood of *Segestria nucula*, in his Verrucaria.

[2] My friend Mr. Willey writes however that in a recent examination of the apothecia of *Staurothele diffractella*, during which he had submitted "the nucleus,

However similar in the characters of their apothecia, the evidence is to me insufficient that *Verrucaria umbrina* can be traced into *Endocarpon pusillum*, or *V. clopima* into *E. pulvinatum*, Th. Fr.; and the points of approach between the two groups may be said perhaps to be no greater than those to be found between *Rinodina* and *Physcia*. And on the other hand the finally indeed blackening, but not carbonaceous perithecium may serve to keep *Staurothele* apart from *Verrucaria* sect. *Polyblastia ;* of which *V. theleodes*, Sommerf. (*Sporodictyon*, Mass.) is so important a type. The group before us is marked by the commonly conspicuous, excipular relation of the thallus to the immersed apothecia; but agrees in this as well with *Segestria* as with *Trypethelium ;* the monocarpous species of which latter genus (as *T. uberinum* (Fée) Nyl., and *T. meristosporum*, Mont.) now closely approach in habit, as does the last-named also in the spores, to the present.

As many as seven species, all rupicoline, have been reckoned by some European writers as referable here ; but the distinctions are slight, and the whole perhaps are included in *Verrucaria umbrina*, Nyl. (*Pyrenoc.* p. 21) as understood by him. This author has since indicated, as belonging here, his *V. subumbrina* (*Lich. Scand.* p. 269). The other species are North American ; the whole genus being northern, though recurring in one of its forms in the Himalayah (Nyl).

S. Drummondii (*Verrucaria*, Tuckerm. *Obs. Lich.* 1. c. 6, p. 286) well distinguished on the light-gray lime-rock (Kingston, Canada, Mr. Drummond) upon which it grows, by the orbicular, dark-brown patches (5–9mm. in diameter) which are radious at the circumference of its verrucose thallus, is a much finer lichen than *Dermatocarpon Ambrosianum*, Mass. (*Lich. Ital.* n. 30) and the spores, so far as these have been yet observed (0,030–40mm. long, and 0,011–20mm. wide) are smaller. There can however be no doubt that the two plants are closely allied to each other, and to *S. umbrina.* —— And the same remark must be made of another North American *Staurothele*, which yet I cannot but distinguish. *S. circinata*, Tuckerm.,[1] occurring abundantly on the lime-rocks of Trenton Falls,

dissected as much as possible from the external parts," to the microscope, "cylindrical, straight spermatia, measuring 0,005–0,007mm. in length, upon simple sterigmata," made their appearance, as if originally included within the perithecium.

[1] *Staurothele circinata* (*sp. nova*) *thallo crustaceo orbiculari tenui contiguo lævigato l. dein rimoso, ambitu zonato, olivaceo-fusco, hypothallo fuscescente fimbriato; apotheciis* (0mm., 3–0mm., **7** *lat.*) *concentrice dispositis protuberantibus. perithecio mox denudato nigro, amphithecio albo. Sporæ* 1–2næ, *ellipsoideæ, muriformi-multiloculares, fuscæ, longit.* 0,034–46mm., *crassit.* 0,016–20mm. On the lime-rock at Trenton Falls, N. Y. The rounded patches exceed at length an inch in diameter. As the patches increase in size, successive lines of growth appear more or less clearly at, and give a zonate aspect to the circumference ; the outermost of these lines being a pale, but finally darkening hypothalline fringe. At the centre the crust becomes chinky, and finally falls away.

33

N. Y., offers orbicular, light olive-brown, zonate and fringed patches of smooth and contiguous thallus, which, like the apothecia, are of twice the dimensions of those of *S. Drummondii.* —— *S. umbrina* (*Verrucaria,* Wahl., Nyl. *Pyrenoc.*) inhabits often inundated, granitic rocks in Vermont (Mr. Russell) and, in the var. *clopima,* Nyl., is found, on similar rocks, near water, in the White Mountains. I have a similar lichen from lime-rocks, Canada (Mr. Drummond). —— *S. diffractella* (*Verrucaria,* Nyl. *Pyrenoc.* p. 33) distinguished by its larger, now subsquamaceous areoles, and larger fruit, the perithecium in which is better developed than in the other species — and distributed formerly by me as *V. tiarodes,* was discovered, on schist, in Vermont (Mr. Frost) and has also occurred in Missouri (Mr. Hall) and Alabama (Mr. Peters).

––––––

Sub-Fam. 2. — TRYPETHELIEI.

Apothecia plura in stromate verrucæformi collecta.

The sub-family before us is most intimately related to the next succeeding one, but derives, in its typical members, a marked distinction, and what we cannot but consider a higher position from the at length curiously developed thalloid warts (*Stroma,* Eschw., Nyl. *Receptaculum verrucæforme e propria substantia colorata formatum,* Ach. *Verruca e thalli substantia medullari formata,* Eschw. *Syst. Excipulum verrucæforme e strato medullari thalli formatum,* Fr., Mont.) in which the (commonly numerous) perithecia are immersed. At its centre then, happily indicated by the species upon which Sprengel established the genus, *Trypethelium* may be reckoned a distinct (subordinate) type, standing in interesting relations to the analogous subtype of *Lecanorei* (*Pertusariei*) as to *Sphæriacei* in Fungi (Fr. *L. E.* p. 429. *S. V. S.* p. 384) but its stroma fails at length to be distinguishable from the thalline envelope of *Staurothele,* as of some species of *Pyrenula;* and points of apparent transition to the latter genus (as *Verrucaria ochroleuca,* Eschw., and compare also *Trypethelium nigritulum,* Nyl., with *Pyrenula aggregata,* Fée, Nyl.) are noticed by authors.

Of the only two known generical types of *Trypetheliei, Astrothelium,* Eschw., not as yet detected within our limits, differs from *Trypethelium* in the convergent and confluent ostioles of the perithecia; or as *Pyrenastrum* from *Pyrenula.*

LXV. — TRYPETHELIUM, Spreng., Ach., Nyl.

Spreng. Anleit. z. Kennt. d. Gewächs. Ach. L. U. p. 58; Syn. p. 104, pro max. p. Trypethelium pro max. p., & Pyrenulæ sp., Eschw. Syst. p. 18; Lich. Bras. p. 154. Trypethelii spp., Fée Ess. p. 65; Monogr. in Ann. Sci. Nat. t. 23; Suppl. (Meissneria, & Pyrenulæ spp. add.)

p. 55. Trypethelium, Fr. S. O. V. p. 261. Mont. in Ann.; Syll. p. 371, pro max. p. Trypethelium & Pyrenulæ sp., Mass. Ric. pp. 143, 163. Trypethelium, Nyl. Pyrenoc. p. 71 ; & in Prodr. Fl. N. Gran. p. 127. Trypethelium & Bathelium, Stizenb. Beitr. l. c. p. 146.

Apothecia (1–00) stromate verrucæformi immersa, perithecio diminuto nigricante, amphithecio nigro, paraphysibus capillaribus. Sporæ ex ellipsoideo oblongæ, quadri-pluriloculares [l. dein muriformi-multiloculares,] fuscescentes l. subincolores. Spermatia haud observata. Thallus hypophlœodes l. obsoletus.

Trypethelium has been often compared with *Pertusaria*, and the former is here considered as filling an analogous place in the present tribe to that of the latter in the *Lecanorei*. In structure, as we look at it, the two groups are notwithstanding most diverse. *Pertusaria* is a compound *Lecanora*, in which a number of hymenia, the full evolution of which has been precluded, and which persist therefore in a nucleiform condition, are enveloped by the common hypothecium, and bordered, as well often by this, as by the thalline, here persistently wart-like, exciple of *Lecanora;* and the whole wart (we refer to the typical *Pertusariæ*) is the apothecium. Not so in the corresponding, compound groups of *Graphidacei* and *Verrucariacei*. Here we have (in the typical species) clusters of *apothecia;* and the whole distinction of the groups turns on the enveloping or margining thalloid stroma.

The exhibition of apothecial structure in *Trypethelium* is comparable with what we find in *Endocarpon :* a commonly much reduced, now coloured, but finally for the most part blackening perithecium, which authors have commonly called ostiole; and a well-marked amphithecium, in the genus before us almost always black, which they have not seldom accepted as the perithecium. The black amphithecium suggests readily enough a comparison with the often similarly coloured part in *Pyrenula*, but the question of comparative rank turns really on the characters of the perithecium; and these, however often obscure, look more frequently towards the *Segestriei*.

Like *Pyrenula*, *Trypethelium* belongs evidently to the coloured spore-series ; a considerable proportion of the species, as reckoned by Nylander, exhibiting the final differentiation of the coloured spore. The sub-family is wholly corticoline.

Nylander, whose revision of the genus (*Pyrenoc.* p. 71) we here follow, enumerates, in all his memoirs known to me, twenty-eight species. Of these, twenty-two are confined to intertropical regions ; three extend from these regions northward so as to come within our limits ; two are known only from our southern states ; and one ascends from these even to Canada.

Trypethelium cruentum, Mont., *determ. ipso.* From tropical America, this reaches northward to the low country of our southern states ; occurring in South Carolina (Mr. Ravenel) Alabama (Mr. Beaumont) Mississippi

(Dr. Veitch) and as far as Wilmington, North Carolina (Rev. Dr. Curtis). —— *T. scoria*, Fée, determ. Nyl. (*T. Carolinianum*, Tuckerm. Suppl. 1, p. 429). Also a tropical lichen, found here in the low country of Carolina (Mr. Ravenel) Alabama (Mr. Beaumont) Louisiana (Hale) and at Hillsborough, North Carolina (Rev. Dr. Curtis). I follow Nylander's determination of *T. scoria*, which includes, according to him, *T. phlyctæna*, Fée. —— *T. pallescens* (Fée) Nyl. (including, according to the latter author, beside the lichen originally so named, *T. erubescens*, *T. Kunzei*, and *T. quassiæcola*, Fée) is near to *T. scoria*, and a specimen from North Carolina (*T. pallescens*, Mont. *in litt.*) proves in fact to be scarcely distinguishable from it. Other southern specimens (Texas, Mr. Ravenel) agree however very closely with the lichen first named (Lindig *Herb. N. Gran.* n. 2663). —— *T. catervarium* (*Verrucaria*, Fée Ess. p. 90, t. 22, f. 1. Nyl. *Pyr.* p. 52). On bark, Brooklyn, Alabama, Mr. Beaumont. Belongs to a cluster of tropical lichens, of which *Verrucaria heterochroa*, Mont., and *Pyrenula cartilaginea*, Fée (*e* Nyl.) are other members, apparently better associable with *Trypethelium* (as compare states of *T. pallescens* and *T. annulare*, as also *T. uberinum*, *T. ochrothelium* and *T. Columbianum*, Nyl.) than with *Pyrenula*.—— *T. scorites* (Tuck.) Nyl. *in Prodr. N. Gran.* p. 128, *not.* (*Verrucaria*, Tuck. *in litt.*). On Hornbeam, North Carolina (Rev. Dr. Curtis). The specimen is too meagre, but the habit of the lichen apparently distinct. In the spores it nearly approaches the next. —— *T. exocanthum*, Tuck. *in litt.*[1] Nyl. *l. c.* p. 127. Low country of Alabama (Mr. Beaumont) and of Louisiana (Hale). Considered by Nylander as near to *T. pallescens;* but the spores associate it closely with the following. —— *T. virens*, Tuck. in Darlingt. Fl. Cest. Nyl. l. c. The most northern exhibition of *Trypethelium*. It occurs in Canada (Mr. Drummond) and is common in the White Mountains; and through the middle states (Dr. Michener) to Virginia; from which it extends southward to the low country of South Carolina (Mr. Ravenel) and Alabama (Mr. Beaumont).—— *T. Sprengelii*, Ach. (*T. Eleutheriæ*, Spreng.!) a tropical species, observed here in Louisiana (Hale). *T. virens* is a coarser plant, and readily distinguishable; it is none the less near to the present, and was at first referred to it by Nylander.

———

Sub-fam. 3. —PYRENULEI.

Apothecia solitaria l. nunc confluentia, perithecio atro.

It is in the groups brought together in the sub-family before us that the

———

[1] *Trypethelium exocanthum (sp. nova) thallo hypophlæode; stromate elevato e hemisphærico subgloboso intus albido; apotheciis nigris. Sporæ in thecis clavato-cylindraceis* 6–8^{næ}, *oblongæ*, 6–10–*loculares, incolores, longit.* 0,041–46^{mm}, *crassit,* 0,009–12^{mm}. *Trunks, in Alabama, and Louisiana. Height of the stroma varying from 1 to nearly* 2^{mm}.

uncertain line of separation between lower Lichens and Fungi finally disappears. So slight indeed are often the indications of thallus in these groups, and so little satisfaction is to be had in the application of any supposed rules of discrimination, that it may well seem nearly indifferent, and to competent enquirers, whether a plant (*Verr. rhyponta*, Ach., Fr. *L. E.* p. 448) shall be saluted as a *Pyrenula* or a *Sphæria*. In this view it is natural to enquire if we cannot eliminate these myco-lichens, all of them corticoline, from the true lichens with which they are still in a tribal sense associable, and have undoubtedly so much in common; and there is no lack of evidence that the thoughts of lichenographers have turned not seldom in this direction. Thus Fries (*S. O. V.* p. 264) concludes his discussion of the insufficiency of the characters by which Acharius attempted to distinguish his *Verrucaria* from his *Pyrenula*, with the observation: '*ne quidem ut tribus*' (*h. e. sectiones*) '*servandæ ; et si restituendæ, plane reformandæ ; terrigenas et saxicolas Pyrenulas, corticolas Verrucarias dicas.*' The important thing here being the suggested discrimination of the saxicoline groups from the corticoline, it is of less consequence that Fée's subsequent restriction of *Pyrenula* to bark-lichens (*Suppl.* p. 76) has since been followed, and *Verrucaria* retained for saxicoline. Fries has not indeed recurred to his early suggestion any further than to distinguish and give prominence in his *Verrucaria* (*L. E.*) to the saxicoline types; those confined to bark being relegated, as inferior, to the end : but Naegeli and Hepp have renewed the generical distinction in their *Pyrenula ;* and there is not a little in modern views of the Lichen-system, as for instance the generally admitted naturalness of the group of rock-*Verrucariæ* (*Verrucaria*, Koerb., *Syst.*) and the close relation to this of such species, otherwise agreeing, as are differenced by bi-quadrilocular (*Thelidium*, Massal., Koerb.) or muriform-multilocular spores (*Polyblastia pro p., Auct.*) which looks the same way. Satisfactory differences for these saxicoline and corticoline groups are still not easily indicated. So reduced is apothecial structure in the present tribe, and so often obscure, that it does not appear to be always sufficient in itself to determine generical relations ; or even to discriminate Lichens from Fungi; and though the naturalness of his results may satisfy the lichenist of the probable value of the subtle distinctions which have led to them, it may be difficult for him to express these in words. Natural genera are notwithstanding to be preferred to artificial ones ; [1] and in the present state of the study of our lower *Verrucariacei*, it is possible that the arrangement now to be proposed shall prove to be of service.

The *Pyrenulei*, as here taken, are readily conceivable as falling into two principal assemblages,—the one (confined to inorganic substrates)

---

[1] " *Unica antiqua et bene evoluta species per omnia evolutionis stadia rite observata majoris momenti est quam novum genus — et genus naturale majoris quam systema artificiale.*" Fr. *S. V. S.* p. 427, *not.*

of true lichens, with a well-marked thallus; and the other (confined to organic substrates) of plants, the thallus of which is more or less obsolete, and the affinity close to Pyrenomycetous Fungi. And a certain appreciable difference in these groups appears further to be recognizable in the general features of their spore-phenomena. In the first we have a very regular and instructive, decolorate exhibition of the modifications of the muriform spore; in the other such a varied and irregular, often fungic as coloured presentation of the same spore-type, as we meet with in *Thelotrema*, the analogous group of the *Lecanorei*. It is not difficult to trace the interlinks which bring together *Thelidium* and *Polyblastia*, or to conceive of these as making one genus with *Verrucaria*. But the case is, as we might expect, otherwise in the corticoline group (*Pyrenula*, as here taken) the irregularity of which is yet paralleled in the higher and more easily determined natural assemblage of Urceolariine *Lecanorei* above referred to; and may prove to be explainable.

These chief assemblages of *Pyrenulei* seem none the less to touch each other in two principal points; and so closely that one very eminent writer (Nyl. *Pyrenoc.*) is not willing to allow of even specific distinction: *Verrucaria conoidea*, Fr., being united by him with *Pyrenula gemmata;* and *V. chlorotica*, Ach., with *Sagedia carpinea*, Mass. In the first case the difficulty is notwithstanding less, possibly, than might appear. It is unknown to me whether or not *V. conoidea* agrees with *P. gemmata* in its spermatia, but in other respects the agreement is scarcely sufficient; bilocular, decolorate spores being (from the point of view of this treatise) to be looked for in either group, and this combined, *a priori*, with general structural congruity. But the questions suggested by *Sagedia*, Massal., Koerb., are much more puzzling. We might take it for possible indeed to refer the rock-*Sagediæ* to *Verrucaria* § *Thelidium*, which Anzi has united to *Sagedia*, and the corticoline, with Naegeli and Hepp, to *Pyrenula* § *Arthopyrenia*, with which last Mudd has associated the whole group; but the agreement of rock- and bark-forms is sufficiently striking, and the often distinct thallus of most of these forms, taken in connexion with their well-characterized spores lends weight rather to the view of Nylander, followed in this by Th. Fries, that a still closer relation exists between *Sagedia* and *Segestria* § *Segestrella*. The latter differs notwithstanding in its coloured perithecium, and, as I have attempted to shew, the colourless spores are probably to be taken for a decolorate exhibition of the modifications of the finally muriform type. In *Sagedia*, on the contrary, the ultimate modification of spore-structure as yet observed (in an American lichen) is the acicular; referring the group to the colourless spore-series, and the right extreme of the sub-family.

Beside *Sagedia*, *Verrucaria*, and *Pyrenula*, this group embraces also some mostly inferior, and more or less questionable modifications of the type of the genus last named, which are commonly kept distinct. *Pyrenastrum* is to *Pyrenula* as *Astrothelium* to *Trypethelium*.——*Endococcus*,

Nyl. (*Tichothecium*, Mass., Koerb. *Parerg.*) a little group of minute parasites on rock- and it now appears (Nyl. *N. Gran.*) on bark-lichens is however, irrespective of its certainly questionable lichenose character (Th. Fr. *Gen.* p. 112) not well to be distinguished from *Pyrenula ;* and was originally referred by Koerber (*Syst.*) to the same cluster which includes *P. thelæna* (*Microthelia*, Koerb.) as it is now by Stizenberger. — *Melanotheca*, Nyl., distinguished by him as differing from *Verrucaria* '*æque ac Glyphis a Graphide*' (*Pyr.* p. 69) includes as well a brown-spored lichen (*Melanotheca* pr. p., Fée) as a cluster of forms with colourless, culminating in acicular spores; and the latter group (*Tomasellia*, Mass.) however associable with the former, should seem, from the point of view of this book, to belong to a different spore-series.——And finally, in *Strigula*, Fr., we reach perhaps the extreme limit of the class in this direction; this little cluster of epiphylline plants, having been originally discribed as a type of pyrenomycetous Fungi, and deserving, now that its lichenose character is allowed, scarcely more than the last place.

LXVI.—SAGEDIA (Mass.) Koerb., emend.

Koerb. Syst. p. 362. Verrucariæ sp., Ach. L. U. p. 51; Syn. pp. 88, 94. Fr. L. E. p. 448. Borr. in E. Bot. Suppl. t. 2597, f. 1. Wallr. Fl. Crypt. Germ. 1, p. 299. Schær. Spicil. p. 342. Leight. Brit. Ang. Lich. pp. 42, 53, t. 18, f. 1, 2 ; t. 23, f. 3. Nyl. Prodr. p. 186; Pyrenoc. p. 36; Lich. Scand. p. 277. Sagediæ spp. (& Porinæ sp. ?) Massal. Ric. pp. 159, 191. Pyrenulæ spp., Naeg. & Hepp in Hepp Flecht. Eur. t. 2. Sagedia pro. p., Anz. Catal. Sondr. p. 106. Segestriæ sect., Th. Fr. Gen. p. 106. Sagedia pro p., (& Porinæ sp. ?) Stizenb. Beitr. l. c. pp. 147, 149. Arthopyreniæ spp., Mudd Man. Brit. Lich. p. 299.

Apothecia innato-superficialia, perithecio distincto atro, amphithecio pallido l. dein nigricante, paraphysibus capillaribus, l. nunc diffluxis. Sporæ e cymbiformi fusiformes l. clavatæ, dein aciculares, quadri-pluriloculares, incolores. Spermatia haud visa. Thallus crustaceus, uniformis, evanidusve.

As compared with the next two following genera, the present, from the point of view at least of this treatise, may seem well distinguishable; but, as in those, almost all the characters are uncertain. A kind of superiority over the merely corticoline assemblage (*Pyrenula*) should seem perhaps to be indicated by the here evident, close affinity of the bark- to the rock-forms, and no less by the generally distinct, lichenose thallus ; and such superiority to be in fact admitted, as well in the place (in his *Verrucaria*) assigned by Nylander to the group, as in Koerber's later reference of one member of it (*Parerg.* p. 325) and Th. Fries's of the whole (*Gen.* p. 106) to *Segestria :* but this difference ceases to be appreciable in certain types which may yet prove to be associable with the genuine *Sagediæ*. The amphithecium is almost always colourless, as in *Segestria*, and so described by Nylander (*Pyrenoc.* p. 36) but *Verruc. quintaria* of this author (in *Prodr. Fl. N. Gran.* p. 115) a Japanese lichen, scarcely indeed differs (the spores proving to be at length 7–8–locular) from *Sagedia olivacea* (Borr.) except in the blackening of the interior exciple. The capillary paraphyses are certainly a distinct feature in *Sagedia*, Koerb., and relied upon, in their dispositions of the group, by the other authors named; but the little dependence really to be put upon this character is indicated in *Pyrenula* § *Arthopyrenia*, where *P. punctiformis*, v. *fallax*, Nyl., with well-marked paraphyses, is inseparable specifically from other forms in which these organs are all but deficient. And even the generally lanceolate outline of the thekes of our group ceases now (as in *S. illinita*, Koerb., Zw. *exs.* n. 36, and *S. lactea*, Koerb., Zw. *exs.* n. 44) to be always available. There remains then, and the remark is equally true of *Verrucaria* and *Pyrenula*, nothing but the spores upon which to predicate generical difference; and even here we are embarrassed, in the case of the two genera last named, by the fact that both belong to the same (typically coloured) series, and offer only different expressions of the same spore-type. Not so, if we do not mistake, with *Sagedia ;* the spores of which are always colourless, and proved to be typically so, and to belong therefore to the colourless series, by their final, unequivocal exhibition (in an American lichen, as in another from Japan) of the acicular type.

There are but few indications of this type in the *Verrucariacei*, and most of the lichens distinguished by it, are perhaps closely akin. Thus *Verrucaria gibba*, Nyl. *Prodr.* p. 185 (*Sarcopyrenia*, Nyl. *Pyrenoc.* p. 69) seems, so far at least as the descriptions extend, to be scarcely separable but by the obsolescence of the paraphyses. *Leptorhaphis Beckhausiana*, Lahm (Koerb. *Pererg.* p. 386) also a rock-lichen, the acicular spores of which are contained in 'fusiform' thekes, differs in the same way; and may carry with it to *Sagedia* the other species of *Leptorhaphis*, growing only on bark; these last appearing to be clearly distinguishable from *Pyrenula* § *Arthopyrenia*, if in nothing else, in their spore-type; and only to differ from *Sagedia* in the imperfect paraphyses. It seems on the whole unlikely that so degenerate a cluster of *Pyrenulæ* as is brought together in *Arthopyrenia*, Massal., should possess saxicoline members; and Koerber himself indicates that the spores of his *A. saxicola* (*Pererg.* p. 387) agree rather with those of *Sagedia ;* while neither the obsoleteness of the paraphyses nor the variation of the thekes (as see above) are perhaps enough to distinguish it. And finally it were to be expected, if the group, as thus hypothetically conceived, is found a natural one, that species referable to it, but differenced by other modifications of the spore-type, should offer themselves: *Lithosphæria*, Beckh. (Koerb. *Pererg.* p. 344) a rock-lichen, with much elongated, 'obliquely biclavate, nebulous-monoblastish' spores in 'fusiform - cylindraceous' thekes, may not impossibly prove better associable with *Sagedia* than with *Verrucaria*.

Of *Sagedia*, Koerb. *Syst.*, this author reckoned ten species (all of them subsumed by Nylander, *Pyrenoc.* p. 36, under his *Verrucaria chlorotica*) and four others are added in his *Parerga*. Beyond Europe and North America, the group is represented in Peru, and Polynesia (Nyl.). Four, more or less distinguishable forms, are known to me as North American.

Sagedia chlorotica (Ach.) Mass. Granitic rocks. The spores are now quadrilocular, measuring 0,015-23$^{mm.}$ long, and 0,0035-45$^{mn.}$ wide; New Bedford (Mr. Willey). But much more commonly we find more elongated, dactyloid-fusiform, 6-8-locular spores, measuring 0,025-40$^{mm.}$ long, and 0,0045-7$^{mm.}$ wide; New Bedford and Weymouth (Mr. Willey) North Carolina (Dr. Curtis). The two forms do not appear to be distinguishable otherwise from each other; or from the European species (*Verr. chlorotica & V. macularis*, Zw. *exs. n.* 152, 153. *Sagedia macularis*, Koerb.).
——No distinction is admitted by Nylander between the corticoline forms subsumed by him under his *Verrucaria chlorotica*, and the saxicoline. And looking only at the European lichens in question, this construction appears to be sustained, in any full comparison, by the spores. Like *Sagedia chlorotica* as here understood, the corresponding bark-lichen, as it occurs in Europe, exhibits broad-fusiform, quadrilocular spores, measuring 15-23 micromill., in length, which pass finally into much longer (Hepp *Abbild.* n. 48) 6-8-locular, finally clavate ones (Leight. *Ang. Lich. t.* 18, *f.* 1) which reach 32-36$^{mmm.}$ in length. These dimensions may well be exceeded in the plant described by Leighton; and we have then, in our North American *Sagedia Cestrensis* (*Verrucaria*, Tuckerm. in Darlingt. *Fl. Cest.* 1853, p. 452)[1] as it commonly appears — in New England, and southward to Pennsylvania (Dr. Michener) North Carolina (Rev. Dr. Curtis) South Carolina (Mr. Ravenel) Alabama (Mr. Peters) and Louisiana (Dr. Hale) — but little beyond possibly larger apothecia, more distinctly conditioned by the thallus, and more evidently and constantly elongated spores (averaging, in my specimens, 30-50$^{mmm.}$, in length, by 2½-5$^{mmm.}$, in width) to distinguish it. The spore-history of our plant is not yet however completed. The long-dactyloid or clavate spore reaches finally, with us, and in forms otherwise inseparable, the full acicular shape, measuring then, in Weymouth and New Bedford specimens (Mr. Willey) 41-57, 53-57, and 53-76$^{mmm.}$, in length, and 2½-3½$^{mmm.}$, in width; and in Alabama ones (Mr. Beaumont) 69-83$^{mmm.}$, in length, and 2½-3$^{mmm.}$, in width. The Massachusetts specimens with longest spores were on Hemlock; and Mr. Willey has recently sent others, from the same bark, the spores of which reach 72-118$^{mmm.}$, in length, and 3-4$^{mmm.}$ in width. I possess what seems the same lichen from Beech trunks in Japan (Mr. Wright) the acicular spores of which measure 41-64$^{mmm.}$, in length, and

---

[1] *V. Cestrica*, as named by me, and cited in Nyl. *Pyrenoc.* p. 36; but changed, as above, by the author of the *Flora Cestrica*.

34

$3-4\frac{1}{2}$mmm., in width. However closely then our plant may probably approach that form of *Verrucaria chlorotica*, Nyl., which was described by Borrer as *V. olivacea*, and figured, as above cited, by Leighton, we are not without reason in keeping it, for the present, apart.——*S. lactea*, Koerb. (Zw. *exs.* n. 44. Rabenh. *Lich. Eur.* n. 599). On various barks. White Mountains (Oakes *herb.*). New Bedford (Mr. Willey). Pennsylvania, in several conditions (Dr. Michener). Apothecia of twice the size of those of the European specimens cited; but in other respects the American lichen scarcely differs, unless indeed that the 6–8–locular spores (averaging 16–27mmm., in length, and 5–7mmm., in width) pass often, from broad-fusiform becoming dactyloid, into oblong conditions. Thekes by no means always lanceolate in my copy of Zw. *exs. n.* 44; and they are rather saccate-clavate in our plant: which, however little it really differ from other corticoline *Sagediæ*, is at once distinguishable from them by its white thallus.——*S. oxyspora* (*Verrucaria*, Nyl. *V. epidermidis, var.*, Ach. *V. albissima*, Nyl. *Scand.*). On bark of Birch, and Oak, Massachusetts (Mr. Willey). Spores varying much in length, and from fusiform to acicular; but other differences scarcely observable in the numerous specimens. The species is rather remarkably separated from the type of *Sagedia* by its indistinct paraphyses.——Thus understood, as inclusive also of *Leptorrhaphis*, Koerb., *Sagedia* may be taken for equivalent to *Endophis*, Norm. *Con.* p. 28 (1852) from which this author, by his observation that the apothecia of his new generic type are those of *Verrucaria*, as limited by Fries, certainly seems to exclude (though he nowhere mentions) *Segestria lectissima*. *Endophis* is then the oldest, but scarcely the preferable name.

LXVII.—VERRUCARIA, Pers., emend.

Verrucaria pro p., & Sphæriæ sp., Pers. in Ust. Ann. Bot.; & Syn. Fung. add., p. xxvii. Verrucaria pro p., & Pyrenulæ spp., Ach. L. U. pp. 51, 64; Syn. pp. 93, 122. Eschw. Syst. p. 16. Fée Ess. p. 40. Verrucaria pro p., Fr. S. O. V. p. 264. Mey. Entwick. p. 329. Schær. Spicil. pp. 53, 332. Sagedia pro p., Verrucaria sect. 1, 2, & Limboriæ sp., Fr. L. E. pp. 413, 430, 457. Mont. Aperç. Morph. p. 11. Thrombii sp., & Verrucariæ spp., Wallr. Fl. Crypt. Germ. 1, pp. 294, 297. Pyrenula pro p., Verrucaria pro p., Thrombii sp., & Limboria, Schær. Enum. p. 208. Sagediæ spp., & Verrucariæ spp., Leight. Brit. Angioc. Lich. pp. 22, 35. Thrombii spp., Verrucaria max. p., Amphoridium, Lithoicea, Bagliettoa, Arthopyreniæ dein Acrocordiæ sp., Thelidium, Porphyriospora, Polyblastiæ spp., & Sporodictyon, Mass. Opp. cit. in locis. Verrucaria, Sagedia pro p., & Thelotrematis spp., Naeg. & Hepp in Hepp Flecht. Eur. t. 2. Verrucaria pro p., & Limboria, Nyl. Pyrenoc. pp. 22, 36, 62; Lich. Scand. p. 270. Verrucaria, Bagliettoa, Acrocordiæ sp., Thelidium, & Sphæromphale pr. p., Koerb. Syst., in locc. Thrombium,

Verrucaria, Bagliettoa, Acrocordiæ sp., Thelidium, Polyblastia max. p., & Sporodictyon, Koerb. Parerg. in locis. Verrucaria, Acrocordiæ sp., Sagedia pro p., & Thelotrematis spp., Anz. Catal. Sondr. in locc. Thrombium, Verrucaria, Acrocordiæ sp., Thelidium, Polyblastia & Sporodictyon, Th. Fr. Gen. in locc. Verrucaria, Thelidium pro p., & Sphæromphale pro p., Mudd Man. Brit. Lich. in locc. Thrombium, Verrucaria, Limboria, Arthopyrenia pro p., Polyblastia, & Sporodictyon, Stizenb. Beitr. 1. c. in locis.

Structuram descripserunt Tulasne Mém. sur les Lich. pp. 51, 57, 90, t. 13, f. 1-13; Fuisting 1. c. p. 45.

Apothecia innato-prominula, perithecio atro, amphithecio pallido 1. dein nigricante, paraphysibus tenuibus plerumque indistinctis 1. diffluxis. Sporæ ovoideo-ellipsoideæ, e simplici bi-quadriloculares, 1. demum muriformi-multiloculares, subincolores. Spermatia (quantum obs.) acicularia; sterigmatibus simplicibus. Thallus crustaceus, sub-tartareus, uniformis, rarius areolato-squamulosus.

The rock- and earth-*Verrucariæ* are not only of distinctly higher rank than the corticoline groups here brought together under *Pyrenula ;* but we find also, if I mistake not, an appreciable, general difference, of which there is no trace in the analogous portions of *Biatorei* and *Eulecideei*, in the spores. We cannot distinguish in this way the saxicoline types of the higher groups just referred to, from the corticoline. But one shall hardly compare the spores of *Verrucaria*, as the genus is understood in this place, exhibiting, with regularity of expression, the successive steps in the differentiation of its spore-type, from the simple (*Verrucaria*, Koerb. *Syst.*) to the bi-quadrilocular (*Thelidium*, Mass.) and finally the muriform-multilocular condition (*Polyblastia* max. p., Mass.) with the heap of varied and irregular forms which characterize *Pyrenula* (Fée, Naeg. & Hepp, *emend.*) without acknowledging that we have, in the groups first and last named, two distinct exhibitions of the (normally) coloured spore.

As here taken, *Verrucaria* is then a group of genuine lichens, with distinct and often conspicuous thallus, and a full and harmonious spore-character, which is regarded as separable from closely related groups, on the one hand by its carbonaceous exciple, and on the other by subtle but appreciable conditions, dependent, it is presumed, on these plants being confined to inorganic substrates.

Only some fifteen or sixteen specific forms of *Verrucaria*, as under-stood here, were recognized by Fries. The number has since been greatly increased; and as now reckoned, in the latest German revisions, exceeds ninety. These have in part been determined since the date of Nylander's monographical exposition of the tribe: in the latter however it is observable that only twenty-seven species are admitted. About two-thirds of these rock-lichens, as described by Koerber, are calcareous; and nearly the whole was first detected in, as a very large part is still confined to, Europe. The North American lime-rocks have as yet been little explored; and are possibly less fertile in *Verrucariœ* than the European. But the whole genus requires study here.

Sect. 1. — SPORES SIMPLE.

V. epigœa (Pers.) Ach. On denuded surfaces of earth; common in Maryland, and Virginia. Illinois (Mr. Hall) Vermont (Mr. Frost) Massachusetts (Mr. Willey) New Jersey (Mr. Austin). The very delicate paraphyses are well distinguishable. —— *V. maura*, Wahl., Th. Fr. Granitic rocks on the sea-shore; Massachusetts (Mr. Russell). I find it common on the Maine coast; and Vahl collected it in Greenland (Th. Fr. *Lich. Arct.* p. 268). — Var. *aractina*, Th. Fr. (*Verr. aractina*, Wahl., Nyl.) differs but little, and has also been recognized by Dr. Fries in Greenland specimens. Paraphyses, as in most of the species, scarcely or only very imperfectly to be made out; running together, so to say, or dissolved at length into an undistinguishable mass. Intermediate gradations between such obscure, and the distinct expression of this structure are not however wanting, and too much weight has with scarcely any doubt been accorded to the difference. In the American *V. muralis* (which is at any rate a genuine *Verrucaria*, Koerb.) I observe the paraphyses now plainly distinguishable; and the author just cited describes them, ' *doch natürlich, dem Gattungs-character gemäss, dabei mucilaginös verschmolzen*,' in several instances. (*Syst.* p. 375. *Parerg.* p. 350). —— *V. ceuthocarpa*, Wahl., Nyl. On granitic rocks often wet by the sea. Greenland, Vahl (Th. Fr. l. c.) and to be looked for here; the lichen of Wahlenberg being described by him (*Fl. Lapp.*) as occurring ' *in foveolis petrarum aquam marinam retinentibus.*' Var. *mucosa*, Nyl. (*Verr. mucosa*, Wahl., Th. Fr.) found '*in petris maritimis sub fluxu semper aqua immersis*' (Wahl. l. c.) is also an inhabitant of Greenland (Th. Fr. l. c.) and it may well be of more southern regions. Spores smaller than in the last species. *V. pinguicula*, Mass. (Arn. *in herb.* Krempelh.!) Lime-rocks. Trenton Falls, New York. A distinct lichen, agreeing also in the spores with the cited European specimens. Nylander (*Pyrenoc.*) reduces it to a variety of *V. plumbea*, Ach. —— *V. margacea*, Wahl., Nyl. Granitic rocks often overflowed by fresh water. Notch of the White Mountains. Also at Weymouth, Mass. (Mr. Willey). —— *V. nigrescens*, Pers. Lime-rocks. Canada (Mr. Drummond). Vermont (Mr. Frost). Pennsylvania (Dr. Michener). Ohio (*V. elœochroa*, Tuck. Syn. N. Eng. p. 87). (Lea). Extending also to other rocks, slightly if at all impregnated with lime. Pebbles in bank-walls, Cambridge. Boulders in walls, Amherst. Old bricks, New Bedford (Mr. Willey). Louisiana (Hale). *Sagedia viridula*, Fr. *L. E.*, is referred here by Th. Fries (*Lich. Arct.*) as by Nylander; and the lighter colour which marks this form is characteristical of most of the American specimens. More distinguishable is the rimose-areolate crust of *Verr. fuscella*, Koerb. (*Sagedia fuscella*, Fr.) represented, if I mistake not, by a lichen from lime- and flint-rocks, Alabama (Mr. Peters) and possibly by others from Vermont (Messrs. Russell and Frost) but reduced also by Nylander to a variety of *V. nigrescens*. From this however the writer just cited still keeps apart his *V. virens* (*Pyrenoc.* p. 24. *Sagedia Novæ Angliæ*, Tuckerm. *in litt.*) occurring on schist in Vermont (Mr. Frost) as on other rocks, also not without trace of lime, in Massachusetts. —— *V. rupestris*, Schrad. Lime-rocks. Canada (Mr. Drummond). Maryland. Virginia (Rev. Dr. Curtis). Texas (Mr. Wright). Var. *purpurascens*, Schær. Alabama (Mr. Peters). —— *V. muralis*, Ach. Old mortar in the old Watertown burying-ground. On mortar, and dead sea-shells, New Bedford (Mr. Willey). A not dissimilar lichen from lime-rocks in New York, and Vermont (Mr. Russell) and Canada West (Mr. Drummond) is perhaps also to be referred here. The species is reduced to a variety of the last (but ill-represented in my American specimens) by Nylander, and Th. Fries.

Sect. 2.—Spores bi-quadri-plurilocular.

V. Nylanderi, Hepp (*Flecht. Eur.* n. 440; Koerb. *Parerg.* p. 350) v. *Hudsonana*, Hepp *l. c.* n. 945. On serpentine, near Hoboken, New York (Hepp, *l. c.*). The lichen is unknown to me. In the European one (Rabenh. *Lich. Eur.* n. 594) I find the paraphyses, however more distinct than in most other *Verrucariæ*, still imperfect. And in this respect an externally similar plant found here on granitic rocks (New Bedford, Mr. Willey) with capillary paraphyses, and smaller, narrower, 2-3-locular spores (0,014-21$^{mm.}$ long, and 0,005-7$^{mm.}$ wide) must be pronounced different. Canadian specimens on limestone (Mr. Drummond) agreeing pretty well with the others named, in general aspect and in the small fruit, offer ovoid, bilocular spores (0,011-23$^{mm.}$ long, and 0,007-9$^{mm.}$ wide) and the paraphyses are undistinguishable. It must be left to further enquiry to determine the rank of these lichens. Nylander (*Pyrenoc.* p. 54) regards Hepp's plant as only a small-fruited form of *V. conoidea*, Fr. —— *V. pyrenophora*, Ach., Nyl. Lime-rocks. Trenton Falls, New York. Also at Chittenango, N. Y. (Mr. Willey) and Missouri (Mr. Hall). Thallus tartareous, continuous and at length rugulose, or now chinky, ash-coloured, variegated more or less with black lines. Spores 4-locular, 0,032-46$^{mm.}$ long, and 0,011-18$^{mm.}$ wide. — From this I cannot but separate a *Verrucaria* of the present section, from lime-rocks in Canada (Mr. Drummond) which presents a thallus of minute, rounded, olivaceous becoming grayish, commonly discrete granules; apothecia scarcely exceeding 0$^{mm.}$ 2, to 0$^{mm.}$ 3, in diameter, or less than half the size of those of *V. pyrenophora;* and ovoid, 4-locular spores, 0,023-30$^{mm.}$ long, and 0,009-11$^{mm.}$ wide. It has unfortunately been collected only once, but may conveniently be distinguished as *V. microbola*.

Sect. 3.— SPORES MURIFORM-MULTILOCULAR.

V. terrestris (Th. Fr. *sub Polyblastia, Lich. Arct.* p. 265, & *herb.*). On the earth. Arctic America (Behring's Straits) Mr. Wright. Apothecia clothed by the thallus; but becoming at length naked. In this species, *Polyblastia*, Mass., appears scarcely to be separable from *Sporodictyon*, Mass., except by the condition of the paraphyses.

LXVIII.—PYRENULA (Ach.) Naeg. & Hepp, emend.

Pyrenula (excl. Sagediis) Naeg. & Hepp in Hepp Flecht. Eur. t. 2, & passim. Pyrenulæ spp., & Verrucariæ spp., Ach. Syn. pp. 117, 87. Eschw. Syst. p. 16. Pyrenula max. p., & Verrucaria max. p., Fée (Ess. p. 40) Suppl. pp. 76, 84. Verrucariæ spp., Turn. & Borr. Lich. Brit. p. 203. Borr. in E. Bot. Suppl. Fr. S. O. V. p. 264; L. E. p. 443. Mey. Entwick. p. 329. Schær. Spicil. p. 54. Mont. Aperç. Morph. p. 11. Tuck. Syn. N. Eng. p. 86. Leight. Brit. Ang. Lich. p. 35. Nyl. Pyrenoc. p. 40, &c.; Lich. Scand. p. 279; in Prodr. Nov. Gran. p. 113; Syn. Lich. N. Caled. p. 84; Add. Nov. ad Lich. Eur. in Flora Ratisb. Pyrenula pro p., & Verrucaria pro p. Schær. Enum. p. 212. Pyrenula, Blastodesmia, Arthopyrenia pro p., Acrocordia pro p., Bunodea, Polyblastiæ spp., & Microthelia, Mass. Opp. var. Acrocordia pro p., Microthelia pro p., Arthopyrenia pro p., Pyrenula, Blastodesmia, & Polyblastiæ spp., Koerb. (Syst.) Parerg. p. 333. Th. Fr. Gen. p. 106. Pyrenula, Acrocordia pro p., Arthopyrenia, & Microthelia, Anz. Catal. Sondr. p. 108. Pyrenula, Thelidium pro p., & Arthopyrenia pro p., Mudd Man. Brit. Lich. p. 297. Sagedia sect. 2, pro p., Arthopyrenia sect. 3, Microthelia pro p., Pyrenula, & Sporodictyon pro p., Stizenb. Beitr. l. c. p. 147.

Structuram exposuerunt Tulasne, Mém. sur les Lich. pp. 58, 192; Fuisting, l. c. p. 51.

Apothecia emerso-denudata, perithecio atro, amphithecio pallido l. dein nigricante, paraphysibus capillaribus nunc diffluxis. Sporæ ex ellipsoideo oblongæ, bi-quadri-pluriloculares, demum et muriformi-multiloculares, fuscescentes l. decolores. Spermatia oblonga, bacillaria, l. acicularia; sterigmatibus simplicibus. Thallus hypophlœodes obsolescens, rarius epiphlœodes.

There can be no doubt that the passage from the *Segestriei* to the subfamily now before us is a descent; or that the carbonaceous exciple is inferior to the coloured. We have seemed however to find that there are some appreciable degrees in this degradation of the Verrucariaceous apothecium. Acicular spores lift up the little group of *Sagediæ* to a higher spore-series than that to which almost the whole remainder of the tribe should seem to be referable; and place it therefore at the head of the *Pyrenulei*. It is not surprising then that this group should embrace as well bark- as rock-lichens. But it is less easy to bring together on terms of equality the two remaining, large assemblages; and we gladly follow Naegeli and Hepp in keeping the corticoline *Pyrenula* separate from the saxicoline *Verrucaria*, as distinguishable, if by nothing else, by its undeniable inferiority. This inferiority is indeed, as already above suggested, of such a nature, as to involve even the fundamental question of class-affinity; and in separating *Verrucaria* therefore from *Pyrenula* we are removing what with all their marked reduction and frequent obscurity of structure are still fully entitled to be called lichens, from what, at the best, deserve no higher name than the equivocal one of myco-lichens. Even as satisfactory a species as *Pyrenula gemmata* (*Acrocordia*, Koerb.) is so close, and the microscopical details scarcely embarrass the evidence, to *Sphæria mastoidea*, Fr. (to which Fries himself regarded his *Verrucaria alba* as 'too near') that Schærer is said by Hepp to have confused the two in his publications. The remark holds equally good of the central assemblage of the genus, with coloured spores (*Pyrenula*, Koerb.) if indeed here the fungic relationship does not become more evident. And when we reach the extremity of *Pyrenula* represented by *P. punctiformis* and *P. rhyponta* (*Arthopyreniæ*, Koerb.) we have arrived where we touch Fungi, according to Fries; or enter among them, according to Wallroth (*Naturgesch. d. Flecht.*, 1, p. 150). Both of these were competent enquirers; and later investigations of the internal structure of the groups referred to, have done little, that I am aware of, to invalidate, in this regard, the earlier.

Pyrenula, as here understood, may appear then to be distinguishable, in a measure, into smaller groups; but these assemblages, though passing in fact for genera with most recent writers, are far from satisfactorily defined. All internal structure of the apothecia, even that of the spores, fails at length to afford sufficient criteria. *Microthelia*, Koerb., in America at least, only adds the (typical) coloration to the spores of *Arthopyrenia ;* and its type (*M. micula*) might well appear, from this point of view, with difficulty separable even in species (Nyl. *Pyr.* p. 61) from a well-known form of the latter. *Arthopyrenia* seems better distinguishable from *Acrocordia* (the type of which was yet originally placed by Massalongo with the former, as it is now by Nylander) but the last exhibits finally, even in *A. gemmata*, a tendency to arthopyreniine modification which becomes distinct in the not rarely quadrilocular *A. biformis* (Borr.!) and we lose at length all hold except on the paraphyses; these being undistinguishable in ordinary conditions of *Pyrenula* (*Arthopyrenia*) *punctiformis*, but yet sufficiently obvious in the v. *fallax*, Nyl. The colourless (or decolorate) spores of *Acrocordia gemmata* contrast, in like manner, sharply, with the coloured ones of *Pyrenula*, Koerb., but both offer only modifications (as shewn by the young spores of *Pyrenula*) of the same type; and *P. hyalospora* (Nyl.) might perhaps as well be considered a quadrilocular *Acrocordia*, as (with Nylander, who especially compares the

American lichen with *Pyrenula leucoplaca*) a decolorate exhibition of the spore-type of the last-named group. *Blastodesmia* is a modification of the *Pyrenula*-spore, looking, as Massalongo saw, towards his *Polyblastiæ corticolæ*, and in fact merging in the latter. As seen indeed in the tropical species, the passage from *Pyrenula*, Koerb., to the bark-*Polyblastiæ* (*Sporodictyon*, Stizenb., *pro p.*) is so nearly imperceptible, that we carry art beyond its province, to disjoin these clusters. There is at least no room for doubt that, excluding species of *Sagedia*, Koerb. (on the ground assumed in this treatise that the acicular or colourless spore-type is of a distinct and higher series than the muriform or coloured) we have in the corticoline section of *Verrucaria*, Fr., into however many subordinate clusters we divide it, a natural group, distinguished from the saxicoline as well generally by a significant deterioration of lichenose character, as specially by the obsolescence of the thallus, and the marked coloration (in the principal and central types) of the spores.

Like *Thelotrema*, with which genus it agrees, as elsewhere already suggested, in some important structural features, as especially in the richness and not unfrequent irregularity in details of its spore-history, *Pyrenula* has its centre and a wide extension in the intertropical regions; the number of northern and austral species recognized by Nylander not much varying perhaps from one-third only of the whole. Several interesting European *Pyrenulæ* are still unknown as North American; but our southern limits include already—and the number will doubtless be extended—some important tropical ones.

North American species with (excepting 1, 2) decolorate spores.

Pyrenula pygmæa (Koerb.) (*Microthelia, dein Tichothecium*, Koerb. *Endococcus erraticus*, Nyl. *Pyr., e Lich. Nov. Gran.*). On the thallus of a *Lecidea*, Greenland, J. Vahl, *e* Th. Fr. *Lich. Arct.* p. 275. The only instance in *Pyrenula* of polysporous thekes; and so close is the relation of the above-reckoned form to another in which the spores are commonly in eights, that authors who have generally accorded systematic weight to the polysporous anomaly, have not attempted it here.——*P. thelæna* (Ach.) (*Verrucaria*, Ach., Nyl.). Trunks, North Carolina (Rev. Dr. Curtis). South Carolina (Mr. Ravenel). Alabama (Mr. Peters). Also (scarcely differing) on White Birch, Massachusetts. Spores bilocular, smaller than in the next species, and always brown. Paraphyses, in our plants, rarely and only imperfectly distinguishable. The European *Verr. cinerella*, Flot., Nyl. 1853 (*Microthelia micula* (Flot.) Koerb.) varies similarly (Nyl.) in this last respect, but is scarcely to be kept apart (Nyl. *Scand.* p. 282). ——*P. punctiformis* (Ach.) Naeg. in Hepp *Flecht. Eur.* 1853 (*Verr. epidermidis*, Nyl. *Arthopyr. analepta*, Koerb.). On various barks, common in New England; and occurring westward to Ohio (Lea) and throughout the southern States (Ravenel, Hale, &c.). The bi-quadrilocular spores larger than in the last, and without colour; but similar lichens occur with smaller spores, which shew colour while yet in the thekes. Paraphyses capillary and quite distinct (v. *fallax*, Nyl.) or more or less obsolescent. In a well-marked form with quadrilocular spores (Illinois, Mr. Hall) and in another, less distinguishable from common states of the species (on Birch, New England) the spore-cells are at length divided longitudinally, as in *Arthopyrenia quercus*, Mass. *Ric.* f. 337 ; thus adding to the evidence afforded by *Arthonia*, and by the similar forms of both groups in which coloration is distinct, that colourless spores of this kind are in fact decolorate exhibitions of the muriform, or coloured type.——*P. quinque-septata* (Nyl.) (*Verrucaria*, Nyl. *Pyr.*). On Holly, South Carolina (Mr. Ravenel). Alabama (Mr. Beaumont). Spores ellipsoid and oblong-ellipsoid, 4-7-locular. Paraphyses not well distinguishable.——*P. subcinerea* (*Verr. chlorotica*, v. *subcinerea*, Nyl. *Pyrenoc.* p. 37). On the bark of *Xanthoxylum*, Texas (Mr. Wright). On *Taxodium*, southern Texas (Mr. Ravenel). Amphithecium black (as observed by Nylander, l. c.) and the lichen appears to be rather akin to the last species, but varies in its quadrilocular, more finger-shaped spores, and in its distinct paraphyses.——*P. Cinchonæ* (Ach.) (*Verrucaria*, Ach., *e* Nyl. *N. Gran. V. prostans*, Mont., Nyl. *Pyr.*). On bark (*determ. cel. Nyl.*). Texas (Mr. Wright). South Carolina (Mr. Ravenel). The bilocular spores now thrice constricted ; and the spore-cells also indicating a tendency to pass into four. Paraphyses distinct. ——*P. subprostans* (Nyl.) (*Verrucaria*, Nyl. *Pyr.*). On Bald Cypress (*determ. cel. Nyl.*). South Carolina (Mr. Ravenel). Differs (in these specimens) from the last in its larger apothecia, and smaller spores. Paraphyses, as in the remaining species, distinct.——*P. tropica* (Ach.) (*Verrucaria*, Ach.). On various barks (*determ. cel. Mont.*). South Carolina (Mr. Ravenel). Alabama (Mr. Peters). Louisiana (Hale). Spores oblong, quadrilocular.——*P. gemmata*, (Ach.) Naeg. in Hepp *Flecht. Eur.* (*Verrucaria*, Ach.). Trunks, common in New England. Spores often short-obtuse-ellipsoid, especially in small-fruited specimens ; but in larger ones the spores are larger, more oblong and acute, often constricted (compare *Acrocordia macrocarpa*, Hepp *in* Kb. *Parerg.* p. 347) and suggesting as well *Arthopyrenia*, as younger, colourless conditions of *Pyrenula*, Koerb. Massalongo's figure (*Ric.* f. 328) of a trilocular spore of this species indicates a tendency which is common to the present group. In *Verrucaria biformis*, Borr.! — probably also to be detected with us, and chiefly differing from smaller forms of the present species in its black amphithecium — trilocular, and even quadrilocular spores are not uncommon.——*P. hyalospora* (Nyl.) (*Verrucaria*, Nyl. *Pyr.*). On various trunks, Massachusetts, New Hampshire, and New York. Pennsylvania (Dr. Michener). Canada (Mr. Drummond). This well-marked North American lichen was first observed by Dr. Nylander, growing with other species sent to him. Spores acutate-ellipsoid or cymbiform, regularly quadrilocular. Most readily placed next to *P. gemmata*, for which alone of our *Pyrenulæ* it is likely to be passed over ; but the spores significantly similar also, except in their want of colour, to those of *P. leucoplaca*, Koerb. (Mass. *Mem.* f. 170) with which the author of the species considers it best associable.

2.—SPECIES WITH COLOURED SPORES.

P. aggregata, Fée *Suppl.* (*Verrucaria*, Fée *Ess.*, Nyl. *Pyr.*). On trunks (*determ.* Nyl.) South Carolina (Mr. Ravenel). Alabama (Mr. Beaumont). Texas (Mr. Ravenel). Spores varying, as in other species of this section, from ellipsoid to cymbiform, or, less commonly, oblong; quadrilocular. The habit of the clustered apothecia is altogether that of *Trypethelium*, and *T. nudum*, Fée, belongs here according to Nylander; nor do the spores at least of *T. nigritulum*, Nyl. (Lindig n. 2794) appreciably differ. Neither of these lichens exhibits any proper stroma.——*P. leucoplaca* (Wallr.) Koerb. (*P. farrea*, Ach. *pr. p.*, Nyl.). Trunks. White Mountains. Vermont (Mr. Frost). Massachusetts (Mr. Willey). New York (Mr. Peck). Spores fuscescent, 4–7–locular, 0,020–0,027$^{mm.}$ long, and 0,005–0,007$^{mm.}$ wide. Paraphyses, as in the other species of this section, distinct. ——*P. glabrata* (Ach.) Mass. (*Verrucaria*, Ach.). Trunks, New England. New Jersey (Mr. Austin). Pennsylvania (Dr. Michener). Spores cocciform, quadrilocular. I have not received it from the south, but a lichen with rather larger, more conical fruit, collected by me in Henrico county, Virginia, was referred here by Dr. Nylander.——*P. mamillana* (Ach.) (*Verrucaria*, Ach., Nyl.) v. *Santensis*, Nyl. (*V. Santensis*, Tuck. *in litt.* Nyl. *Syn. N. Caled.* p. 88). On various barks. South Carolina (Mr. Ravenel). Alabama (Mr. Beaumont). Texas (Mr. Ravenel). The glaucescent apothecia become at length quite naked, as in the ordinary tropical state; and the lichen, though scarcely reaching the same size as the other, and passing here into even minute conditions, differs chiefly in its smaller, more cocciform rather than oblong (quadrilocular) spores. These spores, and the remark is equally applicable to the next species, occur also with sharpened tips, or broad-cymbiform, when they are often colourless; and such states compare with the cocciform and coloured ones, much as the spores of *Thelotrema Bahianum*, &c., with those of *T. cavatum*, &c.——*P. nitida*, Ach. (*Verrucaria*, Ach., & *Auctt.*). Trunks throughout the United States. Common from New England southward to Virginia. Westward (Lea; Hall). Carolina (Curtis; Ravenel) to Louisiana (Hale). Spores more commonly cocciform than those of the European lichen (differing therefore much as *P. mamillana*, β, from α) but occurring also in the ellipsoid and oblong-ellipsoid modifications which characterize the type of the latter; quadrilocular.——Var. *nitidella*, Floerk.! Southern States. South Carolina (Mr. Ravenel). Alabama (Mr. Beaumont). Texas (Mr. Wright). The apothecia smaller than in α, and at length quite immersed (f. *punctella*, Nyl. *Pyr.*).——*P. pachycheila*,[1]

---

[1] *Pyrenula pachycheila (sp. nova) thallo hypophlœode; apotheciis obtectis* (0$^{mm.}$, 7–1$^{mm.}$ *lat.*) *l. solitariis mastoideo-prominulis l. pluribus in verrucas dif-*

(*Verrucaria,* Tuck. *in litt. Trypethelium porosum,* Mont. *in litt. T. pyren-uloides,* Mont., *e* Nyl.). Trunks, South Carolina (Mr. Ravenel). Alabama (Mr. Beaumont). Louisiana (Hale). Texas (Mr. Ravenel). In regard to this, the finest of our *Pyrenulæ,* I find myself compelled to differ from authorities, either of which I should be glad to follow. My late valued friend, Dr. Montagne, referred the Carolina lichen, with an ' *ut videtur,*' to *Trypethelium porosum,* Ach.; and this when his own *T. pyrenuloides,* with which Dr. Nylander associates our plant, was already described. I have no specimen of *T. porosum,* distinguished, according to Nylander, '*perithecio incolore vel tenuissime infuscato,*'—an observation in which however he differs from his cited authorities—but the North American lichen is scarcely a *Trypethelium.* This is equally the view of the author last cited; yet his own reference of the plant to that section of his *Verrucaria (Prodr. Fl. N. Gran.* p. 115) which constitutes *Pyrenastrum,* is perhaps quite as difficult to accept. The specific name is, at any rate, no longer available; and I adopt that under which I long since distributed Carolina specimens. Spores of the North American specimens of *P. pachycheila* before me readily distinguished from those of *Pyrenastrum astroideum* by a more oblong outline; the number of cells in the trans-verse series of spore-cells scarcely exceeding two, while in the *Pyrenastrum* these are commonly from three to five. Perfect spores with eight to ten entire spore-cells occur also; and the passage from these, which are undistinguishable in type from those of *Pyrenula* of Koerber, into the multilocular modification (*Polyblastia pr. p.,* Mass. *Sporodictyon pr. p.,* Stizenb.) is easily seen.——*P. lactea* (Mass.) (*Blastodesmia dein Poly-blastia,* Mass., Koerb. *Pyrenula Naegelii,* Hepp). Trunks, White Moun-tains, on Rock Maple. New Bedford, Mass., on Ash, &c., (Mr. Willey). North Carolina (Rev. Dr. Curtis). South Carolina (Mr. Ravenel). Spores muriform, fuscescent or colourless, contained, very commonly in fours or sixes, in oblong, 'subpedicellate' thekes, and measuring 0,027–46$^{mm.}$ in length, and 0,012–18$^{mm.}$ in width. But they also occur in eights, and smaller; measuring now 0,014–23$^{mm.}$ in length, and 0,003–10$^{mm.}$ in width; corresponding sufficiently thus with the spores of *Polyblastia sericea,* Mass. (*Lich. Ital.* n. 262) which is scarcely distinguishable except by the differences in dimensions. A lichen from Texas (Mr. Wright) scarcely

formes dein aggregatis nigris. Sporæ octonæ, ex ellipsoideo oblongæ, submuri-formi-multiloculares (ser. transv. 8–10, *long.* 2–3) *fuscescentes, longit.* 0,030–69$^{mm.}$, *crassit.* 0,014–23$^{mm.}$, *paraphysibus capillaribus. Verrucaria pyrenuloides,* Nyl., *fide ipsius.*——Trunks at the extreme south; the range of the lichen being similar to that of *Pyrenastrum astroideum,* which often accompanies it, and may even be confounded with it. With iodine, the hymenial gelatine of *P. pachycheila* reddens, for the most part; but not always. Small forms of the species occur; and one of these (*P. thelomorpha, Mihi in litt.*) with apothecia only 0$^{mm.}$,4–0$^{mm.}$,7 in diameter, and spores not exceeding 0,023–30$^{mm.}$ in length, and 0,007–11$^{mm.}$ in width, deserves a separate place.

differs except that the spores—agreeing in their dimensions with the larger ones just cited—are in twos; suggesting a comparison with *Verr. geminella*, Nyl. (*Pyrenoc.* p. 40) from Mexico. Paraphyses well exhibited in most of these plants, but not always (as compare Koerb. *Parerg.* p. 336, with Massalongo and Nylander) and the habit of the species, owing to the colour of the thalline film, and the mostly small apothecia, seems a little alien to that of the present cluster. An Alabama lichen (Mr. Beaumont) is however before me (not well separable from Meissner's specimens of *P. Cinchonæ*, Fée, which is referred by Nylander to *P. nitida*) combining the exact habit of *P. lactea*, with the spores (only smaller) of *P. nitida*.

LXIX.—PYRENASTRUM, Eschw.

Eschw. Syst. p. 16; Lich. Bras. p. 142, pr. p.   Fr. S. O. V. p. 265.   Mey. Entwick. p. 330.   Spreng. Syst. Veg. 4, 1, p. 248, pr. p.   Mont. Aperç. Morph. p. 11; Crypt. Guy., p. 52; Syll. p. 370.   Tuckerm. Suppl. 1, l. c. p. 429.   Parmentaria, Fée Ess. p. 70, t. 20, f. 1; Suppl. p. 67, t. 41, f. 1, 2.   Mass. Ric. p. 144.   Verrucariæ spp., Nyl. Pyrenoc. p. 144; in Prodr. Fl. N. Gran. p. 115.

Apothecia emerso-denudata turbinata, pluribus sæpius in ostiolum commune pallidum desinentibus, perithecio conico-elongato obliquo atro, amphithecio nigricante, paraphysibus capillaribus. Sporæ ex ellipsoideo oblongæ, muriformi-multiloculares, fuscescentes. Spermatia haud visa. Thallus hypophlœodes.

The essential difference (as compare Eschweiler *Lich. Bras.* l. c.) of the type before us, which is distinguished from the analogous *Astrothelium*, in the immediately preceding sub-family, by the absence of a stroma, should seem to lie in the elongation of the more or less oblique, flask-shaped perithecia, quite as much as in the convergence and final confluence of these into a compound apothecium. The compound state may not indeed be reached; but the other features are enough to distinguish our species from all *Pyrenula pachycheila*. The pale ostioles of *Pyrenastrum*, traceable into the inner layer of the apothecium, and now more or less confluent above into a kind of disk, offer another interesting feature; recurring however in the second species of the not dissimilar *Parathelium*, Nyl., as this is described (*Prodr. Fl. N. Gran.* p. 126) though it seems to be wanting in the first.

The whole character of the fructification of *Pyrenastrum* appears to approach closely to that of a type of Pyrenomycetous Fungi (*Sphæriæ incusæ*, Fr. *Syst. Myc.* 2, p. 385, *dein Valsa., S. V. S.* p. 410) with which it is compared by Fries.

Except in so far as it reaches the low country of our southern states, the group is tropical. Fée's indication of the since generally accepted and best-known species (*P. astroideum*) was followed by Eschweiler's recoguition of seven others ; and to these Montagne has added four. Several have since been removed by Nylander to *Astrothelium ;* and the same lichenographer allowed at first (*Pyrenoc.* p. 44) only the rank of a variety of a *Pyrenula*-species, (*Verrucaria,* Nyl.) even to *P. astroideum.* But in a later memoir (*Prodr. Fl. N. Gran.*) he recognizes the '*stirps Pyrenastrorum*' as a section of his *Verrucaria ;* and refers to it his *V. intrusa* (*Pyrenoc.* p. 43) besides once more distinguishing from *P. astroideum* his *V. pyrenuloides.*

    P. astroideum (Fée) Eschw. (*Parmentaria,* Fée. *Pyrenastrum Americanum,* Spreng. *P. gemmeum,* Tuckerm.). On various barks, South Carolina (Mr. Ravenel). Alabama (Mr. Beaumont). Texas (Mr. Wright). Spores in eights, muriform-multilocular, the transverse series of sporecells being from eight to ten, and the longitudinal commonly from three to five. In a common form with simple apothecia (*P. gemmeum,* v. *simplex,* Tuck. *in litt. Verrucaria pyrenuloides,* var., Nyl. *Pyr., V. duplicans,* Nyl. *N. Gran.*) the spores vary from eight to two in the spore sacks, the transverse series reaching, in the larger ones, to from eighteen to twenty ; but it does not appear to offer other points of difference. And this form, if we are right in regarding it as only a subordinate one, is clearly referable, so far at least as the North American specimens go, not at all to our *Pyrenula pachycheila,* but to *Pyrenastrum astroideum ;* to which, under another name, we originally referred it. Nylander remarks of his *Verrucaria* (*Pyrenastrum*) *pyrenuloides* (*Pyr.* p. 44) that it only differs from his *V. aspistea* of that work, of which he took *Pyrenastrum astroideum* for a variety, in the apothecia being more veiled ('*magis obtectis*') and we cannot, even in this respect, distinguish the first-named, as represented in Lindig's collection (n. 716–17, 721, 762) from the last (n. 790).——*P. Ravenelii,* Tuck. Suppl. 1, *l. c.* p. 429. On Linden and Wax Myrtle, low country of South Carolina (Mr. Ravenel). Spores in eights, ellipsoid, muriform-multilocular, the transverse series of sporoblasts from eight to ten, the longitudinal, at the middle, from five to six. We are here in the Debatable Land between Lichens and Fungi ; and it may well chance that we shall lose our way. The plant before us stands however (whatever its systematic relations) in close natural affinity to the foregoing ; and I retain it therefore, not without competent authority, in its present place. And this the more that it bears the name of my valued friend, the accomplished explorer and illustrator of the Lichens and Fungi of South Carolina.

LXX.—STRIGULA, Fr.

    Fr. Syst. Myc. 2, p. 535 ; S. O. V. p. 111. Mont. Pl. Cell. Cub. p. 130, t. 7, f. 1, 2, 3. Mass. Ric. p. 148. Nyl. Pyr. p. 65. Stizenb. Beitr. l. c. p. 146. Squammariées epiphylles, Fée Ess. p. 56, t. 2, f. 1–8, pro p. Stigmatidii spp., Mey. Entwick. p. 328. Verrucariæ sect., Eschw. Lich. Bras. l. c. p. 140.

Apothecia prominula, depresso-globosa, perithecio atro, amphi-thecio incolore 1. dein nigricante, paraphysibus capillaribus. Sporæ oblongo-ovoideæ 1. oblongæ, e simplici bi-quadriloculares, incolores. Spermatia oblonga ; sterigmatibus simplicibus. Thallus hypophlœodes epiphyllus, in crustam tenuem subinde effiguratam demum confluens.

At the very limits of the tribe, and of the class in this direction, *Strigula* offers forms so elegant that we may well at first hesitate as to their real rank. *Segestria epiphylla*, as it grows on the leaves of Cuba, in the midst of the curiously varied forms of *Strigula Féei* and *S. nemathora*, looks rather like a crustaceous lichen environed by effigurate ones ; and it needs a second thought to recognize the former as in fact the higher. We owe to Montagne a full explication of this curious type ; and to Dr. Nylander (1. c.) the more important results of later criticism.

Five species were described by Montagne in the *Plantes Cellulaires* of Cuba ; and this number was afterwards increased, from other tropical regions, by the author of that work, to eight. Three of these have been well united by Dr. Nylander ; and one (*S. rotula*, Mont.) which, if I do not err in considering it represented in Mr. Wright's collections, may be said to combine the thallus of *Strigula* with gymnocarpous, lecanoroid apothecia, has been referred, by the same lichenographer, to *Platygrapha*. Except the very doubtful *S. Babingtonii*, Berk., found on Box and Laurel leaves in England, and since relegated to Fungi by its original describer, the group is a tropical one ; one species appearing however within our limits.

S. complanata (Fée, Mont.) Nyl. (*S. Féei & complanata*, Mont.). On the leaves of *Magnolia grandiflora ;* middle Alabama (Mr. Beaumont, comm. Curtis) and Houston, Texas (Mr. Ravenel). The more or less oblong-ovoid spores of this lichen are colourless ; but suggest a comparison with the decolorate spores of *Pyrenula* sect. *Arthopyrenia*.

CORRIGENDA.

Page 3, line 1, for 2 read 1.

P. 7. DACTYLINA. The spermogones and spermatia of *D. arctica*, as described by Lindsay (on Spermogones, &c., Trans. Edinb. v. 22, p. 133; t. 6, f. 23) approach nearly to those of *D. madreporiformis* (Ibid. p. 132) and are admitted to do so by Nylander (*Recogn. Ramal.* p. 77, 1870) though the latter prefers, in case the two shall hereafter be admitted by him to be congenerical, to bring them together, as Sir W. J. Hooker has already done, in an emended *Dufourea.* Upon this the present writer's remarks (*Obs. Lich.* l. c. 5, p. 396) may be compared. The important discovery, by Dr. J. Müller (*Flora*, 1870, p. 321) of apothecia in the heretofore always reckoned sterile *D. madreporiformis* should seem however to leave no doubt remaining of the very close affinity of this lichen to *D. ramulosa* (upon which compare the descriptions in *Obs. Lich.*, above cited) and the spores of the former are not distinguishable from those of *Cetraria;* with which in fact Müller regards the plant as best associable. This view appears certainly to have much to commend it; but Nylander (*Flora*, 1871, p. 298) prefers rather to insist on the affinity of our lichens in question to *Evernia*, and *Parmelia.* ——A single, young, lateral apothecium, entirely agreeing with similarly situated ones of *D. ramulosa*, has occurred to me in specimens of *D. madreporiformis* from the Rocky Mountains (Dr. Parry) and the mature fruit may therefore be looked for there.——The species last named was mistakenly considered by Acharius to be the same with *Lichen madreporiformis* of Wulfen; upon which, as upon the synonymy in general, compare especially Müller, l. c.

P. 10, and pp. 22-23. CETRARIA. The remark is made, at the place first cited, that the evidence of the spermogones appears to be scarcely sufficient to refer beyond doubt *Parmelia Fendleri* to *Cetraria;* and that the reference to the same genus of *P. Fahlunensis,* may possibly also be questionable. The recent observation of Dr. Th. Fries (*Lich. Scand.* p. 110, 1871) that the spermatia of *Parmelia aleurites,* Ach., do not accord, as asserted by Nylander, with those of *P. hyperopta,* Ach., but rather with those of certain species of *Cetraria,* led me however to a renewed study of the lichen first named, which I had already, under another name, once referred (Syn. Lich. N. Eng. p. 16, 1848) to *Cetraria.* The result was that I found my own, American specimens affording spermatia like those described by Fries; and that I reached at length the better view of these lichens now to be set down. *Cetraria aleurites,* Th. Fr., appears then to be associable, in general, at once with the species next to follow, as especially with *C. aurescens,* Tuckerm.; and to differ, to this extent, from *Parmelia.* Acharius's description of his *Parmelia aleurites* (*L. U.*) seems moreover to point, not to what was afterwards called *P. hyperopta* (Ach. Syn.) but to what Dr. Fries intends by *Cetraria aleurites:* and Dickson's published specimen (from 'old pales, Croft castle, Hereford'!) which is cited by Acharius, is certainly the same plant; as are those of Floerke (herb.!) Fries, Schærer, and Mougeot and Nestler (n. 739). From this, *P. placorodia*, Ach. *Syn.* (*Cetraria*, Tuckerm. l. c.) is not well distinguishable even as a variety; and is fully united (under his *P. placorodia* which is our *Cetr. aleurites*) with the form common to America and Europe, by Nylander (*Scand.*). It is yet worthy of mention that this abundantly fertile v. *placorodia* affords better opportunities of observing that the apothecia are commonly attached as in *Cetraria*, than *a*.——With *C. aleurites* is readily associable *C. Fendleri* (*Parmelia*, Tuckerm. *Platysma*, Nyl.) the condition of which growing on dead wood, with compacter and more complicated thallus, differs from the arboricoline exactly as the corresponding states of *C. ciliaris*, &c. In the tree-form of *C. Fendleri* the spermogones are more strictly marginal, as observed by Nylander, than I have seen them in the other; but their variation in this regard is perhaps no greater than we find in some other *Cetrariæ*.——Next to *C. Fendleri* will follow *C. Fahlunensis* (L.) Schær.; which proves to be, in some respects, not ill-comparable even with *C. ciliaris*.——To this last succeeds *C. sepincola* (Ehrh.) Ach.—— I have never found spermatia in *C. Oakesiana*, belonging, it should seem, with *C. sepincola;* nor in *C. aurescens*, so well comparable with some of the species just named, but belonging, it should seem, with *C. juniperina*.

P. 10. CETRARIA *lacunosa*. The lichen is said to occur also in the Scottish mountains (Leight. Lichen-fl. Gr. Brit. p. 103) and even to have been detected on trees ('*in ramis pinuum,*' Th. Fr. *Lich. Arct.* p. 39; — but this is exactly as *C. glauca* is found) in Norway. A reticulate-lacunose specimen, evidently from rocks, and ticketed by Mr. Borrer, from whom I received it, "Cetraria, Breadalbane mountains," is, in fact, though differing possibly in rather wider lobes, perhaps better referable to *C. glauca* than to the other, properly American lichen. I incline to a similar view of a rock-specimen from Newfoundland, lacunose, like the Scotch one, and similarly black beneath, which Delise (Herb. V. d. Bosch, *e* herb. Spreng.) referred to *C. lacunosa;* and to suspect some of the other localities named above. Whatever its rank, as undoubtedly a very near relative of *C. glauca*, the American *C. lacunosa*, though exceedingly common on trees, and dead wood, is as yet unknown to me as occurring on rocks.

P. 24, line 24, after oblonga, add rarissime elongata, acicularia.

P. 35. The note belongs to *S. Ravenelii*, on the opposite page.

P. 52, line 24. *Pannaria plumbea* was found by me, the past season, in excellent condition, but very sparingly, on an old Oak on Newport Mountain, Mt. Desert, Maine.

P. 72, twelfth line from bottom; read fruticulose.

P. 120, line 13. *L. molybdina* occurred to me not uncommonly, the last year, on maritime rocks of Mt. Desert, Maine.

P. 129. CONOTREMA. Spermogones superficial, black. Sterigmata simple. Spermatia oblong, straight, 0035–004$^{mm.}$ long, and a quarter as wide. (H. Willey *in litt.*)

P. 138. THELOTREMA *subtile*. *T. bicinctulum*, Nyl., to which he referred, as a form (*Consp. Thelotr.*) the earlier *T. subtile*, is unknown to me, and appears now to be regarded distinct in species by its author (*Syn. N. Caled.* p. 34). *T. subtile* is quoted also as an Irish lichen (Leight. Lichen-fl. Gr. Brit. p. 248).

P. 149. *Thamnolia,* Schær., Nyl. Lindsay, who describes and figures the spermogones found by him, and by Nylander, on the *Cladonia vermicularis* of authors, remarks (on Spermogones, &c., l. c. p. 142, t. 5, f. 20–23) that "it is seldom that the spermatia and sterigmata can be found; at least I have examined several dozens of specimens from every variety of habitat, and, though I long suspected these warts of being spermogones, I have only been able to satisfy myself as to their true character — by discovering the spermatia and sterigmata — in a single instance."

P. 163, line 26; read Welwitsch.

P. 167, line 5 of note; read *quernea.*

P. 170, line 30; read *Acolium.*

P. 181, last line; read *Heterothecium.*

P. 187, line 35; read pales.

P. 222, line 21; ARTHONIA *pinguis* should be erased; and the lichen is rather to be taken for an imperfect *Biatora sp. incert.* (H. Willey *in litt.*)

P. 233, line 7; read Christiania.

P. 268, line 10. VERRUCARIA *striatula,* Wahl., was recently detected, in excellent condition, on stones not far from the sea, at Nantasket beach, and also at Weymouth (Mr. Willey). I am unable, at present, to examine a large collection of specimens of maritime *Verrucariæ* of the *maura*-stock, made by me, the past season, on the coast of Maine; but have little doubt that we possess all the published European forms.

INDEX GENERUM.

MEMOIR

OF

EDWARD TUCKERMAN.

1817-1886.

BY

W. G. FARLOW.

READ BEFORE THE NATIONAL ACADEMY, APRIL, 1887.

Judd & Detweiler, Printers, Washington, D. C.

MEMOIR

OF

EDWARD TUCKERMAN.

1817-1886.

BY

W. G. FARLOW.

READ BEFORE THE NATIONAL ACADEMY, APRIL, 1887.

BIOGRAPHICAL MEMOIR OF EDWARD TUCKERMAN.

The sad duty of presenting an account of the life and writings of our lamented associate, EDWARD TUCKERMAN, has been assigned to the writer by order of the Academy.

Edward Tuckerman, the eldest son of Edward Tuckerman, a merchant of Boston, and Sophia (May) Tuckerman, was born in Boston, December 7, 1817. When a boy he attended Ingraham's school, and later fitted for college at the Boston Latin School. He then entered the Sophomore Class of Union College, Schenectady, and received his Bachelor's degree in 1837. After graduation he entered the Harvard Law School and obtained the degree of LL. B. in 1839. He continued to reside in Cambridge for two years longer, pursuing studies in law and also taking a special course at the Divinity School. In 1841–42 he traveled in Europe, extending his journey as far north as Upsala where he formed the acquaintance of the celebrated Prof. Elias Fries. He returned to this country, it would appear, in the summer of 1842, for in the autumn of that year he made a trip to the White Mountains with Prof. Asa Gray. Soon after, he took up his residence at Union College and there received his Master's degree. He returned again to Cambridge in 1844 or 1845 and, wishing to obtain an Academic degree from Harvard, he entered the Senior Class in 1846 and passed the regular examinations with distinction, receiving the degree of A. B. in 1847. Although he had already obtained two degrees from Harvard, he entered the Harvard Divinity School two or three years later and passed through its course of study and prescribed exercises, although it appears from the Harvard Triennial Catalogue that he did not take the degree of Bachelor of Divinity. It should be said in this connection that his family were members of the Protestant Episcopal Church and he himself remained a member of that denomination during his life, although, at the time of his connection with the Harvard Divinity School, it was under the control of the Unitarian denomination.

In May, 1854, he was married in Boston to Sarah Eliza Sigourney Cushing, who still survives him. Soon after his marriage he removed with his wife to Amherst, Mass., where he built a house in a beautiful spot and resided until his death, March 15, 1886. In 1854 he was appointed Lecturer on History in Amherst College, and until 1873 he continued to give instruction in history, during a part of the time filling the chair of Oriental History. In 1858 he was appointed Professor of Botany, a position which he held during the rest of his life, although during his later years he was relieved from class instruction. He received from Amherst the honorary degree of LL. D., was elected a member of this Academy in 1868, and was connected either as an active or honorary member with numerous scientific societies both of this country and of Europe.

As a man, Professor Tuckerman was noted for his sincerity and amiability. He is described by the surviving friends of his earlier years as a most agreeable companion, one whose society was sought by those who prized that good fellowship to which both the heart and head contribute. If he was at times reserved he was also genial when the occasion demanded; if he was often absorbed in his own studies, he unbent when friends sought his society. The writer could repeat many anecdotes told by his old Harvard friends to show how, when students together, they respected his character and enjoyed his companionship. After his removal to Amherst his life was passed in the quiet pursuit of his favorite studies, especially botany, and he rarely left home except to make some botanical excursion. His family relations were most happy, and his wife was not only a devoted companion but also a sympathizer with his work. By his brother professors and, in fact, by the people of Amherst generally, he was highly esteemed as a man and a citizen. As a teacher he inspired the better class of students with an enthusiasm which did not cease with college life, but afterwards developed into an activity of which science in this country has already in part reaped the fruit.

From the first, Professor Tuckerman was of a retiring and sensitive temperament, and, as years passed on, he was forced to become more and more secluded in consequence of a deafness which gradually increased, and at last reached a stage at which conversation became difficult. Although probably never very robust, in his early life he possessed great bodily activity and a degree of venturesomeness and fondness for exploration hardly to have been expected. He made numerous visits to the White Mountains and botanized on the most inaccessible peaks and in the wildest ravines at a time when the White Mountains were as difficult of access as the Rocky

4

Mountains or the Sierras at the present day. With the exception, perhaps, of Oakes, no botanist has ever explored the mountains with the same zeal and success as Professor Tuckerman, and, as far as lichens are concerned, the collections of Oakes are naturally not to be compared with those of Tuckerman.

His natural activity and power of work were unfortunately diminished by sickness during the latter part of his life. A number of years before his death he suffered from a sunstroke from which he probably never quite recovered, and this made it difficult for him to work continuously as had been his habit. For the last few years he failed steadily, and, in the autumn of 1885, he went to Virginia in the hope of restoring his health; but he soon returned to Amherst and continued in comparatively good health, although he was known to be suffering from Bright's disease, until a few days before his death, when complications of the disease confined him to his room, and he at last passed calmly away.

The writings of Professor Tuckerman, apart from his botanical works, relate to historical and theological subjects, and in the present connection do not call for an extended notice. He privately published an edition of Josselyn's "New England's Rarities Discovered," with annotations, including a biography of Josselyn, and a sketch of the earlier sources of our knowledge of New England plants and of some of the people who made them known. In 1832 and 1833 he assisted Mr. Samuel G. Drake in the preparation of his "Book of the Indians" and "Indian Wars." Between 1834 and 1841 he contributed to the New York Churchman no less than fifty-four articles under the title of "Notitia Literaria" and "Adversaria," upon points in history, biography, and theology. He was also a frequent contributor to other religious journals.

Professor Tuckerman's fondness for botany was shown at an early age. When a student at Union College he was appointed curator of the Museum. His acquaintance with William Oakes, of Ipswich, Mass., one of the pioneers of botany in New England, and Dr. T. W. Harris, a noted entomologist and librarian of Harvard College, dates, perhaps, from a still earlier period; at any rate the influence of these two men—the one an indefatigable collector and explorer, the other a thorough student—must have had much to do in forming his tastes and shaping his future career. Of all plants lichens were always the most attractive to him, and his first paper, "An enumeration of some Lichenes of New England," was presented to the Boston

Society of Natural History in 1838–'39, the year after he graduated at Union College, when he was only twenty-one years of age. This was followed by a second paper in 1840, "A Further Enumeration of some New England Lichenes," and a third in 1841, "Further Notice of some New England Lichenes." These papers, it will be noticed, were the work of a young man who had studied only in this country, and relate to a group of plants which, up to that time, can hardly be said to have been studied at all by American botanists; for, if we except Halsey's "Synoptical View of the Lichens growing in the Vicinity of the city of New York," the references to lichens in works by American botanists consisted of lists of species determined by Europeans from specimens sent to them and published often without the names of authorities, and too frequently with glaring typographical errors. Tuckerman's papers, even the earliest, are full of critical notes on structure and distribution, giving the results of his own explorations, especially in the mountainous regions of New England, whose lichen-flora he was the first to investigate.

The most important event of his life, botanically considered, was his journey to Sweden in 1841, where he met Elias Fries, professor of botany at Upsala, the leading lichenologist of his time, and, after Linnaeus, the most distinguished of Sweden's many distinguished botanists. Thirty years later, when the writer was at Upsala, Professor Fries, then a venerable man of eighty with undiminished mental vigor, recalled the days when the enthusiastic young American was at Upsala and related how, when walking together on the famous avenue near the university, Tuckerman discovered a species of lichen which he, the authority on lichens, had not seen there before. The visit to Fries was important because it enabled Tuckerman to acquire, if one may say so, the traditions of the science. In some branches of cryptogamic botany it is almost a necessity that an American should see the species of Europe under the guidance of a botanist trained on the spot if he would clearly recognize the same species when they occur in America. There is an indescribable something, especially in lichens, which certainly is not and probably could not be laid down in books. It is fortunate for our lichenologists that Tuckerman was able to transfer to America and perpetuate on this side of the Atlantic the ideas of classification and specific limitations derived from Fries himself. Certainly

6

during his life he always adhered to the Friesian views of classification, which he preferred to those of later botanists.

While in Europe he did not limit his botanical studies to lichens, but also worked on some of the more difficult genera of phænogams. Before his return to America he contributed to Hooker's Journal of Botany a paper on "*Oakesia*, a new genus of *Empetreae*," and shortly after his return, in 1843, he printed privately at Schenectady his "Enumeratio Methodica Caricum Quarundam," of which Professor Gray says: "He displayed not only his critical knowledge of the large and difficult genus *Carex*, but also his genius as a systematizer, for this essay was the first considerable and a really successful attempt to combine the species of this genus into natural groups." In the American Journal of Science of the same year he published "Observations on some interesting plants of New England," and this was followed in 1848 and 1849 by two papers on similar subjects, including an elaboration of the American species of the difficult genus *Potamogeton*, which he was the first in this country to study critically. These papers include about all that was ever published by Professor Tuckerman on phænogamic plants, if we except the "Catalogue of plants growing without cultivation within thirty miles of Amherst College," issued in 1875, of which he prepared the list of flowering plants. But it should be added that the papers already named do not comprise all that he contributed to phænogamic botany, for he furnished valuable notes on distribution of species to other workers in the same field, which, if they were sometimes properly acknowledged, were, it is to be feared, sometimes absorbed without suitable recognition.

In 1845 he published in the Journal of the Boston Society of Natural History "A further notice of some alpine and other lichenes of New England," and in the same year there appeared at Cambridge his "Enumeration of North American Lichenes, preceded by a general account of lichens and of the Friesian system, together with an essay on the natural systems of Oken, Fries, and Endlicher." In 1847 he presented to the American Academy of Arts and Sciences a "Synopsis of the Lichenes of New England, the other Northern States, and British America," which was issued separately the following year. This work was the first attempt at a systematic description and classification of all lichens known, at that time, in the temperate regions of North America and may be called the lichen-primer of this country. It included 295 species, of which 20 were new. Incomplete as it seems at the present time, it offered to the student of that day the means of recognizing and referring to their proper places in the then accepted system the more prominent species of the eastern portions of the United States and it served as an incentive to the study of lichens which was important. As an adjunct to the synopsis should be mentioned the " Lichenes Americæ Septentrionalis Exsiccati," in three fasciculi, Cambridge, 1847–1855, including specimens of many of the species given in the synopsis and collected mainly by Tuckerman himself.

But the study of lichens soon assumed a new phase. The microscopic characters began to be more carefully studied, new regions were explored, and the number of observers increased rapidly. Naturally, with the increase of collections and a more minute anatomical study, not only did the older descriptive works prove inadequate but the systems of classification themselves required modification. The Western explorers and a new generation of botanists in the East amassed a large amount of material, while the various expeditions to foreign lands brought home rich collections of lichens which were placed in his hands for determination. From 1848 to 1872 he published numerous papers of which the more important were a "Supplement to an Enumeration of North American Lichens," in the Journal of Science in 1858 and 1859, where he described many new species from the Southern States and California; Observationes Lichenologicæ, in four parts, in the Proceedings of the American Academy, 1860 to 1877; the Lichens of the Wilkes Exploring Expedition, and the Lichens of California, Oregon, and the Rocky Mountains; Amherst, 1866. The second and third parts of the Observationes related principally to species collected in Cuba, by Charles Wright, and the range of his studies of exotic forms is shown by the fact that, not including the papers previously named which contained accounts of species from Eastern Asia, the Pacific Islands, the Cape of Good Hope, etc., he also published papers on species from Kerguelen's Land, the Hawaiian Islands, and Arctic America.

The elaboration of this rich material enlarged his views of classification and gave him a broad knowledge of generic types as well as specific forms which he embodied in his "Genera Lichenum," published at Amherst in 1872. This, it seems to the writer, should be regarded as his greatest work. In it he displays a remarkable knowledge of lichen forms and a thorough acquaintance with the literature of systematic lichenology. That it is not more widely read and known is probably due to the prevailing fondness for microscopic details. It must be confessed, however, that the somewhat involved style in which it was written is in part responsible, for it is a hard book to read. It was addressed to experts, not to beginners, and, when it appeared, the older experts were too busy attempting to split up genera and species to an unendurable degree of artificiality, while the younger men, attracted by the writings of Schwendener, Bornet, and Stahl, were too much interested in developmental and physiological questions to care much for systematic works. The Genera Lichenum is a protest against the artificial classifications based almost wholly on the spore characters without regard to other equally important characters, a method first advocated by the Italian lichenologists, with De Notaris at their head, and adopted by the Germans and other continental botanists. Tuckerman advocated the systems of Fries modified by his knowledge of exotic forms. His view of species was a large one, and he recognized numerous varieties of the type but refused to admit that, if a form differed in any visible respect from the type, it must constitute a distinct species. If his classification is at times less easy to follow than that of the modern continental school, it presents ultimately fewer difficulties and is certainly more natural, and hence more scientific.

On the completion of his Genera his whole aim was to complete a descriptive work which should include all the species known in the United States. For this work no living botanist had so ripe an experience or such a mass of valuable material as he. Unfortunately his health failed, and, being the long acknowledged authority on lichens in this country, much of his time was absorbed by correspondents who, at times, ill requited his valuable services. In 1882 there appeared the first volume of his much-desired "Synopsis of the North American Lichens," which comprised the *Parmeliacei*, *Cladoniei*, and *Cænogoniei*. He applied himself industriously to the preparation of the second volume, which it was hoped would soon appear; but death interrupted his task, and it is not now known whether his manuscript is in a state to admit publication.* If not, the loss to American botany will be very great, for

---

*Since the above was written it has been learned that the manuscript of the *Lecidiacei* and *Graphidacei* was left by Professor Tuckerman in condition for printing, and it is the intention of his family to publish it at an early day.

it is certain that he had in his possession a large amount of new material, and no one could so well as he treat the difficult groups *Lecidiacei* and *Verrucariacei*.

A word should be said about Professor Tuckerman's views with regard to the Schwendener theory. Following the earlier indications of De Bary, Schwendener, by a minute study of the thallus of lichens, brought forward proofs to show that the gonidia of lichens had no real genetic connection with the hyphæ, but were, in fact, algæ upon which the hyphæ were parasitic; in other words, what is called a lichen is, properly speaking, a fungus of the order *Ascomycetes*, which is parasitic on some alga; in most cases a species belonging either to the *Palmellaceœ* or the *Nostocaceœ*. The botanical world was divided in opinion, and, for the last fifteen years, the so-called algo-fungal theory of lichens has given rise to endless controversies of a personal and very acrimonious character. As a rule, the systematic lichenologists were opposed to the theory, while the histologists supported it. Professor Tuckerman, who began his studies at a time when microscopic technique had not reached its present perfection, could hardly have been expected to take a very active part in a direction requiring difficult microscopical work. It is said that at first he was inclined to favor the theory, but if so, he soon changed his views and sided with the opponents of the theory. It must be said to his credit that his references to the subject were always courteous and dignified in marked contrast with the course of some other well-known lichenologists. The most definite expression of his opinion in print is to be found in the American Journal of Science and Arts of February, 1879, where, under the title of "The Question of the Gonidia of Lichens," he reviewed the first part of Minks' "Beitraege zur Kenntniss des Baues und Lebens der Flechten." Minks had observed small green bodies in the hyphæ, which finally escaped from them and developed into gonidia. In his review Tuckerman confirms the statement of Minks with regard to the existence of the green bodies called by Minks microgonidia, and remarks that he has observed them himself in *Parmelia tiliacea* v. *flavicans* of Cuba, but he does not go so far as to say that he saw them develop into gonidia. He accepts Minks' statements on this point, however.

The life of our lamented associate was one devoid of some of the incidents which make the lives of many men of science picturesque. It is a simple story, not of struggles against poverty and the enmities of opponents, but of one who, endowed with a fair share of this world's goods and always happy in his family relations, pushed steadily onward in his chosen field—a worker to the last in spite of increasing bodily infirmities. If it was a life so quiet and retired that it may almost be said to have been eventless, it none the less has left its mark. Professor Tuckerman's death has left a gap in the ranks of American botanists which will not be filled for years, and while his contemporaries mourn the loss of a personal friend, the younger generation of botanists feel no less keenly the loss of one whose letters were not only highly instructive and encouraging, but also full of enthusiasm and enlivened by reminiscences of the time when he was young.

The name of Tuckerman is commemorated in a genus of *Compositæ*, dedicated to him by Nuttall, and in several species named in his honor by different botanists. A more widely known memorial is the noble ravine on Mount Washington, the seat of his early explorations, which now bears his name. He will long be remembered by the poor and afflicted relieved by his sympathy and beneficence whose extent, not suspected even by his intimate friends during his life, has been made known only since his death by the grateful recipients of his bounty.

11

LIST OF THE BOTANICAL WRITINGS OF EDWARD TUCKERMAN.

An Enumeration of some Lichenes of New England, with remarks. *Boston Journal of Natural History.* I, 245–262. 1839. Read Dec. 5, 1838.

Note on *Geaster quadrifidus.* *Am. Jour. Sci. and Arts.* XXXVI, 380, July, 1839.

A further Enumeration of some New England Lichenes. *Boston Jour. Nat. Hist.* III, 281–306. 1841. Read March, 1840. Ditto, 438–464. Read March 17, 1841.

Notice of some *Cyperaceæ* of our Vicinity. *Hovey's Magazine of Horticulture and Botany.* VII, 208–210. June, 1841.

On *Oakesia,* a new genus of the order *Empetreæ.* *Hooker's London Journal of Botany.* I, 443–447. 1842.

Observations on some interesting plants of New England. *American Journal of Science and Arts.* XLV, 27–49. 1843.

Enumeratio methodica Caricum quarundam. Species recensuit et secundum habitum pro viribus disponere tentavit Eduardus Tuckerman. Schenectady, 1843. 8vo. Pp. 21.

Descriptions of several new Plants of New England. *Hovey's Mag. Hort. & Bot.* IX, 142, 243. April, 1843.

A further Enumeration of some alpine and other Lichenes of New England. *Boston Jour. Bot.* V, 93–104. 1845.

An Enumeration of North American Lichenes, with a preliminary view of the structure and general history of these plants and of the Friesian System: to which is prefixed an Essay on the Natural Systems of Oken, Fries, and Endlicher. Cambridge, 1845. Small 8vo. Pp. 59.

Observations on some New England Plants, with characters of several new species. *Am. Jour. Sci. & Arts.* VI, N. S., 224–232. 1848.

A Synopsis of the Lichenes of the Northern United States and British America. *Proceedings American Academy of Arts and Sciences.* I, 195–285. 1848. Read Dec. 7, 1847. Reprint, 8vo. Pp. v, 93.

Observations on American species of the genus *Potamogeton,* Linn. *Am. Jour. Sci. & Arts.* VII, N. S., 347–360. 1849.

Lichens in T. G. Lea's Catalogue of Plants, native and naturalized, collected in the vicinity of Cincinnati, O., during the years 1834–1844. Philapdelphia, 1849. Pp. 44–47.

Lichenes: in "Lake Superior, its physical character, vegetation, and animals, compared with those of other and similar regions." By Louis Agassiz. Boston, 1850. Pp. 171–174.

Lichens: in Rept. Exp. and Surveys for a railroad from the Mississippi River to the Pacific Ocean. Vol. VI. Botanical Report, p. 94. Washington, 1857.

Carex argyrantha sp. nov. Privately printed at Amherst, 1859.

Supplement to an Enumeration of North American Lichenes. *Am. Jour. Sci. & Arts.* XXV, N. S., 422–430, May, 1858, and XXVIII, 200–206, Sept., 1859.

The Vegetation of the White Mountains: in the White Hills, their legends, landscape, and poetry by Thomas Starr King. Boston, 1860. Pp. 230–241.

Observations on North American and some other Lichenes. *Proc. Am. Acad. Arts. & Sci.* IV, 383–407, read March 13, 1860: V, 383–422, read April 22, 1862: VI, 263–287, read April 12, 1864: XII, 166–185, read May 29, 1877. Parts 3 and 4 under the title of Observationes Lichenologicæ.

Lichenes: in United States Exploring Expedition during the years 1838–1843, under the command of Charles Wilkes, U. S. N. Vol. XVII. Botany. Philadelphia, 1862 (1874). Pp. 113–152. Pl. 1, 2.

Lichens of California, Oregon, and the Rocky Mountains; so far as yet known. With an appendix. Amherst, 1866. Small 8vo. Pp. 35.

Lichenes: In "Enumeration of Hawaiian Plants," by Horace Mann. *Proc. Am. Acad. Arts and Sci.* VII, 223–234. 1868.

Carex glaucodea in Carices Novæ, by S. T. Olney. *Proc. Am. Acad. Arts. and Sci.* VII, 395. 1868.

Can lichens be identified by chemical tests? *American Naturalist.* II, 104–107. April, 1868.

Lichens: In United States Geological Exploration of the Fortieth Parallel, Clarence King, geologist in charge. Washington, 1871. Pp. 412, 413.

Genera Lichenum: An Arrangement of the North American Lichens. Amherst, 1872. 8vo. Pp. xv, 281.

Two Lichens of Oregon. *Bulletin of the Torrey Botanical Club.* V, 20. April, 1874.

Lecidea elabens. Flora. 1875. Pp. 63, 64. Ratisbon.

Lichens of Kerguelen's Land. *Bull. Torrey Club.* VI, 57–59. October, 1875. Also in Smithsonian Miscellaneous Collections. Vol. XIII; Bulletin U. S. Nat. Museum, I, No. 3, 27–30.

A catalogue of plants growing without cultivation within thirty miles of Amherst College. Amherst, 1875. 8vo. vi, 97. The *Musci, Hepaticæ, Characeæ*, and *Fungi*, by C. C. Frost.

Lichenes: In Report upon United States Geographical Surveys West of the One Hundredth Meridian, in charge of First Lieut. Geo. M. Wheeler. Washington. Vol. VI. Pp. 350, 351. 1878.

List of Lichens collected in the vicinity of Annanactook Harbor, Cumberland Sound, at about Lat. 67° N., Long. 68° 49′ W. (Howgate Expedition). Bull. U. S. Nat. Museum, No. 15. Washington, 1879. Pp. 167, 168. *Smithsonian Misc. Collec.* Vol. XXIII. 1882.

The Question of the Gonidia of Lichens. *Am. Jour. Sci. and Arts.* XVII, 3d ser., 254–256. March, 1879.

Lichens or Fungi? *Bull. Torrey Club.* VII, 66, 67. June, 1881.

Review of Minks's Symbolæ Licheno-Mycologicæ. Beitraege zur Kenntniss der Grenzen zwischen Flechten und Pilzen. *Bull. Torrey Club.* IX, 143. November, 1882.

A Synopsis of the North American Lichens. Part I, comprising the *Parmeliacei, Cladoniei*, and *Cœnogoniei*. Boston, 1882. 8vo. Pp. xx, 262.

New Western Lichens. *Bull. Torrey Club.* X, 21–23. February, 1883.

A new *Ramalina*. *Bull. Torrey Club.* X, 43. April, 1883.

Two Lichens of the Pacific Coast. *Bull. Torrey Club.* XI, 25, 26. March, 1884.

212282

Made in the USA